THE RHODODENDRON SPECIES

Rhododendrons on alpine rocky slopes, Tali Range, Yunnan. Photo J.F. Rock

THE RHODODENDRON SPECIES

VOLUME I • LEPIDOTES

H. H. Davidian,
B.A., B.Sc. (Hons.)

TIMBER PRESS
Portland, Oregon
1982
in cooperation with
THE RHODODENDRON SPECIES FOUNDATION

TIMBER PRESS
P.O. Box 1631
Beaverton, Oregon 97075

Library of Congress Cataloging in Publication Data

Davidian, H. H.
    The Rhododendron species.

    Contents: v. 1. Lepidote Rhododendrons.
    Includes index.
    1. Rhododendron. I. Title.
SB413.R47D258   583'.62   81-23232
ISBN 0-917304-71-3   AACR2

Contents

6

MONGOLIA

CHINA

NEPAL

KATHMANDU ■

SIKKIM

BHUTAN

INDIA

BANGLA
DESH

CALCUTTA ■

BURMA

HANOI ■

LAOS

BAY OF BENGAL

RANGOON ■

THAILAND

MADRAS ■

KHMER REP.

VIETNAM

SRĪ LANKA

KUALALUMPUR

SOUTH EAST ASIA

Scale: 1″ = 370 Miles
1″ = 595 Km.

0   160   320   640   960   1280   1600 Km.

80   185   370   480   740   925 Miles

SUMATRA

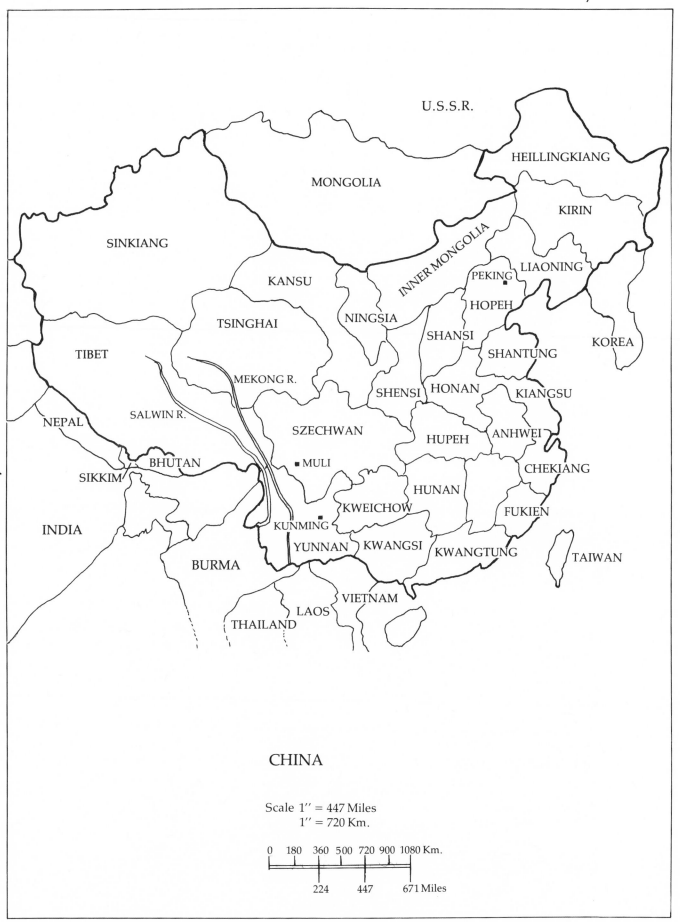

CHINA

Scale 1″ = 447 Miles
1″ = 720 Km.

0   180   360 500 720 900 1080 Km.

224   447   671 Miles

List of Colour Plates

(Following page 48)

List of Black and White Photographs

by J.F. Rock

List of Line Drawings

Foreword

With great satisfaction, we greet this part of Mr. H. H. Davidian's *The Rhododendron Species*. In breadth and thoroughness this study of the genus is without equal. It is the first detailed taxonomic treatment since *The Species of Rhododendron* (1930, 2nd edition 1947), providing technical descriptions of all species, subspecies, and varieties of rhododendron recognized by the author. Combined with this formal botany is a wealth of practical horticulture. Garden use and value, cultural considerations, and notable forms of the species are part of the information offered here. For the Rhododendron Species Foundation, dedicated in part to the dissemination of knowledge about species, this work is welcome indeed.

We also derive pleasure from the publication of this volume by virtue of our own association with Mr. Davidian. On two occasions, first in 1975 soon after the Foundation had moved to our permanent home, and in 1980 after our period of rapid expansion, he spent long days examining our plant collection and providing assessments, innumerable guidelines for identifying species, and recommendations of forms which we should add. Within these few days Mr. Davidian accomplished as much to correct and further the RSF collection as any other individual. Witness to his activity in this region is provided by Peter Cox, writing of *R. elegantulum* in *The Larger Species of Rhododendron* "Rather to my surprise, I saw several plants of this species correctly named in the Seattle area . . ." [p. 270] Now, with *The Rhododendron Species* such valuable assistance is proferred to all.

We applaud the appearance of this work particularly as the culmination of a career devoted to rhododendrons. Mr. H. H. Davidian spent years studying herbarium specimens and reconsidering the taxonomy of the genus and producing, singly and with Dr. J. Macqueen Cowan, several partial revisions while at the Royal Botanic Garden Edinburgh. He has studied many of the living collections in Scotland and England, gaining knowledge of species and forms in cultivation and observing their performance in gardens. How fortunate we are to have the essence of this devotion preserved. And honored we are to sponsor *The Rhododendron Species*, the most comprehensive study ever offered on the genus.

Karen Gunderson
Rhododendron Species Foundation
Federal Way, Washington, U.S.A.

Acknowledgments

I wish to thank Mr. D. M. Henderson, Regius Keeper of the Royal Botanic Garden, Edinburgh, for all his kindness.

My deepest and special gratitude is due to my lawyer Mr. William D. Davidson, W.S. who gave so much of his valuable time in making all the detailed arrangements with the publisher. I appreciate the interest he took in this book, and for devoting so many hours to the reading of the proofs.

I should like to express my deep appreciation to Miss Dorothea E. Purves for all her assistance and proof reading. As Plant Records Officer she was most helpful at all times.

My sincere thanks are extended to Mrs. Eileen M. D. Wood for her excellent and immaculate typing of the whole manuscript, and for so kindly reading the proofs.

I wish to acknowledge a debt of deep gratitude to Miss Helen Jackson for her beautiful line drawings Nos. 2, 3, 4, 5, 6, 9, 10, 11, 12, 13, 14, 15, 16, 17, 18, 19, 20, 21, 23, 24, 25, 26, 27, 28, 29, 30, 33, 34, and to Mrs. Rodella A. Purves for her charming line drawings Nos. 1, 7, 8, 22, 31, 32, 35.

I am also most grateful to Mr. Hamish Gunn for supplying a large number of colour slides.

General Introduction

Much has been written on the classification of the species of Rhododendron. In 1870 Maximowicz provided the taxonomy of 34 species in his *Rhododendrae Asiae Orientalis*, in which he classified the species into seven sections. Another classification was produced by Sir Joseph D. Hooker in 1880 in *Flora of British India*, Vol. III; he dealt with 43 species, the vast majority of which he had discovered in Sikkim in the course of his Himalayan explorations of 1848—1851. Other classifications appeared in the course of years.

It may be noted that during the latter half of the 19th. century the French missionaries in China were responsible for the discovery of several rhododendrons, and these were named and described by Franchet in Paris. As yet the wealth of the flora of western China was still unknown.

In 1899 Wilson collected in Szechuan and Hupeh. In 1904 which is a landmark in the history of plant hunting, Forrest went to Yunnan and in the course of seven expeditions he collected a large number of rhododendrons. He was quickly followed by Kingdon-Ward, Farrer, Rock and later by Ludlow and Sherriff. It was this enterprising and brave band of collectors who were responsible for the great influx of species during the first half of the present century.

Meanwhile Sir Isaac Bayley Balfour, assisted by Sir W. W. Smith and Mr. H. F. Tagg described many new species, named all the magnificent collections arriving in overwhelming quantities, and at the same time worked upon a new classification, laying the foundation of *The Species of Rhododendron*. It may be noted that during the years 1910—1920, some three hundred and twelve new species were described in *Notes from the Royal Botanic Garden, Edinburgh*. Balfour arranged the species in groups or Series, each Series being named after a well-known or representative species, together with those species which appeared to be most closely related to it. It should be noted that during this period there was tremendous enthusiasm and interest in the cultivation of new rhododendrons from China. The gardeners were in need of some kind of a guide to enable them to become acquainted with the large number of rhododendrons they were cultivating. It must be stated that without their untiring efforts the present woodland garden, with its large collection of rhododendrons, would not have been possible. What they have achieved is evident in Caerhays, Exbury, Muncaster, Bodnant, Tower Court, Lochinch, Blackhills, Benmore, and many other gardens.

Balfour's scheme of classification was adopted by the Rhododendron Society. In 1924 a list of species in their Series excluding Malayan, Indonesian and New Guinea species was compiled by Edinburgh and circulated (*The Rhododendron Society Notes*, Vol. II, 1924, pp. 215—227). In 1928, the list was emended (*Rhod. Soc. Notes*, Vol. V, 1928, pp. 209—219), and formed the basis of the classification in *The Species of Rhododendron* which was published in 1930 by the Rhododendron Society. The book was written jointly by Dr. J. Hutchinson of Kew, who dealt with the lepidote rhododendrons, Mr. H. F. Tagg of the Royal Botanic Garden, Edinburgh, who treated the elepidote rhododendrons, and Dr. A. Rehder of the Arnold Arboretum, who was responsible for the azaleas. Much was due to the guidance of Sir W. W. Smith of the Royal Botanic Garden, Edinburgh. The book was published under the editorship of Mr. J. B. Stevenson of Tower Court. In this work, each species was given a description, accompanied sometimes by an illustration, and keys were provided to the species of each Series, but unfortunately no key to the Series themselves was given. The book was universally recognised as the standard work on rhododendrons. It was a magnificent work, an outstanding achievement, and was much used in naming herbarium specimens and plants in cultivation.

After the publication of *The Species of Rhododendron* in 1930, the period of active collecting was continued by Kingdon-Ward, Rock, Ludlow and Sherriff together with Taylor, Hicks or Elliot, and by Yü, who sent large quantities of Rhododendron specimens, and introduced into cultivation a rich harvest of new species and new forms in an ever-increasing stream. By about the middle of the present century it was necessary to make certain changes in *The Species of Rhododendron*; the descriptions of the species had to be emended and amplified, and new keys to the species of each Series had to be provided; some re-arrangement of the present Series and Subseries was apparently necessary. Accordingly, in 1947, Dr. J. M. Cowan and I took up the revision of the same book, involving a detailed examination of herbarium specimens and cultivated plants, and a thorough investigation that a revision requires. In our first review, as a first instalment towards the revision, we reconstituted the Anthopogon and Cephalanthum Series by uniting them into one, to be known as the Anthopogon Series. This was followed by the revisions of the Boothii, Glaucophyllum, Lepidotum, Campanulatum, Fulvum, and Thomsonii Series, and all these were published in the Royal Horticultural Society's *Rhododendron Year Book* of 1947, 1948, 1949, and 1951—1952 respectively.

In 1954 Dr. Cowan retired and left, to be in charge of Inverewe garden, a property of the Scottish National Trust. It now remained to me to continue the whole revision of *The Species of Rhododendron* single-handed. Every year one long Series or two short Series were revised; once again I went over the Series that had already been revised jointly, and the revision of all the Series was completed in the course of years. Some of the early instalments such as, Campylogynum, Saluenense, Lacteum, Triflorum, Auriculatum, Griersonianum, Edgeworthii, Scabrifolium, and Virgatum Series, were published in *The Rhododendron and Camellia Year Book* of 1954, 1956, 1963, and 1964.

Now we must decide upon a choice of a suitable classification for rhododendrons. When *The Species of Rhododendron* is examined, it will be seen that the species are listed in 43 groups or Series according to whether the branchlets, leaves and flowers are scaly or not scaly. The presence or absence of scales has been regarded as a fundamental distinction in the classification of Rhododendrons, a criterion of great importance. Accordingly, the species are divided into two large divisions, Lepidote (scaly) and Elepidote (non-scaly). This arrangement is not explicitly stated, but it is well understood. The question now arises: Are we to accept this classification or are we to substitute some other classification in its place? Before we answer this question, let us investigate this classification and evaluate the merits of the two large divisions as follows:

First. In *The Species of Rhododendron*, as already stated above, 43 Series have been recorded: 23 Lepidote (scaly) Series and 20 Elepidote (non-scaly) Series. Therefore, according to the presence or absence of scales, we have two large divisions of Rhododendrons of almost equal size, namely, Lepidote (scaly) and Elepidote (non-scaly). In other words, two large natural divisions — a natural classification.

Second. Kingdon-Ward, a great collector, who made a thorough study and a detailed examination of a large number of Rhododendron seeds, points out in *The Rhododendron Year Book* 1947, p. 100, that "all Rhododendron seeds belong to one of three well-marked types:

1. Alpine type. (Seed wingless, rounded or angular).
2. Forest type. (Seed flattened, winged all round, about twice as long as broad).
3. Epiphytic type. (Seed spindle shaped, with end tails 4—6 times as long as broad).

Therefore, taking the seed type as a basis of classification, Kingdon-Ward points out that all lepidote (scaly) rhododendrons have Alpine or Epiphytic type of seed, except a few species of the Maddenii Series, and all elepidote (non-scaly) rhododendrons (except Ovatum, Stamineum, Albiflorum Series, and part of Azaleas) have the Forest type of seed. Seed characters are of course very variable. However, it is apparent, with few exceptions, that we have two large natural divisions of Rhododendrons, namely, Lepidote (scaly) and Elepidote (non-scaly).

Third. In 1919 Sir Isaac Bayley Balfour found that there are two types of bud-construction in rhododendrons, convolute in lepidote species, and revolute in elepidote species (*Notes Roy. Bot. Gard. Edin.*, XII (1919) pp. 49—50). He points out that this difference in bud-construction is primary and must be taken into account in any scheme of subdivision of Rhododendrons, and that species with revolute ptyxis must belong to a different division from those with convolute. In 1937, J. Sinclair examined a large number of species of Rhododendron to find out whether this division character was an absolute one and whether any other types of leaf-folding in the bud occurred (*Notes Roy. Bot. Gard. Edin.*, Vol. 19 (1937) pp. 267—271). He found that Lepidote Series have convolute buds, "both scale leaves and foliage leaves are convolute. There is no very sharp differentiation between the last bud-scale and the first foliage-leaf". Whereas the Elepidote Series have revolute buds, "the bud-scales form a definite chamber at the bottom of which the young leaves develop . . . in the centre of this chamber stand the revolute foliage leaves". It is found that the only exception to this rule is *R. pendulum* Hook, f. in the Edgeworthii Series with revolute buds. Sinclair concludes that in the division of Rhododendrons based on the presence or absence of scales, the bud character is equally a fundamental one, and that these two characters, scales and bud-construction, are related one to the other.

In other words, we have two large natural divisions of Rhododendrons based on bud-construction, namely, Lepidote (scaly), and Elepidote (non-scaly).

Fourth. In 1930 when Sir W. W. Smith and assistants produced that invaluable book *The Species of Rhododendron*, we wonder if they realised then how important the two divisions Lepidote and Elepidote would eventually become to the hybridizer. These two divisions of Rhododendron are now well known to the hybridizer. He knows that he can cross Lepidote species with Lepidote, and Elepidote with Elepidote; but he also knows well that he cannot cross Lepidote with Elepidote. So far as is known only one authentic hybrid between a Lepidote and an Elepidote species has ever been crossed, namely, *R. griersonianum* × *R. dalhousiae* 'Grierdal', raised by Admiral Walker Heneage-Vivian in 1937. It is possible that one or two other hybrids between Lepidote and Elepidote species have been produced, but not officially recognised. Many attempts have been made to cross the two groups, but unsuccessfully. It is apparent that Lepidote and Elepidote rhododendrons repel one another and will not cross; they are incompatible. Therefore, we have two large natural divisions of Rhododendrons, Lepidote (scaly) and Elepidote (non-scaly).

Fifth. In 1946 Dr. J. Hutchinson gave an account of "The Evolution and Classification of Rhododendrons" in the *Rhododendron Year Book*, 1946, pp. 42—48. In this article Hutchinson shows the probable course of evolution of the Series of Rhododendron, and his theory is illustrated by a chart in the form of a "family tree". Although the whole subject is speculative, it is interesting to see how far the evidence of the presence or absence of the scale supports Hutchinson's classification of Rhododendrons. From this "family tree", it will be seen that Lepidote (scaly) and Elepidote (non-scaly) Series are two large natural divisions of Rhododendrons.

In 1947 Dr. Hutchinson, when discussing the evolution of Rhododendrons (*The Rhododendron Year Book* 1947, p. 94), refers to the Lepidote and Elepidote Rhododendrons as follows: "Certainly they have diverged sufficiently to render cross-fertilisation between members of the two groups extremely difficult". This point was discussed above.

Sixth. We now come to another interesting distinction between Lepidote and Elepidote Rhododenrons, namely, polyploidy. A detailed account of this subject by Dr. E. K. Janaki Ammal will be found in *The Rhododendron Year Book* 1950, pp. 92—96. Dr. J.

Hutchinson's phylogenetic "family tree" has been used as the framework on which Dr. Janaki Ammal has superimposed the type of polyploidy found in the Series. It will be seen that all the Elepidote Series (excluding *R. canadense* and *R. calendulaceum* in the Azalea Series) are diploids, $2n = 26$; the only other exception is an aberrant triploid seedling which was found in cultivation at Tower Court, namely, *R. diaprepes* 'Gargantua', $2n = 39$. But when the Lepidote Series on the chart is examined, it is noted that polyploids occur in eight out of twenty-four recorded Series. Altogether 78 polyploids have been found representing more than a third of the species in which counts had been made. It is shown that the degree of polyploidy ranges from triploids $2n = 39$ to dodecaploids $2n = 156$, and that the most prevalent type is the tetraploid $2n = 52$, with 44 species, next are the hexaploids $2n = 78$, 22 in number, triploids being rare. It is apparent that strong cytological support is given to Hutchinson's classification of Rhododendrons. In other words, polyploidy is an important aid in classifying Rhododendrons into two large natural divisions, Lepidote (scaly) and Elepidote (non-scaly).

From the above account of the classification of Rhododendrons, it is abundantly and convincingly clear that there are two large natural divisions of almost equal size in Rhododendrons, namely, Lepidote (scaly) and Elepidote (non-scaly).

Within the Elepidote division, there are three other distinct groups of Rhododendrons, namely, Azalea, Azaleastrum, and Camtschaticum.

Azalea. This is a large group of about 78 elepidote species which are characterised by the frequent presence of strigose (unbranched) hairs on the branchlets, leaves, and ovary. The majority of the species are deciduous. The evergreen species have dimorphic leaves consisting of two different forms known as spring leaves and summer leaves. The spring leaves fall off in the autumn. The summer leaves unfold in early summer, and are small and thicker, persisting in winter as clusters at the tips of the shoots. The inflorescence is one- to many-flowered, and the stamens vary in number from 5 to 10. The seeds are variable and fall into Kingdon-Ward's two well-defined groups, Alpine type, as in the Lepidotes, and Forest type, the Elepidotes.

In the "family tree," a chart which is designed to show the probable course of evolution of Rhododendrons (*The Rhododendron Year Book* 1947, p. 46), Dr. Hutchinson points out that it is probable Azaleas have been evolved independently of the other two groups, Lepidote and Elepidote.

According to Dr. E. K. Janaki Ammal (*The Rhododendron Year Book* 1950, pp. 80—81), all the species of Azalea are diploids $2n = 26$, except *R. canadense* and *R. calendulaceum* which are tetraploids $2n = 52$.

Azaleastrum (or "False Azaleas"). This group consists of four elepidote Series. Two of these are deciduous shrubs, namely, Albiflorum and Semibarbatum Series; the other two are evergreen, Ovatum and Stamineum Series. The main diagnostic feature of the group is that the inflorescence is axillary with single or paired flowers, (variable in the Stamineum Series from one to several flowers). The stamens are 5 or 10 in number. The seeds belong to the Alpine and Epiphytic types, as in the Lepidotes. (Seed type of Semibarbatum is unknown). According to Hutchinson's chart showing the probable course of evolution, the Azaleastrums are placed at the bottom of a branch which may have arisen independently of the Elepidote group. The Albiflorum, Ovatum, and Semibarbatum Series are recorded as being diploid $2n = 26$. (There is no record of the chromosome number of the Stamineum Series).

Camtschaticum. This group comprises a single elepidote Series with three species. These are dwarf, low-growing shrubs up to 15 cm. (6 in.) high, with chartaceous, obovate, spathulate-obovate, oval or ovate leaves. The characteristic feature of this group is that the flowers arise singly or up to three at the end of the young leafy shoots of the current year, and not from special buds. *R. camtschaticum* is recorded as being diploid 2n = 26. (The chromosome numbers of the other two species are unknown).

As already stated above, in *The Species of Rhododendron* the species are classified into groups known as Series. The question now arises: Are we to retain the name "Series" or are we to substitute it with another term? Before this question is answered, it would be desirable to investigate more closely the degree of variation within the Series. Although the two large divisions of Rhododendrons, Lepidote (scaly) and Elepidote (non-scaly), are distinguished by hard and fast characters, yet within most of the Series, there is considerable variation in habit and height of growth, in leaf shape and size, in flower shape, size and colour, and in other characters. And indeed, the degree of variation is so great, and the fact that the Series merge into each other to such an extent that it is impossible to draw up an analytical Key to the Series without repeating each Series less than four or five times or more. Extreme variation in most Series is the rule rather than the exception. Having made several attempts, I found it impossible to draw up a concise Key to the Series in view of this great variation. Although I produced a Key on page 42, I had to introduce most of the Subseries in more than one section of the Key.

It may be noted that in the Introduction to *The Species of Rhododendron*, it has been acknowledged that "lines of demarcation between one series and another are sometimes definite, but in other cases very difficult to draw", also "The species in some series fall into line readily and easily; in some they almost defy analysis and alignment". Moreover, throughout the same book, frequent reference is made to "aberrant" species. It is apparent that the authors of *The Species of Rhododendron* were aware of the great variation in each Series and that the Series merged into each other to such an extent that it was impossible to draw hard and fast dividing lines between them. It was due to this merging of the Series that no analytical Key to the Series was provided in *The Species of Rhododendron*. It was this linkage, and indeed it was this continuity between the Series which made the making of a concise Key to the Series impracticable. Accordingly, Sir William W. Smith, and his assistants, had no hesitation in retaining the name "Series" for each group of species. They knew well the meaning of the word "Series" which according to the Oxford Dictionary and other dictionaries, means "join", "succession", "continuity". We ask: what better term is there to denote this unity, succession or continuity of these groups of Rhododendrons than "Series"?

In the proposed new classification by Cullen and Chamberlain, the groups known as Series have been eliminated, and replaced with the term Subsection. It should be emphasised that such terminology as Subsection might imply to gardeners and some others an inflexible, well-defined boundary with no latitude, and this conflicts with the arrangement of the species in groups known as Series which, as already mentioned above, indicates merging, linkage, and continuity.

We are now faced with the problem of classification and the gardeners. It should be noted that during the first quarter of the present century there was a great influx of species from western China. Large quantities of Rhododendron seed were received from collectors, and were distributed to share holders. Records show that from 1910—1914, not only seed but also large numbers of seedlings raised from Forrest's and Wilson's seed were distributed to gardeners. This early period, from the year 1902 onwards, was one of unparalleled activity on the part of gardeners who were raising rhododendrons in the thousands. The achievements of the collectors and the response of the gardeners in raising the plants, produced a complete revolution of gardening. The gardeners raised so many plants that it was found necessary to have these accommodated beyond their garden walls which gradually became the woodland garden as we know it today. It should be mentioned that the gardeners needed a guide to help them with their rhododendrons. Sir Isaac Bayley Balfour now appeared on the scene. He was well aware of the requirements of the gardeners. As already discussed above, he devised a system of classification which would be easy for the gardeners, convenient and of practical use, and applicable at all seasons. He thus laid the foundation of *The Species of Rhododendron*. Balfour's scheme was received with great favour by the gardeners, and was adopted by the Rhododendron Society.

During the past fifty years, *The Species of Rhododendron* has been very helpful and most useful to gardeners. It must be emphasised that during this period the gardeners, propagators, nurserymen, hybridizers, and all those involved in gardening, have found the classification Lepidote (scaly) and Elepidote (non-scaly) immensely useful and most practical in their activities. Moreover, they have found the same classification easy to use. But why has it been found easy to use? The answer is: because it is a natural classification, Lepidote (scaly), Elepidote (non-scaly). Furthermore, all these gardeners are perfectly happy and satisfied with this classification, and during the past fifty years there has hardly been any gardener who has complained about it. Assuming that gardeners were persuaded to change their concept of Rhododendron classification, Lepidote (scaly) and Elepidote (non-scaly), and replace it with an artificial system, undoubtedly they would find the change over most confusing and difficult to understand.

It may be of interest to make a few remarks on some of the items of the revisions suggested by Sleumer, Cullen and Chamberlain, the Philipsons, and the R.H.S. Horticultural Revision.

1. According to Sleumer, in his revision of the Maddenii Series, seven species appear in synonymy under *R. lyi* Lévl. Four of these, namely, *R. johnstoneanum* Watt ex Hutch., *R. parryae* Hutch., *R. ciliipes* Hutch. and *R. scottianum* Hutch. are very distinct species and well merit specific status. Sleumer's decision is not acceptable.

2. In his revision of the Cinnabarinum Series, Cullen has placed *R. concatenans* Hutch., and *R. cinnabarinum* Hook. f. var. *purpurellum* Cowan in synonymy under a combined name "*R. cinnabarinum* subsp. *xanthocodon* (Hutch.) Cullen". This conclusion is impossible to accept. *R. concatenans* with its large apricot bell-shaped flowers cannot be confused with *R. cinnabarinum* nor with the yellow-flowered *R. xanthocodon*. Similarly var. *purpurellum* with its plum-purple flowers is a very distinct plant.

3. According to Cullen, *R. radicans* Balf. f. et Forrest, is now synonymous with a combined name "*R. calostrotum* Balf. f. et Ward subsp. *keleticum* (Balf. f. et Forrest) Cullen". This proposal is inadmissible. *R. radicans* is a creeper only a few inches high. From *R. calostrotum* it is very remote, and from *R. keleticum* it differs markedly in its habit and height of growth.

4. In Chamberlain's revision of the Irroratum Series, *R. hardingii* Forrest, and *R. laxiflorum* Balf. f. et Forrest have been equated with *R. annae* Franch. This suggestion is insupportable. *R. hardingii* and *R. laxiflorum* are so markedly different from *R. annae*, and are so distinctive in cultivation, that they well merit specific rank.

5. In the Philipsons' revision of the Lapponicum Series, *R. paludosum* Hutch. et Ward appears in synonymy under the name "*R. nivale* Hook. f. subsp. *nivale* (Hook. f.)". This decision is not acceptable. *R. paludosum*, in cultivation, is readily distinguished from *R. nivale*, in habit and height of growth, in leaf shape and size, and in the colour of the leaves.

6. In their revision of the Lapponicum Series, the Philipsons have described two new subspecies, namely, "*R. nivale* Hook. f. subsp. *boreale* Philipson et Philipson, and *R. nivale* Hook. f. subsp. *australe* Philipson et Philipson".

Under subsp. *boreale*, ten described species have been placed in synonymy. Four of these names — *R. batangense* Balf. f., *R. oreinum* Balf. f., *R. yaragongense* Balf. f., and *R. vicarium* Balf. f. — have already been reduced by Hutchinson to synonymy under other members of this Series. But the remaining six — *R. nigropunctatum* Bur. et Franch., *R. ramosissimum* Franch., *R. alpicola* Rehd. et Wils., *R. violaceum* Rehd. et Wils., *R. oresbium* Balf. f. et Ward, and *R. stictophyllum* Balf. f. — are so remarkably distinct in cultivation and differ so markedly from *R. nivale*, that each of these definitely merits specific rank. The proposed "subsp. *boreale*" by the Philipsons and the combination of several species in synonymy, is impossible to accept.

As for subsp. *australe*, it is an aggregation of 29 specimens collected by Forrest, Rock, and Yü, and which had been correctly determined as *R. impeditum*, *R. stictophyllum*, *R. diacritum* and other species. All these plants, as in subsp. *boreale*, differing widely in height of growth, in leaf shape and size and in other characters, have been amalgamated by the Philipsons under subsp. *australe* for which there is no justification. Accordingly "subsp. *boreale*" constituted by the Philipsons is definitely not acceptable.

7. According to Sleumer and Chamberlain, the Lacteum Series and Taliense Series are now united into a single large mixed group of 65 species, and all four Subseries in the Taliense Series have been eliminated. This decision cannot be accepted.

8. In Cullen's revision of the Trichocladum Series, *R. viridescens* Hutch. appears as a synonym of *R. mekongense* Franch. This conclusion is not acceptable. *R. viridescens* is a remarkably distinct species and differs so markedly from *R. mekongense* that it well merits specific rank. It should be emphasised that *R. mekongense* is completely deciduous, the flowers are precocious, the corolla is campanulate or tubular-campanulate, the under surface of the leaves is usually slightly glaucous, the branchlets are not bristly or somewhat bristly, and moreover, the flowers appear in May; whereas *R. viridescens* is evergreen, the flowers are not precocious, the corolla is funnel-campanulate, the under surface of the leaves is pale green, the branchlets are moderately or rather densely bristly, and moreover, the plant is a late flowerer, the flowers appearing usually in June.

9. According to R.H.S. Horticultural Revision which is based on Cullen and Chamberlain's classification, it is recommended (*The Rhododendron Handbook* 1980, page 27) that *R. viridescens* should now be known as *R. mekongense* var. *mekongense* Viridescens Group. This recommendation is impossible to accept; similarly Brickell's proposal of the "Group system" is also not acceptable.

It must now be stated that Sleumer's classification of Rhododendrons and revision of the Maddenii Series, Cullen and Chamberlain's classification and revision of the Series, the Philipsons' revision of the Lapponicum Series, and the R.H.S. Horticultural Revision based on Cullen and Chamberlain's classification, are not acceptable in this book, and will not be recognised.

As to the classification of Rhododendrons, excluding Malaysian Rhododendrons, the Series will now be placed in the following groups:

Lepidote (scaly) Rhododendrons
Elepidote (non-scaly) Rhododendrons
Azalea
Azaleastrum, 4 Series: Albiflorum Series, Ovatum Series, Semibarbatum Series, and Stamineum Series.
Camtschaticum, 1 Series, 3 species.

How fortunate we are that men of such eminence, as Sir Isaac Bayley Balfour, Sir William W. Smith, Dr. J. Hutchinson, Dr. Alfred Rehder, and Mr. H. F. Tagg, have been responsible for providing a most useful book, *The Species of Rhododendron*, and laying the foundation of a natural classification of Rhododendrons, Lepidote (scaly) and Elepidote (non-scaly). These men devoted a considerable number of years and much attention to the study of Rhododendrons before they put their profound knowledge into the monumental work, *The Species of Rhododendron*, which they produced in 1930, with the aim of facilitating the recognition of Rhododendrons. These men knew Rhododendrons; they knew well not only herbarium specimens but also cultivated plants. In so far as Rhododendrons and their horticulture is concerned, these men were giants. It is most appropriate to pay tribute to their outstanding achievement, and express our deep gratitude and thanks.

Open situations on the Lichiang Range. Photo J.F. Rock

Glossary

Acuminate. Tapering into a point.

Acute. Pointed.

Adpressed. Lying flat.

Agglutinate. Glued.

Alveola. Cavity.

Anther. The part of the stamen containing the pollen grains.

Apex. Tip.

Appressed. See adpressed.

Auricle. An ear-like appendage.

Axillary. Arising in the angle formed by the junction of leaf and stem.

Bullate. Puckered or blistered.

Campanulate. Bell-shaped.

Capitate. Collected in a dense knob-like head or cluster.

Chromosome. Rod-like portion of the cell-nucleus which determines hereditary characteristics.

Ciliate. With fine hairs.

Clone. The vegetatively produced progeny of a single individual.

Contiguous. Touching.

Cordate. With two round lobes at the base forming a deep recess at the base.

Coriaceous. Leathery.

Crenulate. Margin notched, with rounded teeth, scalloped.

Cultivar. Cultivated variety as distinct from other varieties.

Cuneate. Wedge-shaped.

Decurrent. Extended below the point of insertion.

Deflexed. Bent downwards.

Dichotomous. Divided in pairs.

Eciliate. Without fine hairs.

Eglandular. Not glandular.

Elepidote. Not scaly.

Emarginate. With a notch at the end.

Entire. Margin undivided.

Epiphyte. A plant growing on another plant without being parasitic.

Epiphytic. Growing on another plant without being parasitic.

Fastigiate. With erect branches.

Filament. The stalk bearing the anther.

Floccose. With soft woolly hairs.

Glabrous. Without hairs.

Glandular. With glands.

Glaucous. Covered with greyish waxy bloom.

Globose. Spherical.

Hirsute. Covered with stiff long erect hairs.

Imbricate. Overlapping each other at the margins.

Indumentum. A hairy covering, particularly of the lower surface of the leaves.

Lamina. Blade.

Lepidote. Scaly.

Mucro. A hard sharp point.

Mucronate. Terminated by a hard sharp point.

Nectary. A gland through which a solution of sugar is secreted.

Obtuse. Blunt.

Papillate. Pimpled; covered with minute pimples.

Pedicel. Flower-stalk.

Petiole. Leaf-stalk.

Pilose. Covered wih soft long hairs.

Plastered indumentum. Indumentum skin-like with a smooth, polished surface.

Polyploid. With more than the diploid (2n) number of chromosomes.

Precocious. Flowers produced before the leaves appear.

Puberulous. Minutely pubescent.

Pubescent. Hairy with short soft hairs.

Punctulate. Minutely dotted.

Racemose. Flowers borne on an unbranched main stalk.

Recurved. Curved backwards.

Reflexed. Bent abruptly backwards.

Reticulate. Netted, like a network.

Revolute. Rolled backwards.

Rhachis. The part of the inflorescence bearing the flowers.

Rotate. A very short tube with spreading almost flat petals.

Rugose. Wrinkled.

Rugulose. Somewhat wrinkled.

Salver-shaped. With a long slender tube, and flat spreading petals.
Scabrid. Rough to the touch.
Scale. Minute disc-like object found on branchlets, leaves and flowers.
Sessile. Without a stalk.
Setose. Bristly; with stiff hairs.
Spathulate. With a broadly rounded apex gradually tapering into the stalk.
Stigma. A small pollen-receptive surface at the tip of the style.
Stoloniferous. Bearing runners from near the base of the stem, often below the surface of the soil.

Style. The thread-like part of a gynoecium (pistil) between the ovary and stigma.
Tapered. Lengthening, gradually decreasing in breadth.
Terminal. At the end of a shoot.
Tomentum. Dense hair covering.
Truncate. Straight across.
Undulate. Having a wavy margin.
Ventricose. Swollen on one side.
Villous. With long soft straight hairs.
Zygomorphic. Flower of irregular shape which can be divided into equal halves along one vertical line only.

Leaf Shapes

Linear. Narrow, with parallel opposite sides, the ends tapering, at least 10—12 times as long as broad, e.g. *R. trichostomum.*

Lanceolate. Lance-shaped, widest below the middle, the length of the leaf about three times the breadth, e.g. *R. griersonianum, R. yunnanense.*

Oblanceolate. Base tapering, apex broad, widest above the middle, the length of the leaf about three times the breadth, e.g. *R. fulvum, R. uvarifolium.*

Oblong. The sides more or less parallel, the ends obtuse or somewhat rounded, the length of the leaf is twice the breadth, e.g. *R. selense, R. cerasinum.*

Elliptic. The sides of the leaf are curved tapering equally to tip and base, widest at the middle, the length of the leaf is twice the breadth, e.g. *R. ciliatum* a form, *R. wallichii* a form.

Obovate. The sides are curved, apex rounded, base narrower, widest above the middle, length is about twice the breadth, e.g. *R. lanatum* a form, *R. tsariense* a form.

Ovate. The sides are curved, widest at the base, the tip narrowed, the length is greater than the breadth, e.g. *R. edgeworthii* a form, *R. wasonii.*

Oval. The sides are curved, rounded at both ends, widest at the middle, longer than broad, e.g. *R. callimorphum, R. leucaspis* a form.

Orbicular. Circular, e.g. *R. orbiculare.*

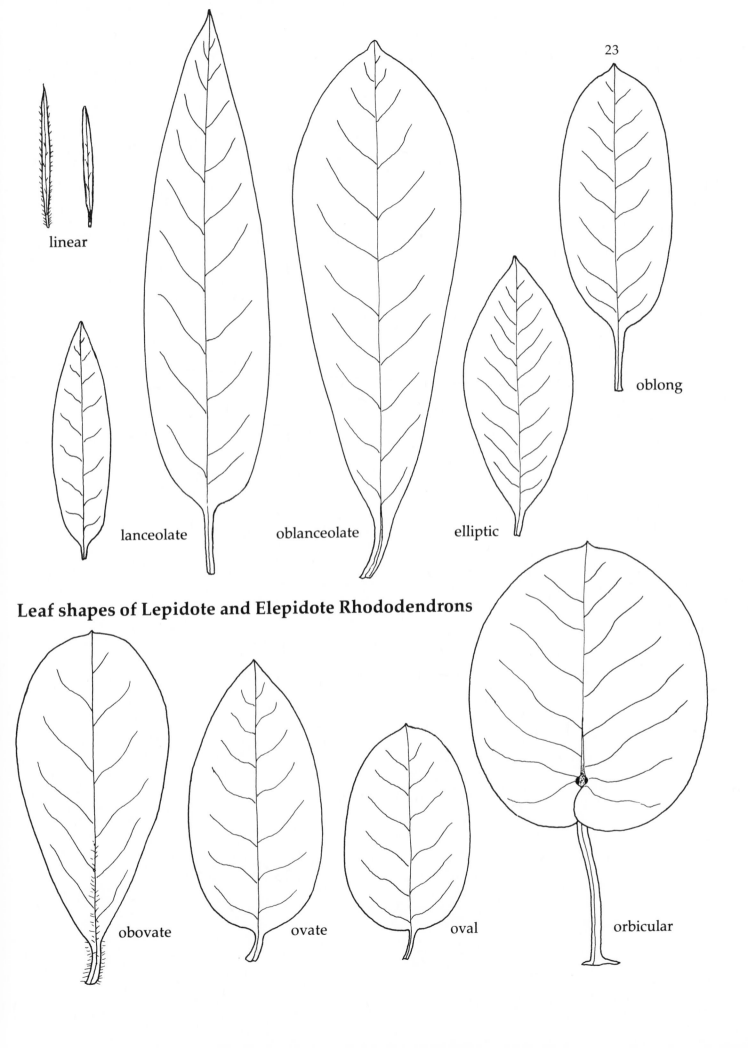

linear

23

oblong

lanceolate   oblanceolate   elliptic

Leaf shapes of Lepidote and Elepidote Rhododendrons

obovate   ovate   oval   orbicular

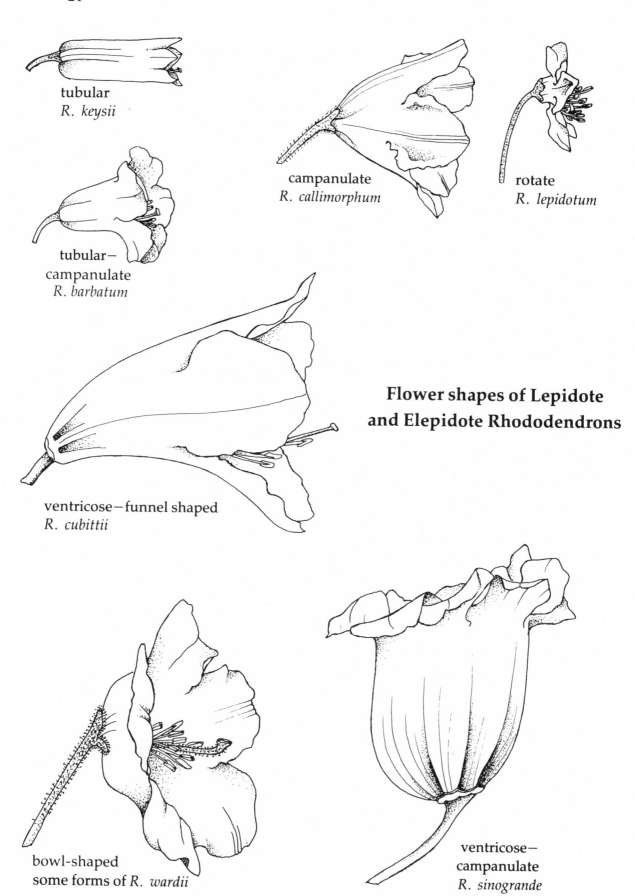

tubular
R. keysii

campanulate
R. callimorphum

rotate
R. lepidotum

tubular—
campanulate
R. barbatum

**Flower shapes of Lepidote
and Elepidote Rhododendrons**

ventricose—funnel shaped
R. cubittii

bowl-shaped
some forms of *R. wardii*

ventricose—
campanulate
R. sinogrande

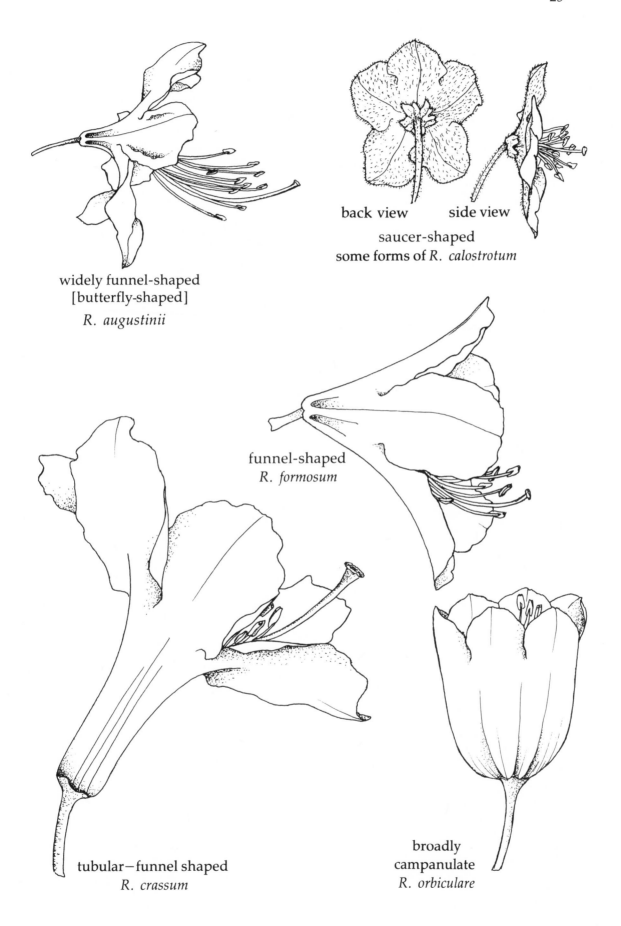

widely funnel-shaped
[butterfly-shaped]
R. augustinii

back view   side view
saucer-shaped
some forms of *R. calostrotum*

funnel-shaped
R. formosum

tubular–funnel shaped
R. crassum

broadly
campanulate
R. orbiculare

Scales

Entire: *R. crassum*

× 125
viewed from above

Undulate: *R. impeditum*

× 137
viewed from above

Lacerate: *R. anthopogon*

× 125
viewed from above

Crenulate: *R. saluenense*

× 125
viewed from above

Vesicular: *R. trichocladum*

× 125
viewed from above

R. trichocladum

× 80
viewed from side

Seeds

Alpine type : *R. cinnabarinum*

× 40 − 50

Alpine type: *R. yunnanense*

× 40 − 50

Epiphytic type: *R. vaccinioides*   × 40 − 50

Epiphytic type: *R. ciliicalyx*

Forest type: *R. falconeri*

   × 40

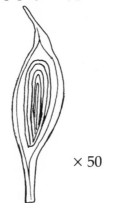

× 50

Forest type: *R. campanulatum*

× 40

Forest type: *R. thomsonii*

Hardiness

H4   Hardy anywhere in the British Isles.
H3   Hardy in the west, east and south, and inland but requires shelter.
H2   Suitable for sheltered gardens in the west coast.
H1   Usually a greenhouse plant.

Award Systems

BRITISH AWARDS

First Class Certificate. F.C.C. Given on the recommendation of the Rhododendron and Camellia Committee to rhododendrons of great excellence. Given at Shows or after trial at Wisley.

Award of Merit. A.M. Given on the recommendation of the Rhododendron and Camellia Committee to rhododendrons which are meritorious. Given at Shows or after trial at Wisley.

Preliminary Commendation. P.C. Given on the recommendation of the Rhododendron and Camellia Committee to a new plant of promise, whether a new introduction from abroad or of garden origin. Given at Shows only.

Award of Garden Merit. A.G.M. Given on the recommendation of the Award of Garden Merit Committee to plants which either are well known to the Council, Committees, Garden Staff and Fellows or have been tested and grown at Wisley in the same manner as they would have been grown in the open in a private garden, are of good constitution, and have proved to be excellent for ordinary garden decoration.

AMERICAN AWARDS

Preliminary Award. P.A. Given for a cut flower truss, with foliage, exhibited at a Show, evaluated by three official judges.

Award of Excellence. A.E. Given by a panel of three judges for a complete plant exhibiting superior foliage, flowers and growth habit.

Test Garden Certificate. T.G.C. Given to a Rhododendron which has been propagated vegetatively and seen in flower by three judges for at least two years in one of the recognised test gardens of the American Rhododendron Society.

History of Rhododendron Introductions, Expeditions, and Collectors

The first rhododendron introduced into cultivation was *R. hirsutum* in 1656 from the European Alps. This initial introduction is credited to John Tradescant the younger. In 1734 Peter Collinson of London who had his own private garden at Mill Hill, brought three American azaleas into cultivation, namely, *R. canescens*, *R. nudiflorum* and *R. viscosum*; in 1736 he also introduced *R. maximum*. About 96 years after *R. hirsutum* was introduced from the European Alps, *R. ferrugineum* arrived from the same region in 1752. The next was *R. ponticum* which was brought from Gibraltar in 1763. About this period Pallas, the well-known German traveller, introduced three rhododendrons from Siberia and eastern Europe, *R. dauricum* in 1780, *R. luteum* in 1793 and *R. chrysanthum* in 1796. By the end of the 18th. century, twelve Rhododendron species were known, and ten of these were in cultivation.

Early in the 19th. century in 1801, *R. camtschaticum* was introduced from Russia. In 1803 another well-known species *R. caucasicum* arrived from Asia Minor, and in the same year *R. obtusum* was introduced by the Directors of the East India Company. During this early period, John Fraser, a native of Inverness, made several journeys to America in order to collect plants, and established a nursery at Sloane Square, Chelsea. In 1808 he discovered *R. catawbiense* in North Carolina, U.S.A., and introduced it in 1809.

Dr. Francis Hamilton, later known as Francis Buchanan-Hamilton, whose home was at Leny, Callander, Scotland, deserves the merit for the first introduction of the crimson *R. arboreum* in 1810. He was a former director of the Botanic Garden at Calcutta, and sent seeds of *R. arboreum* when he was stationed on the borders of Nepal. In 1814 Wallich sent seeds of *R. arboreum* f. *album* from the mountain summit of Sheopore, Nepal, and in 1820 he introduced *R. arboreum* f. *roseum* and *R. campbelliae* also from Nepal. It may be of interest to note that Nathaniel Wallich, a medical doctor from Copenhagen, was Superintendent of the Calcutta Botanic Garden from 1816—1841. He sent seeds of rhododendrons in 1820 from his famous expedition to Nepal. At the time the authorities did not allow visitors to go far afield from the capital, Katmandu. Wallich contacted the Indian pilgrims who were visiting the shrine of Gossain Than at 16,000 feet. The specimens which he acquired from them formed the basis of the famous Wallich Catalogue.

In 1820 a consignment of rhododendron seed arrived, including *R. aromaticum* now known as *R. anthopogon* sent by Dr. Hamilton to William McNab who was then Curator of the Royal Botanic Garden, Edinburgh. Two years later, in 1822, Wallich sent seeds of *R. cinnamomeum* from Nepal. In 1823 *R. molle* (Azalea) arrived from China; in 1825 *R. lapponicum* was introduced from Canada by a Mr. Blair, and in the same year *R. setosum* was received from the Himalayas.

Seeds of the common Himalayan species *R. campanulatum* was first sent by Wallich in 1825. Another common Himalayan species known before Hooker's time, namely, *R. barbatum*, arrived probably in 1829. When the Ceylon records are examined, it will be seen that seeds of the only rhododendron *R. zeylanicum* in the island, were received in 1831. The Madras Rhododendron, *R. nilagiricum* which was discovered in the Nilgiris by the Rev. Schmidt was first introduced in 1840.

The main contribution to the cultivation of rhododendrons came early in the second half of the 19th. century when J.D. Hooker explored Sikkim Himalaya, 1848—1851, and in the course of three years he discovered and introduced 30 different species of Rhododendron. These were described by him and illustrated in *Rhododendrons of the Sikkim Himalayas*. It may be noted that he discovered the vast majority of species that exist in Sikkim. The same area has been frequently explored since then by other collectors but very few new species have been discovered. Hooker's introductions include, amongst others, small rhododendrons such as *R. glaucophyllum, R. ciliatum* and *R. lepidotum*; the deliciously scented *R. edgeworthii*; the medium or large-sized *R. cinnabarinum* and its var. *roylei*; the yellow-flowered *R. lanatum* and *R. campylocarpum*; the beautiful *R. dalhousiae* and *R. maddenii*; the crimson *R. thomsonii* and the lilac *R. wallichii*; and small trees like *R. falconeri, R. hodgsonii*, and *R. grande*. In cultivation plants raised from Hooker's seed, may still be seen as large splendid specimens growing at Caerhays, Lochinch, Stonefield and in a few other gardens. It should be noted that prior to Hooker's expedition to Sikkim, Griffith discovered *R. griffithianum* in Bhutan in 1838—9, although it was later introduced by Hooker from Sikkim.

An important event early in the 19th. century was the journey to Chekiang, China, of Robert Fortune. After training at Edinburgh, he was sent out to China by the Royal Horticultural Society. In 1855 he introduced *R. fortunei* from Chekiang, and he also introduced the tea plant from China to India.

During the latter half of the 19th. century, the French Catholic missionaries who were stationed in Western China were responsible for the introduction of only a few species, *R. delavayi, R. racemosum, R. scabrifolium* and *R. augustinii*. The seeds were sent to the Jardins des Plantes and to Maurice L. de Vilmorin's nursery in Paris, and thence the plants arrived at Kew. The great mass of specimens which the missionaries collected in south-east Tibet, south-west Szechuan and north-west Yunnan were sent to Paris and were named by Franchet who also described species after them — *R. delavayi, R. davidii, R. souliei* and *R. fargesii*. It may be noted that most of the rhododendrons discovered by the French missionaries were later introduced mainly by Wilson and Forrest.

In 1879 Dr. J.E.T. Aitchison discovered *R. afghanicum* in the Kurrum Valley, at Shendtoi and Kaiwas, Afghanistan, and in the following year, 1880, he introduced it into cultivation.

Another well-known traveller and collector during this period was Dr. Augustine Henry, who was medical officer in Chinese Customs, later Professor of Forestry, Dublin. In 1886 he discovered in the Patung district of Hupeh the beautiful blue-flowered rhododendron named after him *R. augustinii*, one of the finest species in cultivation. The plant was first introduced to France by the French missionary Farges.

By the end of the 19th. century some 280 Rhododendron species had been discovered, but only about 45 species were in cultivation. The wealth of the flora of China was still unknown to the world.

Before proceeding to the introductions of the 20th. century, it may be of interest to provide a list of firms of nurserymen who were selling plants from 1850 onwards. These included Lawson & Sons, Edinburgh; Cunningham Fraser & Co. Comely Bank, Edinburgh; T. Methven & Sons, Edinburgh; Standish & Noble, Bagshot; Veitch & Sons, Exeter and Chelsea; Rollinson & Sons, Tooting; Messrs. Jackson, Kingston; Osborn & Son, Fulham Nurseries, London; Sander & Co. St. Albans, and Backhouse & Son, York.

FIRST HALF, THE TWENTIETH CENTURY

The first half of the twentieth century is a period of unparalleled activity in. the introduction of rhododendrons by famous collectors such as Wilson, Forrest, Farrer, Kingdon-Ward, Rock, and Ludlow and Sherriff.

E. H. Wilson made his first expedition in 1899 to West Hupeh and was four times in China (West Hupeh, west and north-west Szechuan). He collected twice for Messrs.

Veitch (1899—1902, and 1903—1905), and then twice for The Arnold Arboretum, Boston, Mass., and subscribers (1907—1909 and 1910—1911). Wilson was born at Chipping Campden, Gloucestershire, in 1876. He worked for a time in the Botanic Gardens, Birmingham, and in 1897 he went to Kew. On his return from his explorations in Japan in 1919, he was appointed assistant director of the Arnold Arboretum. In October 1930, he and Mrs. Wilson were killed in a motor accident in America. Wilson's introductions include *R. sargentianum*, a beautiful rock garden plant; the charming *R. williamsianum*; the early flowerers *R. lutescens*, *R. fargesii*, *R. oreodoxa*, *R. sutchuenense* and *R. praevernum*. Another outstanding species which he introduced is *R. calophytum* with large trusses of up to 30 flowers. Mention must be made of *R argyrophyllum*, *R. davidsonianum*, *R. vernicosum*, and the late flowerer *R. thayerianum*.

In 1904 which is a landmark in the history of plant introduction, George Forrest explored Yunnan and Szechuan, and in the course of seven expeditions, each of two or three years' duration, he discovered and introduced some 250 different species of Rhododendron. Forrest was born at Falkirk in March 1873. After he completed his education in Kilmarnock Academy in Ayrshire, he went to work in a chemist's shop. After a short period, he went to Australia to see his relatives. He returned home in 1902 after having made a short stay in South Africa. He applied for employment to Professor Sir Isaac Bayley Balfour, the Regius Keeper of the Royal Botanic Garden, Edinburgh, and was given a post in the herbarium. At the age of thirty his opportunity for exploration came in 1904. He was offered the chance of exploring Western China for Mr. A. K. Bulley of Neston, Cheshire. This was his first expedition, and lasted from 1904—1907. Some of his well-known introductions include the beautiful dwarf prostrate rhododendron which commemorates his name, *R. forrestii*, and its var. *repens*; the dwarf species in the Lapponicum Series, namely, *R. impeditum*, *R. fastigiatum*, *R. scintillans* and *R. russatum*; two prostrate species *R. radicans* and *R. prostratum* which are excellent rock garden plants; two beautiful dwarf species of the Boothii Series, *R. megeratum* with yellow flowers, and *R. leucaspis* with white flowers; the medium-sized early flowerers *R. fulvum* and *R. fulvoides*. A most outstanding species which Forrest introduced is *R. sinogrande*, the largest-leaved rhododendron, with leaves up to 2½ feet long and large trusses of yellow flowers; another noteworthy plant is *R. giganteum* which grows up to 100 feet high in its native home. Mention must be made of *R. griersonianum* with soft geranium or carmine, almost vermilion, flowers; another remarkable species is *R. taggianum* with large tubular-campanulate white flowers. Among the best known large-leaved rhododendrons which Forrest introduced are *R. arizelum*, *R. basilicum*, *R. praestans* and *R. fictolacteum*. Other well-known introductions include *R. lacteum*, *R. roxieanum* and *R. oreotrephes*.

In November 1930, Forrest started on his seventh expedition which was intended to be his last. He died on January 5th, 1932 while shooting, not far from Tengyueh.

As the Editors of the Scottish Rock Garden Club wrote at the time: "The world deplores the loss of such a man, but Scotland mourns a son."

Forrest was assisted by a number of native collectors who were well trained and most loyal assistants, and often collected far away on their own. Most of them came from a Mosso village in the Lichiang Range. After Forrest's death, his Chinese collectors were employed by Mr. McLaren (later Lord Aberconway) in order to continue plant collecting. They discovered and introduced amongst others, *R. aberconwayi* in the Irroratum Series.

Another collector early in the first half of the twentieth century was Reginald Farrer. He was born in 1880, and was educated at his home at Ingleborough in Yorkshire. It is recorded that from an early age he was interested in alpine plants, and at the age of fourteen he made his first rock garden. After attending Oxford he spent some time in plant collecting in the European Alps. In 1914—15, he went to Kansu, a province of China, and was accompanied by W. Purdom. He found very few rhododendrons in Kansu. In 1919 he went to Upper Burma accompanied by E.H.M. Cox, choosing Hpimaw as their base. From March to mid-November they collected on the high ranges on the

Chinese frontier, and introduced several rhododendrons including two beautiful rock garden plants, *R. calostrotum* and *R. charitopes*, the charming *R. caloxanthum* with yellow flowers, and *R. sperabile*. In the winter of 1919—1920, Cox returned home. Farrer continued alone collecting in the difficult country, and introduced amongst others the crimson-flowered species *R. eriogynum*, *R. kyawi* and *R. mallotum*. Farrer died in Upper Burma on 17th. October 1920. He will always be remembered not only as a collector but also as a vivid writer on horticultural subjects.

A famous collector during this period was Frank Kingdon-Ward. He was born in Manchester in 1885 and educated at St. Paul's School and Christ's College, Cambridge. In 1907 he went to Shanghai as a schoolmaster. In 1909—10 he travelled in the Far East with the Bedford expedition of the Natural History Museum. During the years 1911—1913 he collected in Szechuan and Yunnan for A. K. Bulley who then owned the nursery firm of Bees Ltd., of Liverpool. From 1914—1919 he was in the army. He spent the rest of his life collecting in Upper Burma, north-west Yunnan, Assam, Bhutan and Tibet. Kingdon-Ward introduced a large number of rhododendrons including fine plants suitable for the rock garden, such as, *R. imperator*, *R. pemakoense*, *R. chryseum*, *R. campylogynum* var. *myrtilloides*, *R. calostrotum* var. *calciphilum* and *R. tephropeplum*; the late flowerer *R. venator*; the deliciously scented *R. megacalyx* and the well-known *R. wardii*. Two exceptionally fine rhododendrons which he introduced are *R. macabeanum* and *R. montroseanum*. Mention should be made of other notable species, namely, *R. rhabdotum*, *R. horlickianum*, *R. piercei* and *R. tamaense*. Kingdon-Ward is well-known not only for his introductions, but also for the books he wrote describing his journeys and discoveries.

Another collector in the early part of the present century was Roland Edgar Cooper, born in 1890 at Kingston-on-Thames. In 1913 he was sent out to the Eastern Himalayas by A. K. Bulley. He spent the first year in Sikkim. During 1914 and 1915 he collected in Bhutan and introduced amongst other rhododendrons, *R. argipeplum R. polyandrum* and *R. brachysiphon*. In 1930 he joined the staff of the Royal Botanic Garden, Edinburgh as Assistant Curator, and in 1934 he was appointed Curator. He died in 1962.

An eminent American collector was Joseph Francis Rock, born in Vienna in 1884. From 1907 to 1919 he lived in Hawaii where he was Professor of Botany in the University. In 1920 the U.S. Department of Agriculture sent him to Burma, Assam and Siam (now Thailand) as an agricultural explorer. In 1923—4 and 1927—30 he led expeditions on geographical work for the National Geographic Society of the United States, and in 1924—27 he was off again to China on behalf of Harvard University. During the next thirty years Rock travelled extensively and made large collections of rhododendrons. He had to leave China and returned to Hawaii in 1955; he died in December 1962. Rock discovered and introduced *R. fletcherianum R. adenosum*, *R. arizelum* var. *rubicosum* and the magnificent *R. rothschildii*. He introduced a large number of different forms of the species including beautiful rock garden plants, such as, *R. cephalanthum*, *R. campylogynum* and *R. racemosum*. Also included are *R. haematodes*, *R. citriniflorum* and *R. roxieanum*, and the early flowerers *R. fulvum* and *R. fulvoides*. In the Barbatum Series *R. crinigerum* and *R. glischrum* are worth mentioning. Among the different forms of the large-leaved rhododendrons, *R. praestans*, *R. fictolacteum* and *R. arizelum* deserve attention. Other remarkable introductions include *R. vernicosum*, *R. traillianum* and *R. phaeochrysum*.

Two other well-known collectors during this period were Frank Ludlow and George Sherriff. They made seven expeditions to Bhutan, and south and south-east Tibet. The first was in 1933 to Bhutan and south-east Tibet. In the 1938 expedition they were accompanied by George Taylor, in 1946—47 by Henry Elliot, and in 1949 by J. H. Hicks. Among the best known dwarf species which they introduced, suitable for the rock garden, are *R. ludlowii*, *R. pumilum*, *R. pendulum*, *R. setosum* and *R. megeratum*; special mention should be made of *R. sherriffii*, *R. grothausii*, *R. tsariense*, *R. succothii* and *R. viscidifolium*. Other noteworthy species include *R. tubiforme*, *R. baileyi*, *R wardii*, *R. edgeworthii*, *R. cinnabarinum* and *R. vellereum*. Among the outstanding rhododendrons which they introduced are *R. thomsonii*, *R. pudorosum*, *R. griffithianum*, *R. hodgsonii* and *R. barbatum*.

Another modern collector was T. T. Yü who collected in the course of the expedition to north-west Yunnan and Szechuan organised by Mr. Hu. Yü introduced a good number of different forms of the species, including *R. chameunum*, *R. saluenense*, *R. vesiculiferum*, *R. lukiangense* and *R. diaprepes*.

By the end of the first half of the 20th. century, some 900 Rhododendron species had been discovered, and about 600 of these were in cultivation.

Before we proceed to the second half of the 20th. century, it may be of interest to note that every collector had his own method of working and collecting plants. Forrest believed in bulk collection, and he collected on a larger scale than the others. He was very successful in training a number of native collectors. These faithful and well-trained men covered a larger area of ground than he could have hoped to do himself. Even during the intervals when Forrest came home, these men, who eventually numbered more than twenty, went on collecting plants and seeds. It is apparent why Forrest was able to send large quantities of seed and specimens.

Kingdon-Ward, however, worked entirely single-handed, without the assistance of native collectors. He covered much less ground, but he believed in selecting the best forms of the species. He is well-known not only for the quality of the seeds which he sent, but also for his remarkable field notes.

Farrer's method of collecting was very similar to that of Kingdon-Ward. Except on one occasion when E.H.M. Cox accompanied him, and by others on a few occasions, all his collecting was done by himself. He never employed native collectors. He believed in personal collecting of plants and seeds.

Wilson and Rock collected roughly by the same method as Forrest. They both employed native collectors, but not to such a large extent. Although they covered an enorm-

Camp of J. F. Rock at an elevation of 9,900 feet, north-west Kansu. Photo J.F. Rock

ous mileage, particularly Rock, they were both esteemed for their care in selecting the best forms of plants and for the good quality of seeds they sent home. They relied much more on their own personal selection of plants. Wilson collected in western Szechuan and western Hupeh. As these countries had not been previously explored, he discovered and introduced a good number of new species. Rock went to north-west Yunnan, south-east Tibet, south-west Szechuan and north-west Kansu. Vast areas in these regions had already been covered by Forrest. Consequently Rock discovered only a few species, but he introduced a large number of the best forms of other species. Moreover, he sent most remarkable collections of dried specimens.

Ludlow and Sherriff believed in the personal factor in their collections. Their territory was in Bhutan, and south and south-east Tibet. They selected, as far as possible, the best forms of the species, and sent a large number of specimens accompanied by excellent field notes.

The first half of the twentieth century marks the beginning of a new era in the history of gardening. The remarkable explorations and introductions on a large scale by these explorers produced a complete revolution of gardening in this country. The gardeners were getting bored with the Victorian type of garden which consisted of geometrical planting, regular design, patterns of beds filled with plants and margined with box, topiary work, fountains, terraces and vistas. A great figure early in this period was William Robinson whose book *The English Flower Garden* greatly influenced contemporary gardening. Robinson emphasised the natural garden where plants could be seen as if growing freely in their natural environment. Robinson's style of gardening was shared by Miss Gertrude Jekyll, a distinguished gardener and artist. Another important figure was Reginald Farrer (1880—1920) whose books *My Rock Garden* and two volumes of *The English Rock Garden* made a tremendous impact on gardening, and helped to accelerate the movement towards the natural garden. During this period large consignments of seed were received from the collectors. The enormous number of plants raised from seed by the gardeners had to extend beyond the boundary of garden walls, giving rise eventually to the modern woodland garden.

Another important development during this period was the construction of the rock garden, which became the home of species introduced from alpine regions at elevations of over 10,000 feet. Worthy of special mention were the founding of the Alpine Garden Society in 1929, and the Scottish Rock Garden Club in 1933, to promote the cultivation of alpine plants.

It is to be noted that during the first half of the twentieth century many large private woodland gardens containing fine collections of rhododendrons came into existence. In most of these gardens up to four or five or more working gardeners were employed. A good number of rockeries were constructed for alpine plants, including dwarf rhododendrons ranging from a few inches to about two feet high. Consequently, several new nurseries flourished, propagating rhododendrons in large quantities. It may be said that by about the end of this period, the cultivation of rhododendrons was at its climax.

SECOND HALF, THE TWENTIETH CENTURY

During the Second World War 1939—1945, the expeditions to China and the Himalayas came to an end. The introduction of rhododendrons was now at a standstill. Soon after the War and until recently, China closed its gates to the western world. Moreover, it became difficult to collect in Burma, Sikkim, Bhutan and North India. The only country in the Himalayas still available for expeditions was Nepal which already had been fairly well explored. So it came about that the continuous stream of rhododendron introduction during the first half of this century, now dwindled to a mere trickle.

It may be of interest to record some of the expeditions and introductions of rhododendrons during the past thirty years. In 1949 Polunin discovered *R. cowanianum* in Central Nepal, although it was later introduced by Stainton, Sykes and Williams from the same area in 1954, who also sent seeds of the white form of *R. campanulatum*. In 1950 Col. D. G. Lowndes went to Nepal and discovered *R. lowndesii* in the Marsiandi Valley; the species was introduced by Polunin, Sykes and Williams in 1952.

Another collector during this period was Col. Spring-Smyth who also collected in Nepal and sent seeds of the new varieties, *R. lepidotum* var. *album* and *R. lepidotum* var. *minutiforme*. He also introduced, among others, *R. dalhousiae*, *R. grande*, and forms of *R. arboreum*. In 1965 Cox and Hutchison collected in Assam and Subansiri division, and introduced *R. coxianum* and *R. santapaui* which they discovered, also *R. parryae* and *R. micromeres*. Other collectors include Bowes Lyon, Schilling, George Smith, and Valder.

During the years 1965—1971, F. L. and D. C. Doleshy, the American collectors, went to Japan and introduced *R. makinoi*, *R. metternichii*, *R. japonicum* and *R. keiskei*. About the same time C. C. Hsu and J.J.R. Patrick (Rhododendron Venture) sent from Taiwan seeds of *R. ellipticum*, *R. formosanum*, the dwarf form of *R. pseudochrysanthum*, and other species.

An interesting expedition to Afghanistan in 1969 was made by Per Wendelbo and Ian Hedge who introduced *R. collettianum* and *R. afghanicum* which had been lost to cultivation. In 1971, Beer, Lancaster and Morris sent seeds of several rhododendrons from Nepal, including *R. glaucophyllum* var. *album*, *R. setosum* and *R. anthopogon*.

A most successful expedition in 1976 was made by Mr. & Mrs. Warren Berg (U.S.A.) and Hideo Suzuki (Japan) who discovered and introduced the dwarf form of *R. mucronulatum* growing in abundance on Mt. Halla, on the island of Cheju, Korea.

Some rhododendrons were also introduced in the course of the joint Chinese and British expedition to the Tali Range, Yunnan, in 1981.

It may be desired to add a few remarks on the general conditions in gardens during the latter half of the present century. Soon after the Second World War, in view of the tremendous rise in maintenance costs, large death duties, and high wages of gardeners, hardly any new large woodland garden came into existence. Gone were the days when up to five or more working gardeners were employed in some of the large gardens. At the present time many gardens have only one working gardener, whilst in other gardens the owner himself is the only person who looks after the garden.

It may be noted that during this period a few gardens deteriorated and eventually were neglected after the death of their owners. However, an important development at this time was the tremendous interest shown by the National Trusts throughout the country in acquiring and maintaining gardens with fine collections of rhododendrons which otherwise would have been lost to cultivation. Brodick Castle Gardens, Isle of Arran, may be cited as an example. In 1958 the Castle and garden were accepted by the Scottish National Trust. The garden contains one of the finest collections of rhododendrons in general cultivation.

Another notable feature during this period was the great increase of small "home" gardens varying in size from about one-sixth to half an acre or sometimes up to one or two acres. In most of these gardens the dominant plants are alpines, often with a good collection of dwarf rhododendrons varying in height from a few inches up to about two feet.

We now turn our attention to rhododendrons in the United States. During the latter half of the present century, the phenomenal rise of interest in the cultivation and propagation of rhododendrons in the U.S.A. is well-known everywhere, and is to be greatly admired. The advance in the cultivation of Rhododendron species has been spectacular. The enthusiasm and active co-operation have led to the making of many small, medium-sized and large gardens with good collections of Rhododendron species particularly along the west coast. The tremendous interest in rhododendrons, has been responsible for the formation of the American Rhododendron Society with forty branches (Chapters) and to the publication of the *Quarterly Bulletin* and recently the *Rhododendron and Azalea News*. Two outstanding developments are worth noting: First, the establishment of the Rhododendron Species Foundation, Seattle, Washington in order to encourage the cultivation and introduction of Rhododendron species. Second, the founding of the Berry Botanic Garden, Portland, Oregon, so as to cultivate and propagate not only rhododendrons but also other groups of plants.

Finally, it must be stated that rhododendrons are amongst the important and popular groups of plants in present day horticulture. Credit must be given to all gardeners for their successful achievement in the cultivation of Rhododendron species over the years.

Mekong-Salwin Divide. Dwarf rhododendrons in the foreground. Photo J.F. Rock

List of Lepidote Rhododendron Species and Varieties in their Series

(Q = not known to be in cultivation)

ANTHOPOGON SERIES

anthopogon *D. Don*
anthopogon *D. Don* var. album *Davidian*
anthopogonoides *Maxim.*
cephalanthum *Franch.*
collettianum *Aitch. et Hemsl.*
crebreflorum *Hutch. et Ward*
hypenanthum *Balf. f.*
kongboense *Hutch.*
laudandum *Cowan* Q
laudandum *Cowan* var. temoense *Ward*
    ex Cowan et Davidian
nmaiense *Balf. f. et Ward*
platyphyllum *Balf. f. et W. W. Sm.* Q
pogonophyllum *Cowan et Davidian* Q
primuliflorum *Bur. et Franch.*
primuliflorum *Bur. et Franch.* var.
    cephalanthoides (*Balf. f. et W. W. Sm.*)
    Cowan et Davidian
radendum *Fang* Q
rufescens *Franch.* Q
sargentianum *Rehd. et Wils.*
trichostomum *Franch.*
trichostomum *Franch.* var. hedyosmum
    (*Balf. f.*) *Cowan et Davidian*
trichostomum *Franch.* var. radinum (*Balf.
    f. et W. W. Sm.*) *Cowan et Davidian*

BOOTHII SERIES
BOOTHII SUBSERIES

boothii *Nutt.*
chrysodoron *Tagg ex Hutch.*
dekatanum *Cowan* Q
mishmiense *Hutch. et Ward*
sulfureum *Franch.*

MEGERATUM SUBSERIES

leucaspis *Tagg*
megeratum *Balf. f. et Forrest*

CAMELLIIFLORUM SERIES

camelliiflorum *Hook. f.*
lucidum *Nutt.* Q

CAMPYLOGYNUM SERIES

campylogynum *Franch.*
campylogynum *Franch.* var. celsum
    Davidian
campylogynum *Franch.* var. charopoeum
    (*Balf. f. et Farrer*) *Davidian*
campylogynum *Franch.* var. myrtilloides
    (*Balf. f. et Ward*) *Davidian*
cremastum *Balf. f. et Forrest*

CAROLINIANUM SERIES

carolinianum *Rehder*
carolinianum *Rehder* var. album *Rehder*
chapmanii *Gray*
minus *Michaux*

CILIATUM SERIES

amandum *Cowan* Q
burmanicum *Hutch.*
ciliatum *Hook. f.*
crenulatum *Hutch. ex Sleumer* Q
fletcherianum *Davidian*
valentinianum *Forrest ex Hutch.*
valentinianum *Forrest ex Hutch.* var.
    changii *Fang* Q

CINNABARINUM SERIES

cinnabarinum *Hook. f.*
cinnabarinum *Hook. f.* var. aestivale *Hutch.*
cinnabarinum *Hook. f.* var. blandfordiiflorum
    W. J. Hooker
cinnabarinum *Hook. f.* var. breviforme
    Davidian
cinnabarinum *Hook. f.* var. pallidum *W. J.
    Hooker*
cinnabarinum *Hook. f.* var. purpurellum
    Cowan
cinnabarinum *Hook. f.* var. roylei (*Hook.f.*)
    Hutch.
cinnabarinum *Hook. f.* var. roylei (*Hook.f.*)
    Hutch. forma magnificum *W. Watson*
concatenans *Hutch.*
keysii *Nutt.*
keysii *Nutt.* var. unicolor *Hutch. ex Stearn*
tamaense *Davidian*
xanthocodon *Hutch.*

DAURICIUM SERIES

dauricum *Linn.*
dauricum *Linn.* var. album *DC*
dauricum *Linn.* var. sempervirens *Sims*
mucronulatum *Turcz.*
mucronulatum *Turcz.* var. acuminatum
    Hutch.
mucronulatum *Turcz.* var. albiflorum *Nakai*
    Q
sichotense *Pojark.*

EDGEWORTHII SERIES

edgeworthii *Hook. f.*
pendulum *Hook f.*
seinghkuense *Hutch.*

FERRUGINEUM SERIES

ferrugineum *Linn.*
ferrugineum *Linn.* var. album *D. Don*
ferrugineum *Linn.* var. atrococcineum *Bean*
hirsutum *Linn.*
hirsutum *Linn.* var. albiflorum *Schroet.*
hirsutum *Linn.* var. latifolium *Hoppe* Q
kotschyi *Simonk.*

GLAUCOPHYLLUM SERIES

GENESTIERIANUM SUBSERIES

genestierianum *Forrest*
micromeres *Tagg*

GLAUCOPHYLLUM SUBSERIES

brachyanthum *Franch.*
brachyanthum *Franch.* var. hypolepidotum
    Franch.
charitopes *Balf. f. et Farrer*
glaucophyllum *Rehder*
glaucophyllum *Rehder* var. album *Davidian*
luteiflorum *Davidian*
pruniflorum *Hutch.*
shweliense *Balf. f. et Forrest*
tsangpoense *Ward*
tsangpoense *Ward* var. curvistylum *Ward ex*
    Cowan et Davidian
tubiforme (*Cowan et Davidian*) *Davidian*

HELIOLEPIS SERIES

bracteatum *Rehd. et Wils.*
desquamatum *Balf. f. et Forrest*
fumidum *Balf. f. et W. W. Sm.*
heliolepis *Franch.*
invictum *Balf. f. et Farrer* Q
pholidotum *Balf. f. et W. W. Sm.*
rubiginosum *Franch.*

LAPPONICUM SERIES

CUNEATUM SUBSERIES

cuneatum *W. W. Sm.*

LAPPONICUM SUBSERIES

alpicola *Rehd. et Wils.*
amundsenianum *Hand.-Mazz.* Q
bulu *Hutch.* Q
burjaticum *Malyschev* Q
capitatum *Maxim.*
chryseum *Balf. f. et Ward*
compactum *Hutch.*
complexum *Balf. f. et W. W. Sm.*
dasypetalum *Balf. f. et Forrest*
diacritum *Balf. f. et W. W. Sm.*
drumonium *Balf. f. et Ward*
edgarianum *Rehd. et Wils.*
fastigiatum *Franch.*
fimbriatum *Hutch.*
flavidum *Franch.*
fragariflorum *Ward*
hippophaeoides *Balf. f. et W. W. Sm.*
idoneum *Balf. f. et W. W. Sm.*
impeditum *Balf. f. et W. W. Sm.*
intricatum *Franch.*
lapponicum (*L.*) *Wahlenb.*
litangense *Balf. f. ex Hutch.*
lysolepis *Hutch.*
microleucum *Hutch.*
nigropunctatum *Bur. et Franch.*
nitidulum *Rehd. et Wils.*
nitidulum *Rehd. et Wils.* var. nubigenum
    Rehd. et Wils. Q
nivale *Hook. f.*
oresbium *Balf. f. et Ward*
orthocladum *Balf. f. et Forrest*
paludosum *Hutch. et Ward*
parvifolium *Adams*
parvifolium *Adams* var. albiflorum (*Herder*)
    Maxim. Q
polifolium *Franch.*
polycladum *Franch.* Q
ramosissimum *Franch.*
rupicola *W. W. Sm.*
russatum *Balf. f. et Forrest*
scintillans *Balf. f. et W. W. Sm.*
sclerocladum *Balf. f. et Forrest*
setosum *D. Don*
spilanthum *Hutch.*
stictophyllum *Balf. f.*
tapetiforme *Balf. f. et Ward*
telmateium *Balf. f. et W.W. Sm.*
thymifolium *Maxim.*
tsai *Fang* Q
verruculosum *Rehd. et Wils.*
violaceum *Rehd. et Wils.*
websterianum *Rehd. et Wils.*
yungningense *Balf. f. ex Hutch.*

LEPIDOTUM SERIES
BAILEYI SUBSERIES

baileyi *Balf. f.*

LEPIDOTUM SUBSERIES

cowanianum *Davidian*
lepidotum *Wall. ex G. Don*
lepidotum *Wall. ex G. Don* var. album *Davidian*
lepidotum *Wall. ex G. Don* var. elaeagnoides (*Hook. f.*) *Franch.*
lepidotum *Wall. ex G. Don* var. minutiforme *Davidian*
lepidotum *Wall. ex G. Don* var. obovatum *Hook. f.*
lowndesii *Davidian*

MADDENII SERIES
CILIICALYX SUBSERIES

carneum *Hutch.*
ciliicalyx *Franch.*
ciliipes *Hutch.* Q
coxianum *Davidian*
cubittii *Hutch.*
cuffeanum *Craib ex Hutch.*
dendricola *Hutch.*
fleuryi *Dop* Q
formosum *Wall.*
horlickianum *Davidian*
inaequale (*C. B. Clarke*) *Hutch.*
iteophyllum *Hutch.*
johnstoneanum *Watt ex Hutch.*
lasiopodum *Hutch.*
ludwigianum *Hosseus*
lyi *Lévl.*
notatum *Hutch.* Q
pachypodum *Balf. f. et W. W. Sm.*
parryae *Hutch.*
roseatum *Hutch.*
rufosquamosum *Hutch.* Q
scopulorum *Hutch.*
scottianum *Hutch.*
smilesii *Hutch.* Q
supranubium *Hutch.*
surasianum *Balf. f. et Craib*
taronense *Hutch.*
veitchianum *Hook.*
walongense *Ward.*

MADDENII SUBSERIES

brachysiphon *Balf. f.*
calophyllum *Nutt.* Q
crassum *Franch.*
excellens *Hemsl. et Wils.* Q
maddenii *Hook. f.*
manipurense *Balf. f. et Watt*
odoriferum *Hutch.*
polyandrum *Hutch.*

MEGACALYX SUBSERIES

basfordii *Davidian*
dalhousiae *Hook f.*
goreri *Davidian*
grothausii *Davidian*
headfortianum *Hutch.*
kiangsiense *Fang* Q
levinei *Merrill* Q
liliiflorum *Lévl.* Q
lindleyi *T. Moore*
megacalyx *Balf. f. et Ward*
nuttallii *Booth*
nuttallii *Booth* var. stellatum *Hutch.*
rhabdotum *Balf. f. et Cooper*
taggianum *Hutch.*

MICRANTHUM SERIES

micranthum *Turcz.*

MOUPINENSE SERIES

dendrocharis *Franch.* Q
moupinense *Franch.*
petrocharis *Diels* Q

SALUENENSE SERIES

calostrotum *Balf. f. et Ward*
calostrotum *Balf. f. et Ward* var. calciphilum (*Hutch. et Ward*) *Davidian*
chameunum *Balf. f. et Forrest*
charidotes *Balf. f. et Farrer*
keleticum *Balf. f. et Forrest*
nitens *Hutch.*
prostratum *W. W. Sm.*
radicans *Balf. f. et Forrest*
saluenense *Franch.*

SCABRIFOLIUM SERIES

hemitrichotum *Balf. f. et Forrest*
mollicomum *Balf. f. et W. W. Sm.*
mollicomum *Balf. f. et W. W. Sm.* var. rockii *Tagg* Q
racemosum *Franch.*
scabrifolium *Franch.*
spiciferum *Franch.*
spinuliferum *Franch.*

TEPHROPEPLUM SERIES

auritum *Tagg*
chrysolepis *Hutch.*
tephropeplum *Balf. f. et Farrer*
xanthostephanum *Merr.*

TRICHOCLADUM SERIES

caesium *Hutch.*
lepidostylum *Balf. f. et Forrest*
lithophilum *Balf. f. et Ward*
mekongense *Franch.*
melinanthum *Balf. f. et Ward*
rubrolineatum *Balf. f. et Forrest*
rubroluteum *Davidian*
trichocladum *Franch.*
trichocladum *Franch.* var. longipilosum
    Cowan
viridescens *Hutch.*

TRIFLORUM SERIES
AUGUSTINII SUBSERIES

augustinii *Hemsl.*
augustinii *Hemsl.* var. chasmanthum
    (*Diels*) *Davidian*
bergii *Davidian*
bivelatum *Balf. f.* Q
hardyi *Davidian*
hirsuticostatum *Hand.-Mazz.* Q
trichanthum *Rehder*

HANCEANUM SUBSERIES

afghanicum *Aitch. et Hemsl.*
hanceanum *Hemsl.*
hanceanum *Hemsl.* 'Nanum'

TRIFLORUM SUBSERIES

ambiguum *Hemsl.*
bauhiniiflorum *Watt ex Hutch.*
flavantherum *Hutch. et Ward* Q
kasoense *Hutch. et Ward* Q
keiskei *Miq.*
keiskei *Miq.* 'Yaku Fairy'
  lutescens *Franch.*
triflorum *Hook. f.*
triflorum *Hook. f.* var. mahogani *Hutch.*
wongii *Hemsl. et Wils.*

YUNNANENSE SUBSERIES

amesiae *Rehd. et Wils.*
apiculatum *Rehd. et Wils.* Q
bodinieri *Franch.* Q
concinnoides *Hutch. et Ward* Q
concinnum *Hemsl.*
concinnum *Hemsl.* var. benthamianum
    (*Hemsl.*) *Davidian*
concinnum *Hemsl.* var. pseudoyanthinum
    (*Balf. f. ex Hutch.*) *Davidian*
davidsonianum *Rehd. et Wils.*
hormophorum *Balf. f. et Forrest*
hypophaeum *Balf. f. et Forrest*
longistylum *Rehd. et Wils.*
oreotrephes *W. W. Sm.*
oreotrephes *W. W. Sm.* 'Exquisetum'
polylepis *Franch.*

rigidum *Franch.*
searsiae *Rehd. et Wils.*
siderophyllum *Franch.*
suberosum *Balf. f. et Forrest*
tatsienense *Franch.*
vilmorinianum *Balf. f.*
yunnanense *Franch.*
zaleucum *Balf. f. et W. W. Sm.*
zaleucum *Balf. f. et W. W. Sm.* var.
    flaviflorum *Davidian*

UNIFLORUM SERIES

imperator *Hutch. et Ward*
ludlowii *Cowan*
monanthum *Balf. f. et W. W. Sm.* Q
pemakoense *Ward*
pumilum *Hook. f.*
uniflorum *Hutch. et Ward*

VACCINIOIDES SERIES

asperulum *Hutch. et Ward* Q
emarginatum *Hemsl. et Wils.* Q
euonymifolium *Lévl.* Q
insculptum *Hutch. et Ward* Q
kawakamii *Hayata*
santapaui *Sastry, Kataki,*
    P. Cox, Patricia Cox & P. Hutchison
vaccinioides *Hook. f.*

VIRGATUM SERIES

virgatum *Hook. f.*

Introduction to Keys and Descriptions

Included in this section are a Key to the Series and Subseries followed by Descriptions of Species. It contains 25 Series arranged in alphabetical order. Each Series comprises general characters, distribution, affinity with other Series, a Key to its species, and descriptions of the species.

Each species is given a detailed description based on herbarium specimens and plants in cultivation, with the more important characteristics appearing in italics. The description is followed by notes on the species in relation to the discoverer, collectors, distribution, native habitats and altitudes, affinity with other species, an account of the plant in cultivation, awards, hardiness and flowering months.

KEY TO THE SERIES AND SUBSERIES

1. Under surface of the leaves densely woolly and scaly, the scales obscured; branchlets, petioles, pedicels and ovaries densely woolly .... *Edgeworthii Series*
1. Under surface of the leaves not woolly, the scales exposed; branchlets, petioles, pedicels, and ovaries not woolly.
   2. Corolla salver-shaped, tubular with spreading lobes; inflorescence capitate; under surface of the leaves densely scaly with overlapping scales, spongy — a few layers, scales Lacerate; stamens 5—9 or rarely 10 .. *Anthopogon Series*
   2. Corolla not salver-shaped; inflorescence not capitate; under surface of the leaves not spongy, scales not Lacerate; stamens 10.
      3. Capsule spindle-shaped; seed with an elongated tail at each end; (leaves linear-lanceolate, spathulate-obovate or obovate) .. *Vaccinioides Series*
      3. Capsule conoid, ovoid, oval or oblong; seed without a tail at each end.
         4. Style short, stout, and sharply bent; corolla rotate or campanulate.
            5. Scales on the under surface of the leaves of 2 kinds, smaller pale yellow, larger dark brown; under surface of the leaves conspicuously glaucous .... *Glaucophyllum Series*
            5. Scales on the under surface of the leaves of one kind, brown; under surface of the leaves pale green, pale glaucous green, pale brown or brown (except in *Megeratum Subseries,* sometimes in *Genestierianum Subseries* and *Campylogynum Series*).
               6. Pedicel much longer than the corolla.
                  7. Scales on the under surface of the leaves distinctly Crenulate, overlapping; inflorescence 5—18-flowered .... *Baileyi Series*
                  7. Scales on the under surface of the leaves Entire or Vesicular, overlapping to 6 times their own diameter apart; inflorescence 1—15-flowered.
                     8. Corolla rotate; inflorescence 1—2- or sometimes up to 5-flowered .. *Lepidotum Subseries*
                     8. Corolla campanulate or tubular-campanulate; inflorescence 1—15-flowered.
                        9. Leaves small, laminae 6 mm.—3.7 cm. long, margins crenulate, recurved, the scales on the under surface Vesicular without marginal rim; inflorescence usually 1—4-flowered, umbellate, rhachis 1—2 mm. long; corolla salmon-pink, carmine, plum-purple, almost black-purple or bright red .... *Campylogynum Series*
                        9. Leaves large, laminae 3—15.3 cm. long, margins entire, flat, the scales on the under surface Entire with marginal rim; inflorescence 3—15-flowered, usually distinctly racemose, rhachis 2 mm.—1.5 cm. long; corolla usually deep plum-purple, yellow, greenish-yellow or rarely white .... *Genestierianum Subseries*
               6. Pedicel shorter than the corolla.
                  10. Scales on the under surface of the leaves Entire, slightly overlapping, contiguous or ½—2 times their own diameter apart; leaves evergreen.

11. Inflorescence 1—2- (rarely 3-) flowered; corolla rotate or almost saucer-shaped, rotate-campanulate or campanulate.

    12. Stamens 10; branchlets, petioles, and usually leaf-margins densely or moderately bristly; leaves (laminae) 1.3—5 cm. long; ovary 5-celled ...... *Megeratum Subseries*

    12. Stamens 12—16; branchlets, petioles, and usually leaf-margins not bristly; leaves (laminae) 4.8—12.3 cm. long; ovary 5—10-celled .... *Camelliiflorum Series*

11. Inflorescence 3—15-flowered; corolla campanulate or broadly campanulate.

    13. Inflorescence distinctly racemose, 8—15-flowered, rhachis 2—5 cm. long; corolla small, 8 mm.—1.3 cm. long; branchlets, petioles, and leaf-margins not bristly .... *Hanceanum Subseries*

    13. Inflorescence umbellate, usually 3—8-flowered, rhachis 1—4 mm. long; corolla large, 1.3—4 cm. long; branchlets, petioles, and leaf-margins often bristly .... *Boothii Subseries*

10. Scales on the under surface of the leaves Vesicular, 1—6 times their own diameter apart; leaves deciduous or evergreen ....
.... *Trichocladum Series* (part)

4. Style long, slender and straight; corolla widely funnel-shaped, funnel-shaped, tubular, tubular-campanulate or sometimes campanulate.

    14. Corolla large, 4.5—13.6 cm. long; stamens 10—25; leaves (laminae) up to 26.5 cm. long and 13.1 cm. broad; calyx up to 2.6 cm. long; ovary 5—12-celled; usually tender outdoors .... *Maddenii Series*

    14. Corolla smaller, 0.8—5 cm. long; stamens 10; leaves (laminae) usually up to 12.5 cm. long and 6.5 cm. broad; calyx up to 1.2 cm. long; ovary 5-celled; hardy outdoors.

        15. Scales on the under surface of the leaves Vesicular, 1—6 times their own diameter apart; leaves deciduous or evergreen .... *Trichocladum Series* (part)

        15. Scales on the under surface of the leaves not Vesicular, overlapping contiguous to 8 times their own diameter apart; leaves evergreen, (except in *Dauricum Series* and sometimes in *Yunnanense Subseries*).

            16. Corolla tubular or tubular-campanulate or campanulate.

                17. Scales on the under surface of the leaves of two kinds, smaller pale yellow, larger dark brown; under surface of the leaves conspicuously glaucous ... *Glaucophyllum Subseries*

17. Scales on the under surface of the leaves of one kind, brown or dark brown; under surface of the leaves pale green, pale glaucous green, pale brown or brown.

    18. Corolla contracted at the upper end; under surface of the leaves, ovary, and capsule densely pubescent .... *Scabrifolium Series*
                                                          (R. spinuliferum)

    18. Corolla not contracted at the upper end; under surface of the leaves, ovary, and capsule not pubescent.

        19. Inflorescence distinctly long racemose, 9—28-flowered, rhachis 1.2—2.6 cm. long; style short, shorter than, or as long as, the stamens.

            20. Corolla very small 4—6 mm. long, campanulate, white ....
                .... *Micranthum Series*

            20. Corolla larger 1—2 cm. long, tubular with spreading lobes, crimson-purple, scarlet-purple, rose-purple, rosy-pink or sometimes white .... *Ferrugineum Series*
                                                    (part)

        19. Inflorescence umbellate or very shortly racemose, 1—9-flowered; rhachis usually 1 mm.—1 cm. long; style long, longer than the stamens (except in *Heliolepis Series*, usually as long as the stamens; short in *R. pumilum).*

            21. Inflorescence 1—2- (rarely 3-) flowered; corolla rather densely pubescent on the tube and lobes outside (except in *R. monanthum,* glabrous); dwarf or small shrubs, usually 3—92 cm. (1.2 in.—3 ft.) high .... *Uniflorum Series*
                                                    (part)

            21. Inflorescence 3—9-flowered; corolla not pubescent outside or sometimes pubescent only on the tube; small to large shrubs 30 cm.—7.63 m. (1—25 ft.) high.

                22. Stamens short, as long as the corolla-tube or shorter, usually 4 mm.—1 cm. long; style short, as long as the stamens or shorter. From Europe .. *Ferrugineum Series*
                                                     (part)

                22. Stamens long, longer than the corolla-tube, usually 1.2—4 cm. long; style long, longer than the stamens (except in *Heliolepis Series,* usually as long as the stamens). From Nepal to Upper Burma, Szechuan, and Yunnan.

                    23. Petiole and calyx margin usually moderately or rather densely bristly; branchlets, upper surface and margins of the leaves, and pedicels often moderately or rather densely bristly ....
                    .... *Ciliatum Series*
                                                      (part)

                    23. Petiole, calyx margin, branchlets, upper surface and margins of the leaves, and pedicel not bristly, (calyx margin ciliate or eciliate).

                        24. Corolla moderately or rather densely scaly outside.

                            25. Leaves deciduous or semi-deciduous ...
                          .... *Cinnabarinum Series*
                                                      (part)

                        25. Leaves evergreen.

                            26. Calyx 3—8 mm. long (except in *R. chrysolepis* 0.5—1 mm. long); scales on the under surface of the leaves usually small ....
                            .... *Tephropeplum Series*
                                                     (part)

                            26. Calyx 0.5—3 mm. (rarely 4 mm.) long; scales on the under surface of the leaves large.

27. Inflorescence 4—9- (rarely 3-) flowered; corolla pink, pale or deep rose, lavender, deep lavender-purple, intense bluish-purple, purple or white; leaves aromatic ...... *Heliolepis Series* (part)

27. Inflorescence 2—3-flowered; corolla yellow or pinkish-purple fading to white at the base; leaves not aromatic ... *Triflorum Series* (part)

24. Corolla not scaly outside.

28. Calyx 1—3 mm. or sometimes 4 mm. long, 5-lobed or sometimes a mere rim, not leafy; scales on the under surface of the leaves usually medium-sized and large, usually pale brown, brown or purplish-brown; corolla tubular or tubular-campanulate .... *Cinnabarinum Series* (part)

28. Calyx 4—8 mm. long, 5-lobed, leafy; scales on the under surface of the leaves small, usually black; corolla tubular-campanulate .... *Tephropeplum Series* (part)

16. Corolla widely funnel-shaped (butterfly-shaped) or flat saucer-shaped.

29. Scales on the under surface of the leaves Crenulate, densely overlapping; corolla moderately or rather densely pubescent outside (rarely glabrous) .... *Saluenense Series*

29. Scales on the under surface of the leaves Entire, overlapping to 8 times their own diameter apart; corolla not pubescent or sometimes pubescent outside.

30. Midrib on the under surface of the leaves hairy ... . *Augustinii Subseries*

30. Midrib on the under surface of the leaves glabrous.

31. Inflorescence 1—2-flowered.

32. Leaves completely deciduous or sometimes semi-deciduous; corolla pubescent outside .... *Dauricum Series* (part)

32. Leaves evergreen.

33. Inflorescence axillary in the uppermost few leaves.

34. Branchlets, leaves (laminae), petioles, pedicels, and outside of calyx bristly and/or rather densely pubescent (except in *R. racemosum*, glabrous); under surface of the leaves glaucous or not glaucous *Scabrifolium Series* (part)

34. Branchlets, leaves (laminae), petioles, pedicels, and outside of calyx not bristly, not pubescent; under surface of the leaves not glaucous ... . *Virgatum Series*

33. Inflorescence terminal (except in the *Lapponicum Series* rarely terminal and axillary).

35. Corolla small, 5 mm.—2 cm. long; leaves (laminae) usually 2 mm.
—3.5 cm. long; stamens 5—10 .... *Lapponicum Subseries*
(part)

35. Corolla larger, usually 2—4.8 cm. long; leaves (laminae) usually 2.5—7 cm. long; stamens 10.

 36. Branchlets and petioles moderately or rather densely
bristly; pedicels bristly or not bristly; leaves (laminae)
rigid. Flowering months February—March ....
.... *Moupinense Series*

 36. Branchlets, petioles and pedicels not bristly; leaves
(laminae) not rigid. Flowering months usually April—
May.

  37. Prostrate or dwarf shrubs, 3 in.—1½ feet high;
scales on the under surface of the leaves 1—6
times their own diameter apart; corolla rather
densely pubescent outside .... *Uniflorum Series*
(part)

  37. Medium-sized or large shrubs, usually 3—12 feet
high; scales on the under surface of the leaves
overlapping or contiguous or one-half or twice
their own diameter apart; corolla not pubescent
or pubescent outside.

   38. Calyx large 4 mm.—1.2 cm. long; corolla not
pubescent outside, 1.6—3.4 cm. long;
branchlets, petioles, and pedicels glabrous;
calyx margin usually fringed with long
hairs. From Yunnan and south-west Szechuan .... *Cuneatum Subseries*
(part)

   38. Calyx minute 0.5—1 mm. long; corolla pubescent outside, 1.8—2.1 cm. long; branchlets
rather densely or moderately puberulous,
petioles and pedicels minutely puberulous;
calyx margin glabrous. From eastern
U.S.S.R. .... *Dauricum Series*
(part)

31. Inflorescence 3—8-flowered.

  39. Branchlets, leaves (laminae), petioles,
pedicels, and outside of calyx bristly
and/or rather densely pubescent.

   40. Corolla pale yellow, large 3.6—4.2 cm.
long; calyx large 8 mm.—1 cm.
long; leaf margin crenulate, leaf
base decurrent on the petiole;
petiole narrowly winged on each
side .... *Ciliatum Series*
(part)

   40. Corolla rose, pink, white, reddish-
purple or crimson, smaller 8
mm.—2.8 cm. long; calyx smaller
0.5—6 mm. long, leaf margin entire, leaf base not decurrent on
the petiole; petiole not winged.

41. Inflorescence axillary in the uppermost few leaves; corolla scaly outside .... *Scabrifolium Series*
(part)

41. Inflorescence terminal; corolla usually not scaly outside ... *Lapponicum Series*
(*R. setosum*)

39. Branchlets, leaves (laminae), petioles, pedicels, and outside of calyx not bristly, not pubescent.

42. Corolla small 5 mm.—2 cm. long; leaves (laminae) usually 2 mm.—3.5 cm. long; stamens 5—10; usually dwarf or small shrubs 5 cm.—1.22 m. (2 in.—4 ft.) high.

43. Under surface of the leaves not glaucous; calyx 0.5—6 mm. or rarely 8 mm. long .... *Lapponicum Subseries*
(part)

43. Under surface of the leaves markedly glaucous; calyx 0.5 mm. long .... *Scabrifolium Series*
(*R. racemosum*)

42. Corolla usually larger 2—4.2 cm. long; leaves (laminae) usually 2.5—12.8 cm. long; stamens 10; small, medium-sized or large shrubs, usually 92 cm.—10.37 m. (3—34 ft.) high.

44. Calyx large, 4 mm.—1.2 cm. long; under surface of the leaves densely scaly, the scales similar in size, overlapping or contiguous or nearly contiguous ....
.... *Cuneatum Subseries*
(part)

44. Calyx usually minute or small, 0.5—3 mm. long; under surface of the leaves densely or laxly scaly, the scales unequal, overlapping or contiguous to 8 times their own diameter apart.

45. Corolla deep to pale yellow, greenish-yellow or creamy-white (rarely white).

46. Rhachis 8 mm.—2 cm. long; inflorescence 5—11-flowered; usually small shrub 1—3 ft. high .... *Hanceanum Subseries*
(*R. hanceanum*)

46. Rhachis 0.5—5 mm. long; inflorescence usually 1—6-flowered; small to large shrub 1—20 ft. high .... *Triflorum Subseries*

45. Corolla pink, pale or deep rose, lavender, deep lavender-purple, intense bluish-purple, purple or white.

47. Under surface of the leaves densely scaly, the scales contiguous to their own diameter apart. From the U.S.A. ....
.... *Carolinianum Series*

47. Under surface of the leaves densely or laxly scaly, the scales overlapping to 8 times their own diameter apart. From Yunnan, Kweichow, Upper Burma, Tibet, and Szechuan.

48. Branchlets, petioles, and pedicels not bristly, not puberulous; leaves evergreen, usually aromatic; corolla moderately or rather densely scaly outside; scales on the under surface of the leaves large .... *Heliolepis Series*
(part)

48. Branchlets, petioles, and pedicels bristly or not bristly, puberulous or not puberulous; leaves completely deciduous or semi-deciduous or evergreen, not aromatic; corolla not scaly or moderately or rather densely scaly outside; scales on the under surface of the leaves usually medium-sized or/and small .. *Yunnanense Subseries*

Forest on the Lichiang snow range. Photo J.F. Rock

1. *R. sargentianum.* Photo H. Esslemont

2. *R. anthopogon*

3. *R. trichostomum*. Photo Dr. G. Smith

4. *R. chrysodoron*. Photo H. Gunn

5. *R. leucaspis*
   Photo Miss Sheila Grant

6. *R. campylogynum*
   Photo H. Gunn

7. *R. campylogynum*
   var. *charopoeum*

8. *R. fletcherianum*. Photo H. Gunn

9. *R. ciliatum*. Photo H. Gunn

10. *R. valentinianum*

11. *R. cinnabarinum*. Photo H. Gunn

12. *R. cinnabarinum* var. *roylei*. Photo H. Gunn

13. *R. cinnabarinum* var. *roylei* forma *magnificum*

14. *R. cinnabarinum* var. *blandfordiiflorum*

15. *R. concatenans*

16. *R. concatenans*, young leaves. Photo H. Gunn

17. *R. keysii*

18. *R. mucronulatum*

19. *R. dauricum*

20. *R. edgeworthii*

21. *R. pendulum*
Photo Dr. Florence Auckland

22. *R. hirsutum*
Photo J.T. Aitken

23. *R. glaucophyllum*. Photo H. Gunn

24. *R. charitopes*. Photo H. Gunn

25. *R. luteiflorum*. Photo H. Gunn

26. *R. tubiforme*. Photo H. Gunn

27. *R. brachyanthum* var. *hypolepidotum*
Photo H. Gunn

28. *R. micromeres*

29. *R. rubiginosum*
Photo Dr. Florence Auckland

30. *R. cuneatum*

31. *R. microleucum*

32. *R. complexum*

33. *R. stictophyllum*

34. *R. keiskei*

35. *R. keiskei* 'Yaku Fairy'

36. *R. rupicola*
Photo Mrs. Gwen Bell

37. *R. fimbriatum*

38. *R. chryseum*. Photo H. Gunn

39. *R. lapponicum*

40. *R. impeditum* with dark green leaves.
Photo H. Gunn

41. *R. fastigiatum* with glaucous green leaves. Photo H. Gunn

42. *R. fragariflorum*

43. *R. lepidotum* in Nepal. Photo Dr. G. Smith

44. *R. cubittii*. Photo H. Gunn

45. *R. veitchianum*. Photo H. Gunn

46. *R. rhabdotum*. Photo H. Gunn

47. *R. horlickianum*

48. *R. grothausii*. Photo H. Gunn

49. *R. goreri*. Photo H. Gunn

50. *R. dalhousiae*. Photo H. Gunn

51. *R. johnstoneanum*

52. *R. moupinense*
    Photo H. Gunn

53. *R. calostrotum*

54. *R. calostrotum*
    var. *calciphilum*
    Photo H. Gunn

55. *R. radicans*
   Photo H. Gunn

56. *R. racemosum*

57. *R. tephropeplum*
   Photo H. Gunn

58. *R. lepidostylum*

59. *R. viridescens*. Photo H. Gunn

61. *R. concinnum.* Photo H. Gunn

60. *R. hormophorum.* Photo H. Gunn

62. *R. suberosum*

63. *R. bergii.* Photo H. Gunn

64. *R. rigidum.* Photo H. Gunn

65. *R. davidsonianum.* Photo H. Gunn

66. *R. afghanicum.* Photo Per Wendelbo

67. *R. hanceanum* 'Nanum'. Photo H. Gunn

68. *R. yunnanense*
Photo H. Gunn

69. *R. ambiguum*
Photo H. Gunn

70. *R. oreotrephes*
Photo H. Gunn

71. *R. pemakoense*
Photo H. Gunn

72. *R. uniflorum*

73. *R. ludlowii*

74. *R. imperator*

75. The peat garden, Royal Botanic Garden, Edinburgh.

76. The peat garden in winter, Royal Botanic Garden, Edinburgh.

77. Rhododendrons in Mr. & Mrs. William D. Davidson's garden, Langlea, Jedburgh, Roxburghshire.

78. Rhododendrons in Mr. & Mrs. Hamish Gunn's garden, Edinburgh.

79. Rhododendrons in Younger's Botanic Garden, Benmore, Argyllshire.

80. Dwarf rhododendrons in Mr. & Mrs. J.T. Aitken's garden, Edinburgh.

81. Dwarf rhododendrons in Mr. & Mrs. J. Sutherland's garden, Inverness.

82. The peat garden, Roughhills, nr. Dalbeattie.

83. Harlow Car, Harrogate, Yorkshire.

84. The garden at the Rhodo-dendron Species Foundation, Seattle, Washington, U.S.A.

85. *R. augustinii* in Mr. & Mrs. Lawrence Pierce's garden, Seattle, Washington, U.S.A.

86. Shadehouse at the Rhodo-dendron Species Foundation, Seattle, Washington, U.S.A.

87. Rhododendrons in Cecil Smith's garden, Seattle, Washington, U.S.A.

88. Rhododendrons in Berry Botanic Garden, Portland, Oregon, U.S.A.

89. Ice storm in Berry Botanic Garden, Portland, Oregon, U.S.A.

90. *R. ferrugineum* on the Pyrenees mountains. Photo J.T. Aitken.

91. *R. lapponicum* in the most northerly part of Norway.   Photo E. Sahlin.

92. *R. collettianum* on the mountains, Afghanistan. Photo I. Hedge.

93. Dwarf form of *R. mucronulatum* on Cheju Island, Korea.
Photo Warren Berg.

94. *R. keiskei* 'Yaku Fairy' on the mountains, Japan.

95. Dwarf rhododendrons at 3,660 m. (12,000 ft.) in Nepal. Photo Dr. G. Smith

ANTHOPOGON SERIES

General characters: creeping, prostrate, compact, spreading, or upright, dwarf or small shrubs, 3 cm.—1.80 m. (1.2 in.—6 ft.) or rarely 2.45—2.75 m. (8—9 ft.) high, branchlets densely or sometimes moderately scaly. Leaves evergreen, aromatic, oblong, lanceolate, linear, linear-lanceolate to oval or orbicular, lamina 0.7—5.6 cm. long, 0.2—2.8 cm. broad; *under surface densely scaly with overlapping lacerate scales.* Inflorescence terminal, capitate, often forming a globose cluster, 2—20-flowered; pedicel 1—8 mm. long. Calyx 5-lobed, 0.5—7 mm. long. Corolla narrowly tubular with spreading lobes, 0.8—2.1 cm. long, white, pink, rose, deep red, yellow or greenish. *Stamens 5—9 or rarely 10, 2—9 mm. long, included in the corolla-tube.* Ovary ovoid or conoid, 1—2 mm. long, 5- or rarely 4-celled; *style very short,* thick, straight, *as long as the ovary or shorter or slightly longer,* not scaly, glabrous. Capsule ovoid, conoid or sometimes oblong, 2—5 mm. long, 1—3 mm. broad, densely or sometimes moderately scaly, usually enclosed by the persistent calyx-lobes.

Distribution: Kashmir, Afghanistan, Nepal, Sikkim, Bhutan, Assam, Tibet, Upper Burma, west and north-west Yunnan, western Szechuan and Kansu.

A fairly large Series of 16 species. The main diagnostic features are the densely scaly under surface of the leaves with overlapping lacerate scales, the 5—9 (or rarely 10) stamens included in the corolla-tube, and the very short style.

KEY TO THE SPECIES

A. Leaves bristly.
    B. Leaf-bud scales deciduous; corolla densely scaly outside, 0.8—1 cm. long; calyx 1—2 mm. long; inflorescence 8—10-flowered; under surface of the leaves, and pedicel bristly .... *radendum*
    B. Leaf-bud scales persistent; corolla not scaly or slightly scaly outside, 1.4—1.6 cm. long; calyx 5—6 mm. long; inflorescence 2—3-flowered; under surface of the leaves, and pedicel not bristly .... *pogonophyllum*
A. Leaves not bristly.
    C. Leaves linear, linear-lanceolate or narrowly oblanceolate, 4—5 times as long as broad; calyx 0.5—2 mm. long; capsule not enclosed by the persistent calyx .... *trichostomum*
    C. Leaves orbicular, oval, elliptic, oblong or sometimes lanceolate, length equalling breadth, or up to twice or sometimes 3 times as long as broad; calyx usually 3—5 mm. long; capsule enclosed or rarely partly enclosed by the persistent calyx.
        D. Corolla rather densely or moderately scaly on the tube and lobes outside .... *sargentianum*
        D. Corolla not scaly or rarely only lobes scaly outside.
            E. Corolla-tube densely or moderately hairy outside.
                F. Corolla 0.8—1.1 cm. long, usually deep red, reddish-purple, strawberry-red or deep rose ...... *kongboense*
                F. Corolla usually 1.2—1.6 cm. long, white, pink, creamy-yellow, creamy-white or yellow.
                    G. Leaves usually oval, oblong-oval or elliptic; ovary usually densely hairy all over or in the lower half; calyx densely or moderately scaly outside; scales on the under surface of the leaves often reddish-brown or chocolate or cinnamon-coloured .... *laudandum*
                    G. Leaves usually oblong, oblong-lanceolate, lanceolate or oblong-elliptic; ovary not hairy; calyx moderately scaly or not scaly outside; scales on the under surface of the leaves often dark brown or fawn .... *primuliflorum* var. *cephalanthoides*
            E. Corolla-tube not hairy outside.
                H. Leaf-bud scales persistent.
                    I. Leaves (laminae) usually 3—5 cm. long; leaf-bud scales large, broadly ovate, obovate or rounded, leafy .... *platyphyllum*
                    I. Leaves (laminae) usually 1—2.8 cm. or sometimes up to 4.2 cm. long; leaf-bud scales small, linear or lanceolate, not leafy.
                        J. Corolla white, pink, rose, reddish or rose-crimson.
                          K. Usually upright or spreading or somewhat compact shrub, usually 30 cm.—1.50 m. high.
                            L. Stamens usually 5; scales on the under surface of the leaves often brown or fawn ..... *cephalanthum*

L. Stamens usually 6—9; scales on the under surface of the leaves usually cinnamon or rust-coloured or reddish-brown or dark brown .... *anthopogon*
(part)

K. Very compact or prostrate shrub, 5—15 cm. high ..... *crebreflorum*

J. Corolla yellow, pale yellow, creamy-yellow, lemon-green or creamy-white.

M. Usually upright shrub; leaves (laminae) usually 1.8—4.2 cm. long; stamens 5—8 .... *hypenanthum*

M. Usually compact or spreading shrub; leaves (laminae) 1—2.5 cm. long; stamens usually 5 .... *nmaiense*

H. Leaf-bud scales deciduous.

N. Stamens 10, 6—9 mm. long; leaves (laminae) usually 4—5.6 cm. long. From Afghanistan.. *collettianum*

N. Stamens 5 or sometimes 6—9 (or rarely 10), 2—6 mm. long; leaves (laminae) usually 0.8—3.8 cm. long. From Nepal, Sikkim to Yunnan, Kansu.

O. Inflorescence 5—10-flowered; pedicel densely or moderately scaly, 1—5 mm. long; calyx moderately or densely scaly outside or sometimes not scaly.

P. Scales on the under surface of the leaves usually cinnamon, rust, chocolate-coloured or reddish-brown.

Q. Corolla 1.2—1.9 cm. long; leaves (laminae) 1.3—3.8 cm. long, 0.8—2.5 cm. broad .... *anthopogon*
(part)

Q. Corolla 0.9—1.3 cm. long; leaves (laminae) usually 0.8—2 cm. long, 0.4—1 cm. broad ...... *rufescens*

P. Scales on the under surface of the leaves usually brown or fawn . *primuliflorum*

O. Inflorescence 10—20-flowered; pedicel not scaly, 1—2 mm. long; calyx not scaly outside .... *anthopogonoides*

DESCRIPTION OF THE SPECIES

R. anthopogon D. Don in Mem. Wern. Soc. III (1821) 409; Balf. f. in Notes Roy. Bot. Gard. Edin., IX (1916) 286.

A prostrate, rounded compact, spreading or upright shrub, 15 cm.—1.53 m. (6 in.—5 ft.) high; branchlets densely scaly, glabrous, leaf-bud scales deciduous or persistent. *Leaves* evergreen, orbicular, oval, elliptic, oblong-elliptic or oblong, aromatic, lamina coriaceous, 1.3—3.8 cm. long, 0.8—2.5 cm. broad, apex rounded or obtuse, mucronate, base rounded or obtuse; upper surface dark green, shining, not scaly or scaly, glabrous; margin flat or slightly recurved, glabrous; under surface densely covered with overlapping cinnamon or rust-coloured, reddish-brown, dark brown or brown, lacerate scales (in young leaves creamy-yellow or fawn), glabrous; petiole 3—8 mm. long, densely or moderately scaly, glabrous. *Inflorescence* terminal, capitate, 5—9-flowered, flower-bud scales persistent; rhachis 1—2 mm. long, scaly, glabrous or rarely puberulous; pedicel 2—5 mm. long, densely or moderately scaly, glabrous or rarely puberulous. *Calyx* 5-lobed, 2—5 mm. long, lobes lanceolate or elliptic, outside moderately or densely scaly, margin moderately or densely ciliate. *Corolla* narrowly tubular with spreading lobes, 1.2—1.9 cm. long, 5-lobed, *pink, pale pink, deep rose, reddish or rarely crimson*, outside not scaly, glabrous, inside densely hairy within the tube. *Stamens* 5—9 or rarely 10, unequal, 2—5 mm. long, included in the corolla-tube; filaments glabrous. *Ovary* conoid, 1 mm. long, 5- or rarely 4-celled, moderately or densely scaly, glabrous; style very short, thick, straight, shorter or slightly longer than the ovary, not scaly, glabrous. *Capsule* ovoid or conoid, 2—3 mm. long, 1—2 mm. broad, densely or moderately scaly, glabrous, enclosed by the persistent calyx-lobes.

R. anthopogon was described by D. Don in 1821 from Wallich's Gossain Than specimens. Further gatherings by other collectors show that the plant is widely distributed on the Himalayan range, extending from Kashmir, Nepal, Sikkim and Bhutan to Assam and Tibet. It grows in open pastures, on alpine ridges, on rocky hillsides, on the edge of bigger rhododendron forests, and on dry peaty soil, at elevations of 2,745—5,033 m. (9,000—16,500 ft.). It is recorded as being common in several localities on the Himalayas.

There has been much confusion between *R. anthopogon* with pink or rose flowers and *R. hypenanthum* with yellow flowers. The difficulty was solved by I. Bayley Balfour's description in *Notes Roy. Bot. Gard. Edin., Vol. 9* (1916), pp. 285—292. It is to be noted that a cultivated plant with yellow flowers which has been figured as *R. anthopogon* in the *Botanical Magazine t. 3947* (1842) agrees with *R. hypenanthum*, but has deciduous leaf-bud scales.

The species is very variable in general features, due to its wide geographical distribution, altitudinal range, and diverse habitats in which it is found. It is a prostrate or somewhat compact or spreading or upright shrub, from 6 inches to 5 feet high; the leaves are orbicular, oval, elliptic, oblong-elliptic or oblong, ½—1½ inches long; and the scales on the lower surface of the leaves are cinnamon or rust-coloured, reddish-brown, dark brown or brown.

R. anthopogon shows a strong resemblance to *R. hypenanthum* in general appearance, but is distinguished by the pink, rose or reddish flowers, and often by the deciduous leaf-bud scales. The plant is also allied to *R. collettianum* from which it differs in that the leaves are usually smaller, the corolla is pink, rose or reddish, and the stamens are 5—9 or rarely 10; it further differs in its geographical distribution. The species is diploid with 26 chromosomes.

R. anthopogon was first introduced in 1820. Several forms are in cultivation, including: Form 1. A somewhat compact spreading shrub up to 1 foot high with medium-sized leaves and medium-sized trusses of rosy-pink flowers. Form 2. A broadly upright shrub 1½—2 feet high with large oval leaves and large trusses of reddish flowers. Form 3. A rounded compact shrub, 2 feet high and as much across with medium-sized leaves and small trusses of pale pink flowers. Form 4. A lax upright shrub 1—1½ feet high, with small leaves and small trusses of rosy-pink flowers.

Form 2 is an exceedingly charming plant with large flowers produced freely in trusses of five to nine, and with Form 1 should be a most valuable acquisition to the rock garden and peat walls.

It may be remarked that the leaves of *R. anthopogon* are aromatic and often used as incense in Tibetan monasteries. As the species comes from elevations of up to 16,000 feet, it is hardy in cultivation, nevertheless to obtain the best results some shade and protection from wind should be provided. The plant is difficult to root from cuttings. It was given an Award of Merit when exhibited by Mrs. L.C.R. Messel, Nymans, Handcross, Sussex, in 1955, and again the same Award for a form 'Betty Graham' raised from Ludlow and Sherriff seed (No. 1091) when shown from Glendoick in 1969.

Epithet. With bearded flowers — referring to hairs in floret-tube.
Hardiness 3. April—May. Plate 2.

R. anthopogon D. Don var. **album** Davidian in Quart. Bull. Amer. Rhod. Soc., Vol. 34 (1980) 215.

This plant was first collected by Rohmoo Lepcha in August 1913 at Jongri, Sikkim.

Subsequently it was found by other collectors in Nepal, Bhutan and Tibet. It grows on dry slopes, on open hillsides, and amongst other rhododendrons and small shrubs, at elevations of 3,173—4,575 m. (10,500—15,000 ft.).

The variety differs from the species in that the flowers are white. It is a compact or broadly upright shrub, 30—92 cm. (1—3 ft.) high. The leaves are dark green and shining on the upper surfaces.

It was introduced by Ludlow, Sherriff and Hicks under No. 17550 from Bhutan in 1949 from an elevation of 3,660 m. (12,000 ft.). In cultivation it is quite hardy, free-flowering, and is well worth a place in every collection of rhododendrons.

Epithet. With white flowers.
Hardiness 3. April—May.

R. anthopogonoides Maxim. in Bull. Acad. Petersb. XXIII (1877) 350.

A lax, upright or broadly upright shrub, 92 cm.—1.83 m. (3—6 ft.) high; branchlets densely scaly, and with or without long-stalked scales, glabrous, leaf-bud scales deciduous. *Leaves* evergreen, broadly elliptic, oval or oblong-elliptic, aromatic, lamina coriaceous, 2—4.7 cm. long, 1.4—2.3 cm. broad, apex obtuse or rounded, mucronate, base obtuse or rounded or truncate; upper surface green or bluish-green, matt, not scaly or sparsely or rarely densely scaly, glabrous; margin slightly recurved or flat, glabrous; under surface densely covered with brown, dark brown or rust-coloured, overlapping, lacerate scales, the scales unequal, medium-sized and small, or rarely large; petiole 0.2—1 cm. long, densely scaly, glabrous. *Inflorescence* terminal, capitate, *10—20-flowered*, flower-bud scales persistent; rhachis 2—5 mm. long, scaly, puberulous; *pedicel 1—2 mm. long, not scaly*, glabrous or minutely puberulous. *Calyx* 5-lobed, 3—5 mm. long, lobes oblong, ovate-oblong or elliptic, outside not scaly, margin ciliate. *Corolla* narrowly tubular with spreading lobes, 1—1.4 cm. long, 5-lobed, yellow, greenish, greenish-yellow, greenish-white, whitish-pink or white, outside not scaly, glabrous, inside densely hairy within the tube. *Stamens* 5, unequal, 3—6 mm. long, included in the corolla-tube; filaments glabrous or puberulous at the base. *Ovary* ovoid, 1—2 mm. long, 5-celled, densely scaly, glabrous or rarely puberulous in the lower half; style very short, thick, straight, as long as the ovary or shorter, not scaly, glabrous. *Capsule* conoid, 3—4 mm. long, 3 mm. broad, densely scaly, glabrous, enclosed by the persistent calyx-lobes.

This species was discovered by N.M. Przewalski in 1872 in Kansu. It was later found by other collectors in various localities in Kansu and in eastern Tibet. The plant grows on exposed slopes, in scrub and spruce forests, at elevations of 2,898—3,355 m. (9,500—11,000 ft.).

R. anthopogonoides is a distinct species and is unlikely to be confused with other species of its Series. It is allied to *R. anthopogon* which it resembles in some features, but is readily distinguished by the non-scaly pedicel and calyx, by the 10—20-flowered inflorescence, and usually by the colour of the flowers.

The species has been in cultivation for a long time. It was introduced by Rock in 1925 from eastern Tibet (No. 13279), and from Kansu in the same year (Nos. 13597, 13610, and 13636). In cultivation it is a lax upright shrub up to 3 feet high with oval leaves and greenish-white flowers in trusses of 10—15. The species has been successfully grown outdoors by J.C. Williams at Caerhays, Cornwall, but unfortunately it is now possibly lost to cultivation.

Epithet. Resembling *R. anthopogon*.
Hardiness 3. April—May.

R. cephalanthum Franch. in Bull. Soc. Bot. France, XXXII (1885) 9.

A semi-prostrate, compact, spreading, or upright shrub, 5—92 cm. (2 in.—3 ft.) or sometimes up to 1.53 m. (5 ft.) high; branchlets densely scaly, and with or sometimes without long-stalked scales, glabrous, *leaf-bud scales persistent. Leaves* evergreen, oblong-elliptic, elliptic, oblong, oblong-oval or oval, aromatic, lamina coriaceous, 1—3.5 cm. long, 0.5—1.6 cm. broad, apex rounded or obtuse, mucronate, base rounded or obtuse; upper surface dark green, shining, not scaly, glabrous; margin recurved, glabrous; under surface densely covered with fawn, brown, dark brown, reddish, reddish-brown, chocolate or rust-coloured, overlapping, lacerate scales, glabrous; petiole 2—5 mm. long, densely scaly, and with or without long-stalked scales, glabrous. *Inflorescence* terminal, capitate, 5—10-flowered, flower-bud scales persistent; rhachis 1—2 mm. long, densely or moderately scaly, glabrous; pedicel 2—5 mm. long, densely or moderately scaly, glabrous. *Calyx* 5-lobed, 3—7 mm. long, lobes elliptic, oblong-oval, oblong or lanceolate, outside densely or moderately scaly, margin densely or moderately hairy with long hairs. *Corolla* narrowly tubular with spreading lobes, 1.2—2 cm. long, 5-lobed, white, rose, deep rose, pink, or rose-crimson with white at base, outside not scaly, glabrous or rarely tube hairy, inside densely hairy within the tube. *Stamens* 5—8, unequal, 3—6 mm. long, included in the corolla-tube; filaments glabrous or puberulous at the base. *Ovary* conoid or ovoid, 1—2 mm. long, 5-celled, densely scaly, glabrous; style very short, thick, straight, as long as the ovary or shorter, not scaly, glabrous. *Capsule* ovoid or conoid, 2—4 mm. long, 2—3 mm. broad, rather densely scaly, glabrous, enclosed by the persistent calyx-lobes.

R. cephalanthum was first found by the Abbé Delavay near Lankong and Hokin, Yunnan, in 1884. Subsequent gatherings by other collectors show that the plant is distributed in mid-west and north-west Yunnan, south-west Szechuan, east and southeast Tibet, Upper Burma, and Assam. It is found on rocks, cliffs, boulders, in open stony meadows, in alpine meadows, in peaty moorlands, and at the margins of swamps, at elevations of 2,593—4,575 m. (8,500—15,000 ft.). Farrer records it as being abundant over the high alpine regions in dense drifts like heather at Shing Hong Pass, north-east Upper Burma. According to Kingdon-Ward it is very common, forming thickets 6—9 inches high in Upper Burma, also forming carpets 6 inches high with pink flowers at the Tibet-Yunnan Frontier. Yü points out that it is common in alpine windswept moorland in north-west Yunnan.

R. cephalanthum varies considerably in habit and height of growth, in leaf shape and size, and in the colour of the scales on the lower surface of the leaves. It shows a strong resemblance to *R. anthopogon* in general characters, but is usually distinguished by the conspicuous persistent leaf-bud scales, and very often by the 5 stamens. Moreover, they occupy somewhat different geographical areas. *R. cephalanthum* is a diploid, 2n = 26.

The species was first introduced by Wilson in 1908. It was reintroduced on several occasions by Forrest, Kingdon-Ward, Rock, and Yü. Two distinct forms are in cultivation. Form 1. A compact, rounded or spreading shrub, up to 1 foot high and up to 1½ feet across, a somewhat slow grower, with short annual growths, densely filled with foliage, and with white tinged pink flowers. Form 2. An upright shrub up to 3 feet high, a fairly fast grower, with long rigid annual growths, moderately filled with foliage, and with white or pink flowers. Both forms are characterised by the persistent leaf-bud scales, and aromatic foliage. Form 1 is a delightful plant, free-flowering, and is excellently suited for the rock garden. The species is hardy outdoors, but to be able to grow it satisfactorily, particularly along the east coast, a well-sheltered position should be provided. It received an Award of Merit when shown by Mr. L. de Rothschild in 1934. Another form also received the same Award when exhibited by Mrs. K. Dryden, Sawbridgeworth, Herts., in 1979.

Epithet. With flowers in a head.
Hardiness 3. April—May.

R. collettianum Aitch. et Hemsl. in Journ. Linn. Soc. XVIII (1881) 75.
Illustration. Bot. Mag. Vol. 114 t. 7019 (1888).
An upright or lax somewhat rounded shrub up to 1 m. (3⅓ ft.) high; branchlets densely

scaly, glabrous, leaf-bud scales deciduous. *Leaves* evergreen, lanceolate or oblong-lanceolate, aromatic, lamina coriaceous, *3—5.6 cm. long*, 1.1—2.3 cm. broad, apex acute or obtuse, mucronate, base rounded or obtuse; upper surface dark green or bright green, somewhat shining, not scaly or scaly, glabrous; margin flat or slightly recurved, glabrous; under surface densely covered with *creamy-yellow*, overlapping, lacerate *scales*, glabrous; petiole 0.5—1.4 cm. long, densely scaly, glabrous. *Inflorescence* terminal, capitate, 5—12-flowered, flower-bud scales persistent or deciduous; rhachis 3—5 mm. long, densely scaly, glabrous; pedicel 3—4 mm. long, densely scaly, glabrous. *Calyx* 5-lobed, 3—5 mm. long, lobes unequal, oblong or oblong-oval, outside scaly, glabrous, margin densely ciliate. *Corolla* narrowly tubular-funnel shaped, 1.5—2.4 cm. long, 5-lobed, white or white tinged rose, outside not scaly, glabrous, inside rather densely pubescent within the tube. *Stamens 10*, unequal, *6—9 mm. long*, included in the corolla-tube, the whole filament pubescent above the base or towards the lower two-thirds of its length. *Ovary* conoid or ovoid, 1 mm. long, 5-celled, densely scaly, glabrous; style very short, thick, straight, as long as the ovary or shorter, not scaly, glabrous. *Capsule* conoid or oblong, 3—4 mm. long, 2 mm. broad, densely scaly, glabrous, enclosed or partly enclosed by the persistent calyx-lobes.

This species is an outlier from the known area of distribution of its Series. It was first collected by both Major Collett and Dr. Aitchison on the Safed Kuh and elsewhere in Afghanistan, during the Kurrum Valley Expedition of 1879. In September 1958, J.D.A. Stainton found it in the south-west of Drosh, Urtsun Gol, Chitral, Pakistan, and in June 1969 I. Hedge and P. Wendelbo collected it at Safed Kuh, Mt. Sikaram, Afghanistan. It grows on stony slopes, and forms thickets with masses of juniper, at elevations of 3,050—3,965 m. (10,000—13,000 ft.).

R. collettianum is a distinctive species, one of the finest of the Anthopogon Series. It shows a certain degree of resemblance to *R. anthopogon*, from which it is readily distinguished by the larger lanceolate or oblong-lanceolate leaves, by the 10 stamens, and usually by the creamy-yellow scales on the lower surface of the leaves.

The species was originally introduced by Dr. Aitchison in 1880. It flowered for the first time in the rock garden at Kew in 1888, but eventually the plant was lost to cultivation. It was reintroduced by Hedge and Wendelbo (No. 8975) in 1969, and it flowered in May 1975. The large white flowers up to about one inch in length, are an attractive feature. The plant has proved to be of sturdy habit, fairly fast-growing, and deserves the widest possible recognition.

Epithet. After General Sir Henry Collett, 1836—1901.
Hardiness 3. April—May.

R. crebreflorum Hutch. et Ward in Notes Roy. Bot. Gard. Edin., XVI (1931) 173.

A prostrate spreading or very compact shrub, 5—25 cm. (2—10 in.) high; branchlets densely or moderately scaly, glabrous, leaf-bud scales persistent. *Leaves* evergreen, broadly elliptic, oval or oblong-elliptic, aromatic, lamina 1.3—2.5 cm. long, 0.6—1.7 cm. broad, apex rounded, mucronate, base rounded or obtuse; upper surface reticulate, dark green, shining, not scaly or scaly, glabrous; margin recurved or flat, glabrous; under surface densely covered with dark brown or brown or reddish-brown flaky, overlapping, lacerate scales, glabrous; petiole 2—5 mm. long, scaly, glabrous. *Inflorescence* terminal, capitate, 5—12-flowered, flower-bud scales persistent; rhachis 1—2 mm. long, scaly, glabrous; pedicel 4—5 mm. long, scaly, glabrous. *Calyx* 5-lobed, 3—4 mm. long, lobes oblong or elliptic, outside sparsely or moderately scaly, margin densely or moderately hairy with long hairs. *Corolla* narrowly tubular with spreading lobes, 1.6—2 cm. long, 5-lobed, pale pink, white tinged pink, deep rose or reddish, outside not scaly, glabrous, inside densely hairy within the tube. *Stamens 6*, unequal, 4—5 mm. long, included in the corolla-tube; filaments glabrous. *Ovary* ovoid, 1—2 mm. long, 5-celled, densely scaly, glabrous; style very short, thick, straight, shorter than or as long as the ovary, not scaly, glabrous. *Capsule* ovoid, 3 mm. long, 3 mm. broad, rather densely scaly, glabrous, enclosed by the persistent calyx-lobes.

This dainty little shrublet is undoubtedly one of Kingdon-Ward's finest discoveries in Upper Burma. He first found it at Seinghku Wang, in June 1926, a dwarf twiggy shrub, not rising more than 8—10 inches above the level of the carpet amongst which it was woven, on precipitous slopes, at an elevation of 3,965 m. (13,000 ft.). He collected it again in June 1928 in the Delei Valley, Assam, growing on slabs of rock or on grassy ledges of cliffs, also at 3,965 m. (13,000 ft.).

R. crebreflorum resembles the dwarf form of *R. cephalanthum* in some respects, but differs markedly in that it has a very compact, or prostrate spreading habit of growth, and 6 stamens.

The species was first introduced by Kingdon-Ward in 1926 from Upper Burma (No. 6967). It was reintroduced by him in 1928 from Assam (No. 8337 — the Type number). Two distinct growth forms are in cultivation. Form 1. A very compact rounded shrub up to 6 inches high and as much across, densely filled with foliage. Form 2. A prostrate spreading shrub, up to 3 inches high and up to 3—4 inches wide, moderately filled with foliage. Although the species is a slow grower, it has the advantage of producing the flowers at a young age when raised from seed. It is an exceptionally fine plant, particularly Form 1, when covered with deep rose or reddish flowers in clusters of up to six or more. The plant is hardy outdoors, but to obtain the best results, some shade and protection from wind are essential. It received an Award of Merit when exhibited by Lt.-Col. Messel, Nymans, Sussex, in 1934.

Epithet. Densely-flowered.
Hardiness 3. April—May.

R. hypenanthum Balf. f. in Notes Roy. Bot. Gard. Edin., IX (1916) 291.

A lax upright or dwarf compact shrub, 15—92 cm. (6 in.—3 ft.) high; branchlets densely scaly, glabrous, *leaf-bud scales persistent* or rarely deciduous. *Leaves* evergreen, oval, oblong-oval, oblong-elliptic, elliptic, oblong or orbicular, aromatic, lamina 1—4.2 cm. long, 0.8—2 cm. broad, apex rounded or obtuse, mucronate, base rounded or obtuse; upper surface dark green, shining, not scaly or sparsely or sometimes moderately scaly, glabrous; margin flat or slightly recurved, glabrous; under surface densely covered with reddish-brown, cinnamon, rust-coloured or dark brown, overlapping, lacerate scales, glabrous; petiole 3—7 mm. long, densely or moderately scaly, glabrous. *Inflorescence* terminal, capitate, 5—10-flowered, flower-bud scales persistent; rhachis 1—2 mm. long, scaly or not scaly, glabrous or rarely densely minutely puberulous; pedicel 1—4 mm. long, moderately or densely scaly, glabrous. *Calyx* 5-lobed, 2—4 mm. long, lobes lanceolate, elliptic, oblong-elliptic, oblong or oval, outside scaly or sometimes not scaly, margin densely or sometimes moderately ciliate. *Corolla* narrowly tubular with spreading lobes, 1.1—1.9 cm. long, 5-lobed, *yellow, pale yellow, pale creamy-yellow or lemon-green*, outside not scaly or rarely sparsely scaly, glabrous, inside densely pubescent within the tube. *Stamens* 5—8, unequal, 2—5 mm. long, included in the corolla-tube; filaments glabrous. *Ovary* ovoid or conoid, 1 mm. long, 5-celled, moderately or densely scaly, glabrous; style very short, thick, straight, as long as the ovary or slightly longer, not scaly, glabrous. *Capsule* ovoid or conoid, 2—5 mm. long, 2—3 mm. broad, moderately or densely scaly, glabrous, enclosed or partly enclosed by the persistent calyx-lobes.

R. hypenanthum was described by Isaac Bayley Balfour in 1916. It has a wide geographical distribution, extending from Kashmir and Punjab to Nepal, Sikkim and Bhutan. The plant grows in scrub, in open birch wood, on open hillsides, amongst rocks, and in open moorland, at elevations of 3,173—4,270 m. (10,500—14,000 ft.) or sometimes up to 5,490 m. (18,000 ft.). It is said to form low thickets one foot high in some localities.

It is very closely allied to *R. anthopogon*. There is a marked similarity between them in habit and height of growth, and in the shape and size of the leaves. The main distinction between them is that in R. *hypenanthum* the corolla is yellow, pale yellow or lemon-green, whereas in R. *anthopogon* it is pink, rose, reddish or rarely crimson. Moreover, in the former the leaf-bud scales are persistent or rarely deciduous, whilst in the latter they are usually deciduous. On the basis of these distinctions R. *hypenanthum* might well be regarded as a variety. However, the extremes of these plants are so dissimilar in cultivation that it may be desirable to retain the name R. *hypenanthum*.

The species was first introduced in 1820. It was reintroduced by Stainton, Sykes and Williams (No. 9090) in 1954 from Nepal at an elevation of 3,660 m. (12,000 ft.). The plant is recorded as having flowered in 1842 in the Countess of Rosslyn's garden at Dysart House, Fife, Scotland, with yellowish-white flowers produced abundantly in the open air. Two distinct growth forms are in cultivation. Form 1. A somewhat lax upright shrub up to 3 feet high. Form 2. A dwarf compact shrub 1—1½ feet high. The flowers are produced freely in clusters of five to ten. The dwarf compact forms are charming plants, and should be valuable acquisitions to the rock garden. A clone 'Annapurna' (Stainton, Sykes & Williams No. 9090) was given an Award of Merit when shown from Glendoick in 1974.

Epithet. Bearded flowers.
Hardiness 3. April—May.

R. kongboense Hutch. in Bot. Mag. Vol. 160 t. 9492 (1937).
A broadly upright shrub, 15 cm.—2.44 m. (6 in.—8 ft.) high; branchlets short twiggy, or long, densely scaly, and with long-stalked scales, glabrous, leaf-bud scales deciduous. *Leaves* evergreen, oblong, oblong-elliptic, oblong-lanceolate, oblong-oval or oval, aromatic, lamina coriaceous, 0.9—2.8 cm. long, 0.4—1.1 cm. broad, apex obtuse or rounded, mucronate, base obtuse or rounded; upper surface dark green, matt or somewhat shining, densely or rarely sparsely scaly, glabrous; margin flat or slightly recurved, glabrous; under surface densely covered with chocolate, cinnamon, rust-coloured, dark brown, brown or fawn, overlapping, lacerate scales, the scales unequal, large and/or medium-sized; petiole 2—6 mm. long, densely scaly, glabrous. *Inflorescence* terminal, capitate, 6—12-flowered, flower-bud scales persistent or deciduous; rhachis 1—2 mm. long, scaly or not scaly, densely or moderately puberulous or glabrous; pedicel 1—4 mm. long, moderately or densely scaly, glabrous. *Calyx* 5-lobed, *3—5 mm. long, large for the size of the flower*, greenish or reddish-purple, lobes oblong, elliptic, oblong-elliptic or oblong-oval, outside densely scaly down the middle of the lobes, glabrous, margin ciliate. *Corolla* narrowly tubular with spreading lobes, *0.8—1.1 cm. long*, 5-lobed, rose, pink, almost white flushed pink, strawberry red, deep red or reddish-purple, outside not scaly, *tube densely or rarely moderately hairy outside*, inside densely hairy within the tube. *Stamens* 5, unequal, 3—4 mm. long, included in the corolla-tube; filaments glabrous. *Ovary* ovoid, 1 mm. long, 5-celled, densely scaly, glabrous; style very short, thick, straight, shorter or longer than the ovary, not scaly, glabrous. *Capsule* ovoid, 3 mm. long, 2—3 mm. broad, densely scaly, glabrous, enclosed by the persistent calyx-lobes.

This species was discovered by Kingdon-Ward in June 1924 at Doshong La, Tibet-Bhutan Border. Subsequently it was found by him again, and by Ludlow, Sherriff, and Elliot or Taylor in various localities in Tibet. It grows among boulders, on limestone cliffs, in marshy ground, in rhododendron and oak forest, and on dry ground at elevations of 3,173—4,575 m. (10,500—15,000 ft.).

The species is very variable in habit and height of growth due to the various environmental conditions in which it is found. In south-east Tibet where it grows on rocks, it is a dwarf shrub 6 inches high, while in the same region, in rhododendron and oak forest, it forms an erect shrub 8 feet high.

The characteristic features of this plant are the short corolla 0.8—1.1 cm. long, densely hairy on the tube outside, and the large calyx 3—5 mm. long which is large for the size of the corolla. The scales on the lower surface of the leaves are chocolate, cinnamon or rust-coloured, or dark brown, brown or fawn.

R. kongboense shows a resemblance to *R. primuliflorum* var. *cephalanthoides* in its general appearance, but is distinguished by its shorter and usually deep red corolla, and by the densely scaly calyx down the middle.

The species was first introduced by Kingdon-Ward in June 1924 (No. 5850 — the Type number) from an elevation of 3,660—3,965 m. (12,000—13,000 ft.). It was reintroduced by him in July of the same year (No. 6020). Ludlow, Sherriff and Elliot sent seed in September 1947 (No. 13269). In cultivation it is broadly upright, up to 3 or 4 feet or sometimes 5 feet high with dark green, highly aromatic leaves. It is a pleasing shrub, a vigorous grower, with deep red flowers produced freely in clusters of six to twelve. Although the species is hardy, a sheltered position should be provided.

Epithet. From Kongbo, S.E. Tibet.
Hardiness 3. April—May.

R. laudandum Cowan in Notes Roy. Bot. Gard. Edin., Vol. 19 (1937) 222.

A rounded somewhat compact, or broadly upright and somewhat spreading shrub, 15 cm.—1.22 m. (6 in.—4 ft.) high; branchlets densely scaly, and with or without long-stalked scales, glabrous, leaf-bud scales deciduous. *Leaves* evergreen, oblong-oval, oval, elliptic or oblong, aromatic, lamina coriaceous, 0.9—1.8 cm. long, 0.4—1 cm. broad, apex rounded or obtuse, mucronate, base rounded or obtuse or cuneate; upper surface dark green or pale green, shining or matt, not scaly or rather densely scaly (in young leaves densely scaly) glabrous; margin slightly recurved or flat, glabrous; under surface densely covered with *dark reddish-brown, chocolate or cinnamon-coloured*, dark brown or fawn, overlapping, lacerate scales, the scales unequal, large and medium-sized; petiole 2—4 mm. long, densely scaly, glabrous. *Inflorescence* terminal, capitate, 5—10-flowered, flower-bud scales persistent; rhachis 1—2 mm. long, scaly or not scaly, puberulous or glabrous; pedicel 3—6 mm. long, densely scaly, glabrous. *Calyx* 5-lobed, unequal, 4—5 mm. long, lobes lanceolate, oblong, elliptic, oblong-oval or oval, outside densely or moderately scaly, margin densely or moderately ciliate. *Corolla* narrowly tubular with spreading lobes, 1.3—1.5 cm. long, 5-lobed, pale pink, pink, white or rarely creamy-yellow, *outside* not scaly, *tube densely or moderately hairy* or rarely glabrous, inside densely hairy within the tube. *Stamens* 5, unequal, 3—5 mm. long, included in the corolla-tube; filaments glabrous. *Ovary* ovoid, 1—2 mm. long, 5-celled, scaly, *densely hairy all over or in the lower half*; style very short, thick, straight, shorter than, or as long as, the ovary, not scaly or scaly, glabrous. *Capsule* ovoid, 2—4 mm. long, 2—3 mm. broad, scaly, hairy or glabrous, enclosed by the persistent calyx-lobes.

Kingdon-Ward discovered this plant in June 1924 at Temo La, southern Tibet. He collected it again in July 1935 in the same region. In June 1936, Ludlow and Sherriff found it in south Tibet. It grows on rocks and hillsides at elevations of 4,270—4,575 m. (14,000—15,000 ft.). Kingdon-Ward records it as forming a compact low tangled undergrowth. According to Ludlow and Sherriff it is common on hillsides.

A remarkable feature of this plant is often the chocolate-coloured scales on the lower surface of the leaves, by which the species is readily distinguished from most other members of its Series.

It is closely related to *R. rufescens*. There is a strong similarity between them in general characters. *R. laudandum* differs from its ally in that the corolla-tube is densely hairy outside, and the ovary is hairy all over or in the lower half.

The species is recorded as having been introduced under Kingdon-Ward No. 5733 from his 1924—1925 expedition to Tibet and Bhutan. Unfortunately, the plant under this number has not been seen in cultivation.

Epithet. Praiseworthy.
Not in cultivation.

R. laudandum Cowan var. **temoense** Ward ex Cowan et Davidian in The Rhododendron Year Book (1947) 73.

This plant was first collected by Kingdon-Ward in June 1924 at Doshong La, Tibet-Bhutan border. It was later found by Ludlow, Sherriff and Elliot in various localities in south-east Tibet. The plant grows on steep alpine slopes, on hillsides, and on moraines, at elevations of 2,898—4,728 m. (9,500—15,500 ft.). Kingdon-Ward records it as forming masses 6—9 inches deep on the more sheltered flank of the mountain at Doshong La, with many other species.

The variety differs from the species in that the leaf-bud scales are usually persistent, and the ovary is glabrous and densely scaly.

The plant was introduced by Kingdon-Ward in June 1924 (No. 5848 — the Type number) from 3,660—3,965 m. (12,000—13,000 ft.) In its native home it grows from 6 inches to 4 feet high; in cultivation it is a rounded somewhat compact, or broadly upright and somewhat spreading shrub, up to 2 feet high, with aromatic foliage. It is fairly fast-growing, and one of its chief merits is that it flowers at a remarkably early age. The plant is easy to grow, and is not difficult to increase from cuttings. It is free-flowering, and seldom fails to put forth a profusion of flowers in clusters of five to eight. The plant is hardy outdoors, but to be able to grow it satisfactorily, particularly along the east coast and in gardens inland, a well-sheltered position should be provided.

Epithet. From Temo La, southern Tibet.

Hardiness 3. April—May.

R. nmaiense Balf. f. et Ward in Notes Roy. Bot. Gard. Edin., Vol. 9 (1916) 252.

A somewhat compact and spreading, or bushy shrub, 15—92 cm. (6 in.—3 ft.) high; branchlets densely or moderately scaly, and with or without long-stalked scales, glabrous, leaf-bud scales persistent. *Leaves* evergreen, oblong, oval, orbicular, elliptic or oblong-oval, aromatic, lamina coriaceous, 1—2.5 cm. long, 0.8—1.3 cm. broad, apex rounded, mucronate, base rounded or obtuse; *upper surface* dark green, *shining,* scaly or not scaly, glabrous; margin recurved or flat, glabrous; under surface densely covered with rust-coloured, dark brown or reddish-brown, overlapping, flaky, lacerate scales, glabrous; petiole 2—5 mm. long, densely or moderately scaly, glabrous. *Inflorescence* terminal, capitate, 5—8-flowered, flower-bud scales persistent; rhachis 1—2 mm. long, scaly, glabrous; pedicel 2—5 mm. long, densely or moderately scaly, glabrous. *Calyx* 5-lobed, 4—5 mm. long, lobes oblong, oblong-oval or elliptic, outside densely or moderately scaly, margin densely or moderately scaly or not scaly, eciliate or ciliate. *Corolla* narrowly tubular with spreading lobes, 1.3—2 cm. long, 5-lobed, *sulphur-yellow, lemon-yellow or creamy-white, tube often deep yellow* outside not scaly or rarely lobes sparsely scaly, glabrous, inside densely hairy within the tube. *Stamens 5 or sometimes 6,* unequal, 4—5 mm. long, included in the corolla-tube; filaments glabrous. *Ovary* ovoid, 1—2 mm. long, 5-celled, densely scaly, glabrous; style very short, thick, straight, as long as the ovary or shorter, not scaly, glabrous. *Capsule* ovoid, 2—4 mm. long, 2—3 mm. broad, rather densely scaly, glabrous, enclosed by the persistent calyx-lobes.

R. nmaiense was described from a specimen (No. 1791) collected by Kingdon-Ward in July 1914 on the ridge of Naung Chaung, east Upper Burma. It was afterwards collected by Forrest, and by Ludlow, Sherriff and Elliot in various localities in south-east Tibet. It grows amonst bamboo brake, amongst granite boulders, on cliffs, on boulder slopes, on rocks, and in open moorland, at elevations of 3,050—4,118 m. (10,000—13,500 ft.).

In general appearance, the species shows a resemblance to *R. cephalanthum,* but differs in that the corolla is sulphur-yellow, lemon-yellow or creamy-white, and the stamens are 5 or sometimes 6.

The plant has been in cultivation for a long time, and was possibly introduced by Kingdon-Ward. In its native home, it grows from 6 inches up to 3 feet in height, but in cultivation it is a neat somewhat compact and spreading shrub up to 1 foot high and

1—1½ feet across with oblong-oval aromatic leaves, dark green and very shining on the upper surface. It is a pleasing shrub, and provides a fine display with its sulphur-yellow flowers in trusses of five to eight. The plant is rare in cultivation, but is worthy of a place in every rock garden.

Epithet. From the Nmai Hka, Upper Burma.

Hardiness 3. April—May.

R. platyphyllum Balf. f. et W.W. Sm. in Notes Roy. Bot. Gard. Edin., Vol. 9 (1916) 259.

A semi-prostrate or upright shrub, 15 cm.—1.53 m. (6 in.—5 ft.) high; branchlets short, twiggy, densely scaly, and with long-stalked scales, glabrous, *leaf-bud scales persistent, large, broadly ovate, obovate or rounded, leafy. Leaves* evergreen, broadly elliptic, elliptic, oblong-elliptic, oblong-oval or oval, *lamina* coriaceous, *2.6—5 cm. long, 1.5—2.8 cm. broad*, apex rounded or obtuse, emarginate, mucronate, base obtuse or rounded; upper surface dark green, shining, not scaly, glabrous; margin slightly recurved, glabrous; under surface densely covered with brown, dark brown or rust-coloured, overlapping, lacerate scales, the scales unequal, large and medium-sized; petiole 3—5 mm. long, densely or moderately scaly, and with long-stalked scales, glabrous. *Inflorescence* terminal, capitate, 6—10-flowered, flower-bud scales persistent; rhachis 2—3 mm. long, scaly or not scaly, glabrous; pedicel 3—5 mm. long, scaly, glabrous. *Calyx* 5-lobed, *4—7 mm. long*, lobes oblong or elliptic, outside scaly, margin sparsely or densely hairy with long hairs. *Corolla* narrowly tubular with spreading lobes, *1.8—2 cm. long*, 5-lobed, white, creamy-white, occasionally faintly flushed rose, pale rose or white flushed rose, outside not scaly, glabrous, inside densely hairy within the tube. *Stamens* 5, unequal, 5—6 mm. long, included in the corolla-tube; filaments glabrous or slightly puberulous towards the base. *Ovary* ovoid or conoid, 1 mm. long, 5-celled, densely scaly, glabrous; style very short, thick, straight, as long as the ovary, not scaly, glabrous. *Capsule* ovoid or conoid, 3 mm. long, 2—3 mm. broad, densely scaly, glabrous, enclosed by the persistent calyx-lobes.

R. platyphyllum is a native of Yunnan. It was first collected by the Abbé Delavay in June 1887 on the Tali Range. Subsequently it was found by Forrest, McLaren's collectors, and Rock in various localities in the same region. The plant grows on cliffs and crags, in bamboo brakes, and in open alpine pasture amongst rocks, at elevations of 3,050—4,423 m. (10,000—14,500 ft.).

The species is very variable in habit and height of growth. It is a semi-prostrate or upright shrub, from 6 inches up to 5 feet high. The large broad leaf to which the specific name refers, is a distinctive character. The broadly ovate or rounded, leafy, persistent leaf-bud scales are its remarkable features. Other notable characters are the large calyx, 4—7 mm. long, and the large corolla, 1.8—2 cm. long. In some respects, the species resembles *R. cephalanthum*, from which it is readily distinguished by well-marked features.

R. platyphyllum was first introduced by Forrest in July 1914 (No. 13526). It was reintroduced by him in 1919 (No. 18041), and again in 1929 (No. 28241). Unfortunately the species has now been lost to cultivation.

Epithet. Broad-leaved.

Not in cultivation.

R. pogonophyllum Cowan et Davidian in The Rhododendron Year Book (1947) 75.

A *prostrate creeping shrub, 3—10 cm. (1.2—4 in.) high;* branchlets scaly, hairy, leaf-bud scales persistent. *Leaves* evergreen, obovate or ovate, lamina coriaceous 0.7—1 cm. long, 4—6 mm. broad, apex rounded, emarginate, base cuneate or obtuse; *upper surface* green, shining, rugulose, not scaly, *bristly; margin* recurved, *bristly;* under surface densely covered with brown, overlapping, lacerate scales, not bristly; *petiole* 1—3 mm. long, moderately or rather densely scaly, *bristly* or not bristly. *Inflorescence* terminal, *umbellate, 2—3-flowered,* flower-bud scales persistent; pedicel 2—4 mm. long, sparsely or moderately scaly, not bristly. *Calyx* 5-lobed, *5—6 mm. long,* lobes oblong, outside not scaly or sparsely scaly, glabrous or sparsely hairy, margin ciliate. *Corolla* narrowly tubular with spreading lobes, 1.4—1.6 cm. long, 5-lobed, white or pale pink, outside not scaly or slightly scaly, glabrous, inside rather densely pubescent within the tube. *Stamens 6,* unequal, 3—4 mm. long, included in the corolla-tube; filaments glabrous. *Ovary* ovoid or conoid, 1 mm. long, 5-celled, moderately or sparsely scaly, glabrous; style very short, thick, straight, as long as the ovary or slightly longer, not scaly, glabrous. *Capsule:* —

The distribution of *R. pogonophyllum* is restricted to Central Bhutan. The plant was discovered by Ludlow and Sherriff in June 1937 at Tang Chu, Ritang. They collected it again later in June at Rinchen Chu, Chore, in the same region. It is found creeping along rocks and on rocky thin soil, and over rocks, on open hillsides, at elevations of 4,270—4,575 m. (14,000—15,000 ft.).

A remarkable feature of this plant is the prostrate creeping habit of growth, 1—4 inches high, by which the species is readily distinguished from all other members of its Series. Other diagnostic characters are the bristly nature of the leaves and petioles, and the umbellate 2—3-flowered inflorescence.

The species is related to *R. radendum* from which it differs markedly in that it is a prostrate creeping shrub, the leaf-bud scales are persistent, the calyx is large, 5—6 mm. long, the inflorescence is 2—3-flowered, the pedicel is not bristly, the corolla is not scaly or slightly scaly outside, and the stamens are 6. It further differs in its geographical distribution. The plant has not been introduced into cultivation.

Epithet. With bearded leaves — referring to the bristles on the leaves and petioles.
Not in cultivation.

R. primuliflorum Bur. et Franch. in Journ. de Bot. V (1891) 95.

A matted, prostrate, cushion or broadly upright shrub, 5 cm.—1.83 m. (2 in.—6 ft.) or rarely 2.44—2.75 m. (8—9 ft.) high; branchlets short twiggy or long, densely scaly, and with or without long-stalked scales, glabrous, *leaf-bud scales deciduous. Leaves* evergreen, oblong, elliptic, oblong-elliptic, oblong-lanceolate, lanceolate or oval, aromatic, lamina coriaceous, 0.8—3.4 cm. long, 0.5—1.3 cm. or rarely 1.5 cm. broad, apex obtuse or rounded, mucronate, base obtuse or rounded; upper surface dark green, shining, not scaly or rarely scaly (in young leaves densely scaly), glabrous; margin slightly recurved or flat, glabrous; under surface densely covered with brown, dark brown, fawn or rust-coloured, overlapping, lacerate scales, the scales unequal, large and medium-sized; petiole 2—4 mm. long, densely scaly, glabrous. *Inflorescence* terminal, capitate, 5—10-flowered, flower-bud scales persistent or deciduous; rhachis 1—3 mm. long, scaly or not scaly, minutely puberulous or glabrous; pedicel 1—4 mm. long, scaly, glabrous. *Calyx* 5-lobed, 2—5 mm. long, lobes lanceolate, oblong, ovate, oblong-oval or oval, outside scaly or not scaly, glabrous or rarely puberulous, margin ciliate or eciliate. *Corolla* narrowly tubular with spreading lobes, 1—1.6 cm. long, 5-lobed, white, white with yellow tube, pale rose, pink, deep rose-pink, white tinged orange at base, creamy-yellow, creamy-white or yellow, outside not scaly or rarely lobes rather densely or moderately scaly, glabrous, inside densely hairy within the tube. *Stamens 5,* unequal, 3—5 mm. long, included in the corolla-tube; filaments glabrous or puberulous at the base. *Ovary* ovoid or conoid, 1 mm. long, 5-celled, densely scaly, glabrous; style very short, thick, straight, as long as the ovary or shorter, not scaly, glabrous. *Capsule* ovoid or conoid, 3—4 mm. long, 3 mm. broad, densely scaly, glabrous, enclosed by the persistent calyx-lobes.

R. primuliflorum was described by Bureau and Franchet in 1891 from a plant collected by Bonvalot and Prince H. D'Orléans between Lhassa and Batang, Tibet in May 1890. It has a wide distribution extending from Eastern Siberia, south-east and east Tibet, Kansu, and south-west Szechuan to north-west and mid-west Yunnan. It is found on rocks, on limestone cliffs, on boulders, in open alpine moorland, and in rocky pastures, at elevations of 3,050—5,185 m. (10,000—17,000 ft.). It is recorded as being common in north-west Yunnan.

The species varies considerably in general features. It is a matted, prostrate, cushion or broadly upright shrub, ranging from 2 inches up to 6 feet or rarely up to 8 or 9 feet high; the leaves are lanceolate, oblong to oval, (laminae) ⅓—1⅓ inches long; the scales on the lower surface are fawn, brown, dark brown or rust-coloured; and the inflorescence is 5—10-flowered. The plant bears a resemblance to *R. cephalanthum*, from which it is readily distinguished by the deciduous leaf-bud scales and often by the 5 stamens.

R. primuliflorum was first introduced by Forrest in 1910 (No. 5866) from the eastern flank of the Lichiang Range, Yunnan, at 3,355—3,660 m. (11,000—12,000 ft.). Forrest later sent seeds on many occasions from other localities. It was also introduced by Kingdon-Ward, Rock, and Yü. In cultivation it is a broadly upright shrub up to 3 or 4 feet high, fairly well-filled with dark green aromatic leaves. It is a robust grower, with rigid branchlets, and does not seem particular as to position in the rock garden and peat walls. The plants vary widely in their freedom of flowering; some do not flower freely, but make pleasant and useful evergreen shrubs. The species is difficult to increase from cuttings.

Epithet. Primrose-flowered.
Hardiness 3. April—May.

R. primuliflorum Bur. et Franch. var. **cephalanthoides** (Balf. f. et W.W. Sm.) Cowan et Davidian in The Rhododendron Year Book (1947) 79.

Syn. *R. cephalanthoides* Balf. f. et W.W. Sm. in Notes Roy. Bot. Gard. Edin., Vol. 9 (1916) 216.

This plant was first collected by Forrest in May 1906 on the eastern flank of the Lichiang Range, north-west Yunnan. It was afterwards found by him and by other collectors in north-west Yunnan, south-east Tibet and south-west Szechuan. The plant grows on ledges and in clefts of limestone cliffs, on rocky slopes, in open moorland, in rocky alpine pastures, in swamps, and in spruce forests, at elevations of 3,355—4,728 m. (11,000—15,500 ft.). Ludlow and Sherriff record it as growing extensively in the alpine moorland in Tibet.

The variety differs from the species in that the corolla-tube is moderately or rather densely puberulous outside.

The plant was first introduced by Forrest in 1917 (No. 15088) from north-west Yunnan at 3,660 m. (12,000 ft.). It was reintroduced by him and by Rock from the same region, and by Ludlow, Sherriff and Taylor from south-east Tibet. It is a vigorous, fairly fast-growing shrub up to two or three feet in height with aromatic foliage. The plant is hardy, and is easily adaptable to any position in the garden. It flowers freely, and provides a fine display with its rose-pink flowers in clusters of three to eight. The plant is difficult to root from cuttings.

Epithet. Like *R. cephalanthum*.
Hardiness 3. April—May.

R. radendum Fang in Contrib. Biol. Lab. Sc. Soc. China, XII (1939) 62.

A small shrub up to 1 m. (3⅓ ft.) high; branchlets densely scaly, *densely bristly*, leaf-bud scales deciduous. *Leaves* evergreen, ovate-lanceolate or obovate-lanceolate, 1—1.8 cm. long, 3—6 mm. broad, apex acute or obtuse, base obtuse; upper surface green, shining, scaly, *bristly*; margin revolute; under surface densely scaly with brownish scales, *bristly*; petiole about 3 mm. long, scaly, *bristly*. *Inflorescence* terminal, capitate, 8—10-flowered; pedicel 2—3 mm. long, scaly, *bristly*. *Calyx* 5-lobed, small, 1—2 mm. long, lobes ovate, outside scaly, *bristly*, margin ciliate. *Corolla* narrowly tubular with spreading lobes, 0.8—1 cm. long, 5-lobed, purplish-white, *outside densely scaly*, inside hairy. Stamens 5, included; filaments glabrous. *Ovary* ovoid, 1 mm. long, scaly; style very short, as long as the ovary, glaborus. *Capsule: —*

R. radendum is known from a single collection made in May 1930 by the Chinese collector W.C. Cheng near Tatsienlu, Sikang (now western Szechuan), at an elevation of 3,050 m. (10,000 ft.).

The bristly character of the branchlets, leaves, petioles, pedicels, and calyx, is its most remarkable feature. The species is related to *R. pogonophyllum* from which it differs in that it grows up to 3 feet high, the calyx is small, 1—2 mm. long, the inflorescence is 8—10-flowered, the corolla is small, 0.8—1 cm. long, densely scaly outside, and the stamens are 5. It further differs in its geographical distribution. The plant has not been introduced into cultivation.

Epithet. Scraped; smooth.

Not in cultivation.

R. rufescens Franch. in Journ. de Bot. IX (1895) 396.

A small shrub, 30 cm.—1.25 m. (1—4 ft.) high; branchlets short, twiggy, densely scaly, and with or without long-stalked scales, glabrous, leaf-bud scales deciduous. *Leaves* evergreen, obovate, oval, oblong-oval, oblong-elliptic or oblong, aromatic, lamina coriaceous, 0.8—2.8 cm. long, 0.4—1.6 cm. broad, apex rounded or obtuse, mucronate, base rounded or obtuse; upper surface dark green, shining, not scaly, glabrous; margin slightly recurved or flat, glabrous; *under surface* densely covered with *chocolate, cinnamon or rust-coloured or dark reddish-brown* scales, the scales unequal, medium-sized or large; petiole 1—4 mm. long, densely scaly, glabrous. *Inflorescence* terminal, capitate, 5—8-flowered, flower-bud scales persistent; rhachis 1—2 mm. long, scaly or not scaly, glabrous; pedicel 1—4 mm. long, scaly, glabrous. *Calyx* 5-lobed, 2—5 mm. long, greenish or dark reddish-purple, lobes oblong, oblong-elliptic or oblong-oval, outside sparsely or moderately scaly or not scaly, margin sparsely or densely ciliate. *Corolla* narrowly tubular with spreading lobes, *0.9—1.3 cm. long*, 5-lobed, white or rose, outside not scaly or rarely lobes scaly, glabrous, inside densely hairy within the tube. *Stamens 5*, unequal, 3—4 mm. long, included in the corolla-tube; filaments glabrous. *Ovary* ovoid or conoid, 1 mm. long, 5-celled, densely scaly, glabrous; style very short, thick, straight, as long as the ovary or longer, not scaly, glabrous. *Capsule* ovoid or conoid, 3 mm. long, 2—3 mm. broad, densely scaly, glabrous, enclosed by the persistent calyx-lobes.

R. rufescens is a distinct species of comparatively restricted distribution in Szechuan. It was first collected by the Abbé Soulié in 1892 in south-west Szechuan. Subsequently it was found by Wilson, and Rock in other localities in the same region, and by Harry Smith in north Szechuan. It grows in grasslands and in alpine regions at elevations of 3,050—4,865 m. (10,000—15,950 ft.).

A diagnostic feature of this plant is the chocolate or cinnamon-coloured or dark reddish-brown scales on the lower surface of the leaves. The species is closely allied to *R. anthopogon* from which it is distinguished usually by the 5 stamens, by the smaller leaves and smaller corolla. It is very similar to *R. laudandum* in the chocolate or cinnamon-coloured scales on the lower surface of the leaves, but differs in distinctive features. The plant has not been introduced into cultivation.

Epithet. Becoming reddish.

Not in cultivation.

R. sargentianum Rehd. et Wils. in Plantae Wilsonianae (1913) 504.

Illustration. Bot. Mag. Vol. 146 t. 8871 (1920). (Not satisfactory).

A *compact shrub,* 30—60 cm. (1—2 ft.) high; branchlets short, twiggy, densely scaly, and with long-stalked scales, glabrous, *leaf-bud scales persistent.* Leaves evergreen, broadly elliptic, oval or oblong-elliptic, aromatic, lamina coriaceous, 0.8—1.6 cm. or rarely 2 cm. long, 0.5—1.1 cm. broad, apex rounded or obtuse, mucronate, base rounded or obtuse; upper surface dark green, shining, not scaly, glabrous; margin recurved, glabrous; under surface densely covered with rust-coloured, dark brown or brown, overlapping, lacerate scales, the scales unequal, large and medium-sized; petiole 2—4 mm. long, densely or moderately scaly, glabrous. *Inflorescence* terminal, capitate, 5—7- or rarely 12—flowered, flower-bud scales deciduous or persistent; rhachis 1—2 mm. long, scaly, glabrous; pedicel 5—8 mm. long, densely scaly, glabrous. *Calyx* 5-lobed, 2—4 mm. long, lobes oval, oblong-oval, oblong or lanceolate, outside moderately or densely scaly, margin hairy with long hairs. *Corolla* narrowly tubular with spreading lobes, 1.2—1.6 cm. long, 5-lobed, *lemon-yellow, pale yellow or white, outside rather densely or moderately scaly on the tube, moderately scaly on the lobes,* glabrous, inside densely hairy within the tube. *Stamens* 5, unequal, 3—5 mm. long, included in the corolla-tube; filaments glabrous. *Ovary* ovoid, 1 mm. long, 5-celled, densely scaly, glabrous; style very short, thick, straight, as long as the ovary or shorter, not scaly, glabrous. *Capsule* ovoid or conoid, 3—4 mm. long, 3 mm. broad, densely scaly, glabrous, enclosed by the persistent calyx-lobes.

This species is a native of western Szechuan. It was discovered by Wilson in July 1903 at Washan, when collecting for Messrs. Veitch and Sons. He found it again in October 1904 without precise locality, also in June and October 1908 and in 1910 at Mupin in the same region. It grows on exposed rocks and cliffs at elevations of 3,000—4,300 m. (9,836—14,098 ft.). The plant is of uncommon occurrence; no other collector has found it in its native home.

R. sargentianum is a distinct species, and cannot be confused with any species of its Series. It is easily recognised by its very compact habit of growth, by the persistent leaf-bud scales, by the corolla being rather densely scaly outside, and by the small broadly elliptic or oval, aromatic leaves. In some respects it resembles *R. nmaiense* from which it is readily distinguished by the very compact habit of growth and by the rather densely scaly corolla. It is also allied to the compact form of *R. cephalanthum* but differs in that the stamens are 5 and the corolla is rather densely scaly outside.

The species is undoubtedly one of the finest of all dwarf rhododendrons in cultivation. It was first introduced by Wilson in 1903—1904 (No. 1208 — the Type number, and No. 1888). The plant was reintroduced by him in 1908 (No. 3454) and in 1910 (No. 4237). In cultivation it is a very compact shrub up to 2 feet high and as much across, densely filled with dark green, aromatic foliage. It is a slow grower with short annual growths, but it has the advantage of flowering at an early age. Two colour forms are in cultivation, yellow and white. The two forms vary in the size of the leaves, and in freedom of flowering. In some gardens, the species flowers fairly freely; in a few gardens it is a shy flowerer, but in some other gardens, particularly in the Royal Botanic Garden, Edinburgh, it is very free-flowering and provides an admirable display with a profusion of yellow or white flowers in clusters of five to seven. *R. sargentianum* is hardy in sheltered positions, and is an exceptionally fine plant for the rock garden.

A form with pale yellow flowers was given an Award of Merit when shown by Lady Aberconway and the Hon. H.D. McLaren, Bodnant, in 1923. Another form 'Whitebait' with nearly white flowers received the same Award when exhibited by E.H.M. Cox and P.A. Cox, Glendoick, in 1966.

Epithet. After C.S. Sargent, Director of the Arnold Arboretum, Mass., who died in 1927.

Hardiness 3. April—May. Plate 1.

R. trichostomum Franch. in Journ. de Bot. IX (1895) 396.

Illustration. Bot. Mag. Vol. 146 t. 8831 (1920), as *R. ledoides.*

A low somewhat compact rounded and spreading, or broadly upright, or a lax upright shrub, 20 cm.—1.22 m. (8 in.—4 ft.) or rarely 2 m. (6½ ft.) high; branchlets short, twiggy, or long, densely scaly, and with or without long-stalked scales, glabrous, *leaf-bud scales*

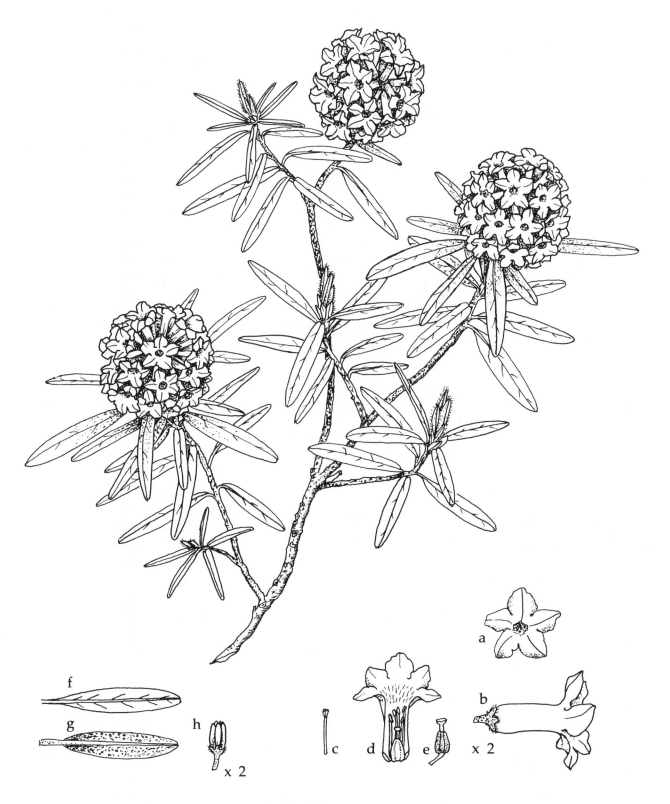

1. **R. trichostomum**
nat. size

a. petal. b. flower. c. stamen. d. section. e. ovary, style. f. leaf (upper surface).
g. leaf (lower surface). h. capsule.

deciduous or rarely persistent. *Leaves* evergreen, *narrowly oblanceolate, linear or linear-lanceolate*, aromatic, lamina coriaceous, 0.8—3 cm. long, 2—8 mm. broad, apex rounded, obtuse or acute, mucronate, base tapered or obtuse; upper surface dark green, matt, scaly or not scaly, glabrous; margin recurved, glabrous; under surface densely covered with dark brown, brown, fawn or rust-coloured, overlapping, lacerate scales, the scales unequal, large and medium-sized; petiole 1—4 mm. long, densely scaly, glabrous. *Inflorescence* terminal, capitate, *globose, 8—20-flowered*, flower-bud scales persistent; rhachis 0.2—1.3 cm. long, scaly, minutely puberulous or glabrous; pedicel 1—7 mm. long, moderately or densely scaly, glabrous. *Calyx* 5-lobed, 0.5—2 mm. long, lobes lanceolate, oblong, ovate or oval, outside scaly or not scaly, margin ciliate or rarely eciliate. *Corolla* narrowly tubular with spreading lobes, 0.8—1.6 cm. long, 5-lobed, white, pink, rose, deep rose, or rarely creamy-white tinged salmon-pink, tube deep pink, outside not scaly or rarely lobes sparsely scaly, glabrous, inside densely hairy within the tube. *Stamens* 5, unequal, 3—6 mm. long, included in the corolla-tube; filaments glabrous or minutely puberulous towards the base. *Ovary* conoid or ovoid, 1 mm. long, 5-celled, densely scaly, glabrous; style very short, thick, straight, longer or shorter than the ovary, not scaly, glabrous. *Capsule* conoid, ovoid or oblong, 3—5 mm. long, 2—3 mm. broad, densely scaly, glabrous, calyx persistent.

R. trichostomum was described by Franchet in 1895 from a specimen collected by the Abbé Delavay in May 1887 near Lankong in western Yunnan. Subsequent gatherings by other collectors show that the plant is distributed in western Yunnan, western and south-western Szechuan, growing in pine and oak forests, in open stony pastures, in thickets, in alpine meadows, and amongst rocks, at elevations of 2,500—4,300 m. (8,196—14,098 ft.).

A diagnostic feature of this plant is the linear, narrowly oblanceolate or linear-lanceolate leaves by which the species is readily distinguished from all other members of its Series. Another remarkable character is the large, rounded, capitate inflorescence of 8—20 flowers. In general appearance it shows a resemblance to *R. primuliflorum* from which it is distinguished by the shape of the leaves, usually by the smaller calyx and larger truss.

R. trichostomum was first introduced by Wilson in 1908 from western Szechuan (No. 1328). It was reintroduced by Forrest a few times, including No. 11246 as *R. ledoides* (now a synonym of *R. trichostomum*) in 1913. Kingdon-Ward sent seed in 1921 under No. 4465. The species first flowered in cultivation in 1917 raised from Forrest's seed. In its native home it grows usually 1½—4 feet high. Wilson found a plant in 1908 west of Tatsienlu, western Szechuan, and it was up to 6½ feet tall. Three distinct forms are in cultivation. Form 1. A low, somewhat compact, rounded and spreading shrub up to 1½—2 feet high, a rather slow grower with short annual growths. Form 2. A broadly upright shrub up to 2—3 feet high with short or somewhat long annual growths. Form 3. A lax upright fast-growing shrub up to 4—4½ feet high with long slender branches. In cultivation the flowers are white, pink, rose or deep rose. The species varies in hardiness, and to be able to grow it satisfactorily, particularly along the east coast, a sheltered position should be provided. It is a late flowerer, the flowers appearing in May and June. The species is free-flowering, and is an unusually attractive sight when covered with large globose trusses of up to 20 flowers. It received an Award of Merit when exhibited as *R. ledoides* by A.K Bulley, Neston, in 1925. A form 'Quarry Wood' was given the same Award when shown as *R. trichostomum* var. *ledoides* by Mr. and Mr. Martyn Simmonds, Quarry Wood, Newbury, in May 1971, and again to another form 'Lakeside' when exhibited under the same varietal name, by the Crown Estate Commissioners, Windsor Great Park, in 1972. It also received a First Class Certificate when shown as *R. trichostomum* var. *ledoides* by The Lady Anne Palmer, Torrington, Devon, in 1976.

Epithet. Hairy-mouthed.
Hardiness 3. May—June. Plate 3.

R. trichostomum Franch. var. **hedyosmum** (Balf. f.) Cowan et Davidian in The Rhododendron Year Book (1947) 84.

Syn. *R. hedyosmum* Balf. f. in Notes Roy. Bot. Gard. Edin., Vol. 9 (1916) 234.

Illustration. Bot. Mag. Vol. 153 t. 9202 (1930). Figured as *R. hedyosmum.*

This plant is a native of western Szechuan. It appeared in cultivation in the Royal
Botanic Garden, Edinburgh in 1909, where it flowered for the first time in 1916, raised
from Wilson's seed No. 1208, the type of *R. sargentianum.*

The variety differs from the species in that the corolla is large, 1.9—2.1 cm. long, with
a long tube, and the leaves are oblong. The plant has now possibly been lost to
cultivation.

Epithet of the variety. Sweet-scented.

Hardiness 3. May—June.

R. trichostomum Franch. var. **radinum** (Balf. f. et W.W. Sm.) Cowan et Davidian in The
Rhododendron Year Book (1947) 84.

Syn. *R. radinum* Balf. f. et W.W. Sm. in Notes Roy. Bot. Gard. Edin., Vol. 9 (1916) 268.

This plant was first collected by Forrest in June 1913 on the Lichiang Range, western
Yunnan. It was later found by him and by other collectors in other localities in Yunnan
and south-west Szechuan. The plant grows in alpine pastures, in pine and spruce
forests, on cliffs, on open rocky slopes, in open scrub, and among rocks, at elevations of
2,593—4,423 m. (8,500—14,500 ft.). Kingdon-Ward records it as being a bushy undershrub not above 8 or 10 inches high, growing in masses like heather on the rocky slopes
amongst scattered pine trees at 3,050 m. (10,000 ft.) at Yung-ning, western Yunnan.

The variety differs from the species in that the corolla is scaly all over the tube and
lobes or on the lobes, and the leaves are often densely scaly on the upper surface.

The plant was first introduced by Forrest in 1913 from the Lichiang Range, western
Yunnan (No. 10278 — the Type number). He reintroduced it on many occasions from
other localities. Kingdon-Ward sent seeds in 1921 under No. 3998. Rock also introduced
it in 1923—1924 (No. 59196), and again in 1932. It is a charming plant for the rock garden,
and is most effective when laden with white or rose flowers. An Award of Merit was
given to a clone 'Sweet Bay' when shown by the Crown Estate Commissioners, Windsor
Great Park in 1960, and again to another clone when exhibited by Mr. and Mrs. Martyn
Simmonds, Quarry Wood, Newbury, in May 1972.

Epithet of the variety. Slender.

Hardiness 3. May—June.

BOOTHII SERIES

General characters: small to medium shrubs, often epiphytic, 20 cm.—2.45 m. (8 in.—8 ft.), or rarely 8—10 cm. (3.2—4 in.) or 3 m. (10 ft.) high; branchlets moderately or densely bristly or sometimes not bristly. Leaves elliptic, obovate, oblong-elliptic, ovate, oval, nearly orbicular or oblong, lamina 1.3—5 cm. long, 0.8—6.2 cm. broad; under surface pale glaucous green or glaucous, densely scaly, the scales ½—2 times their own diameter apart or sometimes contiguous; petiole moderately or rather densely bristly or not bristly. Inflorescence terminal, 1—10-flowered; pedicel 0.6—2.5 cm. long, moderately or rather densely bristly or not bristly. Calyx 5-lobed, 0.3—1.3 cm. long (in *R. chrysodoron* an undulate rim, 1 mm. long). *Corolla campanulate, rotate-campanulate or rotate,* 1.3—4 cm. long, 5- (or rarely 4-) lobed, yellow, lemon-yellow, sulphur-yellow or white, without or sometimes with reddish-brown spots, outside moderately or rather densely scaly on the tube and lobes. Stamens 10. Ovary ovoid or conoid, 2—7 mm. long, 5-celled (in *R. chrysodoron* and sometimes in *R. boothii* 6-celled), densely scaly; *style short, stout and sharply bent.* Capsule oval, oblong-oval, ovoid or conoid, 0.6—1.7 cm. long, 0.5—1.3 cm. broad, moderately or densely scaly, calyx-lobes persistent.

Distribution: Assam, south-east and east Tibet, north-east Upper Burma, west and north-west Yunnan.

The Boothii Series is allied to the Glaucophyllum Series, and it also shows some affinity with the Camelliiflorum Series, in which, however, the stamens are 12—16, and the ovary is 10-celled.

KEY TO THE SUBSERIES

A. Inflorescence 1—2- (or rarely 3-) flowered; scales on the under surface of the leaves
  bladder-like or almost bladder-like with very narrow rim ... *Megeratum Subseries*
A. Inflorescence 3—10- (or rarely 2-) flowered; scales on the under surface of the leaves
  saucer-shaped with broad rim, Entire .... *Boothii Subseries*

BOOTHII SUBSERIES

General characters: small to medium shrubs, often epiphytic, 20 cm.—2.45 m. (8
in.—8 ft.) or rarely 3 m. (10 ft.) high; branchlets often bristly. Leaves elliptic, obovate,
oblong-elliptic, ovate, ovate-elliptic, oval or oblong, lamina 2.6—12.6 cm. long, 1.3—6.2
cm. broad; under surface pale glaucous green or pale glaucous, densely scaly, *the scales
saucer-shaped*, ½—2 times their own diameter apart or sometimes contiguous; petiole
often bristly. *Inflorescence terminal, 3—10- (or rarely 2-) flowered*; pedicel 0.6—2.5 cm.
long, bristly or not bristly. Calyx 5-lobed, 0.3—1.3 cm. long (in *R. chrysodoron* an undulate rim, minute, 1 mm. long). *Corolla broadly campanulate or campanulate*, 1.3—4 cm. long,
5-lobed, yellow, bright lemon-yellow or sulphur-yellow, without or sometimes with
reddish-brown spots, outside moderately or rather densely scaly on the tube and lobes.
Stamens 10. Ovary ovoid or conoid, 2—7 mm. long, 5-celled (in *R. chrysodoron* and
sometimes in *R. boothii* 6-celled); style short, stout and sharply bent. Capsule oval,
oblong-oval or conoid, 0.6—1.7 cm. long, 0.5—1.3 cm. broad, calyx-lobes persistent.

KEY TO THE SPECIES

A. Calyx an undulate rim, minute, 1 mm. long; ovary 6-celled .... *chrysodoron*
A. Calyx with large leafy lobes, 0.3—1.3 cm. long; ovary 5-celled (except in *R. boothii*
  sometimes 6-celled).
  B. Leaves acutely acuminate or acuminate at the apex; pedicel moderately or
    densely bristly; branchlets and petioles densely bristly; midrib on the upper
    surface of the leaves and/or margin usually bristly.
    C. Corolla unspotted; inflorescence 7—10-flowered; pedicel moderately
      bristly, 1—1.3 cm. long .... *boothii*
    C. Corolla usually heavily spotted with reddish-brown; inflorescence 3—4-
      flowered; pedicel densely woolly, 1.6—2.5 cm. long .... *mishmiense*
  B. Leaves rounded or obtuse at the apex; pedicel not bristly; branchlets and
    petioles not bristly or sometimes moderately bristly; midrib on the upper
    surface of the leaves and margin not bristly.
      D. Corolla 1.3—1.6 cm. or sometimes up to 2 cm. long; calyx 3—6 mm.
        long; inflorescence 4—8-flowered; scales on the under surface of
        the leaves usually uniform, small, one-half to their own diameter
        apart .... *sulfureum*
      D. Corolla 2—2.6 cm. long; calyx 6—8 mm. long; inflorescence 2—3-
        flowered; scales on the under surface of the leaves markedly
        unequal in size, large and medium-sized, contiguous ....
        .... *dekatanum*

DESCRIPTION OF THE SPECIES

R. boothii Nutt. in Hook. Kew Journ. Bot. Vol. 5 (1853) 356.
  Illustration. Bot. Mag. Vol. 116 t. 7149 (1890).
  An upright or broadly upright or rounded shrub, usually epiphytic, 1.53—2.44 m.
(5—8 ft.) or sometimes 3 m. (10 ft.) high; branchlets scaly, densely hairy, leaf-bud scales

deciduous. *Leaves* evergreen, ovate, ovate-elliptic or elliptic, lamina coriaceous, very thick, 8.2—12.6 cm. long, 3.5—6.2 cm. broad, apex acutely acuminate, mucronate, base rounded or obtuse; upper surface bright green or green, somewhat shining, not scaly, midrib hairy or glabrous; margin hairy or glabrous; under surface pale glaucous green, densely scaly, the scales unequal, medium-sized, dark brown, their own diameter apart; *petiole 0.6—1 cm. long, scaly, densely woolly. Inflorescence* terminal, shortly racemose, *7—10-flowered*, flower-bud scales deciduous; rhachis 3—4 mm. long, scaly, hairy or glabrous; *pedicel* stout, *1—1.3 cm. long,* densely scaly, *bristly* with long bristles. *Calyx* 5-lobed, large, leafy, 0.8—1.3 cm. long, lobes ovate or rounded, outside moderately or sparsely scaly, margin ciliate or eciliate. *Corolla* broadly campanulate with 5 spreading lobes, 2—3.1 cm. long, yellow, bright lemon-yellow or sulphur-yellow *without spots,* outside rather densely scaly, glabrous. *Stamens* 10, unequal, 1—1.8 cm. long, shorter than the corolla; filaments hairy in the lower one-third to one-half of their length. *Ovary* conoid, 4—5 mm. long, 5—6-celled, densely scaly, glabrous; style short, stout and sharply bent, not scaly or scaly at the base, glabrous. *Capsule* oval, 1—1.7 cm. long, 0.9—1.3 cm. broad, densely scaly, glabrous, calyx-lobes persistent.

R. *boothii* was discovered by T.J. Booth in 1849 on the Gascherong Hills, in Assam. Subsequently it was collected by Kingdon-Ward at Lagam in Assam in 1938, and by Ludlow, Sherriff and Elliot at Pemakochung in south-east Tibet in 1947. It grows as an epiphyte on oak and Abies trees at elevations of 1,525—3,050 m. (5,000—10,000 ft.) Kingdon-Ward records it as being a common epiphyte in forests on sheltered slopes at 2,135—2,440 m. (7,000—8,000 ft.) in Assam.

A diagnostic feature is the broadly bell-shaped, bright lemon-yellow or yellow, unspotted corolla. Other outstanding characters are the broadly ovate or ovate-elliptic leaves, acutely acuminate at the apex, hairy on the margins and on the midrib above, and 7—10-flowered inflorescence. It is very closely allied to R. *mishmiense,* from which it is distinguished by the unspotted corolla, by the 7—10-flowered inflorescence, and by the shorter bristly pedicel. The species is diploid, 2n = 26.

The plant was introduced by T.J. Booth in 1852. In cultivation it is a broadly upright or rounded shrub up to 5 feet high. Along the west coast it is hardy outdoors only in well-sheltered gardens. It has been in cultivation in a few gardens in Cornwall. Along the east coast it is tender and is suitable for a cool greenhouse. The plant was successfully grown in the glasshouse in the Royal Botanic Garden, Edinburgh; it was a rounded shrub 4 feet high and as much across, free-flowering, but unfortunately it was accidentally destroyed in 1950.

Epithet. After T.J. Booth who collected in Bhutan, about 1850.

Hardiness 1—2. April—May.

R. chrysodoron Tagg ex Hutch. in Gard. Chron., XCV (1934) 276.

Illustration. Bot. Mag. Vol. 159 t. 9442 (1936).

A broadly upright or bushy shrub, sometimes epiphytic, 20 cm.—1.83 m. (8 in.—6 ft) high; *branchlets* scaly, *bristly with long, slender bristles,* or sometimes not bristly, leaf-bud scales deciduous. *Leaves* evergreen, broadly elliptic, obovate or oblong-elliptic, lamina coriaceous, 4.8—8 cm. long, 2—4.1 cm. broad, apex rounded or obtuse, conspicuously mucronate, base rounded or obtuse; upper surface bright green or dark green, shining, not scaly or slightly scaly; margin not bristly (in young leaves bristly or not bristly); under surface pale glaucous green, densely scaly, the scales unequal, large and medium-sized, brown, 1—2 times their own diameter apart; *petiole 0.6—1.5 cm. long, scaly, bristly with long, slender bristles,* or sometimes not bristly. *Inflorescence* terminal, shortly racemose, 3—6-flowered, flower-bud scales deciduous; rhachis 2—4 mm. long, scaly, glabrous; pedicel stout, 0.7—1.1 cm. long, densely scaly, not bristly. *Calyx saucer-like, an undulate rim,* 5-lobed, *minute, 1 mm. long,* lobes triangular or broadly ovate, outside densely scaly, margin moderately or densely bristly with long, slender bristles. *Corolla* broadly campanulate, 3—4 cm. long, 5-lobed, tube 5-pouched at the base, bright canary yellow or yellow, without spots, outside scaly on the tube and lobes, glabrous or tube hairy at the base. *Stamens* 10, unequal, 2—3 cm. long, shorter than the corolla; filaments densely hairy in the lower one-third to two-thirds of their length. *Ovary* ovoid or conoid, 4—6 mm. long, *6-celled*, densely scaly, glabrous; style short, stout and sharply bent, 1.7—2 cm. long, scaly at the base, glabrous. *Capsule* oblong or oblong-oval, 1—1.2 cm. long, 6—8 mm. broad, scaly, calyx persistent.

This species was described in 1934 from a plant raised from Forrest's seed under number 25446 (in part) collected in 1924 in western Yunnan; the dried specimen under this number is *R. ciliicalyx*. It was first flowered by the Earl of Stair in 1931 who sent it to Edinburgh. It was named by Tagg *R. chrysodoron* or the "golden gift".

In 1931 Kingdon-Ward found a plant in the Adung Valley, north-east Upper Burma (No. 9221 = 9371) which he named provisionally *R. butyricum*. It flowered in the glasshouse of the Royal Botanic Garden, Edinburgh some years ago, and it is identical with *R. chrysodoron*. Kingdon-Ward describes this plant as "a small bushy shrub, epiphytic in the forest, or on rocks in the river bed . . . . In bloom from early February to late May, according to altitude." Kingdon-Ward reintroduced *R. chrysodoron* in 1953 from the Triangle, North Burma (No. 20878).

In cultivation the plant grows up to 6 feet or more in height. It is a distinctive species, and is easily recognised by the large yellow unspotted corolla, the stout, sharply bent style, the saucer-like, minute calyx 1 mm. long, and usually by the bristly branchlets and petioles. It is related to *R. sulfureum*, but is readily distinguished by well-marked characters.

It is an early flowerer, the flowers appearing in February or March. The plant is hardy outdoors only in well-sheltered gardens in the west coast; in the east coast it is tender and requires a cool greenhouse. It is a pleasing shrub, and is of great beauty with its yellow flowers produced freely in trusses of three to six. It received an Award of Merit when exhibited by Lord Aberconway, in 1934.

Epithet. Golden gift — referring to the yellow-flowered plant given by Lord Stair to the Royal Botanic Garden, Edinburgh.

Hardiness 1—2. February—April. Plate 4.

R. dekatanum Cowan in Notes Roy. Bot. Gard. Edin., Vol. 19 (1937) 226.

A shrub, 60 cm.—1.22 m. (2—4 ft.) high; branchlets scaly, not bristly, leaf-bud scales deciduous. *Leaves* evergreen, oval, obovate, oblong-oval, oblong-obovate or broadly oblong, lamina coriaceous, 3—6 cm. long, 2—3.5 cm. broad, apex rounded, mucronate, base rounded or obtuse; upper surface olive-green, matt, not scaly; margin slightly recurved, glabrous; under surface pale glaucous, densely scaly, *the scales markedly unequal in size, large and medium-sized*, dark brown and brown, *contiguous*; petiole 5—6 mm. long, densely scaly, not bristly. *Inflorescence* terminal, umbellate, *2—3-flowered*, flower-bud scales deciduous; rhachis 1—2 mm. long, scaly or not scaly, glabrous or sparsely hairy; pedicel 6—8 mm. long, thick, densely scaly, glabrous. *Calyx* 5-lobed, *6—8 mm. long*, lobes rounded or oval, outside moderately or sparsely scaly, glabrous, margin glabrous. *Corolla* broadly campanulate, *2—2.6 cm. long*, 5-lobed, bright lemon-yellow, outside scaly on the tube and lobes, glabrous. *Stamens* 10, unequal, 1.4—1.7 cm. long, shorter than the corolla; filaments densely villous towards the lower half to two-thirds of their length. *Ovary* ovoid, 4 mm. long, 5-celled, densely scaly, glabrous; style short, stout and sharply bent, scaly at the base, glabrous. *Capsule:* —

This plant is known only from a single collection made in April 1936 by Ludlow and Sherriff, at Chayul Chu, southern Tibet. It grows in rhododendron and bamboo forest at an elevation of 3,508 m. (11,500 ft.).

It is a small shrub, 2—4 feet high with oval to oblong leaves, and bright lemon-yellow flowers. The plant shows a strong resemblance to R. *sulfureum* in general appearance, but differs in the larger calyx and corolla, in the 2—3-flowered inflorescence, and particularly in that the scales on the lower surface of the leaves are very markedly different in size, contiguous. Moreover, it differs in its geographical distribution. The species has not been introduced into cultivation.

Epithet. After Mrs. De Kat.

Not in cultivation.

R. mishmiense Hutch. et Ward in Notes Roy. Bot. Gard. Edin., Vol. 16 (1931) 173.

A small shrub, usually epiphytic, up to 1.22 m. (4 ft.) high; branchlets scaly, densely bristly, leaf-bud scales deciduous. *Leaves* evergreen, elliptic, oblong-elliptic, ovate or ovate-elliptic, lamina coriaceous, very thick, 6.8—11 cm. long, 3—4.7 cm. broad, apex acuminate, mucronate, base obtuse or rounded; upper surface bright green or green, somewhat shining, not scaly, midrib hairy; margin hairy or glabrous; under surface pale green or pale glaucous green, densely scaly, the scales unequal, medium-sized, dark brown, their own diameter apart; petiole 0.6—1 cm. long, scaly, densely bristly. *Inflorescence* terminal, shortly racemose, *3—4-flowered*, flower-bud scales deciduous; rhachis 2—3 mm. long, scaly, hairy or glabrous; *pedicel 1.6—2.5 cm. long*, sparsely scaly, *densely woolly. Calyx* 5-lobed, large, leafy,0.4—1.3 cm. long, lobes ovate or rounded, outside scaly, margin bristly. *Corolla* broadly campanulate with 5 spreading lobes, 2.2—3.2 cm. long, bright lemon-yellow, yellow or sulphur-yellow, *the upper lobes heavily spotted with reddish-brown*, outside rather densely scaly, hairy on the tube or glabrous. *Stamens* 10, unequal, 1.3—1.7 cm. long, shorter than the corolla; filaments densely hairy in the lower one-third to two-thirds of their length; anthers 6—8 mm. long. *Ovary* conoid, 5—7 mm. long, 5-celled, densely scaly, glabrous; style short, stout and sharply bent, not scaly, glabrous. *Capsule* conoid, 1.3 cm. long, 1 cm. broad, scaly, calyx-lobes persistent.

R. *mishmiense*, as the name suggests, is a native of the Mishmi Hills, in Assam. It was first collected by Kingdon-Ward at Chibaon in April 1928. He found it again later in the same month in other localities in the same region. The plant grows in scrub, on rock faces amidst a tangle of rhododendrons, on granite or gneiss cliffs, on ridges in rhododendron thickets, and as an epiphyte in the forest, at elevations of 1,830—2,745 m. (6,000—9,000 ft.). According to Kingdon-Ward, it is a fairly common epiphyte in the temperate rain forest at 1,830—2,135 m. (6,000—7,000 ft.).

The species resembles R. *boothii* in general characters, but differs in that the upper lobes of the corolla are heavily spotted reddish-brown, the inflorescence is 3—4-flowered, and the pedicel is longer, 1.6—2.5 cm. long and densely woolly.

The plant was first introduced by Kingdon-Ward in 1928 (No. 8113), and again in the same year (No. 8592). It comes from comparatively low elevations, and in cultivation it usually requires the protection of a greenhouse. The species has always been rare in gardens. In 1940 an Award of Merit was given to a plant under the name R. *mishmiense* with an 8-flowered inflorescence and slightly spotted on the three upper lobes of the corolla; the plant would appear to be R. *boothii*. The species is now possibly lost to cultivation.

Epithet. From the Mishmi Hills, Assam.

Hardiness 1. April—May.

R. sulfureum Franch. in Bull. Soc. Bot. France, XXXIV (1887) 283.

Illustration. Bot. Mag. Vol. 148 t. 8946 (1922).

A compact rounded, or broadly upright shrub, often epiphytic, 30 cm.—1.53 m. (1—5 ft.) high; branchlets rather densely or moderately scaly, bristly or not bristly, leaf-bud scales deciduous. *Leaves* evergreen, obovate, oblong-obovate, elliptic, oblong-elliptic, oblong or oval, lamina coriaceous, 2.6—8.6 cm. long, 1.3—4.2 cm. broad, apex rounded or obtuse, mucronate, base obtuse or rounded; upper surface bright or dark green, somewhat shining, not scaly or sometimes sparsely scaly; margin glabrous; under surface glaucous, densely scaly, the *scales* unequal, *small or somewhat small*, dark brown or brown, *one-half to their own diameter apart*; petiole 0.3—1.4 cm. long, moderately or rather densely scaly, not bristly or bristly. *Inflorescence* terminal, umbellate, *4—8-flowered*, flower-bud scales deciduous; rhachis 1—3 mm. long, scaly or not scaly, glabrous; pedicel 0.6—1.3 cm. or sometimes 2 cm. long, rather densely or moderately scaly, glabrous. *Calyx* 5-lobed, *3—6 mm. long*, lobes oblong, oblong-oval, oval or orbicular, outside moderately or rather densely scaly, glabrous, margin ciliate or eciliate. *Corolla* campanulate, *1.3—1.6 cm. or sometimes 2 cm. long*, 5-lobed, bright or deep yellow, bright or deep sulphur-yellow, greenish-yellow or rarely greenish-orange, outside scaly on the tube and lobes, glabrous or sometimes sparsely hairy on the tube. *Stamens* 10, unequal, 0.7—1.3 cm. long, shorter than the corolla; filaments densely hairy towards the base or the lower half. *Ovary* ovoid or conoid, 2—3 mm. long, 5-celled, densely scaly, glabrous; style short, stout and sharply bent, scaly at the base, glabrous. *Capsule* oval or oblong-oval, 0.6—1.1 cm. long, 5—7 mm. broad, moderately or densely scaly, glabrous, calyx-lobes persistent.

R. *sulfureum* was discovered by the Abbé Delavay in April 1886 on Mount Tsang-chan, above Tali, western Yunnan. It was later collected by Forrest, Farrer, Rock, and Kingdon-Ward in various localities in west and north-west Yunnan, and north-east Upper Burma. The plant grows on cliffs, on rocks, in open situations amongst scrub, on boulders, and often as an epiphyte on trees in forests, at elevations of 2,135—3,849 m. (7,000—12,620 ft.).

The species is very variable in habit and height of growth ranging from 1 to 5 feet high, often growing as an epiphyte, in leaf shape from oblong, oblong-oval, obovate to oval, and in leaf size from 1 inch up to 3.4 inches long. The short, stout and sharply bent style is a striking feature of the species and of all the members of its Series. The plant bears a resemblance to R. *dekatanum* in some features, but is readily distinguished by notable characters.

R. *sulfureum* was first introduced by Forrest in 1910 (No. 6777). It was reintroduced by him several times from Yunnan. Farrer sent seeds in 1919 from Upper Burma. Kingdon-Ward also introduced it in 1953 from The Triangle, North Burma (No. 21001). The species first flowered at Caerhays, Cornwall, in April 1920. In cultivation it is a compact rounded, or broadly upright shrub, 1—4 feet high, usually well-filled with bright green leaves. It is successfully grown outdoors in some gardens along the west coast, but in the east coast and inland it is tender and should be grown in a cool greenhouse. It is a charming plant, free-flowering, with trusses of 4—8 bright yellow, bell-shaped flowers. The species was given an Award of Merit when shown by Lord Stair, Lochinch, Wigtownshire, in 1937, as R. *commodum*.

Epithet. Sulphur-coloured.
Hardiness 1—2. April—May.

MEGERATUM SUBSERIES

General characters: small to medium shrubs, often epiphytic, 30—92 cm. (1—3 ft.) or rarely 8—10 cm. (3.2—4 in.) or sometimes 1.22—1.83 m. (4—6 ft.) high; branchlets moderately or densely bristly. Leaves elliptic, obovate-elliptic, obovate, oval, oblong-oval or nearly orbicular, lamina 1.3—5 cm. long, 0.8—3.4 cm. broad; under surface glaucous, densely scaly, the *scales* small and medium-sized, *bladder-like or almost bladder-like*, sunk in pits, ½—1½ times their own diameter apart; petiole moderately or rather densely bristly. *Inflorescence* terminal 1—2- (or rarely 3-) *flowered*; pedicel 0.6—1.1 cm. long, moderately or rather densely bristly or not bristly. Calyx 5-lobed, 0.6—1 cm. long.

Corolla campanulate, rotate-campanulate, rotate, or almost saucer-shaped, 1.6—3.2 cm. long, 5- (or rarely 4-) lobed, yellow, deep yellow, pale lemon-yellow, creamy-yellow, white or sometimes white with a pinkish tinge, without spots or rarely with purple spots on the upper lobes. Stamens 10. Ovary ovoid or conoid, 3—4 mm. long, 5-celled, densely scaly; style short, stout and sharply bent. Capsule oblong-oval, ovoid or oval, 0.7—1 cm. long, 5—6 mm. broad, densely or moderately scaly, calyx-lobes persistent.

KEY TO THE SPECIES

A. Corolla yellow, pale lemon-yellow or creamy-yellow (or rarely white); pedicel moderately or rather densely bristly, not scaly or rarely sparsely scaly; upper surface of the leaves not bristly; corolla campanulate or rotate-campanulate; under surface of the leaves markedly glaucous .... *megeratum*

A. Corolla white (or sometimes white with a pinkish tinge); pedicel not bristly or rarely slightly bristly, rather densely or moderately scaly; upper surface of the leaves bristly; corolla rotate or almost saucer-shaped; under surface of the leaves glaucous .... *leucaspis*

DESCRIPTION OF THE SPECIES

R. leucaspis Tagg in Gard. Chron., Vol. 85 (1929) 128, 135, 308, fig. 67.
Illustration. Bot. Mag. Vol. 164 t. 9665 (1944).

A compact rounded, bushy, broadly upright or straggly shrub or sometimes more or less prostrate with ascending branches, sometimes epiphytic, 30—92 cm. (1—3 ft.) or sometimes 1.22—1.53 m. (4—5 ft.) high; branchlets scaly, rather densely or moderately bristly, leaf-bud scales persistent or deciduous. Leaves evergreen, nearly orbicular, oval, oblong-oval, obovate or elliptic, lamina coriaceous, 2.8—5 cm. long, 1.5—3.4 cm. broad, apex rounded, mucronate, base rounded or obtuse; *upper surface* dark green, shining, rather densely or moderately scaly or not scaly, *bristly*; margin recurved, rather densely or moderately bristly; *under surface glaucous*, densely scaly, the scales varying in size, small and medium-sized, brown, bladder-like or almost bladder-like, sunk in pits, one-half to their own diameter apart; petiole 4—9 mm. long, moderately or rather densely scaly, bristly. *Inflorescence* terminal, umbellate, 1—2- (or rarely 3-) flowered, flower-bud scales persistent or deciduous; rhachis 0.5—1 mm. long, scaly or not scaly, hairy or glabrous; *pedicel* 0.6—1 cm. long, thick, *rather densely or moderately scaly*, puberulous or rarely not puberulous, *not bristly* or rarely slightly bristly. *Calyx* 5-lobed, 6—8 mm. long, lobes obovate, oval or oblong-oval, outside moderately or slightly scaly at the base, or rarely scaly on the lobes, margin densely hairy. *Corolla rotate or almost saucer-shaped*, 2.3—3.2 cm. long, 5-lobed, *white* or sometimes with a pinkish tinge, outside scaly on the tube and lobes, glabrous. *Stamens* 10, unequal, 1.5—2.1 cm. long, shorter than the corolla; filaments densely or moderately hairy towards the lower half or three-fourths of their length. *Ovary* conoid or ovoid, 3—4 mm. long, 5-celled, densely scaly, glabrous; style short, stout and sharply bent, moderately or slightly scaly at the base, glabrous or rarely puberulous at the base. *Capsule* oval or oblong-oval, 0.8—1 cm. long, 5—6 mm. broad, scaly, calyx-lobes persistent.

This extremely fine plant was discovered by Kingdon-Ward in November 1924 (No. 6273) at Musi La, Tsangpo Gorge, south-east Tibet. It was growing as a bushy undershrub, sometimes more or less prostrate with ascending branches, or erect 1—2 feet high, amongst bamboo and other rhododendrons on steep grassy slopes, or on cliffs. Later in the same month, he found it again in the Tsangpo Gorge (No. 6291) a small, bushy or straggly undershrub of 1—3 feet, with long loose branches, also epiphytic on big moss-clad trees in the middle forest. He also collected it in July 1926 in the Di Chu Valley in the same region (No. 7171), where it formed sprawling tangles in well-shaded thickets in rather swampy ground. In 1947, Ludlow, Sherriff and Elliot found it growing on cliff faces in the Tsangpo Gorge, south-east Tibet. The plant grows at elevations of 2,440—3,050 m. (8,000—10,000 ft.).

A diagnostic feature is the white, rotate or almost saucer-shaped corolla, by which the species is readily distinguished from all the other members of its Series. Other remarkable characters are the densely or moderately bristly branchlets, petioles, the upper surface and margins of the leaves, and the glaucous lower surface of the leaves, densely scaly, the scales being one-half to their own diameter apart. The species is related to *R. megeratum*, but the latter has a yellow campanulate or rotate-campanulate corolla, moderately or rather densely bristly pedicels, and leaves which are non-bristly on the upper surface.

R. leucaspis was first introduced by Kingdon-Ward in 1924 (No. 6273 — the Type number), and it first flowered in cultivation in the spring of 1928. It was reintroduced by him in 1926 under No. 7171. In cultivation along the east coast it is a compact rounded, or bushy shrub, 2—3 feet high and as much across or wider, but along the west coast in view of heavier rainfall and higher degree of humidity, it often forms a somewhat lax broadly upright shrub up to 4 or even 5 feet high. It is an early flowerer, the flowers appearing in February to April, but these are liable to be destroyed by early spring frosts. It may be remarked that in some cold gardens prolonged frosts not only split the bark of the plant but also sometimes destroy the whole plant as happened in the winters of 1948 and 1963. An interesting feature is that the species flowers quite young when raised from seed, often in four or five years. When it escapes the frost, it is of exquisite beauty when adorned with a profusion of white flowers in clusters of 1—2. The species is highly rated, and received an Award of Merit when exhibited by Mr. Lionel de Rothschild in 1929 (K.W. No. 6273), and a First Class Certificate when shown by Mr. E. de Rothschild, in 1944 (K.W. No. 7171).

Epithet. White shield.
Hardiness 2—3. February—April. Plate 5.

R. megeratum Balf. f. et Forrest in Notes Roy. Bot. Gard. Edin., Vol. 12 (1920) 140.
Illustration. Bot. Mag. Vol. 152 t. 9120 (1927).

A dwarf, prostrate cushion, compact rounded, or broadly upright shrub, often epiphytic, 8—92 cm. (3 in.—3 ft.) or rarely 1.53—1.83 m. (5—6 ft.) high; branchlets scaly, moderately or densely bristly, leaf-bud scales persistent or semi-persistent. *Leaves* evergreen, elliptic, obovate-elliptic or oval, lamina coriaceous, 1.3—4 cm. long, 0.8—2 cm. broad, apex rounded or obtuse, mucronate, base rounded or obtuse; *upper surface* dark green, shining, not scaly, *not bristly*; margin recurved, bristly or sometimes not bristly; *under surface very glaucous*, densely scaly, the scales varying in size, small and sometimes medium-sized, brown, bladder-like or almost bladder-like, sunk in pits, 1—1½ times their own diameter apart; petiole 0.3—1.1 cm. long, moderately or rather densely scaly, moderately or rather densely bristly. *Inflorescence* terminal, umbellate, 1—2- (or rarely 3-) flowered, flower-bud scales deciduous; rhachis 0.5—1 mm. long, scaly or not scaly, glabrous; *pedicel* 0.8—1.1 cm. long, *not scaly or rarely sparsely scaly, moderately or rather densely bristly*. *Calyx* almost membranous, 5-lobed, divided as far as the middle or beyond, 0.6—1 cm. long, lobes oval or oblong-oval, outside not scaly or rarely slightly scaly, margin eciliate or sometimes sparsely ciliate. *Corolla campanulate or rotate-campanulate*, 1.6—2.5 cm. long, 5- (or rarely 4-) lobed, *yellow, deep yellow, pale lemon-yellow, creamy-yellow* or rarely white, without spots or rarely with purple spots on the upper lobes, outside moderately or rather densely scaly on the tube and lobes, glabrous. *Stamens* 10, unequal, 1—1.5 cm. long, shorter than the corolla; filaments densely hairy towards the base or to two-thirds of their length. *Ovary* ovoid, 3 mm. long, 5-celled, densely scaly, glabrous; style short, stout and sharply bent, slightly or moderately scaly at the base, glabrous. *Capsule* oblong-oval, ovoid or oval, 0.7—1 cm. long, 5—6 mm.

broad, densely scaly, glabrous, enclosed by the persistent calyx-lobes.

R. megeratum was first found by Forrest in August 1914 on the Kari Pass, Mekong-Yangtze divide, north-west Yunnan. Subsequent gatherings by other collectors show that the plant is distributed in north-west Yunnan, north-east Upper Burma, south, south-east and east Tibet, and Assam. It grows on ledges and crevices of cliffs, on boulders, on rocky slopes, on and among rocks, and as an epiphyte in forests, at elevations of 2,440—4,000 m. (8,000—13,111 ft.). Farrer describes it as growing on ledges of alpine cliffs, forming low wide masses a few inches high at 3,173 m. (10,500 ft.) on the Chaw-ji Pass, north-east Upper Burma, also forming a low almost prostrate cushion in the high alpine granitic precipices at 3,660—3,965 m. (12,000—13,000 ft.) on the Chimili Cliffs. Kingdon-Ward records it as being a common epiphyte, generally in masses with long hanging shoots at 3,050—3,355 (10,000—11,000 ft.) in Assam.

The outstanding characters of this plant are the yellow campanulate or rotate-campanulate corolla, the short, stout and sharply bent style, the markedly glaucous lower surfaces of the leaves densely scaly with bladder-like or almost bladder-like scales sunk in pits, 1—1½ times their own diameter apart, and the densely or moderately bristly branchlets, petioles and pedicels. It is allied to *R. leucaspis* from which it is readily distinguished by its yellow campanulate or rotate-campanulate corolla, by the markedly glaucous lower surface of the leaves, by the moderately or rather densely bristly pedicels, and by the leaves without bristles on the upper surfaces.

R. megeratum was first introduced by Forrest in 1914 (No. 12942 — the Type number). He later sent seeds on several occasions from north-west Yunnan. The species was also introduced by Kingdon-Ward, Rock, Yü, and Ludlow and Sherriff. In its native home it grows from a few inches up to 3 feet or rarely 5—6 feet high. Two distinct forms are in cultivation. Form 1. A compact rounded shrub, up to 3 or 4 feet high, and as much across, densely branched, and densely filled with foliage. Form 2. A low, somewhat lax and spreading shrub, up to 1½—2 feet high, with larger flowers. The species is very particular as to position in the garden. It may be remarked that the plant varies widely in hardiness. Along the west coast it has proved hardy in the open in sheltered gardens. Along the east coast and inland, some forms are hardy and succeed admirably outdoors in well-sheltered positions; other plants in some gardens are somewhat tender, slow growers, difficult to cultivate, and need almost greenhouse conditions. Moreover, some forms are susceptible to bark-split and are sometimes killed by prolonged heavy frosts. The species also varies considerably in its freedom of flowering. Some plants flower abundantly and provide an impressive display, whilst other forms are shy flowerers and hardly produce more than a few flowers every year. The flowers appear in March or April, but are apt to succumb to early spring frosts. However, it should be stated that a successfully grown plant with dark green foliage, covered with large yellow flowers is, as the specific name suggests, "lovely in the highest degree", and is worthy of a place in every collection of rhododendrons. The species was given an Award of Merit when shown by Lord Swaythling in April 1935, and again for another form when exhibited by Lord Aberconway and the National Trust, in April 1970.

Epithet. Passing lovely.
Hardiness 2—3. March—April.

CAMELLIIFLORUM SERIES

General characters: small or medium shrubs, often epiphytic, 60 cm.—1.83 m. (2—6 ft.) high. Leaves evergreen, oblong, oblong-lanceolate, lanceolate, oblong-elliptic or ovate-elliptic, lamina 4.8—12.3 cm. long, 1.5—3.9 cm. broad; under surface densely scaly, the scales contiguous or slightly overlapping or one-half to their own diameter apart. *Inflorescence* terminal, *1—2-flowered*; pedicel 4—8 mm. long, densely or rarely moderately scaly. Calyx 5-lobed, 0.5—1.1 cm. long. Corolla campanulate with spreading lobes, 1.5—2.5 cm. long, white, white tinged pink, red or deep wine-red; 5-lobed. *Stamens 12—16.* Ovary ovoid or rarely conoid, 2—3 mm. long, 5—10-celled, densely scaly; *style short, stout and sharply bent.* Capsule short stout, oval or oblong-oval, 0.8—1.3 cm. long, 6—8 mm. broad, densely scaly.

Distribution: Nepal, Sikkim, and Bhutan.

A small Series of two species. It shows a resemblance to the Boothii Series and Maddenii Series.

KEY TO THE SPECIES

A. Leaf apex obtuse or acute; scales on the under surface of the leaves contiguous or slightly overlapping or one-half their own diameter apart .... *camelliiflorum*

A. Leaf apex acutely acuminate; scales on the under surface of the leaves about their own diameter apart .... *lucidum*

DESCRIPTION OF THE SPECIES

R. camelliiflorum Hook. f. in Rhod. Sikkim Himal. t. 28 (1849).

Illustration. Bot. Mag. Vol. 82 t. 4932 (1856).

A rounded, bushy, broadly upright, or lax straggly shrub, often epiphytic, 60 cm.— 1.83 m. (2—6 ft.) high; branchlets rather densely scaly with large scales. *Leaves* evergreen, oblong, oblong-lanceolate, lanceolate or oblong-elliptic, lamina coriaceous, 4.8—12.3 cm. long, 1.5—3.8 cm. broad, apex obtuse or acute, mucronate, base obtuse, rounded or tapered; upper surface dark green, not scaly or rarely scaly; under surface densely scaly, the scales large, unequal, dark brown, contiguous or slightly overlapping or one-half their own diameter apart, with or without larger darker brown or brown scales widely scattered; petiole 0.3—1.2 cm. long, grooved above, densely scaly with large scales. *Inflorescence* terminal, umbellate, *1—2-flowered*; rhachis 1—2 mm. long, densely scaly; pedicel 4—8 mm. long, thick, densely or rarely moderately scaly with large scales. *Calyx* deeply 5-lobed, 0.5—1.1 cm. long, lobes oblong-oval, oval or oblong, outside sparsely or moderately scaly with large scales, margin not ciliate. *Corolla* campanulate with 5 spreading orbicular or oblong-oval lobes, 1.5—2.5 cm. long, fleshy, white, white tinged pink, red or deep wine-red, outside scaly with large scales, inside densely hairy within the throat with long hairs. *Stamens 12—16*, unequal, 0.9—2 cm. long; filaments densely hairy towards the base with long hairs. *Ovary* ovoid or rarely conoid, 2—3 mm. long, 5—10-celled, densely scaly, glabrous; *style short, stout and sharply bent,* not scaly, glabrous. *Capsule* short stout, oval or oblong-oval, 0.8—1.3 cm. long, 6—8 mm. broad, densely scaly with large scales, glabrous, calyx-lobes persistent.

This species was discovered by J.D. Hooker in 1848 in Sikkim Himalaya. Further gatherings by other collectors show that the plant is distributed in Nepal, Sikkim, and Bhutan, growing on rocks, in dense jungle, on cliff edges, among shrubs, on boulders, in mixed forest, and often as an epiphyte in forests, at elevations of 2,745—3,660 m. (9,000—12,000 ft.).

In the shape of the corolla and the short, stout, sharply bent style, *R. camelliiflorum* resembles the species of the Boothii Series. It also shows a resemblance to some of the species of the Maddenii Series in the shape and size of the leaves, and in the size and distribution of the scales on the lower surfaces. From its ally, *R. lucidum*, it is distinguished by the obtuse or acute leaf apex, and by the distribution of the scales on the lower surface of the leaves.

The species was first introduced by J.D. Hooker in 1851. It was reintroduced by Ludlow and Sherriff on many occasions. Spring-Smyth sent seeds under several numbers from Nepal. In cultivation it is a rounded shrub up to 5 feet high and as much across, or broadly upright or a lax straggly shrub up to 6 feet high. Two colour forms are in cultivation, white tinged pink, and deep red. Although it grows at high altitudes in its native home, in cultivation it is tender outdoors along the east coast and needs the protection of a greenhouse, but it grows well in sheltered gardens along the west coast. The plant is fairly fast-growing, free-flowering, the flowers being produced in May, June or sometimes in July.

Epithet. With Camellia-like flowers.

Hardiness 1—2. May—July.

R. lucidum Nutt. in Hook. Journ. Bot. V (1853) 363.

A shrub; branchlets sparingly scaly. *Leaves* ovate-elliptic or oblong-lanceolate, 5—10 cm. (2—4 in.) long, 2.5—3.8 cm. (1—1½ in.) broad, apex acutely acuminate, somewhat narrowed to the base; upper surface finely reticulate, under surface glaucous, densely scaly, the scales unequal, about their own diameter apart, lateral veins distinct about 8 pairs; petiole 0.6—1.3 cm. long, scaly. *Inflorescence* terminal, (flowers not seen), winter-buds ellipsoid, 1.9 cm. long, bud-scales ovate-orbicular, mucronate, about 6 mm. long, loosely scaly on the back, minutely ciliate. *Calyx* oblong-oval, glabrous. *Ovary* 5—8-celled. *Capsule* ovate.

R. lucidum was described by Nuttall in 1853 from a single rather inadequate specimen collected by Booth in Bhutan. It grows on mountains beyond the Bhorelli, amongst pines and other hardy plants of the higher regions.

The plant would appear to be related to *R. camelliiflorum*, but differs in that the leaf apex is acutely acuminate, and the scales on the lower surface of the leaves are about their own diameter apart. There is no record of its occurrence in cultivation.

Epithet. Shining.

Not in cultivation.

CAMPYLOGYNUM SERIES

General characters: dwarf, prostrate or compact or small erect shrubs, 2.5 cm.—1.22 m. (1 in.—4 ft.) or sometimes up to 1.83 m. (6 ft.) high. Leaves evergreen, obovate, oblong-obovate or oblanceolate, lamina 0.6—3.7 cm. long, 0.3—1.8 cm. broad; *margin crenulate*, recurved; under surface scaly, the *scales vesicular*, 1—6 times their own diameter apart. Inflorescence terminal, 1—4- (or rarely 5-) flowered; pedicel very long, 1.8—5 cm. long. Calyx 1—6 mm. long. Corolla campanulate, 0.8—2.4 cm. long, nodding, pale rose-purple, salmon-pink, carmine to deep plum-purple, almost black-purple or bright red. Stamens 10 or rarely 8. Ovary conoid, 2—5 mm. long, densely or moderately scaly, 5-celled; *style thick, bent or sharply bent*. Capsule ovoid or conoid, 5—9 mm. long, 4—6 mm. broad.

Distribution: west and north-west Yunnan, east and north-east Upper Burma, south-east and east Tibet, and Assam.

A small Series of two species allied to the Glaucophyllum Series, with a general tendency towards the Lepidotum and Uniflorum Series.

KEY TO THE SPECIES

A. Upper surface of the leaves dark green, lower surface usually glaucous; corolla deep plum-purple, almost black-purple, pale rose-purple, carmine, rose or pink; dwarf, prostrate, matted or compact, or sometimes erect shrub ... *campylogynum*

A. Both surfaces of the leaves pale green, lower surface not glaucous; corolla usually bright red; erect shrub .... *cremastum*

DESCRIPTION OF THE SPECIES

R. campylogynum Franch. in Bull. Soc. Bot. France, XXXII (1885) 10.

A dwarf, prostrate, semi-prostrate matted, cushion, compact, somewhat spreading, or small erect shrub, 2.5—45 cm. (1 in.—1½ ft.) or rarely 60 cm. (2 ft.) high; branchlets short, scaly with short, thick stalked scales, glabrous or minutely puberulous, leaf-bud scales persistent or subpersistent or rarely deciduous. *Leaves* evergreen, obovate, oblong-obovate or oblanceolate, lamina coriaceous, 0.6—2.5 cm. long, 0.3—1.8 cm. broad, apex rounded, mucronate, base tapered or obtuse; upper surface dark green, shining, *not scaly* or rarely scaly; margin crenulate, recurved, scaly; under surface glaucous or sometimes not glaucous, scaly, the scales 1—6 times their own diameter apart (sometimes they soon fall off); petiole 1—4 mm. long, scaly or not scaly. *Inflorescence* terminal, umbellate, 1—3- (or rarely up to 5-) flowered, flower-bud scales deciduous or persistent; pedicel very long, 1.8—5 cm. long, scaly. *Calyx* 5-lobed to base, 1—6 mm. long, lobes rounded or ovate, outside and margin not scaly or sometimes scaly, glaucous or not glaucous, *glabrous*, pinkish-purple, plum-purple or yellowish-green. *Corolla* campanulate, *1.4— 1.8 cm. long*, 5-lobed, fleshy, nodding, thinly glaucous outside, pale rose-purple, salmon-pink, carmine to deep plum-purple and almost black-purple, *not scaly outside*. *Stamens* 10 or rarely 8, unequal, alternately long and short, 0.6—1.4 cm. long, shorter than the corolla; filaments puberulous at the base or to their whole length. *Ovary* conoid, 2—4 mm. long, moderately or densely scaly, 5-celled; *style thick, bent*, slightly longer or shorter than the corolla, not scaly, glabrous or rarely puberulous at the base, crimson or purple. *Capsule* ovoid, short, 5—9 mm. long, 4—6 mm. broad, sparsely or moderately scaly, calyx persistent.

This species was discovered by the Abbé Delavay in June 1883 on Mount Tsang Chan, Tali Range, western Yunnan. Subsequent gatherings by other collectors show that the plant is distributed in west and north-west Yunnan, east and north-east Upper Burma, and in south-east Tibet. It grows in moist stony moorland, on ledges of cliffs, on boulders, in stony meadows, on rocks, on open hillsides, amongst scrub, and on the margins of rhododendron thickets, at elevations of 3,050—4,575 m. (10,000—15,000 ft.). Kingdon-Ward describes it as a dwarf shrub of 2—4 inches forming carpets with other dwarf species on the summits of granite mountains above bamboo and tree limit, at about 3,965 m. (13,000 ft.), N'mai Divide, East Burma. He also records it as forming carpets 6—9 inches thick, covering the granite rocks and slopes, and as being one of the commonest dwarf rhododendrons of Imaw Bum at 3,660—3,965 m. (12,000—13,000 ft.), East Burma.

R. campylogynum is a very variable plant due to the various environmental conditions in which it is found. It is a dwarf, prostrate or semi-prostrate matted shrub, or a cushion, compact or somewhat spreading shrub, or a small erect shrub; it grows from 2.5 to 45 cm. (1 in.—1½ ft.) high; the leaves (laminae) are 0.7—2.5 cm. (¼—1 in.) long; the scales on the lower surface of the leaves are 1—6 times their own diameter apart (or sometimes they fall off); and the flower colour is pale rose-purple, salmon-pink, carmine to deep plum-purple and almost black-purple.

A characteristic feature of this plant is the campanulate corolla with a thick bent style, nodding on a very long pedicel which is usually two or three times the length of the

2. R. campylogynum
nat. size
a. section. b. stamen. c. ovary, style. d. capsule.

corolla. Another distinctive character is its prostrate, compact or spreading habit of growth, usually up to 45 cm. (1½ ft.) high. The species is related to *R. cremastum* from which it is distinguished by the habit and height of growth, by the smaller leaves dark green on the upper surface, usually glaucous on the lower surface, and usually by the colour of the flowers.

The species was first introduced by Forrest in 1912 (No. 13518). It was reintroduced by him, and by Kingdon-Ward, Rock, Ludlow, Sherriff and Elliot, and Yü from various localities in Yunnan and Tibet. In cultivation it is a compact or somewhat spreading shrub up to one foot high with short branchlets. The plant is a late flowerer, the flowers appearing in May or June. Although a slow grower, one of its merits is that it flowers at a fairly early age when raised from seed. It is hardy, free-flowering, and is an excellent plant for the rock garden. An Award of Merit was given to a salmon-pink form 'Thimble', and again to another form 'Baby Mouse' when exhibited by Capt. Collingwood Ingram, in 1966 and 1973 respectively. The same Award was given to a form 'Beryl Taylor' when shown by Lord Aberconway and the National Trust in 1975. A form with white flowers, known as 'Leucanthum' raised and exhibited as *R. campylogynum* var. *leucanthum* by Capt. Collingwood Ingram, was also given an Award of Merit in 1973.

Epithet. With bent ovary.

Hardiness 3. May—June. Plate 6.

R. campylogynum Franch. var. **celsum** Davidian in The Rhododendron and Camellia Year Book (1954) 83.

Forrest first collected this plant in June—July 1906 on the eastern flank of the Tali Range, west Yunnan. He found it again later in that month in the same region. It grows in open situations amongst cane scrub, at elevations of 2,745—3,660 m. (9,000—12,000 ft.).

This variety is readily distinguished from the species by its erect habit and height of growth, 45 cm.—1.83 m. (1½—6 ft.) high. The leaves are small to medium size, 0.7—2.5 cm. in length, and the flowers are of medium size, 1.4—1.8 cm. long.

The plant was introduced by Forrest in 1906 from west Yunnan (No. 4152). In cultivation it is an upright shrub up to 75 cm. (2½ ft.) high, with deep plum-purple or deep purple flowers. It is hardy, free-flowering, and easy to grow. The plant is uncommon in cultivation, but is worthy of being widely grown.

Epithet of the variety. High.

Hardiness 3. May—June.

R. campylogynum Franch. var. **charopoeum** (Balf. f. et Farrer) Davidian in The Rhododendron and Camellia Year Book (1954) 83.

Syn. *R. charopoeum* Balf. f. et Farrer in Notes Roy. Bot. Gard. Edin., Vol. 13 (1922) 245.

Illustration. Bot. Mag. Vol. 158 t. 9407A (1935). Figured as *R. campylogynum*.

This plant was first collected by the Abbé Soulié in July 1903 at Tsekou, east Tibet. It was afterwards found by other collectors in east and south-east Tibet, north-east Upper Burma, and north-west and mid-west Yunnan. The plant grows on alpine slopes, at the margins of rhododendron scrub, on ledges of cliffs, in alpine meadows, on rocks, in stony moorland, and in thickets, at elevations of 3,350—4,270 m. (10,983—14,000 ft.). It is recorded as being common in thickets in north-west Yunnan.

The variety differs from the species in its larger flowers, 1.9—2.4 cm. (¾—1 in.) long.

The plant was first introduced by Forrest in 1930 from north-west Yunnan (No. 30883). It was reintroduced by Yü in 1937 (No. 8630). In cultivation it is a very compact spreading shrub up to 1½ feet high with short annual growths, and densely filled with dark green shining leaves. The plant has two distinct colour forms, deep plum-purple and pale rose. It is hardy, free-flowering, and provides an admirable display with its large bell-shaped flowers in clusters of 1—3. The plant is easy to grow, and should be a most valuable acquisition to any rock garden.

Epithet of the variety. Causing joy.

Hardiness 3. May—June. Plate 7.

R. campylogynum Franch. var. **myrtilloides** (Balf. f. et Ward) Davidian in The Rhododendron and Camellia Year Book (1954) 84.

Syn. *R. myrtilloides* Balf. f. et Ward in Notes Roy. Bot. Gard. Edin., Vol. 13 (1922) 276.

Kingdon-Ward discovered this plant in July 1914 on the ridge of Naung Chaung in N'mai Divide, north-east Upper Burma. Subsequently it was collected by him and by Farrer, Forrest, and Rock in other localities in north-east Upper Burma, mid-west and north-west Yunnan, south-east Tibet, and Assam. It grows on granite cliffs, among rocks and boulders, in open barren rocky pasture, in moist stony alpine meadows and moorland, and on screes, at elevations of 2,440—4,728 m. (8,000—15,500 ft.). Kingdon-Ward records it as forming heath-like masses on slaty rocks in the open river bed, and as being common on steep granite slabs and precipices in north-east Upper Burma, also as forming carpets 6 inches high on sheltered slopes in south-east Tibet.

This variety is distinguished from the species by its smaller flowers, 0.8—1.4 cm. long. It is a dwarf compact or somewhat spreading shrub up to 30 cm. (12 in.) high.

It was first introduced by Kingdon-Ward in 1919 from north-east Upper Burma (No. 3172). It was reintroduced by him later in that year from the same region (No. 3303). Farrer sent seeds in 1919 from the Hpimaw Ridge (Nos. 1046 and 1046a). Forrest also introduced it in 1924 and 1925 from west Yunnan (Nos. 24587 and 27357). In cultivation it

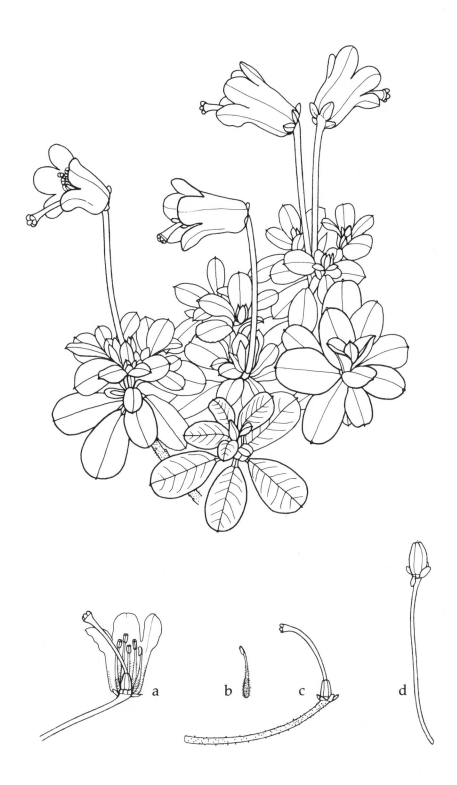

3. **R. campylogynum** var. **charopoeum**
nat. size

a. section. b. stamens. c. ovary, style. d. capsule.

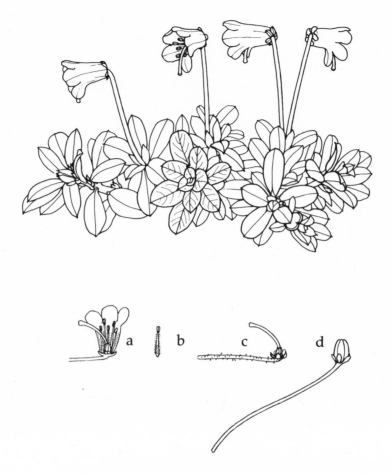

4. R. campylogynum var. **myrtilloides**

nat. size

a. section. b. stamens. c. ovary, style. d. capsule.

is a neat, very compact shrub, 6 in.—1 ft. high with short annual growths and densely filled with dark green leaves. It shows a wide range of colour, from black-purple, deep plum-purple, bright wine-red, rose-purple to rose or pink. Although a slow grower, it often flowers when only a few inches high. It is a delightful small shrub, and is most attractive when covered with tiny bells on very long pedicels in clusters of 1—3. The plant is hardy, and is a most desirable plant for every rock garden. It is very highly rated, and well deserved the Award of Merit which it received when exhibited by Mr. Lionel de Rothschild in 1925, and a First Class Certificate when shown by Mr. Edmund de Rothschild in 1943.

Epithet of the variety. Myrtle-like.

Hardiness 3. May—June.

R. cremastum Balf. f. et Forrest in Notes Roy. Bot. Gard. Edin., Vol. 13 (1920) 39.

A broadly upright shrub, 60 cm.—1.83 m. (2—6 ft.) high; branchlets scaly, glabrous, leaf-bud scales persistent or deciduous. *Leaves* evergreen, obovate or oblong-obovate, lamina coriaceous, 2—3.7 cm. long, 1.2—1.6 cm. broad, apex rounded, mucronate, base cuneate or obtuse; *upper surface pale green*, matt, scaly or not scaly; margin crenulate, recurved, scaly or not scaly; *under surface pale green*, *not glaucous*, scaly, the scales unequal, medium-sized, brown, 3—5 times their own diameter apart, midrib prominent, lateral veins raised; petiole 1—4 mm. long, scaly, glabrous. *Inflorescence* terminal, umbellate, 1—4-flowered, flower-bud scales persistent or deciduous; pedicel very long, 2.5—4.5 cm. long, scaly. *Calyx* 5-lobed, 4—6 mm. long, purple, lobes ovate or rounded, outside densely scaly at the base, or not scaly, margin not scaly, glabrous. *Corolla* campanulate, 1.4—2 cm. long, 5-lobed, nodding, *light plum-rose or bright red or deep wine-red*, not scaly outside. *Stamens* 10, unequal, 1—1.3 cm. long, as long as the corolla or shorter; filaments densely pubescent at the base or to two-thirds their length. *Ovary* conoid, 4—5 mm. long, densely scaly, glabrous, 5-celled; style thick, sharply bent or bent, not scaly, glabrous, plum-rose or purple. *Capsule* conoid or ovoid, 0.5—1 cm. long, 5—6 mm. broad, scaly, calyx-lobes persistent.

This species was discovered by Forrest in July 1917 in the Mekong-Salwin Divide, north-western Yunnan. It was found by him again in the same year in south-east Tibet. The plant grows in open situations amongst rocks and dwarf scrub at an elevation of 3,355 m. (11,000 ft.).

R. cremastum resembles *R. campylogynum* in the shape of the leaves, and in the very long pedicels, but is readily distinguished by its habit and height of growth, by the pale green upper and lower surfaces of the leaves, not glaucous below, usually by the larger leaves and by the bright red flowers.

The species was possibly first introduced by Forrest from north-west Yunnan. It was perhaps reintroduced by Kingdon-Ward during his 1931 expedition to north-east Upper Burma. In cultivation it is a broadly upright shrub up to 6 feet high with large leaves, pale green on both surfaces. The plant has also been known as "*R. campylogynum* var. *rubrum*" and "Bodnant Red". It is a pleasing species, free-flowering and has proved to be most attractive in flower. Although it is hardy, a sheltered position should be provided along the east coast and inland. An Award of Merit was given to a clone 'Bodnant Red' when shown by the Crown Estate Commissioners, Windsor Great Park, in 1971.

Epithet. Suspended.

Hardiness 3. May—June.

CAROLINIANUM SERIES

General characters: shrubs, 60 cm.—6 m. (2—20 ft.) or rarely 9.16 m. (30 ft.) high; branchlets moderately or densely scaly. Leaves evergreen, elliptic, ovate, oval, oblong-oval, ovate-elliptic, ovate-lanceolate or lanceolate, lamina 2—11.8 cm. long, 1.1—6.5 cm. broad; *under surface densely scaly*, the *scales* medium-sized, unequal, *contiguous to their own diameter apart*. Inflorescence terminal, or terminal and axillary in the uppermost one or two leaves, 4—12-flowered; pedicel 0.5—1.6 cm. long. Calyx 5-lobed, 0.5—2 mm. long. Corolla narrowly or widely funnel-shaped or tubular funnel-shaped, 2—3.4 cm. long, pink, rose, pale pinkish-purple, pale rosy-purple or white, with or without brownish-red or greenish spots. Stamens 10. Ovary conoid or rarely oblong, 2—4 mm. long, 5-celled, densely scaly; style slender, straight. Capsule oblong, 0.6—1.3 cm. long, 3—4 mm. broad, densely scaly.

Distribution: east and south-east U.S.A.

A small American Series of three species, allied to the Heliolepis Series.

KEY TO THE SPECIES

A. Leaf apex acuminate, acute or rarely obtuse; leaves ovate, elliptic, ovate-elliptic, ovate-lanceolate or lanceolate, lamina usually 5—11.8 cm. long, flat, midrib on the upper surface hairy.

    B. Corolla-tube longer than the lobes; corolla narrowly tubular funnel-shaped or narrowly funnel-shaped; a straggly or upright shrub 1.22—6 m. (4—20 ft.) or rarely 9.15 m. (30 ft.) high .... *minus*

    B. Corolla-tube shorter than, or as long as, the lobes; corolla widely funnel-shaped; a compact or somewhat compact shrub, 92 cm.—2.44 m. (3—8 ft.) high .... *carolinianum*

A. Leaf apex rounded or broadly obtuse; leaves oval or oblong-oval, lamina 2—5 cm. long, revolute, midrib on the upper surface glabrous .... *chapmanii*

DESCRIPTION OF THE SPECIES

R. carolinianum Rehder in Rhodora, Vol. 14 (1912) 99.

    Illustration. Bot. Reg. 1, t. 37 (1815), as *R. punctatum* var.

    A *compact or somewhat compact* shrub, 92 cm.—2.44 m. (3—8 ft.) high; branchlets moderately or rather densely scaly, leaf-bud scales deciduous. *Leaves* evergreen, ovate, ovate-elliptic, elliptic, ovate-lanceolate or lanceolate, lamina coriaceous, 4.6—10.8 cm. long, 1.8—4.6 cm. broad, apex acuminate, acute or obtuse, mucronate, base obtuse; upper surface convex or flat, dark green or paler green, scaly or not scaly, midrib hairy; under surface densely scaly, the scales medium-sized, unequal, brown, contiguous to their own diameter apart; petiole 0.7—2 cm. long, densely scaly, glabrous. *Inflorescence* terminal, shortly racemose, 4—12-flowered; rhachis 3—5 mm. long, moderately or densely scaly; pedicel 0.8—1.5 cm. long, rather densely or moderately scaly, glabrous. *Calyx* 5-lobed, unequal or equal, 0.5—2 mm. long, lobes ovate or triangular, outside and margin densely or moderately scaly, margin eciliate or ciliate. *Corolla widely funnel-shaped*, 2—3 cm. long, pink or pale rosy-purple, with or without faint spots, outside scaly on the tube and lobes or rarely tube not scaly, *tube* 0.9—1.3 cm. long, *shorter than, or as long as, the lobes*, 5-lobed, lobes 1.2—1.8 cm. long. *Stamens* 10, unequal, 1.3—3 cm. long, as long as the corolla or shorter; filaments densely hairy towards the base. *Ovary* conoid or rarely oblong, 2—4 mm. long, 5-celled, densely scaly, glabrous; style slender, straight, not scaly or rarely scaly at the base, glabrous. *Capsule* oblong, 1—1.3 cm. long, 3—4 mm. broad, densely scaly, glabrous, calyx persistent.

    R. carolinianum is a native of the eastern U.S.A. It is found on the mountains of North and South Carolina and of Tennessee, growing in woodland and on hill slopes.

    The plant was at first regarded as a variety of *R. minus*, but in 1912 Rehder gave it specific status. It is very closely allied to *R. minus*. There is a definite resemblance between them in the shape, size and densely scaly lower surface of the leaves, in the terminal inflorescence of up to 12 flowers, in the minute calyx, and in the size, colour and degree of scaliness of the corolla. When the extremes of these plants are compared, the main distinctions between them are that *R carolinianum* is a compact or somewhat compact shrub 3—8 feet high, the leaves are usually ovate to ovate-lanceolate, the corolla is widely funnel-shaped, the corolla-tube is shorter than or as long as the lobes, the tube being 0.9—1.3 cm. long, and the lobes 1.2—1.8 cm. long; whereas *R. minus* is a straggly or upright shrub 4—10 or 20 feet or rarely 30 feet high, the leaves are often lanceolate, narrow, pointed, the corolla is narrowly tubular funnel-shaped or narrowly funnel-shaped, the corolla-tube is longer than the lobes, the tube being 1.6—2.2 cm. long, and the lobes 0.8—1.2 cm. long. It may be remarked that although these distinctions are evident when the extremes are compared, the adequate collections now available and

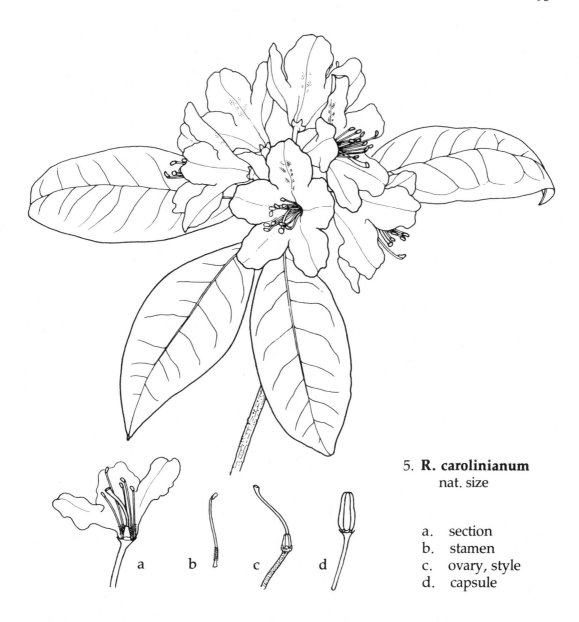

5. **R. carolinianum**
nat. size

a. section
b. stamen
c. ovary, style
d. capsule

plants in cultivation show that these distinctions are inconstant and unreliable. The species merge into each other, and many specimens and plants in cultivation may be given either name.

R. carolinianum was first introduced about 1810. In cultivation it is a small, somewhat compact, rounded shrub up to 3 feet high, or a medium-sized, broadly upright shrub up to 5 or 6 feet. It is a useful plant in that it is a late flowerer, the flowers appearing in May and June. It is free-flowering, and one of its chief merits is that it flowers at a young age when raised from seed. The plant is hardy, and is worthy of a place in every garden. It was given an Award of Merit when shown by Col. N.R. Colville, Launceston, Cornwall, in 1968.

In 1958 *R. carolinianum* Rehder f. *luteum* Frisbie, was described from a plant which appeared in cultivation with mimosa-yellow flowers. The origin of this plant is unknown. It is said to have come from "mountains of North Carolina". The plant would appear to be of hybrid origin.

Epithet. From Carolina.

Hardiness 3. May—June.

R. carolinianum Rehder var. **album** Rehder in Manual of Cultivated Trees and Shrubs (1940) 707.

This name was given by Rehder to a plant from North Carolina, eastern U.S.A.

The variety differs from the species in that the flowers are white or whitish, with or without greenish spots.

The plant was first introduced in 1895. In cultivation it is usually a rounded shrub up to 92 cm. or 1.22 m. (3 or 4 ft.) high. The leaves are variable from ovate-lanceolate to lanceolate. The plant is hardy and is well worth a place in every collection of rhododendrons.

Epithet of the variety. With white flowers.

Hardiness 3. May—June.

R. chapmanii Gray in Proc. Am. Acad. Vol. 12 (1876) 61.

A shrub, 60 cm.—2 m. (2—6½ ft.) high; branchlets erect, rigid, densely or moderately scaly, leaf-bud scales deciduous. *Leaves evergreen, oval or oblong-oval, lamina* somewhat rigid, *revolute, 2—5 cm. long,* 1.1—2.5 cm. broad, *apex rounded or broadly obtuse,* notched or entire, base obtuse; upper surface pale green or bright green, matt or somewhat lustrous, scaly or not scaly, *midrib glabrous;* under surface densely scaly, the scales medium-sized, unequal, brown, contiguous or one-half their own diameter apart; petiole 3—6 mm. long, densely scaly. *Inflorescence* terminal, shortly racemose, 5—8-flowered; rhachis 3—4 mm. long, scaly; pedicel 0.5—1.5 cm. long, rather densely scaly, glabrous. *Calyx* 5-lobed, minute, 0.5—1 mm. long, outside and margin densely or moderately scaly, margin ciliate. *Corolla* tubular funnel-shaped, 2.5—3 cm. long, pink or rose, outside scaly on the tube and lobes or not scaly, tube 1.3—2 cm. long, longer than the lobes, 5-lobed, lobes 0.6—1.2 cm. long, margin crinkled or entire. *Stamens* 10, unequal, 2—3 cm. long, shorter than the corolla; filaments rather densely pubescent towards the base. *Ovary* conoid or oblong, 2—3 mm. long, 5-celled, densely scaly, glabrous; style slender, straight, not scaly, glabrous. *Capsule* oblong, 0.7—1 cm. long, 3—4 mm. broad, densely scaly, glabrous, calyx persistent.

R. chapmanii is a native of west Florida, U.S.A., growing in coastal sandy plains and on sand dunes. It is said to be rare in its native home.

It is a distinct species, and grows up to 2 m. (6½ ft.) high. The plant shows a certain degree of resemblance to *R. carolinianum* and *R. minus,* but differs in that the leaves are oval or oblong-oval, revolute and rigid, with rounded or broadly obtuse apex, and are usually smaller 2—5 cm. long.

It was first introduced in 1936. In cultivation along the east coast the plant is too tender outdoors, and is liable to be destroyed by heavy frosts. It is suitable only for well-sheltered gardens along the west coast.

Epithet. After A.W. Chapman, American botanist; 1809—99.

Hardiness 1—2. April—May.

R. minus Michaux in Journ. Hist. Nat. (1792) 412.

Illustration. Bot. Mag. Vol. 49 t. 2285 (1822). Figured as *R. punctatum.*

A *straggly or upright shrub,* 1.22—6 m. (4—20 ft.) or rarely 9.15 m. (30 ft.) high; branchlets scaly, leaf-bud scales deciduous. *Leaves evergreen, elliptic, ovate-elliptic, oblong-lanceolate or lanceolate, lamina coriaceous,* 5.8—11.8 cm. long, 2.3—6.5 cm. broad, apex acuminate or acute, mucronate, base obtuse; upper surface convex or flat, dark green or paler green, scaly or not scaly, midrib hairy; under surface densely scaly, the scales medium-sized, unequal, brown, one-half to their own diameter apart; petiole 0.8—1.4 cm. long, densely scaly. *Inflorescence* terminal, or terminal and axillary in the uppermost one or two leaves, shortly racemose, 6—12-flowered; rhachis 0.3—1 cm. long, scaly; pedicel 0.8—1.6 cm. long, rather densely or moderately scaly, glabrous. *Calyx* 5-lobed, minute, 0.5—1 mm. long, lobes ovate or triangular, outside sparsely or densely scaly, margin scaly or not scaly, ciliate. *Corolla narrowly tubular funnel-shaped or narrowly funnel-shaped*, 2.6—3.4 cm. long, pink, rose, pale pinkish-purple or sometimes white, with or without brownish-red or greenish spots, outside scaly on the tube and lobes, *tube* 1.6—2.2 cm. long, *longer than the lobes*, 5-lobed, lobes 0.8—1.2 cm. long, margin not crinkled or sometimes crinkled. *Stamens* 10, unequal, 2—3.1 cm. long, as long as the corolla or shorter; filaments densely or moderately hairy towards the base. *Ovary* conoid, 2—3 mm. long, 5-celled, densely scaly, glabrous; style slender, straight, not scaly, glabrous. *Capsule* oblong, 0.6—1 cm. long, 3—4 mm. broad, densely scaly, glabrous, calyx persistent.

This plant was described by Michaux in 1792. It is a native of east and south-east U.S.A., and grows on the lower mountains and plains from North and South Carolina to Georgia and Alabama.

R. minus varies considerably in habit and height of growth, and in the shape and size of the leaves. It is a straggly or upright shrub, 1.22—6 m. (4—20 ft.) or rarely 9.15 m. (30 ft.) high. The leaves are elliptic, ovate-elliptic, oblong-lanceolate or lanceolate, (laminae) 5.8—11.8 cm. long, 2.3—6.5 cm. broad. It is closely allied to *R. carolinianum*; the distinctions between them are discussed under the latter.

The plant was first introduced in 1786. In cultivation it is a broadly upright shrub up to 6 feet high. It is a late flowerer, extending the flowering season into May and June. The species is hardy, fairly fast-growing, and is easy to grow.

Epithet. Smaller.

Hardiness 3. May—June.

CILIATUM SERIES

General characters: small or medium-sized shrubs, 30 cm.—1.83 m. (1—6 ft.) high; *branchlets moderately or rather densely bristly* or sometimes not bristly. Leaves evergreen, elliptic, oblong-elliptic, oval, oblong-oval, oblanceolate, obovate or oblong-lanceolate, *lamina* 2—8.6 cm. long, 1—4 cm. broad; upper surface bristly or not bristly; *margin rather densely or moderately bristly* or sometimes not bristly; under surface scaly, the scales slightly overlapping or contiguous to 6 times their own diameter apart, midrib bristly or bristly at the base or not bristly; *petiole moderately or rather densely bristly* or sometimes not bristly. Inflorescence terminal, 1—6- or rarely 10-flowered; pedicel 0.4—2 cm. long, moderately or rather densely bristly or not bristly. *Calyx* 5-lobed, 0.5 mm.—1 cm. long, *margin moderately or rather densely bristly* or rarely slightly bristly. Corolla tubular-campanulate or tubular with spreading lobes or campanulate or widely funnel-shaped, 2.6—5 cm. or rarely 2.1 cm. long, 5-lobed, white, white tinged pink or red, pale pink, yellow, creamy-yellow, greenish-yellow or greenish-white, outside not scaly or moderately or rather densely scaly. Stamens 10. Ovary conoid, ovoid, oblong or ovate, 2—6 mm. long, 5—6-celled, densely scaly; style slender, straight. Capsule conoid, ovoid or oblong-oval, 0.6—1.3 cm. long, 0.5—1 cm. broad, densely scaly.

Distribution: Nepal, Sikkim, Bhutan, south and south-east Tibet, south-west Burma, north-east Upper Burma, south-east Szechuan, and Laos.

This Series consists of six species, allied to the Tephropeplum Series. It also shows a certain degree of resemblance to the Ciliicalyx Subseries, Maddenii Series.

KEY TO THE SPECIES

A. Corolla white, white tinged pink or red, or pale pink; stem and branches with smooth, flaking bark .... *ciliatum*

A. Corolla yellow, creamy-yellow, greenish-yellow or greenish-white; stem and branches with rough bark.

> **B.** Corolla not scaly or rarely sparsely scaly outside, widely funnel-shaped; under surface of the leaves laxly scaly, the scales 3—6 times their own diameter apart; ovary and capsule pilose in the upper half ...*fletcherianum*
>
> **B.** Corolla moderately or rather densely scaly on the tube and lobes outside, tubular with spreading lobes, tubular-campanulate or campanulate; under surface of the leaves densely scaly, the scales slightly overlapping, contiguous or sometimes 1½—2 times their own diameter apart; ovary and capsule glabrous.
>
> > **C.** Leaf margin crenulate; leaf base decurrent on the petiole; corolla 2.1—3 cm. long; leaves (laminae) 2.8—3.2 cm. long, scales on the under surface 1½—2 times their own diameter apart; calyx 1—2 mm. long .... *crenulatum*
> >
> > **C.** Leaf margin entire; leaf base not decurrent or sometimes slightly decurrent on the petiole; corolla 2.6—5 cm. long; leaves (laminae) 2—8.5 cm. long, scales on the under surface slightly overlapping, contiguous or one-half their own diameter apart; calyx 0.5 mm.—1 cm. long.
> >
> > > **D.** Pedicel bristly; margin of the leaves rather densely setose, lamina usually 2—4 cm. long; corolla-tube moderately or rather densely pubescent outside, pubescent inside; branchlets rather densely setose .... *valentinianum*
> > >
> > > **D.** Pedicel not bristly; margin of the leaves not bristly or sometimes sparsely or moderately bristly, lamina usually 4.6—8.5 cm. long; corolla-tube not pubescent or sometimes moderately pubescent at the base outside, glabrous inside; branchlets not bristly or sparsely or moderately bristly.
> > >
> > > > **E.** Calyx 0.5—3 mm. or rarely 4—6 mm. long; inflorescence 4—6- or rarely 10-flowered; style scaly in the lower one-third or one-half or rarely at the base, or rarely scaly throughout to the tip; midrib on the upper surface of the leaves not bristly; branchlets slightly or moderately bristly .... *burmanicum*
> > > >
> > > > **E.** Calyx 0.7—1 cm. long; inflorescence 2—3-flowered; style not scaly; midrib on the upper surface of the leaves moderately or sparsely bristly; branchlets not bristly .... *amandum*

DESCRIPTION OF THE SPECIES

R. amandum Cowan in Notes Roy. Bot. Gard. Edin., Vol. 19 (1937) 245.

A shrub, 1.22—1.53 m. (4—5 ft.) high; *branchlets* moderately or rather densely scaly, *not bristly. Leaves* evergreen, elliptic or oblong-elliptic, lamina coriaceous, 5—8.5 cm. long, 2—3.5 cm. broad, apex obtuse, mucronate, base obtuse, not decurrent; upper surface olive-green, shining, scaly, sparsely bristly, *midrib moderately or sparsely bristly;* margin entire, flat or slightly recurved, sparsely or moderately bristly near the base or not bristly; under surface densely scaly, the scales medium-sized, unequal, brown, one-half their own diameter apart, not bristly, midrib not bristly or slightly bristly; petiole 4—5 mm. long, margin not winged, densely scaly, bristly. *Inflorescence* terminal, umbellate or shortly racemose, *2—3-flowered*; rhachis 2—3 mm. long, scaly, rather densely pubescent, not bristly; pedicel 0.6—1 cm. long, somewhat thick, densely scaly, not bristly. *Calyx* 5-lobed, *0.7—1 cm. long*, lobes oval or oblong-oval or ovate, red, outside scaly, not bristly, margin rather densely bristly, inside densely hairy with white hairs. *Corolla* campanulate, 3—3.2 cm. long, 5-lobed, pale lemon-yellow, outside scaly on the tube and lobes, glabrous, inside glabrous. *Stamens* 10, unequal, 1.9—2.4 cm. long, shorter than the corolla; filaments rather densely or moderately pubescent at the base. *Ovary* ovate, 5 mm. long, 5-celled, densely scaly, glabrous; *style* slender, straight, shorter than the corolla, longer than the stamens, *not scaly*, glabrous. *Capsule:* —

This species is known from a single collection made in April 1936 by Ludlow and Sherriff at Chayul Chu, Natrampa, southern Tibet. It is found on steep rocks, among other small rhododendrons at an elevation of 3,508 m. (11,500 ft.).

It is a small shrub, 1.22—1.53 m. (4—5 ft.) high with elliptic or oblong-elliptic leaves. The species shows a resemblance to *R. burmanicum* in its appearance but differs in that the calyx is large, 0.7—1 cm. long, the inflorescence is 2—3-flowered, the style is not scaly, the midrib on the upper surface of the leaves is moderately or sparsely bristly, and the branchlets are not bristly. It is also allied to *R. ciliatum* but is distinguished by well-marked characters. There is no record of its occurrence in cultivation.

Epithet. Sending out of the way.

Not in cultivation.

R. burmanicum Hutch. in Kew Bull. (1914) 185.

An upright or broadly upright shrub, 92 cm.—1.83 m. (3—6 ft.) high, stem and branches with rough bark; branchlets densely or moderately scaly, slightly or moderately bristly. *Leaves* evergreen, *oblanceolate, obovate or oblong-obovate*, lamina coriaceous, 4—8 cm. long, 1.6—4 cm. broad, apex obtuse or rounded, mucronate, base tapered or obtuse, slightly decurrent on the petiole or not decurrent; upper surface dark or bright green, shining, moderately or rather densely scaly, not bristly, midrib not bristly; margin entire, flat or slightly recurved, bristly or not bristly; under surface densely scaly, the *scales* somewhat large or medium-sized, unequal, brown, *slightly overlapping or contiguous or one-half their own diameter apart*, with or without widely or closely scattered larger scales, not bristly, midrib not bristly or sparsely bristly at the base; petiole 0.5—1.5 cm. long, margin narrowly winged near the base of the lamina or ridged on each side, densely scaly, moderately or slightly bristly or rarely not bristly. *Inflorescence* terminal, umbellate or shortly racemose, 4—6- or rarely 10-flowered; rhachis 2—4 mm. long, scaly, pubescent or glabrous, not bristly; pedicel 0.5—2 cm. long, densely scaly, not bristly. *Calyx* 5-lobed, *0.5—3 mm.* or rarely 4—6 mm. *long*, lobes ovate, triangular, oblong-oval or oval, outside densely or moderately scaly, not bristly, margin moderately or slightly bristly. *Corolla* tubular-campanulate, 2.8—5 cm. long, 5-lobed, yellow, creamy-yellow, greenish-yellow or greenish-white, outside moderately or rather densely scaly on the tube and lobes, glabrous or pubescent at the base of the tube, inside glabrous. *Stamens* 10, unequal, 1.3—4 cm. long, shorter than the corolla; filaments rather densely pubescent in the lower one-third. *Ovary* oblong or conoid, 4—6 mm. long, 6-celled, densely scaly, glabrous; style slender, straight, as long as the corolla or slightly longer or shorter, scaly in the lower one-third or one-half or rarely at the base, or rarely scaly throughout to the tip, glabrous or rarely pubescent at the base. *Capsule* ovoid or conoid, 0.9—1.2 cm. long, 0.6—1 cm. broad, rather densely scaly, glabrous, calyx persistent.

R. burmanicum was described by Hutchinson in 1914 from a plant grown in the Glasnevin Botanic Garden, Dublin, raised from seed collected by Lady Wheeler Cuffe on Mount Victoria, south-west Burma. Subsequently it was collected on the same mountain by Unwin in April 1926, and by Kingdon-Ward in April 1956. It grows along the margins of forests at elevations of 2,745—3,020 m. (9,000—9,900 ft.).

The characteristic features of this plant are the oblanceolate, obovate or oblong-obovate leaves, densely scaly on the lower surface, the scales being slightly overlapping or contiguous or one-half their own diameter apart, the 4—6- or rarely 10-flowered inflorescence, usually the small calyx, and the tubular-campanulate, yellow, creamy-yellow or greenish-yellow corolla, moderately or rather densely scaly outside. It is allied to *R. amandum*; the relationship between them is discussed under the latter. In some respects it resembles *R. ciliatum* which, however, differs in that the corolla is white or pale pink, the leaves are bristly on the upper surface and margins, and the bark of the stem and branches is smooth and flaking.

In cultivation *R. burmanicum* is an upright or broadly upright shrub 92 cm.—1.22 m. (3—4 ft. high), although in its native home it reaches a height of 1.83 m. (6 ft.). A compact form in cultivation under the name *R. burmanicum,* is in fact, *R. burmanicum* hybrid. Along the east coast, the species is tender and is suitable for a cool greenhouse; in the west coast and N. Ireland it is successfully grown outdoors in sheltered gardens. It is free-flowering, and makes a fine show with its yellow flowers in trusses of four to six.

Epithet. From Burma.
Hardiness 1—2. March—May.

R. ciliatum Hook. f. Rhod. Sikkim Himal. t. 24 (1851).
Illustration. Bot. Mag. Vol. 78 t. 4648 (1852). Figured as *R. ciliatum* var. *roseo-album.*
An upright, broadly upright or somewhat compact rounded, sometimes semi-prostrate or straggly shrub, 30 cm.—1.53 m. (1—5 ft.) or rarely 1.83 m. (6 ft.) high; *stem and branches with smooth, brown, flaking bark; branchlets* scaly, *moderately or rarely rather densely setose. Leaves* evergreen, elliptic, oblong-elliptic or oblong-lanceolate, lamina coriaceous, 3.6—8.6 cm. long, 1.8—3.6 cm. broad, apex acute, obtuse or acuminate, mucronate, base rounded or obtuse, not decurrent; *upper surface* dark or bright green, shining, scaly, *moderately or sparsely setose, midrib moderately or sparsely setose, margin* entire, flat or slightly recurved, *rather densely to sparsely setose; under surface* pale green, scaly, the scales somewhat large or medium-sized, unequal, brown or pale brown, 2—3 times their own diameter apart, not setose, *midrib moderately or sparsely setose; petiole* 0.3—1 cm. long, margin not winged, scaly, *moderately or rather densely setose. Inflorescence* terminal, shortly racemose or umbellate, 2—5-flowered; rhachis 2—3 mm. long, scaly or not scaly, puberulous or glabrous, not bristly; *pedicel* 0.5—1 cm. long, scaly, *moderately or rather densely setose. Calyx* 5-lobed, 0.4—1 cm. long, lobes ovate or rounded or ovate-oblong, veined, pale green or red, outside scaly or scaly in the lower half or at the base, sparsely bristly or not bristly, margin bristly. *Corolla* tubular-campanulate, 2.6—5 cm. long, 5-lobed, *white, white tinged pink or red, or pale pink,* outside not scaly, glabrous, inside glabrous; lobes emarginate. *Stamens* 10, unequal, 1.2—3.1 cm. long, shorter than the corolla; filaments densely pubescent towards the base. *Ovary* conoid, 3—5 mm. long, 5—6-celled, densely scaly, glabrous; style slender, straight, as long as the corolla or slightly longer or shorter, longer than the stamens, not scaly, glabrous. *Capsule* short stout, or ovate, 1—1.3 cm. long, 0.7—1 cm. broad, ribbed, rather densely scaly, glabrous, calyx-lobes persistent.

This species was discovered by J.D. Hooker in 1849 in Sikkim. It was later found by other collectors in various localities in Sikkim, Nepal, Bhutan, south and south-east Tibet. The plant grows in pine and rhododendron forests, at the margin of rain forests, on open hillsides, on rocks, in swamps, and in boggy ground, at elevations of 2,440—3,965 m. (8,000—13,000 ft.).

R. ciliatum is very variable in habit and height of growth. It is an upright, broadly upright or somewhat compact rounded shrub, sometimes semi-prostrate, spreading or straggly, and it grows from 1 up to 5 or rarely 6 feet high.

The outstanding features of this plant are the white or pale pink flowers, and the smooth, brown, flaking bark of the stem and branches. In these respects, it is readily

6. **R. ciliatum**
nat. size

a. section. b. stamen. c. ovary, style. d. capsule (enclosed). e. capsule.

distinguished from all the other members of its Series. Other diagnostic characters are the moderately or rather densely setose branchlets, leaves (laminae), petioles, and pedicels. The species is related to *R. burmanicum*, *R. fletcherianum*, and *R. amandum*, from all of which it differs markedly in distinctive features.

A cultivated plant figured as *R. modestum* in the *Botanical Magazine* Vol. 125 t. 7686 (1899), and which is said to be most nearly allied to *R. ciliatum*, would appear to be *R. ciliatum* hybrid.

R. ciliatum was first introduced by J.D. Hooker in 1850. It was reintroduced several times by Ludlow and Sherriff, and with Taylor or Hicks, and by other collectors. In cultivation it grows up to 3 or 4 feet or rarely up to 6 feet. Amongst the several forms in gardens, one which is somewhat compact and wide spreading, up to 2½ feet in height, is of great beauty and generally considered to be the best. The species has a long flowering season; it provides colour from March to the end of May, although an early spring frost takes its heavy toll. The plant is hardy, and is easily adaptable to any position in the garden. It seeds itself freely in some gardens along the west coast. The species received an Award of Merit when exhibited by Col. Lord Digby, Minterne, Dorset, in 1953.

Epithet. Fringed.

Hardiness 3. March—May. Plate 9.

R. crenulatum Hutch. ex Sleumer in Blumea, Suppl. IV, Dr. H.J. Lam Jubilee Vol. 2. X. 1958.

A low shrub, 1 m. (3⅓ ft.) high; *branchlets* scaly, *rather densely pubescent*, not bristly, leaf-bud scales deciduous. *Leaves* evergreen, elliptic or oblong-elliptic, lamina coriaceous, 2.8—3.2 cm. long, 1.4—2 cm. broad, apex obtuse, mucronate, *base* obtuse or cuneate, *decurrent on the petiole*; upper surface dark green, shining, not scaly, glabrous, not bristly, midrib puberulous, not bristly; *margin crenulate*, not bristly; under surface scaly, the scales medium-sized, brown, 1½—2 times their own diameter apart; *petiole* 2—4 mm. long, flat, scaly, *narrowly winged or ridged on each side*, pubescent, not bristly. *Inflorescence* terminal, shortly racemose, 3—4-flowered, flower-bud scales persistent, ovate, outside scaly, glabrous, margin densely puberulous; pedicel 0.8—1 cm. long, rather densely scaly, glabrous, not bristly. *Calyx* 5-lobed, 1—2 mm. long, lobes ovate, outside scaly, glabrous, margin ciliate. Corolla funnel-campanulate, *2.1—3 cm. long*, 5-lobed, pale yellow, outside rather densely scaly all over the tube and lobes, pubescent on the tube or glabrous. *Stamens 10*, unequal, 1.2—2 cm. long, as long as the corolla or shorter; filaments pubescent towards the base. *Ovary* conoid, 5 mm. long, densely scaly; style slender, straight, about as long as the corolla, longer than the stamens, glabrous. *Capsule* broadly oblong, 1—1.3 cm. long, 4 mm. broad, scaly, calyx persistent.

The only collection of *R. crenulatum* was made by A.F.G. Kerr in April 1932 at Pu Bia, Laos, at an elevation of 2,800 m. (9,180 ft.).

It is a small shrub 1 m. (3⅓ ft.) high, and shows a certain degree of resemblance to *R. valentinianum*, but differs in that the margins of the leaves are crenulate, the base of the lamina is decurrent on the petiole, the branchlets, leaves, petioles and pedicels are not bristly, the corolla is funnel-campanulate, and the petiole is flat, narrowly winged or ridged on each side. In its crenulate leaf margin and decurrent leaf base, it resembles *R. fletcherianum*, but is readily distinguished by well-marked characters. The plant has not been introduced into cultivation.

Epithet. Scalloped, referring to the crenulate leaf margin.

Not in cultivation.

R. fletcherianum Davidian in The Rhododendron and Camellia Year Book (1962) 103.

Compact and somewhat spreading when young, ultimately a broadly upright

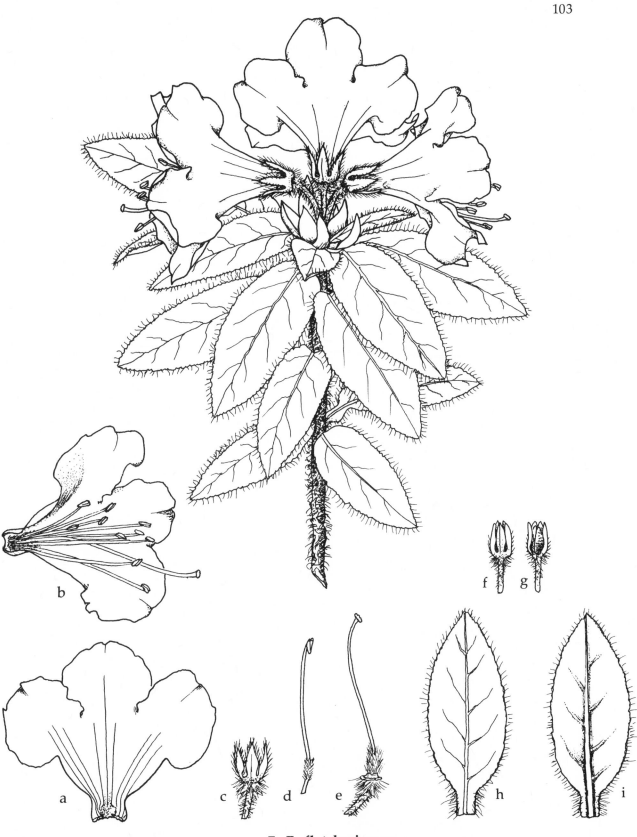

7. R. fletcherianum
nat. size

a. petal. b. section. c. calyx. d. stamen. e. ovary, style. f. capsule (enclosed).
g. capsule. h. leaf (upper surface). i. leaf (lower surface).

shrub, 60 cm.—1.22 m. (2—4 ft.) high, stem and branches with rough bark; branchlets scaly, bristly. *Leaves* evergreen, elliptic, oblong-elliptic or oblong-lanceolate, lamina coriaceous, 2.3—5.6 cm. long, 1.1—2.8 cm. broad, apex obtuse or acute, mucronate, *base* obtuse or cuneate, *decurrent on the petiole*; upper surface dark green, shining, scaly or not scaly, not bristly, midrib not bristly; *margin crenulate*, bristly; under surface pale green, scaly, the scales medium-sized, unequal, pale brown or pale greenish-brown, *3—6 times their own diameter apart*, not bristly, midrib not bristly; *petiole* 0.4—1 cm. long, *narrowly winged on each side*, flat and grooved above, scaly, bristly. *Inflorescence* terminal, umbellate or shortly racemose, 2—4- or rarely 5-flowered; rhachis 2—3 mm. long, not scaly or slightly scaly, glabrous, not bristly; pedicel 0.4—1.6 cm. long, sparsely scaly, rather densely or moderately pilose. *Calyx* 5-lobed, 0.8—1 cm. long, lobes oblong or oblong-ovate, pale green, outside scaly at the base, not bristly, margin rather densely or moderately pilose. *Corolla widely funnel-shaped*, 3.6—4.2 cm. long, 5-lobed, pale yellow, *outside not scaly or sparsely scaly*, glabrous, inside glabrous. *Stamens* 10, unequal, 1.6—3.2 cm. long, shorter than the corolla; filaments densely villous towards the base. *Ovary* conoid or ovoid, 3 mm. long, 5-celled, rather densely scaly, pilose in the upper half; style slender, straight, as long as the corolla or slightly longer, longer than the stamens, not scaly, glabrous. *Capsule* conoid, ovoid or oblong-oval, 6—9 mm. long, 5—7 mm. broad, rather densely scaly, bristly in the upper half, enclosed by the persistent calyx-lobes.

Rock discovered this species in May—June 1932 in the Province of Tsarung, southeast Tibet. He collected it again later in August—October of the same year in the same area. It grows in forests and alpine regions at elevations of 4,118—4,270 m. (13,500—14,000 ft.). The herbarium specimens and cultivated plants were previously under the tentative name *R. valentinianum* aff. The plant is of rare occurrence for it was found only by Rock in south-east Tibet.

R. fletcherianum is a distinctive species and is easily recognised by its habit of growth, by the widely funnel-shaped pale yellow flowers, and by the bristly branchlets, petioles, and pedicels. Other diagnostic features are the decurrent leaf-base, the petiole being flat above and narrowly winged on each side, the crenulate margin of the leaves, and the laxly scaly lower surface of the leaves, the scales being 3—6 times their own diameter apart. The species is related to *R. ciliatum* and *R. burmanicum*, but is distinguished from both by important characteristics.

The plant was introduced by Rock in 1932 (No. 22302 — the Type number). In cultivation it is at first compact and somewhat spreading, ultimately developing into a broadly upright shrub up to 4 feet high. The plant has been known as "Rock's form of *R. valentinianum*". It is hardy, and is easy to increase from cuttings. One of its merits is that it flowers at a remarkably early age when raised from seed. It is one of the finest of the yellow-flowered small rhododendrons, and is extremely charming when covered with a profusion of flowers in trusses of two to four. A form 'Yellow Bunting' was given an Award of Merit when shown by E.H.M. Cox and P.A. Cox in April 1964.

Epithet. After H.R. Fletcher, Regius Keeper, Royal Botanic Garden, Edinburgh, 1956—1970.

Hardiness 3. March—May. Plate 8.

R. valentinianum Forrest ex Hutch. in Notes Roy. Bot. Gard. Edin., Vol. 12 (1919) 45.
Illustration. Bot. Mag. Vol. 179 n.s.t. 623 (1972).

A compact rounded or compact spreading or rarely upright shrub, 30 cm.—1.22 m. (1—4 ft.) high, stem and branches with rough bark; *branchlets* scaly, *rather densely brown setose*. *Leaves* evergreen, elliptic, oblong-elliptic, oval or oblong-oval, lamina coriaceous, 2—4.6 cm. long, 1—2.9 cm. broad, apex rounded or obtuse, mucronate, base rounded or obtuse, not decurrent; upper surface dark green, shining, scaly, not setose or sparsely or moderately setose, midrib setose or setose at the base or in the lower half; *margin* entire, recurved, *rather densely brown setose*; under surface pale green, densely

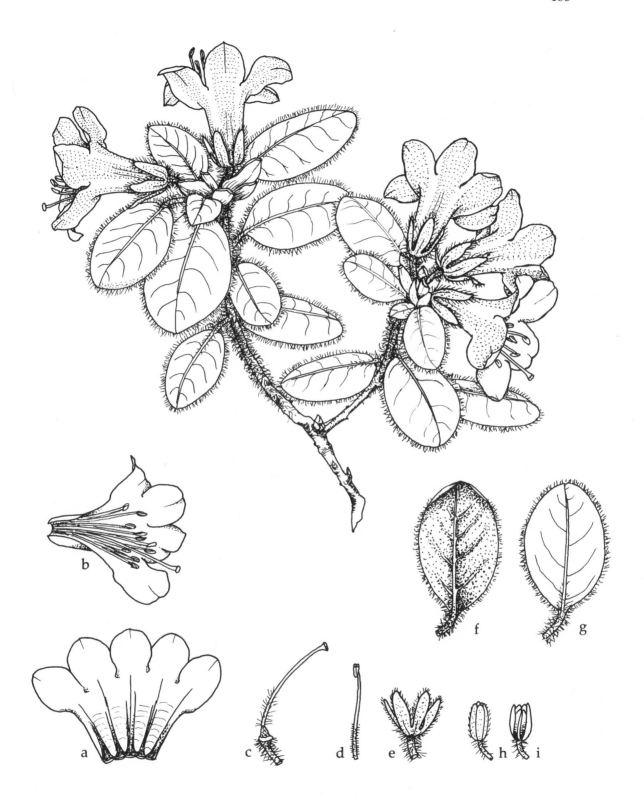

8. R. valentinianum
nat. size

a. petal. b. section. c. ovary, style. d. stamen. e. calyx. f. leaf (lower surface).
g. leaf (upper surface). h. capsule (enclosed). i. capsule.

scaly, the scales somewhat large or medium-sized, unequal, brown, contiguous or one-half their own diameter apart, not setose, midrib not setose or setose at the base; *petiole* 0.3—1 cm. long, margin not winged, scaly, *rather densely brown setose. Inflorescence* terminal, shortly racemose or umbellate, 1—4- or sometimes 5—6-flowered, flower-bud scales persistent or deciduous; rhachis 1—3 mm. long, scaly, bristly or not bristly; *pedicel* 4—7 mm. long, thick, scaly, *bristly. Calyx* 5-lobed, 5—8 mm. long, lobes oblong, outside moderately or rather densely scaly, not bristly, margin rather densely bristly. *Corolla tubular with spreading lobes or tubular-campanulate,* 2.6—3.5 cm. long, 5-lobed, bright yellow or bright sulphur-yellow, outside moderately or rather densely scaly on the tube and lobes, *moderately or rather densely pubescent on the tube,* glabrous on the lobes, margin of the lobes scaly or not scaly, inside pubescent in the tube, glabrous in the lobes. *Stamens* 10, unequal, 1.6—2.8 cm. long, shorter than the corolla; filaments rather densely pubescent in the lower one-third. *Ovary* conoid, 2—3 mm. long, 5-celled, densely scaly, not bristly or rarely bristly; style slender, straight, as long as the corolla, longer than the stamens, scaly at the base, glabrous or rarely minutely puberulous at the base. *Capsule* conoid or ovoid, 7—9 mm. long, 5—6 mm. broad, ribbed, densely scaly, glabrous, enclosed by the persistent calyx-lobes.

R. valentinianum was first collected by Forrest in May—June 1917 on the Shweli-Salwin Divide, west Yunnan. It was later found by him again in other localities in the same region and mid-west Yunnan. In June 1919, Kingdon-Ward collected it in north-east Upper Burma. The plant grows in open scrub, on cliffs and rocky slopes, and in alpine meadows, at elevations of 2,745—3,660 m. (9,000—12,000 ft.).

The outstanding characters of this plant are usually the compact habit of growth, the rather densely setose branchlets, petioles, and pedicels, and the dark green leaves rather densely setose on the margins and densely scaly on the lower surface. Another notable feature is the tubular corolla with spreading lobes, or tubular-campanulate, bright yellow or bright sulphur-yellow, moderately or rather densely scaly outside, and moderately or rather densely pubescent on the tube. The species is related to *R. ciliatum* but differs markedly in conspicuous characters.

The species was first introduced by Forrest in 1917 (No. 15899 — the Type number). It was reintroduced by him on several occasions from Yunnan. Along the east coast and inland, the plant is difficult to cultivate outdoors; moreover, it is a slow grower, and takes many years to reach flowering stage. Nevertheless, it is successfully grown in the rock garden, Royal Botanic Garden, Edinburgh, where it forms a compact and spreading shrub 1½ feet high and 2 feet across, and flowers moderately or sometimes freely. Along the west coast the species has proved hardy in the open and succeeds well in sheltered gardens. A fine example of the plant is at Caerhays, Cornwall, where it forms a compact shrub 4 feet high and as much across, densely filled with dark green foliage. A well-grown compact plant can be most attractive when covered with bright yellow flowers in clusters of two to six. The species received an Award of Merit when exhibited by the Hon. H.D. McLaren, Bodnant, in 1933.

Epithet. After Père S.P. Valentin, Tsedjong Mission, China.
Hardiness 1—2. April—May. Plate 10.

R. valentinianum Forrest ex Hutch. var. **changii** Fang in Contrib. Biol. Lab. Sci. Soc. China, Vol. XII (1939) 71.

The variety was described by Fang in 1939 from a plant collected in thickets in south-east Szechuan, at an elevation of 2,000 m. (6,557 ft.).

It differs from the species in that the pedicel and margin of the calyx-lobes are not bristly. Moreover, it differs in its geographical distribution. The plant has not been introduced into cultivation.

Epithet of the variety. After Chang, a collector.
Not in cultivation.

CINNABARINUM SERIES

General characters: medium-sized shrubs or trees, 1.22—7.63 m. (4—25 ft.) or rarely 60 cm. (2 ft.) high. Leaves evergreen (in *R. tamaense* deciduous or semi-deciduous), oblong, elliptic, oblong-lanceolate, lanceolate, to obovate or oval, lamina 2.5—15.5 cm. long, 1.5—5 cm. broad; upper surface glaucous or not glaucous; under surface glaucous or not glaucous, densely scaly, the scales nearly contiguous or one-half their own diameter apart (in *R. tamaense* laxly scaly, the scales 2—5 times their own diameter apart). Inflorescence terminal, or terminal and axillary in the uppermost 1—3 leaves, 2—9-flowered; pedicel 0.4—2.5 cm. long. *Calyx* 5-lobed or sometimes a mere rim, *1—4 mm. long. Corolla tubular or tubular-campanulate*, rarely funnel-campanulate or campanulate, 1.5—4.6 cm. long, cinnabar-red, orange, yellow, apricot, salmon-pink to deep plum-crimson or rich plum-purple, *outside not scaly* (in *R. tamaense* moderately or sparsely scaly). Stamens 10. Ovary oblong, conoid or sometimes narrow slender, 2—5 mm. long; style long, slender, straight. Capsule oblong or oblong-oval, 0.5—1.3 cm. long, 3—6 mm. broad.

Distribution: Nepal, Sikkim, Bhutan, south and south-east Tibet, and North Burma.

A small distinct Series usually with tubular or tubular-campanulate corolla, and long, slender and straight style. The affinity of the Series is mainly with the Tephropeplum Series.

KEY TO THE SPECIES

A. Leaves deciduous or semi-deciduous; under surface of the leaves laxly scaly, the scales usually 2—5 times their own diameter apart .... *tamaense*
A. Leaves evergreen; under surface of the leaves densely scaly, the scales nearly contiguous or one-half their own diameter apart.
    B. Inflorescence terminal; corolla tubular-campanulate or widely funnel-campanulate or tubular slightly widened towards the top with spreading lobes, not ventricose, 2.5—4 cm. long.
        C. Corolla cinnabar-red, salmon-pink, rose, pale pinkish-purple, bright pinkish-mauve, deep plum-crimson or rarely orange ... *cinnabarinum* and varieties (part)
        C. Corolla yellow, creamy-yellow or apricot.
            D. Corolla tubular, slightly widened towards the top with spreading lobes, yellow .... *cinnabarinum* (part)
            D. Corolla tubular-campanulate, creamy-yellow or apricot.
                E. Corolla creamy-yellow; upper surface of the young and adult leaves olive-green, slightly glaucous; upper surface of the adult leaves moderately or rather densely scaly, under surface pale glaucous green or pale green .... *xanthocodon*
                E. Corolla apricot; upper surface of the young leaves markedly bluish-green, glaucous; upper surface of the adult leaves bluish-green or dark green, not scaly, under surface tinged purple, or purplish-brown or pale purplish-brown .... *concatenans*
    B. Inflorescence terminal and axillary in the uppermost 1—3 leaves; corolla tubular with erect lobes, not spreading, slightly ventricose, 1.5—2.5 cm. long .... *keysii*

DESCRIPTION OF THE SPECIES

R. cinnabarinum Hook. f. Rhod. Sikkim Himal. t. 8 (1849).

A compact rounded or spreading, broadly upright or upright shrub, 1.22—5.49 m. (4—18 ft.) high; branchlets purplish or green, moderately or sparsely scaly. *Leaves* evergreen, oval, ovate-elliptic, obovate-elliptic, oblong-obovate, elliptic, oblong, oblong-lanceolate or lanceolate, lamina coriaceous, 3.2—9 cm. long, 1.8—5 cm. broad, apex rounded or obtuse, mucronate, base rounded or obtuse; upper surface bluish-green, pale bluish-green, olive-green or greyish-green, moderately or slightly glaucous, not scaly or sometimes scaly; under surface glaucous green, pale glaucous green, pale brown or brown, densely scaly, the scales unequal, medium-sized or sometimes small, brown, one-half their own diameter apart or nearly contiguous or sometimes their own diameter apart, without or sometimes with large scattered, dark brown scales; petiole 0.8—2 cm. long, sparsely or moderately or rarely rather densely scaly. *Inflorescence* terminal, shortly racemose, 3—9-flowered; rhachis 0.3—1 cm. long, not scaly or sparsely or moderately scaly, glabrous or rarely pubescent; pedicel 0.5—1.6 cm. long, moderately or rather densely scaly. *Calyx* 5-lobed or sometimes a mere rim, *1—2 mm. long*, lobes unequal or equal, triangular or ovate or rarely oblong, outside and margin not scaly or moderately or densely scaly, glabrous. *Corolla tubular, slightly widened towards the top, the lobes spreading, or tubular-campanulate*, 2.6—3.8 cm. long, 5-lobed, cinnabar-red, salmon-pink tinged yellow, salmon-pink, yellow or rarely orange, *outside not scaly*. *Stamens* 10, unequal, 1.8—3.4 cm. long, shorter than the corolla; filaments pubescent towards the base. *Ovary* oblong or conoid, 3—5 mm. long, 5-celled, densely scaly; style slender straight, longer or slightly shorter than the corolla, not scaly, pubescent at the base or glabrous. *Capsule* oblong or rarely oblong-oval, 0.8—1.3 cm. long, 3—6 mm. broad, straight, densely scaly, calyx-lobes persistent.

9. **R. cinnabarinum**
nat. size
a. section. b. capsule.

R. cinnabarinum has a wide geographical distribution, extending from Nepal, Sikkim and Bhutan to south and south-east Tibet. It was discovered by J.D. Hooker in April and May 1849 in Sikkim. The plant grows in pine, oak, Abies or rhododendron forests, in bamboo forests, in scrub jungle, and on open hillsides, at elevations of 2,135—4,118 m. (7,000—13,500 ft.). Ludlow and Sherriff record it as being very common in rhododendron forests on steep hillsides and in dense jungles in Bhutan.

As would be expected from the wide geographical distribution, diverse habitats and altitudinal range, *R. cinnabarinum* varies considerably in several of its features. It is a compact rounded, spreading, or upright shrub, 1.22—3 m. (4—10 ft.) or sometimes up to 5.49 m. (18 ft.) high; the leaves are oval, ovate-elliptic, elliptic to oblong, oblong-lanceolate or lanceolate, (laminae) 3.2—9 cm. long, 1.8—5 cm. broad; and the corolla is cinnabar-red, rose, pinkish-purple, deep plum-crimson, orange, or yellow. Some of the extreme forms have been given varietal status.

A marked feature of the species is usually the tubular corolla, 2.6—3.8 cm. long, although in its varieties the corolla shape varies from tubular to widely funnel-campanulate. The minute calyx 1—2 mm. long and the non-scaly corolla are constant characters of the species and its varieties.

R. cinnabarinum was first introduced by J.D. Hooker in 1849. It was reintroduced by Ludlow and Sherriff and by other collectors from the Himalayas. Several forms are in cultivation, varying in habit and height of growth, in leaf shape and size, and in flower colour. The more distinctive forms are: Form 1. A compact rounded or spreading shrub up to 6 feet high and as much across, with bluish-green leaves and narrowly tubular cinnabar-red corolla. Form 2. A tall broadly upright shrub up to 10 feet high, with greyish-green leaves; corolla same as the previous form. Form 3. A broadly upright shrub up to 8 feet high with narrowly tubular, yellow corolla, rare in cultivation. Form 4. A broadly upright shrub up to 6 feet high with broadly tubular-campanulate, deep salmon-pink corolla. All these forms are charming plants and are greatly admired when laden with flowers in trusses of three to nine. They are also extremely useful plants in that they are late flowerers, prolonging the flowering season into June and July. Some forms often produce good fertile seed in plenty.

It may be observed that some plants in cultivation under the name *R. cinnabarinum*, raised from seed introduced from the Himalayas, would appear to be natural hybrids.

A form with coral flowers bright red outside, raised from Ludlow, Sherriff and Taylor seed (No.6560) has been called *R. cinnabarinum* 'Cuprea'. It was given an Award of Merit when shown by Capt. Collingwood Ingram, in 1954.

Epithet. Cinnabar-red.

Hardiness 3. April—July. Plate 11.

R. cinnabarinum Hook. f. var. **aestivale** Hutch. in Gard. Chron. Vol. 92 (1932) 98.

This plant was described by Hutchinson in 1932 from a plant raised by Colonel Stephenson R. Clarke at Borde Hill, Sussex.

The variety differs from the species in its narrow, oblong-lanceolate leaves, and in its later flowering in July. It is hardy, but is rare in cultivation.

Epithet of the variety. Summer-flowering.

Hardiness 3. July.

R. cinnabarinum Hook. f. var. **blandfordiiflorum** W.J. Hooker in Bot. Mag. Vol. 82 t. 4930 (1856).

J.D. Hooker discovered this plant in 1849 in Sikkim. It is recorded as being not uncommon in valleys, on mountain-tops and ridges, at elevations of 3,050—3,660 m. (10,000—12,000 ft.).

It differs from the species in that the tubular corolla is 5—6.3 cm. (2—2½ in.) long, usually about twice as long as that of the species; it is red outside, yellow or greenish-yellow within.

The plant was introduced by J.D. Hooker in 1849. In cultivation it is a broadly upright shrub, usually up to 3 m. (10 ft.) high. It is fairly fast-growing, and is of great beauty when covered with tubular flowers. The plant was given an Award of Merit when shown by Lord Aberconway in 1945.

Epithet. Blandfordia-flowered.

Hardiness 3. May—July. Plate 14.

R. cinnabarinum Hook. f. var. **breviforme** Davidian in Quart. Bull. Amer. Rhod. Soc. Vol. 35, January 1982.

Ludlow, Sherriff and Hicks discovered this plant in fruit under No. 21283 in October 1949, at Lao, Lao Chu, north-east Bhutan, growing in mixed rhododendron and Abies forest at an elevation of 3,173 m. (10,500 ft.). They introduced it in the same year.

This variety is readily distinguished by the short tubular corolla, 3—3.5 cm. long, bright red outside, deep yellowish inside and at the margin of the lobes.

In cultivation, the plant has been known as *R. cinnabarinum* "var. Nepal". It is a broadly upright shrub, somewhat compact, 1.22—1.53 m. (4—5 ft.) high, densely filled with foliage. The plant is free-flowering and should be included in every collection of rhododendrons. It received an Award of Merit when exhibited by Hydon Nurseries Ltd. Surrey, in 1977 (L. S. & H. No. 21283 — the Type number).

Epithet of the variety. A form with shorter corolla.

Hardiness 3. June—July.

R. cinnabarinum Hook. f. var. **pallidum** W.J. Hooker in Bot. Mag. Vol. 80 t. 4788 (1854).

This plant was described by Sir William J. Hooker in 1854 from a plant raised at Kew, from seed collected by J.D. Hooker in Sikkim.

The variety is distinguished by the widely funnel-campanulate corolla, narrowed at the base, and with spreading lobes, rose or pale pinkish-purple in colour.

It is a broadly upright shrub up to 1.83 m. (6 ft.) high with rigid branchlets. The plant is rare in cultivation.

Epithet of the variety. Pale.

Hardiness 3. June—July.

R. cinnabarinum Hook. f. var. **purpurellum** Cowan in Notes Roy. Bot. Gard., Edin., Vol. 21 (1953) 147.

This plant was discovered by Ludlow and Sherriff at Natrampa, Chayul Chu, south Tibet, growing in rhododendron and bamboo forest at an elevation of 3,050 m. (10,000 ft.). It is recorded as being common in its native home.

The variety differs from the species in that the corolla is short, campanulate, rich plum-purple or bright pinkish-mauve, and the leaves are usually smaller.

The plant was first introduced by Ludlow and Sherriff in 1936 (No. 1354 — the Type number). In its native home it grows from 2.44—3.66 m. (8—12 ft.) high, but in cultivation it is a somewhat rounded shrub, up to 1.83 m. (6 ft.) in height. It is very hardy, free-flowering, and gives a delightful colour display with trusses of three to six flowers. The plant received an Award of Merit when exhibited by Capt. Collingwood Ingram, in May 1951.

Epithet of the variety. Purple.

Hardiness 3. May—July.

R. cinnabarinum Hook. f. var. **roylei** (Hook. f.) Hutch. in The Species of Rhododendron (1930) 222.

Syn. *R. roylei* Hook. f. Rhod. Sikkim Himal. t.7 (1849).

J.D. Hooker discovered this plant in 1849 in Sikkim. Further gatherings by other collectors show that the plant is distributed in Nepal, Sikkim and Bhutan. It is found amongst hillside shrubs, in open woodland, and in Abies and rhododendron forests, at elevations of 2,898—3,813 m. (9,500—12,500 ft.).

The variety is distinguished by the deep plum-crimson corolla, with a glaucous sheen.

The plant was first introduced by J.D. Hooker in 1851. It was reintroduced several times by other collectors. In cultivation it grows up to 5.49 m. (18 ft.) or even 6 m. (20 ft.) high. The flowers are produced very freely, for which the bluish-green leaves provide a charming contrast. It may be of interest to note that the whole plant is particularly attractive with sunlight behind it producing a glistening and shining effect. The plant is very hardy, and is well worth a place in every garden.

Epithet of the variety. After Dr. Royle.

Hardiness 3. May—July. Plate 12.

R. cinnabarinum Hook. f. var. **roylei** (Hook. f.) Hutch. forma **magnificum** W. Watson in Gard. Chron. Vol. LXIV, (1918) 38, Fig. 15.

This name was given to a plant raised from seed by Mr. Reuthe, and it received an Award of Merit when exhibited in May 1918 under the name *roylei magnificum*.

The forma differs from the variety in that the corolla is exceptionally large, 4—5.3 cm. long, with a broad tube.

In cultivation it is a broadly upright shrub varying from 1.53 m. (5 ft.) up to 2.44 m. (8 ft.) high. It is of sturdy habit, fairly fast-growing, and makes a wonderful show with its large deep plum-crimson flowers. Several remarkable specimens are to be seen at Crarae, Argyllshire, Scotland where they reach a height of 6—8 feet and flower freely with trusses of 3—6. A form 'Vin Rose' was also given an Award of Merit when shown by the Crown Estate Commissioners, Windsor Great Park, in May 1953.

Epithet of the forma. Magnificent.

Hardiness 3. June—July. Plate 13.

R. concatenans Hutch. in Gard. Chron. XCVII (1935) 376.

Illustration. Bot. Mag. Vol. 179 n.s.t. 634 (1973).

A broadly upright or somewhat rounded shrub, 1.53—2.14 m. (5—7 ft.) high; branchlets green, moderately or rather densely scaly. *Leaves* evergreen, elliptic or oblong-elliptic, lamina coriaceous, 4—8.7 cm. long, 2—5 cm. broad, apex rounded or obtuse, mucronate, base rounded or obtuse; *upper surface bluish-green or dark green*, not glaucous or glaucous, shining or matt (*in young leaves markedly bluish-green glaucous*, matt), not scaly; under surface tinged purple or purplish-brown or pale purplish-brown (in young leaves glaucous), densely scaly, the scales unequal, medium-sized and large, purplish-brown or brown, nearly contiguous or one-half their own diameter apart, without or with large, scattered dark brown scales; petiole 0.6—1.2 cm. long, rather densely or moderately scaly. *Inflorescence* terminal, shortly racemose, 3—8-flowered; rhachis 0.3—1 cm. long, scaly or not scaly, glabrous; pedicel 0.5—1.5 cm. long, moderately or rather densely scaly. *Calyx* 5-lobed, unequal, 1—4 mm. long, lobes ovate, triangular or lanceolate, outside moderately or rather densely scaly, margin scaly, eciliate or ciliate. *Corolla* tubular-campanulate, 3—4 cm. long, 5-lobed, *apricot*, faintly tinged with pale purple outside or not tinged, not scaly outside. *Stamens* 10, unequal, 1.6—2.6 cm. long, shorter than the corolla; filaments pubescent in the lower one-third or one-half of their length. *Ovary* conoid, 3—4 mm. long, 5-celled, densely scaly; style slender, straight, as long as the corolla or longer, not scaly, puberulous at the base or glabrous. *Capsule* oblong-oval, 0.8—1 cm. long, 4—5 mm. broad, rather densely scaly, calyx-lobes persistent.

R. concatenans was described by Hutchinson in 1935 from a plant grown by Lt.-Col. L.C.R. Messel, Nymans, Handcross, Sussex, raised from seed collected by Kingdon-Ward under No. 5874. The species was discovered by Kingdon-Ward in June 1924 at Doshong La, south-east Tibet, growing on steep rocky slopes among rhododendron scrub at elevations of 3,660—3,965 m. (12,000—13,000 ft.). He describes the plant as "Bush of 6 feet . . . foliage (October) bright glaucous, visible from afar; a most striking bush".

A diagnostic feature is the large, apricot, tubular-campanulate corolla up to 4 cm. long, prominently veined, by which the species is readily distinguished from its nearest ally *R. xanthocodon* and from all the other species of its Series. Another notable character is the large elliptic or oblong-elliptic leaf, up to 8.7 cm. long and 5 cm. broad, upper surface bluish-green or dark green, with or without a marked glaucous sheen, lower surface purple, purplish-brown or pale purplish-brown.

It may be remarked that some later introductions growing in gardens under the name *R. concatenans*, would appear to be natural hybrids. These plants have been mainly responsible for the confusion in distinguishing between *R. concatenans* and *R. cinnabarinum*.

In cultivation *R. concatenans* is a broadly upright or a somewhat rounded shrub, up to about 7 feet in height. Two distinct forms are grown in gardens. In Form 1, the adult leaves are large up to 8.7 cm. long, with or without a faint glaucous sheen on the upper surface. In Form 2, the adult leaves are smaller up to 6 cm. long, with a marked glaucous sheen on the upper surface, the leaf appearing silvery-white. An exceedingly attractive feature of the species is the bluish-green young growths, covered with a glaucous sheen. The plant is hardy, but to be able to grow it satisfactorily particularly along the east coast and in gardens inland, a well-sheltered position is essential. A well-grown healthy plant is extremely charming when covered with a profusion of flowers in trusses of three to eight. It received a First Class Certificate when exhibited by Lt.-Col. L.C.R. Messel, Nymans, Sussex, in 1935.

Epithet. Linking together.

Hardiness 3. April—May. Plate 15.

R. keysii Nutt. in Hook. Journ. Bot. Vol. 5 (1853) 353.

Illustration. Bot. Mag. Vol. 81 t. 4875 (1855).

A lax upright shrub or tree, sometimes epiphytic, 60 cm.—6 m. (2—20 ft.) high; branchlets purplish or green, moderately or rather densely scaly. *Leaves* evergreen, lanceolate, oblong, oblong-lanceolate, or sometimes oblong-elliptic, elliptic or obovate, lamina 5—15.5 cm. or rarely 3—4 cm. long, 1.5—3.6 cm. or rarely 1—1.1 cm. broad, apex acute, obtuse or rarely rounded, mucronate, base obtuse or tapered or rarely rounded; upper surface dark green, not glaucous, shining, moderately or sparsely scaly; under surface pale green, not glaucous, densely scaly, the scales unequal, medium-sized and large, brown or dark brown, one-half or their own diameter apart or rarely twice their own diameter apart, with or sometimes without large, scattered, dark brown scales; petiole 0.5—1.6 cm. long, rather densely or moderately scaly. *Inflorescence terminal and axillary in the uppermost 1—3 leaves*, shortly racemose, 2—6-flowered; rhachis 0.5—1 cm. long, moderately or sparsely scaly or not scaly, glabrous; pedicel 4—9 mm. long, rather densely or moderately scaly or not scaly. *Calyx* 5-lobed, equal or unequal, minute, 1 mm. long, lobes triangular, ovate or oblong-oval, outside not scaly or scaly, margin scaly or not scaly, eciliate or ciliate. *Corolla tubular, slightly ventricose, 1.5—2.5 cm. long*, 5-lobed, *lobes erect, small*, orange, coral, salmon-pink or deep scarlet, with yellow or yellowish lobes, outside not scaly. *Stamens* 10 or rarely 12, unequal, 1.2—2.5 cm. long, slightly longer or shorter than the corolla; filaments pubescent in the lower one-third or one-half of their length. *Ovary* oblong or narrow slender or conoid, 2—4 mm. long, 5-celled, densely scaly; style slender straight, longer than, or as long as, the corolla, pubescent at the base or in the lower one-third or rarely glabrous. *Capsule* oblong, 5—8 mm. long, 3 mm. broad, straight, rather densely scaly, calyx-lobes persistent.

This species was described by Nuttall in 1853. It is distributed in Bhutan, Assam, south and south-east Tibet, growing in thickets, in Picea and Tsuga forests, in rhododendron and mixed forests, and in dense rhododendron jungle, at elevations of 2,440—3,660 m. (8,000—12,000 ft.). Ludlow and Sherriff record it as being very common in a few localities in Bhutan.

The species is easily recognised by the slightly ventricose, short tubular corolla 1.5—2.5 cm. long, with small erect lobes, and by the inflorescence of 2—6 flowers which are terminal and axillary in the uppermost few leaves. In these respects, it differs markedly from its nearest ally *R. cinnabarinum*, and from all the other species of its Series. The plant is hexaploid with 78 chromosomes.

In 1937, *R. igneum* was described by J.M. Cowan from a specimen No. 2334 collected by Ludlow and Sherriff at Chayul Chu, southern Tibet. When this specimen is examined it is seen that in leaf shape and size, in the distribution of the scales on the lower surface, in flower shape, size and colour, and in all other morphological details, *R. igneum* agrees with *R. keysii*.

R. keysii was first introduced by Booth in 1851. It was reintroduced by Cooper, Kingdon-Ward, and Ludlow, Sherriff and Hicks. In its native home it is a shrub or tree, sometimes epiphytic, 2—20 feet high, but in cultivation it is a lax upright shrub up to 8 or 9 feet. A notable characteristic is the inflorescence of 2 to 6 flowers produced from a terminal bud and several axillary buds in the uppermost few leaves, often clustered forming a large compound inflorescence of 15 to 25 flowers. It is a useful plant in that it is a late flowerer, the flowers appearing in June or July. It is hardy, fairly fast-growing, and is easy to grow.

Epithet. After a Mr. Keys.

Hardiness 3. June—July. Plate 17.

R. keysii Nutt. var. **unicolor** Hutch. ex Stearn in Journ. Roy. Hort. Soc. Vol. LIX (1934) 39.

This name was given to a plant raised by Mr. Lionel de Rothschild at Exbury in 1926 from Kingdon-Ward's seed No. 6257 collected in Pemako, south-east Tibet. It should be noted that under this number two distinct plants have appeared in cultivation, namely, *R. keysii* var. *unicolor*, and *R. trichocladum* form.

The variety differs from the species in that the corolla is deep red, rarely the tips of the short erect lobes being slightly yellowish. Moreover, the lanceolate leaves are often longer, the laminae up to 15.5 cm. The plant is rare in cultivation but is worthy of being widely grown. It was given an Award of Merit when shown by Mr. Lionel de Rothschild in 1933 (Kingdon-Ward No. 6257).

Epithet of the variety. Uniform flower colour.

Hardiness 3. June—July.

R. tamaense Davidian in The Royal Horticultural Society's Rhododendrons (1972) 54.

A broadly upright shrub, often epiphytic at least when young, 92 cm.—1.83 m. (3—6 ft.) high or a small tree; branchlets scaly. *Leaves deciduous or semi-deciduous*, elliptic, oblong-oval, oblong-lanceolate or oblong, lamina coriaceous 2.5—5.8 cm. long, 1.5—2.6 cm. broad, apex rounded, obtuse or acute, mucronate, base rounded or obtuse, upper surface green, not scaly; *under surface* pale glaucous green or brown, scaly, *the scales* unequal, medium-sized and small, or large, brown, pale brown or reddish-brown, *2—5 times their own diameter apart* or rarely their own diameter apart; petiole 0.5—1 cm. long, scaly. *Inflorescence* terminal, shortly racemose, 2—5-flowered; rhachis 1—3 mm. long, scaly; pedicel 0.5—1.9 cm. long, scaly with large scales. *Calyx* a mere rim or 5-lobed, minute, 1 mm. long, lobes rounded, outside and margin densely scaly. *Corolla* tubular, widened towards the top, or tubular-campanulate, 3—4.6 cm. long, fleshy, 5-lobed, deep royal purple, purple or pale lavender, outside moderately or sparsely scaly. *Stamens* 10, unequal, 1.5—3.1 cm. long, shorter than the corolla; filaments villous at the base. *Ovary* conoid or oblong, 3—5 mm. long, 5-celled, densely scaly; style slender, straight, as long as the corolla or a little longer, not scaly. *Capsule* oblong, 0.9—1 cm. long, 3—5 mm. broad, straight, rather densely or moderately scaly, calyx persistent.

Kingdon-Ward discovered this plant in May 1953 in Kachin State, North Triangle, North Burma. He found it again later in that year at Tama Bum in the same region. It grows in thickets on the fringes of forests, and in rhododendron-silver fir forests, often epiphytic at least when young, at elevations of 2,745—3,173 m. (9,000—10,500 ft.). Kingdon-Ward records it as being common along the ridge in rhododendron moss forests.

R. tamaense is a remarkably distinct species. The diagnostic features of this plant are the deciduous or semi-deciduous leaves, laxly scaly on the lower surface, the scales being 2—5 times their own diameter apart, or rarely their own diameter apart. In these respects, it is readily distinguished from its nearest ally *R. cinnabarinum* and from all the other members of its Series. Another distinctive character is the tubular corolla widened

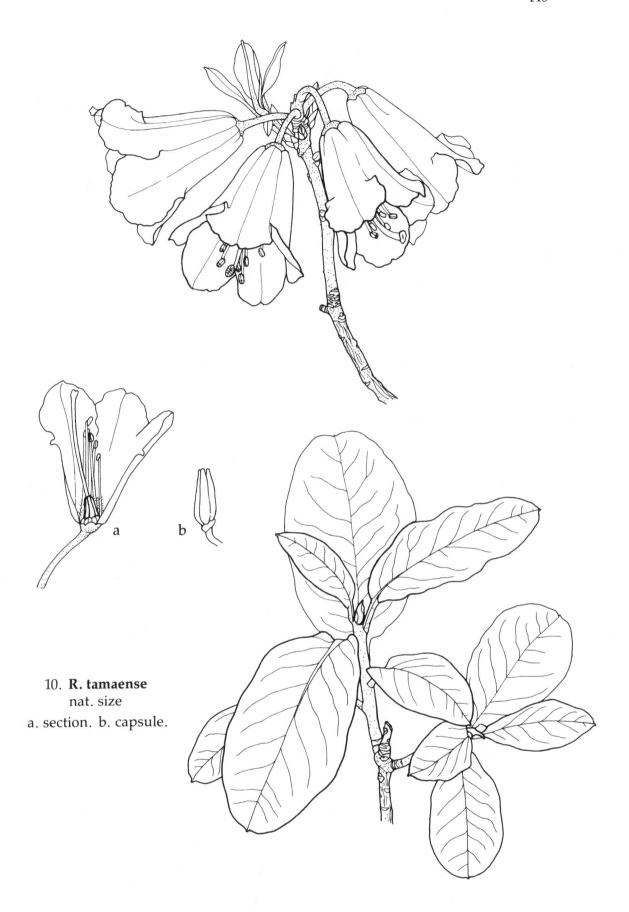

10. **R. tamaense**
nat. size
a. section. b. capsule.

towards the top, or tubular-campanulate, up to 4.6 cm. long, deep royal purple, purple or pale lavender. The species shows a certain degree of resemblance to *R. oreotrephes* in the Triflorum Series, but differs markedly in outstanding features.

The plant was introduced by Kingdon-Ward in 1953 (No. 21021 — the Type number, and No. 21003). In its native home it is a medium-sized shrub or a small tree, often an epiphyte; in cultivation it is a broadly upright shrub up to 6 feet high but likely to grow taller. It produces good fertile seed occasionally. The plant is hardy, free-flowering, and is well worth a place in every collection of rhododendrons.

Epithet. From Tama, North Triangle, North Burma.
Hardiness 3. April—May.

R. xanthocodon Hutch. in Gard. Chron. Vol. XCV (1934) 409.

A broadly upright shrub or tree, 1.83—7.63 m. (6—25 ft.) high; branchlets green, rather densely or moderately scaly. *Leaves* evergreen, elliptic, oblong-elliptic, obovate, oval or oblong, *lamina* coriaceous, 3—7.5 cm. long, 1.6—4.5 cm. broad, apex rounded or obtuse, mucronate, base rounded or obtuse; *upper surface olive-green, not glaucous* or slightly glaucous, shining, (*in young leaves olive-green*, slightly glaucous, matt), moderately or rather densely scaly; *under surface pale glaucous green or pale green*, densely scaly, the scales unequal, medium-sized and large, or medium-sized, or small, dark brown or brown or pale brown, one-half or their own diameter apart, without larger dark brown scattered scales; petiole 0.8—1.5 cm. long, rather densely or moderately scaly. *Inflorescence* terminal, shortly racemose, 2—6- or rarely 8-flowered; rhachis 0.3—1.2 cm. long, rather densely or moderately scaly, glabrous; pedicel 1—2.5 cm. long, scaly. *Calyx* 5-lobed, unequal or equal, 1—2 mm. long, lobes triangular or ovate, outside and margin densely or moderately scaly, glabrous. *Corolla* tubular-campanulate, 2.5—3.2 cm. long, 5-lobed, *creamy-yellow*, without spots, outside not scaly. *Stamens* 10, unequal, 0.9—2.8 cm. long, shorter than the corolla; filaments pubescent towards the base. *Ovary* conoid, 3—4 mm. long, 5-celled, densely scaly; style slender, straight, longer than, or as long as, the corolla, not scaly, glabrous. *Capsule* oblong, 1—1.3 cm. long, 3—4 mm. broad, straight, densely scaly, calyx-lobes persistent.

R. xanthocodon was described by Hutchinson in 1934 from a plant raised by Lord Aberconway at Bodnant, Wales, and from Kingdon-Ward's dried specimen under No. 6026. Kingdon-Ward discovered it in July 1924 at Nam La, Tibet. Subsequently it was collected by Ludlow, Sherriff and Hicks, at Peipe La, Bhutan. It grows in mixed forests and in fir forests, at elevations of 3,355—3,660 (11,000—12,000 ft.).

Hutchinson placed the species in the Triflorum Series, but in *The Rhododendron and Camellia Year Book* 1954, p. 68, it was correctly assigned to the Cinnabarinum Series.

In some respects, the species resembles *R. cinnabarinum* from which it differs markedly in that the upper surface of the leaves is olive-green, usually not glaucous, and the corolla is tubular-campanulate, creamy-yellow.

The plant was introduced by Kingdon-Ward in 1924 (No. 6026 — the Type number). In its native home it is a shrub or a slender tree, 6 to 25 feet high, but in cultivation it is a broadly upright shrub up to 8 or 9 feet. It is a robust grower, free-flowering, and provides a fine display with trusses of two to six flowers. The plant is hardy, but requires some shade and protection from wind, for the best results to be obtained. It received an Award of Merit when exhibited by Mr. Lionel de Rothschild in 1935 (K.W. No. 6026).

Epithet. Yellow bell.
Hardiness 3. May.

DAURICUM SERIES

General characters: shrubs, 1—4 m. (3⅓—13 ft.) high; branchlets densely to sparsely scaly. *Leaves deciduous or evergreen*, elliptic, oblong-elliptic, oblong-oval, oval, almost orbicular, elliptic-lanceolate or lanceolate, lamina 1—4 cm. long, 0.6—3.6 cm. broad; under surface scaly, the scales overlapping to 4 times their own diameter apart. Inflorescence terminal, or terminal and axillary in the uppermost 1—3 leaves, 1—2-flowered; pedicel 0.3—1 cm. long. Calyx 5-lobed, minute, 0.5—1 mm. long. *Corolla widely funnel-shaped*, 1.3—2.8 cm. long, 5-lobed, pink, rose, rose-purple, reddish-purple, pale pinkish-purple or white, *outside not scaly* or rarely sparsely scaly, *pubescent* or rarely glabrous. Stamens 10. Ovary conoid or oblong, 2—4 mm. long, 5-celled, densely scaly; style slender, straight. Capsule oblong, 0.9—1.6 cm. long, 2—5 mm. broad, rather densely scaly.

Distribution: from the Altai Mountains, U.S.S.R. east to Siberia, north Mongolia, Manchuria, north and north-east China, Korea, Japan, and Sakhalin island.

A small Series with widely funnel-shaped flowers, showing a certain degree of resemblance to the species of the Triflorum Series.

KEY TO THE SPECIES

A. Leaves evergreen or semi-evergreen.
　　B. Leaves (laminae) usually 1.6—2.8 cm. broad; pedicel densely scaly; corolla pale pinkish-purple or rose .... *sichotense*
　　B. Leaves (laminae) 0.6—2 cm. broad; pedicel moderately scaly; corolla reddish-purple or dark purple .... *dauricum* var. *sempervirens*
A. Leaves deciduous.
　　C. Under surface of the leaves densely scaly, the scales overlapping or contiguous or ½ or sometimes 1½ times their own diameter apart; leaf apex rounded or broadly obtuse; corolla 1.3—2.3 cm. long; leaves (laminae) 1—3.4 cm. long, 0.6—2 cm. broad .... *dauricum*
　　C. Under surface of the leaves laxly scaly, the scales 2—4 times their own diameter apart; leaf apex acute, acuminate or obtuse; corolla 2.3—2.8 cm. long; leaves (laminae) 3.2—8 cm. long, usually 1.6—3.6 cm. broad .... *mucronulatum*

DESCRIPTION OF THE SPECIES

R. dauricum Linn. Sp. Pl. (1753) 392.
　　Illustration. Bot. Mag. Vol. 17 t. 636 (1803).
　　A shrub, 1.53—2.44 m. (5—8 ft.) high; branchlets rather densely to sparsely scaly, rather densely minutely puberulous, leaf-bud scales persistent or deciduous. *Leaves deciduous,* elliptic, oblong-elliptic, oblong-oval or oval, *lamina thin, 1—3.4 cm. long, 0.6—2 cm. broad, apex rounded or broadly obtuse,* mucronate, base rounded or obtuse; upper surface dark green or bright green, shining, rather densely or moderately scaly, midrib puberulous or glabrous; margin crenulate; *under surface densely scaly, the scales* medium-sized, unequal, brown, *overlapping or contiguous or ½ or sometimes 1½ times their own diameter apart;* petiole 2—8 mm. long, scaly, rather densely or moderately minutely puberulous. *Inflorescence* terminal, or terminal and axillary in the uppermost one or two leaves, umbellate, 1—2-flowered, flower-bud scales deciduous or persistent; rhachis 1 mm. long, scaly or not scaly; pedicel 3—8 mm. long, scaly, rather densely or moderately minutely puberulous. *Calyx* 5-lobed, minute, 0.5—1 mm. long, lobes ovate or triangular, outside densely or moderately scaly, margin densely scaly, glabrous. *Corolla* widely funnel-shaped, *1.3—2.3 cm. long,* precocious, 5-lobed, pink, rose-purple, reddish-purple or dark purple, *outside not scaly* or rarely sparsely scaly, *pubescent* or rarely glabrous. *Stamens* 10, unequal, 1—2 cm. long, shorter than the corolla; filaments pubescent at the base. *Ovary* conoid or oblong, 2—3 mm. long, 5-celled, densely scaly, glabrous; style slender, straight, longer than the corolla, longer than the stamens, not scaly, glabrous. *Capsule* oblong, 0.9—1.3 cm. long, 4—5 mm. broad, straight or slightly curved, rather densely scaly, glabrous, calyx persistent.

　　R. dauricum was described by Linnaeus in 1753. It has a wide area of distribution, extending from the Altai Mountains U.S.S.R. east to Siberia, north Mongolia, Manchuria, north-east China, Korea, Japan and Sakhalin island. The sub-Alpine tracts in the northern parts of Siberia between the Lena and Yenisei rivers, are said to be empurpled by the flowers of this species in May.

　　In 1917, *R. fittianum* Balf. f. was described from a cultivated plant which appeared as a stray in seedpans of *R. radinum* (now *R. trichostomum* var. *radinum*) under Forrest No. 10278, at Werrington Park, Cornwall. The plant is a natural hybrid of *R. racemosum.*

　　The distinctive features of *R. dauricum* are the deciduous, oval to oblong-elliptic leaves, rounded or broadly obtuse at the apex, and the widely funnel-shaped, pink, rose-purple, reddish-purple or dark purple corolla, pubescent on the outside. It is closely allied to *R. mucronulatum;* the distinctions between them are discussed under the latter.

The plant was first introduced in 1780. In cultivation it is a lax broadly upright shrub up to 6 feet high, with short branchlets. It is one of the earliest of rhododendrons to burst into bloom, usually in January and February, sometimes in December. The plant is free-flowering, and it has the added advantage of producing the flowers quite young when raised from seed. It is perfectly hardy, but unfortunately the flowers are sometimes completely destroyed by early spring frosts. The plant is easy to grow, and is greatly admired when covered with pink or rose-purple flowers in clusters of 1—2.

Epithet. From Dauria, part of S.E. Siberia, east of Lake Baikal, N.E. Asia, now partly in U.S.S.R. and partly in China.

Hardiness 3—4. Jan.—Feb.—March, sometimes in December. Plate 19.

R. dauricum Linn. var. album DC Prodr. VII (1839) 725.

This plant was described by De Candolle in 1839. The variety differs from the species in the white flowers. It was introduced into cultivation from Japan. The plant is hardy and free-flowering.

Epithet of the variety. With white flowers.

Hardiness 3—4. Jan.—Feb.—March.

R. dauricum Linn. var. sempervirens Sims in Bot. Mag. Vol. 44 t. 1888 (1817).

Illustration. Bot. Mag. Vol. 147 t. 8930 (1921).

This plant was described by Sims in 1817. It is widely distributed from Siberia to north-east China and Japan.

The variety is distinguished from the species by the evergreen or semi-evergreen leaves. It differs further in that in cultivation it flowers in March and April, whereas the species flowers usually in January and February, sometimes in December.

A plant which was given the name *R. dauricum* Linn. var. *atrovirens* Hort. in 1817, is identical with var. *sempervirens* in every respect. In 1936, *R. ledebourii* Pojark. was described from a plant collected on the Altai Mountains, Russia. It agrees with var. *sempervirens* in general characters and in every morphological detail.

The variety is said to have been introduced by Thomas Bell in 1798 from Russia. Perhaps the finest example of var. *sempervirens* is in the Royal Botanic Garden, Edinburgh, consisting of a large group of plants up to 6 feet high, with dark green semi-evergreen leaves. In March the plants provide a most delightful colour display with reddish-purple flowers, but occasionally a devastating spring frost takes its heavy toll. The plant was given an Award of Merit in March 1963, and a First Class Certificate in February 1969 for a form 'Midwinter' when shown on both occasions by the Crown Estate Commissioners, Windsor Great Park.

Epithet of the variety. Evergreen.

Hardiness 3—4. March—April.

R. mucronulatum Turcz. in Bull. Soc. Nat. Mosc. (1937) 155.

Illustration. Bot. Mag. Vol. 136 t. 8304 (1910).

A broadly upright shrub, 1—4 m. (3⅓—13 ft.) or sometimes up to 30 cm. (1 ft.) high; branchlets long slender, scaly, not bristly or sometimes bristly, not puberulous or rarely minutely puberulous, leaf-bud scales deciduous. *Leaves deciduous*, elliptic, elliptic-lanceolate or lanceolate, *lamina* thin, *3.2—8 cm. long, 1.3—3.6 cm. broad, apex acute, acuminate or sometimes obtuse*, mucronate, base obtuse or tapered; upper surface bright green, shining or matt, scaly, not bristly or sometimes bristly with appressed bristles, midrib puberulous or glabrous; margin crenulate, not bristly or sometimes bristly; *under surface* pale green, *scaly, the scales* medium-sized, unequal, brown, *2—4 times their own diameter apart*, not bristly or sometimes moderately or sparsely bristly; petiole 0.2—1 cm. long, moderately or rather densely scaly, not bristly or sometimes bristly, not puberulous or minutely puberulous. *Inflorescence* terminal, or terminal and axillary in the uppermost 1—3 leaves, umbellate, 1—2- or sometimes 3-flowered, flower-bud scales per-

11. **R. mucronulatum**
nat. size

a. flower. b. stamen. c. ovary, style.
d. capsule.

a b c d

sistent; rhachis 1 mm. long, scaly; pedicel 0.8—1 cm. long, scaly, not bristly or sometimes bristly, not puberulous or minutely puberulous. *Calyx* 5-lobed, minute, 0.5—1 mm. long, lobes ovate or triangular, outside moderately or densely scaly, not bristly or sometimes bristly, margin not scaly or scaly, bristly or not bristly. *Corolla* widely funnel-shaped, *2.3—2.8 cm. long*, precocious, 5-lobed, rose, rose-purple, pale rose-purple or reddish-purple, without spots, *outside not scaly*, *pubescent*. *Stamens* 10, unequal, 1.6—2.7 cm. long, shorter than the corolla; filaments moderately or densely pubescent at the base. *Ovary* oblong or conoid, 2—4 mm. long, 5-celled, densely scaly, glabrous; style slender, straight, longer than, or as long as, the corolla, longer than the stamens, not scaly, glabrous. *Capsule* oblong, 1.2—1.6 cm. long, 4—5 mm. broad, straight or slightly curved, rather densely scaly, glabrous, calyx persistent.

R. mucronulatum was described in 1837. It is distributed in south-east Siberia, Manchuria, northern China, Korea, and Japan.

The remarkable features of this plant are the completely deciduous large leaves, and the large corolla pubescent on the outside. The flowers are terminal, or terminal and axillary in the uppermost one to three leaves. The species is allied to *R. dauricum*. The main distinctions between them are that in *R. mucronulatum* the leaf apex is usually acute or acuminate, the corolla is large 2.3—2.8 cm. long, the lower surface of the leaves is laxly scaly, the scales being 2—4 times their own diameter apart, the leaves (laminae) are large, 3.2—8 cm. long, usually 1.6—3.6 cm. broad, and the branchlets are long slender; whereas in *R. dauricum* the leaf apex is rounded or broadly obtuse, the corolla is smaller 1.3—2.3 cm. long, the lower surface of the leaves is densely scaly, the scales are overlapping or contiguous or one-half their own diameter apart, the leaves (laminae) are smaller 1—3.4 cm. long, 0.6—2 cm. broad, and the branchlets are short twiggy. However, it is to be noted that when a large number of plants in cultivation are examined, it is found that these distinctions are not constant, and the species are linked by intergrading forms.

It is of interest to point out that Mr. and Mrs. Warren Berg and Mr. Hideo Suzuki collected a dwarf form of *R. mucronulatum* on the island of Cheju, Korea in May 1976. They found it growing in abundance on Mt. Halla at elevations of 1,373—1,830 m. (4,500—6,000 ft.). The plant was introduced by them into cultivation in 1976. It first flowered in Mr. and Mrs. John Wood's garden in Edinburgh.

R. mucronulatum was first introduced to the Arnold Arboretum by Dr. Bretschneider (surgeon to the Russian Embassy in Peking, China) in 1882 from Peking. In 1907, Kew reintroduced it from a Yokohama nursery in Japan. In cultivation it is a broadly upright shrub usually up to 8 feet high with large elliptic, elliptic-lanceolate or lanceolate, bright green leaves. It is the harbinger of spring, free-flowering, and when it escapes the frost, it heralds spring with a blaze of purple colour in February or in January or sometimes towards the end of December. The plant is very hardy, and it sometimes flowers when the ground is covered with snow. It is fairly fast-growing, and should be a most valuable acquisition to every garden.

As evidence of its merit as a garden plant, it may be mentioned that an Award of Merit was three times given to it: when shown by Kew in 1924 to a form with rich purplish-rose flowers, in 1935 to a form known as 'Roseum', and in 1965 to a form 'Cornell Pink'. A form 'Winter Brightness' received a First Class Certificate when exhibited by the Crown Estate Commissioners, Windsor Great Park, in 1957.

Epithet. With a small point.
Hardiness 3—4. Jan.—Feb.—March, sometimes in December. Plate 18.

R. mucronulatum Turcz. var. **acuminatum** Hutch. in The Species of Rhododendron (1930) 227.

This name was given by Hutchinson in 1930 to a plant raised in cultivation.

The variety differs from the species in that it flowers several weeks later than the species. Moreover, the leaves are lanceolate with matt upper surfaces, and the corolla is pale pinkish-purple.

It was introduced from Japan in 1907. The plant is broadly upright up to 2.44 m. (8 ft.) high. It is perfectly hardy and free-flowering.

Epithet of the variety. Tapering to a point.

Hardiness 3—4. March—April.

R. mucronulatum Turcz. var. **albiflorum** Nakai in Flora Koreana, II (1911) 76.

This plant was described by Nakai in 1911. It is a native of Korea, and is recorded as being of rare occurrence.

The variety is distinguished by the white flowers, spotted with green. It has not been introduced into cultivation.

Epithet of the variety. White-flowered.

Not in cultivation.

R. sichotense Pojark. in Komarov, Flora URSS Vol. XVIII (1952) 722.

A shrub, 1.22—1.83 m. (4—6 ft.) high; branchlets scaly, rather densely or moderately puberulous, leaf-bud scales deciduous. *Leaves evergreen*, oval, oblong-oval or almost orbicular, *lamina* somewhat coriaceous, *2.3—4 cm. long, 1.3—2.8 cm. broad,* apex rounded, mucronate, base rounded or obtuse; upper surface bright green, shining, moderately or rather densely scaly, midrib puberulous or glabrous; margin crenulate; under surface pale green, densely scaly, the scales medium-sized, unequal, brown, overlapping or contiguous or one-half or twice their own diameter apart; petiole 3—6 mm. long, scaly, minutely puberulous. *Inflorescence* terminal, or terminal and axillary in the uppermost one or two leaves, umbellate, 1—2-flowered, flower-bud scales persistent or deciduous; rhachis 0.5—1 mm. long, scaly; *pedicel 3—6 mm. long, densely scaly,* minutely puberulous. *Calyx* 5-lobed, minute, 0.5—1 mm. long, lobes ovate or triangular, outside and margin densely scaly, glabrous. *Corolla* widely funnel-shaped, 1.8—2.1 cm. long, 5-lobed, *pale pinkish-purple or rose,* outside not scaly, pubescent. *Stamens* 10, un-equal, 1—2 cm. long, shorter than the corolla; filaments rather densely pubescent at the base. *Ovary* conoid or oblong, 2 mm. long, 5-celled, densely scaly, glabrous; style slender, straight, as long as, or longer than, the corolla, longer than the stamens, not scaly, glabrous. *Capsule* oblong, 0.9—1.3 cm. long, 2—3 mm. broad, straight or slightly curved, rather densely scaly, glabrous, calyx persistent.

This plant was described by Pojarkova from a plant collected in eastern U.S.S.R. It grows in woods in river valleys, north of the Olga River.

R. sichotense shows a strong resemblance to *R. dauricum* var. *sempervirens*, particularly in the shape of the leaves and distribution of the scales on the lower surface, in the inflorescence, and in the shape and size of the corolla. It differs from its ally in that the leaves are usually larger, the pedicels are densely scaly, and the flowers are pale pinkish-purple or rose. Whether these distinctions are important enough to keep *R. sichotense* specifically distinct, is a matter of some doubt. Nevertheless, the name may be allowed to stand until more is known of this plant.

The plant has now been introduced into cultivation. It is broadly upright, 3—4 feet high, and free-flowering.

Epithet. From Sikhote-Alin, easternmost U.S.S.R.

Hardiness 3—4. March—April.

EDGEWORTHII SERIES

General characters: shrubs, often epiphytic, 30 cm.—3.66 m. (1—12 ft.) high; *branchlets densely woolly*. Leaves evergreen, ovate, elliptic, ovate-elliptic, oblong-elliptic, ovate-lanceolate, oblong-lanceolate or oblong; lamina 2.3—14 cm. long, 1.2—5.6 cm. broad; upper surface strongly or moderately bullate (in *R. pendulum* not bullate); *under surface densely woolly, scaly*, the scales ½—2 times their own diameter apart; *petiole densely woolly*. Inflorescence terminal, 1—4-|(or rarely up to 6-) flowered; *pedicel* 0.6—2.1 cm. long, *densely wooly*. Calyx 0.5—1.9 cm. long. Corolla campanulate or funnel-campanulate or rotate-campanulate, 1.5—7.6 cm. long, white or white tinged pink or sulphur-yellow. Stamens 10. *Ovary* ovate, oval or oblong, 2—8 mm. long, *densely woolly*, scaly; style long, straight or sharply bent. Capsule oval, ovate or oblong, 0.8—2.2 cm. long, 0.6—1.3 cm. broad, densely or sometimes moderately woolly, rather densely or moderately scaly.

Distribution: Nepal, Sikkim, Bhutan, Assam, south and south-east Tibet, Upper Burma, north-west Yunnan, and south-west Szechuan.

A small distinct Series of three species, widely distributed, showing no particular affinity with any other Series. A diagnostic feature of importance is the densely woolly and scaly lower surface of the leaves.

KEY TO THE SPECIES

A. Style long, straight; corolla large, 3.2—7.6 cm. long; calyx large, usually 1—1.9 cm. long; flowers scented .... *edgeworthii*
A. Style short, sharply bent; corolla small, 1.5—2.5 cm. long; calyx small, 5—9 mm. long; flowers not scented.
    B. Upper surface of the leaves bullate; flowers sulphur-yellow; upper surface of the leaves not convex, margins not recurved; calyx pale green .... *seinghkuense*
    B. Upper surface of the leaves not bullate; flowers white or white tinged pink or rarely pale yellow; upper surface of the leaves convex, margins slightly recurved; calyx red or tinged red .... *pendulum*

DESCRIPTION OF THE SPECIES

R. edgeworthii Hook. f. Rhod. Sikkim Himal., t. 21 (1851).
    Illustration. Bot. Mag. Vol. 82 t. 4936 (1856).
    A straggly shrub, often epiphytic, 30 cm.—3.60 m. (1—12 ft.) high; branchlets densely woolly with brown or rust-coloured or whitish wool, not scaly or sparsely scaly. *Leaves* evergreen, ovate, elliptic, ovate-elliptic, oblong-elliptic, ovate-lanceolate or oblong-lanceolate, lamina coriaceous, 4—14 cm. long, 2—5.6 cm. broad, apex acuminate or acutely acuminate or rarely acute, mucronate, base rounded or sometimes broadly obtuse; *upper surface strongly or moderately bullate*, glabrous or with vestiges of hairs, not scaly or sometimes scaly, midrib deeply grooved, woolly ⅓ to its entire length or glabrous, primary veins impressed; *under surface densely woolly* with brown or rust-coloured or fawn wool, *densely scaly*, the scales very small, more or less equal, pale brown or brown, one-half or their own diameter apart, midrib prominent, primary veins raised or obscured by the indumentum; petiole 0.6—2.5 cm. long, densely woolly with brown or fawn or rust-coloured wool, not scaly or rarely scaly. *Inflorescence* terminal, umbellate or shortly racemose, 1—3- (or sometimes 4- or rarely up to 6-) flowered; rhachis 1—3 mm. long, tomentose, not scaly or rarely sparsely scaly; pedicel 0.6—2.1 cm. long, densely woolly with brown or rust-coloured or fawn wool, not scaly or sometimes scaly. *Calyx* deeply 5-lobed, *0.6—1.9 cm. long*, red or tinged red, lobes unequal, ovate or rounded or obovate, outside glabrous or moderately or densely or sometimes sparsely hairy, scaly or rarely not scaly, margin densely hairy, not scaly. *Corolla* campanulate or funnel-campanulate, *very fragrant*, 5-lobed, *3.2—7.6 cm. long*, white, or white tinged pink, or rose, with or without a yellow blotch at the base, outside glabrous or hairy, moderately or rather densely scaly. *Stamens* 10, unequal, 1.5—5 cm. long; filaments densely villous in the lower ⅓—½ of their lengths. *Ovary* ovate or oval or oblong, 3—8 mm. long, 5—6-celled, densely woolly with brown wool, moderately or sparsely scaly; *style long, straight*, longer than the stamens, densely woolly and scaly in the lower ¼—⅓ of its length, (rarely not scaly). *Capsule* oval or oblong or short stout, 1—2.2 cm. long, 0.8—1.2 cm. broad, densely or sometimes moderately woolly with brown wool, rather densely or moderately scaly, calyx-lobes persistent.

    This species was discovered by J.D. Hooker in the Sikkim Himalaya in 1849. Subsequent gatherings by other collectors show that the species has a wide area of distribution, extending from Nepal, Sikkim, Bhutan and Assam to south and east Tibet, north-east Upper Burma, north-west Yunnan, and south-west Szechuan. It grows on cliffs, on rocks, on humus-covered boulders, in open rocky situations amongst dwarf scrub in side valleys, in deciduous forests, in mixed forests, and in thickets, often as an epiphyte, at elevations of 1,830—3,965 m. (6,000—13,000 ft.). Kingdon-Ward records it as being abundant on open granite ridges at 2,440 m. (8,000 ft.) at Laktang, north-east Upper Burma. According to Farrer it is abundant as an epiphyte occupying the tops of almost

12. **R. edgeworthii**
nat. size

a. flower. b. stamen. c. ovary, style.
d. capsule (enclosed). e. capsule.

every tree in the alpine zone at Shing Hong, Nyitadi and elsewhere at 2,745—3,050 m. (9,000—10,000 ft.) also in north-east Upper Burma.

R. edgeworthii is a very variable plant in view of its wide geographical distribution, altitudinal range, and diverse habitats in which it is found. It grows from 30 cm. to 3.60 m. (1—12 ft.) high; the leaves are ovate, elliptic, oblong-elliptic, ovate-lanceolate or oblong-lanceolate, laminae 4—14 cm. long, 2—5.6 cm. broad; the calyx is 0.6—1.9 cm. long; and the corolla is 3.2—7.6 cm. long.

It may be noted that in 1887, *R. bullatum* Franch. was described from a plant collected by Delavay in north-west Yunnan, and in 1917 the name *R. sciaphyllum* Balf. f. et Ward was given to a plant from east Burma. In 1964 both names were relegated to synonymy under *R. edgeworthii* (*The Rhododendron and Camellia Year Book*, 1964, p. 104).

A diagnostic criterion of significance is the densely woolly as well as the densely scaly lower surface of the leaves, by which *R. edgeworthii* and the other members of its Series are readily distinguished from the species of all other Series. Other remarkable characters of this species are the markedly bullate upper surface of the leaves, and the large calyx and corolla. From its allies *R. pendulum* and *R. seinghkuense*, it differs by well-marked characteristics.

R. edgeworthii was first introduced by J.D. Hooker in 1851. It was reintroduced on many occasions by Forrest, Farrer, Kingdon-Ward, Rock, Ludlow and Sherriff, McLaren, Yü, and Cox and Hutchison. In its native home it grows from 1 up to 12 feet high, but in cultivation it reaches 3 or 4 feet or sometimes 5 or 6 feet. The species varies considerably in cultivation in leaf shape and size, in the size of the corolla from 3.2—7.6 cm. long, and in the size of the calyx. In some forms a large red calyx up to 1.9 cm. long, is a conspicuous feature. There are three distinct colour forms: Form 1. White strongly tinged red. Form 2. White tinged pink. Form 3. White. The plant is characterised by the deliciously scented flowers. As it comes from elevations of 6,000 to 13,000 feet, it varies in hardiness. Along the west coast the species is hardy outdoors in well-sheltered gardens; in the east coast and inland it is tender and is suitable for a cool greenhouse. It is to be noted that two plants of this species in the Royal Botanic Garden, Edinburgh, have proved hardy and are successfully grown outdoors in the woodland, and amongst other rhododendrons; these plants are three to four feet high, free-flowering with large, white strongly tinged red flowers. The species is a fairly vigorous grower, and is of exquisite beauty with its large campanulate or funnel-campanulate flowers in trusses of one to three or sometimes four.

R. edgeworthii is very highly rated. A white form received an Award of Merit when exhibited by T.H. Lowinsky, Sunninghill in 1923 under the name of *R. bullatum* (Farrer No. 842), and again in 1946 for a white flushed rose form also under the same name, when shown by Lord Aberconway, Bodnant. It also rceived a First Class Certificate when exhibited by Lt.-Col. L.C.R. Messel, Handcross, Sussex in 1933, and again in 1937 under the name *R. bullatum* (Forrest No. 26618) when shown by Mr. Lionel de Rothschild, Exbury, in 1937.

Epithet. After M.P. Edgeworth, Bengal Civil Service; 1812—81.
Hardiness 1—2. April—May. Plate 20.

R. pendulum Hook. f. Rhod. Sikkim Himal. t. 13 (1849).

An upright or bushy or somewhat compact rounded shrub, sometimes epiphytic, 30 cm.—1.22 m. (1—4 ft.) high; branchlets densely woolly with brown or fawn wool, sparsely scaly or not scaly, leaf-bud scales persistent or deciduous. *Leaves* evergreen, oblong, elliptic, oblong-elliptic or rarely oval, lamina coriaceous, 2.3—5 cm. long, 1.2—2.5 cm. broad, apex obtuse or rounded, mucronate, base obtuse or rounded; *upper surface convex, not bullate,* glabrous or with vestiges of hairs, not scaly or sparsely scaly, midrib deeply grooved, tomentose at the base or one-half its length or entire length, primary veins impressed; margins slightly recurved; *under surface densely woolly* with brown or fawn wool, *densely scaly,* the scales very small or medium-sized, brown, one-half or their

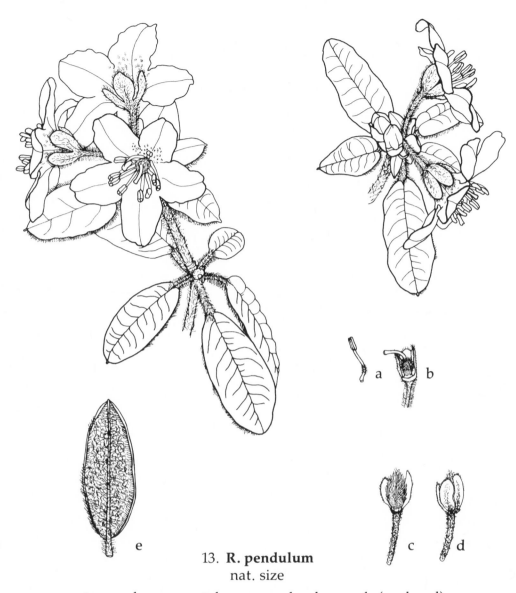

13. R. pendulum
nat. size

a. stamen. b. ovary, style. c. capsule. d. capsule (enclosed).
e. leaf (Lower surface).

own diameter apart, midrib prominent, primary veins obscured by the indumentum; petiole 0.4—1.2 cm. long, densely woolly with brown or fawn wool, scaly or not scaly. *Inflorescence* terminal, shortly racemose or umbellate, 1—3-flowered; rhachis 1—2 mm. long, tomentose, sparsely scaly or not scaly; pedicel 0.6—1.6 cm. long, densely woolly with brown wool, not scaly or sparsely scaly. *Calyx* 5-lobed, 5—9 mm. long, *red or tinged red*, lobes obovate or rounded or oval, outside moderately or sparsely tomentose, moderately or sparsely scaly or not scaly, margin densely tomentose, not scaly. *Corolla* rotate-campanulate, 5-lobed, 1.5—2.2 cm. long, *white or white tinged pink or pale yellow*, with or without brown or reddish-brown spots, outside glabrous or sparsely hairy, rather densely or moderately scaly. *Stamens* 10, unequal, 0.9—1.4 cm. long; filaments densely villous towards the base. *Ovary* ovate, 2—3 mm. long, 5-celled, densely woolly with fawn or brown wool, moderately or densely scaly; *style short, sharply bent*, tomentose and scaly at the base. *Capsule* ovate or oval, 1—1.3 cm. long, 6—8 mm. broad, densely woolly with brown wool, rather densely scaly, calyx-lobes persistent.

R. pendulum was discovered by J.D. Hooker in 1849 in Sikkim. It was later found by other collectors in Nepal, Sikkim, Bhutan, and south and south-east Tibet. The plant grows on rocks, on cliffs, on rocks in river beds, and in forests, often as an epiphyte on rhododendrons and conifers, at elevations of 2,288—3,660 m. (7,500—12,000 ft.). Ludlow, Sherriff and Hicks record it as being common locally, always on cliffs, at Rudo La, in Bhutan.

The notable features of this plant are the oblong to oval leaves, with convex non-bullate upper surfaces, densely woolly and densely scaly lower surfaces, the densely woolly branchlets and petioles, the rotate-campanulate corolla, white or white tinged pink or pale yellow, and the short sharply bent style. In some respects it resembles *R. seinghkuense*, but is distinguished by the non-bullate upper surface of the leaves, by the colour and to an extent by the shape of the corolla, and by the red calyx. It is also allied to *R. edgeworthii* from which it differs in the size and shape of the corolla, in the short, sharply bent style, in the non-bullate upper surface of the leaves, usually in the smaller calyx, and in the scentless flowers.

In the rotate-campanulate corolla and in the short sharply bent style, *R. pendulum* resembles the species of the Boothii Series, but differs markedly in important characters.

The species was first introduced possibly by J.D. Hooker in 1850. It was reintroduced by Ludlow and Sherriff in 1936 (No. 2898), and with Taylor in 1938 (No. 6660). It is a slow grower, and in some cold gardens inland it is difficult to establish. The plant is uncommon in cultivation. Perhaps the finest example is in the rock garden of the Royal Botanic Garden, Edinburgh; it is a somewhat compact rounded shrub, 3 feet high and as much across, free-flowering, with trusses of 1—3 flowers. The species varies in hardiness, and to be able to grow it satisfactorily, particularly along the east coast and in gardens inland, a well-sheltered position should be provided.

Epithet. Hanging.

Hardiness 1—3. April—May. Plate 21.

R. seinghkuense Hutch. in The Species of Rhododendron (1930) 234.

An upright or sometimes prostrate shrub, usually epiphytic, 30—92 cm. (1—3 ft.) high; branchlets densely or sometimes moderately woolly with brown or rust-coloured wool, scaly or not scaly, leaf-bud scales persistent or subpersistent. *Leaves* evergreen, ovate, ovate-lanceolate, oblong-lanceolate, oblong-elliptic or elliptic, lamina coriaceous, 3—8 cm. long, 1.6—4 cm. broad, apex acuminate or acute or obtuse, mucronate, base rounded or broadly obtuse; *upper surface bullate, not convex,* glabrous or with vestiges of hairs or rarely tomentose, scaly or not scaly, midrib deeply grooved, glabrous or tomentose at the base or one-half of its length, primary veins impressed; *under surface densely woolly* with brown wool, *scaly,* the scales very small, more or less equal, brown or pale brown, 1—2 times their own diameter apart, midrib prominent, primary veins raised; petiole 0.4—1.3 cm. long, densely woolly with brown or rust-coloured or whitish wool, scaly or not scaly. *Inflorescence* terminal, umbellate, 1— (or rarely 2-) flowered; rhachis 1—2 mm. long, tomentose, not scaly or sparsely scaly; pedicel 1—2 cm. long, densely woolly with brown wool, not scaly or sparsely scaly. *Calyx* 5-lobed, 5—8 mm. long, *pale green,* lobes rounded, outside and margin densely woolly with brown wool, not scaly. *Corolla* rotate-campanulate, 5-lobed, 2—2.5 cm. long, *sulphur-yellow,* outside glabrous or tube sparsely hairy, rather densely scaly. *Stamens* 10, unequal, 1.3—2 cm. long; filaments densely villous in the lower ⅓—⅔ of their lengths. *Ovary* ovate, 4 mm. long, 5—6-celled, densely woolly with brown wool, scaly; style short, sharply bent, glabrous or woolly at the base, not scaly. *Capsule* rounded or oval, 0.8—1.4 cm. long, 0.8—1.3 cm. broad, densely woolly with rust-coloured or brown wool, scaly, calyx-lobes persistent.

R. seinghkuense was described from a plant collected by Kingdon-Ward in May 1926 at Seinghku Wang in Upper Burma. He found it again later on the Burma-Tibet Frontier. Yü

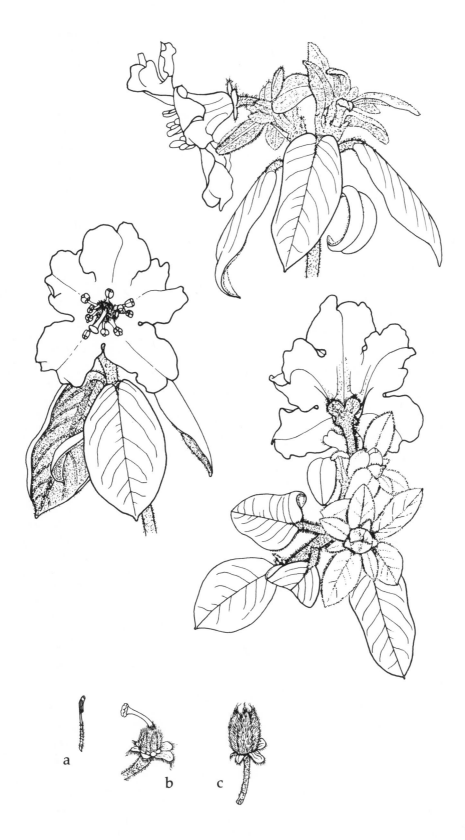

14. R. seinghkuense
nat. size

a. stamen. b. ovary, style. c. capsule.

collected it in 1938 in north-west Yunnan. It grows on rocks, on cliffs, on steep rocky slopes, in forests and in woods, often as an epiphyte, at elevations of 1,830—3,050 m. (6,000—10,000 ft.). Kingdon-Ward records it as being abundant at Seinghku Wang in Upper Burma.

A diagnostic feature of importance which the species shares with its two allies, is the densely woolly and scaly lower surface of the leaves. *R. seinghkuense* resembles *R. pendulum* in some features; the distinctions between them are discussed under the latter. In the bullate upper surface of the leaves, it agrees with *R. edgeworthii* from which it is readily distinguished by the shape, size and colour of the corolla, by the short sharply bent style, and usually by the smaller calyx.

R. seinghkuense also shows a resemblance to the species of the Boothii Series in the rotate-campanulate corolla and in the short sharply bent style. From this Series, however, it is remote in other characters.

The species was first introduced by Kingdon-Ward in 1922 (No. 5440). It was reintroduced by him in 1926 (No. 6993 — the Type number), and in 1931 (No. 9254 = 9543). In its native home it is an upright or prostrate shrub up to 3 feet in height, but in cultivation it grows usually up to about one foot. The plant is too tender outdoors and is suitable for a cool greenhouse. It is a delightful little shrub with single or paired sulphur-yellow flowers. The species is rare in cultivation, but is worthy of being widely grown. It was given an Award of Merit when shown by the Crown Estate Commissioners, Windsor, in 1953.

Epithet. From the Seinghku Valley, Upper Burma.
Hardiness 1. March—April.

FERRUGINEUM SERIES

General characters: small shrubs, 30 cm.—1.22 m. (1—4 ft.) high; branchlets densely or moderately scaly. Leaves evergreen obovate, oval, oblong-oval, oblong, oblanceolate, oblong-lanceolate or lanceolate, *lamina* 0.8—2.6 cm. long, 0.4—1.6 cm. broad; *margin crenulate* or sometimes entire; under surface densely or laxly scaly, the scales overlapping to 4 times their own diameter apart. Inflorescence racemose or umbellate, 3—16-flowered; pedicel 0.6—2.5 cm. long, densely or moderately scaly. Calyx 5-lobed, 0.5—5 mm. long. *Corolla tubular, with spreading lobes,* 1—2 cm. long, 5-lobed, crimson-purple, scarlet-purple, rose-purple, rosy-pink or white, outside densely to sparsely scaly. *Stamens* 10, 0.4—1.2 cm. long, *as long as the corolla-tube or shorter or slightly longer.* Ovary conoid or ovoid, 2—3 mm. long, 5—6-celled, densely scaly; *style* slender, straight, *short,* as long as the stamens or shorter, 1¼—2½ times as long as the ovary or shorter. Capsule conoid, ovoid or oblong, 3—7 mm. long, 2—4 mm. broad, moderately or densely scaly.

Distribution: mountains of Southern and Central Europe from the Pyrenees to the Transylvanian Alps and Northern Bulgaria.

The Series consists of three European species, bearing no affinity with the species of any other Series.

KEY TO THE SPECIES

A. Margins of the leaves bristly, under surface laxly scaly, the scales 2—4 times their own diameter apart; calyx 2—5 mm. or rarely 1 mm. long, lobes usually lanceolate or oblong; petiole moderately or slightly bristly .... *hirsutum*

A. Margins of the leaves not bristly, under surface densely scaly, the scales overlapping or contiguous or one-half their own diameter apart; calyx minute, 0.5—1 mm. long, lobes triangular or ovate; petiole usually not bristly.

    B. Corolla not hairy outside or sometimes puberulous on the tube; style usually 1¼ times to twice as long as the ovary; stamens usually as long as the corolla-tube or slightly longer; corolla-tube broad; pedicel usually glabrous; scales on the under surface of the leaves usually overlapping...*ferrugineum*

    B. Corolla-tube rather densely pubescent outside, lobes moderately pubescent; style usually shorter than the ovary; stamens shorter than the corolla-tube, included; corolla-tube slender; pedicel usually rather densely or moderately minutely puberulous; scales on the under surface of the leaves usually contiguous or one-half their own diameter apart .... *kotschyi*

DESCRIPTION OF THE SPECIES

R. ferrugineum Linn. Sp. Pl. (1753) 392.

A broadly upright or somewhat compact rounded shrub, 30 cm.—1.22 m. (1—4 ft.) high; *branchlets* densely scaly, glabrous, *not bristly*, leaf-bud scales deciduous. *Leaves* evergreen, oblanceolate, lanceolate or oblong, lamina coriaceous, 1.6—4.3 cm. long, 0.6—1.6 cm. broad, apex obtuse, rounded or acute, mucronate, base tapered or obtuse, slightly decurrent on the petiole or not decurrent; upper surface dark green, shining, not scaly, not bristly; margin crenulate or entire, not bristly; under surface densely scaly, the scales somewhat large or medium-sized, unequal, brown or dark brown or reddish-brown, overlapping or rarely contiguous, not bristly; *petiole* 2—8 mm. long, narrowly winged near the base of the lamina or ridged on each side, densely or moderately scaly, glabrous, *not bristly* or rarely sparsely bristly. *Inflorescence* terminal, racemose, 5—16-flowered; rhachis 0.5—2 cm. long, rather densely or moderately scaly or not scaly, glabrous or rather densely minutely puberulous, not bristly; pedicel 0.6—1.7 cm. long, rather densely or moderately scaly, glabrous or rarely minutely puberulous. *Calyx* 5-lobed, minute, 0.5—1 mm. long, lobes triangular or ovate, outside densely or moderately scaly, margin scaly or not scaly, hairy with long hairs. *Corolla* tubular, with spreading lobes, 1.3—1.7 cm. long, 5-lobed, crimson-purple, rose-scarlet, rose-purple or deep rose, *outside* moderately or rather densely scaly, *glabrous or puberulous on the tube*; margin of the lobes glabrous or rarely hairy; inside rather densely or moderately pubescent. *Stamens* 10, unequal, 4—8 mm. long, *as long as the corolla-tube or shorter or slightly longer*; filaments pubescent in the lower half or at the base. *Ovary* conoid, 2 mm. long, 5—6-celled, densely scaly, glabrous; *style* slender, straight, short, shorter than, or as long as, the stamens, or shorter than the taller 5 or 6 stamens, *1¼ or 1½ times or twice as long as the ovary*, or rarely as long as the ovary, not scaly, glabrous or rarely puberulous at the base. *Capsule* conoid or oblong, 4—7 mm. long, 3—4 mm. broad, moderately or densely scaly, glabrous, calyx persistent.

R. ferrugineum was described by Linnaeus in 1753. It is widely distributed on the European Alps, the Pyrenees, the Austrian Alps, and on the mountains of west Yugoslavia. The plant, known as the "Alpine Rose", is found in abundance in various localities in its native home.

The species varies in height of growth from 1 foot up to 4 feet, and in the colour of the flowers from rosy-pink, deep rose to rose-scarlet and crimson-purple. It is easily recognised by the oblanceolate, lanceolate or oblong leaves up to 4.3 cm. long, densely scaly on

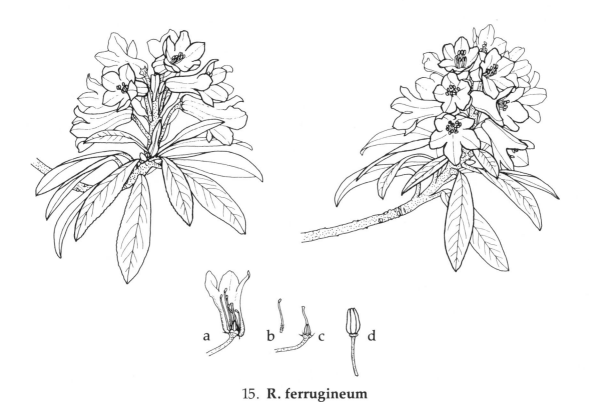

15. R. ferrugineum
nat. size

a. section. b. stamen. c. ovary, style. d. capsule.

the lower surface by dark brown or reddish-brown scales, by the minute calyx, and by the tubular corolla with spreading lobes, moderately or rather densely scaly outside. In general appearance it shows considerable resemblance to *R. hirsutum* from which it is readily distinguished by the non-bristly branchlets and leaves, by the densely scaly lower surface of the leaves, and by the smaller calyx. Natural hybrids often occur between the two species in their native home.

R. ferrugineum is said to have been in cultivation in 1739. It is also recorded as having been first introduced in 1752 which has been regarded as probably the date of the second introduction from Switzerland. In cultivation it forms a somewhat compact rounded, or broadly upright shrub up to 3 or 4 feet high and often as much across. The plant is very hardy, and is easily adaptable to any position in the garden. Although a slow grower, it flowers quite young when raised from seed. It is a valuable plant in that it is a late flowerer, prolonging the flowering season into June and July. The plant is free-flowering, easy to grow, and well suited for the rock garden.

Epithet. Rusty-coloured.
Hardiness 3—4. June—July.

R. ferrugineum Linn. var. album D. Don.
The variety is distinguished from the species by the white flowers. The plant is said to be rare in its native home.

In cultivation it is a rounded shrub, up to 60 cm. (2 ft.) high and almost as much across, very hardy and free-flowering. It was given an Award of Merit when exhibited by the Crown Estate Commissioners, Windsor Great Park, in 1969.

Epithet of the variety. With white flowers.
Hardiness 3—4. June—July.

R. ferrugineum Linn. var. **atrococcineum** Bean in Trees and Shrubs Hardy in the British Isles, Vol. III (1951) 65.

This name was given by W.J. Bean in 1933 to a plant raised in cultivation.

The variety differs from the species in that the flowers most nearly approach scarlet. It is a broadly upright shrub up to 2 feet high, and is most attractive when covered with a profusion of flowers in June and July.

Epithet of the variety. Deep scarlet.

Hardiness 3—4. June—July.

R. hirsutum Linn. Sp. Pl. (1753) 392.

Illustration. Bot. Mag. Vol. 43 t. 1853 (1816).

A small somewhat compact or broadly upright shrub, 30 cm.—1 m. (1—3½ ft.) high; *branchlets* scaly, minutely puberulous or glabrous, *bristly* or not bristly, leaf-bud scales deciduous. *Leaves* evergreen, obovate, oval, oblong-oval, oblong, oblanceolate or oblong-lanceolate, lamina coriaceous, 0.8—2.6 cm. long, 0.4—1.3 cm. broad, apex rounded or obtuse, mucronate, base rounded, obtuse or tapered, slightly decurrent on the petiole or not decurrent; upper surface dark green, shining, not scaly or sparsely scaly, not bristly; *margin crenulate, bristly; under surface* pale green, *laxly scaly, the scales* somewhat large, unequal, thick, dark brown or brown, *2—4 times their own diameter apart*, not bristly; *petiole* 2—4 mm. long, narrowly winged near the base of the lamina or ridged on each side, scaly, not puberulous, *moderately or slightly bristly. Inflorescence* terminal, racemose, 4—12-flowered; rhachis 0.5—3 cm. long, moderately or sparsely scaly, rather densely minutely puberulous, not bristly; pedicel 1—2.5 cm. long, scaly, rather densely minutely puberulous or glabrous, not hairy or sometimes hairy with long hairs. *Calyx* 5-lobed, *2—5 mm.* or rarely 1 mm. *long, lobes lanceolate or oblong*, or rarely ovate and triangular, outside scaly, margin not scaly, hairy with long hairs. *Corolla* tubular, with spreading lobes, 1—2 cm. long, 5-lobed, rose-pink, scarlet or crimson, outside scaly, glabrous or puberulous on the tube; *margin of the lobes hairy*; inside rather densely or moderately pubescent. *Stamens* 10, unequal, 0.4—1.2 cm. long, *as long as the corolla-tube or shorter or slightly longer*; filaments moderately or rather densely pubescent at the base or in the lower half. *Ovary* conoid or ovoid, 2—3 mm. long, 5-celled, densely scaly, glabrous; *style* slender, straight, *short*, as long as the stamens or shorter than the taller 5 or 6 stamens, *1½ times or twice or rarely 2½ times as long as the ovary*, not scaly, puberulous at the base. *Capsule* conoid or ovoid, 3—7 mm. long, 3—4 mm. broad, moderately or densely scaly, glabrous, calyx persistent.

This species was described by Linnaeus in 1753. It is a native of the Central European Alps, the Austrian Alps, and the mountains of north-west Yugoslavia, growing on limestone formation.

The plant resembles *R. ferrugineum* in general features, but differs in that the margins of the leaves and usually the branchlets and petioles are bristly, the lower surfaces of the leaves are laxly scaly, the scales being 2—4 times their own diameter apart, the calyx is larger usually 2—5 mm. long, and the margin of the corolla-lobes is hairy. A characteristic feature of this species and generally of the other members of its Series, is the crenulate margin of the leaves.

R. hirsutum is of historical importance because it was the first rhododendron introduced into cultivation in 1656; this introduction is credited to John Tradescant, the younger. In cultivation it is a small, somewhat compact or broadly upright shrub, usually up to 2 feet high. Although in its native home it grows on limestone formation, in cultivation it succeeds in acid soil. With its oval to oblong-lanceolate, dark green shining leaves, it makes a very pleasant evergreen for the rock garden. Like its ally, *R. ferrugineum*, it is also a useful plant in that it is a late flowerer, the flowers appearing in June and July. The plant is free-flowering, and is greatly admired when covered with scarlet or crimson or rose-pink flowers in trusses of 4 to 12. It is very hardy, and is an excellent plant for the rock garden.

A double-flowered form of garden origin is known as *R. hirsutum* 'Flore Pleno'.

Epithet. Hairy.

Hardiness 3—4. June—July. Plate 22.

R. hirsutum Linn. var. **albiflorum** Schroet. Das Pflanz. der Alpen (1926) 180.

This variety is distinguished from the species by its white flowers. In its native home it grows on limestone formation, and is said to be of rare occurrence.

In cultivation it is a somewhat compact and spreading shrub up to 60 —92 cm. (2—3 ft.) high. The plant is uncommon in gardens. It is perfectly hardy, and is easy to grow.

Epithet of the variety. White-flowered.

Hardiness 3—4. June—July.

R. hirsutum Linn. var. **latifolium** Hoppe.

This variety differs from the species in that the leaves are broad, almost rounded. The plant has not been introduced into cultivation.

Epithet of the variety. Broad-leaved.

Not in cultivation.

R. kotschyi Simonk. Enum. Fl. Transylv. (1886) 389.

Illustration. Bot. Mag. Vol. 152 t. 9132 (1928).

A small somewhat compact and spreading shrub, 30—45 cm. (1—1½ ft.) high; branchlets rather densely or moderately scaly, glabrous or puberulous, not bristly, leaf-bud scales deciduous. *Leaves* evergreen, oblong, oblong-obovate, oblanceolate or oblong-elliptic, lamina coriaceous, 0.9—2.3 cm. long, 5—8 mm. broad, apex rounded or obtuse, mucronate, base obtuse or tapered, slightly decurrent on the petiole or not decurrent; upper surface dark green, shining, not scaly, not bristly; margin crenulate, not bristly; under surface densely scaly, the scales somewhat large or medium-sized, unequal, dark brown, contiguous or slightly overlapping or one-half their own diameter apart, not bristly; petiole 1—5 mm. long, narrowly winged near the base of the lamina or ridged on each side, densely or moderately scaly, glabrous, not bristly. *Inflorescence* terminal, umbellate or shortly racemose, 3—7-flowered; rhachis 2—3 mm. long, not scaly or slightly scaly, glabrous, not bristly; *pedicel* 0.8—2 cm. long, moderately or rarely rather densely scaly, *rather densely or moderately minutely puberulous* or rarely glabrous. *Calyx* 5-lobed, minute, 1 mm. long, lobes ovate or triangular or oblong, outside scaly or not scaly, margin scaly, hairy with long hairs or glabrous. *Corolla* tubular, *tube slender*, with spreading lobes, 1.3—2 cm. long, 5-lobed, crimson-purple, scarlet-purple, rosy-pink or rarely white, outside sparsely or moderately scaly, *rather densely or rarely moderately pubescent on the tube, moderately pubescent on the lobes*; margin of the lobes glabrous or rarely hairy; inside rather densely or moderately pubescent. *Stamens* 10, unequal, 4—7 mm. long, *included, shorter than the corolla-tube*; filaments pubescent at the base. *Ovary* conoid or ovoid, 2—3 mm. long, 5—6-celled, densely scaly, glabrous; *style* slender, straight, short, shorter than the stamens, *shorter than*, or rarely as long as, *the ovary*, not scaly, glabrous. *Capsule* conoid or ovoid, 3—5 mm. long, 2—3 mm. broad, densely scaly, glabrous, calyx persistent.

R. kotschyi was described by Simonkai in 1886. It is a native of the Transylvanian and Carpathian mountains and the mountains of Bulgaria and Yugoslav Macedonia. It is found at elevations of 1,500—2,400 m. (4,918—7,868 ft.) often growing on limestone.

The species is allied to *R. ferrugineum* which it resembles in some features but differs markedly in that the corolla-tube is slender, the corolla, both tube and lobes, are rather densely or moderately pubescent outside, the style is usually shorter than the ovary, and the stamens are included, shorter than the corolla-tube. The flower colour is crimson-purple, scarlet-purple, rosy-pink or rarely white.

The plant was first introduced in 1846. In cultivation it is a neat little shrub, somewhat compact and spreading, up to 1 or 1½ feet high, with short branchlets and dark green shining leaves crenulate at the margins. Although a slow grower, one of its merits is that it flowers at a young age when raised from seed. Like its allies, it is a late flowerer, the flowers appearing in June, July or sometimes in May, the date being dependent on the season. The plant is hardy, free-flowering, and often produces good fertile seed. The species is uncommon in cultivation, but is well worth a place in every rock garden.

Epithet. After Theodor Kotschy, 1913—66, Austrian botanist.

Hardiness 3. May—July.

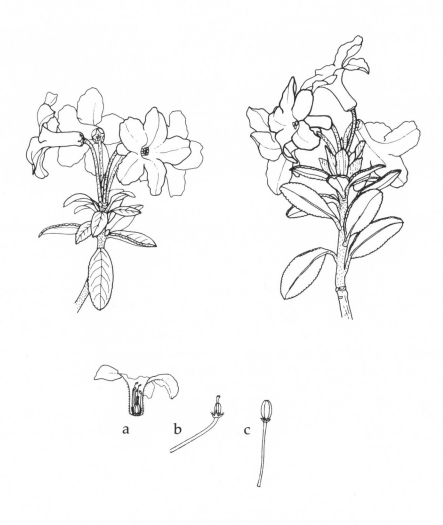

16. **R. kotschyi**

nat. size

a. section. b. ovary, style. c. capsule.

GLAUCOPHYLLUM SERIES

General characters: small or medium-sized shrubs or rarely small trees, sometimes epiphytic, 23 cm.—4.58 m. (9 in.—15 ft.) high, stem and branches usually with smooth, brown, flaking bark. Leaves evergreen, lanceolate, oblong-lanceolate to obovate, oval, lamina 1.3—15.3 cm. long, 0.6—4.5 cm. broad; *under surface usually markedly glaucous, densely or laxly scaly, the scales of 2 kinds, the smaller pale yellow scales overlapping to 10 times their own diameter apart, the larger dark brown scales widely or sometimes closely separated* (in Genestierianum Subseries the scales of one kind, ½—10 times their own diameter apart). Inflorescence terminal, or sometimes terminal and axillary in the uppermost one or two leaves, umbellate or racemose, 3—10- (in Genestierianum Subseries up to 15-) flowered; pedicel 1.6—4.2 cm. long. Calyx 5-lobed, 0.1—1.3 cm. long. Corolla campanulate or sometimes rotately campanulate or sometimes tubular, 0.8—2.6 cm. or rarely 3.8 cm. long, 5-lobed, pink, rose, plum-purple, cerise-coloured, yellow, greenish-yellow or sometimes white. Stamens 10 or rarely 8—9. Ovary conoid, ovoid or oblong-oval, 2—5 mm. long, 5-celled, densely scaly; *style short, stout and sharply bent or deflexed* (in *R. tubiforme* long, slender and straight). Capsule conoid, ovoid, oblong-oval, oblong or slender, 0.4—1.6 cm. long, 3—6 mm. broad, rather densely or moderately scaly, often enclosed by the persistent calyx-lobes.

Distribution: Nepal, Sikkim, Bhutan, Assam, south, south-east and east Tibet, Upper and north-east Upper Burma, mid-west, west and north-west Yunnan.

The Series consists of ten species wih campanulate, or sometimes rotately campanulate or tubular corolla. Its affinity is with the Boothii and less closely with the Campylogynum and Tephropeplum Series.

The Glaucophyllum Series is divided into two Subseries. In the Glaucophyllum Subseries, the scales on the under surface of the leaves (though similar in structure) are of two kinds. The Genestierianum Subseries contains one aberrant species, more appropriately placed in this than any other group.

KEY TO THE SUBSERIES

A. Scales on the under surface of the leaves of one kind, brown or pale brown or rarely yellow .... *Genestierianum Subseries*
A. Scales on the under surface of the leaves of two kinds, smaller pale yellow, and larger brown .... *Glaucophyllum Subseries*

GENESTIERIANUM SUBSERIES

General characters: small or medium-sized shrubs or sometimes small trees, sometimes epiphytic, 92 cm.—4.58 m. (3—15 ft.) high. Leaves lanceolate, oblanceolate, oblong or oblong-elliptic, lamina 3.2—15.3 cm. long, 1.4—4.5 cm. broad; *under surface* markedly glaucous or pale glaucous green, *scaly, the scales of one kind, brown or pale brown* or rarely pale yellow, ½—10 times their own diameter apart; petiole 0.5—2 cm. long. Inflorescence 3—15-flowered; pedicel usually slender, 1.6—4.2 cm. long, longer than the corolla. Calyx 5-lobed, 1—4 mm. long. Corolla tubular-campanulate or rotately campanulate, 0.8—1.8 cm. long, 5-lobed, deep plum-purple, pale yellow, yellow, greenish-yellow or rarely white. Stamens 10 or sometimes 8—9. Ovary conoid or ovoid, 2—4 mm. long, 5-celled, densely scaly; style short, stout and sharply bent or deflexed. Capsule ovoid, conoid, oblong, oblong-oval, oblong or slender, 0.5—1.6 cm. long, 3—6 mm. broad, calyx persistent.

KEY TO THE SPECIES

A. Scales on the under surface of the leaves minute, widely spaced, 4—10 times their own diameter apart or rarely more; leaf apex acutely acuminate; corolla not scaly outside, covered with a glaucous bloom, deep plum-purple ..... *genestierianum*
A. Scales on the under surface of the leaves varying much in size, large to small, densely set, ½—1½ times their own diameter apart; leaf apex obtuse or rounded; corolla-tube and lobes rather densely scaly outside, not glaucous, pale yellow, yellow, greenish-yellow or rarely white, with or without green spots .... *micromeres*

DESCRIPTION OF THE SPECIES

R. genestierianum Forrest in Notes Roy. Bot. Gard. Edin., Vol. 12 (1920) 122.
Illustration. Bot. Mag. Vol. 156 t. 9310 (1933).

A broadly upright shrub or sometimes a small tree, 1.22—4.58 m. (4—15 ft.) high; *branchlets purplish or reddish-brown*, glaucous or not glaucous, (young growths reddish-purple, glaucous), sparsely scaly, glabrous, leaf-bud scales deciduous. *Leaves* evergreen, lanceolate or oblanceolate, lamina coriaceous, 5.5—15.3 cm. long, 1.4—4.5 cm. broad, *apex acutely acuminate*, mucronate, base obtuse or tapered; upper surface olive-green or dark green, matt or somewhat shining, not scaly; under surface markedly glaucous, laxly scaly, *the scales* unequal, *small*, brown or pale brown, *4—6 times or rarely 10 or more times their own diameter apart*, without larger brown scales; petiole 0.5—2 cm. long, glaucous or not glaucous, sparsely scaly, glabrous. *Inflorescence* terminal, or rarely terminal and axillary in the uppermost one or two leaves, *racemose, 6—15-flowered*, flower-bud scales deciduous; rhachis 1—1.5 cm. or rarely 3 mm. long, glaucous or somewhat glaucous, not scaly or sparsely scaly, glabrous; *pedicel* slender, 1.6—3 cm. long, longer than the corolla, *glaucous* or somewhat glaucous, not scaly or sparsely scaly, glabrous. *Calyx* a shallow fleshy cup, shortly 5-lobed, 1—2 mm. long, lobes erect, broadly ovate or ovate, deep plum-purple, *covered with a glaucous bloom*, outside not scaly or sparsely or moderately scaly, margin eciliate. *Corolla* tubular-campanulate, 1.2—1.8 cm. long, 5-lobed, fleshy, *deep plum-purple, covered with a glaucous bloom, outside not scaly.* Stamens 8—10, 1—1.7 cm. long, slightly longer or shorter than the corolla; filaments glabrous. *Ovary* conoid or ovoid, 2—4 mm. long, 5-celled, densely scaly, glabrous; style short, stout and sharply bent or deflexed, glaucous, not scaly, glabrous. *Capsule* conoid or ovoid, 5—7 mm. long, 4—6 mm. broad, rather densely or moderately scaly, glabrous, calyx persistent.

R. genestierianum was discovered by Forrest in April 1919 in the N'Maikha-Salwin Divide, north-east Upper Burma. It was later found by him again and by other collectors in the same region and in mid-west Yunnan, eastern and south-eastern Tibet. It grows on the margins of forests, in cane brakes, on open rocky slopes, and in mixed thickets, at elevations of 2,000—4,423 m. (6,557—14,500 ft.). It is recorded as being common in woods in Upper Kiukiang Valley, Narktai, Yunnan.

The diagnostic features of this plant are the distinctly racemose inflorescence of usually 9 to 15 deep plum-purple flowers, and the lanceolate or oblanceolate leaves acutely acuminate at the apex. In these respects it usually differs markedly from all the other members of its Series. Other distinguishing characters are the laxly scaly lower surface of the leaves, the scales being 4—10 times their own diameter apart or rarely more, the purplish or reddish-brown branchlets, the long pedicels 1.6—3 cm. in length, longer than the corolla, the tubular-campanulate corolla, the calyx and pedicels covered with a glaucous bloom, and the glabrous stamens.

The species was first introduced by Forrest in 1919 (No. 17824 — the Type number). It was reintroduced by him on several occasions, and by Kingdon-Ward, Rock, and Yü. Although it comes from higher elevations of 3,050—3,965 (10,000—13,000 ft.), in cultivation along the east coast it is tender outdoors and is suitable for a cool greenhouse. It is worth noting that even in the glasshouse it is somewhat difficult to grow. In the west coast, it is successfully grown outdoors in well-sheltered gardens in mild areas. A most remarkable feature of the plant is the reddish-purple young growths which always attract attention. It is a charming rhododendron, fairly fast-growing, and is well worth attempting. A good example of the species is at Brodick Castle Gardens, Island of Arran, consisting of a group of plants flourishing in a sheltered position, raised from seed introduced by Kingdon-Ward from The Triangle, North Burma, in 1953.

Epithet. After Père A. Genestier, b. 1858, of the French R.C. Tibetan Mission, friend of G. Forrest.

Hardiness 1—2. April—May.

R. micromeres Tagg in Notes Roy. Bot. Gard. Edin., Vol. 16 (1931) 211.

A lax upright or straggly or spreading shrub, often epiphytic, 92 cm.—2 m. (3—6½ ft.) high; branchlets scaly, glabrous, leaf-bud scales deciduous. *Leaves* evergreen, oblong-lanceolate, lanceolate, oblong, oblong-elliptic, oblong-obovate or elliptic, lamina coriaceous, 3.2—8 cm. long, 1.5—3.6 cm. broad; *apex obtuse or rounded*, mucronate, base obtuse or cuneate; upper surface bright green, somewhat matt, scaly or not scaly; *under surface* pale glaucous green or glaucous, *densely scaly, the scales* unequal, *varying much in size, small to large,* brown, sunk in pits ½—1½ *times their own diameter apart*, without larger brown scales; petiole 0.5—1 cm. long, densely scaly, glabrous. *Inflorescence* terminal, or rarely terminal and axillary in the uppermost one or two leaves, racemose or umbellate, 3—11-flowered; flower-bud scales deciduous; rhachis 2—7 mm. long, scaly, glabrous; pedicel slender, 2—4.2 cm. long, longer than the corolla, lengthening considerably in fruit, scaly, glabrous. *Calyx* 5-lobed, 2—4 mm. long, *lobes reflexed* or sometimes erect, rounded or ovate, outside scaly, margin eciliate. *Corolla rotately campanulate*, 0.8—1.4 cm. long, 5-lobed, *yellow, pale yellow, greenish-yellow or rarely white,* with or without green spots, *outside not glaucous, rather densely scaly on the tube and lobes. Stamens* 10, unequal, 0.5—1 cm. long, as long as the corolla or shorter; filaments densely or moderately hairy in the lower one-third or nearly to the apex. *Ovary* conoid, 2—4 mm. long, 5-celled, densely scaly, glabrous; style very short, stout and sharply bent, scaly at the base, or not scaly, glabrous. *Capsule* oblong or slender, 1.1—1.6 cm. long, 3—5 mm. broad, curved or straight, densely scaly, glabrous, calyx-lobes persistent.

Forrest discovered this plant in fruit in June 1922 in the Salwin Kiu-Chiang Divide, south-eastern Tibet. Further gatherings by him and by other collectors show that the plant has a wide area of distribution extending from south-east and east Tibet, north-west Yunnan, North Burma to Assam and east Bhutan. It grows in mixed forests, in spruce forest, on ledges of cliffs, and on rocks, often as an epiphyte, at elevations of 2,440—4,300 m. (8,000—14,098 ft.). Kingdon-Ward records it as being one of the commonest epiphytic species in the mixed forests in Assam, and at the Burma-Tibet Frontier, also in rhododendron moss forests in North Triangle, North Burma.

R. micromeres is a somewhat aberrant species in the Glaucophyllum Series. It differs from the other species of this Series in that the lower surfaces of the leaves are not markedly glaucous, and the scales are of one colour varying much in size.

The characteristic features of the species are the small rotately campanulate yellow or greenish-yellow corolla 0.8—1.4 cm. long, the long pedicels 2—4.2 cm. in length, lengthening considerably in fruit, and often the reflexed calyx. Its nearest ally is *R. genestierianum* which it resembles in some features, but differs in that the corolla is yellow or greenish-yellow or rarely white, densely scaly but not glaucous outside, the lower surface of the leaves is densely scaly, the scales being ½—1½ times their own diameter apart, and the leaves are obtuse or rounded at the apex.

The species was first introduced by Forrest in 1922 (No. 21811 — the Type number). It was reintroduced by him on two other occasions. Kingdon-Ward sent seed several times including No. 21007 in 1953 from the North Triangle, North Burma. The plant was also introduced by Rock, Ludlow, Sherriff and Taylor or Hicks, Yü, and Cox and Hutchison. In 1931 it flowered at Bulstrode Gardens, Gerrard's Cross, Bucks., raised by Sir John Ramsden from seed (No. 6251) collected by Kingdon-Ward in 1924 at Pemako during his exploration of the Tsangpo Gorge. It may be observed that the flower characters given in the description of the species by Tagg were based largely upon this plant which was sent to Edinburgh for naming. In cultivation along the east coast, the species is tender outdoors and needs the protection of the glasshouse; in the west coast it is likely to succeed outdoors in well-sheltered gardens in mild areas. It is a lax upright shrub up to about 2 feet high or more, with small yellow flowers.

Epithet. With small parts.
Hardiness 1—2. May—June. Plate 28.

GLAUCOPHYLLUM SUBSERIES

General characters: small or medium-sized shrubs, 23 cm.—2.14 m. (9 in.—7 ft.) high; stem and branches with smooth, brown flaking bark. Leaves lanceolate, oblong-lanceolate, oblong-obovate, obovate or oval, lamina 1.3—9 cm. long, 0.6—2.6 cm. broad; *under surface* markedly glaucous, densely or laxly *scaly, the scales of 2 kinds, the smaller pale yellow scales overlapping to about 10 times their own diameter apart, the larger dark brown scales widely or sometimes closely separated*, petiole 0.2—1.3 cm. long. Inflorescence 3—10- or sometimes 2-flowered; pedicel 0.8—4 cm. long. Calyx 5-lobed, 0.2—1.3 cm. long. Corolla campanulate (in *R. tubiforme*, tubular), 0.8—2.6 cm. or sometimes 3.8 cm. long, pink, pinkish-purple, rose, plum-purple, nearly crimson, cerise-coloured, violet, yellow, greenish-yellow or rarely white. Stamens 10. Ovary conoid or ovoid, 2—5 mm. long, 5-celled, densely scaly; style short, stout and sharply bent or deflexed or rarely almost straight (in *R. tubiforme*, long, slender and straight). Capsule conoid, ovoid or oblong-oval, 0.4—1 cm. long, 3—6 mm. broad, enclosed or sometimes partly enclosed by the persistent calyx-lobes.

KEY TO THE SPECIES

A. Corolla yellow or greenish-yellow (or rarely white).
>   **B.** Pedicel slender, 2.6—4 cm. long, longer than the corolla; calyx-lobes rounded or oval or broadly elliptic; corolla 0.8—1.5 cm. or rarely 1.9 cm. long; style short, stout and sharply bent or sometimes deflexed .... *brachyanthum*
>   **B.** Pedicel stout, 0.8—1 cm. long, shorter than the corolla; calyx-lobes lanceolate or ovate-lanceolate; corolla 2—2.3 cm. long; style somewhat long, stout and sharply bent .... *luteiflorum*

A. Corolla pink, rose, pinkish-purple, plum-purple, cerise-coloured or sometimes white.
>   **C.** Calyx-lobes lanceolate or ovate-lanceolate, apex markedly pointed; leaves lanceolate, oblong-lanceolate, elliptic or sometimes oblong, apex often acute; style short, stout and sharply bent or deflexed, or long, slender and straight.
>>   **D.** Corolla campanulate, 1.4—2.6 cm. long; style usually short, stout and sharply bent or deflexed; shrub up to 1.22m. (4 ft.) or sometimes 1.52 m. (5 ft.) high .... *glaucophyllum*
>>   **D.** Corolla tubular, 2.3—3.8 cm. long; style long, slender and straight; shrub up to 2.14 m. (7 ft.) high .... *tubiforme*
>   **C.** Calyx-lobes rounded, oval, ovate, oblong-oval or oblong, apex rounded or obtuse (in *R. charitopes* sometimes pointed); leaves oval, obovate, oblong-obovate or oblong, apex rounded or obtuse; style short, stout and sharply bent or deflexed.
>>   **E.** Corolla pink, rose, pinkish-purple, plum-purple, cerise-coloured, violet or rarely white, lobes unspotted or spotted pink, outside not scaly or sparsely scaly; style glabrous.
>>>   **F.** Under surface of the leaves laxly scaly, the scales 2—6 or more times or sometimes their own diameter apart .... *tsangpoense*
>>>   **F.** Under surface of the leaves densely scaly, the scales slightly overlapping or contiguous or ½—1½ times their own diameter apart.
>>>>   **G.** Corolla 1—1.6 cm. long, campanulate; calyx 3—5 mm. long; scales on the under surface of the leaves usually slightly overlapping or contiguous or ½ their own diameter apart ...... *pruniflorum*
>>>>   **G.** Corolla 1.8—2.6 cm. long, usually broadly campanulate or almost saucer-shaped; calyx 0.6—1 cm. long; scales on the under surface of the leaves ½—1½ times their own diameter apart .... *charitopes*
>>   **E.** Corolla pale pink tinged yellow, upper three lobes spotted pink, outside rather densely or moderately or slightly scaly; style puberulous or glabrous .... *shweliense*

DESCRIPTION OF THE SPECIES

R. brachyanthum Franch. in Bull. Soc. Bot. France, XXXIII (1886) 234.
   Illustration. Bot. Mag. Vol. 144 t. 8750 (1918).
   A small or medium-sized, broadly upright or spreading shrub, 30 cm.—1.83 m. (1—6 ft.) high; stem and branches with smooth, brown flaking bark; branchlets scaly, leaf-bud scales deciduous. *Leaves* evergreen, oblong, lanceolate, oblong-obovate or obovate, strongly aromatic, lamina coriaceous, 2—6.5 cm. or rarely 8 cm. long, 1—2.6 cm. or rarely 3.2 cm. broad, apex obtuse, rounded or acute, mucronate, base obtuse or tapered; upper surface bright green or dark green, shining, scaly or not scaly; *under surface* usually markedly glaucous, *laxly scaly*, the scales unequal, medium-sized or somewhat large,

pale yellow *scales 4—10 times or rarely 3 times their own diameter apart or sometimes more*, brown scales widely separated; petiole 0.3—1 cm. long, scaly. *Inflorescence* terminal, or rarely terminal and axillary in the uppermost one or two leaves, umbellate or shortly racemose, 3—10-flowered, flower-bud scales deciduous or persistent; rhachis 2—5 mm. long, scaly or not scaly; *pedicel slender, 1.4—4 cm. long, longer than the corolla*, moderately or rather densely scaly. *Calyx* 5-lobed, leafy, 3—8 mm. long, *lobes rounded, oval, oblong-oval or broadly elliptic*, outside scaly, margin eciliate or slightly ciliate. *Corolla* campanulate, 0.8—1.5 cm. or rarely 1.9 cm. long, 5-lobed, *yellow, pale or deep yellow, greenish-yellow* or rarely white, outside not scaly or sparsely scaly. *Stamens* 10, unequal, 0.6—1.3 cm. long, as long as the corolla or shorter; filaments densely or moderately hairy in the lower one-half or nearly to the apex. *Ovary* conoid, 2—3 mm. long, 5-celled, densely scaly, glabrous; *style short, stout and sharply bent or sometimes deflexed*, not scaly or sometimes scaly at the base, glabrous. *Capsule* conoid, oblong-oval or oval, 4—7 mm. long, 4—5 mm. broad, rather densely scaly, glabrous, enclosed or sometimes partly enclosed by the persistent calyx-lobes.

This species was discovered by the Abbé Delavay in June 1887 on the mountain Tsang-chan near Tali in Yunnan. It was later found by Forrest and by McLaren's collectors in other localities in west Yunnan, and by Ludlow and Sherriff and also Elliott in south and south-east Tibet. The plant grows in open rocky situations amongst scrub, in rhododendron thickets, and on steep rocky hillsides, at elevations of 3,000—3,355 m. (9,836—11,000 ft.).

R. brachyanthum is a distinctive species and is unlikely to be confused with any other rhododendron. The outstanding features of this plant are the campanulate, deep or pale yellow or greenish-yellow flowers in trusses of 3—10, the long slender pedicels 1.4—4 cm. in length, longer than the corolla, and the widely spaced scales on the lower surface of the leaves, the scales being usually 4—10 times their own diameter apart. A remarkable feature of this species and usually of all the other members of its Series is the short, stout and sharply bent or sometimes deflexed style. The plant resembles *R. luteiflorum* in some features, but differs markedly in distinctive features.

The species was first introduced by Forrest in 1917—1919 (No. 15487). It was reintroduced by him in 1930—1931 (No. 28266). In cultivation it is a broadly upright or spreading shrub up to about 5 feet high. A characteristic feature is the strongly aromatic foliage. Other well-marked characters are the smooth brown flaking bark of the stem and the branches, and the oval capsule usually enclosed by the large, leafy, persistent calyx. It is a valuable plant in that it is a late flowerer, extending the flowering season into June and July. The plant is very hardy, a fairly vigorous grower, and free-flowering. A form 'Jaune' received an Award of Merit when shown by Capt. Collingwood Ingram, Benenden, in 1966.

Epithet. With short flowers.
Hardiness 3. May—June.

R. brachyanthum Franch. var. **hypolepidotum** Franch. in Journ. de Bot., XII (1898) 262.
   Syn. *R. hypolepidotum* (Franch.) Balf. f. et Forrest in Notes Roy. Bot. Gard. Edin., Vol. 13 (1922) 266.
   Illustration. Bot. Mag. Vol. 155 t. 9259 (1931). Figured as *R. hypolepidotum*.
   This plant was first collected by the Abbé Soulié in July 1903 on Mt. Sela, near Tsekou, south-east Tibet. Subsequently it was found by other collectors in the same region and in east Tibet, north-west Yunnan, and north-east Upper Burma. It grows in pine forests, in open scrub, in open alpine meadows, amongst boulders, on cliffs and rocky slopes, at elevations of 2,745—4,423 m. (9,000—14,500 ft.). Kingdon-Ward records it as growing in compact masses, being very common, forming thickets a foot thick, at Imaw Bum, north-east Upper Burma at elevations of 3,355—3,660 m. (11,000—12,000 ft.).
   In 1922, *R. charitostreptum* Balf. f. et Ward was described from a plant collected by

Kingdon-Ward in north-east Upper Burma. In 1948 the name was placed in synonymy under *R. brachyanthum* var. *hypolepidotum* (*The Rhododendron Year Book*, 1948, p. 83).

The variety differs from the species in that the lower surface of the leaves is densely scaly, pale yellow scales being contiguous to 1½ times their own diameter apart, and brown scales widely or closely separated.

The plant was first introduced by Forrest in 1914 (No. 13302). It was reintroduced by him on many occasions and by Kingdon-Ward, Rock, Ludlow, Sherriff and Taylor, and Yü. Two distinct growth forms are in cultivation. Form 1. A somewhat compact, rounded and spreading shrub up to 60 cm. (2 ft.) high. Form 2. A broadly upright shrub up to 1.53 m. (5 ft.) in height. Form 1 and the smaller plants of Form 2 are well worth acquiring for every rock garden. Both forms are hardy and free-flowering. A clone 'Blue Light' was given an Award of Merit when shown by the Crown Estate Commissioners, Windsor Great Park, in 1951.

Epithet of the variety. Scaly beneath.

Hardiness 3. May—June. Plate 27.

R. charitopes Balf. f. et Farrer in Notes Roy. Bot. Gard. Edin., Vol. 13 (1922) 243.

Illustration. Bot. Mag. Vol. 157 t. 9358 (1934).

A somewhat compact rounded shrub, 23—92 cm. (9 in.—3 ft.) or sometimes up to 1.22 or 1.53 m. (4 or 5 ft.) high; stem and branches with smooth, brown, flaking bark or sometimes with rough bark; branchlets rather densely or moderately scaly, glabrous, leaf-bud scales deciduous or persistent. *Leaves* evergreen, *obovate or oblong-obovate*, aromatic, lamina coriaceous, 2.6—7 cm. long, 1.3—2.9 cm. broad, apex rounded, mucro-nate, base obtuse, cuneate or rarely rounded; upper surface dark green, somewhat shining, sparsely or moderately or rarely rather densely scaly or not scaly; under surface markedly glaucous, densely scaly, the scales unequal, medium-sized or somewhat large, pale yellow *scales ½—2 times their own diameter apart*, larger brown scales widely separated; petiole 4—6 mm. long, densely or moderately scaly, glabrous. *Inflorescence* terminal, umbellate, 3—4- or sometimes 2- or 6-flowered, flower-bud scales deciduous or persistent; rhachis 1—6 mm. long, scaly or not scaly, glabrous or puberulous; pedicel slender or somewhat slender, 1.4—3 cm. long, shorter or longer than the corolla, rather densely or moderately scaly, glabrous. *Calyx* 5-lobed, leafy, *0,6—1 cm. long*, lobes ovate, oblong-oval, oval or rounded, apex rounded or sometimes acute, outside moderately or rather densely scaly, margin eciliate or sometimes ciliate. *Corolla* campanulate or *broadly campanulate or almost saucer-shaped*, *1.8—2.6 cm. long*, 5-lobed, apple-blossom pink, speckled with crimson; or rose, deep rose-crimson or rose-crimson, without spots, outside not scaly or sometimes sparsely scaly, glabrous or sometimes sparsely hairy. *Stamens* 10, unequal, 1—1.9 cm. long, shorter than the corolla; filaments densely hairy in the lower two-thirds or nearly to the apex. *Ovary* conoid or ovoid, 4—5 mm. long, 5-celled, densely scaly, glabrous; style short, stout and sharply bent or deflexed, not scaly or rarely scaly at the base, glabrous. *Capsule* oblong-oval, conoid or ovoid, 0.8—1 cm. long, 5—6 mm. broad, densely scaly, glabrous, enclosed by the persistent calyx-lobes.

R. charitopes was discovered by Farrer in June 1920 in the Shing Hong Pass, in north-east Upper Burma. It was later found by Forrest in other localities in the same region and in north-west Yunnan. The plant grows amongst dwarf scrub, on cliffs, on rocky slopes, and on humus-covered boulders in side valleys, at elevations of 3,173—4,270 m. (10,500—14,000 ft.).

The species resembles *R. tsangpoense* in some features, but is readily distinguished by the larger calyx, usually by the larger broadly campanulate or almost saucer-shaped corolla, and very often by the broadly obovate leaves. The flower colour varies from apple-blossom pink speckled with crimson, to rose or deep rose-crimson or rose-crimson, without spots.

R. charitopes was first introduced by Forrest in July 1924 from the Salwin-Kiu Chiang Divide, north-west Yunnan, from an elevation of 3,355 m. (11,000 ft.) (No. 25570), and again in the same month from the same locality from 4,270 m. (14,000 ft.) (No. 25581). It flowered for the first time in April 1929. In cultivation it is a somewhat compact rounded shrub up to 3 feet or sometimes up to 4 or even 5 feet high with dark green aromatic foliage. The plant is hardy outdoors, but to be able to grow it satisfactorily along the east coast and in gardens inland, it should be given a sunny aspect and protection from wind. A healthy compact plant up to 2 feet high and as much across, is of exquisite beauty when covered with large broadly campanulate or saucer-shaped flowers of apple-blossom pink speckled with crimson. As the specific name suggests, the plant is "graceful of aspect" and is worthy of being widely cultivated. Farrer records pure albinos on the Chawchi Pass, north-east Upper Burma, but these have not yet been introduced into cultivation. A clone 'Parkside' received an Award of Merit when exhibited by the Crown Estate Commissioners, Windsor Great Park, in 1979.

Epithet. Graceful of aspect.

Hardiness 3. April—May. Plate 24.

R. glaucophyllum Rehder in Journ. Arn. Arb., XXVI (1945) 23.

Syn. *R. glaucum* Hook. f. Rhod. Sikkim Himal., t. 17 (1849).

Illustration. Bot. Mag. Vol. 79 t. 4721 (1853). Figured as *R. glaucum*.

A broadly upright or somewhat rounded or bushy or sometimes spreading shrub, 30 cm.—1.22 m. (1—4 ft.) or sometimes 1.5 m. (5 ft.) high; stem and branches with smooth, brown, flaking bark; branchlets scaly, glabrous, leaf-bud scales deciduous. *Leaves* evergreen, oblong, *lanceolate, oblong-lanceolate*, elliptic or obovate, aromatic, lamina coriaceous, 3—9 cm. long, 1—2.6 cm. broad, apex acute or obtuse, mucronate, base obtuse or tapered; upper surface dark green, shining, rather densely or moderately scaly; under surface markedly glaucous, densely scaly, the smaller pale yellow scales ½—2 times or rarely 3 times their own diameter apart, larger brown scales widely or closely separated; petiole 0.4—1.3 cm. long, rather densely or moderately scaly, glabrous. *Inflorescence* terminal, or sometimes terminal and axillary in the uppermost one or two leaves, umbellate, 4—10-flowered, flower-bud scales deciduous; rhachis 2—3 mm. long, scaly or not scaly; pedicel somewhat slender, 0.8—2.7 cm. long, as long as the corolla or shorter or rarely longer, rather densely or moderately scaly. *Calyx* 5-lobed, *leafy, 0.5—1 cm. long, lobes ovate-lanceolate, lanceolate* or rarely ovate, *apex markedly pointed* or rarely obtuse, outside rather densely or moderately scaly, margin eciliate or rarely ciliate. *Corolla* campanulate, 1.4—2.6 cm. long, 5-lobed, pink, rose, pinkish-purple or reddish-purple, outside not scaly or sparsely or moderately scaly. *Stamens* 10, unequal, 0.9—2.1 cm. long, as long as the corolla or shorter; filaments densely or moderately hairy in the lower one-third to two-thirds of their length. *Ovary* conoid or ovoid, 2—3 mm. long, 5-celled, densely scaly, glabrous; style short, stout and sharply bent or deflexed, or somewhat slender almost straight, shorter or longer than the corolla, not scaly, glabrous. *Capsule* ovoid or conoid, 5—8 mm. long, 5—6 mm. broad, rather densely scaly, glabrous, enclosed by the persistent calyx-lobes.

This well-known species was discovered by J.D. Hooker in May 1849 in the Sikkim Himalaya. Subsequently it was found by other collectors in Nepal, Sikkim, and Bhutan. It grows amongst rocks, on ridges, in pine and rhododendron forests, at elevations of 2,745—3,660 m. (9,000—12,000 ft.).

R. glaucophyllum is a very variable plant. It grows from 30 cm. to 1.22 m. (1—4 ft.) or sometimes 1.5 m. (5 ft.) high; the leaves are lanceolate to elliptic or obovate, (laminae) 3—9 cm. long; the inflorescence is 4—10-flowered; the corolla is 1.4—2.6 cm. long, pink, rose, pinkish-purple or reddish-purple, and the style is short, stout and sharply bent or deflexed or sometimes almost straight. A diagnostic feature is the large leafy calyx, ovate-lanceolate or lanceolate, markedly pointed, 0.5—1 cm. long. In general appear-

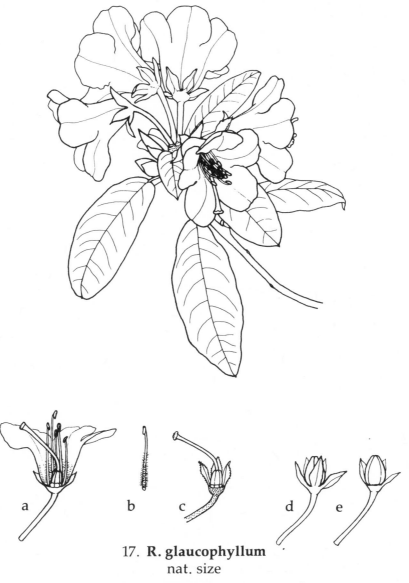

17. **R. glaucophyllum**
nat. size

a. section. b. stamen. c. ovary, style.
d. capsule (enclosed). e. capsule.

ance the species shows a resemblance to *R. tsangpoense* from which it is readily distinguished by the shape and usually by the size of the calyx, usually by the shape of the leaves and by the densely scaly lower surface. It also differs in its geographical distribution. Moreover *R. glaucophyllum* is a diploid 2n = 26, whereas *R. tsangpoense* is a tetraploid 2n = 52.

The plant was first introduced by J.D. Hooker in 1850. It was reintroduced several times by other collectors. There are at least six distinct forms in cultivation varying in habit and height of growth, in leaf shape and size, in flower size and colour. A broadly upright form up to 2 or 2½ feet high with large leaves up to 3 inches long, and large reddish-purple flowers 1 inch long, is generally considered to be one of the best. The striking features of all these forms are the markedly glaucous lower surfaces of the leaves, and the smooth brown flaking bark of the stem and branches. Another characteristic feature is the oval or oblong-oval capsule enclosed by the large persistent calyx-lobes. Moreover, the leaves when crushed have a distinct resinous smell. The species is hardy, free-flowering, and easy to grow. The smaller forms up to 2 or 2½ feet high are charming plants for the rock garden.

Epithet. With bluish-grey leaf.
Hardiness 3. April—May. Plate 23.

R. glaucophyllum Rehder var. **album** Davidian in Quart. Bull. Amer. Rhod. Soc., Vol. 35, January, 1981.

This plant was first collected by Beer, Lancaster, and Morris in November 1971 at Barun Khola, Nepal (No. 12319). It grows on rocky banks, in the open well drained localities, at an elevation of 3,050 m. (10,000 ft.).

The variety differs from the species in that the flowers are white, usually smaller up to 2 cm. long.

The plant was introduced by Beer, Lancaster, and Morris under seed No. 315 (= 12319). In its native home it is an erect shrub, 3 feet high; in cultivation it is somewhat compact spreading up to 1½ feet high and is likely to grow taller. It is hardy and free-flowering. A form was given the cultivar name 'Len Beer' when exhibited in 1977.

R. luteiflorum Davidian in Quart. Bull. Amer. Rhod. Soc. Vol. 32, (1978), No. 2, pp. 82—84.

A rounded spreading or broadly upright shrub, 60 cm.—1.53 m. (2—5 ft.) high; stem and branches with smooth brown flaking bark; branchlets scaly. *Leaves* evergreen, lanceolate, oblanceolate or oblong-lanceolate, aromatic, lamina coriaceous, 4—6.8 cm. long, 1.5—2.6 cm. broad, apex rounded or obtuse, mucronate, base tapered, obtuse or rounded, slightly decurrent on the petiole or not decurrent; upper surface dark green, shining, not scaly or scaly; *under surface* markedly glaucous, *laxly scaly*, the smaller pale yellow *scales 3—8 times their own diameter apart*, the larger dark brown scales widely separated; petiole 0.7—1.2 cm. long, margins slightly winged or ridged or rounded, moderately or rather densely scaly. *Inflorescence* terminal, umbellate or shortly racemose, 3—6-flowered, flower-bud scales deciduous; rhachis 3—5 mm. long, scaly; pedicel 0.8—1.5 cm. long, shorter than the corolla, rather densely or moderately scaly. *Calyx large, leafy*, 5-lobed, *6—8 mm. long, lobes lanceolate or ovate-lanceolate, apex acute*, outside scaly, margin not ciliate. *Corolla* campanulate, 2—2.2 cm. long, 5-lobed, *lemon-yellow or greenish-yellow*, without spots, outside scaly or not scaly. *Stamens* 10, unequal, 1—1.5 cm. long, shorter than the corolla; filaments densely pubescent at the base or in the lower two-thirds of their length. *Ovary* conoid or oblong, 5 mm. long, 5-celled, densely scaly; style somewhat long, stout and sharply bent, shorter than the corolla, not scaly. *Capsule* conoid or oblong-oval, 5—7 mm. long, 5—6 mm. broad, rather densely scaly, enclosed by the persistent calyx-lobes.

This plant was first described as *R. glaucophyllum* var. *luteiflorum*.

Kingdon-Ward discovered it in June 1953 at Tama Bum, North Triangle, North Burma. He found it again later in November of the same year at Uring Bum, above Akhail in the same region. It grows in dense bushy thickets on open granite ridges, at elevations of 2,898—3,355 m. (9,500—11,000 ft.).

It shows a resemblance to *R. glaucophyllum* in general features, but is readily distinguished by its lemon-yellow or greenish-yellow flowers, by the laxly scaly lower surface of the leaves, the scales being 3—8 times their own diameter apart, somewhat by its habit of growth, and usually by the larger leaves. It also differs in its geographical distribution. *R. luteiflorum* comes from North Burma, whereas *R. glaucophyllum* is known from Nepal, Sikkim and Bhutan.

The species was introduced by Kingdon-Ward under No. 21040, in 1953. In cultivation it is a spreading or broadly upright shrub up to 2 or 3 feet high, and usually as much across, with dark green aromatic leaves. It is undoubtedly one of the finest yellow-flowered dwarf rhododendrons in cultivation. Striking features are the markedly glaucous lower surfaces of the leaves and the large leafy lanceolate or ovate-lanceolate calyx, as well as the charming smooth brown flaking bark of the stem and branches. The plant is hardy, but along the east coast is should be given a well-sheltered position in the garden. It is free-flowering, and is exceedingly beautiful when laden with large bells in trusses of three to six. A clone 'Glen Cloy' received an Award of Merit in 1960 and a First Class Certificate in 1966 when shown on both occasions as *R. glaucophyllum* var. *luteiflorum* by the National Trust for Scotland, Brodick Castle Gardens, Isle of Arran.

Epithet. With yellow flowers.

Hardiness 3. April—May. Plate 25.

R. pruniflorum Hutch. in The Species of Rhododendron (1930) 302.

A compact spreading or rounded shrub, 30 cm.—1.22 m. (1—4 ft.) high; stem and branches with smooth brown flaking bark; branchlets rather densely or moderately scaly, glabrous, leaf-bud scales deciduous. *Leaves* evergreen, obovate, oblong-obovate or oblong, aromatic, lamina coriaceous, 1.5—5 cm. long, 1—2.6 cm. broad, apex rounded or obtuse, mucronate, base rounded, obtuse or cuneate; upper surface dark green or olive-green, shining, not scaly or scaly; *under surface* markedly or sometimes slightly glaucous, *densely scaly*, the scales unequal, large or medium-sized, the smaller pale yellow *scales contiguous or slightly overlapping or ½ their own diameter apart* (or rarely their own diameter apart), the larger brown scales widely or closely separated; petiole 2—8 mm. long, rather densely or moderately scaly, glabrous. *Inflorescence* terminal, or rarely terminal and axillary in the uppermost one or two leaves, umbellate or shortly racemose, 3—7-flowered, flower-bud scales deciduous; rhachis 2—7 mm. long, densely or moderately scaly, glabrous; pedicel slender, 1.3—3.5 cm. long, longer than the corolla or rarely equalling it, rather densely or moderately scaly, glabrous. *Calyx* 5-lobed, 3—5 mm. long, lobes oblong-oval, oval, ovate, rounded or elliptic, apex rounded or rarely obtuse, outside rather densely or moderately scaly or not scaly, margin eciliate or rarely sparsely ciliate. *Corolla* campanulate, 1—1.6 cm. long, 5-lobed, nearly crimson, plum-purple, cerise-coloured, violet, lavender-purple or rarely pink, outside not scaly or rarely sparsely scaly. *Stamens* 10, unequal, 0.6—1.5 cm. long, as long as the corolla or shorter; filaments densely hairy in the lower one-half or nearly to the apex. *Ovary* conoid or ovoid, 2—3 mm. long, 5-celled, densely scaly, glabrous; style short, stout and sharply bent or deflexed, not scaly or rarely scaly at the base, glabrous. *Capsule* conoid, 5—6 mm. long, 4—5 mm. broad, densely scaly, glabrous, enclosed by the persistent calyx-lobes.

Kingdon-Ward first collected this plant in June 1926 at Seinghku Wang in northeastern Burma. He found it again, in Assam in 1928 and in 1950. Ludlow and Sherriff collected it in south Tibet in 1936, and again with Elliot in south-east Tibet in 1947. It grows in dense rhododendron thickets, on rocky hillsides, in scrub, and in Abies forests at elevations of 3,355—4,270 m. (11,000—14,000 ft.).

The species is closely allied to *R. tsangpoense* which it resembles in leaf shape and size, and in the shape of the corolla, but is readily distinguished by the densely scaly lower surface of the leaves, the scales being overlapping or contiguous or ½ or rarely their own diameter apart, usually by the smaller corolla, and often by the more compact habit of growth.

The plant was first introduced by Kingdon-Ward in 1926 from north-eastern Burma (No. 6924). He reintroduced it later from the same region and from Assam. In cultivation it is a compact spreading or rounded shrub up to 3 or 4 feet high and as much across, a robust grower, and well-filled with dark green or olive-green foliage. A striking feature is the smooth brown flaking bark of the stem and branches. Another characteristic is the strongly aromatic foliage. The plant is perfectly hardy, and is well adapted to the rock garden.

Epithet. Plum-flowered.

Hardiness 3. May—June.

R. shweliense Balf. f. et Forrest in Notes Roy. Bot. Gard. Edin., Vol. 13 (1922) 293.

A somewhat compact rounded small shrub, 30—76 cm. (1—2½ ft.) high; stem and branches with smooth brown flaking bark or rarely with rough bark; branchlets rather densely or moderately scaly, glabrous, leaf-bud scales deciduous. *Leaves* evergreen, obovate, oblong or oblong-obovate, aromatic, lamina coriaceous, 1.3—4.7 cm. long, 0.6—1.8 cm. broad, apex rounded or obtuse, mucronate, base obtuse or tapered; upper surface dark or pale green, matt, scaly or not scaly; under surface markedly or sometimes very thinly glaucous, scaly, the scales unequal, medium-sized or somewhat large, pale yellow scales ½—4 times their own diameter apart, larger brown scales closely or widely separated; petiole 0.3—1 cm. long, rather densely or moderately scaly, glabrous. *Inflorescence* terminal, umbellate, 2—4-flowered, flower-bud scales deciduous; rhachis 1—3 mm. long, scaly, glabrous; pedicel slender, 1.5—2.3 cm. long, longer than the corolla, scaly, glabrous. *Calyx* 5-lobed, 4—7 mm. long, lobes oblong-oval, oval or ovate, outside glaucous or not glaucous, scaly, margin eciliate or sparsely ciliate. *Corolla* campanulate, 1.3—1.5 cm. long, 5-lobed, *pale pink tinged yellow, upper three lobes spotted pink, outside rather densely or moderately or slightly scaly*. *Stamens* 10, unequal, 1—1.5 cm. long, as long as the corolla or shorter; filaments densely or moderately hairy in the lower one-half or throughout their whole length. *Ovary* conoid or ovoid, 2 mm. long, 5-celled, densely scaly, glabrous; style short, stout and sharply bent or deflexed, scaly at the base or not scaly, puberulous or glabrous. *Capsule* ovoid or conoid, 4—5 mm. long, 3—4 mm. broad, densely scaly, glabrous, enclosed by the persistent calyx-lobes.

The distribution of *R. shweliense* is restricted to western Yunnan. It was discovered by Forrest in June 1919 in the Shweli-Salwin Divide. It was found by him again in May 1924 in the same region. The plant grows on open cliffs and rocky slopes at elevations of 3,050—3,355 m. (10,000—11,000 ft.).

The species bears a resemblance to *R. brachyanthum* var. *hypolepidotum* in leaf shape and size, and in the size of the calyx, but differs markedly in the colour of its flowers, usually in the corolla being densely or moderately scaly outside, and in the shorter pedicels.

R. shweliense was introduced by Forrest in 1924 (No. 24154). In cultivation it is a somewhat compact rounded shrub up to 2 feet high, with smooth brown flaking bark and aromatic foliage. In its native home, the lower surface of the leaves is markedly glaucous, although in cultivation it is pale green and very thinly glaucous. The plant is quite hardy, free-flowering, and easy to grow. It is uncommon in cultivation, but is worthy of being widely grown.

Epithet. From the Shweli River.

Hardiness 3. April—May.

R. tsangpoense Ward in Gard. Chron. LXXXVI (1929) 504.

A somewhat compact or rounded shrub, 30 cm.—1.22 m. (1—4 ft.) high; stem and branches with smooth, brown flaking bark; branchlets scaly, glabrous, leaf-bud scales deciduous. *Leaves* evergreen, obovate, oblong-obovate, elliptic, oblong or oval, aromatic, lamina coriaceous, 1.3—5.2 cm. long, 0.6—2.6 cm. or rarely 3.2 cm. broad, apex rounded or obtuse, mucronate, base obtuse, cuneate or rounded; upper surface dark green, shining, scaly or not scaly; *under surface* markedly glaucous, *scaly*, the scales unequal, medium-sized or somewhat large, the smaller pale yellow *scales 1—6 (usually 2—6) times or rarely 10 times their own diameter apart*, the larger brown scales widely or closely separated; petiole 2—6 mm. long, moderately or rather densely scaly, glabrous. *Inflorescence* terminal, umbellate or shortly racemose, 3—6- or rarely 2-flowered, flower-bud scales deciduous; rhachis 2—5 mm. long, scaly, glabrous; pedicel slender, 1.3—3 cm. long, as long as the corolla or longer, moderately or rather densely scaly, glabrous. *Calyx* 5-lobed, 2—7 mm. long, lobes rounded, ovate, oval or oblong-oval, apex rounded or rarely acute, outside slightly or moderately scaly or not scaly, margin eciliate or rarely ciliate. *Corolla* campanulate, 1.3—2.6 cm. long, 5-lobed, pink, reddish-purple, pinkish-purple or rarely cerise, outside not scaly or rarely slightly scaly. *Stamens* 10, unequal, 0.8—1.7 cm. long, shorter than the corolla; filaments densely hairy in the lower one-half or nearly to the apex. *Ovary* ovoid or conoid, 3—4 mm. long, 5-celled, densely scaly, glabrous; style short, stout and sharply bent or sometimes deflexed, not scaly or sometimes scaly at the base, glabrous. *Capsule* conoid, 5—6 mm. long, 4—5 mm. broad, densely scaly, glabrous, enclosed or partly enclosed by the persistent calyx-lobes.

This plant was first found by Kingdon-Ward in June 1924 at Doshong La in south-east Tibet. It was later found by Ludlow and Sherriff, also with Elliot, in other localities in the same region. The plant grows on steep alpine slopes and among rocks, at elevations of 2,440—4,118 m. (8,000—13,500 ft.). Kingdon-Ward records it as forming scrub 1—2 feet high on steep alpine slopes mixed with other species.

R. tsangpoense is related to *R. pruniflorum*; the distinctions between them are discussed under the latter. It is also allied to *R. charitopes* which it resembles in general appearance, but is distinguished by the smaller calyx, usually by the smaller campanulate corolla and narrowly obovate to oblong-elliptic leaves. It further differs from *R. charitopes* and from all the other members of its Series in that it is tetraploid with 52 chromosomes. All the others are diploid with 26 chromosomes.

The species was introduced by Kingdon-Ward in 1924 (No. 5844—the Type number). In cultivation it is a somewhat compact or rounded shrub up to 3 or 4 feet high and as much across, with campanulate corolla and aromatic foliage. Another marked feature is the smooth brown flaking bark of the stem and branches. The plant is hardy outdoors and is most attractive when covered with pinkish-purple flowers in clusters of 3—6. The clone 'Cowtype' was given an Award of Merit when exhibited by Major A.E. Hardy, Sandling Park, in 1972.

Epithet. From the Tsangpo River.
Hardiness 3. May—June.

R. tsangpoense Ward var. **curvistylum** Ward ex Cowan et Davidian in The Rhododendron Year Book (1948) 90.

Syn. *R. curvistylum* Ward, nomen nudum.

This plant was first collected by Kingdon-Ward in June 1924 at Doshong La, in south-east Tibet, forming dense tangled scrub 30—60 cm. (1—2 ft.) high with other species on the side of the mountain, at 3,660—3,965 m. (12,000—13,000 ft.).

The variety differs from the species in that the corolla is smaller, narrowly tubular-campanulate, deep cerise-coloured.

The plant was introduced by Kingdon-Ward in 1924 (No. 5843 — the Type number). In cultivation it is a small spreading shrub up to 45 cm. (1½ ft.) high. It is hardy, and flowers freely with clusters of two to six flowers.

Epithet of the variety. Curved style.
Hardiness 3. May—June.

R. tubiforme (Cowan et Davidian) Davidian in Quart. Bull. Amer. Rhod. Soc., Vol. 35, January (1981).

A broadly upright shrub, 30 cm.—2.14 m. (1—7 ft.) high; stem and branches with smooth, brown, flaking bark; branchlets rather densely or moderately scaly. *Leaves* evergreen, obovate, oblong-obovate, oblong, lanceolate or oblanceolate, aromatic, lamina coriaceous, 3.2—6 cm. long, 1.3—2.5 cm. broad, apex rounded, obtuse or acute, mucronate, base obtuse, tapered or rounded; upper surface dark green, shining, rather densely or moderately scaly; under surface markedly glaucous, densely scaly, the smaller pale yellow scales 1—2 times or sometimes 3 (or rarely 4) times their own diameter apart, the larger dark brown scales closely or widely separated; petiole 0.4—1 cm. long, rather densely or moderately scaly, glabrous. *Inflorescence* terminal, or rarely terminal and axillary in the uppermost one or two leaves, umbellate or shortly racemose, 3—5-flowered; rhachis 2—3 mm. long, scaly or not scaly; pedicel 0.8—1.6 cm. long, shorter than the corolla, rather densely scaly. *Calyx* 5-lobed, leafy, 5—8 mm. or rarely 1.1—1.3 cm. long, lobes ovate-lanceolate or lanceolate, apex markedly pointed or rarely obtuse, outside rather densely or moderately scaly, margin scaly, not ciliate. *Corolla tubular, 2.3—3.8 cm. long*, 5-lobed, pink, deep rose, or pink with white lobes, with or without darker spots, outside moderately or sparsely scaly or not scaly. *Stamens* 10, unequal, 1.6—3 cm. long, as long as the corolla or a little shorter; filaments densely hairy in the lower half. *Ovary* conoid or ovoid, 2—4 mm. long, 5-celled, densely scaly; *style long, slender, straight*, longer than, or as long as, the corolla, not scaly, glabrous. *Capsule* conoid or ovoid, 5—7 mm. long, 4—5 mm. broad, moderately or rather densely scaly, enclosed or rarely partly enclosed by the persistent calyx-lobes.

R. tubiforme was discovered by Kingdon-Ward in May 1935 at Manda La, Assam frontier. It was later found by him again at Poshing La, Assam. The plant was also collected by Ludlow and Sherriff, and together with Elliot or Hicks in east Bhutan and in south-east Tibet. It grows in conifer-rhododendron forests, in open rhododendron forests, in mixed rhododendron and bamboo forests, on rocks, and on precipitous slopes, at elevations of 2,745—3,660 m. (9,000—12,000 ft.). It is recorded as being common on rock faces in rhododendron forests in Bhutan.

The diagnostic features of this plant are the tubular corolla, 2.3—3.8 cm. long, and the long, slender and straight style, as long as the corolla or longer. In these respects it is readily distinguished from its nearest ally *R. glaucophyllum*. It also differs in that it grows up to 7 feet high, whereas *R. glaucophyllum* reaches a height of 4 feet.

The species was introduced by Ludlow and Sherriff in 1936 from east Bhutan (No. 2856). In cultivation it is a broadly upright shrub, up to 5 or 6 feet high, well-filled with dark green foliage. It is fairly fast-growing, and provides an admirable display with its deep rose flowers produced freely in clusters of three to five. The plant is hardy, but to be able to grow it satisfactorily, particularly along the east coast and in gardens inland, a well-sheltered position should be provided.

Epithet. With tubular flowers.

Hardiness 3. April—May. Plate 26.

HELIOLEPIS SERIES

General characters: shrubs or trees, 60 cm.—9.15 m. (2—30 ft.) high. Leaves ever-green, ovate-lanceolate, elliptic-lanceolate, lanceolate, oblong-lanceolate, elliptic, oblong or ovate, lamina 1.3—12.5 cm. long, 0.9—4.6 cm. broad; under surface scaly, the *scales large*, overlapping or contiguous to 4 or rarely 5—6 times their own diameter apart. Inflorescence terminal, or sometimes terminal and axillary in the uppermost one or two leaves, 2—9-flowered; pedicel 0.4—2.5 cm. or rarely 3 cm. long. Calyx 5-lobed or sometimes undulately lobed, 0.5—1 mm. or sometimes 2—4 mm. long. Corolla funnel-shaped, funnel-campanulate, campanulate, widely funnel-shaped or tubular-campanulate, 1.2—4.2 cm. long, 5-lobed, pink, pale or deep rose, deep lavender, lavender, intense bluish-purple, purple or white, with or without a crimson blotch at the base, and with or rarely without crimson spots, outside moderately or rather densely scaly. Stamens 10. Ovary oblong or conoid, 3—5 mm. long, 5-celled, densely scaly; *style slender, straight*. Capsule oblong or rarely oblong-oval, 0.8—1.7 cm. long, 3—5 mm. broad, densely scaly.

Distribution: west and south-west Szechuan, mid-west, west, north-west and north-east Yunnan, east and north-east Upper Burma, south-east and east Tibet.

The main features of this Series are the tubular-campanulate, campanulate, funnel-shaped or widely funnel-shaped corolla, the long, slender and straight style, the large scales, and the aromatic foliage.

The species with tubular-campanulate or campanulate corollas bear some resemblance to the Tephropeplum Series, whilst those with widely funnel-shaped corollas are allied to the Triflorum Series.

KEY TO THE SPECIES

A. Corolla large, 1.6—4.2 cm. long; leaf-bud scales deciduous; leaves (laminae) 3—12.5 cm. long.

    B. Style glabrous (or rarely puberulous at the base); scales on the under surface of the leaves usually overlapping or contiguous or nearly contiguous, with or without widely or closely scattered larger darker scales.

        C. Corolla 1.6—3.1 cm. long, 1.5—3.5 cm. across, funnel-shaped, funnel-campanulate, campanulate or tubular-funnel shaped.

            D. Scales on the under surface of the leaves overlapping or contiguous or nearly contiguous; style longer than the stamens; rhachis of the inflorescence glabrous; stamens puberulous towards the base or sometimes glabrous . . . . *rubiginosum*

            D. Scales on the under surface of the leaves one-half their own diameter apart; style as long as the stamens or shorter; rhachis of the inflorescence puberulous; stamens densely villous towards the base . . . . *fumidum*

        C. Corolla usually 3—4.2 cm. long, 3.5—6 cm. across, usually almost saucer-shaped or widely funnel-shaped . . . . *desquamatum*

    B. Style rather densely or moderately pubescent in the lower one-half or one-third or at the base (or rarely glabrous); scales on the under surface of the leaves nearly contiguous to 4 (or rarely 5—6) times their own diameter apart, without scattered larger darker scales.

        E. Corolla moderately or rather densely scaly all over the outside; stamens shorter than the corolla; style shorter than the corolla; branchlets and petioles glabrous.

            F. Corolla usually campanulate or tubular-campanulate, regular; scales on the under surface of the leaves nearly contiguous to 4 (or rarely 5—6) times their own diameter apart; plant hexaploid with 78 chromosomes . . . . *heliolepis*

            F. Corolla funnel-campanulate, slightly zygomorphic; scales on the under surface of the leaves one-half their own diameter apart; plant octoploid with 104 chromosomes . . . . *pholidotum*

        E. Corolla scaly on one side; stamens as long as the corolla or longer; style longer than the corolla; branchlets and petioles minutely puberulous . . . . *invictum*

A. Corolla small, 1.2—1.5 cm. long; leaf-bud scales persistent; leaves (laminae) 1.3—4.2 cm. long . . . . *bracteatum*

DESCRIPTION OF THE SPECIES

R. bracteatum Rehd. et Wils. in Plantae Wilsonianae (1913) 519.

    Illustration. Bot. Mag. Vol. 150 t. 9031 (1924).

A broadly upright or somewhat compact shrub, 92 cm.—3 m. (3—10 ft.) high; branchlets purple, minutely puberulous or glabrous, scaly, *leaf-bud scales persistent*. *Leaves* elliptic-oblong, elliptic, oblong, ovate-oblong, ovate-lanceolate, oblong-oval or ovate, aromatic, *lamina* coriaceous, *1.3—4.2 cm. long*, 0.9—1.7 cm. broad, apex obtuse or rounded, mucronate, base rounded or obtuse; upper surface dark green or olive-green, reticulate, scaly, glabrous, midrib glabrous; under surface scaly, the scales unequal, very large, yellowish or pale brown, 1—4 times their own diameter apart, without scattered larger darker scales; petiole 0.3—1.2 cm. long, glabrous, moderately or rather densely scaly. *Inflorescence* terminal, shortly racemose, 3—6-flowered, flower-bud scales deciduous; rhachis 1—3 mm. long, minutely puberulous or glabrous, scaly; pedicel slender, 1.3—2 cm. or rarely 2.5 cm. long, as long as the corolla or longer, scaly. *Calyx* 5-lobed,

1—2 mm. long, lobes ovate or triangular, outside scaly, margin ciliate or eciliate, scaly. *Corolla* campanulate, *1.2—1.5 cm. long,* 1.5—2 cm. across, 5-lobed, white or white tinged pink, with or without a crimson blotch at the base, and with crimson spots, outside glabrous, scaly, inside rather densely pubescent at the base of the tube. *Stamens* 10, unequal, 0.9—1.3 cm. long, as long as the corolla or shorter; filaments densely villous in the lower one-half or one-third. *Ovary* oblong or conoid, 3—4 mm. long, 5-celled, densely scaly, glabrous; style slender, straight, as long as the corolla or shorter, as long as the stamens, glabrous or pubescent at the base, not scaly. *Capsule* oblong, 0.8—1.5 cm. long, 3—4 mm. broad, straight, glabrous, rather densely scaly, calyx persistent.

Wilson discovered this plant in July 1908 near Wen-ch'uan Hsien, in western Szechuan. He collected it again in October 1910 at Mupin, in the same region. The plant grows in woodlands and on cliffs at elevations of 2,600—3,300 m. (8,525—10,820 ft.).

In the original diagnosis *R. bracteatum* is associated with *R. yanthinum* (now a synonym of *R. concinnum*), and in *The Species of Rhododendron* it is placed in the Oreotrephes Subseries, Triflorum Series. From this Series, it is very remote. *R. bracteatum* shows a marked similarity to the species of the Heliolepis Series, particularly in flower shape and in the large-sized scales; in 1963 it was transferred to this Series when the Triflorum Series was revised (*The Rhododendron and Camellia Year Book* 1963, p. 157).

The diagnostic features of this plant are the persistent leaf-bud scales, the small corolla 1.2—1.5 cm. long, and the small leaves 1.3—4.2 cm. long. In these respects, it is readily distinguished from its nearest ally *R.|heliolepis*, and from all the other members of its Series. The very large scales (¼ mm. in diameter, 3—4 in a sq. mm. of surface), particularly on the lower surfaces of the leaves, are a remarkable character of this species and most of its allies in its Series.

The species was introduced by Wilson in 1910 (No. 4253). In cultivation it is a broadly upright or somewhat compact shrub, 3—10 feet high with aromatic foliage. The plant appears to have a restricted distribution in western Szechuan. It has not been found by any other collector. It is a useful plant in that it is a late flowerer, the flowers appearing in June—July. The plant is uncommon in cultivation. It is perfectly hardy, free-flowering, and provides a fine display with trusses of three to six flowers.

Epithet. Furnished with bracts.
Hardiness 3. June—July.

R. desquamatum Balf. f. et Forrest in Notes Roy. Bot. Gard. Edin., Vol. 13 (1920) 40.
  Illustration. Bot. Mag. Vol. 160 t. 9497 (1937).
  A broadly upright or spreading shrub or tree, 1.53—8 m. (5—26 ft.) high; branchlets densely or moderately scaly, leaf-bud scales deciduous. *Leaves* evergreen, ovate-lanceolate, ovate, elliptic-lanceolate, oblong-lanceolate or lanceolate, not aromatic, lamina coriaceous, 4.5—12.5 cm. long, 1.5—4.5 cm. broad, apex acute or acutely acuminate, mucronate, base obtuse, tapered or rounded; upper surface dark green or olive-green, scaly or not scaly, glabrous, midrib glabrous; under surface densely scaly, the scales unequal, large and medium-sized, dark brown or brown or rust-coloured, overlapping or contiguous or nearly contiguous, with widely or closely scattered larger darker scales; petiole 0.5—1.8 cm. long, densely scaly. *Inflorescence* terminal, or terminal and axillary in the uppermost one or two leaves, shortly racemose, 3—7-flowered, flower-bud scales deciduous; rhachis 2—4 mm. long, glabrous or puberulous, densely or moderately scaly; pedicel 0.5—2.3 cm. long, shorter than the corolla, rather densely or moderately scaly. *Calyx* 5-lobed, minute, 0.5—1 mm. long, lobes ovate or triangular, outside densely or moderately scaly, margin eciliate or rarely ciliate, densely or moderately scaly. *Corolla widely funnel-shaped or almost saucer-shaped* or funnel-shaped, *3—4.2 cm.* (or rarely 2.3 cm.) *long,* 3.5—6 cm. (or rarely 3.2 cm.) *across,* 5-lobed, deep rose, pink, deep rose-lavender, deep purple-rose, intense bluish-purple, lavender-purple, lavender, purple, pinkish-purple or white, with crimson spots, outside scaly, inside mod-

erately or rather densely puberulous at the base of the tube. *Stamens* 10, unequal, 1.3—3.2 cm. long, shorter than the corolla; filaments puberulous towards the base. *Ovary* oblong or conoid, 3—5 mm. long, 5-celled, densely scaly, glabrous or rarely puberulous at the apex; style slender, straight, as long as the corolla or longer, longer than the stamens, glabrous, not scaly. *Capsule* oblong or rarely oblong-oval, 0.8—1.7 cm. long, 3—5 mm. broad, straight or slightly curved, densely scaly, calyx persistent.

Forrest first found this plant in July 1917 in the Shweli-Salwin Divide, western Yunnan. Further gatherings by him and other collectors show that the species is widely distributed in west and north-west Yunnan, north-east Upper Burma, south-west Szechuan and south-east Tibet. It grows in rhododendron thickets and forests, in pine and spruce forests, in mixed forests, and in cane brakes, at elevations of 2,500—4,270 m. (8,197—14,000 ft.). It is said to be common in bamboo forests, in thickets, in mixed forests, and in woods in western Yunnan.

The species is closely related to *R. rubiginosum*. There is a strong resemblance between them in habit and height of growth, in the shape and size of the leaves, in the densely scaly lower surface of the leaves, and in flower colour. *R. desquamatum* differs markedly from its ally in that the corolla is large, usually widely funnel-shaped or almost saucer-shaped, 3—4.2 cm. long, 3.5—6 cm. across. It is worth noting that *R. desquamatum* is a tetraploid with 52 chromosomes, while *R. rubiginosum* is hexaploid with 78 chromosomes or tetraploid with 52 chromosomes.

R. desquamatum was first introduced by Forrest in 1917 from western Yunnan (No. 15761 — the Type number). He later sent seeds on several occasions from north-west Yunnan and north-east Upper Burma. The species was also introduced by Farrer (No. 875), by Rock (No. 59506), and by Yü (No. 10961). In its native home, it is a medium-sized shrub or tree, 5-26 feet high, but in cultivation it is a broadly upright or spreading shrub, usually up to 10 feet. A good example of this plant is to be seen at the Younger Botanic Garden, Benmore, Argyllshire. Some plants produce a few capsules of good fertile seeds nearly every year. The species is very hardy, a vigorous grower, and has proved to be most attractive when covered with deep rose-purple flowers with crimson spots, in trusses of three to seven. It received an Award of Merit when shown by Capt. A.M. Talbot Fletcher, Margam Castle, Port Talbot, S. Wales, in 1938, raised from Forrest seed (No. 24535).

Epithet. Bereft of scales.
Hardiness 3. April—May.

R. fumidum Balf. f. et W.W. Sm. in Notes Roy. Bot. Gard. Edin., Vol. 10 (1917) 112.

A broadly upright shrub, 1.53—2 m. (5—6½ ft.) high; branchlets moderately or rather densely scaly, leaf-bud scales deciduous. *Leaves* evergreen, lanceolate or ovate-lanceolate, not aromatic, lamina coriaceous, 4.4—7.5 cm. long, 1.5—2.9 cm. broad, apex acutely acuminate, mucronate, base obtuse or rounded; upper surface dark green, not scaly, glabrous, midrib puberulous or glabrous; *under surface* scaly, the *scales* unequal, large, dark brown or brown, *one-half their own diameter apart*, without scattered larger darker scales; petiole 0.6—1.5 cm. long, moderately or rather densely scaly. *Inflorescence* terminal, shortly racemose, 4—7-flowered; *rhachis* 2—7 mm. long, *puberulous*, scaly; pedicel 1—1.6 cm. long, shorter than the corolla, rather densely scaly. *Calyx* 5-lobed, minute, 1 mm. long, lobes triangular or ovate, outside scaly, margin ciliate or eciliate, scaly. *Corolla* funnel-shaped or campanulate, 1.6—2.5 cm. long, 1.8—2.7 cm. across, 5-lobed, pale violet or pale lavender-purple, outside rather densely scaly, inside rather densely pubescent at the base of the tube. *Stamens* 10, unequal, 1.1—2.2 cm. long, shorter than the corolla; *filaments densely villous towards the base. Ovary* oblong, 3—5 mm. long, 5-celled, densely scaly, glabrous; *style* slender, straight, shorter than the corolla, *as long as the stamens or shorter*, glabrous, not scaly. *Capsule* oblong, 1.5 cm. long, 4 mm. broad, straight, rather densely scaly, calyx persistent.

Maire discovered this plant in June 1911 on the summit of Io-chow, in north-east Yunnan. He found it again in 1913 on the plateau of Te-ma-Tchouan in the same region. It grows at elevations of 3,200—3,400 m. (10,492—11,148 ft.).

R. fumidum resembles *R. rubiginosum* in general features, but differs in that the scales on the lower surface of the leaves are one-half their own diameter apart, the style is as long as the stamens or shorter, the stamens are densely villous towards the base, and the rhachis of the inflorescence is puberulous. It also differs in its geographical distribution. *R. fumidum* is known from north-east Yunnan, while *R. rubiginosum* comes from west and north-west Yunnan, south-east Tibet, and south-west Szechuan.

The plant has been in cultivation for a long time. It is a broadly upright shrub, 5 feet high, with pale lavender-purple flowers. The plant is hardy, with rigid branchlets, and is free-flowering. It is rare in cultivation.

Epithet. Smoke-covered.

Hardiness 3. May—June.

R. heliolepis Franch. in Bull. Soc. Bot. France, XXXIV (1887) 283.

Illustration. Bot. Mag. Vol. 147 t. 8898 (1938). Figured as *R. brevistylum*.

A broadly upright or sometimes a straggly shrub, or tree, 60 cm.—5.49 m. (2—18 ft.) high; branchlets glabrous, moderately or rather densely scaly, leaf-bud scales deciduous. *Leaves* evergreen, ovate-lanceolate, elliptic-lanceolate, lanceolate, oblong-lanceolate or ovate, *aromatic* or rarely not aromatic, lamina coriaceous, 4—11.5 cm. long, 1.5—4.6 cm. broad, apex acute or acuminate, mucronate, base rounded, obtuse or tapered; upper surface dark green, reticulate, moderately or densely scaly, glabrous, midrib moderately or rather densely puberulous or glabrous; *under surface scaly*, the *scales* unequal, *very large*, yellowish, or yellowish and brown, or brown, *nearly contiguous 4 times or rarely 5—6 times their own diameter apart*, without scattered larger darker scales, petiole 0.6—1.8 cm. long, glabrous, moderately or densely scaly. *Inflorescence* terminal, shortly racemose, 4—9-flowered, flower-bud scales deciduous; rhachis 0.3—1.5 cm. long, rather densely or moderately minutely puberulous or glabrous, moderately or rather densely scaly; pedicel 0.8—2.5 cm. or rarely 3 cm. long, shorter than the corolla, moderately or rather densely scaly. *Calyx* 5-lobed or rarely undulately lobed, 1—4 mm. long, lobes ovate, triangular or oblong-oval, outside densely or moderately scaly, margin ciliate or eciliate, densely or moderately scaly. *Corolla tubular-campanulate, funnel-campanulate, widely campanulate or campanulate,* 1.8—3 cm. long, 1.6—3.5 cm. across, 5-lobed, rose, deep rose, red, deep or pale lavender-rose, lavender-purple, purple, pink, white or white flushed rose, with or without a crimson blotch at the base, and with or rarely without a few or numerous crimson or greenish spots, outside glabrous or rarely pubescent, moderately or rather densely scaly, inside rather densely pubescent at the base of the tube. *Stamens* 10, unequal, 0.8—2.6 cm. long, shorter than the corolla; filaments densely villous in the lower one-half or one-third. *Ovary* conoid or oblong, 3—5 mm. long, 5-celled, densely scaly, pubescent at the apex, or glabrous; style slender, straight, shorter than the corolla, as long as the stamens or shorter than the taller 2—5 stamens, moderately or rather densely pubescent at the base or in the lower one-third or one-half or rarely glabrous, not scaly. *Capsule* oblong, 0.9—1.5 cm. long, 3—5 mm. broad, straight, glabrous or pubescent at the apex, rather densely scaly, calyx persistent.

This species was first collected by the Abbé Delavay in July 1886 near Hokin, western Yunnan. It was later found by other collectors in mid-west and west Yunnan, east and north-east Upper Burma, and east and south-east Tibet. It grows in rhododendron thickets and forests, in mixed scrub, on alpine slopes, and in conifer, spruce, Abies and pine forests, at elevations of 3,000—3,813 m. (9,836—12,500 ft.). It is recorded as being common in and at the margins of Abies forests and in rhododendron forests in western Yunnan.

In 1898, *R. brevistylum* Franch. was described from a specimen (No. 1008) collected by

18. **R. heliolepis**
nat. size

a. flower. b. section. c. ovary, style. d. stamen. e. capsule.

Soulié in western Szechuan. It was said to differ from *R. heliolepis* in that the style is much shorter than the stamens, and the leaves are narrowed to the base. These characters are common to both species. In 1917, *R. oporinum* Balf. f. et Ward was founded on a specimen (No. 1906) collected by Kingdon-Ward in east Upper Burma. When this specimen is examined, it will be seen that it is identical with *R. heliolepis* in every respect.

R. heliolepis is a very variable plant. It is a shrub or tree, and grows from 2 feet up to 18 feet high; the leaves are lanceolate, oblong-lanceolate to ovate, the laminae are 4—11.5 cm. long, 1.5—4.6 cm. broad, the scales on the lower surfaces are nearly contiguous to 4 times or rarely 5—6 times their own diameter apart; the pedicel is 0.8—2.5 cm. long; and the flower colour varies from pink or white to red or deep lavender-purple. *R. heliolepis* is a hexaploid with 78 chromosomes, or sometimes tetraploid with 52 chromosomes.

The species was first introduced by Forrest in 1912 (No. 8938). It was reintroduced by him on several occasions. Seeds were sent by Farrer, Kingdon-Ward, Rock, McLaren's collectors, and Yü. Features worth noting are the very large, glistening, yellowish or brown scales on both surfaces of the leaves, and the strongly aromatic foliage. Four colour forms are in cultivation, namely, pink, rose, reddish-purple, and white, usually with a crimson blotch at the base. It is an extremely useful plant in that it is a late flowerer, prolonging the flowering season into June and July. The plant is very hardy, a vigorous grower, and free-flowering. A form with white flowers with green and brown spots, was given an Award of Merit when exhibited by Mrs. R. Stevenson, Tower Court, Ascot, in 1954, under Forrest No. 26961.

Epithet. With glittering scales.
Hardiness 3. June—July.

R. invictum Balf. f. et Farrer in Notes Roy. Bot. Gard. Edin., Vol. 10 (1917) 116.

A shrub, 1.22—2.14 m. (4—7 ft.) high; *branchlets minutely puberulous*, scaly, leaf-bud scales deciduous. *Leaves* evergreen, elliptic or oblong-elliptic, lamina coriaceous, 4.4—4.6 cm. long, 2.3—2.5 cm. broad, apex obtuse, mucronate, base obtuse or rounded; upper surface dark green, reticulate, not scaly, glabrous, midrib rather densely puberulous; under surface scaly, the scales unequal, very large, yellowish, one-half their own diameter apart, without scattered larger darker scales; *petiole* 0.8—1 cm. long, *minutely puberulous*, scaly. *Inflorescence* terminal, shortly racemose, 2- or more-flowered, flower-bud scales deciduous; rhachis 1—2 mm. long, glabrous, scaly; pedicel 6—8 mm. long, shorter than the corolla, glabrous scaly. *Calyx* 5-lobed, minute, 1 mm. long, lobes ovate or triangular, *outside* and margin *puberulous*, scaly. *Corolla* funnel-campanulate, *slightly zygomorphic*, 2.2—2.6 cm. long, 2.6 cm. across, 5-lobed, purple, outside glabrous, *scaly on one side*, inside rather densely pubescent at the base of the tube. *Stamens* 10, unequal, 1.2—2.5 cm. long, *as long as the corolla or longer*; filaments densely villous in the lower third. *Ovary* oblong or conoid, 3 mm. long, 5-celled, densely scaly, puberulous at the apex; *style* slender, straight, *longer than the corolla*, longer than the stamens, puberulous at the base, not scaly. *Capsule* 1.2 cm. long, 4 mm. broad, scaly.

R. invictum was discovered by Farrer and Purdom in April—May 1916 in the alpine coppice of the Siku-Satanee Ranges in Kansu, at elevations of 2,440—2,745 m. (8,000—9,000 ft.). It is recorded as being not uncommon in its native home.

A remarkable feature of the plant is the slightly zygomorphic corolla. In this respect and in general appearance, *R. invictum* bears a resemblance to *R. pholidotum*, from which it differs in that the branchlets, petioles, and the outside of the calyx are puberulous, the pedicel is short, 6—8 mm. long, the corolla is scaly only on one side, the stamens are as long as the corolla or longer, and the style is longer than the corolla. It also differs in its geographical distribution. *R. invictum* is a native of Kansu, but *R. pholidotum* comes from north-west Yunnan. The species has not been introduced into cultivation.

Epithet. Unconquered.
Not in cultivation.

R. pholidotum Balf. f. et W.W. Sm. in Notes Roy. Bot. Gard. Edin., Vol. 10 (1917) 132.

A shrub, 92 cm.—2.44 m. (3—8 ft.) high; branchlets glabrous, rather densely or moderately scaly, leaf-bud scales deciduous. *Leaves* evergreen, ovate-lanceolate, oblong-lanceolate, lanceolate or elliptic-lanceolate, aromatic, lamina coriaceous, 4—7.3 cm. long, 1.6—2.8 cm. broad, apex acute or acuminate, mucronate, base obtuse or rounded; upper surface dark green, shining, reticulate, moderately or rather densely scaly, glabrous, midrib rather densely puberulous; *under surface* scaly, the *scales* unequal, very large, yellowish or pale brown, or yellowish and brown, *one-half their own diameter apart*, without scattered larger darker scales; petiole 0.6—1.3 cm. long, glabrous, moderately or rather densely scaly. *Inflorescence* terminal, shortly racemose, 4—8-flowered, flower-bud scales deciduous; rhachis 3—4 mm. long, minutely puberulous or glabrous, scaly or not scaly; pedicel 1.3—2 cm. long, shorter than the corolla, glabrous, moderately or rather densely scaly. *Calyx* 5-lobed, 1—3 mm. long, lobes ovate or triangular, outside glabrous, moderately or densely scaly, margin puberulous or ciliate or glabrous. *Corolla funnel-campanulate or widely funnel-campanulate, slightly zygomorphic,* 2.2—3 cm. long, 2.3—3.4 cm. across, 5-lobed, rose-purple, rose or deep purple, with reddish spots, outside glabrous, rather densely scaly, inside rather densely pubescent at the base of the tube. *Stamens* 10, unequal, 1.3—1.9 cm. long, shorter than the corolla; filaments densely villous in the lower one-half or one-third. *Ovary* conoid or oblong, 3—5 mm. long, 5-celled, densely scaly, pubescent at the apex; style slender, straight, shorter than the corolla, shorter than the taller 2—4 stamens, puberulous at the base or rather densely pubescent in the lower third or glabrous, not scaly. *Capsule* oblong or oblong-oval, 0.8—1 cm. long, 3—4 mm. broad, straight, glabrous or slightly pubescent at the apex, rather densely scaly, calyx persistent.

Forrest first collected this plant in August 1906, on the eastern flank of the Tali Range, north-west Yunnan. He found it again later in the same region. It grows amongst scrub at elevations of 3,050—3,660 m. (10,000—12,000 ft.).

The slightly zygomorphic corolla of *R. pholidotum* is a feature of interest. Moreover, the plant is an octoploid with 104 chromosomes. In this respect it differs markedly from all the other members of its Series. The species is allied to *R. heliolepis* which it resembles in general features, but is distinguished by the widely funnel-campanulate corolla, and by the densely scaly lower surface of the leaves, the scales being one-half their own diameter apart. It is also related to *R. invictum*; the relationship between them is discussed under the latter.

R. pholidotum was introduced by Forrest in 1910 (No. 6762 — the Type number). In cultivation it is a broadly upright shrub up to 6 feet high, well-filled with dark green aromatic leaves, shining on the upper surface, and with very large scales on the lower surface. The flowers appear late in the season, in June and July. The plant is hardy, free-flowering with trusses of 4—8 deep purple flowers with reddish spots. It is uncommon in cultivation, but is worthy of being widely grown.

Epithet. Scaly.
Hardiness 3. June—July.

R. rubiginosum Franch. in Bull. Soc. Bot. France, XXXIV (1887) 282.

Illustration. Bot. Mag. Vol. 124 t. 7621 (1898).

A compact rounded, spreading, bushy, broadly upright or upright shrub, or tree, 60 cm.—9.15 m. (2—30 ft.) high; branchlets densely or moderately scaly, leaf-bud scales deciduous. *Leaves* evergreen, ovate-lanceolate, elliptic-lanceolate, lanceolate or oblong-lanceolate, not aromatic, lamina coriaceous, 3—9 cm. long, 1.3—4.2 cm. broad, apex acute or acutely acuminate, mucronate, base obtuse, rounded or tapered; upper surface dark green, or sometimes paler green, shining or somewhat matt, scaly or not scaly, glabrous, midrib glabrous; *under surface densely scaly*, the *scales* unequal, large, or large and medium-sized, rust-coloured or dark brown or brown, *overlapping or contiguous or nearly contiguous*, with or without widely scattered larger darker scales; petiole 0.5—1.8 cm. long, densely scaly. *Inflorescence* terminal, or sometimes terminal and axillary in the uppermost one to three leaves, shortly racemose, 4—8-flowered, flower-bud scales deciduous; rhachis 2—4 mm. long, glabrous, scaly; pedicel 0.4—1.8 cm. long, shorter than the corolla, rather densely or moderately scaly. *Calyx* 5-lobed or undulately lobed, minute, 0.5—1 mm. long, lobes triangular or ovate, outside densely or moderately scaly, margin eciliate or rarely ciliate, densely or moderately scaly. *Corolla funnel-shaped or funnel-campanulate or tubular-funnel shaped*, 1.6—3.1 cm. long, 1.5—3.5 cm. across, 5-lobed, pink, pale rose, lilac-rose, deep lavender-rose, deep lavender, purple, deep purple, pinkish-purple, lavender-purple or white, with crimson spots, outside scaly, inside rather densely or moderately puberulous at the base or glabrous. *Stamens* 10, unequal, 0.9—2.8 cm. long, shorter than the corolla; filaments puberulous towards the base or sometimes glabrous. *Ovary* oblong or conoid, 3—5 mm. long, 5-celled, densely scaly, glabrous; style slender, straight, as long as the corolla or longer, longer than the stamens, glabrous or rarely puberulous at the base, not scaly. *Capsule* oblong or rarely oblong-oval, 0.9—1.7 cm. long, 3—5 mm. broad, straight, densely scaly, calyx persistent.

19. R. rubiginosum

nat. size

a. flower. b. ovary, style. c. stamen. d. capsule.

R. rubiginosum was described by Franchet in 1887 from a specimen collected by the Abbé Delavay in 1886 on Tsang-chan mountain in west Yunnan. Subsequent gatherings by other collectors show that the plant is distributed in west and north-west Yunnan, south-east Tibet and south-west Szechuan. It grows in open situations in forests, in rhododendron forests, in thickets, in cane brakes, in open mountain pastureland, in spruce, oak, and pine forests, and on granite boulders, at elevations of 2,440—4,270 m. (8,000—14,000 ft.). Forrest records it as forming thickets in side valleys in north-west Yunnan. According to Kingdon-Ward it grows in mixed forests in considerable numbers in the same region. Yü records it as being common at Chungtien and on the Lichiang Snow Range, Yunnan.

In 1913 *R. leclerei* Lévl. was described from a plant collected by E.E. Maire in May 1912, on the high plateau of Ta-Hai-Tse in west Yunnan. It agrees with *R. rubiginosum* in general characters and in morphological details. The only difference between them is that in *R. rubiginosum* the corolla is 2—3.1 cm. long, whereas in *R. leclerei* it is 1.6—2 cm. long. On this distinction alone, *R. leclerei* does not merit specific status.

R. rubiginosum varies considerably in several of its features. It is a shrub or tree, 2—30 feet high; the leaves are ovate-lanceolate to lanceolate, (laminae) 3—9 cm. long, 1.3—4.2 cm. broad; the inflorescence is 4—8-flowered; and the corolla is 1.6—3.1 cm. long. The species is hexaploid with 78 chromosomes, also tetraploid with 52 chromosomes. It is closely allied to *R. desquamatum*; the relationship between them is discussed under the latter.

The species was first introduced to Paris by the Abbé Delavay in 1889. It was reintroduced on several occasions by Forrest, Kingdon-Ward, Rock, and Yü. In its native home it is a shrub or tree, 2—30 feet high. Several forms are in cultivation. At one extreme, the species is a compact rounded shrub, 5 feet high and as much across, densely filled with dark green, ovate-lanceolate leaves, and with deep purple flowers; at the other extreme it is an upright shrub 20 feet high, moderately filled with paler green, lanceolate leaves, and with pink flowers. These extremes are linked with intergrading forms varying in habit and height of growth, in the shape and size of the leaves and flowers, and in flower colour from pink, rose, lilac-rose, deep purple, deep lavender-purple to white, with crimson spots. A common feature of all these forms is the densely scaly lower surface of the leaves with large, overlapping or contiguous or nearly contiguous, rust-coloured or dark brown scales, and with or without widely scattered larger darker scales. One of the best forms is a compact rounded or a broadly upright shrub, 6—8 feet high, well-filled with dark green foliage, with a terminal truss and five or six axillary trusses in the uppermost few leaves, forming a large closely packed compound inflorescence of 25 to 30 flowers. The species often produces good fertile seed in plenty. One of its chief merits is that it flowers at a young age when raised from seed. It is hardy, free-flowering, and is a most desirable plant for every garden. A clone 'Wakehurst' received an Award of Merit when shown by Sir Henry Price Bt., Wakehurst Place, Sussex, in 1960.

Epithet. Reddish-brown.
Hardiness 3. April—May. Plate 29.

R. rubiginosum at 8,700 feet, western Yunnan. Photo J.F. Rock

LAPPONICUM SERIES

General characters: *dwarf or small* (or sometimes medium-sized or large) erect, cushion, compact, or prostrate *shrubs*, 5 cm.—1.22 m. (2 in.—4 ft.) or sometimes up to 3.70 m. (12 ft.) high; branchlets short or long, densely scaly, not bristly, or rarely bristly. Leaves evergreen, oblong, lanceolate linear to obovate, oval or nearly orbicular, *lamina 0.2—2.5 cm.* or sometimes up to 7 cm. *long*, 0.1—1 cm. or sometimes up to 2.8 cm. broad; upper surface densely scaly; under surface densely scaly, the scales overlapping to twice (or rarely up to 4 or 6 times) their own diameter apart. Inflorescence terminal, or rarely terminal and axillary in the uppermost 1—6 leaves, 1—6- or rarely up to 14-flowered; pedicel 0.5—6 mm. or sometimes up to 1.6 cm. long, densely or sometimes moderately scaly. Calyx 5-lobed, 0.5—6 mm. or sometimes up to 1.2 cm. long. *Corolla widely funnel-shaped* or rarely tubular-funnel shaped, *slightly zygomorphic*, 0.5—2 cm. or rarely up to 3.4 cm. long, 5-lobed, yellow, pink, rose, white, purple, pinkish-purple, deep plum—crimson, lavender, lavender-blue to deep violet-purple. Stamens 5—10, long-exserted or rarely included in the corolla-tube. Ovary conoid, rarely ovoid or oblong, 1—2 mm. or rarely 3 mm. long, 5- or rarely 6-celled; *style long or short, slender and straight.* Capsule conoid or oblong or sometimes ovoid, 2—7 mm. or rarely up to 1.4 cm. long, 2—4 mm. or rarely 5 mm. broad.

Distribution: north of Sweden and Norway, Greenland, north-east U.S.A., Canadian Arctic; eastern U.S.S.R.; Siberia to north-east China, Nepal, Sikkim, Bhutan to Assam, Tibet, Upper Burma, Yunnan, Szechuan, Kansu, Japan.

A large Series of fifty species, divided into Cuneatum Subseries and Lapponicum Subseries. The species are dwarf or small shrubs, except *R. cuneatum* (Cuneatum Subseries) a medium-sized or large shrub, and are usually characterised by the widely funnel-shaped, slightly zygomorphic corolla and long-exserted slender straight style.

A distinct Series showing a tendency towards the Saluenense Series.

KEY TO THE SUBSERIES

A. Dwarf or small shrubs up to 1.53 m. (5 ft.) high; leaves (laminae) usually 0.2—4 cm. long; calyx usually up to 6 mm. long; corolla 0.5—2 cm. long *Lapponicum Subseries*

A. Medium or large shrub up to 3.70 m. (12 ft.) high; leaves (laminae) 1.4—7 cm. long; calyx up to 1.2 cm. long; corolla 1.6—3.4 cm. long .... *Cuneatum Subseries*

CUNEATUM SUBSERIES

General characters: usually a large shrub, 30 cm.—3.70 m. (1—12 ft.) high; branchlets long or short, thick, densely scaly. Leaves evergreen, oval, oblong-oval to oblong or lanceolate, lamina 1.4—7 cm. long, 0.6—2.8 cm. broad, upper surface densely scaly; under surface densely scaly, the scales contiguous or overlapping or nearly contiguous. Inflorescence terminal, 1—6-flowered; pedicel 0.2—1.6 cm. long, moderately or densely scaly. Calyx 5-lobed, 0.4—1.2 cm. long. Corolla tubular-funnel shaped or widely funnel-shaped, slightly zygomorphic, 1.6—3.4 cm. long, 5-lobed, deep rose, rose, rose-lavender to lavender-blue. Stamens 10, long-exserted. Ovary conoid, 2—3 mm. long, 5-celled. Style long, slender and straight. Capsule conoid or oblong, 0.6—1.4 cm. long, 4—5 mm. broad.

DESCRIPTION OF THE SPECIES

R. cuneatum W.W. Sm. in Notes Roy. Bot. Gard. Edin., Vol. 8 (1914) 200.
Illustration. Bot. Mag. Vol. 162 t. 9561 (1939). Figured as *R. ravum*.

A broadly upright spreading, or somewhat compact or bushy shrub, *usually large*, 30 cm.—3.70 m. (1—12 ft.) high; branchlets long or short, thick, densely scaly with flaky scales, glabrous, leaf-bud scales deciduous. *Leaves* evergreen, oblong-lanceolate, oblong, oblong-elliptic, oblong-oval, oval or lanceolate, *large*, lamina 1.4—7 cm. long, 0.6—2.8 cm. broad, apex obtuse, rounded or rarely acute, mucronate, base obtuse or rounded; upper surface pale green, matt, densely scaly, the scales one-half to their own diameter apart or contiguous or overlapping; under surface densely scaly, the *scales are characteristic, similar in size and colour*, large, brown or dark brown or fawn or creamy-yellow or rarely cinnamon-red, contiguous or overlapping or nearly contiguous, without or rarely with closely scattered dark brown scales; petiole 0.2—1.5 cm. long, densely scaly. *Inflorescence* terminal, umbellate, 1—6-flowered, flower-bud scales subpersistent or persistent or deciduous; rhachis 1—5 mm. long, not scaly or scaly, puberulous or glabrous; pedicel 0.2—1.6 cm. long, moderately or densely scaly, glabrous. *Calyx* 5-lobed, *large* 0.4—1.2 cm. long, reddish, pink or greenish, lobes oblong-oval, oval, elliptic, oblong-lanceolate or oblong, outside scaly along the middle or rarely not scaly, glabrous, margin not scaly or rarely scaly, fringed with long hairs or rarely glabrous. *Corolla* tubular-funnel shaped or widely funnel-shaped, slightly zygomorphic, *large*, 1.6—3.4 cm. long, 5-lobed, rose-lavender, deep rose, rose, deep rose-purple, purple, lavender, purple-lavender or lavender-blue, with or without deeper spots, outside scaly on the lobes or not scaly, glabrous. *Stamens* 10, unequal, long-exserted, long, as long as the corolla or a little shorter or longer, 1.2—3 cm. in length; filaments villous towards the base. *Ovary* conoid, 2—3 mm. long, 5-celled, densely scaly, glabrous or rarely with a tuft of hairs at the apex; style long, slender, straight, longer than the stamens, longer than the corolla, not scaly, pubescent at the base or rarely glabrous. *Capsule* conoid or oblong,

20. R. cuneatum
nat. size

a. petals. b. stamens. c. ovary, style. d. capsule. e. capsule (enclosed).

0.6—1.4 cm. long, 4—5 mm. broad, densely scaly, glabrous or sometimes hairy at the apex, enclosed by the persistent calyx-lobes or sometimes not enclosed.

R. cuneatum was discovered by Forrest in October 1910 on the eastern flank of the Lichiang Range, western Yunnan. It was later found by him and other collectors in other localities in mid-west and north-west Yunnan and in south-west Szechuan. The plant grows on rocky slopes, on limestone cliffs, amongst rocks and scrub, in thickets and cane brakes, in pastures, in pine and oak forests, at elevations of 2,745—4,270 m. (9,000—14,000 ft.).

In 1916 *R. ravum* Balf. f. et W. W. Sm. was described from a specimen No. 10423 collected by Forrest in July 1913 on the mountains in the north-east of the Yangtze bend, Yunnan, and in 1919 *R. cheilanthum* Balf. f. et Forrest was founded on Forrest's No. 10435 from the same locality. These species agree with *R. cuneatum* in the shape and size of the leaves, in the shape, size and colour of the flowers, and in all other characters they are identical. *R. habaense* Balf. f. et Forrest nomen is synonymous with *R. cuneatum*. *R. cuneatum* is a hexaploid with 78 chromosomes.

The species was first introduced by Forrest in 1913 (No. 10423). It was reintroduced several times by him and by Kingdon-Ward, Rock, McLaren, and Yü. It first flowered at Caerhays and elsewhere in April 1917. In cultivation it is a broadly upright spreading or somewhat compact shrub up to 6 feet high with thick branchlets, although in its native home it reaches 12 feet in height. The plant is very hardy and fairly fast-growing. It is free-flowering, and provides a fine display with its deep rose, rose or purple flowers in clusters of three to six.

Epithet. Wedge-shaped.
Hardiness 3. April—May. Plate 30.

R. cuneatum is an aberrant species in the Lapponicum Series. It has little in common with the species of this Series. It differs markedly in its height of growth up to 3.70 m. (12 ft.), in the size of the leaves (laminae) up to 7 cm. long and 2.8 cm. broad, in the size of the calyx up to 1.2 cm. long, and in the size of the corolla up to 3.4 cm. long. In some respects it is comparable with the species of the Triflorum Series and Heliolepis Series; in other features it does not conform to the members of these Series, particularly in its large calyx. *R. cuneatum* is so distinctive that it does not fit well into any known Series. Accordingly, it is now placed in a Subseries by itself in the Lapponicum Series.

LAPPONICUM SUBSERIES

General characters: dwarf or small, erect or compact or cushion or prostrate shrubs, 5 cm.—1.53 m. (2 in.—5 ft.) high; branchlets short or long, densely scaly. Leaves evergreen, oblong, lanceolate, linear, obovate, elliptic, oblong-oval, oval, ovate or nearly orbicular, lamina 0.2—3.5 cm. or sometimes 4 cm. or rarely up to 6.5 cm. long, 0.1—1.1 cm. or sometimes up to 2.3 cm. broad, upper surface densely scaly; under surface densely scaly, the scales overlapping to twice (or rarely up to 4 or 6 times) their own diameter apart. Inflorescence terminal, or rarely terminal and axillary in the uppermost 1—6 leaves, 1—6- or sometimes up to 8- or rarely 14-flowered; pedicel 0.5—5 mm. or sometimes up to 9 mm. or rarely 1.2 cm. long, densely or sometimes moderately scaly. Calyx 5-lobed, 0.5—6 mm. or rarely 8 mm. long. Corolla widely funnel-shaped, rarely tubular-funnel shaped or flat, slightly zygomorphic, 0.5—2 cm. long, 5-lobed, yellow, pink, rose, white, purple, deep plum-crimson, lavender, lavender-blue to deep violet-purple. Stamens 5—10, long-exserted or sometimes included in the corolla-tube. Ovary conoid, rarely ovoid or oblong, 1—2 mm. or rarely 3 mm. long, 5- or rarely 6-celled; style long or short, slender and straight. Capsule conoid or oblong, or sometimes ovoid, 2—7 mm. long, 2—4 mm. broad.

KEY TO THE SPECIES

1. Flowers yellow.

    2. Upper surface of the leaves greyish-green or pale green, matt; branchlets not puberulous; scales on the under surface of the leaves overlapping or contiguous or one-half their own diameter apart, bicolorous, dark brown and yellow, or sometimes unicolorous, dark brown; stamens 5—10. .. *chryseum*

    2. Upper surface of the leaves dark green, shining; branchlets rather densely puberulous (or rarely glabrous); scales on the under surface of the leaves one-half to twice their own diameter apart, unicolorous, dark brown or brown, stamens 10 .... *flavidum*

1. Flowers white, pink, rose, purple, lavender to deep violet-purple.

    3. Flowers white.

        4. Corolla scaly outside the lobes; scales on the under surface of the leaves characteristic, similar in size and colour, creamy-yellow or fawn (densely set) with closely or widely scattered dark brown scales .... *bulu*
                                                                       (part)

        4. Corolla not scaly outside; scales on the under surface of the leaves brown, fawn or greenish (densely set) without scattered dark brown scales.

            5. Compact rounded shrub; style medium in length, as long as the stamens; calyx 0.5 mm. long; corolla 0.8—1 cm. long; stamens short, 6—8 mm. long .... *microleucum*

            5. Usually broadly upright shrub; style long, longer than the stamens; calyx 1—2 mm. long; corolla 1—1.3 cm. long; stamens long, 0.8—1.3 cm. in length .... *parvifolium*
                                                                  var. *albiflorum*

    3. Flowers pink, rose, purple, lavender to deep violet-purple.

        6. Branchlets, petioles and usually leaf margins moderately or rather densely bristly; under surface of the leaves, and pedicels bristly or not bristly .... *setosum*

        6. Branchlets, petioles, margins and under surface of the leaves, and pedicels not bristly.

            7. Corolla-tube and the base of the lobes puberulous outside .... *dasypetalum*

            7. Corolla-tube and the lobes not puberulous outside.

                8. Stamens and style very short, usually included, concealed in the corolla-tube; corolla tubular-funnel shaped.

                    9. Usually an upright lax shrub; scales on the under surface of the leaves characteristic, similar in size and colour, pale greyish (whitish); corolla usually lavender-blue, or pale or dark blue .. *intricatum*

                    9. Compact rounded, or low spreading shrub; scales on the under surface of the leaves brown or pale brown, or yellowish and brown; corolla deep rose-purple, very pale purple, pink or rosy-violet.

                        10. Compact rounded shrub; scales on the under surface of the leaves brown or pale brown; stamens 5 or 6, 3—5 mm. long. North-west Yunnan species ..... *complexum*

10. Low spreading shrub; scales on the under surface of the leaves yellowish and brown; stamens 5—10, 7—8 mm. long. U.S.S.R. species ...... *burjaticum*

8. Stamens and style short or long, exserted from the corolla-tube; corolla widely funnel-shaped.

11. Scales on the under surface of the leaves characteristic, all similar in size and colour, creamy-yellow or fawn, overlapping, without scattered dark brown scales.

12. Style and stamens short, ½ or sometimes ⅔ the length of the corolla; style shorter than, or sometimes as long as, the stamens.

13. Stamens 5, 3—4 mm. long; corolla small, 5 mm. long .... *tsai*

13. Stamens 10 (or rarely 8), usually 5 mm.—1.4 cm. long; corolla larger, usually 6 mm.—1.1 cm. (or rarely 1.5 cm.) long.

14. Flower sessile or nearly sessile; pedicel hardly 0.5 mm. long; corolla flat with very short tube; ovary completely exposed, visible .... *thymifolium* (part)

14. Flower not sessile; pedicel 0.5—5 mm. long; corolla widely funnel-shaped with distinct tube, not flat; ovary concealed within the corolla-tube, not visible.

15. Inflorescence 3—8-flowered; pedicel 2—5 mm. long; leaves (laminae) 1—4 cm. long .... *hippophaeoides*

15. Inflorescence usually 1—2-flowered; pedicel 0.5—1 mm. long; leaves (laminae) usually 3 mm.—1 cm. long.

16. Leaves lanceolate, oblanceolate or oblong; corolla-lobes not scaly outside .. *spilanthum* (part)

16. Leaves oval, ovate, elliptic, oblong-ovate or rarely oblong; corolla-lobes scaly outside along the middle .... *diacritum* (part)

12. Style and stamens long, protruding; stamens as long as the corolla or a little longer; style longer than both the stamens and the corolla.

17. Leaves lanceolate, oblong-lanceolate, oblong or oblong-oval; broadly upright or very lax upright shrub up to 4½ feet high; corolla not scaly outside.

18. Leaves (laminae) usually 1.8—3.5 cm. long, 6 mm.—1.5 cm. broad; pedicel usually 4—9 mm. long... .... *fimbriatum*

18. Leaves (laminae) usually 3 mm.—1.6 cm. long, 2—5 mm. broad; pedicel 0.5—5 mm. long.

19. Corolla 1—1.7 cm. long; pedicel 1—5 mm. long; calyx 1—4 mm. long; shrub 1—4½ ft. high .... *websterianum*

19. Corolla usually 6—9 mm. long; pedicel 0.5—1 mm. long; calyx 0.5—1 mm. long; shrub 1—2 feet high .. *polifolium*

17. Leaves ovate or oval; compact rounded shrub up to 1½ feet high; corolla-lobes usually scaly outside .... *idoneum* (part)

11. Scales on the under surface of the leaves dissimilar or similar in size and colour, dark brown, brown, cinnamon-brown (or rarely fawn), overlapping, contiguous to 6 times their own diameter apart, with or without closely or widely scattered dark brown scales.

    20. Corolla not scaly outside (to p. 173).

        21. Style short, much shorter than the stamens.

            22. Scales on the under surface of the leaves ½ to twice their own diameter apart . . . . *lysolepis*
(part)

            22. Scales on the under surface of the leaves usually overlapping or nearly contiguous.

                23. Leaves lanceolate, linear-lanceolate, oblanceolate or sometimes oblong.

                    24. Rounded somewhat compact or broadly upright shrub; scales on the under surface of the leaves usually dark brown, brown or cinnamon-brown, pedicel 1—3 mm. long; leaf apex acute or obtuse . . . . *orthocladum*
(part)

                    24. Upright somewhat lax shrub; scales on the under surface of the leaves fawn; pedicel 0.5—1 mm. long; leaf apex rounded or obtuse . . . . *spilanthum*
(part)

                23. Leaves usually ovate, oval, elliptic or oblong-elliptic.

                    25. Usually compact rounded shrubs up to 3½ feet high; leaves (laminae) up to 2 cm. long; scales on the under surface of the leaves overlapping to ½ their own diameter apart.

                        26. Inflorescence 1—2- or sometimes 3—4-flowered; corolla usually 8 mm.—1 cm. long; shrub up to 2 feet high . . . . *oresbium*

                        26. Inflorescence usually 3—6-flowered; corolla usually 1—1.5 cm. long; shrub up to 3½ feet high . . . .
. . . . *yungningense*
(part)

                    25. Usually broadly upright shrubs up to 1 foot high; leaves (laminae) up to 8 mm. long; scales on the under surface of the leaves overlapping or nearly contiguous.

                        27. Corolla usually 1.4 cm. long, lavender-purple; calyx 2 mm. long; stamens 10; scales on the under surface of the leaves overlapping . . . .
. . . . *alpicola*

                        27. Corolla 8 mm.—1.2 cm. long; usually purplish-red; calyx 0.5—2 mm. long; stamens 8—10; scales on the under surface of the leaves overlapping or nearly contiguous . . *ramosissimum*
(part)

        21. Style medium or long, as long as the stamens or longer.

                    28. Style medium, as long as the stamens.

                        29. Robust shrub up to 3½ feet high with thick branchlets; leaves (laminae) up to 2 cm. long, upper surface greyish-green, matt; inflorescence usually 3—6-flowered . . . . *yungningense*
(part)

                        29. Shrub usually up to 2 feet high with slender branchlets; leaves (laminae) up to 1 cm. long, upper surface dark or pale green, shining or sometimes matt; inflorescence 1—2-flowered.

30. Usually rounded somewhat compact shrub; upper surface of the leaves dark green, shining; corolla usually deep rose-purple; scales on the under surface of the leaves often ½ to twice their own diameter apart .... *stictophyllum* (part)

30. Usually broadly upright shrub; upper surface of the leaves pale green, matt; corolla usually purplish-red; scales on the under surface of the leaves overlapping or nearly contiguous .... *ramosissimum* (part)

28. Style long, longer than the stamens.

31. Under surface of the leaves laxly scaly, the scales 1½—6 times their own diameter apart; margins of the leaves crenulate; branchlets rather densely puberulous; pedicels 5—8 mm. long; dwarf shrub, 4 inches to 1 foot high .... *fragariflorum*

31. Under surface of the leaves usually densely scaly, the scales overlapping, contiguous, ½ or sometimes up to twice their own diameter apart; margins of the leaves entire; branchlets usually glabrous; pedicels usually 0.5—5 mm. long, usually small or large shrubs up to 5 feet high.

32. Inflorescence 3—14-flowered (to p. 171).

33. Usually large shrub, up to 5 feet high; leaves (laminae) up to 6.5 cm. long; inflorescence usually 4—14-flowered; calyx 3—6 mm. (or rarely 1 mm.) long; scales on the under surface of the leaves often bicolorous, dark brown and yellow .... *russatum*

33. Usually small shrubs up to 3 feet high; leaves (laminae) up to 2.6 cm. long; inflorescence usually 3—5-flowered; calyx usually 0.5—3 mm. long; scales on the under surface of the leaves unicolorous, dark brown, brown, pale brown or sometimes cinnamon-brown.

34. Corolla usually deep reddish, bright rose, rose-purple or pink; pedicels usually 4 mm.—1 cm. long. From the Arctic, circumpolar; and N.E. Asia, from Siberia to Alaska.

35. Usually a prostrate or spreading shrub, usually 5—30 cm. (2 in.—1 ft.) high, leaves (laminae) up to 1.5 cm. long; corolla up to 1 cm. long; stamens 5—10. From the Arctic, circumpolar.. *lapponicum*

35. Rounded or broadly upright shrub, 30 cm.—1 m. (1—3⅓ ft.) high; leaves (laminae) up to 2.5 cm. long; corolla up to 1.3 cm. long; stamens 10. From N.E. Asia, from Siberia to Alaska .... *parvifolium*

34. Corolla usually deep blue-purple, bluish-purple, violet-mauve, lavender or pale rose-purple; pedicels 0.5—3 mm. long (except *R. scintillans* 1—5 mm.). From Yunnan, Szechuan and Kansu.

36. Inflorescence usually terminal and axillary in the uppermost 1—6 leaves, forming a compound inflorescence of 20—25 flowers, compact; broadly upright shrub with thick stiff upright branchlets 10—12 cm. (4—5 in.) long .... *compactum*

36. Inflorescence terminal, not axillary, not forming a compact group; compact, cushion, spreading or broadly upright shrubs, with short branchlets (except in *R. scintillans*).

37. Spreading shrub, with slender upright branchlets 7—15 cm. (3—6 in.) long; leaves lanceolate or oblong; scales on the under surface of the leaves ½ their own diameter apart or nearly contiguous .... *scintillans*

37. Broadly upright or upright or compact or cushion shrubs, usually with short branchets 1—5 cm. (0.4—2 in.) long; leaves ovate, oval, elliptic, oblong-oval, oblong (or rarely lanceolate in *R. polycladum*); scales on the under surface of the leaves overlapping, nearly contiguous or ½ their own diameter apart.

    38. Calyx usually 0.5—3 mm. long.

        39. Somewhat lax upright shrub; upper surface of the leaves olive-green, lamina usually 1.2—2.4 cm. long; pedicel 0.5—1 mm. long . . . .
. . . . *capitatum*

        39. Very compact or compact or broadly upright shrubs; upper surface of the leaves dark green, glaucous-green or greyish-green, lamina usually 5 mm.—1.5 cm. long; pedicel 0.5—3 mm. long.

            40. Corolla 1—1.6 cm. long, purple, lavender, deep or pale rose-purple or deep blue-purple; leaves usually oblong, oblong-oval, elliptic or lanceolate.

                41. Very compact or compact or sometimes broadly upright shrubs; upper surface of the leaves dark green or markedly glaucous-grey; calyx usually 2—5 mm. long; scales on the under surface of the leaves ½ their own diameter apart or nearly contiguous or overlapping.

                    42. Very compact spreading or rounded shrub; upper surface of the adult and young leaves dark green, not glaucous . . . . . . *impeditum* (part)

                    42. Compact or broadly upright shrub; upper surface of the adult and particularly of the young leaves markedly glaucous-grey . . *fastigiatum* (part)

                41. Broadly upright shrubs; upper surface of the leaves greyish-green; calyx 0.5—1 mm. long; scales on the under surface of the leaves usually overlapping.

                    43. Corolla 1—1.6 cm. long; leaves elliptic, oblong-oval, oblong-elliptic or oblong . . *tapetiforme* (part)

                    43. Corolla 1 cm. long; leaves oblong or lanceolate . . . .
. . . . *polycladum*

            40. Corolla usually 1 cm. long, violet-purple; leaves usually oval or ovate . . . *violaceum* (part)

    38. Calyx 4—5 mm. long . . . . *amundsenianum*

32. Inflorescence 1—2-flowered (from p. 170).

44. Under surface of the leaves densely scaly, the scales overlapping.
    45. Leaves (laminae) usually 1—1.5 cm. long.
        46. Leaves oblong, oblong-oval or oblong-elliptic, upper surface greyish-green, matt, laminae up to 1.5 cm. long; calyx 0.5—1 mm. long; corolla usually pink, pale purple, pale rose-purple or purple-blue ....
        .... *tapetiforme*
        (part)
        46. Leaves usually ovate, oval, or elliptic, upper surface dark green, shining, laminae up to 1.2 cm. long; calyx 0.5—3 mm. long; corolla violet-purple or pinkish-violet.
            47. Corolla usually 9 mm.—1.1 cm. long; pedicel 0.5—3 mm. long; stamens 10 .... *violaceum*
            (part)
            47. Corolla 1.2—1.3 cm. long; pedicel 1 mm. long; stamens 8—10 .....
            .... *nitidulum*
    45. Leaves (laminae) usually 2—9 mm. long.
        48. Corolla usually 1.2—1.7 cm. long; shrubs up to 1.22 m. (4 ft.) high.
            49. Upper surface of the leaves pale greyish-green, matt; calyx 0.5—2 mm. long; corolla usually purple-blue or purple .... *edgarianum*
            (part)
            49. Upper surface of the leaves dark green, shining; calyx 2—4 mm. long; corolla rose-lilac ..... *nitidulum* var.
            nubigenum
        48. Corolla usually 8 mm.—1 cm. long; shrubs up to 60 cm. (2 ft.) high.
            50. Shrubs up to 60 cm. (2 ft.) high; upper surface of the leaves dark green, shining, under surface of the leaves usually without scattered dark brown scales.
                51. Usually rounded or somewhat compact shrub; calyx 0.5—3 mm. long; corolla usually deep rose-purple .... *stictophyllum*
                (part)
                51. Broadly upright shrub; calyx 0.5—1 mm. long; corolla usually pink ...... *nigropunctatum*
                (part)
             50. Shrub often up to 25 cm. (10 in.) high; upper surface of the leaves pale greyish-green, matt, under surface with closely or widely scattered dark brown scales .... *nivale*
            (part)
44. Under surface of the leaves laxly scaly, the scales ½ to twice their own diameter apart or rarely nearly contiguous.
            52. Scales on the under surface of the leaves brown or pale brown, with closely or widely scattered dark brown scales.
                53. Usually rounded somewhat compact shrub up to 76 cm. (2½ ft.) high; upper surface of the leaves dark green, somewhat shining; leaves (laminae) 3 mm.—1.4 cm. long; corolla usually violet, bluish-purple or lavender .....
                .... *paludosum*

53. Usually straggly or upright shrub, often up to 25 cm. (10 in.) high; upper surface of the leaves pale greyish-green, matt; leaves (laminae) 2 mm.—1 cm. long; corolla usually reddish-purple, deep purple or deep pink .
.... *nivale*
(part)

52. Scales on the under surface of the leaves brown or dark brown, without scattered darker brown scales.

> **54.** Very compact spreading or rounded shrub, with short thick branchlets; scales on the under surface of the leaves ½ their own diameter apart .... *impeditum*
> (part)

> **54.** Broadly upright or upright or sometimes bushy shrubs, with long slender or sometimes short thick branchlets; scales on the under surface of the leaves ½ to twice their own diameter apart.

>> **55.** Upper surface of the leaves pale greyish-green, matt; corolla 1.5—2.5 cm. across .... *edgarianum*
>> (part)

>> **55.** Upper surface of the leaves dark green, shining; corolla usually 1—1.5 cm. across.

>>> **56.** Calyx 0.5—1 mm. long; leaves (laminae) 5—9 mm. long; corolla usually pink; scales on the under surface of the leaves ½ their own diameter apart .... *nigropunctatum*
>>> (part)

>>> **56.** Calyx usually 2—4 mm. long; leaves (laminae) usually 8 mm.—1.5 cm. long; corolla purple-violet, dark purple, pinkish-purple, reddish-purple to plum-purple; scales on the under surface of the leaves ½ to twice their own diameter apart.

>>>> **57.** Corolla 8—9 mm. long, often pinkish-purple; stamens 6—9 mm. long .... *lysolepis*
>>>> (part)

>>>> **57.** Corolla 1—1.5 cm. long, often plum-purple; stamens 7 mm.—1.2 cm. long ... *litangense*

20. Corolla scaly outside the lobes (from p. 169).

>> **58.** Style short, shorter than, or sometimes as long as, the stamens.

>>> **59.** Flower sessile or nearly sessile; pedicel hardly 0.5 mm. long; corolla flat with very short tube; ovary completely exposed, visible .
>>> .... *thymifolium*
>>> (part)

>>> **59.** Flower not sessile; pedicel 0.5—2 mm. long; corolla widely funnel-shaped with distinct tube, not flat; ovary concealed within the corolla-tube, not visible ....
>>> .... *drumonium*

>> **58.** Style long, longer than the stamens.

>>> **60.** Inflorescence 3—8 flowered; calyx usually 3—6 mm. long.

>>>> **61.** Scales on the under surface of the leaves usually bi-colorous, dark brown and yellow; corolla deep plum-purple, plum-purple, deep plum-crimson or black-purple .... *rupicola*

    61. Scales on the under surface of the leaves unicolorous, dark or pale brown; corolla deep purple-blue, purplish-blue, lavender-rose or purplish-rose.

        62. Compact or broadly upright shrub; adult and particularly young leaves markedly glaucous-grey; corolla 1—1.5 cm. long; scales on the under surface of the leaves pale brown to dark brown, overlapping or nearly contiguous or ½ their own diameter apart .... *fastigiatum* (part)

        62. Upright shrub; adult and young leaves dark green; corolla 1.4—1.8 cm. long; scales on the under surface of the leaves dark brown or rufescent, overlapping .... *sclerocladum*

60. Inflorescence 1—2- (or rarely 3-) flowered; calyx 0.5—2 mm. or sometimes 3 mm. long.

        63. Scales on the under surface of the leaves brown, overlapping, usually with closely or widely scattered dark brown scales; corolla usually 7 mm.—1.1 cm. long.

            64. Leaves usually oval, ovate, oblong-ovate or elliptic; usually broadly upright and spreading shrub .... *diacritum* (part)

            64. Leaves lanceolate, oblanceolate, oblong-lanceolate or oblong; upright shrub .... *telmateium*

        63. Scales on the under surface of the leaves usually creamy-yellow or fawn, ½ their own diameter apart or nearly contiguous or overlapping, or without closely or widely scattered dark brown scales; corolla 1.1—1.6 cm. long.

            65. Branchlets pilose; stamens 7—8; scales on the under surface of the leaves ½ or their own diameter apart .. .. *verruculosum*

            65. Branchlets not pilose; stamens 10; scales on the under surface of the leaves overlapping or nearly contiguous.

                66. Compact rounded shrub, 15—45 cm. (6 in.—1½ ft.) high with short branchlets; leaves ovate or oval, (laminae) 5 mm.—1.4 cm. long .... *idoneum* (part)

                66. Upright shrub, 30 cm.—1.53 m. (1—5 ft.) high, usually with long branchlets; leaves oblong, oblong-oval or oblong-elliptic, (laminae) 9 mm.—2.3 cm. long .... *bulu* (part)

DESCRIPTION OF THE SPECIES

R. alpicola Rehd. et Wils. in Plantae Wilsonianae (1913) 506.

    A small somewhat rounded or sometimes broadly upright shrub, 30 cm.—1.37 m. (1—4½ ft.) high; branchlets short, densely scaly, leaf-bud scales deciduous. *Leaves* evergreen, ovate, elliptic or rarely oval, lamina 5—8 mm. long, 2—5 mm. broad, apex obtuse, base rounded or broadly cuneate; upper surface densely scaly; under surface densely scaly, the scales pale yellowish-red, overlapping; petiole 1—2 mm. long, scaly. *Inflorescence* terminal, 1- or sometimes 2—3-flowered, flower-bud scales deciduous; pedicel very short. *Calyx* 5-lobed, 2 mm. long, lobes oblong or rounded, densely scaly, margin sparsely ciliate. *Corolla* funnel-shaped, 1.2—1.4 cm. long, lavender-purple, outside not scaly, glabrous. *Stamens* 10, unequal, exserted, slightly shorter than the corolla, 7—9 mm. long; filaments villous towards the base. *Ovary* conoid, about 2 mm. long, 5-celled, densely scaly; *style short, shorter than the stamens*, pubescent in the lower part or sometimes glabrous. *Capsule* ovoid, about 4 mm. long, densely scaly.

This species was discovered by Wilson in July 1908, north of Tatsienlu, western Szechuan, growing in moorlands at elevations of 4,000—5,000 m. (13,111—16,393 ft.)

In 1913, *R. alpicola*, Rehd. et Wils. var. *strictum*, Rehd. et Wils. was described from a specimen also collected by Wilson in the same month in the same region. It was said to differ from the species in its more fastigiate habit, in the nearly equal calyx-lobes, and in the glabrous style. However, in these and in all other characters the variety agrees with *R. alpicola* under which it will now be placed in synonymy.

R. alpicola shows a strong resemblance to *R. ramosissimum*, particularly in the shape and size of the leaves, and in the short style, but is distinguished by the larger corolla, usually by the larger calyx, and by the colour of the scales on the lower surface of the leaves.

The species was introduced by Wilson possibly in 1908. In cultivation it is a small, somewhat rounded shrub, 1½ feet high with short branchlets and tiny leaves. It is very hardy, and the single lavender-purple flowers are produced freely. The plant is well suited for the rock garden. It is rare in cultivation.

Epithet. A dweller in high mountains.
Hardiness 3—4. April—May.

R. amundsenianum Hand.-Mazz. in Anz. Akad. Wiss. Wien, No. 4—5 (1921).

A shrub 30 cm. (1 ft.) high; branchlets short, densely scaly with flaky scales, glabrous, leaf-bud scales deciduous. *Leaves* oblong-oval or elliptic, lamina 0.9—1.5 cm. long, 5—7 mm. broad, apex rounded, mucronate, base rounded or obtuse; upper surface green, matt, densely scaly, the scales overlapping; under surface densely scaly, the scales large, dark brown, overlapping or contiguous; petiole 1—2 mm. long, densely scaly, glabrous. *Inflorescence* terminal, umbellate, 3-flowered, flower-bud scales persistent; pedicel 2—3 mm. long, densely scaly. *Calyx 4—5 mm. long*, lobes ovate, outside scaly, margin densely ciliate. *Corolla* and stamens not seen. *Ovary* densely scaly; style long, densely pilose at the base. *Capsule* 3 mm. long.

R. amundsenianum is represented by a single rather inadequate specimen. It was collected by Handel-Mazzetti in April 1914 on Mount Lose-schan, near Ningyuen, Szechuan, at an elevation of 3,900—4,250 m. (12,787—13,934 ft.).

In the original diagnosis it is associated with *R. pycnocladum* (now a synonym of *R. diacritum*) and *R. nitidulum*. There would appear to be very little difference between *R. amundsenianum* and *R. nitidulum* also from Szechuan, but the scanty material is insufficient as conclusive evidence. The plant has not been introduced into cultivation.

Epithet. After E. Amundsen, a missionary in Yunnanfu.
Not in cultivation.

R. bulu Hutch. in Rhod. Soc. Notes, Vol. 3, No. 5 (1929—31) 280.

An upright shrub, 30 cm.—1.53 m. (1—5 ft.) high; branchlets long or short, densely scaly with flaky scales, glabrous, leaf-bud scales deciduous. *Leaves* evergreen, oblong, oblong-oval or oblong-elliptic, lamina 0.9—2.3 cm. long, 3—8 mm. broad, apex obtuse or rounded, mucronate, base obtuse or tapered; upper surface pale green, matt, densely scaly, the scales nearly contiguous or overlapping; *under surface densely scaly, the scales are characteristic*, similar in size and colour, large, *creamy-yellow or fawn, nearly contiguous or overlapping, with closely or widely scattered dark brown scales*; petiole 1—2 mm. long, densely scaly, glabrous. *Inflorescence* terminal, or rarely terminal and axillary in the uppermost two or three leaves, umbellate, 1—3-flowered, flower-bud scales subpersistent or persistent; rhachis 0.5—1 mm. long, scaly or not scaly, glabrous; pedicel 1—2 mm. long, densely scaly, glabrous or rarely rather densely puberulous. *Calyx* 5-lobed, 1—3 mm. long, pink or reddish, lobes ovate, lanceolate or oblong-oval, outside moderately or densely scaly, glabrous, margin scaly, eciliate or ciliate. *Corolla* widely funnel-shaped, slightly zygomorphic, 1.1—1.6 cm. long, 5-lobed, pure white, bright purple, magenta, deep violet-magenta, purplish or pinkish-purple, outside scaly along the middle of the lobes, glabrous. *Stamens* 10, unequal, exserted, long, as long as the corolla or a little longer, 1—1.5 cm. in length; filaments villous towards the base. *Ovary* conoid, 2 mm. long, 5-celled, densely scaly, glabrous; style long, longer than the stamens, scaly at the base or rarely not scaly, glabrous or rarely puberulous at the base. *Capsule* conoid, 3—4 mm. long, 2 mm. broad, densely scaly, glabrous, calyx-lobes persistent.

Kingdon-Ward discovered this plant in May 1924 at Chake, Tsangpo Valley below Nang Dzong, south-east Tibet. He found it again later in the same month at Lusha, in the same region. In 1936 Ludlow and Sherriff collected it in south Tibet; later, with Taylor or Elliot, they found it again in other localities in south-east Tibet. It grows in birch copse, in oak woods, in larch, Abies and pine forests, and amongst rocks by rivers, at elevations of 2,989—3,813 m. (9,800—12,500 ft.). Ludlow, Sherriff and Elliot record it as being a very common plant at Miling, in the Tsangpo Valley, Kongbo.

The species varies considerably in height of growth, ranging from 30 cm. to 1.53 m. (1—5 ft.), in leaf size from 9 mm. to 2.3 cm. long, and in flower colour from pure white, pinkish-purple, bright purple to deep violet-magenta. It resembles *R. websterianum* in leaf shape and size, in the creamy-yellow or fawn overlapping scales on the lower surface of the leaves, in the 1—3-flowered inflorescence, and in the size of the corolla, but is distinguished by the scaly corolla-lobes, usually by the shorter pedicels, and by the superimposed closely or widely scattered dark brown scales on the lower surface of the leaves. There is no record of its occurrence in cultivation.

Epithet. A native name in Assam.

Not in cultivation.

R. burjaticum Malyschev in Not. Syst. Herb. Inst. Bot. Acad. Sci. U.S.S.R. XXI (1961) 455—458.

A low spreading, much branched shrub, up to 15 cm. (6 in.) high; branchlets densely scaly, glabrous, leaf-bud scales deciduous. *Leaves* elliptic or ovate, lamina coriaceous, 0.7—1.2 cm. long, 3—6 mm. broad, apex obtuse or rounded, mucronate, base obtuse or rounded; upper surface dark green, matt, densely scaly, the scales overlapping; margin slightly recurved; under surface densely scaly, the scales medium-sized, yellowish and brown, overlapping; petiole 1—3 mm. long, densely scaly, glabrous. *Inflorescence* terminal, umbellate, 2—5-flowered, flower-bud scales deciduous; rhachis 0.5—1 mm. long, scaly, glabrous; pedicel 1—3 mm. long, densely scaly, glabrous. *Calyx* 5-lobed, minute, 0.5 mm. long, lobes ovate or triangular, outside not scaly or scaly, margin ciliate. *Corolla tubular-funnel shaped*, 0.9—1.5 cm. long, 5-lobed, rosy-violet, outside not scaly, glabrous. *Stamens* 5—10, unequal, exserted from the corolla-tube, *short, shorter than the corolla, 7—8 mm. long*; filaments puberulous at the base. *Ovary* conoid, 2 mm. long, 5-celled, densely scaly, glabrous; *style very short, shorter than the stamens, 3—5 mm. long*, not scaly, glabrous. *Capsule* conoid, 4 mm. long, 2—3 mm. broad, densely scaly, glabrous, calyx-lobes persistent.

This species was discovered by Malyschev in June 1958 on the eastern Sajan mountains, U.S.S.R., growing in moist places in larch woods near the upper limit of tree growth.

The diagnostic features of *R. burjaticum* are the short stamens, 7—8 mm. long, shorter than the corolla, the very short style, 3—5 mm. long, shorter than the stamens, and the tubular-funnel shaped corolla. In these respects it shows a strong resemblance to *R. complexum* from north-west Yunnan, and to *R. intricatum* from west and south-west Szechuan and north-west Yunnan. From *R. lapponicum* and *R. parvifolium* it is readily distinguished by the fore-mentioned characters. The plant has not been introduced into cultivation.

Epithet. From the Buryat area, south of Lake Baikal, U.S.S.R.

Not in cultivation.

R. capitatum Maxim. in Melang. Biolog. IX (1877) 773.

A *somewhat lax upright shrub*, 30—92 cm. (1—3 ft.) high; branchlets long or short, densely scaly with flaky scales, glabrous, leaf-bud scales deciduous. *Leaves* oblong, oblong-elliptic or oblong-oval, lamina 1—2.4 cm. long, 3—9 mm. broad, apex obtuse or rounded, minutely mucronate, base obtuse or rounded; upper surface *pale green or olive-green*, matt, densely scaly, the scales overlapping or contiguous; under surface densely scaly, the scales large, pale yellow and dark brown, or dark brown, overlapping or one-half their own diameter apart; petiole 1—4 mm. long, densely scaly, glabrous. *Inflorescence* terminal, umbellate, 2—5-flowered, flower-bud scales deciduous or persistent; rhachis 0.5—1 mm. long, scaly or not scaly, glabrous; pedicel very short, 0.5—1 mm. long, moderately or rarely densely scaly or rarely not scaly, minutely puberulous or glabrous. *Calyx* 5-lobed, 1—3 mm. long, yellowish, lobes oval, oblong-oval, lanceolate or oblong, outside not scaly or scaly, glabrous or rarely puberulous, margin not scaly, ciliate or eciliate. *Corolla* widely funnel-shaped, slightly zygomorphic, 1.3—1.7 cm. long, 5-lobed, bluish-purple, deep purplish-red or purplish-lavender, outside not scaly, glabrous. *Stamens* 10, unequal, exserted, long, as long as the corolla or a little shorter, 0.9—1.2 cm. in length; filaments villous towards the base. *Ovary* conoid, 1—2 mm. long, 5-celled, densely scaly, glabrous; style long, longer than, or rarely as long as the stamens, not scaly, puberulous at the base or glabrous. *Capsule* conoid, 4 mm. long, 2—3 mm. broad, scaly, puberulous, calyx-lobes persistent.

This plant was first collected by Przewalski in 1872 in Kansu. It was later found by other collectors in various localities in the same region. The plant grows in alpine meadows and in rocky and alpine slopes, at elevations of 2,745—3,660 m. (9,000—12,000 ft.).

R. capitatum shows a strong resemblance to *R. bulu* in habit and height of growth, in the shape and size of the leaves, and in the size of the corolla. It differs markedly from its ally in that the inflorescence is up to 5-flowered, the corolla is not scaly outside, and the stamens are usually shorter, 0.9—1.2 cm. long. The plant is tetraploid with 52 chromosomes.

The species was first introduced by Rock in 1925 from Kansu (No. 13600). He sent seeds under several numbers from his 1925 expedition including No. 13605 which is now in general cultivation. It may be remarked that Farrer also collected the plant in 1915 in Kansu under Nos. 511 and 512 in flower, but these were not introduced into cultivation. The species is easily recognised by its somewhat lax upright habit of growth, 2—3 feet high, with long branchlets and olive-green leaves, and large bluish-purple flowers in clusters of 2—5. The plant is very hardy, fairly fast-growing, and is not difficult to increase from cuttings.

Epithet. With flowers in a head.
Hardiness 3—4. April—May.

R. chryseum Balf. f. et Ward in Notes Roy. Bot. Gard. Edin., Vol. 9 (1916) 219.

Illustration. Bot. Mag. Vol. 154 t. 9246 (1931).

A rounded spreading or broadly upright or compact or lax straggly shrub, 15—92 cm. (6 in.—3 ft.) or rarely up to 1.53 m. (5 ft.) high; *branchlets* densely scaly, scales flaky or rarely not flaky, *glabrous*, leaf-bud scales deciduous. *Leaves* oblong-oval, obovate, oblong, oval, ovate, elliptic or oblong-elliptic, lamina 0.8—2 cm. long, 0.4—1 cm. broad, apex rounded or obtuse, mucronate, base obtuse or rounded; *upper surface greyish-green or pale green, matt*, densely scaly, the scales contiguous or overlapping; *under surface* densely scaly, the *scales* large, *bicolorous, dark brown and yellow, or sometimes unicolorous, dark brown*, ½ *their own diameter apart or contiguous or overlapping*; petiole 1—3 mm. long, densely scaly, glabrous. *Inflorescence* terminal, umbellate, 1—6-flowered, flower-bud scales deciduous; rhachis 1—2 mm. long, scaly or not scaly, glabrous; pedicel 1—5 mm. long, densely or rarely moderately scaly, glabrous. *Calyx* 5-lobed, 1—6 mm. long, yellow, pink or red, lobes oblong, ovate or rounded, outside densely or rarely moderately scaly, glabrous, margin scaly or not scaly, ciliate or rarely eciliate. *Corolla* widely funnel-shaped, slightly zygomorphic, 0.9—1.7 cm. long, 5-lobed, *bright yellow, yellow, greenish, golden-yellow, deep or pale yellow,* outside moderately or sometimes sparsely scaly on the lobes, glabrous. *Stamens* 5—10, unequal, long-exserted, long or medium, as long as the corolla or a little longer, 0.8—1.4 cm. long; filaments villous towards the base. *Ovary* conoid, 1—2 mm. long, 5-celled, densely scaly, glabrous or rarely puberulous; style long, longer than the stamens, not scaly, glabrous or puberulous at the base. *Capsule* conoid or ovoid, 3—4 mm. long, 2—3 mm. broad, densely scaly, glabrous or puberulous, calyx-lobes persistent.

Kingdon-Ward discovered this plant in June 1913 in Ka-gwr-pw Valley, Tibet-Yunnan frontier. Further gatherings by other collectors show that the plant is widely distributed in north-west Yunnan, south-east Tibet and south-west Szechuan. It grows on granite screes, on cliffs and rocks, in open alpine meadows and pastures, in moorlands, in conifer forests, amongst scrub, and in pine forests, at elevations of 3,355—4,770 m. (10,000—15,639 ft.).

R. chryseum shows considerable variation in general features, particularly in habit and height of growth, in leaf shape and size, in the inflorescence, and in the size of the corolla. It may be a compact or rounded and spreading or broadly upright or lax straggly shrub, 15—92 cm. (6 in.—3 ft.) or rarely up to 1.53 m. (5 ft.) high; the leaves are oval, ovate, obovate to oblong, 0.8—2 cm. long, the inflorescence is 1—6-flowered, and the corolla is 0.9—1.7 cm. long.

In 1919, *R. muliense* Balf. f. et Forrest was described from a specimen No. 16252 collected by Forrest in June 1918 in south-west Szechuan. It is said to differ from *R. chryseum* in that the style is pubescent towards the base, and the stamens are 10. From the ample material now available and plants in cultivation it can be seen that these distinctions are inconstant and unreliable. In *R. chryseum* the style is glabrous or puberulous at the base, and the stamens are 5, 6, 8 or 10. These species are very much alike in habit and height of growth, in leaf shape and size, in flower shape, size and colour, and in all other respects they agree.

In 1922, *R. chamaezelum* Balf. f. et Forrest was founded on Forrest's No. 14074 from north-west Yunnan. It is stated to differ from *R. chryseum* in that the stamens are 8, and the inflorescence is 1-flowered. These distinctions are evident when the two type specimens are compared, but the adequate material and plants in cultivation show that the species merge into each other, and no constant character can be found to separate them. It may be noted that in the original description of *R. chamaezelum* the inflorescence is said to be 2—3-flowered, and the stamens are 10.

It must be emphasized that the diagnostic criteria which were used in separating the species are not constant, and the whole material under the above names represents a single variable unit. *R. chryseum*, being the oldest described species, is the valid name.

The characteristic features of *R. chryseum* are the bicolorous scales, dark brown and yellow, (or sometimes unicolorous, dark brown) on the lower surface of the leaves, and the greyish-green or pale green, matt, upper surface. The plant is diploid with 26 chromosomes.

The species was first introduced possibly by Forrest from north-west Yunnan. It was reintroduced by him on several occasions including No. 13947 in 1917. Kingdon-Ward sent seeds in 1921 (No. 4023) and again in 1931. The species was also introduced by Rock, and Yü. The plant first flowered at Caerhays, Cornwall at the end of March 1918. Several forms are in cultivation, including Form 1. A dwarf very compact shrub, 6 inches high and as much across with golden-yellow flowers. Form 2. A somewhat compact spreading shrub, 1½ feet high and up to 2 feet across, with pale yellow flowers. Form 3. A broadly upright shrub up to 2 feet high with sulphur-yellow flowers. Form 4. A broadly upright shrub up to 2 feet high with greenish flowers. Form 5. A very lax straggly shrub up to 2 feet high with long branches, and with sulphur-yellow or pale greenish-yellow flowers. Form 6. A large, somewhat rounded shrub 3 feet high with large leaves up to 2 cm. long and 1 cm. broad, and with yellow flowers. The species is one of the finest dwarf rhododendrons in cultivation, particularly Form 1, an exceptionally fine plant. All the forms are free-flowering, and they have the added advantage of producing the flowers at a remarkable early age when raised from seed. Some forms produce a few capsules of good fertile seed nearly every year. The species is difficult to increase from cuttings except Forms 2, 5, and sometimes Form 4. *R. chryseum* is hardy, and is an excellent plant for the rock garden.

Epithet. Golden-yellow.

Hardiness 3—4. April—May. Plate 38.

R. compactum Hutch. in Gard. Chron. Vol. 91 (1932) 326.

A broadly upright shrub, 70 cm.—1 m. (2⅓—3⅓ ft.) high; *branchlets thick, stiff, upright 10—12 cm. long*, densely scaly with flaky scales, glabrous, leaf-bud scales deciduous. *Leaves* oblong, oblong-lanceolate or lanceolate, lamina 1.2—2.6 cm. long, 4—8 mm. broad, apex rounded or obtuse, mucronate, base tapered or obtuse; upper surface bright green or greyish-green, shining or matt, densely scaly, the scales overlapping or contiguous; under surface densely scaly, the scales large, dark brown, ½ their own diameter apart; petiole 2—4 mm. long, densely scaly, glabrous. *Inflorescence* 4—6-flowered, umbellate, terminal, or *terminal and axillary in the uppermost 1—6 leaves forming a compact large compound inflorescence of 20—25 flowers*, flower-bud scales deciduous or subpersistent; rhachis 1 mm. long, scaly or not scaly, glabrous; pedicel 1—3 mm. long, densely scaly, glabrous. *Calyx* 5-lobed, 0.5—2 mm. long, yellowish or greenish, lobes ovate, rounded or lanceolate, outside scaly or not scaly, glabrous, margin not scaly, ciliate. *Corolla* widely funnel-shaped, slightly zygomorphic, 1—1.5 cm. long, 5-lobed, violet-mauve or purplish-mauve, outside not scaly, glabrous. *Stamens* 10, unequal, long-exserted, medium or long, as long as the corolla, 0.9—1.2 cm. long; filaments villous towards the base. *Ovary* conoid, 1—2 mm. long, 5—6-celled, densely scaly, glabrous; style long, longer than the stamens, not scaly, glabrous. *Capsule* oblong, 5—6 mm. long, 2—3 mm. broad, rather densely scaly, glabrous, calyx-lobes persistent.

This species was described by Hutchinson in 1932 from a plant grown by Lord Headfort at Kells, County Meath, Eire, from Forrest's seed under number 13905, probably collected in north-western Yunnan in 1918. The herbarium specimen under this number is the Type specimen of *R. dasypetalum*.

There are two main characters of this plant. One is the broadly upright habit of growth up to 1 m. (3⅓ ft.) high with thick, stiff, erect branchlets 4—5 inches long; the other is the 4—6-flowered terminal, or terminal and axillary inflorescence in the uppermost 1—6 leaves which forms a compact large compound inflorescence of 20—25 flowers to which the specific name refers. The plant bears a resemblance to *R. scintillans* in some features, but is readily distinguished by its habit of growth and compact inflorescence. It is a tetraploid with 52 chromosomes.

The species was reintroduced by Forrest from north Yunnan in 1925 (No. 25555). It is very hardy, a robust grower, and is easy to increase from cuttings. The plant has proved to be most attractive in flower and would be well worth acquiring for every rock garden.

Epithet. Compact.

Hardiness 3—4. April—May.

R. complexum Balf. f. et W.W. Sm. in Notes Roy. Bot. Gard. Edin., Vol. 9 (1916) 222.

A small matted or *compact rounded shrub*, 30—60 cm. (1—2 ft.) high; branchlets short, densely scaly with flaky scales, glabrous, leaf-bud scales deciduous. *Leaves* elliptic, oblong-elliptic, ovate or oval, small, lamina 4—9 mm. long, 2—5 mm. broad, apex rounded or obtuse, mucronate, base rounded or obtuse; upper surface pale greyish-green, matt, densely scaly, the scales overlapping; *under surface* densely scaly, the *scales large, brown or pale brown,* overlapping or rarely ½ their own diameter apart; petiole 1—2 mm. long, densely scaly, glabrous. *Inflorescence* terminal, umbellate, 2—4-flowered, flower-bud scales persistent or deciduous; rhachis 0.5—1 mm. long, scaly or not scaly, glabrous; pedicel 1—2 mm. long, densely scaly, glabrous. *Calyx* 5-lobed, minute, 0.5—1 mm. long, pink, reddish or greenish, lobes triangular, ovate or oblong, outside scaly or not scaly, glabrous, margin not scaly, hairy with long hairs. *Corolla tubular-funnel* shaped, slightly zygomorphic, small, 0.9—1.3 cm. long, 5-lobed, *deep rose-purple, very pale purple almost white, or pink,* outside not scaly, glabrous. *Stamens 5 or 6,* unequal, *included in the corolla-tube, very short,* shorter than the corolla, *3—5 mm long;* filaments villous or puberulous towards the base. *Ovary* conoid, 1 mm. long, 5-celled, densely scaly, glabrous; *style very short, shorter than the stamens,* one-half or two-thirds the length of the stamens, *as long as, or twice as long as the ovary,* not scaly, glabrous. *Capsule* conoid, 3—4 mm. long, 2—3 mm. broad, moderately or rather densely scaly, glabrous, calyx-lobes persistent.

This species was discovered by Forrest in June 1914 on the Chungtien plateau, Yunnan. Subsequently it was found by him again, and by Rock in other localities in north-west Yunnan. It grows in open stony pastures and on stony slopes at elevations of 3,355—4,270 m. (11,000—14,000 ft.).

The very short stamens included in the corolla-tube are a marked characteristic of this plant. Other distinctive features are the very short style, shorter than the stamens, as long as or twice as long as the ovary, and the tubular-funnel shaped corolla. In these respects the species is very similar to its ally *R. intricatum,* from which it is distinguished by the brown or pale brown scales on the lower surface of the leaves, by the deep or pale rose-purple or pink flowers, by the 5—6 stamens, and by the compact rounded habit of growth. It is hexaploid with 78 chromosomes.

The species was first introduced by Forrest in 1917 (No. 15392). It was reintroduced by Rock in 1922 (No. 3970). In cultivation it is a small compact rounded shrub, 30—45 cm. (1—1½ ft.) high and almost as much across, with short annual growths and rose-purple flowers. The plant is very hardy, free-flowering, and is not difficult to root from cuttings. It is rare in cultivation, but should be a valuable acquisition to any rock garden.

Epithet. Interwoven.

Hardiness 3—4. April—May. Plate 32.

R. dasypetalum Balf. f. et Forrest in Notes Roy. Bot. Gard. Edin., Vol. 11 (1919) 45.

A small rounded shrub, 30—76 cm. (1—2½ ft.) high; branchlets long, densely scaly with flaky scales, glabrous, leaf-bud scales deciduous. *Leaves* oblong, oblong-elliptic, oblong-oval or oblong-lanceolate, lamina 1—2 cm. long, 4—9 mm. broad, apex obtuse or rounded, mucronate, base obtuse or rounded; *usually V-shaped;* upper surface dark green, shining, densely scaly, the scales ½—2 times their own diameter apart or overlapping; under surface densely scaly, the scales large, brown or dark brown or fawn, overlapping, without or rarely with closely or widely scattered darker brown scales; petiole 1—3 mm. long, densely scaly, glabrous. *Inflorescence* terminal, umbellate, 1—4-flowered, flower-bud scales persistent or deciduous; rhachis 1 mm. long, scaly, minutely puberulous or glabrous; pedicel 0.4—1.2 cm. long, densely scaly, glabrous or rarely puberulous. *Calyx* 5-lobed, 2—4 mm. long, crimson-purple, reddish, pink or greenish, lobes lanceolate, ovate, oblong or oblong-oval, outside moderately or sparsely scaly, puberulous, margin not scaly, hairy with long hairs. *Corolla* widely funnel-shaped, slightly zygomorphic, *1.5—2 cm. long,* 5-lobed, bright purplish-rose, outside not scaly, *puberulous on the tube and at the base of the lobes outside. Stamens 10,* unequal, long-exserted, long, as long as the corolla or a little shorter, 0.8—1.6 cm. in length; filaments villous towards the base. *Ovary* conoid, 2—3 mm. long, 5-celled, densely scaly, glabrous or rarely puberulous at the base; style long, longer than the stamens, not scaly, puberulous at the base or glabrous. *Capsule* conoid, 4—7 mm. long, 2—3 mm. broad, densely scaly, glabrous or rarely puberulous, calyx-lobes persistent.

This plant is known from a single collection made in June 1917 by Forrest on the Li-ti-ping, in north-west Yunnan, growing in open stony pasture at an elevation of 3,355 m. (11,000 ft.).

As the name suggests, a diagnostic feature is the corolla puberulous outside on the tube and at the base of the lobes. In this respect the species is readily distinguished from all the other species of its Series. It shows a certain degree of resemblance to *R. scintillans*, from which is differs markedly in distinctive features. Moreover, *R. dasypetalum* is a tetraploid with 52 chromosomes, while *R. scintillans* is a diploid with 26 chromosomes.

R. dasypetalum was introduced by Forrest in 1917 (No. 13905 — the Type number). In cultivation it is a compact rounded shrub up to 2 feet high and almost as much across with dark green shining leaves. A notable character which is usually constant is the bending up of the two halves of the leaf, forming a broad V with the midrib in cross section. Another marked feature is the large widely funnel-shaped corolla up to 2 cm. long, and up to 2.5 cm. across. The species is hardy, a vigorous grower, and is most effective when covered with bright purplish-rose flowers in clusters of two to four. It is uncommon in cultivation, but is well worth a place in every rock garden.

Epithet. With hairy petals.

Hardiness 3—4. April—May.

R. diacritum Balf. f. et W.W. Sm. in Notes Roy. Bot. Gard. Edin., Vol. 9 (1916) 225.

A matted or spreading or semi-prostrate or broadly upright somewhat spreading shrub, 8 cm.—1.07 m. (3 in.—3½ ft.) high; branchlets short or long, densely scaly with flaky scales, glabrous, leaf-bud scales deciduous. *Leaves elliptic, oval, ovate, oblong-ovate* or rarely oblong-oval, *tiny or small, lamina 0.3—1 cm. long, 2—5 mm. broad*, apex obtuse or rounded, mucronate, base obtuse or rounded, upper surface greyish-green or green, matt or somewhat shining, densely scaly, the scales overlapping or nearly contiguous; *under surface densely scaly, the scales are characteristic, similar in size and colour*, large, *brown, overlapping*, with or without closely or widely scattered dark brown scales; petiole 1—2 mm. long, densely scaly, glabrous. *Inflorescence* terminal, umbellate, 1—2-flowered, flower-bud scales deciduous or rarely persistent; rhachis 0.5—1 mm. long, scaly or not scaly, glabrous; pedicel 0.5—2 mm. long, densely scaly, glabrous. *Calyx* 5-lobed, 0.5—3 mm. long, purple, pink, crimson-purple or greenish, lobes ovate, oblong or lanceolate, outside densely or moderately scaly, glabrous, margin scaly or not scaly, ciliate or eciliate. *Corolla* widely funnel-shaped, slightly zygomorphic, small or rarely large, 0.8—1.1 cm. or rarely 1.5 cm. long, 5-lobed, deep rose-purple, purplish-blue, deep blue-purple or purplish-red, outside scaly along the middle of the lobes or rarely not scaly, glabrous. *Stamens* 10, unequal, exserted, medium or long, as long as the corolla or a little shorter or longer, 0.7—1.4 cm. long; filaments villous towards the base. *Ovary* conoid, 1—2 mm. long, 5-celled, densely scaly, glabrous or rarely puberulous at the base or at the apex; style longer than the stamens and the corolla, not scaly, glabrous. *Capsule* conoid, 3—5 mm. long, 2—3 mm. broad, densely scaly, glabrous, calyx-lobes persistent.

R. diacritum was first collected by Forrest in May 1906 on the eastern flank of the Lichiang Range, north-west Yunnan. Subsequently it was collected by him again, also by Rock and by Yü, in other localities in north-west and mid-west Yunnan, and south-west Szechuan. It grows on cliffs and boulders, in alpine meadows, and in open moorland, at elevations of 3,050—4,660 m. (10,000—15,279 ft.).

In 1916 *R. pycnocladum* Balf. f. et W.W. Sm. was described from a specimen No. 2181 collected by Forrest in north-west Yunnan. In *The Species of Rhododendron* 1930, the name has correctly been placed in synonymy under *R. diacritum* Balf. f. et W.W. Sm.

The diagnostic features of this species are the oval, ovate to elliptic, tiny or small leaves, 3 mm.—1 cm. long, 2—5 mm. broad, densely scaly on both surfaces, the lower surface with large, overlapping, characteristic brown scales, similar in size and colour, usually with closely or widely separated dark brown scales, and the 1—2-flowered inflorescence. The species is closely allied to R. drumonium but is distinguished by the longer style, usually by the larger calyx, and often by the broadly upright somewhat spreading habit of growth. It is also related to R. telmateium, but differs markedly in its oval, ovate or elliptic leaves, and usually in its habit of growth; moreover, it is a robust grower with long or short thick branchlets, but R. telmateium is a delicate upright shrub with short slender branchlets.

R. diacritum was first introduced by Forrest in 1910 (No. 5879). He later sent seeds several times from Yunnan. The species was also introduced by Rock and by Yü. In cultivation it is a broadly upright somewhat spreading shrub, 2 feet high and almost as much across, although in its native home it forms a matted or semi-prostrate or spreading or broadly upright shrub, 3 inches to 3½ feet high. It is fairly fast-growing with single or paired deep rose-purple flowers produced in great profusion. The plant is hardy, but is rare in cultivation. It is a charming plant for the rock garden, and should be in every collection of rhododendrons.

Epithet. Distinguished.
Hardiness 3—4. April—May.

R. drumonium Balf. f. et Ward in Notes Roy. Bot. Gard. Edin., Vol. 9 (1916) 226.

A matted or *very compact spreading* or broadly upright shrub, 8 cm.—1.07 m. (3 in.—3½ ft.) high; branchlets long or short, densely scaly with flaky scales, glabrous, leaf-bud scales deciduous. *Leaves* elliptic, oval, oblong-ovate, ovate or rarely oblong, *tiny or small, lamina 3—8 mm. or rarely 1 cm. long, 2—4 mm. broad*, apex obtuse or rounded, mucronate, base obtuse or rounded; upper surface greyish-green or dark green, matt or somewhat shining, densely scaly, the scales overlapping; *under surface densely scaly, the scales are characteristic, similar in size and colour*, large, *brown, overlapping*, with or rarely without closely or widely scattered dark brown scales; petiole 1—2 mm. long, densely scaly, glabrous. *Inflorescence* terminal, umbellate 1- or rarely 2-flowered, flower-bud scales deciduous or persistent; rhachis 0.5 mm. long, scaly or not scaly, glabrous; pedicel very short, 0.5—1 mm. long, densely scaly, glabrous. *Calyx* 5-lobed, *0.5—1 mm. or rarely 2 mm. long*, pink, purple, crimson-purple or greenish, lobes rounded, ovate or oblong, outside moderately or densely scaly, glabrous, margin scaly or not scaly, eciliate or ciliate. *Corolla* widely funnel-shaped, slightly zygomorphic, small, 0.7—1.1 cm. long, 5-lobed, deep purplish-blue, purple-blue or deep rose-purple, outside scaly along the middle of the lobes, glabrous. *Stamens* 10 or rarely 8, unequal, exserted, short or medium, as long as the corolla or a little shorter, 0.6—1 cm. long; filaments villous towards the base. *Ovary* conoid, 1—2 mm. long, 5-celled, densely scaly, glabrous or rarely puberulous at the base; *style medium or short, as long as the stamens or shorter*, not scaly, glabrous. *Capsule* conoid, 3—4 mm. long, 2 mm. broad, densely scaly, glabrous, calyx-lobes persistent.

This species was first collected by Kingdon-Ward in May 1913 in the Valley of Chung River, Yunnan. It was afterwards found by him again, also by Forrest and by Rock in the same region and in south-west Szechuan and south-east Tibet. It grows in open pine forests, in open stony pastures, and on cliffs, at elevations of 3,173—4,270 m. (10,500—14,000 ft.).

It shows a strong resemblance to R. diacritum in general characters, but is distinguished by its shorter style, usually by the smaller calyx, and often by the very compact spreading habit of growth. The species is a tetraploid with 52 chromosomes.

The plant was first introduced by Forrest in 1913 (No. 10434). He reintroduced it on several occasions from Yunnan. Rock sent seeds in 1923 from the same region. In cultivation it is a dwarf, very compact spreading shrub, 6—8 inches high and 10—12 inches across, or broadly upright 1—1½ feet high, with tiny oval greyish-green or dark green leaves. It is very hardy, produces flowers freely, and is easy to grow. The plant is rare in cultivation. but is well worth a place in every rock garden.

Epithet. From woods.

Hardiness 3—4. April—May.

R. edgarianum Rehd. et Wils. in Plantae Wilsonianae (1913) 508.

A small *broadly upright* or matted shrub, 30—92 cm. (1—3 ft.) high; branchlets short or long, densely scaly, scales flaky or not flaky, glabrous, leaf-bud scales deciduous. *Leaves* oval, ovate, elliptic or oblong-oval, lamina 0.4—1.3 cm. long, 2—7 mm. broad, apex rounded or obtuse, mucronate, base rounded or obtuse; *upper surface pale greyish-green, matt*, densely scaly, the scales overlapping or their own diameter apart; under surface densely scaly, the scales large, brown or dark brown, overlapping or their own diameter apart, with or without closely scattered dark brown scales; petiole 1—3 mm. long, densely scaly, glabrous. *Inflorescence* terminal, umbellate, *1—2-flowered*, flower-bud scales deciduous; rhachis 0.5 mm. long, scaly or not scaly, glabrous; pedicel 1—2 mm. long, densely scaly, glabrous. *Calyx* 5-lobed, 0.5—2 mm. long, greenish, pink or purple, lobes oval, ovate or oblong-oval, outside scaly, glabrous, margin not scaly or scaly, ciliate or eciliate. *Corolla* widely funnel-shaped, slightly zygomorphic, 1.1—1.7 cm. long, 1.5—2.5 cm. across, 5-lobed, rose-purple, purple, deep purplish-blue or purple-blue, outside not scaly, glabrous. *Stamens* 10 or rarely 8, unequal, exserted, long, as long as the corolla or a little shorter, 0.8—1.2 cm. in length; filaments densely villous towards the base. *Ovary* conoid, 1—2 mm. long, 5-celled, densely scaly, glabrous; *style long, longer than*, or rarely as long as, *the stamens*, not scaly, glabrous. *Capsule* ovoid or conoid, 3—5 mm. long, 3—4 mm. broad, densely scaly, glabrous, calyx-lobes persistent.

This species was discovered by Wilson in June 1908 in the vicinity of Tatsienlu, western Szechuan. It was found by him again later in July and October of the same year in the same region. The plant was also collected by Forrest in 1918 and by Rock in 1923, in north-west Yunnan. It grows in moorlands at elevations of 3,600—5,000 m. (11,803—16,393 ft.). Wilson records it as forming heaths north of Tatsienlu, in western Szechuan.

R. edgarianum is a very distinct species, and cannot be confused with any species of its Series. It bears a resemblance to *R. oresbium* in some features, but differs markedly in its habit of growth, in the pale greyish-green colour of the leaves, usually in the 1—2-flowered inflorescence, and in the long style, longer than or rarely as long as, the stamens. The species is tetraploid with 52 chromosomes.

The plant was introduced by Forrest from an elevation of 4,423 m. (14,500 ft.), in north-west Yunnan (No. 16450). In its native home it grows from 1 to 3 feet high. In cultivation it is easily recognised by its broadly upright habit of growth up to 2½ feet with pale greyish-green leaves. It is fairly fast-growing, and is most attractive when covered with purplish-blue flowers. The plant is hardy, and is a valuable species for the rock garden.

Epithet. After Rev. J.H. Edgar, China Inland Mission.

Hardiness 3—4. April—June.

R. fastigiatum Franch. in Bull. Soc. Bot. France, Vol. XXXIII (1886) 234.

A *compact spreading, cushion, matted, broadly upright or upright* shrub, 15 cm.—1.22 m. (6 in.—4 ft.) high; branchlets short or sometimes long, thick, densely scaly, scales not flaky or flaky, glabrous, leaf-bud scales deciduous. *Leaves* oblong, elliptic, ovate, oblong-elliptic or oblong-oval, lamina 0.6—1.8 cm. long, 2—8 mm. broad, apex obtuse or rounded, mucronate, base obtuse or rounded; *upper surface glaucous-grey or pale glaucous-green (in young leaves markedly glaucous-grey)*, matt, densely scaly, the scales overlapping or nearly contiguous or one-half their own diameter apart; under surface densely scaly, the scales large, pale brown or brown or dark brown, overlapping or nearly contiguous or one-half their own diameter apart; petiole 1—3 mm. long, densely scaly, glabrous. *Inflorescence* terminal, umbellate, 2—5-flowered, flower-bud scales deciduous; rhachis 0.5—2 mm. long, scaly or not scaly, glabrous; pedicel 1—3 mm. long, densely scaly, glabrous. *Calyx* 5-lobed, 3—5 mm. long, pink, purple, greenish or reddish, lobes oblong, oblong-lanceolate or oblong-oval, outside sparsely to rather densely scaly, glabrous, margin not scaly, fringed with long hairs. *Corolla* widely funnel-shaped, slightly zygomorphic, 1—1.5 cm. long, 5-lobed, lavender-rose, bright lavender-blue, purplish-blue, deep purple-blue, deep lavender or deep blue, outside not scaly or sometimes scaly on the lobes, glabrous. *Stamens* 10, unequal, long-exserted, long, as long as the corolla or a little longer, 0.9—1.7 cm. in length; filaments villous towards the base. *Ovary* conoid, 1—2 mm. long, 5-celled, densely scaly, glabrous or rarely puberulous at the apex; style long, longer than the stamens, not scaly, glabrous or rarely puberulous at the base. *Capsule* conoid, 3—6 mm. long, 2—4 mm. broad, densely scaly, glabrous or rarely puberulous at the base or at the apex, calyx-lobes persistent.

This species was first collected by the Abbé Delavay in June 1883 on mount Tsang-chan, above Tali, Yunnan. Further gatherings by other collectors show that the plant is distributed in mid-west and north-west Yunnan. It grows on rocky slopes, on cliffs, on screes, in alpine moorlands, in open pastures, and in pine forests, at elevations of 3,200—4,423 m. (10,492—14,500 ft.).

R. fastigiatum varies considerably in habit and height of growth. It may be a compact spreading, cushion, matted, broadly upright or upright shrub, and it grows from 15 cm. to 1.22 m. (6 in.—4 ft.) high. The species is allied to *R. impeditum* which it resembles in leaf shape and size, in the distribution and colour of the scales on the lower surface, in flower shape and size, and in the long stamens and style. It differs markedly from its ally in that the adult leaves and particularly the young leaves are very glaucous-grey, and its habit of growth varies from compact spreading to upright; whereas in *R. impeditum* both the adult and young leaves are dark green, not glaucous, and its habit of growth is very compact spreading.

The species was first introduced by Forrest in 1906 from western Yunnan (No. 4149). It was reintroduced by him several times from the same region including Nos. 5847 and 6757. Rock sent seeds from north-west Yunnan in 1948. Three distinct forms are in cultivation. Form 1. A compact spreading shrub 1 foot high and 2 feet across with glaucous-grey leaves. Form 2. A compact rounded shrub 1 foot high and as much across, with smaller markedly glaucous-grey leaves, introduced by Rock. Form 3. A broadly upright shrub 2 feet high with somewhat long branches, and with glaucous-grey leaves. The species is very hardy, free-flowering, and easy to grow. A most remarkable feature is the markedly glaucous-grey young foliage. Although a slow grower, it is an excellent plant for the rock garden. It was given an Award of Merit when exhibited by G. Reuthe, Keston, in 1914.

Epithet. Erect.
Hardiness 3—4. April—May. Plate 41.

R. fimbriatum Hutch. in Gard. Chron., Vol. 91 (1932) 438.

A broadly upright shrub, 60 cm.—1.22 m. (2—4 ft.) high; branchlets long, erect, densely scaly with flaky scales, glabrous, leaf-bud scales deciduous. *Leaves* lanceolate, oblong-lanceolate or oblong, lamina 1.5—3.5 cm. long, 0.5—1.5 cm. broad, apex obtuse or rounded, mucronate, base obtuse or tapered; upper surface pale green, matt, densely scaly, the scales overlapping or nearly contiguous; *under surface densely scaly, the scales are characteristic,* similar in size and colour, large, *fawn* or *creamy-yellow,* or rarely fawn and brown, *overlapping or nearly contiguous;* petiole 3—6 mm. long, densely scaly, glabrous. *Inflorescence* terminal, shortly racemose, 3—9-

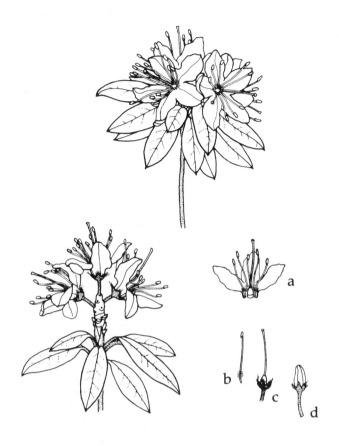

21. R. fimbriatum
nat. size

a. section. b. stamen. c. ovary, style. d. capsule.

flowered, flower-bud scales deciduous; rhachis 2—3 mm. long, moderately or densely scaly, glabrous; pedicel 3—9 mm. long, densely scaly, glabrous. *Calyx* 5-lobed, 1 mm. long, pink, lobes ovate, rounded or triangular, outside moderately or densely scaly, glabrous, margin scaly or not scaly, hairy with long hairs. *Corolla* widely funnel-shaped, slightly zygomorphic, 1.2—1.6 cm. long, 5-lobed, deep mauve-purple or purple, outside not scaly, glabrous. *Stamens* 10, unequal, long-exserted, *long, as long as the corolla or a little longer*, 0.8—1.3 cm. in length; filaments villous towards the base. *Ovary* conoid, 1—2 mm. long, 5-celled, densely scaly, glabrous or hairy at the apex; *style long, longer than the stamens and the corolla*, not scaly or scaly at the base, glabrous. *Capsule* conoid or oblong, 4—7 mm. long, 3—4 mm. broad, densely scaly, glabrous, calyx-lobes persistent.

This species was described by Hutchinson from a plant grown by Lord Headfort at Kells, County Meath, Eire, from Forrest's seed under No. 22197. The corresponding herbarium specimen in fruit has been named *R. cheilanthum* which is now a synonym of *R. cuneatum*. It was collected in August 1922 in south-west Szechuan, growing on open rocky slopes in open conifer forests at an elevation of 3,660 m. (12,000 ft.). In September 1922 Forrest found the true specimen of *R. fimbriatum* (No. 23149) in the Chienchuan-Mekong Divide, north-west Yunnan, growing in boggy pasture on the margins of forests at 3,660 m. (12,000 ft.).

A distinctive feature of the species is the characteristic fawn or creamy-yellow scales, similar in size and colour, overlapping or nearly contiguous on the lower surface of the leaves. In some respects, R. fimbriatum shows a resemblance to R. hippophaeoides, from which it is readily distinguished by the long stamens, as long as the corolla or a little longer, by the very long protruding style, much longer than the stamens and the corolla, and often by the larger corolla. In R hippophaeoides the stamens and style are very short, much shorter than the corolla, and the corolla is often smaller. Moreover, in R. fimbriatum the flowers are usually purple, while in R. hippophaeoides they are usually lavender-blue or sometimes bright rose. R. fimbriatum is also allied to R. websterianum, from which it differs markedly in the larger leaves, usually in the inflorescence up to 9-flowered, and usually in the longer pedicels.

In cultivation R. fimbriatum is a broadly upright shrub up to 2 or 3 feet high with long erect branchlets and purple flowers produced freely in clusters of three to nine. It is a charming plant and is not difficult to increase from cuttings. The plant is hardy, and is well suited for the rock garden.

Epithet. Minutely fringed.

Hardiness 3—4. April—May. Plate 37.

R. flavidum Franch. in Journ. de Bot. IX (1895) 395.

Illustration. Bot. Mag. Vol. 136 t. 8326 (1910).

A broadly upright or bushy shrub, 45—92 cm. (1½—3 ft.) or rarely 2 m. (6½ ft.) high; *branchlets* moderately or densely scaly with flaky scales, *rather densely puberulous* or rarely glabrous, leaf-bud scales deciduous. *Leaves* oblong, lanceolate, oblong-oval or oval, lamina 0.8—1.8 cm. long, 0.4—1 cm. broad, apex obtuse or rounded, mucronate, base obtuse or rounded; *upper surface dark green, shining,* moderately or densely scaly, the scales nearly contiguous or overlapping; *under surface* scaly, the *scales* large, unicolorous, dark brown or brown, *one-half to twice their own diameter apart;* petiole 1—2 mm. long, densely or moderately scaly, puberulous or glabrous. *Inflorescence* terminal, umbellate, 3—5-flowered, flower-bud scales deciduous; rhachis 1 mm. long, scaly or not scaly, glabrous; pedicel 2—4 mm. long, scaly, puberulous or glabrous. *Calyx* 5-lobed, 1—4 mm. long, greenish or pink, lobes oblong, oblong-lanceolate, ovate or rounded, outside moderately or rather densely scaly or not scaly, glabrous, margin not scaly or sparsely scaly, ciliate. *Corolla* widely funnel-shaped, slightly zygomorphic, 1—1.5 cm. long, 5-lobed, *pale yellow, outside not scaly* or rarely scaly on the lobes, glabrous. *Stamens* 10, unequal, long-exserted, long, as long as the corolla or a little longer, 0.8—1.7 cm. in length; filaments villous or rarely puberulous towards the base. *Ovary* conoid, 2 mm. long, 5-celled, densely scaly, glabrous; style long, longer than the stamens, not scaly, puberulous at the base or rarely glabrous. *Capsule* conoid, 5 mm. long, 3 mm. broad, densely scaly, glabrous, calyx-lobes persistent.

R. flavidum was described by Franchet in 1895 from a specimen collected by the Abbé Soulié in 1893 in western Szechuan. It was later found by other collectors in the same region. The plant grows in forests and moorlands, and on rocks, at elevations of 3,300—4,300 m. (10,820—14,098 ft.). Wilson records it as being common in alpine regions around Tatsienlu.

R. primulinum Hemsley, which was described in 1910, has correctly been referred to *R. flavidum.* In 1913 *R flavidum* Franch. var. *psilostylum* Rehd. et Wils. was described from a plant No. 3452 collected by Wilson in western Szechuan. It is said to differ from the species in the colour of the leaves, in the scaly flowers, in the smaller calyx, in the glabrous style, and in the smaller and more globose fruit. These features are shared by *R. flavidum.*

The diagnostic features of *R. flavidum* are the dark green leaves, shining on the upper surface, and usually the rather densely puberulous branchlets. In these respects, it is readily distinguished from its ally, *R. chryseum.* It further differs in that the scales on the lower surface of the leaves are usually widely spaced, their own diameter up to twice their own diameter apart, unicolorous, dark brown or brown, and the corolla is usually not scaly outside. The plant is a hexaploid with 78 chromosomes or diploid with 26 chromosomes.

The species was first introduced by Wilson in 1905 (No. 1773 as *R. primulinum*). The plant first flowered in April 1909 (Wilson No. 1773), with J. Veitch and Sons in their nursery at Coombe Wood. It was reintroduced by him in 1908 (No. 1202). In its native home it grows 1½—3 feet high. Wilson found a plant, north of Tatsienlu, 3—6 feet in height. In cultivation it is a broadly upright shrub up to 3 or 4 feet, with long slender branchlets, and dark green shining leaves. Unlike its ally *R. chryseum*, it is not difficult to increase from cuttings. It is quite hardy, free-flowering, and is a valuable plant for the rock garden.

Epithet. Somewhat yellow.
Hardiness 3—4. April—May.

R. fragariflorum Ward in Gard. Chron. Ser. 3, LXXXVI (1929) 504.

A dwarf upright spreading, or straggly or rounded or compact prostrate spreading shrub, 10—30 cm. (4 in.—1 ft.) high; *branchlets* very short, somewhat thick, moderately or rather densely scaly, *rather densely puberulous*, not bristly, leaf-bud scales deciduous. *Leaves* obovate, obovate-elliptic, elliptic, oval, oblong-oval or oblong, lamina 0.5—1.6 cm. long, 3—7 mm. broad, apex rounded, mucronate, base rounded or obtuse; upper surface dark green or bright green, shining, rather densely scaly, the scales somewhat large, yellowish or brown, shining; *margin* recurved, *crenulate*, bristly or not bristly; *under surface* scaly, the *scales* somewhat large, dark brown and yellow, or dark brown, *Entire*, *1½—6 times their own diameter apart*; petiole 1—2 mm. long, scaly, not bristly or rarely bristly. *Inflorescence* terminal, umbellate, 2—6-flowered, flower-bud scales deciduous; rhachis 0.5—1 mm. long, scaly or not scaly, puberulous or glabrous; pedicel 5—8 mm. long, crimson-purple, moderately or rather densely scaly, moderately or rather densely minutely puberulous. *Calyx* 5-lobed to base, 3—8 mm. long, lobes crimson, crimson-purple or pink, ovate, oval, elliptic or oblong, outside scaly, margin scaly, ciliate or eciliate, *Corolla* widely funnel-shaped or almost rotate, slightly zygomorphic, 1—1.7 cm. long, 5-lobed, purple or "crushed strawberry" colour, dark purple, plum-purple, pinkish-purple or purplish-crimson, outside sparsely scaly along the middle of the lobes or not scaly, glabrous. *Stamens* 10, unequal, long-exserted, long, as long as the corolla or a little shorter, 0.8—1.2 cm. in length; filaments villous towards the base. *Ovary* conoid, 2 mm. long, 5-celled, densely scaly, glabrous; style red, long, longer than the stamens, longer than, or as long as, the corolla. *Capsule* conoid, 5—7 mm. long, 3—4 mm. broad, scaly, glabrous, calyx-lobes persistent.

R. fragariflorum has been tentatively included in the Saluenense Series. In habit and height of growth, in the shape and size of the leaves, in the shape and colour of the corolla, and in the long stamens and style, it resembles both the Saluenense and the Lapponicum Series. When the more adequate material and plants in cultivation are examined in detail, it becomes apparent that in its small corolla glabrous outside, in the short pedicels, in the laxly spaced scales on the lower surface of the leaves, and particularly in its Entire type of scale, *R. fragariflorum* shows a marked similarity to the species in the Lapponicum Series; in these respects it is readily distinguished from the species in the Saluenense Series. It may be remarked that the main distinction between the Saluenense and Lapponicum Series is one of scale type. In the Saluenense Series the scales are of the Crenulate type in which the margin of the scale is distinctly scalloped. This is a noteworthy feature because crenulate scales, although they occur elsewhere in rhododendrons, are typical of the Saluenense Series. In the Lapponicum Series, the scales are often of the Undulate type, or sometimes of the Entire type with a broad or narrow marginal zone. In *R. fragariflorum* the scale is Entire, with a narrow marginal zone, broad intermediate zone, and a fairly large centre zone. Accordingly, *R. fragariflo-rum* with an Entire type of scale, is now placed in the Lapponicum Series, the main distinction between the two Series thus being maintained.

R. fragariflorum was discovered by Kingdon-Ward in June 1924 at Temo La, southern Tibet. It was collected by him again later in the same region and on the Bhutan frontier in Assam. Afterwards it was found by Ludlow and Sherriff, together with Taylor, Elliot, or Hicks, in south and south-east Tibet, and in Bhutan. It grows on open rocky hillsides, on turf slopes, in swamps, and in open marshy pastures within Abies-Rhododendron forests, at elevations of 3,660—4,575 m. (12,000—15,000 ft.). Kingdon-Ward records it as growing all over the alpine region in southern Tibet, forming hassocks and continuous carpets not above six inches high.

The species shows a resemblance to *R. setosum* in the shape and size of the leaves, in the distribution of the scales on the lower surface of the leaves, in the size of the calyx, and in the colour of the corolla. It is readily distinguished from its ally by the non-bristly branchlets, petioles, and usually leaves.

The plant was first introduced by Kingdon-Ward in 1924 (No. 5734). It was re-introduced by Ludlow, Sherriff and Elliot in 1947 (No. 15828). Two distinct growth forms are in cultivation. Form 1. A rounded somewhat spreading shrub up to 1 foot high. Form 2. A compact, prostrate spreading shrub, up to 5 inches high and up to 12 inches across. The species is a slow grower with short, somewhat thick annual growths, and dark green shiny leaves. It is hardy, but tends to be difficult to increase from cuttings. It is uncommon in cultivation, but is a useful plant for the rock garden.

Epithet. Strawberry-flowered.
Hardiness 3. May—June. Plate 42.

R. hippophaeoides Balf. f. et W.W. Sm. in Notes Roy. Bot. Gard. Edin., Vol. 9 (1916) 236.
Illustration. Bot. Mag. Vol. 152 t. 9156 (1928).

A broadly upright shrub, 23 cm.—1.22 m. (9 in.—4 ft.) or rarely 1.53 m. (5 ft.) high; branchlets long or short, densely scaly with flaky scales, glabrous, leaf-bud scales deciduous. *Leaves* oblong, oblong-oval, oblong-lanceolate or rarely lanceolate, lamina 1—4 cm. long, 0.4—1.7 cm. broad, apex obtuse, rounded or rarely acute, mucronate, base obtuse, tapered or rounded; upper surface pale greyish-green, matt, densely scaly, the scales contiguous; *under surface densely scaly, the scales characteristic, similar in size and colour*, large, *creamy-yellow, overlapping* or rarely contiguous; petiole 2—5 mm. long, densely scaly, glabrous. *Inflorescence* 3—8-flowered, umbellate, terminal, or terminal and axillary in the uppermost 1—3 leaves forming a compact large compound inflorescence of 12—20 flowers; flower-bud scales deciduous or rarely persistent; rhachis 1—2 mm. long, scaly or not scaly, glabrous; pedicel 2—5 mm. long, densely scaly, glabrous. *Calyx* 5-lobed, 1—2 mm. long, pink or reddish, lobes ovate or rounded, outside moderately or rarely densely scaly, glabrous, margin not scaly or scaly, hairy with long hairs or glabrous. *Corolla* widely funnel-shaped, slightly zygomorphic, *1—1.3 cm. long*, 5-lobed, *lavender-blue, pale lavender-blue, purplish-blue* or sometimes bright rose, outside not scaly, glabrous. *Stamens* 10 or rarely 8, unequal, exserted, *short, one-half or two-thirds the length of the corolla*, 0.6—1 cm. long; filaments villous or puberulous towards the base. *Ovary* conoid, 1—2 mm. long, 5-celled, densely scaly, glabrous; *style short, shorter than the corolla, as long as the stamens or shorter*, not scaly, glabrous. *Capsule* conoid or oblong, 4—6 mm. long, 3—4 mm. broad, densely scaly, glabrous, calyx-lobes persistent.

R. hippophaeoides was discovered by Kingdon-Ward in May 1913 in the valley of the Chung River, north-west Yunnan. It was later found by other collectors in various localities in the same region and in south-west Szechuan. It grows in pine forests, in boggy peaty meadows, in open situations in alpine scrub, in moist stony pastures, in open grassy marshes, and in open bogs in pine forest, at elevations of 2,400—4,270 m. (7,868—14,000 ft.). According to Kingdon-Ward it is a dwarf shrub forming carpets or separate tufts 9 inches to a foot high in open pine forests at 3,173 m. (10,500 ft.) in north-west Yunnan.

The diagnostic features of this plant are the densely scaly lower surface of the leaves with characteristic creamy-yellow, overlapping scales similar in size and colour, the very short stamens and style, much shorter than the corolla, and usually the pale lavender-blue flowers. It is allied to R. *fimbriatum*; the distinctions between them are discussed under the latter.

R. *hippophaeoides* was first introduced by Forrest in 1903 (No. 10333). He later sent seeds on many occasions from north-west Yunnan. It was reintroduced by Rock, and Yü. In cultivation it is a broadly upright shrub up to 2 or 3 feet high, often with long annual growths. The species varies in leaf shape and size, from oblong-lanceolate to oblong-oval, the lamina being 1 cm. up to 4 cm. in length. The inflorescence is terminal, or terminal and axillary in the uppermost 1—3 leaves, 3—8-flowered. The best form is one with a group of several trusses clustered at the end of the branchlet forming a compact large compound inflorescence of 12—20 flowers. The species often produces good fertile seed in plenty. It is free-flowering even as a small plant. It is hardy, and is a most desirable plant for the rock garden. The species received an Award of Garden Merit in 1925. A form with lavender-blue flowers was given an Award of Merit when exhibited by Lady Aberconway and the Hon. H.D. McLaren, Bodnant, in 1927.

Epithet. Resembling sea buckthorn.
Hardiness 3—4. April—May.

R. idoneum Balf. f. et W.W. Sm. in Notes Roy. Bot. Gard. Edin., Vol. 9 (1916) 237.

A small *compact rounded*, cushion, matted or spreading shrub, *15—45 cm.* (*6 in.—1½ ft.) high; branchlets short, thick*, densely scaly with flaky scales, glabrous, leaf-bud scales deciduous. *Leaves* ovate, oval or rarely ovate-oblong, lamina 0.5—1.4 cm. long, 3—7 mm. broad, apex rounded or obtuse, mucronate, base rounded; upper surface green, shining, densely scaly, the scales overlapping or rarely one-half their own diameter apart; *under surface densely scaly, the scales characteristic, similar in size and colour*, large, *creamy-yellow or fawn, overlapping* or rarely contiguous, without or sometimes with widely or closely scattered dark brown scales; petiole 1—3 mm. long, densely scaly, glabrous. *Inflorescence* terminal, umbellate, *1—2-flowered*, flower-bud scales deciduous; rhachis 0.5 mm. long, scaly or not scaly, glabrous; pedicel 1 mm. long, densely scaly, glabrous. *Calyx* 5-lobed, 2—3 mm. long, purple, pink or greenish, lobes lanceolate, oblong or ovate, outside scaly, glabrous, margin not scaly, hairy with long hairs. *Corolla* widely funnel-shaped, slightly zygomorphic, 1.1—1.4 cm. long, 5-lobed, deep purplish-blue or purplish-blue, outside scaly along the middle of the lobes or not scaly, glabrous. *Stamens* 10 or rarely 8, unequal, long-exserted, long, as long as the corolla or a little longer, 0.9—1.4 cm. in length; filaments villous towards the base. *Ovary* conoid, 1 mm. long, 5-celled, densely scaly, glabrous; style long, longer than the stamens and the corolla, not scaly, glabrous or puberulous at the base. *Capsule* conoid, 3—5 mm. long, 2—4 mm. broad, densely scaly, glabrous or rarely hairy at the apex, calyx-lobes persistent.

Forrest first collected this plant in July 1914 on the mountains of the Chungtien plateau, north-west Yunnan. He found it again later in other localities in the same region. In 1932, McLaren's collectors also found it in north-west Yunnan. It grows on open ledges of cliffs and in stony pastures at elevations of 3,660—4,270 m. (12,000—14,000 ft.).

R. *idoneum* is a remarkably distinct species and cannot be confused with any species of its Series. It is easily recognised by its compact rounded habit of growth, by the ovate or oval leaves, densely scaly on the lower surface with characteristic creamy-yellow or fawn, overlapping scales similar in size and colour, by the 1—2-flowered inflorescence, by the long stamens as long as the corolla or a little longer, and by the long style longer than the corolla. The species is allied to R. *polifolium*, but is distinguished by the compact habit of growth, the short thick branchlets, the shape of the leaves, and by the larger calyx and corolla.

The species was first introduced by Forrest in 1914 (No. 12623 — the Type number). He later sent seeds under Nos. 15645 and 21577. In 1932 McLaren reintroduced it under Nos. S127 and S131. It flowered for the first time in May 1919 in the Royal Botanic Garden, Edinburgh. In cultivation it is a small compact rounded shrub, 12 inches high and as much across, although in its native home it is a matted or spreading shrub, 6 inches to 1½ feet high. It sets good fertile seeds nearly every year. Although a slow grower, it flowers at a fairly young age. It is hardy, free-flowering, and is well suited for the rock garden. The plant is rare in cultivation, but is worthy of being widely grown.

Epithet. Suitable.

Hardiness 3—4. April—May.

R. impeditum Balf. f. et W.W. Sm. in Notes Roy. Bot. Gard. Edin., Vol. 9 (1916) 239.

A small, matted or *very compact spreading or rounded*, or cushion shrub, 10—76 cm. (4 in.—2½ ft.) high; *branchlets short, thick*, densely scaly, scales flaky or not flaky, glabrous, leaf-bud scales deciduous. *Leaves* elliptic, ovate, oblong-oval, oblong or oblong-elliptic, lamina 0.5—1.6 cm. long, 3—6 mm. broad, apex obtuse or rounded, mucronate, base obtuse or rounded; *upper surface dark green in both the adult and young leaves*, not glaucous, somewhat shining, scaly, the scales one-half to their own diameter apart or contiguous; under surface densely scaly, the scales large, brown or dark brown, one-half their own diameter apart or rarely contiguous; petiole 1—3 mm. long, densely scaly, glabrous. *Inflorescence* terminal, umbellate, 1—3- or rarely 4-flowered, flower-bud scales deciduous; rhachis 0.5—1 mm. long, scaly or not scaly, glabrous; pedicel 1 mm. long, densely or rarely moderately scaly, glabrous. *Calyx* 5-lobed, 2—3 mm. or rarely 1 mm. long, pink, purple or greenish, lobes oblong, oblong-oval or oblong-lanceolate, outside moderately or sparsely scaly or rarely not scaly, glabrous, margin not scaly or rarely scaly, fringed with long hairs. *Corolla* widely funnel-shaped, slightly zygomorphic, 0.9—1.6 cm. long, 5-lobed, light or deep purplish-blue, pale or deep purple, pale or deep rose-purple, intense blue-purple, bright violet or lavender, outside not scaly, glabrous. *Stamens* 10, unequal, long-exserted, long, as long as the corolla or a little longer, 0.9—1.5 cm. in length; filaments villous towards the base. *Ovary* conoid, 1—2 mm. long, 5-celled, densely scaly, glabrous or sometimes puberulous at the apex; style long, longer than the stamens, not scaly, glabrous or rarely puberulous at the base. *Capsule* conoid, 3—5 mm. long, 2—3 mm. broad, moderately or densely scaly, glabrous or rarely puberulous at the base.

R. impeditum was discovered by Forrest in June 1910 on the eastern flank of the Lichiang Range, Yunnan. Subsequently it was found by him and by other collectors in mid-west and north-west Yunnan and in south-west Szechuan. The plant grows in open peaty pasture, in alpine meadows, in open moorland, on rocky slopes, on limestone cliffs, and in grassland, at elevations of 3,660—4,880 m. (12,000—16,000 ft.). It is recorded as being common in grassland, also as forming dense matted shrub a foot deep on the open rocks and ridges, in north-west Yunnan.

A conspicuous character of this plant is the very compact habit of growth with short thick branchlets, densely filled with foliage. Another distinguishing feature is the dark green upper surface of both the adult and young leaves. The species is allied to *R. fastigiatum*. The relationship between them is discussed under the latter.

R. impeditum was first introduced by Forrest in 1910 (No. 5863 — the Type number). It was reintroduced by him several times including Nos. 5876, 15076 and 20492. Rock sent seeds in 1924 under Nos. 11303 and 11469. Two distinct growth forms are in cultivation, both forms having a very compact habit of growth. Form 1 is a small rounded shrub, 6—8 inches high and as much across with tiny leaves. This form is rare in cultivation. Form 2 is a larger spreading shrub, 1½ feet high and 2—3 feet across with larger leaves. In cultivation the flower colour varies from deep blue-purple, pale purple to rose-purple. A form with deep blue-purple flowers is generally considered to be the best. The species is free-flowering, and one of its chief merits is that it flowers at a remarkably early age. It is hardy, and is a first class plant for the rock garden. A form under Rock No. 59263 received an Award of Merit when shown by the Sunningdale Nurseries in 1944.

Epithet. Tangled.

Hardiness 3—4. April—May. Plate 40.

R. intricatum Franch. in Journ. de Bot. IX (1895) 395.

Illustration. Bot. Mag. Vol. 133 t. 8163 (1907).

A somewhat *lax broadly upright* or bushy or matted shrub, 15—92 cm. (6 in.—3 ft.) high; branchlets long or short, densely scaly with flaky scales, glabrous, leaf-bud scales deciduous. *Leaves* ovate, oblong-oval, elliptic, oblong-elliptic, oval or rarely oblong, lamina 0.5—1.4 cm. or rarely 1.5—2 cm. long, 0.3—1 cm. broad, apex rounded or obtuse, mucronate, base rounded or obtuse; *upper surface pale greyish-green, matt*, densely scaly, the scales overlapping; *under surface* densely scaly, the *scales are characteristic, similar in size and colour*, large, *pale greyish, overlapping* or rarely nearly contiguous; petiole 1—3 mm. or rarely up to 5 mm. long, densely scaly, glabrous. *Inflorescence* terminal, umbellate, 2—5- or rarely 7—10-flowered; flower-bud scales persistent or rarely deciduous; rhachis 0.5—2 mm. long, scaly or not scaly, glabrous or rarely puberulous; pedicel 1—2 mm. or rarely up to 4 mm. long, densely scaly, glabrous. *Calyx* 5-lobed, minute, 0.5—1 mm. long, reddish, pink or greenish, lobes triangular, ovate or oblong-oval, outside not scaly or rarely scaly, glabrous, margin scaly or not scaly, hairy with long hairs or glabrous. *Corolla tubular-funnel shaped*, slightly zygomorphic, small, 0.7—1.3 cm. or rarely 2.3 cm. long, 5-lobed, dark purplish-blue, dark blue, *lavender-blue, pale lavender-blue*, purple-blue, deep violet-mauve or rarely rose-pink, outside not scaly, glabrous. *Stamens 7—10* or rarely 11, unequal, *included in the corolla-tube, very short*, shorter than the corolla, *3—6 mm. long*; filaments villous or moderately or slightly puberulous towards the base. *Ovary* conoid, 1—2 mm. long, 5-celled, densely scaly, glabrous; *style very short, shorter than the stamens*, one-half or one-third the length of the stamens, *as long as, or one-half as long as the ovary*, not scaly, glabrous. *Capsule* conoid, ovoid or oblong, 2—4 mm. long, 2—3 mm. broad, moderately or densely scaly, glabrous, calyx-lobes persistent.

This species was first collected by the Abbé Soulié in June 1891 around Tatsienlu, western Szechuan. Further gatherings by other collectors show that the plant is distributed in west and south-west Szechuan, and in north-west Yunnan. It is found in open pastures, in moist situations by streams, in marshy stony meadows, on grassy hills, and in dry moorland, at elevations of 3,355—4,600 m. (11,000—15,082 ft.). It is said to be a very common alpine shrub in the neighbourhood of Tatsienlu, western Szechuan. Kingdon-Ward records it as being common on the east flank of the Litang River Divide, north-west Yunnan.

In 1895, *R. blepharocalyx* Franch. was described from a specimen collected by Soulié in western Szechuan. The isotype and the ample material now available show that it is identical with *R. intricatum* in every respect.

In 1932, *R. peramabile* Hutch. was founded on a specimen grown by Lord Headfort at Kells, County Meath, Eire, under Forrest seed No. 20463. The corresponding herbarium specimen under the same number is the Type specimen of *R. yungningense*. Hutchinson points out that *R. peramabile* is a luxuriant form of *R. intricatum*. It is worth noting that cultivated specimens under Forrest No. 20463 are identical with *R. intricatum* in every character.

The diagnostic features of *R. intricatum* are the tubular-funnel shaped corolla, the very short stamens concealed in the corolla-tube, and the very short style, shorter than the stamens. In these respects it differs markedly from all the other species of its Series, except *R. complexum*, its nearest ally. Another well-marked character is the densely scaly lower surface of the leaves with characteristic pale greyish scales, overlapping or rarely nearly contiguous, similar in size and colour. It is allied to *R. complexum*; the distinctions between them are discussed under the latter.

R. intricatum was first introduced by Wilson for Messrs. Veitch in 1904 from western Szechuan (No. 3934). It was reintroduced by Forrest on several occasions from north-west Yunnan, including No. 20450. Kingdon-Ward sent seeds from the Yunnan-Szechuan border under No. 4184. Rock reintroduced it from north-west Yunnan, under Nos. 03757 and 03838. The plant flowered for the first time in Messrs. Veitch's nursery in April 1907. In cultivation it is a somewhat lax broadly upright shrub up to 3 feet high with pale greyish-green leaves. The species is hardy, a fairly fast grower, and provides a delightful colour display with its pale lavender-blue flowers produced freely in clusters of two to five. It was given a First Class Certificate when exhibited by Messrs. J. Veitch, Chelsea, in 1907.

Epithet. Entangled.
Hardiness 3—4. April—May.

R. lapponicum (L.) Wahlenb., Fl. Lapp. (1812) 104.
Illustration. Bot. Mag. Vol. 58 t. 3106 (1831).

A dwarf, *prostrate or spreading* or somewhat upright shrub, 5—45 cm. (2 in.—1½ ft.) or sometimes 60—92 cm. (2—3 ft.) high; branchlets short, densely scaly, scales flaky or not flaky, puberulous or glabrous, leaf-bud scales deciduous. *Leaves* elliptic, oblong-elliptic, oblong-oval, oblong-obovate, oblong or rarely ovate, lamina 0.5—1.5 cm. long, 2—5 mm. broad, apex obtuse or rounded, mucronate, base obtuse or rounded; upper surface pale green, matt, densely scaly, the scales overlapping or nearly contiguous; under surface densely scaly, the scales large, dark brown or brown or pale brown, overlapping; petiole 1—2 mm. long, densely scaly, glabrous. *Inflorescence* terminal, umbellate, 2—5-flowered, flower-bud scales deciduous; rhachis 0.5—2 mm. long, scaly or rarely not scaly, glabrous or rarely puberulous; pedicel 0.4—1 cm. long, densely scaly, glabrous or rarely puberulous. *Calyx* 5-lobed, minute, 0.5—1 mm. long, reddish, crimson-purple or pink, lobes ovate, triangular or rounded, outside densely or moderately scaly, glabrous, margin not scaly or rarely scaly, hairy with long hairs. *Corolla* widely funnel-shaped, slightly zygomorphic, small, 0.7—1 cm. long, 5-lobed, rose-purple, pinkish-purple, pink or purplish, outside not scaly, glabrous. *Stamens* 5—10, unequal, exserted, long or medium, as long as the corolla or a little longer, 0.5—1 cm. long; filaments villous or puberulous towards the base. *Ovary* conoid, 1 mm. long, 5-celled, densely scaly, glabrous; style long, longer than the stamens, not scaly, glabrous. *Capsule* conoid or oblong, 3—5 mm. long, 2—3 mm. broad, rather densely scaly, glabrous or rarely rather densely puberulous at the base, calyx-lobes persistent.

R. lapponicum is found in Arctic regions, in Lapland, in the north of Sweden and Norway, in Greenland, in Labrador, in the north-east U.S.A., and in the Canadian Arctic. It grows in peat, moss, clay-like soil, on limestone, on igneous or serpentine rocks, in bogs and damp places, at elevations from sea level up to 1,830 m. (6,000 ft.).

It is a dwarf prostrate or spreading or somewhat upright shrub 2 inches to 1½ feet or sometimes 2—3 feet high. The species shows a strong resemblance to *R. parvifolium* in the shape of the leaves, and in the shape and colour of the flowers, but is distinguished usually by the habit and height of growth, and often by the smaller leaves, the smaller corolla, and 5—10 stamens. It is a diploid with 26 chromosomes or tetraploid with 52 chromosomes.

R. lapponicum was first introduced by a Mr. Blair in 1825 from Canada. It flowered for the first time in July 1830 in Mr Cunningham's nursery at Comely Bank, now part of Edinburgh. Although it has been introduced several times, it is still a rare plant in cultivation. A group of four rooted plants introduced from Mount Washington, New Hampshire, U.S.A., in December 1936, were successfully grown in the rock garden of the Royal Botanic Garden, Edinburgh. They were dwarf prostrate plants, 3—4 inches high, and provided a fine display with purplish flowers in clusters of two to five; unfortunately these plants gradually deteriorated and died in August 1974. In September 1978, two little rooted plants, two to three inches high, were introduced from Newfoundland, but although they were well looked after, they were unable to adapt themselves to the new environment, and were alive for only three weeks. The species is a slow grower and is difficult to increase from cuttings; moreover, it hardly sets seed. It is a very difficult plant particularly in the south; it should be grown in cold gardens along the east coast and inland. Although the plant is rare, it is worthy of a place in every rock garden where it can be grown.

Epithet. From Lapland.

Hardiness 3—4. March—April. Plate 39.

R. litangense Balf. f. ex Hutch. in The Species of Rhododendron (1930) 411.

A *broadly upright* or bushy shrub, 30 cm.—1.22 m. (1—4 ft.) high; branchlets long or short, densely scaly with flaky scales, glabrous or rarely minutely puberulous, leaf-bud scales deciduous. *Leaves* oblong-elliptic, oblong-oval, elliptic, oblong or rarely oval, lamina 0.5—1.5 cm. long, 3—7 mm. broad, apex obtuse or rounded, mucronate, base obtuse or rounded; *upper surface dark green*, shining, scaly, the scales one-half to their own diameter apart; *under surface* scaly, the *scales* large, brown or dark brown, *one-half to twice their own diameter apart*; petiole 1—3 mm. long, densely scaly, glabrous. *Inflorescence* terminal, umbellate, 1—2- or rarely 3-flowered, flower-bud scales subpersistent or deciduous; rhachis 0.5—1 mm. long, scaly or not scaly, glabrous; pedicel 1—2 mm. long, moderately or densely scaly, glabrous. *Calyx* 5-lobed, 1—3 mm. long, pale green, purple or reddish, lobes oblong or ovate, outside moderately or sparsely scaly or rarely not scaly, glabrous, margin not scaly, hairy with long hairs. *Corolla* widely funnel-shaped, slightly zygomorphic, 1—1.5 cm. long, 5-lobed, *plum-purple*, deep purplish-blue, bluish-purple, *deep purple*, purple, *reddish-purple* or lavender-blue, outside not scaly or rarely sparsely scaly on the lobes, glabrous. *Stamens* 10, unequal, long-exserted, long, as long as the corolla or a little longer, 0.7—1.2 cm. in length; filaments villous towards the base. *Ovary* conoid, 2 mm. long, 5-celled, densely scaly, glabrous; style long, longer or rarely a little shorter than the stamens, not scaly, puberulous at the base or glabrous. *Capsule* conoid, 3—5 mm. long, 2—3 mm. broad, densely scaly, glabrous, calyx-lobes persistent.

This species was discovered by Forrest in June 1918 on the Muli mountains, valley of the Litang, south-west Szechuan. It was later found by Kingdon-Ward in Yunnan-Szechuan border, and by Rock in south-west Szechuan and in north-west Yunnan. The plant grows in open alpine pastures, in cane brakes, amongst boulders, on rocky slopes, in spruce and oak forests, at elevations of 3,050—4,875 m. (10,000—15,984 ft.).

R. litangense is a distinct species and cannot be confused with any other species in the Lapponicum Series. It is easily recognised by its broadly upright habit of growth up to 4 feet high, by the oblong-oval to oblong dark green shining leaves, usually by the laxly scaly lower surface of the leaves, and often by the plum-purple flowers. The species shows a certain degree of resemblance to *R. capitatum* from Kansu, but differs markedly in its habit of growth, in the smaller dark green shining leaves, usually in the laxly spaced scales on the lower surface, and usually by the colour of the flowers. It further differs in its geographical distribution. In some respects it also resembles *R. lysolepis*, but is distinguished by well-marked characters.

The species was first introduced by Forrest in 1918 from 3,965—4,270 m. (13,000—14,000 ft.) in south-west Szechuan (No. 16277 — the Type number). It was reintroduced by him from the same region at 3,660 m. (12,000 ft.) (No. 16284). Rock sent seeds in 1929 from north-west Yunnan (No. 03839) and in 1932 from south-west Szechuan (No. 24369). In cultivation it is a broadly upright shrub, 3—4 feet high with dark green shining leaves, and usually with plum-purple flowers produced freely in clusters of 1—3. The plant is hardy, fairly fast-growing, and sets good fertile seed. It is uncommon in cultivation, but would be well worth acquiring for every rock garden.

Epithet. From Litang, S.W. Szechuan.

Hardiness 3—4. April—May.

R. lysolepis Hutch. in The Species of Rhododendron (1930) 412.

A broadly upright or bushy shrub, 45 cm.—1.22 m. (1½—4 ft.) high; branchlets densely scaly with flaky scales, glabrous or minutely puberulous, leaf-bud scales deciduous. *Leaves* elliptic or oblong-oval, lamina 0.5—2 cm. long, 3—8 mm. broad, apex obtuse or rounded, mucronate, base obtuse or rounded; upper surface dark green, shining, densely scaly, the scales nearly contiguous or one-half their own diameter apart; *under surface* scaly, the *scales* large, brown, *one-half to twice their own diameter apart*; petiole 1—3 mm. long, densely scaly, glabrous. *Inflorescence* terminal, umbellate, 1—3-flowered, flower-bud scales deciduous or persistent; rhachis 0.5—1 mm. long, scaly or not scaly, glabrous; pedicel 1—2 mm. long, moderately or densely scaly, glabrous. *Calyx* 5-lobed, 2—4 mm. long, crimson-purple or pale green, lobes oblong-oval or oblong, outside scaly, glabrous, margin not scaly, hairy with long hairs. *Corolla* widely funnel-shaped, slightly zygomorphic, *small, 8—9 mm. long*, 5-lobed, purple-violet, pinkish-violet, dark purple or pinkish-purple, outside not scaly, glabrous. *Stamens* 10, unequal, long-exserted, *short*, as long as the corolla or a little shorter, 6—9 mm. long; filaments villous towards the base. *Ovary* conoid, 1—2 mm. long, 5-celled, densely scaly, glabrous; *style short or long, shorter or longer than the stamens*, not scaly, glabrous or puberulous at the base. *Capsule* conoid, 3 mm. long, 2 mm. broad, densely scaly, glabrous, calyx-lobes persistent.

This species was described by Hutchinson in 1930 from plants cultivated at Kew. Their origin has not been indicated. These plants are very similar to a specimen No. 4456 collected by Kingdon-Ward in July 1921 above the Litang River at Muli, south-west Szechuan, growing in oak forest at an elevation of 3,660 m. (12,000 ft.). Kingdon-Ward sent seeds of this plant in 1921, and it is probable that the Kew plants were raised from these seeds.

R. lysolepis is a distinctive species. It shows a resemblance to *R. orthocladum* and *R. stictophyllum* in habit and height of growth, but is readily distinguished from both by well-marked characters.

In its native home it grows up to 4 feet high; in cultivation it is a broadly upright shrub up to 2 feet in height with slender branchlets, dark green shining leaves, laxly scaly beneath, with small flowers 8—9 mm. long, with short stamens, and usually with a short style. It is a fairly common plant in cultivation. One of its chief merits is that in some gardens it has a long flowering season extending from about the middle of April to about the middle or end of July. It is a delightful small shrub, free-flowering, and is easy to increase from cuttings.

Epithet. With loose scales.

Hardiness 3—4. April—July.

R. microleucum Hutch. in Gard. Chron. Vol. XCIII (1933) 333.

Illustration. Bot. Mag. Vol. 168, n.s. t. 171A (1951).

A small *compact rounded shrub, 45—60 cm. (1½—2 ft.) high and as much across*; branchlets short or long, densely scaly with flaky scales, glabrous, leaf-bud scales deciduous. *Leaves* narrowly oblanceolate, oblong or lanceolate, lamina 0.8—1.5 cm. long, 2—5 mm. broad, apex obtuse, minutely mucronate, base obtuse or tapered; upper surface green, somewhat shining, densely scaly, the scales overlapping or nearly contiguous; under surface densely scaly, the scales large, brown or fawn, nearly contiguous or one-half their own diameter apart; petiole 1—2 mm. long, densely scaly, glabrous. *Inflorescence* terminal, umbellate, 1—4-flowered, flower-bud scales persistent or sub-persistent; rhachis 0.5—1 mm. long, scaly or not scaly, glabrous; pedicel 1—4 mm. long, densely scaly, glabrous. *Calyx* 5-lobed, minute, 0.5 mm. long, pale green, lobes rounded, triangular or ovate, outside densely scaly, glabrous, margin scaly or not scaly, ciliate or eciliate. *Corolla* widely funnel-shaped, slightly zygomorphic, small, 0.8—1 cm. long, 5-lobed, *pure white*, outside not scaly, glabrous. *Stamens* 10, unequal, exserted, *short*, as long as the corolla or a little shorter, *6—8 mm. long*; filaments puberulous towards the base. *Ovary* conoid, 1—2 mm. long, 5-celled, densely scaly, glabrous; *style medium, as long as the stamens,* not scaly or scaly at the base, glabrous. *Capsule* conoid or ovoid, 3—4 mm. long, 2—3 mm. broad, densely or moderately scaly, glabrous, calyx-lobes persistent.

This species was described by Hutchinson in 1933 from a plant grown in the rock garden at Exbury, raised from Forrest's seed of unknown origin, presumably collected in western China.

R. microleucum is an albino of the Lapponicum Series. In some respects it resembles *R. orthocladum*. The main distinctions between them are that *R. microleucum* is a compact rounded shrub, up to 2 feet high and as much across, the corolla is white, the style is medium in length, as long as the stamens, and the leaves vary from oblong to lanceolate; whereas *R. orthocladum* is a broadly upright, or rounded somewhat compact shrub, up to 4 feet high, the corolla is lavender, pale or deep purplish-blue or purple, the style is very short, shorter than the stamens, and the leaves vary from lanceolate to linear. They further differ usually in the distribution of the scales on the lower surface of the leaves.

R. microleucum has been associated with *R. scintillans*. From this species it differs markedly in its habit and height of growth, in the smaller leaves and corolla, in the flower colour, and in the shorter stamens and style.

The species is very free-flowering, and is exceedingly attractive with its white flowers in clusters of one to four. It is very hardy, and is an exceptionally fine plant for the rock garden. The plant is highly rated, and received a First Class Certificate when shown by Mr. L. de Rothschild in 1939.

Epithet. Small and white.
Hardiness 3—4. April—May. Plate 31.

R. nigropunctatum Bureau et Franch. in Journ. de Bot. V (1891) 95.
Illustration. Bot. Mag. Vol. 139 t. 8529 (1913).
A small *broadly upright shrub, 25—60 cm. (10 in.—2 ft.) high*; branchlets short or long, densely scaly, scales flaky or not flaky, glabrous, leaf-bud scales deciduous. *Leaves* ovate, elliptic or oblong-elliptic, *tiny or small, lamina 5—9 mm. long,* 3—5 mm. broad, apex obtuse or rounded, mucronate, base obtuse or rounded; upper surface dark green, shining, densely scaly, the scales overlapping or contiguous or one-half to their own diameter apart; under surface densely scaly, the scales large, pale brown or brown, overlapping or contiguous or one-half to their own diameter apart, with or without closely scattered dark brown scales; petiole 1—2 mm. long, densely or moderately scaly, glabrous. *Inflorescence* terminal, umbellate, *1—2-flowered,* flower-bud scales persistent or subpersistent; rhachis 0.5—1 mm. long, scaly or not scaly, glabrous; pedicel 1 mm. long, densely scaly, glabrous. *Calyx* 5-lobed, *minute, 0.5—1 mm. long,* greenish or pink, lobes ovate, rounded or oblong-oval, outside scaly, glabrous, margin not scaly or scaly, ciliate or eciliate. *Corolla* widely funnel-shaped, slightly zygomorphic, *small, 0.8—1.2 cm. long,* 5-lobed, pale purple or pink, outside not scaly, glabrous. *Stamens* 10, unequal, exserted, short or long, *as long as the corolla or a little longer,* 0.6—1.1 cm. long; filaments villous towards the base. *Ovary* conoid, 1 mm. long, 5-celled, densely scaly, glabrous or rarely puberulous at the apex; *style long, longer than the stamens,* not scaly, glabrous or rarely puberulous at the base. *Capsule* conoid or oblong, 3—5 mm. long, 2 mm. broad, moderately or rather densely scaly, glabrous or rather densely puberulous, calyx-lobes persistent.

R. nigropunctatum was discovered by Bonvalot and Prince Henri d'Orléans in May 1890 between Lhassa and Batang, west Szechuan, growing at elevations of 3,050—4,575 m. (10,000—15,000 ft.).

The main features of this plant are the broadly upright habit of growth, 10 inches to 2 feet high,. the tiny or small leaves, lamina 5—9 mm. long, dark green and shining above, densely scaly beneath, the single or paired small flowers, 0.8—1.2 cm. long, pale purple or pink, usually the long stamens, and the long style, longer than the stamens.

The original diagnosis associates it with *R. thymifolium*. From this species it is very remote. It is allied to *R. stictophyllum* which it resembles in some features, but is readily distinguished usually by its flower colour, the long protruding style, the smaller calyx, and usually by the habit of growth.

The species was introduced by Wilson from west Szechuan. It is a charming small shrub with slender branchlets, and well-filled with foliage. The plant is fairly fast-growing, and seldom fails to provide a fine show with its pink flowers produced with great freedom. It is hardy, easy to grow, and well worth a place in every rock garden.

Epithet. Marked with black spots.

Hardiness 3—4. April—May.

R. nitidulum Rehd. et Wils. in Plantae Wilsonianae (1913) 509.

A broadly upright shrub, 60 cm.—1.53 m. (2—5 ft.) high; branchlets short, thick, densely scaly with flaky scales, glabrous, leaf-bud scales deciduous. *Leaves ovate or elliptic*, lamina 0.7—1.2 cm. long, 5—7 mm. broad, apex obtuse, mucronate, base rounded; upper surface dark green, shining, densely scaly, the scales contiguous or nearly contiguous; under surface densely scaly, the scales large, brown, contiguous or overlapping; petiole 1—2 mm. long, densely scaly, glabrous. *Inflorescence* terminal, umbellate, *1—2-flowered*, flower-bud scales subpersistent; rhachis 0.5 mm. long, scaly or not scaly, glabrous; pedicel 1 mm. long, densely scaly, glabrous. *Calyx* 5-lobed, 1—3 mm. long, pink, lobes ovate or oblong-oval, outside scaly, glabrous, margin not scaly, ciliate. *Corolla* widely funnel-shaped, slightly zygomorphic, *1.2—1.3 cm. long*, 5-lobed, violet-purple, outside not scaly, glabrous. *Stamens* 8—10, unequal, exserted, long, as long as the corolla or a little shorter, 0.8—1 cm. in length; filaments villous towards the base. *Ovary* conoid, 2 mm. long, 5-celled, densely scaly, glabrous; style long, longer than the stamens, not scaly, glabrous. *Capsule:* —

This species was first collected by Wilson in June 1908 growing in uplands at Mupin, western Szechuan, at elevations of 3,300—4,000 m. (10,820—13,111 ft.). It appears to have a restricted distribution in its native home.

R. nitidulum shows a resemblance to *R. capitatum* and *R. violaceum* in its appearance, but is distinguished from both usually by the shape of the leaves. It also differs from the former usually in the 1—2-flowered inflorescence, and from the latter in the larger flowers.

The plant was in cultivation for a long time. It is a small broadly upright shrub, 2 feet high with short thick branchlets and violet-purple flowers. The species is now possibly lost to cultivation.

Epithet. Shining.

Hardiness 3—4. April—May.

R. nitidulum Rehd. et Wils. var. **nubigenum** Rehd. et Wils. in Plantae Wilsonianae (1913) 510.

This plant was first found by Wilson in July 1908 in the vicinity of Tatsienlu, western Szechuan, growing in moorlands at elevations of 4,300—5,000 m. (14,098—16,393 ft.).

The variety differs from the species in that it is a smaller plant, 10—30 cm. (4 in.—1 ft.) high, usually with smaller leaves, 4—8 mm. long, 2—5 mm. broad. It is recorded as being the most alpine of all the rhododendrons growing in the neighbourhood of Tatsienlu. The plant has not been introduced into cultivation.

Epithet of the variety. Near the clouds.

Not in cultivation.

R. nivale Hook. f. Rhod. Sikkim Himal. t. 26 (1851).

A small prostrate, straggly, broadly upright, cushion or somewhat compact rounded shrub, *8—30 cm. (3 in.—1 ft.)* or sometimes 60—92 cm. (2—3 ft.) or rarely up to 1.53 m. (5 ft.) *high*; branchlets short, densely scaly, scales not flaky or flaky, glabrous, leaf-bud scales deciduous. *Leaves* elliptic, ovate, oval or oblong-oval, tiny or small, *lamina 0.2—1 cm. long*, 2—6 mm. broad, apex rounded or obtuse, minutely mucronate, base rounded or obtuse; *upper surface pale greyish-green, matt*, densely scaly, the scales overlapping; under surface densely scaly, the scales large, brown or pale brown, overlapping or nearly contiguous or one-half their own diameter apart, with closely or widely scattered dark brown scales; petiole 0.5—2 mm. long, densely scaly, glabrous. *Inflorescence* terminal, umbellate, 1- or sometimes 2-flowered, flower-bud scales persistent or deciduous; rhachis 0.5—1 mm. long, scaly or not scaly, glabrous; pedicel very short, 0.5—1 mm. long, densely or rarely moderately scaly, glabrous. *Calyx* 5-lobed, 2—3 mm. or rarely 1 mm. long, crimson-purple, purple, pink or greenish, lobes oblong, oblong-oval, ovate or lanceolate, outside moderately or densely scaly, glabrous, margin eciliate or ciliate. *Corolla* widely funnel-shaped, slightly zygomorphic, small, 0.8—1.1 cm. long, 5-lobed, reddish-purple, purple, lilac, *deep purple or deep pink*, outside not scaly or sometimes scaly along the middle of the lobes, glabrous. *Stamens* 10 or rarely 8, unequal, exserted, medium, as long as the corolla or a little longer, 0.7—1.1 cm. long; filaments villous towards the base. *Ovary* conoid, 1—2 mm. long, 5-celled, densely or rarely moderately scaly, glabrous or densely minutely puberulous in the lower half or all over; style long, longer than the stamens, not scaly, glabrous or sometimes puberulous at the base. *Capsule* conoid, 3 mm. long, 2 mm. broad, moderately or densely scaly, minutely puberulous, calyx-lobes persistent.

This species was discovered by J.D. Hooker in 1849 on the bare slopes of the mountains on the Tibetan frontier in Sikkim Himalaya. Further gatherings by other collectors show that the distribution of the plant extends from Nepal and Sikkim to Bhutan and Tibet. It grows on dry slopes, on open rocky hillsides, on rocks, in damp meadows, in open moorland, and occasionally in swamps, at elevations of 3,050—5,490 m. (10,000—18,000 ft.), and even 5,795 m. (19,000 ft.) — being the highest elevation of all rhododendrons. Ludlow, Sherriff and Hicks record it as forming extensive drifts in the alpine moorland at 4,270 m. (14,000 ft.) and as being common above the Abies zone at 3,965 m. (13,000 ft.) in Bhutan.

R. nivale is a distinctive species and cannot be confused with any other species of its Series. It shows a certain degree of resemblance to *R. nigropunctatum* and *R. stictophyllum*; however, from these and other species it is very remote.

The species was introduced by R.E. Cooper in 1915 from Bhutan, said to be under seed No. 2487. It first flowered in the Royal Botanic Garden, Edinburgh, on 26th. March 1920. In its native home it grows usually from 3 inches up to 3 feet high; in cultivation it is a dwarf somewhat compact rounded shrub 10 inches high, with short branchlets and pale greyish-green leaves with matt upper surfaces. The species is difficult to cultivate and is reputed to be a slow grower. It is very hardy, and a well-grown plant is most attractive with its single or paired reddish-purple flowers produced in great profusion. It does best in cold gardens, kept fairly moist at the root, and with a sunny aspect. The plant is rare in cultivation, but is well suited for the rock garden.

Epithet. Snowy.
Hardiness 3—4. April—May.

R. oresbium Balf. f. et Ward in Notes Roy. Bot. Gard. Edin., Vol. 9 (1916) 253.

A small cushion or *compact rounded shrub*, 15—60 cm. (6 in.—2 ft.) high; branchlets short, densely scaly with flaky, black or dark brown scales, glabrous, leaf-bud scales deciduous. *Leaves* ovate, oval, elliptic, oblong-elliptic or oblong, lamina 0.4—1.3 cm. long, 3—6 mm. broad, apex rounded or obtuse, mucronate, base rounded or obtuse;

upper surface greyish-green or dark greenish, matt, densely scaly, the scales overlapping or ½ their own diameter apart; under surface densely scaly, the scales large, dark brown or brown, overlapping or ½ their own diameter apart, without scattered darker brown scales; petiole 0.5—3 mm. long, densely scaly, glabrous. *Inflorescence* terminal, umbellate, *1—2- or sometimes 3—4-flowered*, flower-bud scales deciduous; rhachis 0.5 mm. long, scaly or not scaly, glabrous; pedicel 1 mm. long, densely scaly, glabrous. *Calyx* 5-lobed, 0.5—2 mm. long, greenish or purple, lobes ovate or ovate-oblong, outside densely scaly or not scaly, glabrous, margin not scaly, densely ciliate or eciliate. *Corolla* widely funnel-shaped, slightly zygomorphic, 0.8—1.3 cm. long, 1.2—1.5 cm. across, 5-lobed, purple-blue or pinkish-lavender, outside not scaly, glabrous. *Stamens* 10, unequal, exserted, long or medium, as long as the corolla or a little shorter, 0.6—1.3 cm. long; filaments puberulous towards the base. *Ovary* conoid, 1—2 mm. long, 5-celled, densely scaly, glabrous; *style short, shorter than, or as long as, the stamens*, not scaly, glabrous. *Capsule* conoid, 4 mm. long, 3 mm. broad, densely scaly, glabrous, calyx-lobes persistent.

R. oresbium was first collected by Kingdon-Ward in 1913 at Doker La, on the Tibet-Yunnan frontier. It was later found by Forrest in south-east Tibet, and by Rock in north-west Yunnan. The plant grows in open stony moorlands and on hillsides, at elevations of 3,965—4,575 m. (13,000—15,000 ft.).

The characteristic features of this plant are the compact rounded habit of growth, the greyish-green or darkish green leaves, and the short style, shorter than, or as long as, the stamens. It is allied to *R. edgarianum*; the distinctions between them are discussed under the latter.

The plant has been in cultivation for a long time. In its native home it grows from 6 inches to 2 feet high, but in cultivation it is a compact shrub 2 feet high and almost as much across, with short, thick branchlets. It is quite hardy, free-flowering, and easy to grow. The plant is uncommon in cultivation, but should be a valuable acquisition to any rock garden.

Epithet. Mountain-dwelling.
Hardiness 3—4. April—May.

R. orthocladum Balf. f. et Forrest in Notes Roy. Bot. Gard. Edin., Vol. 11 (1919) 104.

A *rounded somewhat compact or broadly upright* or bushy *shrub*, 30 cm.—1.22 m. (1—4 ft.) high; branchlets densely scaly with flaky scales, glabrous, leaf-bud scales deciduous. *Leaves lanceolate, linear-lanceolate, linear* or rarely oblong, *lamina 0.5—2 cm. long*, 1—4 mm. broad, apex acute, obtuse or rarely rounded, mucronate, base tapered or obtuse; upper surface green or pale green, shining or matt, densely scaly, the scales overlapping or sometimes nearly contiguous; under surface densely scaly, the scales large, brown, fawn, cinnamon-brown or dark brown, overlapping or nearly contiguous, with or without closely or widely scattered dark brown scales; petiole 1—2 mm. long, densely scaly, glabrous. *Inflorescence* terminal, umbellate, 1—4-flowered, flower-bud scales persistent or deciduous; rhachis 0.5—1 mm. long, scaly or not scaly, glabrous; pedicel 1—3 mm. long, densely scaly, glabrous. *Calyx* 5-lobed, minute, 0.5—1 mm. long, reddish or pink, lobes rounded or triangular, outside densely or moderately scaly, glabrous, margin scaly or not scaly, glabrous or hairy with long hairs. *Corolla* widely funnel-shaped, slightly zygomorphic, 0.8—1 cm. or rarely 1.3 cm. long, 5-lobed, *lavender, pale purplish-blue, deep blue-purple or purple*, outside not scaly or rarely sparsely scaly on the lobes, glabrous. *Stamens* 10, unequal, exserted, short, shorter than, or rarely as long as, the corolla, 5—8 mm. long; filaments villous towards the base. *Ovary* conoid, 1—2 mm. long, 5-celled, densely scaly, glabrous; *style very short, shorter than*, or rarely as long as, *the stamens*, not scaly or rarely scaly at the base, glabrous. *Capsule* conoid, 3—4 mm. long, 2 mm. broad, densely scaly, glabrous, calyx-lobes persistent.

R. orthocladum was discovered by Forrest in July 1913 on the mountains in the north-east of the Yangtze bend, north-west Yunnan. Subsequently it was collected by him again, by Rock, and also by Kingdon-Ward in other localities in the same region and in south-west Szechuan. The plant grows in open situations on ledges of limestone cliffs, amongst rocks, in stony alpine meadows, and in open pasture on the margins of pine forests, at elevations of 2,745—4,270 m. (9,000—14,000 ft.). Kingdon-Ward records it as forming broom-like thickets a foot or two deep on the open mountain summits at Yung-ning.

A diagnostic feature of this plant is the narrowly lanceolate or linear-lanceolate or linear leaves, laminae 0.5—2 cm. long, and 1—4 mm. broad. Another notable character is the very short style, shorter than the stamens. The species is allied to R. spilanthum from which it is readily distinguished by its rounded somewhat compact or broadly upright habit of growth, usually by the colour of the scales on the lower surface of the leaves, and usually by the longer pedicels. It is also related to R. microleucum; the distinctions between them are discussed under the latter. Moreover, it shows a certain degree of resemblance to R. scintillans, but differs markedly in its habit of growth, its very short style, its short stamens, and often in its smaller corolla.

The species was first introduced by Forrest in 1913 (No. 10481 — the Type number). It was reintroduced by him on several occasions. Two distinct forms are in cultivation. Form 1. A rounded somewhat compact shrub, 3 feet high and almost as much across with lanceolate leaves. Form 2. A broadly upright shrub, 2 feet high with linear leaves. The species is free-flowering, and one of its merits is that it flowers at an early age. It is fairly fast-growing, and is not particular as to position in the garden. The plant is hardy and should be in every collection of rhododendrons.

Epithet. With straight twigs.
Hardiness 3—4. April—May.

R. paludosum Hutch. et Ward in Notes Roy. Bot. Gard. Edin., Vol. 16 (1931) 175.

A small *rounded somewhat compact or broadly upright shrub*, 23—76 cm. (9 in.—2½ ft.) high; branchlets short or somewhat long, densely scaly, scales not flaky or rarely flaky, glabrous, leaf-bud scales deciduous. *Leaves elliptic, ovate, oblong-oval or oval*, tiny or small, lamina 0.3—1.4 cm. long, 0.2—1.1 cm. broad, apex obtuse or rounded, minutely mucronate, base obtuse or rounded; *upper surface dark green, somewhat shining*, densely scaly, the scales overlapping; under surface densely scaly, the scales large, pale brown, nearly contiguous, rarely one-half or their diameter apart, with closely or widely scattered dark brown scales; petiole 1—2 mm. long, densely scaly, glabrous. *Inflorescence* terminal, umbellate, 1—2- or sometimes 3-flowered, flower-bud scales deciduous or persistent; rhachis 0.5 mm. long, scaly or not scaly, glabrous; pedicel 0.5—2 mm. long, densely scaly, glabrous. *Calyx* 5-lobed, 2—4 mm. or rarely 1 mm. long, yellowish, reddish or crimson-red, lobes oblong or ovate-oblong, outside moderately or rather densely scaly, glabrous, margin scaly, glabrous or rarely hairy with long hairs. *Corolla* widely funnel-shaped, slightly zygomorphic, small, 0.8—1.3 cm. long, 5-lobed, *violet, lavender, bluish-purple* or purple, outside not scaly or rarely scaly on the lobes, glabrous. *Stamens* 8—10, unequal, long-exserted, medium in length, as long as the corolla or a little longer, 0.7—1.2 cm. long; filaments villous towards the base. *Ovary* conoid, 1—2 mm. long, 5-celled, densely scaly, glabrous; style long, longer than the stamens, not scaly, minutely puberulous at the base or glabrous. *Capsule* conoid, 3 mm. long, 2 mm. broad, densely scaly, glabrous, calyx-lobes persistent.

This species was discovered by Kingdon-Ward in June 1924 at Tsela Dzong, south Tibet. It was later found by him again in the same region. In 1936, Ludlow and Sherriff collected it in other localities in south Tibet. The plant grows in bogs, on rocks amongst mixed scrub, and in boggy pastures, at elevations of 3,660—4,575 m. (12,000—15,000 ft.). Kingdon-Ward records it as forming masses in open bogs in birch copse or in the open valleys, also as forming dense colonies in boggy pastures at the foot of the hills.

R. paludosum is a remarkably distinctive species and cannot be confused with *R. nivale* or with any other species in its Series. The main features of this plant are the rounded somewhat compact or broadly upright habit of growth up to 2½ feet high, the elliptic to ovate leaves up to 1.4 cm. long, and up to 1.1 cm. broad, dark green and somewhat shining on the upper surface, the 1—2- or sometimes 3-flowered inflorescence, the corolla up to 1.3 cm. long, and the long style.

The species was first introduced by Kingdon-Ward in 1924 (Nos. 5729, 5777, 5778, and 5792 — the Type number). It was reintroduced by him under Nos. 7058 and 10595. In its native home it grows 9—12 inches high, but in cultivation it is a robust, rounded somewhat compact, or broadly upright shrub 2—2½ feet in height and usually almost as much across. A diagnostic feature in cultivation is the large broadly ovate leaves, laminae 1.2—1.4 cm long, and 0.8—1.1 cm. broad, dark green and somewhat shining above. In these respects alone, *R. paludosum* is easily distinguished from its ally *R. nivale* which is a dwarf shrub in cultivation, up to 10 inches high with tiny leaves, laminae 2—9 mm. long, and 2—5 mm. broad, pale greyish-green and matt above. Moreover, *R. paludosum* is fairly fast-growing usually with somewhat long branchlets, whereas *R. nivale* is a slow grower with short branchlets.

R. paludosum often sets good fertile seed, and is easy to increase from cuttings. It is hardy, free-flowering, and provides a fine display with its bluish-purple flowers. The plant is uncommon in cultivation, but is worthy of being widely grown.

Epithet. Marshy.
Hardiness 3—4. April—May.

R. parvifolium Adams in Mém. Soc. Nat. Mosc. IX (1834) 237.

Illustration. Bot. Mag. Vol. 154 t. 9229 (1931).

A *rounded or broadly upright shrub*, 30—92 cm. (1—3 ft.) high; branchlets long, densely scaly, scales not flaky or flaky, puberulous or glabrous, leaf-bud scales deciduous. *Leaves* oblong, oblong-lanceolate, oblong-elliptic, oblong-oval or elliptic, *lamina 0.6—2.5 cm. long*, 0.3-1 cm. broad, apex obtuse or rounded, mucronate, base obtuse or tapered; upper surface pale green, matt, densely scaly, the scales contiguous or overlapping; under surface densely scaly, the scales large, brown or fawn or greenish, overlapping or continuous or one-half their own diameter apart; petiole 2—4 mm. long, densely scaly, glabrous. *Inflorescence* terminal, umbellate, 2—5-flowered, flower-bud scales deciduous; rhachis 1—3 mm. long, scaly or not scaly, puberulous or glabrous; pedicel 2—6 mm. long, densely scaly, puberulous or glabrous. *Calyx* 5-lobed, 1—2 mm. long, pink or reddish, lobes ovate, triangular or lanceolate, outside densely or moderately scaly, glabrous, margin not scaly or scaly, hairy with long hairs or glabrous. *Corolla* widely funnel-shaped, slightly zygomorphic, *1—1.3 cm. long*, 5-lobed, deep reddish, bright rose, rose-purple or pale rose-magenta, outside not scaly, glabrous. *Stamens* 10, unequal, long-exserted, long, as long as the corolla or a little longer, 0.8—1.3 cm. in length; filaments puberulous or villous towards the base, deep reddish-purple or rose. *Ovary* conoid, 1 mm. long, 5-celled, densely scaly, glabrous; style long, longer than the stamens, not scaly, glabrous, deep reddish-purple, purple or rose. *Capsule* conoid, 5 mm. long, 3—4 mm. broad, rather densely scaly, glabrous, calyx-lobes persistent.

R. parvifolium was described by Adams in 1834 from plants growing around Lake Baikal, Siberia. It is a native of North-east Asia, extending from Siberia to North-east China, North Korea, Sakhalin, the north island of Japan, the Aleutians and Alaska.

It shows a resemblance to *R. lapponicum* in general features but is distinguished usually by the taller habit of growth up to 3 feet high, often by the larger leaves and larger corolla, and 10 stamens. In *R. lapponicum* the stamens are 5—10.

The species was introduced about 1877 from Siberia. A fine example of this rhododendron is growing in the rock garden of the Royal Botanic Garden, Edinburgh. It is a rounded shrub, 3 feet high and almost as much across. The species has proved to be of sturdy habit, fairly fast-growing, with long thick branchlets. It is an early flowerer, the flowers appearing in January—March. When it escapes the frost, it provides an admirable display with its rose-purple flowers produced freely in clusters of 2—5. The species is rare in cultivation. It is a charming plant for the rock garden, and is worthy of more general cultivation.

Epithet. With small leaves.

Hardiness 3—4. January—March.

R. parvifolium Adams var. **albiflorum** (Herder) Maxim. Rhod. As. Orient (1870) 17.

This plant is a native of Siberia. It differs from the species in its white flowers. The plant has not been introduced into cultivation.

Epithet of the variety. With white flowers.

Not in cultivation.

R. polifolium Franch. in Journ. de Bot. IX (1895) 397.

A small upright shrub, *30—60 cm. (1—2 ft.) high*; branchlets long or short, densely scaly with flaky scales, glabrous, leaf-bud scales deciduous. *Leaves* oblong, oblong-oval, elliptic or oblong-elliptic, small or tiny, lamina 0.3—1 cm long, 2—5 mm. broad, apex obtuse or rounded, mucronate, base obtuse or rounded; upper surface pale green, matt, densely scaly, the scales overlapping; *under surface densely scaly*, the *scales are characteristic, similar in size and colour*, large, *creamy-yellow or fawn, overlapping*; petiole 1—2 mm. long, densely scaly, glabrous. *Inflorescence* axillary in the uppermost one or two leaves and terminal, or terminal, umbellate, 1—3-flowered, flower-bud scales persistent or deciduous; rhachis 0.5 mm. long, scaly or not scaly, glabrous; *pedicel very short, 0.5—1 mm. long*, densely scaly, glabrous. *Calyx* 5-lobed, *minute, 0.5—1 mm. long*, pink, lobes rounded or ovate, outside scaly, glabrous, margin scaly or not scaly, eciliate or ciliate. *Corolla* widely funnel-shaped, slightly zygomorphic, *small, 0.6—1 cm. long*, 5-lobed, deep purplish-blue or purplish-blue, outside not scaly, glabrous. *Stamens* 10, unequal, exserted, medium or long, as long as the corolla or a little longer, 0.6—1 cm. long; filaments villous towards the base. *Ovary* conoid, 1 mm. long, 5-celled, densely scaly, glabrous; style medium or long, as long as the stamens or longer, not scaly, glabrous. *Capsule* conoid, 3 mm. long, 2 mm. broad, densely scaly, glabrous, calyx-lobes persistent.

This species was first collected by the Abbé Soulié in 1893 near Tatsienlu, western Szechuan. It was later found by other collectors in the same region. The plant grows on hillsides at elevations of 2,745—4,600 m. (9,000—15,082 ft.).

R. polifolium is an upright shrub 1—2 feet high with tiny leaves, 0.3—1 cm. long. A distinctive feature is the densely scaly lower surface of the leaves with characteristic creamy-yellow or fawn overlapping scales, similar in size and colour. It resembles *R. thymifolium* in some features, but is readily distinguished by the long style, as long as the stamens or longer, usually by the non-scaly corolla, and usually by its habit and height of growth.

The species has long been in cultivation. It is a small shrub, 1½ feet high with somewhat slender branchlets and small purplish-blue flowers in clusters of 1—3. The plant is now rare.

Epithet. Many-leaved.

Hardiness 3—4. April—May.

R. polycladum Franch. in Bull. Soc. Bot. France XXXIII (1886) 234.

A small shrub; branchlets short, densely scaly with flaky scales, glabrous, leaf-bud scales deciduous. *Leaves oblong or lanceolate*, lamina 0.6—1.2 cm. long, 2—4 mm. broad, apex obtuse or acute, mucronate, base obtuse; upper surface dark green, shining, densely scaly, the scales nearly contiguous; under surface densely scaly, the scales large, dark brown, overlapping or nearly contiguous; petiole 1—2 mm. long, densely scaly, glabrous. *Inflorescence* terminal, umbellate, 2—3-flowered, flower-bud scales deciduous; rhachis 0.5 mm. long, scaly or not scaly, glabrous; pedicel very short, 0.5—1 mm. long, densely scaly, glabrous. *Calyx* 5-lobed, minute, 0.5—1 mm. long, purple or pink, lobes rounded or ovate, outside scaly, glabrous, margin not scaly, ciliate. *Corolla* widely funnel-shaped, slightly zygomorphic, small, 1 cm. long, 5-lobed, purple, outside not scaly, glabrous. *Stamens* 10, unequal, exserted, medium or long, as long as the corolla, 0.8—1 cm. long; filaments villous towards the base. *Ovary* conoid, 1 mm. long, 5-celled, densely scaly, glabrous; *style long, longer than the stamens*, not scaly, glabrous. *Capsule:* —

This plant was discovered by the Abbé Delavay in May 1884 at Koulapo, Hokin, north-west Yunnan, growing in pastures and on rocks at an elevation of 3,000 m. (9,836 ft.).

The original diagnosis makes no reference to its affinity. In the shape and size of the leaves, in the size of the corolla, and in the long style, *R. polycladum* shows a strong resemblance to *R. fastigiatum*. The herbarium material of this plant is scanty. Meanwhile, the name *R. polycladum* may be allowed to stand until further specimens are available. The plant has not been introduced into cultivation.

Epithet. With many branches.

Not in cultivation.

R. ramosissimum Franch. in Journ. de Bot. XII (1898) 264.

A small, compact or broadly upright or bushy shrub, 10 cm.—1 m. (4 in.—3⅓ ft.) high; *densely branched*, branchlets short, densely scaly, scales not flaky or rarely flaky, glabrous, leaf-bud scales deciduous. *Leaves* ovate, elliptic or oval, *tiny or small, lamina 3—7 mm. long*, 2—4 mm. broad, apex obtuse or rounded, mucronate, base rounded or obtuse; upper surface pale green, matt, densely scaly, the scales overlapping; under surface densely scaly, the scales large, dark to pale brown, overlapping or nearly contiguous, with or without closely or widely scattered dark brown scales; petiole 1—2 mm. long, densely scaly, glabrous. *Inflorescence* terminal, umbellate, *1—2- or rarely 3-flowered*, flower bud scales persistent or deciduous; rhachis 0.5—1 mm. long, scaly or not scaly, glabrous; pedicel very short, 0.5—1 mm. long, densely or moderately scaly, glabrous. *Calyx* 5-lobed, 0.5—2 mm. long, reddish, lobes ovate, oblong or oval, outside moderately or densely scaly, glabrous, margin scaly or rarely not scaly, glabrous or rarely hairy with long hairs. *Corolla* widely funnel-shaped, slightly zygomorphic, *small, 0.8—1.2 cm. long*, 5-lobed, dark purplish-blue, purplish-red, deep bluish or purple, outside not scaly or rarely scaly on the lobes, glabrous. *Stamens* 8—10, unequal, exserted, short, as long as the corolla or a little shorter, 0.5—1 cm. long; filaments villous towards the base or rarely glabrous. *Ovary* conoid, 1—2 mm. long, 5-celled, densely scaly, glabrous; *style short, shorter than, or as long as, the stamens*, not scaly, glabrous. *Capsule* conoid, 3 mm. long, 2 mm. broad, densely scaly, minutely puberulous at the base or glabrous, calyx-lobes persistent.

R. ramosissimum was described by Franchet in 1898 from a plant collected by R.P. Mussot in the south of Tatsienlu, western Szechuan. It was later collected by Soulié, Wilson, and Rock in other localities in the same region, and by Kingdon-Ward in the Yunnan-Szechuan Border. The plant grows in moorlands, on limestone screes, and in alpine regions, at elevations of 3,050—4,900 m. (10,000—16,066 ft.).

In 1920, *R. yaragongense* Balf. f. was described from a specimen collected by Soulié in west Szechuan. It is identical with *R. ramosissimum* in every respect, and in *The Species of Rhododendron* 1930, p. 422, it has been placed correctly in synonymy under the latter.

R. ramosissimum is a distinct species, and cannot be mistaken for *R. nivale* or any other species of its Series. The main features of this plant are the compact or broadly upright habit of growth, densely branched with tiny leaves, the 1—2- or rarely 3-

flowered inflorescence, the small flowers 0.8—1.2 cm. long, and the short style, shorter than, or as long as, the stamens. The species is tetraploid with 52 chromosomes. It resembles *R. alpicola* and *R. stictophyllum* in some features, but differs from both in distinctive characters.

The species was first introduced by Wilson in 1908 (Nos. 3468 and 3469). In its native home it grows from 4 inches to 3⅓ feet high, but in cultivation it is a small shrub of 1½—2 feet. The plant is very hardy, with small purplish-red flowers produced in great profusion. It is rare in cultivation, but should be a valuable acquisition to any rock garden.

Epithet. Very branched.

Hardiness 3—4. April—May.

R. rupicola W.W. Sm. in Notes Roy. Bot. Gard. Edin., Vol. 8 (1914) 203.

A matted, cushion, compact rounded, rounded, broadly upright or upright shrub, 8 cm.—1.22 m. (3 in.—4 ft.) high; branchlets short or long, densely scaly with flaky scales, glabrous, leaf-bud scales deciduous. *Leaves* elliptic, oblong-elliptic, obovate, oblong-oval, oval or nearly orbicular, lamina 0.8—2.5 cm. long, 0.4—1.4 cm. broad, apex rounded or obtuse, mucronate, base rounded or obtuse; upper surface green, matt, densely scaly, the scales overlapping or contiguous; *under surface* densely scaly, the *scales large, bicolorous, dark brown and yellow, or rarely unicolorous, dark brown, overlapping or nearly contiguous*; petiole 2—3 mm. long, densely scaly, glabrous. *Inflorescence* terminal, umbellate, 2—8-flowered, flower-bud scales deciduous or persistent; rhachis 1—3 mm. long, scaly or not scaly, glabrous or rarely puberulous; pedicel 1—4 mm. long, densely scaly, glabrous. *Calyx* 5-lobed, 2—5 mm. long, deep crimson-purple or crimson-purple or rarely pink, lobes ovate, oblong-oval, oval, oblong or lanceolate, outside densely or rarely moderately scaly along the middle, glabrous or rarely puberulous, margin not scaly or rarely scaly, ciliate. *Corolla* widely funnel-shaped, slightly zygomorphic, 1—1.6 cm. long, 5-lobed, *deep plum-purple, deep plum-crimson, plum-purple, black-purple, deep magenta-red* or purplish-rose, outside scaly along the middle of the lobes, glabrous. *Stamens* 10 or sometimes 5—8, unequal, long-exserted, long, as long as the corolla or a little longer, 0.9—1.5 cm. in length; filaments villous towards the base. *Ovary* conoid, 1—2 mm. long, 5-celled, densely or sometimes moderately scaly, puberulous at the base or in the lower half and sometimes at the apex, or glabrous; style long, longer than the stamens, not scaly, glabrous or puberulous at the base. *Capsule* conoid, 3—6 mm. long, 2—3 mm. broad, rather densely scaly, puberulous in the lower half or at the base or rarely all over, calyx-lobes persistent.

This species was discovered by Forrest in June 1910 on the western flank of the Lichiang Range, Yunnan. Subsequently it was found by him again, and by other collectors in north-west Yunnan, east and north-east Upper Burma, and south-west Szechuan. It grows on rocks, limestone cliffs, screes and boulders, in open alpine pastures, in stony meadows and moorland, at elevations of 3,355—4,270 m. (11,000—14,000 ft.).

In 1916, *R. achroanthum* Balf. f. et W.W. Sm. was described from a specimen (No. 12581) collected by Forrest on the mountains of the Chungtien plateau, Yunnan. The original diagnosis associated it with *R. rupicola*. However, the ample material now available and plants in cultivation show that it is identical with *R. rupicola* in every respect.

A noteworthy feature of *R. rupicola* is the deep plum-purple or deep plum-crimson or black-purple flowers, by which the species is readily distinguished from its nearest ally *R. russatum*, and usually from all the other members of its Series. It further differs from *R. russatum* in that the corolla lobes are scaly outside, and the leaves are often smaller. A well-marked character of *R. rupicola* is the bicolorous scales, dark brown and yellow, densely set on the lower surface of the leaves, overlapping or nearly contiguous. The plant is diploid with 26 chromosomes or tetraploid with 52 chromosomes.

R. rupicola was first introduced by Forrest in 1910 (No. 5865 — the Type number). It was reintroduced by him on several occasions. Rock sent seeds in 1929 from north-west Yunnan. In cultivation it is usually a small broadly upright shrub 2 feet high, although in its native home it is an upright, matted, cushion or compact rounded shrub 3 inches to 4 feet high. Two distinct forms are in cultivation. Form 1. A broadly upright spreading shrub 2 feet high with oval or nearly orbicular leaves, and deep plum-crimson flowers. Form 2. An upright shrub up to 2 feet high with lanceolate leaves and somewhat pale plum-crimson flowers. Form 1 is generally regarded as being the better form. It is very hardy, and is exceedingly attractive when adorned with a profusion of flowers in clusters of 2—8. The plant is uncommon in cultivation, but is an excellent rhododendron for the rock garden.

Epithet. Dweller in stony places.
Hardiness 3—4. April—May. Plate 36.

R. russatum Balf. f. et Forrest in Notes Roy. Bot. Gard. Edin., Vol. 11 (1919) 126.
Illustration. Bot. Mag. Vol. 148 t. 8963 (1922). Figured as *R. cantabile*.

An upright, compact rounded, cushion, semi-prostrate or straggly shrub, *15 cm.— 1.53 m. (6 in.—5 ft.) high*; branchlets densely scaly, scales flaky or rarely not flaky, glabrous, leaf-bud scales deciduous. *Leaves* oblong-elliptic, oblong-oval, oval, oblong-ovate, oblong or oblong-lanceolate, *lamina 0.8—6.5 cm. long*, 0.4—2.3 cm. broad, apex rounded, obtuse or rarely acute, mucronate, base obtuse or rounded; upper surface dark or pale green, matt or shining, densely scaly, the scales nearly contiguous or one-half their own diameter apart or overlapping; *under surface* densely scaly, the *scales large, bicolorous, dark-brown and yellow, or unicolorous, cinnamon-red or dark brown or brown*, contiguous or overlapping or one-half their own diameter apart; petiole 1—9 mm. long, densely scaly, glabrous. *Inflorescence* terminal, umbellate, *3—6- or sometimes up to 10- or rarely 14-flowered*, flower-bud scales persistent or deciduous; rhachis 1—3 mm. long, scaly or not scaly, puberulous or glabrous; pedicel 1—4 mm. long, densely or rarely sparsely scaly, glabrous or rarely puberulous. *Calyx* 5-lobed, *3—6 mm. or rarely 1 mm. long*, greenish, pink, reddish or crimson-purple, lobes oblong, oblong-oval, rounded or ovate, outside moderately or sparsely scaly or not scaly, glabrous, margin not scaly or rarely scaly, hairy with long hairs or rarely glabrous. *Corolla* widely funnel-shaped, slightly zygomorphic, 1.3—2 cm. long, 5-lobed, deep purple-blue, deep rose-purple, rose-purple, deep violet-purple, light purple or violet, *outside not scaly*, glabrous or rarely puberulous on the tube. *Stamens* 10 or sometimes 5—8, unequal, long-exserted, long, as long as the corolla or a little longer, 0.9—2 cm. in length; filaments villous towards the base. *Ovary* conoid, 2 mm. long, 5-celled, densely scaly, glabrous, or sometimes pubescent all over or at the apex; style long, longer than the stamens, not scaly, hairy up to one-half its length or glabrous. *Capsule* conoid, 4—6 mm. long, 3—4 mm. broad, densely or moderately scaly, pubescent or glabrous, calyx-lobes persistent.

This well-known species was first collected by Forrest in June 1917 in the Kari Pass, north-west Yunnan. Further gatherings by him and other collectors show that the plant is distributed in north-west and mid-west Yunnan, north-east Upper Burma, and south-west Szechuan. It grows in stony pastures, on cliffs and rocky slopes, on boulders and screes, in the crevices of limestone cliffs, in cane brakes, in rhododendron scrub, open boggy meadows on the margin of conifer forests, in alpine moorland, and by streams, at elevations of 3,355—4,270 m. (11,000—14,000 ft.).

In 1922, *R. cantabile* Balf. f. was described from a plant raised from seed by J.C. Williams of Caerhays Castle, Cornwall. Forrest's specimen No. 16583 which has been cited, is *R. rupicola*. When *R. cantabile* is compared with *R. russatum*, it will be seen that in height and habit of growth, in leaf shape and size, in the size and colour of the flowers, and in all other characters these two plants agree.

R. russatum is a very variable plant. It is an upright, compact rounded, cushion, semi-prostrate or straggly shrub, and grows from 6 inches to 5 feet high; the leaves are oval, oblong-oval to oblong-lanceolate, 0.8—6.5 cm. long, 0.4—2.3 cm. broad; the flower colour varies from deep violet-blue, through deep rose-purple to light purple. It is a tetraploid with 52 chromosomes. The species is related to *R. rupicola*. The relationship between them is discussed under the latter.

The species was first introduced by Forrest in 1917 (No. 13915 — the Type number). It was reintroduced many times by him and by Rock. Several distinct forms are in cultivation, including: Form 1. An upright shrub, 5 feet high, with large leaves up to 6.5 cm. long and 2.3 cm. broad, with purplish-blue flowers. Form 2. A broadly upright shrub 3 feet high with smaller leaves up to 2.5 cm. long, with purplish-blue or rose-purple flowers. Form 3. A broadly upright shrub 2 feet high with deep violet-blue flowers. Form 4. A somewhat compact rounded shrub 1½—2 feet high with purple-blue flowers. Form 5. A small straggly shrub 1½ feet high with small leaves 1 cm. long. All these forms are attractive plants, but Form 3 bearing a profusion of deep violet-blue flowers is of great beauty and is generally considered to be the best. The species is very hardy and should be in every collection.

The plant is highly rated, and an Award of Merit was given to a form with intense violet-blue flowers, when exhibited by A.M. Williams, Launceston, in May 1927, and a First Class Certificate to a form with intense purple flowers when shown by Lionel de Rothschild in 1933. It was given an Award of Garden Merit in 1938.

Epithet. Reddened.
Hardiness 3—4. April—May.

R. scintillans Balf. f. et W.W. Sm. in Notes Roy. Bot. Gard. Edin., Vol. 9 (1916) 271.

A *spreading* or rarely cushion *shrub*, 15 cm.—1.07 m. (6 in.—3½ ft.) high; *branchlets upright, slender, 8—15 cm. (3—6 in.) long*, densely scaly with flaky scales, glabrous, leaf-bud scales deciduous. *Leaves lanceolate or oblong*, rarely oblong-elliptic or oblong-oval, lamina 0.8—2.3 cm. long, 2—7 mm. broad, apex obtuse, acute or rounded, mucronate, base tapered or obtuse; upper surface dark green, shining, densely scaly, the scales overlapping or contiguous or nearly contiguous; *under surface* densely scaly, the *scales* large, dark brown or brown or sometimes cinnamon-brown, *one-half their own diameter apart or nearly contiguous* or rarely overlapping; petiole 1—4 mm. long, densely scaly, glabrous. *Inflorescence* terminal, umbellate, 2—5-flowered, flower-bud scales deciduous or subpersistent; rhachis 0.5—1 mm. long, scaly or not scaly, glabrous; pedicel 1—5 mm. long, densely scaly, glabrous. *Calyx* 5-lobed, 0.5—2 mm. or rarely 4 mm. long, purple, reddish, yellowish or pink, lobes ovate, rounded or sometimes lanceolate, outside scaly or not scaly, glabrous, margin not scaly or scaly, ciliate. *Corolla* widely funnel-shaped, slightly zygomorphic, 1—1.5 cm. long, 5-lobed, lavender-blue, deep or pale purplish-blue, deep blue-purple, pale rose-purple or dark purplish-red, outside not scaly, glabrous. Stamens 10, unequal, long-exserted, medium or long, as long as the corolla or a little longer, 0.7—1.2 cm. long; filaments villous towards the base. *Ovary* conoid, 1—2 mm. long, 5-celled, densely scaly, glabrous or rarely hairy at the apex; style long, longer than the stamens, not scaly, glabrous or rarely puberulous at the base. *Capsule* conoid or oblong, 4—5 mm. long, 2—3 mm. broad, moderately or densely scaly, glabrous or rarely puberulous at the base, calyx-lobes persistent.

R. scintillans was discovered by Forrest in May 1913 on the summit of the Lankong-Hoching Pass, Yunnan. It was afterwards found by him again, by McLaren's collectors, and by Rock in various localities in mid-west and north-west Yunnan. The plant grows in marshy and boggy pastures, in rocky alpine meadows, amongst scrub, on rocky slopes, in alpine moorland, on cliffs and rocks, in and on the margins of oak and conifer forests, at elevations of 3,355—3,965 m. (11,000—13,000 ft.).

In 1975, *R. gemmiferum* M.N. et W.R. Philipson was described from specimens collected by Forrest and Rock in Yunnan. When the Type specimen under Forrest No. 13902 is examined, it is seen that in height of growth, in the shape and size of the leaves and in the distribution of the scales on the lower surfaces, in the shape, size and colour of the corolla, and in all other details, *R. gemmiferum* is identical with *R. scintillans* under which it will now be placed in synonymy. The other specimens which have been regarded as *R. gemmiferum* are in leaf; they would appear to be possibly *R. russatum*, *R. litangense*, and *R. scintillans*.

A characteristic feature of *R. scintillans* is its spreading habit of growth with upright slender branchlets varying in length from 8 to 15 cm. (3—6 in.). Another well-marked character is its lanceolate or oblong leaves 0.8—2.3 cm. long. It bears a resemblance to *R. orthocladum* in some features, but is readily distinguished by its habit of growth, by the larger corolla, and by the longer stamens and style.

The species was first introduced by Forrest in 1913 (No. 10014 — the Type number). It was reintroduced by him on several occasions. Rock sent seed in 1923 (No. 11319). In its native home it grows from 6 inches to 3½ feet high, but in cultivation it is 2—3 feet in height. Several forms are in cultivation varying in leaf size and flower colour. The best form is one with deep blue-purple flowers. It is a pleasing shrub, free-flowering, and provides a fine display with clusters of 2—5 flowers.

A form with purplish-rose flowers received an Award of Merit when shown by Lady Aberconway and the Hon. H.D. McLaren, Bodnant, in 1924, and a First Class Certificate was awarded for a form with lavender-blue flowers when exhibited by L. de Rothschild, Exbury, in 1934.

Epithet. Sparkling.
Hardiness 3—4. April—May.

R. sclerocladum Balf. f. et Forrest in Notes Roy. Bot. Gard. Edin., Vol. 11 (1919) 133.

A broadly upright shrub, 92 cm.—1.53 m. (3—5 ft.) high; branchlets densely scaly with flaky scales, glabrous, leaf-bud scales deciduous. *Leaves* oblong-oval or oblong, lamina 0.9—1.5 cm. long, 4—6 mm. broad, apex rounded or obtuse, mucronate, base obtuse; *upper surface dark green*, matt, densely scaly, the scales nearly contiguous or overlapping; *under surface* densely scaly, the *scales* large, *dark brown or rufescent*, overlapping; petiole 1—2 mm. long, densely scaly, glabrous. *Inflorescence* terminal, umbellate, 3—4-flowered, flower-bud scales subpersistent; rhachis 1—2 mm. long, scaly or not scaly, glabrous; pedicel 2—3 mm. long, densely scaly, glabrous. *Calyx* 5-lobed, *4—5 mm. long*, crimson-purple, reddish or pink, lobes oblong or oblong-oval, outside scaly, glabrous, margin not scaly, hairy with long hairs. *Corolla funnel-shaped*, slightly zygomorphic, *1.4—1.8 cm. long*, 5-lobed, purplish-rose, outside scaly on the lobes, glabrous. *Stamens* 10, unequal, long-exserted, long, as long as the corolla or a little longer, 1.4—1.7 cm. in length; filaments villous towards the base. *Ovary* conoid, 2 mm. long, 5-celled, densely scaly, glabrous; style long, longer than the stamens, not scaly, pubescent at the base. *Capsule* oblong, 6—8 mm. long, 3—4 mm. broad, straight, densely scaly, glabrous, calyx-lobes persistent.

This plant is known from a single collection made in July 1914 by Forrest on the mountains of the Chungtien plateau, north-west Yunnan. It grows in open rocky pasture and on the margins of pine forests at an elevation of 3,355 m. (11,000 ft.).

In *The Species of Rhododendron* 1930, p. 433, *R. sclerocladum* has been placed in synonymy under *R. ravum* (now a synonym of *R. cuneatum*.) From this species it usually differs markedly in its smaller leaves, in the shorter pedicel, in the smaller calyx and corolla, in the shorter stamens, and usually in its habit of growth.

The species (No. 12665 — holotype) has not been introduced into cultivation. It may be observed that some plants in cultivation labelled "R. ravum" of unknown origin, possibly introduced by Rock, show a strong resemblance to *R. sclerocladum* and could be regarded as extreme forms of this species. These plants are broadly upright in growth, 3—5 feet high with oblong-oval leaves and purplish-rose flowers in clusters of 2—4. They are hardy and fairly fast-growing.

Epithet. Rigid branches.
Hardiness 3. April—May.

R. setosum D. Don in Mem. Wern. Soc. III (1821) 408.
Illustration. Bot. Mag. Vol. 139 t. 8523 (1913).
A broadly upright shrub, 15 cm.—1.22 m. (6 in.—4 ft.) high; *branchlets* long, densely or moderately scaly with flaky scales, *moderately or rather densely bristly*, rather densely or moderately puberulous or sometimes not puberulous, leaf-bud scales deciduous. *Leaves* oval, obovate, oblong-obovate, oblong-oval, oblong or oblong-elliptic, lamina 0.6—1.7 cm. long, 4—7 mm. broad, apex rounded or obtuse, mucronate, base obtuse or rounded; upper surface pale greyish-green or dark green, matt, densely scaly, the scales nearly contiguous or one-half their own diameter apart; *margin* recurved, *sparsely or moderately bristly; under surface* scaly, the *scales* large, brown or yellow or pale brown, or yellow and dark brown, *1—4 times* or rarely one-half *their own diameter apart, not bristly or bristly; petiole* 1—3 mm. long, scaly, *bristly*, puberulous or not puberulous. *Inflorescence* terminal, umbellate, 3—6-flowered, flower-bud scales deciduous; rhachis 1—3 mm. long, scaly or not scaly, glabrous; *pedicel* 2—8 mm. long, densely or moderately scaly, *not bristly or moderately or rather densely bristly*, moderately or rather densely puberulous or sometimes not puberulous. *Calyx* 5-lobed, *4—6 mm. long, reddish or crimson-purple*, lobes oblong, ovate or oval, outside scaly, glabrous or rarely rather densely puberulous, margin scaly or rarely not scaly, glabrous or rarely hairy with long hairs. *Corolla* widely funnel-shaped, slightly zygomorphic, 1.3—2 cm. long, 5-lobed, purple, reddish-pink, pink, wine red, bright purple-pink or reddish-purple, outside not scaly or rarely scaly on the lobes, glabrous or rarely puberulous on the tube. *Stamens* 8—10, unequal, long-exserted, long, as long as the corolla or a little shorter, 0.8—1.3 cm. in length; filaments villous towards the base. *Ovary* conoid, 2 mm. long, 5-celled, densely scaly, glabrous or rarely rather densely puberulous; style long, longer than the stamens, not scaly, glabrous or rarely puberulous at the base. *Capsule* conoid, 5—6 mm. long, 3—5 mm. broad, densely or moderately scaly, glabrous or sometimes rather densely puberulous, enclosed by the persistent calyx-lobes or rarely not enclosed.

R. setosum was described by D. Don in 1821. It is widely distributed in Nepal, Sikkim, Bhutan, and south Tibet. The plant grows on ridges and boulders, in open stony and rocky places, in meadows, and in scrub jungle, at elevations of 2,745—5,033 m. (9,000—16,500 ft.). It is recorded as being very common in Nepal and Sikkim.

Diagnostic features of this plant are the bristly branchlets, petioles and margins of the leaves. Another marked character is the reddish or crimson-purple large calyx, 4—6 mm. long. The leaves vary from oval, obovate to oblong, and the scales on the lower surface are usually 1—4 times their own diameter apart. The species shows a certain degree of resemblance to *R. fragariflorum*, but differs in distinctive features. It is a diploid with 26 chromosomes.

It was first introduced in 1825. It was reintroduced by Ludlow, Sherriff and Hicks in 1949 from Bhutan (No. 17543). In cultivation it is a small shrub, 1—1½ feet high with pale greyish-green leaves, matt on the upper surface. In its native home the flowers are purple, reddish-pink, pink, wine-red or bright purple-pink, but in cultivation they are usually reddish-purple. The plant is most attractive when covered with flowers in clusters of 3—6, and is excellently suited for the rock garden.

Epithet. Bristly.
Hardiness 3—4. April—May.

R. spilanthum Hutch. in Rhod. Soc. Notes, Vol. 3, No. 5 (1929 - 31) 287.
A small *upright shrub*, 60—92 cm. (2—3 ft.) high; *branchlets somewhat slender, erect*, densely scaly with flaky scales, glabrous or rarely puberulous, leaf-bud scales deciduous. *Leaves lanceolate, oblanceolate or oblong, lamina 0.6—1.3 cm. long, 2—4 mm. broad,*

apex obtuse or rounded, mucronate, base obtuse or tapered; upper surface pale green, matt, densely scaly, the scales overlapping; under surface densely scaly, the scales are often characteristic, similar or dissimilar in size and colour, large, creamy-yellow or fawn, overlapping or nearly contiguous, with or without closely or widely scattered dark brown scales; petiole 1—2 mm. long, densely scaly, glabrous. *Inflorescence* terminal, umbellate, 1—3-flowered, flower-bud scales persistent; rhachis 0.5—1 mm. long, scaly or not scaly, glabrous; pedicel very short, 0.5—1 mm. long, densely scaly, glabrous. *Calyx* 5-lobed, minute, 0.5—1 mm. long, pink, lobes rounded or ovate, outside scaly, glabrous, margin scaly, ciliate. *Corolla* widely funnel-shaped, slightly zygomorphic, *small, 0.8—1 cm. long*, 5-lobed, blue-purplish, outside not scaly, glabrous. *Stamens* 10, unequal, exserted, *short or medium, shorter than the corolla*, 6—9 mm. long; filaments villous towards the base. *Ovary* conoid, 1 mm. long, 5-celled, densely scaly, glabrous; *style short, shorter than the stamens*, not scaly, glabrous. *Capsule* conoid or oblong, 3—5 mm. long, 2—3 mm. broad, densely scaly, glabrous, calyx-lobes persistent.

This species was discovered by Rock in June 1922 at Muli, south-west Szechuan. It was found by him again in the same region in 1932.

It is a distinct species and cannot be mistaken for any other species of its Series. The diagnostic features of this plant are its upright habit of growth, 2—3 feet high with somewhat slender erect annual growths, the lanceolate, oblanceolate or oblong leaves, laminae 0.6—1.3 cm. long, 2—4 mm. broad, the small corolla 0.8—1 cm. long, and the short style, shorter than the stamens. *R. spilanthum* is allied to *R. orthocladum* but is distinguished by its upright habit of growth, by the creamy-yellow or fawn scales on the lower surface of the leaves, and usually by the shorter pedicels. It is also related to *R. thymifolium* from which it differs in its habit of growth, and in its widely funnel-shaped corolla with a distinct tube concealing the ovary; in *R. thymifolium* the corolla is flat sessile or almost sessile, hardly with a tube, and the ovary is completely exposed.

R. spilanthum was introduced by Rock in 1932 (No. 24320). In cultivation it is a small shrub 2 feet high, and makes a fine show with its blue-purplish flowers produced freely in clusters of 1—3. The plant is uncommon in cultivation, but is well worth acquiring for every rock garden.

Epithet. With spotted flowers.
Hardiness 3—4. April—May.

R. stictophyllum Balf. f. in Notes Roy. Bot. Gard. Edin., Vol. 11 (1919) 139.

A small, matted, cushion, *rounded somewhat compact or broadly upright shrub*, 15—60 cm. (6 in.—2 ft.) high; branchlets short, densely or rarely moderately scaly, scales not flaky or flaky, glabrous or rarely minutely puberulous, leaf-bud scales deciduous. *Leaves* oval, elliptic, oblong-elliptic, ovate-oblong or ovate, *small or tiny, lamina 0.3—1 cm. long*, 2—5 mm. broad, apex rounded or obtuse, minutely mucronate, base rounded or obtuse; upper surface dark green, shining, scales overlapping or rarely up to their own diameter apart; under surface densely scaly, the scales large, pale or dark brown, overlapping or rarely one-half to twice their own diameter apart, with or without closely scattered dark brown scales; petiole 1—2 mm. long, densely or rarely moderately scaly, glabrous. *Inflorescence* terminal, umbellate, *1—2-flowered*, flower-bud scales persistent or deciduous; rhachis 0.5—1 mm. long, scaly or not scaly, glabrous; pedicel very short, 0.5—1 mm. long, densely scaly, glabrous. *Calyx* 5-lobed, 0.5—3 mm. long, reddish, lobes rounded, ovate, triangular or oblong-oval, outside densely or moderately scaly, glabrous, margin scaly or not scaly, glabrous or hairy with long hairs. *Corolla* widely funnel-shaped, slightly zygomorphic, *small, 0.8—1.2 cm. long*, 5-lobed, deep purplish-blue, *deep rose-purple*, pale purple or rose, outside not scaly or rarely slightly scaly on the lobes, glabrous. *Stamens* 10, unequal, exserted, short, as long as the corolla or a little shorter, 0.6—1.2 cm. long; filaments puberulous or villous towards the base or rarely glabrous. *Ovary* conoid, 1—2 mm. long, 5-celled, densely scaly, glabrous; *style short or medium, as long as the stamens or longer*, not scaly, glabrous. *Capsule* conoid, 3 mm. long, 2 mm. broad, densely or rarely moderately scaly, glabrous, calyx-lobes persistent.

This species was first collected by the Abbé Soulié on high mountains at Batang, in western Szechuan. It was later collected by Forrest, and Rock in various localities in south-west Szechuan, south-east Tibet and north-west Yunnan. The plant grows in open moorland, in rocky pasture, in moist alpine meadows, on cliffs and screes, and on boulders, at elevations of 3,965—4,575 (13,000—15,000 ft.).

R. stictophyllum is a distinctive species and cannot be confused with *R. nivale* or with any other species of its Series. It is easily recognised by its rounded somewhat compact or broadly upright habit of growth, by the tiny leaves, laminae 0.3—1 cm. long, dark green, shining above, by the 1—2-flowered inflorescence, by the small corolla 0.8—1.2 cm. long, and by the short or medium style, as long as the stamens or longer. In some respects, it shows a resemblance to *R. nigropunctatum*; the distinctions between them are discussed under the latter.

The species was first introduced by Forrest in 1921 from north-west Yunnan (No. 20462). It was reintroduced by him later in 1922. Rock sent seeds in 1932 from the same region (No. 24385). Although in its native home it grows from 6 inches to 2 feet high, in cultivation it is a small shrub of 2 feet with short annual growths, and dark green leaves. The plant is very hardy, and provides a delightful colour display with its deep rose-purple flowers produced in great profusion. It is easy to increase from cuttings, and should be a most valuable acquisition to any rock garden.

Epithet. With spotted leaves.

Hardiness 3—4. April—May. Plate 33.

R. tapetiforme Balf. f. et Ward in Notes Roy. Bot. Gard. Edin., Vol. 9 (1916) 279.

A small, matted, cushion, upright or *broadly upright shrub*, 12—60 cm. (5 in.—2 ft.) high; branchlets short or long, densely scaly, scales flaky or not flaky, glabrous, leaf-bud scales deciduous. *Leaves* elliptic, oblong-oval, oblong, oblong-elliptic or rarely oval, lamina 0.6—1.5 cm. long, 0.3—1 cm. broad, apex rounded or obtuse, mucronate, base obtuse or rounded; upper surface greyish-green, matt, densely scaly, the scales overlapping; under surface densely scaly, the scales large, dark brown or brown, overlapping or rarely contiguous, rarely with closely or widely scattered dark brown scales; petiole 1—3 mm. long, densely scaly, glabrous. *Inflorescence* terminal, umbellate, 1—3-flowered, flower-bud scales deciduous; rhachis 0.5—1 mm. long, scaly or not scaly, glabrous or rarely puberulous; pedicel 1—2 mm. long, densely scaly, glabrous or rarely puberulous. *Calyx* 5-lobed, minute, 0.5—1 mm. long, pink, purple or greenish, lobes ovate, rounded or oblong-oval, outside not scaly or scaly, glabrous or rarely puberulous, margin not scaly or scaly, hairy with long hairs or rarely glabrous. *Corolla* widely funnel-shaped, slightly zygomorphic, 1—1.6 cm. long, 5-lobed, pink, pale purple, pale rose-purple, purple-blue, dark or pale purple-blue or red, outside not scaly, glabrous. *Stamens* 10, unequal, long-exserted, long, as long as the corolla or a little longer, 0.6—1.5 cm. in length; filaments villous towards the base. *Ovary* conoid, 1—2 mm. long, 5-celled, densely scaly, glabrous or rarely puberulous; *style long* or medium, *longer than*, or rarely as long as *the stamens, longer* or rarely a little shorter *than the corolla*, not scaly, glabrous or rarely puberulous at the base. *Capsule* conoid, 3—5 mm. long, 2—4 mm. broad, densely scaly, glabrous or rarely puberulous at the base, calyx-lobes persistent.

R. tapetiforme was discovered by Kingdon-Ward in July 1913 forming a carpet at Ka-gwr-pw at the Tibet-Yunnan frontier. Subsequently it was collected by Forrest and by Rock in various localities in north-west and west Yunnan. It grows on cliffs, boulders and dry slopes, in alpine moorland, and in meadows, at elevations of 3,355—4,728 m. (11,000—15,500 ft.).

The species shows considerable resemblance to *R. yungningense*, particularly in the shape and size of the leaves, and in the shape, size and colour of the flowers. It differs markedly from its ally in its habit of growth, and usually in the long style, longer than the stamens and the corolla. The plant is a hexaploid with 78 chromosomes.

R. tapetiforme was first introduced by Forrest in 1917 (No. 15356). This number is wrongly recorded as *R. hippophaeoides* in cultivation. It was reintroduced by him in 1921. In its native home it forms a matted, cushion or upright shrub, 5 inches to 2 feet high, but in cultivation it is a broadly upright shrub 2 feet high, usually with short thick annual growths. It is a vigorous grower, and attracts attention when covered with purple-blue flowers in clusters of 1—3. The plant is uncommon in cultivation.

Epithet. Carpet-like.
Hardiness 3—4. April—May.

R. telmateium Balf. f. et W.W. Sm. in Notes Roy. Bot. Gard. Edin., Vol. 9 (1916) 280.

A small *upright* or rarely matted *shrub*, 10—92 cm. (4 in.—3 ft.) high; branchlets short, slender, densely scaly with flaky scales, glabrous or sometimes minutely puberulous, leaf-bud scales deciduous. *Leaves lanceolate, oblong, oblanceolate, oblong-lanceolate or rarely oblong-elliptic, tiny or small*, lamina 0.3—1.1 cm. or rarely 1.3 cm. *long, 2—3 mm.* or rarely 5 mm. broad, apex acute, obtuse or rounded, mucronate, base obtuse or tapered; upper surface green, somewhat shining, densely scaly, the scales overlapping; *under surface densely scaly, the scales* large, *pale brown or brown, overlapping, with closely or widely scattered dark brown scales*; petiole 1—2 mm. long, densely scaly, glabrous. *Inflorescence* terminal, umbellate, 1—2-flowered, flower-bud scales deciduous or persistent; rhachis 0.5 mm. long, scaly or not scaly, glabrous; pedicel 0.5—2 mm. long, densely scaly, glabrous. *Calyx* 5-lobed, 1—2 mm. or rarely 0.5 mm. long, pink, purple or pale green, lobes oblong, lanceolate or ovate, outside densely or moderately scaly, glabrous, margin scaly, eciliate or sometimes ciliate. *Corolla* widely funnel-shaped, slightly zygomorphic, *small, 0.8—1.1 cm.* or rarely 1.3 cm. *long*, 5-lobed, rose-purple, deep rose-purple, lavender, purplish-blue or deep indigo blue, outside scaly along the middle of the lobes, scaly in bands or not scaly on the tube, glabrous or rarely puberulous on the tube. *Stamens* 8—10, unequal, exserted, short or medium or long, as long as the corolla or a little shorter or rarely a little longer, 0.5—1.2 cm. long; filaments villous towards the base. *Ovary* oblong or conoid, 1—2 mm. long, 5-celled, densely scaly, glabrous; *style long, longer than the stamens and the corolla*, not scaly or rarely scaly at the base, glabrous or sometimes puberulous at the base. *Capsule* oblong or conoid, 3—4 mm. long, 2 mm. broad, densely scaly, glabrous or sometimes puberulous, calyx-lobes persistent.

Forrest discovered this plant in June 1914 on the mountains west of Fengkow Valley, Yunnan. Further gatherings by him and other collectors show that the plant is distributed in north-west Yunnan and south-west Szechuan. It grows in rocky situations in pine forests, in stony meadows, amongst alpine scrub, in moorland, in boggy situations, on boulders, on ledges of cliffs, and on screes, at elevations of 2,600—4,575 m. (8,525—15,000 ft.).

The diagnostic features of this plant are the lanceolate to oblong-lanceolate, tiny leaves, laminae 0.3—1.1 cm. long, 2—3 mm. broad, densely scaly on the lower surface with pale brown or brown overlapping scales, with closely or widely scattered dark brown scales, the small corolla 0.8—1.1 cm. or rarely 1.3 cm. long, scaly on the lobes outside, scaly or not scaly on the tube, and the long style longer than the stamens and the corolla.

The species resembles *R. diacritum* in some features, but is readily distinguished by the lanceolate, oblong, oblanceolate or oblong-lanceolate leaves; in *R. diacritum* they are oval, ovate or elliptic. Moreover, *R. telmateium* is a delicate upright shrub with slender branchlets, whereas *R. diacritum* is a robust grower, usually broadly upright and spreading, with long or short thick branchlets.

R. telmateium was first introduced by Forrest in 1914 (No. 12568) and again a few times in 1921 from north-west Yunnan. It was reintroduced by Kingdon-Ward in 1921, and by Rock in 1923. In its native home it grows from 4 inches to 3 feet high, but in cultivation it is an upright shrub 1½—2 feet in height. It is a charming little plant which no one can fail to admire when covered with single or paired rose-purple flowers. The plant is very hardy, easy to grow, and worthy of a place in every rock garden.

Epithet. From the marshes.

Hardiness 3—4. April—May.

R. thymifolium Maxim. in Bull. Acad. Petersb. XXIII (1877) 351.

A broadly upright or a very lax upright shrub, 30 cm.—1.22 m. (1—4 ft.) high; branchlets thin, densely scaly, scales not flaky or flaky, glabrous, leaf-bud scales deciduous. *Leaves* oblong, oblanceolate, oblong-lanceolate, elliptic or sometimes oval, lamina 0.4—1.8 cm. long, 2—7 mm. broad, apex obtuse or rounded, mucronate, base obtuse or tapered; upper surface greyish-green, matt, densely scaly, the scales overlapping; *under surface densely scaly, the scales are usually characteristic, similar in size and colour,* large *pale brown or creamy-yellow,* overlapping, without or sometimes with scattered dark brown scales; petiole 1—2 mm. long, densely scaly, glabrous. *Inflorescence* terminal, umbellate, 1- or sometimes 2-flowered, flower-bud scales persistent or deciduous; rhachis 0.5 mm. long, scaly or not scaly, glabrous; the *flowers sessile or almost sessile, pedicel very short,* 0.5—1 mm. long, densely scaly, glabrous. *Calyx* 5-lobed, minute, 0.5—1 mm. long, pink or reddish, lobes triangular, rounded or ovate, outside scaly, glabrous, margin scaly or not scaly, hairy with long or short hairs or rarely glabrous. *Corolla* widely funnel-shaped, *flat, tube very short,* slightly zygomorphic, *small, 5—9 mm. long,* 5-lobed, lavender-blue, purple, blue or purplish-lavender, outside scaly or not scaly on the tube and the lobes, glabrous. *Stamens* 10, unequal, exserted, *short,* as long as the corolla or shorter, *4—8 mm. long;* filaments villous towards the base. *Ovary* conoid or ovoid, *completely exposed, visible,* 1 mm. long, 5-celled, densely scaly, glabrous; *style very short, shorter than the stamens,* not scaly, glabrous or rarely puberulous at the base. *Capsule* conoid or ovoid, 2—3 mm. long, 2 mm. broad, densely scaly, glabrous, calyx-lobes persistent.

R. thymifolium was first collected by Przewalski in 1873 in Kansu. It was later found by other collectors in the same region and in eastern Tibet. The plant grows on rocky moist slopes, amongst bushes and pine trees, and in moorland, at elevations of 2,900—4,270 m. (9,508—14,000 ft.). It is recorded as being abundant in valleys and in moorlands.

The most striking character of this plant is the sessile or almost sessile flower, with a flat corolla and very short tube, the ovary being completely exposed and visible. Other notable features are the densely scaly lower surface of the leaves usually with characteristic creamy-yellow or fawn overlapping scales, similar in size and colour, without or sometimes with scattered dark brown scales, the very short stamens, and the very short style, shorter than the stamens. The species is allied to *R. polifolium* and *R. spilanthum*, but is readily distinguished from both by important characters.

R. thymifolium has been in cultivation for a long time. It was introduced possibly by Farrer in 1915, and by Kingdon-Ward in 1922, and again by Yü in 1937 (No. 14803). Two distinct forms are in cultivation. Form 1. A broadly upright shrub 1½—2 feet high, with short annual growths, small leaves and small flowers. Form 2. A very lax upright shrub 2—2½ feet high with long annual growths, and larger leaves and flowers. Form 1 is a dainty little shrub, free-flowering, and well suited for the rock garden. The species is rare in cultivation.

Epithet. With leaves like thyme.

Hardiness 3—4. April—May.

R. tsai Fang in Contrib. Biol. Lab. Sci. Soc. Vol. XII (1939) 66.

A small shrub, 30 cm. (1 ft.) high; branchlets long, densely scaly, scales not flaky or flaky, glabrous, leaf-bud scales deciduous. *Leaves* oblong, oblong-oval, elliptic or oblong-elliptic, lamina 0.6—1.1 cm. long, 3—5 mm. broad, apex obtuse or rounded, mucronate, base obtuse or tapered; upper surface pale green, matt, densely scaly, the scales overlapping; *under surface densely scaly, the scales are characteristic, similar in size and colour,* large, *fawn, overlapping*; petiole 1 mm. long, densely scaly, glabrous. *Inflorescence* terminal, umbellate, 5—7-flowered, flower-bud scales deciduous; rhachis 1 mm. long, scaly or not scaly, glabrous; pedicel 1—2 mm. long, densely scaly, glabrous. *Calyx* 5-lobed, minute, 0.5—1 mm. long, pink, lobes ovate or rounded, outside scaly, glabrous, margin scaly, eciliate or ciliate. *Corolla* widely funnel-shaped, slightly zygomorphic, *small, 5 mm. long,* 5-lobed, purplish-white, outside not scaly, glabrous. *Stamens 5,* unequal, exserted, *short,* shorter than the corolla, *3—4 mm. long,* filaments glabrous. *Ovary* conoid, 1 mm. long, 5-celled, densely scaly, glabrous; *style very short, shorter than, or nearly as long as the stamens,* not scaly, glabrous. *Capsule: —*

The only collection of this species was made by Tsai in May 1932 at Chao-tung Hsien, Yunnan, growing in open moss land at an elevation of 2,900 m. (9,508 ft.). It is recorded as being very common in its native home.

The species shows a resemblance to *R. polifolium* in general features, but differs in the 5—7-flowered inflorescence, in the smaller corolla 5 mm. long, in the 5 short stamens 3—4 mm. long, and in the very short style. The plant has not been introduced into cultivation.

Epithet. After H.T. Tsai, a Chinese collector.

Not in cultivation.

R. verruculosum Rehd. et Wils. in Plantae Wilsonianae (1913) 507.

A broadly upright or compact shrub, 60—90 cm. (1—3 ft.) high; *branchlets* short, scaly, *pilose,* leaf-bud scales deciduous. *Leaves* oval, elliptic-ovate, broadly elliptic or oblong, lamina 0.7—1.5 cm. long, 5—8 mm. broad, apex rounded, mucronate, base broadly cuneate or rounded; upper surface dark green, scaly; under surface scaly, the scales one-half or their own diameter apart; petiole 1—3 mm. long, scaly. *Inflorescence* terminal, *1—2-flowered,* flower-bud scales subpersistent; pedicel 1—2 mm. long, densely scaly. *Calyx* 5-lobed, 1—2 mm. long, brown, lobes ovate or rounded, outside scaly, margin densely ciliate. *Corolla* widely funnel-shaped, 1.2—1.4 cm. long, 5-lobed, purple or deep purple, outside scaly on the lobes. *Stamens 7—8,* exserted, shorter than the corolla, 7—8 mm. long; filaments villous towards the base. *Ovary* conoid, 1—2 mm. long, 5-celled, densely scaly, glabrous; *style long, longer than the stamens,* not scaly, glabrous. *Capsule* oblong or conoid, 4—5 mm. long, 3 mm. broad, densely scaly, glabrous, calyx-lobes persistent.

This species is known from a single collection made in June 1908 by Wilson in western Szechuan, growing in sunny places among rocks, at an elevation of 3,300 m. (10,820 ft.).

The main features of this plant are the pilose branchlets, the oval, broadly elliptic or oblong leaves, laminae 0.7—1.5 cm. long, the 1—2-flowered inflorescence, the corolla-lobes scaly outside, the 7—8 stamens, and the long style, longer than the stamens. The original diagnosis associates it with *R. polycladum.* From this species it differs in the pilose branchlets, usually in the shape of the leaves, in the larger corolla, scaly on the lobes, and in the 7—8 stamens. It is also related to *R. bulu,* but is distinguished by the pilose branchlets, by the smaller leaves, and by the 7—8 stamens. Moreover, it shows a resemblance to *R. impeditum* but differs usually in distinctive features.

The species has been in cultivation for a long time, and was possibly introduced by Wilson from western Szechuan. A well-grown plant is most effective when covered with purple flowers. It is rare in cultivation but is well worth a place in every rock garden. It was given an Award of Merit when exhibited by Col. Stephenson R. Clarke, Borde Hill, in 1932.

Epithet. With small warts.

Hardiness 3—4. April—May.

R. violaceum Rehd. et Wils. in Plantae Wilsonianae (1913) 511.

A broadly upright or bushy shrub, 23 cm.—1.22 m. (9 in.—4 ft.) high; branchlets short, densely scaly with flaky scales, glabrous, leaf-bud scales deciduous. *Leaves oblong-oval, elliptic, oval or ovate*, small, lamina 0.5—1.2 cm. long, 3—6 mm. broad, apex rounded or obtuse, mucronate, base rounded or obtuse; upper surface dark green, shining, densely scaly, the scales overlapping; under surface densely scaly, the scales large, brown, overlapping or nearly contiguous, with or without closely scattered dark brown scales; petiole 1—3 mm. long, densely scaly, glabrous. *Inflorescence* terminal, umbellate, 1—3-flowered, flower-bud scales deciduous; rhachis 0.5—1 mm. long, scaly or not scaly, glabrous; pedicel 0.5—3 mm. long, densely scaly or not scaly, glabrous or minutely puberulous. *Calyx* 5-lobed, 0.5—3 mm. long, pink, lobes rounded, ovate or oblong-oval, outside densely or moderately scaly or not scaly, glabrous, margin scaly or not scaly, ciliate. *Corolla* widely funnel-shaped, slightly zygomorphic, 0.9—1.2 cm. long, 5-lobed, *violet-purple or pinkish-violet*, outside not scaly, glabrous. *Stamens* 10, unequal, exserted, medium or long, as long as the corolla or a little longer, 0.8—1.2 cm. long; filaments villous towards the base. *Ovary* conoid, 1—2 mm. long, 5-celled, densely scaly, glabrous; style long, longer than the stamens, not scaly, glabrous or puberulous at the base. *Capsule* ovoid, about 5 mm. long, scaly, calyx-lobes persistent.

Wilson discovered this plant in June 1908 in western Szechuan, and found it again later in the same region. Farrer also collected it in 1914 in Kansu. It grows in moorlands and in alpine turf at elevations of 3,355—4,500 m. (11,000—14,754 ft.). Farrer records it as being a bush of 9—12 inches or more, abundant as heather in the high alpine turf of the Thundercrown range at 3,355—3,660 m. (11,000—12,000 ft.).

In the original diagnosis it is associated with *R. polycladum*. From this plant it is distinguished by the shape of the leaves, usually by the larger calyx, and by the colour of the flowers. It is also related to *R. nitidulum* but differs markedly in the smaller corolla. The plant is a tetraploid with 52 chromosomes.

The species was first introduced by Wilson in 1910 from western Szechuan (No. 4269). It was reintroduced by Farrer in 1914 from Kansu (No. 119). In cultivation it is a broadly upright shrub up to 2 feet high with violet-purple flowers. The plant is hardy, fairly fast-growing, and is not difficult to increase from cuttings. It is rare in cultivation, but is worthy of being widely cultivated.

Epithet. Violet-coloured.

Hardiness 3—4. April—May.

R. websterianum Rehd. et Wils. in Plantae Wilsonianae (1913) 511.

A broadly upright or a very lax upright shrub, 30 cm.—1.37 m. (1—4½ ft.) high; branchlets densely scaly, scales flaky or not flaky, glabrous, leaf-bud scales deciduous. *Leaves oblong, lanceolate, linear-lanceolate or oblong-oval, lamina 0.5—2 cm. long*, 2—9 mm. broad, apex obtuse, rounded or acute, mucronate, base tapered or obtuse; upper surface pale green, matt, densely scaly, the scales overlapping; *under surface densely scaly*, the *scales are characteristic, similar in size and colour*, large, *creamy-yellow or fawn, overlapping*; petiole 1—5 mm. long, densely scaly, glabrous. *Inflorescence* terminal, umbellate, 1—3- or rarely up to 6-flowered, flower-bud scales subpersistent or deciduous; rhachis 1 mm. long, scaly or not scaly, glabrous; pedicel 1—5 mm. long, densely scaly, glabrous. *Calyx* 5-lobed, 1—4 mm. long, yellowish, purple, reddish or pink, lobes oblong, oval or ovate, outside scaly or not scaly, glabrous, margin not scaly or rarely scaly, ciliate or rarely eciliate. *Corolla* widely funnel-shaped, slightly zygomorphic, 1—1.7 cm. long, 5-lobed, rosy-purple, bright rose, rose-lavender, purple-blue, deep lavender-blue or lavender-blue, outside not scaly, glabrous. *Stamens* 10, unequal, long-exserted, *long, as long as the corolla or a little longer* or rarely slightly shorter, 0.8—1.7 cm. in length; filaments villous towards the base. *Ovary* conoid, 2 mm. long, 5-celled, densely scaly, glabrous; *style long, longer than the stamens*, scaly at the base or not scaly, glabrous or puberulous at the base.

Capsule conoid or oblong, 4—7 mm. long, 2—3 mm. broad, densely scaly, glabrous, calyx-lobes persistent.

R. *websterianum* was first collected by Wilson in June 1908 at Tatsienlu, western Szechuan. Further gatherings by him, Forrest, Rock, and McLaren's collectors show that the plant is distributed in western and south-western Szechuan, mid-west and north-west Yunnan. It grows in moorlands, in stony alpine meadows, in open boggy pastures, amongst scrub, on cliffs, and on rocky slopes, at elevations of 3,300—4,900 m. (10,820—16,066 ft.).

The main features of this plant are the oblong, lanceolate, linear-lanceolate or sometimes oblong-oval leaves, densely scaly on the lower surfaces with characteristic creamy-yellow or fawn overlapping scales similar in size and colour, the long stamens, and the long style longer than the stamens. The species is very variable in leaf size, 0.5—2 cm. long, and 2—9 mm. broad. It shows a resemblance to R. *fimbriatum* in general appearance, but is distinguished by the smaller leaves, usually by the fewer-flowered inflorescence and the shorter pedicels.

The species was first introduced by Wilson in 1908 (No. 1225 — the Type number). It was reintroduced many times by Forrest. Two distinct forms are in cultivation. Form 1. A broadly upright shrub, 3—4½ feet high, somewhat densely branched, fairly well-filled with lanceolate leaves, and free-flowering. Form 2. A very lax upright shrub up to 2 feet high with few branches and narrow linear-lanceolate leaves, less floriferous. The species is uncommon in cultivation. Form 1 is a pleasing shrub and should be in every collection of rhododendrons.

Epithet. After F.G. Webster, of Boston, U.S.A.
Hardiness 3—4. April—May.

R. yungningense Balf. f. ex Hutch. in The Species of Rhododendron (1930) 436.

A *rounded somewhat compact shrub*, 30 cm.—1.07 m. (1—3½ ft.) high; branchlets short or somewhat long, thick, erect, scaly with flaky scales, glabrous, leaf-bud scales deciduous. *Leaves* oblong-lanceolate, oblong-elliptic, oblong, elliptic, lanceolate, oblong-oval or ovate, *lamina* 0.6—2 cm. long, 0.2—1 cm. broad, apex obtuse or rounded, mucronate, base obtuse or rounded; *upper surface greyish-green, matt*, densely scaly, the scales overlapping or nearly contiguous; under surface densely scaly, the scales large, brown or dark brown or cinnamon-red, nearly contiguous or overlapping or rarely one-half their own diameter apart, without or rarely with closely scattered dark brown scales; petiole 1—5 mm. long, densely scaly, glabrous. *Inflorescence* terminal, umbellate, 1—6-flowered, flower-bud scales deciduous or persistent; rhachis 0.5—2 mm. long, scaly or not scaly, glabrous; pedicel 1—2 mm. long, densely scaly, glabrous. *Calyx* 5-lobed, 0.5—2 mm. long, pink or purple or crimson-purple, lobes ovate or rounded, outside scaly or not scaly, glabrous, margin scaly or not scaly, ciliate or eciliate. *Corolla* widely funnel-shaped, slightly zygomorphic, 0.9—1.5 cm. long, 5-lobed, deep purple, deep blue-purple, pale bluish-purple or deep purplish-red, outside not scaly, glabrous. *Stamens* 10, unequal, exserted, long or medium in length, as long as the corolla or a little shorter, 0.7—1.3 cm. long; filaments villous or puberulous towards the base. *Ovary* conoid or ovoid, 1—2 mm. long, 5-celled, densely scaly, glabrous or rarely puberulous at the apex; *style medium or short, as long as the stamens or shorter* or rarely slightly longer, not scaly, glabrous or rarely puberulous at the base. *Capsule* conoid or oblong, 4—5 mm. long, 2—4 mm. broad, moderately or densely scaly, glabrous, calyx-lobes persistent.

Forrest discovered this plant in June 1921 on the mountains east of Yungning, south-west Szechuan. He found it again later in the same region and in west and north-west Yunnan. It grows on alpine slopes, in meadows, rhododendron scrub and stony moorland, on cliffs, and rocks, at elevations of 3,355—4,270 m. (11,000—14,000 ft.).

In 1932, *R. glomerulatum*, Hutch. was described from a plant grown by Lord Headfort at Kells, County Meath, Eire, raised from Forrest seed No. 21297. The ample material now available and plants in cultivation show that *R. glomerulatum* agrees with *R. yungningense* in height and habit of growth, in the shape and size of the leaves, in the shape and colour of the flowers. In all other characters they are identical.

R. yungningense shows a strong resemblance to *R. tapetiforme* in some features, but is readily distinguished by its habit of growth, and by the short style, as long as the stamens or shorter.

The species was first introduced by Forrest in 1922 from south-west Szechuan. He reintroduced it later a few times from west Yunnan. In cultivation it is a rounded somewhat compact shrub up to 3½ feet high and almost as much across, with short or somewhat long, thick, erect branchlets. It is perfectly hardy, a vigorous grower, and provides a fine display with its pale bluish-purple flowers produced in great profusion. The plant is uncommon in cultivation but is worth growing in any collection.

Epithet. From Yungning, Szechuan.

Hardiness 3—4. April—May.

LEPIDOTUM SERIES

General characters: small or medium-sized shrubs, 5 cm.—2.44 m. (2 in.—8 ft.) high; branchlets rather densely or sometimes slightly scaly. Leaves evergreen or deciduous, oblanceolate, oblong-obovate, obovate, oval or elliptic, lamina 0.3—7 cm. long, 0.2—3.3 cm. broad; under surface densely or laxly scaly, the scales entire or crenulate, overlapping to 5 times their own diameter apart. Inflorescence terminal, or rarely terminal and axillary in the uppermost one or two leaves, umbellate or racemose, 1—12- or sometimes up to 18-flowered; *pedicel slender*, 1—4.3 cm. long, *longer than the corolla*, moderately or densely scaly. Calyx 5-lobed, 1—8mm. long. *Corolla rotate or rotate-campanulate*, 0.8—1.8 cm. long, 5-lobed, pink, purple, rose, scarlet, crimson, crimson-purple, yellow or white, with or without crimson or deep rose or greenish spots. Stamens 8—10 or rarely 11. Ovary conoid or ovoid, 2—4 mm. long, 5-celled, densely scaly; *style short, stout and sharply bent.* Capsule oblong, conoid, oblong-oval or ovoid, 4—9 mm. long, 3—5 mm. broad, densely scaly, calyx-lobes persistent.

Distribution: Kashmir, Punjab, Nepal, Sikkim, Bhutan, Assam, south and south-east Tibet, north-east Upper Burma, and north-west Yunnan.

A small distinctive Series of four species divided into Baileyi Subseries and Lepidotum Subseries. The main diagnostic features are the slender pedicel longer than the corolla, the rotate or rotate-campanulate corolla, and the short, stout and sharply bent style.

The nearest affinity of the Series is with the Glaucophyllum Series, but there is a tendency towards the Campylogynum Series. The crenulate type of scale which occurs in the Baileyi Subseries and is characteristic of the Saluenense Series, suggests a definite relationship between the latter and the Lepidotum Series.

KEY TO THE SUBSERIES

A. Inflorescence 1—3- or sometimes 4—5-flowered, umbellate, rhachis usually 0.5—3 mm. long; scales on the under surface of the leaves entire, brown or yellowish-green; leaves evergreen or deciduous; corolla pink, purple, rose, crimson, yellow or white, with or without crimson or deep rose or greenish spots .... *Lepidotum Subseries*

A. Inflorescence 5—12- or sometimes up to 18-flowered, racemose, rhachis 3 mm.—2.5 cm. long; scales on the under surface of the leaves crenulate, cinnamon or rust-coloured or sometimes brown; leaves evergreen; corolla deep purple, deep reddish-purple, reddish-purple, crimson-purple or purple, with or without darker spots .... *Baileyi Subseries*

BAILEYI SUBSERIES

General characters: small or medium-sized shrub, 60 cm.—1.83 m. (2—6 ft.) or rarely 30 cm. (1 ft.) high; branchlets rather densely scaly. Leaves evergreen, oblong, obovate, oblong-obovate, elliptic, oblong-oval or oval, lamina 2.2—7 cm. long, 0.8—3.3 cm. broad; *under surface* densely scaly, the *scales crenulate, overlapping*; petiole 0.3—1.5 cm. long, densely scaly. *Inflorescence* terminal, or rarely terminal and axillary in the uppermost one or two leaves, racemose, *5—12- or sometimes up to 18-flowered; rhachis 0.3—2.5 cm. long*; pedicel slender, 1.2—3.5 cm. long, longer than the corolla, rather densely scaly. Calyx 5-lobed, 2—4 mm. long. *Corolla* rotate, 0.8—1.6 cm. long, 5-lobed, *deep purple, deep reddish-purple, reddish-purple, crimson-purple or purple*, with or without darker spots. Stamens 10. Ovary conoid or ovoid, 2—3 mm. long, 5-celled, densely scaly; style short, stout and sharply bent. Capsule conoid, ovoid or oblong, 5—8 mm. long, 3—4 mm. broad, densely scaly, calyx-lobes persistent.

DESCRIPTION OF THE SPECIES

R. baileyi Balf. f. in Notes Roy. Bot. Gard. Edin., Vol. 11 (1919) 23.
  Illustration. Bot. Mag. Vol. 148 t. 8942 (1922).
  An upright lax, or spreading somewhat rounded, or straggly shrub, 60 cm.—1.83 m. (2—6 ft.) or rarely 30 cm. (1 ft.) high; branchlets rather densely scaly, not bristly. *Leaves* evergreen, oblong, obovate, oblong-obovate, elliptic, oblong-oval or oval, lamina coriaceous, 2.2—7 cm. long, 0.8—3.3 cm. broad, apex obtuse or rounded, mucronate, base obtuse, cuneate or rounded; upper surface dark or pale green, matt or shining, densely or sometimes moderately scaly; *under surface* densely scaly, the *scales* unequal, large and medium-sized, *crenulate, cinnamon, rust-coloured or brown, overlapping*; petiole 0.3—1.5 cm. long, densely scaly, not bristly. *Inflorescence* terminal, or rarely terminal and axillary in the uppermost one or two leaves, *racemose, 5—12-or sometimes up to 18-flowered; rhachis 0.3—2.5 cm. long*, scaly or not scaly, rather densely puberulous; pedicel slender, 1.2—3.5 cm. long, longer than the corolla, rather densely scaly, not bristly. *Calyx* 5-lobed, 2—4 mm. long, reddish or rarely greenish, lobes unequal, ovate, oblong, oval or oblong-oval, outside densely scaly, margin eciliate or ciliate. *Corolla* rotate, 0.8—1.6 cm. long, 5-lobed, *deep purple, deep reddish-purple, reddish-purple, crimson-purple or purple*, with or without darker spots, outside rather densely or moderately scaly. *Stamens* 10, unequal, 0.6—1 cm. long, exserted from the tube; filaments densely hairy towards the base or to two-thirds of their length. *Ovary* conoid or ovoid, 2—3 mm. long, 5-celled, densely scaly, glabrous; style short, stout and sharply bent, not scaly, glabrous or rarely puberulous. *Capsule* conoid, ovoid or oblong, 5—8 mm. long, 3—4·mm. broad, densely scaly, glabrous, calyx-lobes persistent.

R. baileyi was discovered by Lt.-Col. F.M. Bailey during his survey of the Tsangpo river in south Tibet in 1913. He preserved no specimen, but the species was described by Sir Isaac Bayley Balfour in 1919 from plants raised from Bailey's seed by J.C. Williams of Caerhays Castle at Werrington Park, and at the Royal Botanic Garden, Edinburgh, where the plant flowered in the spring of 1918. The species was later found by other collectors in Sikkim, Bhutan, and south-east Tibet. It grows in fir forest, in bamboo-Abies forest, among junipers, on dry hill slopes, on mossy rocks and boulders, at elevations of 2,440—4,270 m.(8,000—14,000 ft.). Ludlow, Sherriff and Elliot record it as being very common in spruce and Tsuga forests on steep hillsides at Nyam Jang Chu Gorge, south-east Tibet.

The species resembles *R. lepidotum* in its rotate corolla and short stout sharply bent style. The main distinctions between them are that in *R. baileyi* the inflorescence is racemose, 5—12- or sometimes up to 18-flowered, the rhachis is 3 mm.—2.5 cm. long, the leaves are large, laminae usually 3—7 cm. long, and the plant is tetraploid with 52 chromosomes, whereas in *R. lepidotum* the inflorescence is umbellate, 1—2- or sometimes 3- or rarely 4-flowered, the rhachis is minute 0.5—1 mm. long, the leaves are small, laminae usually 3 mm.—3 cm. long, and the plant is diploid with 26 chromosomes. Moreover, an important diagnostic feature of *R. baileyi* is the Crenulate scale; in this respect the species differs markedly from *R. lepidotum* and from all other species of its Series where the scale is Entire. The Crenulate scale is also noted in the Saluenense Series.

R. baileyi was reintroduced by Ludlow and Sherriff No. 2896, with Taylor No. 6656, and also a few times with Hicks. Two growth forms are in cultivation. Form 1. An upright lax shrub, 4—5 feet high. Form 2. A spreading, somewhat rounded shrub 2—3 feet high and as much across. The flower colour varies from crimson-purple to purple. The species is fairly fast-growing and free-flowering. Although it is hardy, some forms require a sheltered position particularly along the east coast and inland. The smaller forms are well suited for the rock garden. The plant was given an Award of Merit when shown by A.C. and J.F.A. Gibson, Glenarn, Rhu, Dunbartonshire, in 1960.

Epithet. After Lt.-Col. F.M. Bailey, traveller in Tibet.

Hardiness 3. April—May.

LEPIDOTUM SUBSERIES

General characters: small or medium-sized shrubs, 5 cm.—2.44 m. (2 in.—8 ft.) high; branchlets slightly to rather densely scaly. Leaves evergreen or deciduous, oblanceolate, lanceolate, oblong-obovate, obovate or elliptic, lamina 0.3—6 cm. long, 0.2—2.9 cm. broad; *under surface* densely or laxly scaly, the *scales Entire*, overlapping to 4 times their own diameter apart; petiole 1—5 mm. long, densely or moderately scaly. *Inflorescence* terminal, *umbellate or sometimes shortly racemose, 1—3- or sometimes 4—5- flowered*; pedicel slender, 1—4.3 cm. long, longer than the corolla, moderately or densely scaly. Calyx 5-lobed, 1—8 mm. long. *Corolla* rotate or rotate-campanulate, 0.8—1.8 cm. long, 5-lobed, *pink, purple, rose, scarlet, crimson, crimson-purple, yellow or white*, with or without crimson or deep rose or greenish spots. Stamens 8—10 or rarely 11. Ovary conoid, 2—4 mm. long, 5-celled, densely scaly; style short, stout, and sharply bent. Capsule oblong, conoid, oblong-oval or ovoid, 4—9 mm. long, 3—5 mm. broad, densely scaly, calyx-lobes persistent.

KEY TO THE SPECIES

A. Margins of the leaves (laminae), branchlets and petioles not bristly; under surface of the leaves densely scaly, the scales overlapping to one-half or rarely their own diameter apart; leaves evergreen or sometimes deciduous; leaf base not decurrent on the petiole .... *lepidotum*

A. Margins of the leaves (laminae) bristly, branchlets and petioles often bristly; under surface of the leaves laxly scaly, the scales usually 2—5 times their own diameter apart; leaves deciduous; leaf base decurrent on the petiole.

  B. Corolla pale yellow, with carmine spots on the posterior side; dwarf shrublet 5—12 cm. (2—5 in.) or rarely 30 cm. (1 ft.) high; pedicel bristly or rarely not bristly; inflorescence 1—2-flowered; leaves (laminae) 9 mm.—2.8 cm. long, 4 mm.—1.2 cm. broad .... *lowndesii*

  B. Corolla reddish-purple, crimson-purple or pink, with or without darker spots; medium-sized shrub, 92 cm.—2.44 m. (3—8 ft.) high; pedicel not bristly; inflorescence 2—5-flowered; leaves (laminae) usually 2.5—6 cm. long, 1.4—2.9 cm. broad .... *cowanianum*

DESCRIPTION OF THE SPECIES

R. cowanianum Davidian in Notes Roy. Bot. Gard. Edin., Vol. 21 (1952) 99.

An upright lax, or spreading shrub, *92 cm.—2.44 m. (3—8 ft.) high*; branchlets scaly, minutely puberulous or glabrous, sparsely bristly or not bristly. *Leaves deciduous*, obovate or oblong-obovate, *lamina chartaceous, 2.3—6 cm. long, 1.2—2.9 cm. broad*, apex rounded, mucronate, base obtuse or cuneate, decurrent on the petiole; upper surface bright green, shining, rather densely or moderately scaly, moderately or rather densely puberulous or glabrous, not bristly or rarely sparsely bristly, midrib moderately or rather densely pubescent or glabrous, not bristly; *margin bristly; under surface* pale green, scaly, the *scales* unequal, large and medium-sized, *Entire*, yellowish-green or pale brown, *1—4 times their own diameter apart*, not bristly; *petiole* 3—5 mm. long, narrowly winged or ridged on each side, scaly, rather densely pubescent or not pubescent, *bristly. Inflorescence* terminal, umbellate or shortly racemose, 2—5-flowered; rhachis 1—4 mm. long, scaly or not scaly; pedicel slender, 1—1.8 cm. long, longer than the corolla, rather densely or moderately scaly, not bristly. *Calyx* 5-lobed, 4—8 mm. long, lobes rounded, ovate, oblong-oval or oval, outside scaly, margin ciliate or eciliate. *Corolla* rotate-campanulate, 1.3—1.8 cm. long, 5-lobed, *reddish-purple, crimson-purple or pink*, with or without darker spots, outside not scaly or rarely slightly scaly. *Stamens* 10, unequal, 0.8—1.4 cm. long, exserted from the tube; filaments densely hairy towards the base or to three-fourths their length. Ovary conoid, 3—4 mm. long, 5-celled, densely scaly, glabrous; style short, stout and sharply bent, not scaly, glabrous. *Capsule* conoid or oblong-oval, 6—8 mm. long, 4—5 mm. broad, densely scaly, glabrous, calyx-lobes persistent.

This species was first collected by O. Polunin in June 1949 in Langtang lateral valley, Central Nepal. Subsequently it was found by Stonor, and by Stainton, Sykes and Williams in other localities in Nepal. The plant grows on the edge of forests, in clearings in forests, on scree slopes in open Betula-Rhododendron forest, and among rocks in river-beds, at elevations of 3,050—3,965 m. (10,000—13,000 ft.). Polunin records it as being frequent in birch forests, in the Langtang valley, Central Nepal.

R. cowanianum is very similar to the species of the Lepidotum Series, particularly in the rotate corolla and in the short stout sharply bent style. It further agrees with the species of the Lepidotum Subseries in the Entire scale with a marginal rim. The plant also resembles the species of the Trichocladum Series in its deciduous leaves, but differs markedly in the shape and colour of the corolla, and in the Entire scale; in the Trichocladum Series the scale is Vesicular, that is, bladder-like. *R. cowanianum* will now be placed in the Lepidotum Series.

It shows a resemblance to *R. lepidotum* in some features, but differs in that it is a taller plant up to 8 feet high, the leaves are usually larger, laminae up to 6 cm. long, the leaf margin and petiole are bristly, and the scales on the lower surface of the leaves are laxly spaced, 1—4 times their own diameter apart. *R. cowanianum* is also allied to *R. baileyi* from which it is readily distinguished by the deciduous leaves, laxly scaly on the lower surface, by the bristly leaf margin and petiole, by the fewer-flowered inflorescence, and by the Entire scale.

The species was introduced by Stainton, Sykes and Williams in 1954 (No. 9097). In cultivation it is upright in growth or spreading, up to 3 feet high. A distinctive feature is its large deciduous leaves which often provide good autumn colour. The plant often produces fertile seed in plenty. Worth noting is the fact that nearly all the seedlings when raised from open-pollinated seed come true to type. Although hardy, it is particular as to position in the garden. In some gardens it is difficult. To obtain the best results, some shade and protection from wind are essential.

Epithet. After Dr. J.M. Cowan, 1892—1960.

Hardiness 3. April—May.

R. lepidotum Wall. ex G. Don in Royle Ill. Bot. Himal. p. 260 t. 64, fig. 1 (1835).

Illustrations. Hook. f. Rhod. Sikkim Himal. t. XXIII A (1951), figured as *R. salignum*. Bot. mag. Vol. 78 t. 4657 (1852); and ibid. Vol. 80 t. 4802 (1854), figured as *R. lepidotum* var. *chloranthum*.

A small, broadly upright, or compact rounded, or lax shrub, 5—92 cm. (2 in.—3 ft.) or sometimes up to 1.53 m. (5 ft.) high; branchlets often twiggy, *warty*, rather densely or moderately scaly, not bristly. *Leaves* evergreen or sometimes deciduous, oblanceolate, lanceolate, oblong-obovate, obovate or elliptic, lamina coriaceous, 1—3.2 cm. long, 0.4—1.1 cm. broad, apex rounded, obtuse or rarely acute, mucronate, base obtuse, tapered or rounded; upper surface dark or pale green, somewhat matt or shining, densely scaly; under surface pale glaucous green, densely scaly, the scales unequal, large and medium-sized, *Entire*, brown, overlapping to one-half or rarely their own diameter apart; petiole 1—5 mm. long, densely or moderately scaly, not bristly. *Inflorescence* terminal, umbellate, *1—2- or sometimes 3-* or rarely *4-flowered*; rhachis minute, 0.5—1 mm. long, scaly; *pedicel slender*, 1.3—3 cm. or sometimes up to 3.8 cm. long, *longer than the corolla*, moderately or densely scaly, not bristly. *Calyx* 5-lobed, 1—4 mm. long, reddish-purple, purple or greenish-purple, lobes rounded, ovate, oblong-oval or oval, outside moderately or densely scaly, margin eciliate or ciliate. *Corolla rotate*, 1—1.6 cm. long, 5-lobed, pink, purple, rose, scarlet, crimson or yellow, with or without crimson or deep rose or greenish spots, outside rather densely or sometimes moderately scaly. *Stamens* 8—10, unequal, 0.5—1 cm. long, exserted from the tube; filaments densely pubescent towards the base or to two-thirds of their length. *Ovary* conoid, 2—3 mm. long, 5-celled, densely scaly, glabrous; *style short, stout and sharply bent*, not scaly, glabrous. *Capsule* oblong, conoid or oblong-oval, 4—9 mm. long, 3—4 mm. broad, densely scaly, glabrous, calyx-lobes persistent.

The name *R. lepidotum* first appeared in Wallich's Catalogue 758, and it was figured in Royle's *Illustrations of Himalayan Plants* in 1835. In 1848 J.D. Hooker collected it in the Sikkim Himalaya. Further gatherings by various collectors show that the species has a wide area of distribution extending from Kashmir, Punjab, Nepal, Sikkim, Bhutan, Assam to south and south-east Tibet, north-east Upper Burma, and north-west Yunnan. It grows on cliffs, boulders, rocks and stony slopes, amongst scrub, on grass slopes, in open pasture, on hillsides, by streams, in pine forests, in Quercus-Ilex forest, and in Abies forest, at elevations of 2,440—4,880 m. (8,000—16,000 ft.).

R. lepidotum is a very variable plant. It grows from 2 inches to 3 feet or sometimes up to 5 feet high; the leaves are evergreen or deciduous, lanceolate to obovate and oval, laminae 3 mm.—3.8 cm. long, 2 mm.—1.8 cm. broad, the corolla is 8 mm.—1.6 cm. long,

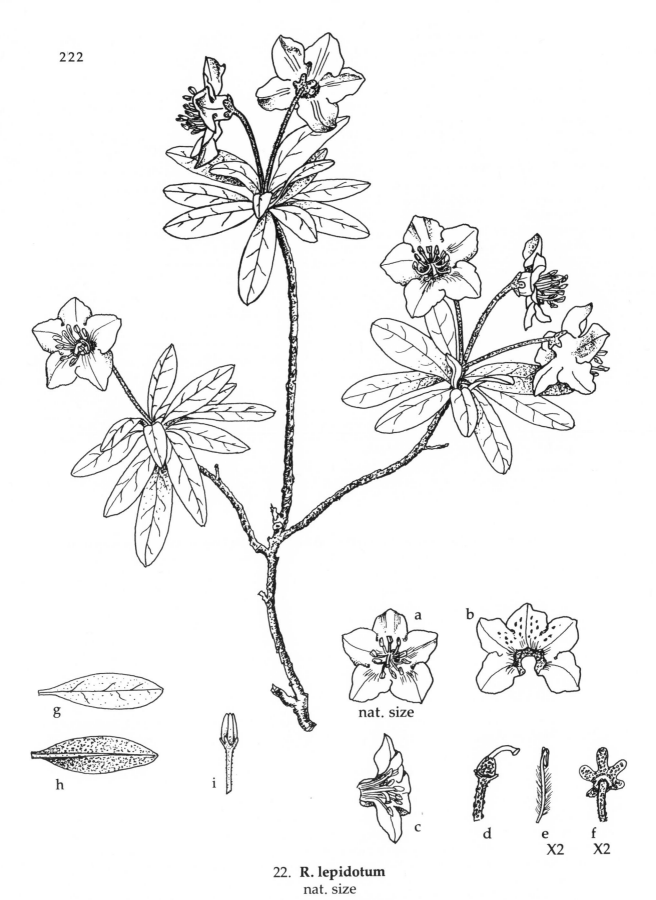

22. R. lepidotum
nat. size

a. flower. b. petals. c. section. d. ovary, style. e. stamen. f. calyx. g. leaf (upper surface). h. leaf (lower surface). i. capsule.

and the flower colour is pink, purple, rose, scarlet, crimson, yellow, greenish-yellow, or white. The species is allied to *R. baileyi*. The relationship between them is discussed under the latter.

The species was first introduced by J.D. Hooker in 1850. It was reintroduced many times by other collectors. Some ten or more different forms are in cultivation. The more distinctive forms are: Form 1. A shrub up to 3 or 4 feet high, leaves evergreen, usually lanceolate or oblanceolate, up to 3.2 cm. long, up to 1.1 cm. broad, corolla large up to 1.6 cm. long, pink, scarlet or crimson. Form 2. A shrub similar to No. 1 but with yellow flowers. Form 3. A robust shrub up to 4 feet high with stout branchlets, leaves evergreen, obovate or oval, large, up to 3.8 cm. long and up to 1.8 cm. broad, corolla same as No. 1, known as *R. obovatum* or *R. lepidotum* var. *obovatum*. Form 4. A dwarf shrublet, 2 inches to 1 foot high, leaves usually deciduous, tiny, corolla small, yellow, pale yellow or greenish-yellow, known as *R. elaeagnoides* or *R. lepidotum* var. *elaeagnoides*. Form 5. A shrub 1—2 feet high, leaves evergreen, lanceolate or oblanceolate up to 2.5 cm. long, corolla white or white slightly tinged pink. Form 6. A shrub 1—2 feet high, leaves deciduous, tiny, corolla tiny, red or crimson-purple.

These six extremes are so distinct in cultivation, that it would seem desirable to distinguish Forms 3—6 as varieties, although they are linked with intermediates.

The plant varies in hardiness. It is extremely useful in that it is a late flowerer, prolonging the flowering season into June. The species and all its varieties are well suited for the rock garden. A form 'Reuthe's Purple', with large purplish-red flowers received an Award of Merit when exhibited by Messrs. G. Reuthe Ltd., Foxhill Nurseries, Keston, Kent, in 1967.

Epithet. Beset with scales.
Hardiness 2—3. April—June. Plate 43.

R. lepidotum Wall. ex G. Don var. **album** Davidian in Quart. Bull. Amer. Rhod. Soc., Vol. 35, January (1982).

This plant (Form No. 5) was first collected by Major Lall Dhevoj in 1930 in Nepal. It was later found by Ludlow, Sherriff and Hicks in Bhutan in 1949, and by Col. Spring-Smyth in Nepal in 1961. It grows on open grassy banks and in crevices of cliffs at elevations of 2,288—4,270 m. (7,500—14,000 ft.).

The variety differs from the species in that the corolla is white or white slightly tinged pink. It is a small, broadly upright or spreading shrub, 30—60 cm. (1—2 ft.) high. The leaves are evergreen, lanceolate or oblanceolate, up to 2.5 cm. long, and the corolla is up to 1.5 cm. long.

It was introduced into cultivation by Col. Spring-Smyth in 1961 from Nepal (No. 51).
Epithet of the variety. With white flowers.
Hardiness 3. May—June.

R. lepidotum Wall. ex G. Don var. **elaeagnoides** (Hook. f.) Franch. in Bull. Bot. Soc. France, XXXIII (1886) 234.

Illustration. Hook. f. Rhod. Sikkim Himal. t. 23B Fig. 2 (1851). Figured as *R. elaeagnoides*.

J.D. Hooker discovered this plant (Form No. 4) in 1848 in Sikkim Himalaya. Subsequently it was found by other collectors in Nepal, Sikkim, Bhutan and south-east Tibet. It grows amongst stones and boulders, on cliffs, on open rocky hillsides, and in gravelly river-beds, at elevations of 3,813—4,575 (12,500—15,000 ft.). Ludlow, Sherriff and Hicks record it as being a low-growing shrub forming mats in the alpine zone in Bhutan.

In this variety the leaves are usually deciduous, tiny, laminae 3—9 mm. long, 2—7 mm. broad; the corolla is yellow, pale yellow or greenish-yellow, with or without darker spots, 8 mm.—1.3 cm. long. It is a dwarf compact shrub, 5—30 cm. (2 in.—1 ft.) high.

The plant has been in cultivation for a long time, having possibly been first introduced by J.D. Hooker in 1850.

Epithet of the variety. Resembling Elaeagnus.

Hardiness 3. May—June.

R. lepidotum Wall. ex G. Don var. **minutiforme** Davidian in Quart. Bull. Amer. Rhod. Soc., Vol. 35, January 1981.

This plant (Form No. 6) was first found by Lakshman Mali in 1927 in Nepal. It was afterwards collected by Stainton, Sykes and Williams in 1954 and by Col. Spring-Smyth in 1961 in the same region. It grows in damp places and on boulders at an elevation of 3,965 m. (13,000 ft.).

The variety is distinguished by the minute corolla, 5—9 mm. long, red or crimson-purple. The leaves are deciduous, tiny, laminae 3—7 mm. long, 2—4 mm. broad. It is a small, rounded compact, or broadly upright shrub, 30—60 cm. (1—2 ft.) high.

The plant has long been in cultivation. It was reintroduced by Col. Spring-Smyth in 1961 (No. 35).

Epithet of the variety. With minute flowers and leaves.

Hardiness 3. May—June.

R. lepidotum Wall. ex G. Don var. **obovatum** Hook. f. in Bot. Mag. Vol. 105 t. 6450 (1879).

J.D. Hooker discovered this plant (Form No. 3) in 1848 in Sikkim Himalaya. It was afterwards found by other collectors in Sikkim, Nepal, Bhutan and north-west Yunnan. The plant grows in rocky places, on dry clay banks and humus-covered boulders, and on open hillsides, at elevations of 3,050—3,965 m. (10,000—13,000 ft.).

In this variety the leaves are obovate or oval, large, 2—3.8 cm. long, 1—1.8 cm. broad. The corolla is purple, dark red or deep rose, up to 1.6 cm. long. It is a robust shrub, 30 cm.—1.22 m. (1—4 ft.) high with stout branchlets.

The plant was introduced possibly by J.D. Hooker in1850. It is rare in cultivation.

Epithet of the variety. Obovate, referring to obovate leaves.

Hardiness 3. May—June.

R. lowndesii Davidian in Notes Roy. Bot. Gard. Edin., Vol. 21 (1952) 99.

A *dwarf, creeping or spreading or somewhat rounded shrublet, 5—12 cm. (2—5 in.) or rarely 30 cm. (1 ft.) high;* branchlets short or long, thin, slightly or moderately scaly, moderately or rather densely pubescent, *pilose. Leaves* deciduous, obovate, oblong-obovate or oblanceolate, lamina chartaceous, 0.9—2.8 cm. long, 0.4—1.2 cm. broad, apex rounded or obtuse, mucronate, *base* obtuse or tapered, *decurrent on the petiole;* upper surface bright green, somewhat shining, scaly or not scaly, moderately or rather densely puberulous; *margin bristly;* under surface pale green, scaly, the *scales* unequal, medium-sized, *Entire,* yellowish-green, *2—5 times their own diameter apart,* sparsely bristly or not bristly; *petiole* 1—2 mm. long, narrowly winged or ridged on each side, scaly, *slightly or moderately bristly. Inflorescence* terminal, umbellate, 1—2-flowered; rhachis minute, 0.5—1 mm. long, slightly scaly or not scaly; *pedicel* slender, 1.6—4.3 cm. long, longer than the corolla, scaly, *bristly* or rarely not bristly. *Calyx* 5-lobed, 2—5 mm. long, crimson or reddish, lobes rounded, ovate or oblong-ovate, outside scaly or rarely not scaly, margin ciliate. *Corolla* rotate-campanulate, 1.3—1.7 cm. long, 5-lobed, *pale yellow,* with carmine or greenish-yellow spots on the posterior side, outside scaly. *Stamens* 10 or rarely 11, 0.6—1 cm. long, exserted from the tube; filaments densely hairy towards the base or to two-thirds of their length. *Ovary* conoid, 2—3 mm. long, 5-celled, densely scaly, glabrous; style short, stout and sharply bent, not scaly, glabrous. *Capsule* conoid or ovoid, 4—7 mm. long, 3 mm. broad, rather densely scaly, glabrous, calyx-lobes persistent.

R. lowndesii was discovered by Col. D.G. Lowndes in July 1950 in Marsiandi Valley, Nepal. Subsequently it was collected by Polunin, Sykes and Williams, also by Stainton, Sykes and Williams, and by George Smith in other localities in Nepal. The plant grows in rock crevices, on peaty banks, on rock ledges, amongst rocks on grass slopes, and on cliff ledges, at elevations of 3,050—4,575 m. (10,000—15,000 ft.).

The species resembles *R. lepidotum* var. *elaeagnoides* in its deciduous leaves and pale yellow flowers, but is readily distinguished by the bristly branchlets, margins of leaves, petiole and pedicel, by the distribution of the scales on the lower surface of the leaves, the scales being laxly spaced, 2—5 times their own diameter apart, and usually by the larger leaves.

The plant flowered for the first time towards the end of May 1956 in the Royal Botanic Garden, Edinburgh. It was raised from seed taken from a herbarium fruiting specimen under No. 3486 collected by Polunin, Sykes and Williams in Nepal in 1952. It was reintroduced by Stainton, Sykes and Williams, and by George Smith of Manchester University. In cultivation it is a somewhat rounded, spreading shrub with short branchlets, although in its native home it is often a prostrate creeping shrub with very long branchlets. The plant is a slow grower and is reputed to be difficult. Although it is deciduous and comes from elevations of 10,000—15,000 feet, it is advisable to cover the plant in cultivation outdoors during the winter months. In many gardens it has failed to establish. But it has been successfully grown in some gardens, particularly along the east coast. It provides a fine display with its single or paired pale yellow flowers situated on long flower-stalks, and are often produced freely.

Epithet. After Col. D.G. Lowndes, who discovered it in 1950.

Hardiness 3. May—June.

MADDENII SERIES

General characters: small to large shrubs or sometimes small trees, often epiphytic, 60 cm.—9.15 m. (2—30 ft.) high. Leaves evergreen, linear, linear-lanceolate, lanceolate, oblong to elliptic, obovate, oblong-oval or almost oval, lamina 2—26.5 cm. long, 0.5—13 cm. broad, under surface densely or laxly scaly, the scales contiguous or rarely overlapping to 5 times their own diameter apart. Inflorescence terminal, usually umbellate, 1—9- or rarely up to 12-flowered; pedicel 0.3—3.5 cm. long, thick or somewhat thick. Calyx 5-lobed or sometimes an undulate rim, usually 0.1—2.6 cm. long. *Corolla tubular-funnel shaped or funnel-shaped or tubular-campanulate*, often waxy, *4.5—13.6 cm.* or rarely 4 cm. *long*, white, creamy-white, yellow, rose or pink, outside rather densely or moderately scaly all over or at the base of the tube, or sometimes not scaly. *Stamens 10—25* (rarely 8). Ovary usually conoid, ovoid or oblong, apex tapered into the style or truncate, 0.4—1 cm. or rarely 1.5 cm. long, 5—12-celled. Capsule usually oblong, oblong-oval or oval, 0.9—7.2 cm. long, 0.5—2.5 cm. broad.

Distribution: Nepal, Sikkim, Bhutan, Assam, south, south-east and east Tibet, north-west, north, north-east Upper Burma and Lower Burma, mid-west, west, north-west and south-west Yunnan, Kweichow, Thailand, Vietnam, and Laos.

This is a large Series comprising fifty species with a wide area of distribution. It is divided into three Subseries, Ciliicalyx Subseries, Maddenii Subseries, and Megacalyx Subseries. The main features of the Series are the large tubular-funnel shaped or funnel-shaped or tubular-campanulate corolla, often waxy, 4.5—13.6 cm. long, and the 10—25 stamens. The species are often epiphytic in their native home. In cultivation the vast majority are tender along the east coast and inland, and require the protection of a greenhouse, although most of them are successfully grown outdoors in sheltered gardens along the west coast, particularly in Cornwall and Northern Ireland.

KEY TO THE SUBSERIES

A. Stamens 15—25 or rarely 12; ovary 10—12-celled (except in *R. excellens*, 5-celled);
petiole grooved above .... *Maddenii Subseries*
A. Stamens 10 or rarely 8 or rarely 11—14; ovary 5—6- or rarely 7-celled; petiole convex
not grooved, or grooved above.
    B. Calyx large, 7 mm.—2.6 cm. long; petiole convex, not grooved above (except in
R. megacalyx and rarely in *R. basfordii*, grooved above); corolla not pubescent
(or rarely pubescent on the tube) outside; ovary tapered into the style
(except in *R. megacalyx* and rarely in *R. nuttallii*, apex truncate) ....
.... *Megacalyx Subseries*
    B. Calyx small, usually 1—6 mm. long; petiole grooved above; corolla pubescent
at the base of the tube or sometimes all over the tube and lobes outside (or
rarely not pubescent); ovary usually truncate at the apex. *Ciliicalyx Subseries*

CILIICALYX SUBSERIES

General characters: small, medium-sized or large shrubs or sometimes small trees, often epiphytic, 60 cm.—4.58 m. (2—15 ft.), rarely 30 cm. or 7.63 m. (1 or 25 ft.) high. Leaves elliptic, oblong-elliptic, obovate, oblong-obovate, oblong-oval, ovate, oblong-lanceolate, oblanceolate, lanceolate, linear-lanceolate or linear, lamina 2—13 cm. long, 0.5—6.8 cm. broad, under surface densely or laxly scaly, the scales ½—5 times their own diameter apart, or sometimes contiguous, or rarely overlapping; *petiole* 0.3—1.8 cm. or sometimes up to 2.5 cm. long, *grooved above*. Inflorescence 1—6-flowered; pedicel 0.3—2.3 cm. long, thick or sometimes somewhat thick. *Calyx* 5-lobed or an undulate rim, oblique, *0.5—2 mm. or sometimes 3—7 mm.* or rarely 1 cm. *long.* Corolla funnel-shaped, sometimes widely funnel-shaped or tubular-funnel shaped, 4.5—9.3 cm. or rarely 4 cm. long, 5-lobed, fragrant or not fragrant, white or white tinged pink or sometimes white with pink bands outside along the middle of the tube and lobes, rarely pink or rose, with or without a yellow or greenish or orange blotch at the base, moderately or laxly scaly all over the outside, rarely sparsely scaly or not scaly, *pubescent at the base of the tube outside or sometimes all over the tube and lobes*, rarely not pubescent. *Stamens* 10 or rarely 11—14, 2.3—6.8 cm. long. *Ovary* conoid or sometimes oblong, *apex truncate*, sometimes somewhat tapered or tapered into the style, 4—7 mm. or rarely 0.8—1 cm. long, *5—6- or rarely 7-celled*; style long, straight or curved in the upper part, scaly in the lower ⅓—¾ (or rarely ¼) its length. Capsule oblong-oval, oblong or sometimes oval, oblique at the base, 1.2—3 cm. long, 0.6—1.6 cm. broad, densely or rarely moderately scaly.

KEY TO THE SPECIES

1. Under surface of the leaves densely scaly, the scales ½ their own diameter apart, or sometimes contiguous or overlapping.
    2. Leaves linear, linear-lanceolate, narrowly lanceolate or narrowly oblanceolate, laminae usually 0.5—1.2 cm. broad; leaf base decurrent on the petiole; petiole with narrow wings at the margins .... *iteophyllum*
    (part)
    2. Leaves elliptic, oblong-elliptic, obovate, oblong-obovate, ovate, or sometimes broadly lanceolate or broadly oblanceolate, laminae usually 1.5—6.8 cm. broad; leaf base not decurrent on the petiole (except sometimes in *R. lyi*); petiole without narrow wings at the margins (except sometimes in *R. lyi*).
        3. Branchlets and petioles moderately or rather densely bristly; margin of leaves often bristly.
            4. Leaves elliptic, obovate or oblong-elliptic, apex obtuse or rounded, laminae 2—4.6 cm. broad; corolla yellow, pale yellow, white tinged yellow, or sometimes white or white tinged pink .... *johnstoneanum*
            4. Leaves oblanceolate, oblong-lanceolate, lanceolate (or rarely oblong-obovate), apex acute or shortly acute or abruptly acute, laminae usually 1.3—2.8 cm. broad; corolla white .... *lyi*
            (part)
        3. Branchlets and petioles not bristly (except sometimes in *R. supranubium* and *R. surasianum* bristly); margin of leaves not bristly.
            5. Corolla small, 3.6—4.5 cm. long; a large tree or shrub, 5—6.10 m. (16—20 ft.) high, not epiphytic.
                6. Leaves obovate-oblanceolate or oblong-oblanceolate, laminae 4.5—6.5 cm. long, 1.8—2.5 cm. broad; pedicel 3 mm. long; rhachis of the inflorescence villous .... *smilesii*
                6. Leaves elliptic or oblong-elliptic, laminae 6—7.6 cm. long, 2.8—4 cm. broad; pedicel 7 mm.—1.5 cm. long; rhachis of the inflorescence glabrous .... *fleuryi*
            5. Corolla large, 4.6—9.3 cm. long; usually small, medium-sized or large shrubs, sometimes epiphytic, 60 cm.—4.58 m. (2—15 ft.) high.
                7. Leaves broadly oblanceolate, broadly lanceolate or oblong-lanceolate, apex acuminate or acute.
                    8. Corolla tubular-funnel shaped, 7 cm. long, white; scales on the under surface of the leaves medium-sized; branchlets not bristly .... *rufosquamosum*
                    8. Corolla funnel-shaped, 5—6.5 cm. long, white flushed rose or purplish outside, or rarely white; scales on the under surface of the leaves large; branchlets sometimes bristly .... *supranubium*
                    (part)
                7. Leaves elliptic, oblong-elliptic, obovate, oblong-obovate or ovate, apex rounded, obtuse, usually abruptly acute or abruptly acuminate.
                    9. Leaves (laminae) very thick, leathery, rigid, apex rounded or obtuse; branchlets closely or widely warted with leaf-scars; old leaves including petiole usually turn crimson-purple; Thailand species .... *ludwigianum*
                    (part)

9. Leaves (laminae) not very thick, not rigid, apex abruptly acute or acuminate; branchlets not warted with leaf-scars; old leaves including petiole remain green; North Burma or West Yunnan species (except *R. surasianum* North Thailand species).

    10. Corolla large, usually 7.5—8.5 cm. long; style 7—9 cm. long; calyx margin often glabrous .... *lasiopodum* (part)

    10. Corolla smaller, usually 4.6—7.2 cm. (or rarely 2.8 cm.) long; style 4.2—7 cm. (or rarely 3 cm.) long; calyx margin usually hairy with long hairs or bristly.

        11. Leaves usually ovate or ovate-elliptic, laminae usually widest below the middle .... *roseatum*

        11. Leaves usually elliptic, oblong-elliptic, obovate, oblong-obovate, oblong-lanceolate or rarely broadly lanceolate, laminae usually widest at or above the middle.

            12. Corolla usually 4.6—5 cm. long, often yellow or with a streak of yellow on the upper lobe; pedicel 5 mm.—1 cm. long. .... *pachypodum*

            12. Corolla usually 5.8—7.2 cm. long, white, white tinged pink or crimson, or pale pink; pedicel usually 1—1.5 cm. long.

                13. Corolla pale pink; Northern Thailand species .... *surasianum*

                13. Corolla white, or white tinged pink or crimson; Northern Burma or Western Yunnan species.

                    14. Leaves elliptic or oblong-elliptic, apex abruptly acuminate; style 4.8—6 cm. long; shrub often epiphytic; Northern Burma species .. *dendricola* (part)

                    14. Leaves usually obovate or oblong-obovate, apex abruptly acute; style 6—7 cm. long; shrub not epiphytic; Western Yunnan species .. *scottianum*

1. Under surface of the leaves laxly scaly, the scales usually 1½—5 times or sometimes their own diameter apart.

                15. Branchlets and petioles usually moderately or sparsely bristly (except *R. cuffeanum* and *R. walongense*, not bristly); leaves linear, linear-lanceolate, lanceolate, oblanceolate or oblong-lanceolate, apex acute or acuminate, base usually tapered.

                    16. Leaves linear, linear-lanceolate, narrowly lanceolate or narrowly oblanceolate, usually 5 mm.—1.2 cm. broad; leaf base decurrent on the petiole; petiole with narrow wings at the margins .... *iteophyllum* (part)

                    16. Leaves usually broadly lanceolate, broadly oblanceolate, or oblong-lanceolate, usually 1.3—4.4 cm. broad; leaf base not decurrent (except in *R. lyi*, *R. coxianum* and *R. formosum*); petiole often without narrow wings at the margins.

                        17. Calyx large, 2—7 mm. or rarely up to 1 cm. long; calyx margin bristly.

18. Leaves narrow, usually 1.5—2 cm. broad, oblanceolate; under surface of the leaves laxly scaly, the scales 2—5 times their own diameter apart; Assam species .... *coxianum*

18. Leaves broad, usually 2.5—4.4 cm. broad, oblong-lanceolate or broadly oblanceolate; under surface of the leaves somewhat densely scaly, the scales 1½ or sometimes 2 times their own diameter apart; Western Yunnan or South-western Burma species.

> **19.** Branchlets and petioles usually bristly; inflorescence 2—4-flowered; corolla usually not scaly outside, widely funnel-shaped or funnel-shaped; leaf apex acute or obtuse; Western Yunnan species .. *ciliicalyx* (part)

> **19.** Branchlets and petioles not bristly; inflorescence 4—5-flowered; corolla laxly scaly on the tube and on the lobes outside, tubular-campanulate or tubular-funnel shaped; leaf apex acuminate; South-western Burma species .... *cuffeanum*

17. Calyx small 1 mm. or sometimes 2 mm. long; calyx margin not bristly or bristly.

> **20.** Corolla widely funnel-shaped, usually 7.5—8.3 cm. long; stem and branches with smooth, brown, flaking bark; early flowering, the flowers appearing in February or early March .. *cubittii*

> **20.** Corolla funnel-shaped, usually 4—7 cm. long; stem and branches with rough bark; later-flowering, the flowers appearing usually in March—June.

>> **21.** Corolla usually not scaly outside .... *ciliicalyx* (part)

>> **21.** Corolla moderately or rarely sparsely scaly all over the outside.

>>> **22.** Leaves (laminae) 10—13 cm. long; corolla creamy or creamy-white, pubescent all over the tube outside .... *walongense*

>>> **22.** Leaves (laminae) usually 2—9.5 cm. long; corolla white or white flushed rose, pubescent at the base of the tube outside or glabrous.

>>>> **23.** Leaves usually 1.3—1.6 cm. broad, leaf-base decurrent or slightly decurrent on the petiole, margin of lamina bristly or not bristly; petiole with narrow wings or ridges at the margins .. *formosum*

>>>> **23.** Leaves usually 1.5—4 cm. broad, leaf-base not decurrent on the petiole (except sometimes in *R. lyi*), margin of lamina usually not bristly; petiole without wings or ridges at the margins.

>>>>> **24.** Scales on the under surface of the leaves their own diameter apart .... *lyi* (part)

>>>>> **24.** Scales on the under surface of the leaves 2—4 times their own diameter apart.

>>>>>> **25.** Corolla white, laxly or sparsely scaly all over the outside, glabrous or pubescent at the base of the tube outside .... *inaequale* (part)

>>>>>> **25.** Corolla white flushed rose or purplish outside, or rarely white, moderately scaly all over the outside, pubescent at the base of the tube outside .... *supranubium* (part)

15. Branchlets and petioles not bristly (except in *R. ciliipes*); leaves elliptic, obovate, ovate, ovate-lanceolate, elliptic-lanceolate or oblong-obovate, (rarely oblong-lanceolate or oblanceolate), apex obtuse, rounded, abruptly acuminate, abruptly acute, acute or sometimes acuminate, base rounded or obtuse or cuneate.

26. Calyx 4—6 mm. long, 5-lobed; leaves ovate-lanceolate or ovate; inflorescence usually 1-flowered; branchlets and petioles bristly .... *ciliipes*

26. Calyx 1 mm. or sometimes 2—3 mm. long, an undulate rim or 5-lobed; leaves elliptic, obovate, oblong-obovate, elliptic-lanceolate or rarely oblong-lanceolate; inflorescence 2—6-flowered; branchlets and petioles often not bristly.

27. Leaves (laminae) very thick, leathery, rigid, apex rounded or obtuse; branchlets closely or widely warted with leaf-scars; old leaves including petiole usually turn crimson-purple; Thailand species ...... *ludwigianum*
(part)

27. Leaves (laminae) not very thick, usually not rigid, apex abruptly acuminate or acute (except in *R. scopulorum*, rounded or obtuse); branchlets not warted with leaf-scars; old leaves including petiole remain green; Burma, Tibet, Yunnan and Assam species, (except sometimes in *R. veitchianum* from Thailand).

28. Corolla large, usually 7.5—8.5 cm. long; style 5.8—9 cm. long.

29. Calyx usually an undulate rim; style 7—9 cm. long; scales on the under surface of the leaves 1—3 times their own diameter apart; Yunnan species .... *lasiopodum*
(part)

29. Calyx 5-lobed, lobes ovate; style 5.8—6.8 cm. long; scales on the under surface of the leaves 1—2 times their own diameter apart; Assam species .... *parryae*

28. Corolla smaller, usually 4.5—7.2 cm. long; style usually 3.8—6.8 cm. long.

30. Under surface of the leaves very glaucous; margins of the corolla-lobes usually crinkled .... *veitchianum*

30. Under surface of leaves pale glaucous green or pale green (except in *R. carneum*, glaucous); margins of the corolla-lobes entire.

31. Corolla pink or rose; under surface of the leaves glaucous .... *carneum*

31. Corolla white or creamy-white or white tinged pink (except in *R. scopulorum* rarely apple blossom pink); under surface of the leaves pale glaucous green or pale green.

32. Leaf apex rounded or obtuse; calyx 2 mm. long, 5-lobed; corolla pubescent all over the tube and lobes outside .... *scopulorum*

32. Leaf apex abruptly acuminate or abruptly acute or acute; calyx 1 mm. or rarely 2 mm. long, a mere rim or 5-lobed; corolla pubescent at the base of the tube outside or sometimes glabrous.

33. Corolla 4.5—5.4 cm. long; scales on the under surface of the leaves 3—5 times their own diameter apart.

34. Leaves usually obovate, oblong-obovate or obovate-elliptic, apex abruptly acute; pedicel not puberulous; corolla white with purplish-pink bands on the angles outside, with a yellow blotch at the base; scales on the under surface of the leaves medium-sized . .
.... *notatum*

34. Leaves elliptic, elliptic-lanceolate or oblong-lanceolate, apex acuminate or acutely acuminate or acute; pedicel rather densely puberulous; corolla white, without purplish-pink bands

outside, with or without a yellow
blotch at the base; scales on the under
surface of the leaves large . . .*taronense*

33. Corolla usually 5.8—7.2 cm. long; scales on the
under surface of the leaves 1—3 times their
own diameter apart.

35. Leaves elliptic-lanceolate, oblong-
lanceolate, obovate-lanceolate
or oblanceolate, apex acutely or
shortly acuminate or acute, base
cuneate or tapered or obtuse.

36. Corolla white or creamy-
white, with pink bands outside the lobes, rather densely or moderately pubes-
cent outside; leaf-apex acutely or shortly acuminate;
style is as long as the corolla or shorter; North
Burma species . . . .
. . . . *horlickianum*

36. Corolla white, without pink
bands outside the lobes,
not pubescent or pubescent
only at the base of the tube
outside; leaf-apex usually
acute or obtuse; style is
longer than the corolla; Assam species . . . . . *inaequale*
(part)

35. Leaves elliptic or oblong-elliptic,
apex abruptly acuminate, base
rounded or obtuse . . . *dendricola*
(part)

DESCRIPTION OF THE SPECIES

R. carneum Hutch. in Bot. Mag. Vol. 141 t. 8634 (1915).

A somewhat lax, broadly upright shrub, 92 cm.—1.83 m. (3—6 ft.) high; branchlets
rather densely or moderately scaly, not bristly. *Leaves* elliptic, obovate-elliptic or obovate, lamina coriaceous, 5—10 cm. long, 2.7—4.3 cm. broad, apex obtuse or acute,
mucronate, base rounded or obtuse; upper surface dark green, somewhat shining, scaly
or not scaly, midrib grooved, primary veins 5—10 on each side, deeply impressed;
margin not bristly; *under surface glaucous*, scaly, the scales unequal, large and medium-
sized, brown, 1—2 times their own diameter apart, midrib prominent, primary veins
raised; petiole 0.8—1.4 cm. long, grooved above, densely scaly, not bristly. *Inflorescence*
terminal, umbellate or shortly racemose, 3—6-flowered; rhachis 5—6 mm. long, scaly;

pedicel 0.8—1 cm. long, thick, densely scaly, not bristly. *Calyx* 5-lobed, oblique, *minute, 1 mm. long*, lobes ovate or triangular, outside densely scaly, margin hairy with long hairs. *Corolla* funnel-shaped, 4.5—5 cm. long, 5-lobed, margins of lobes entire, *pink or rose*, with a yellow blotch at the base, *scaly all over the outside*, pubescent at the base of the tube outside. *Stamens* 10—12, unequal, 2.4—3.7 cm. long, shorter than the corolla; filaments densely hairy in the lower ⅓—½ their length. *Ovary* conoid, apex truncate, 4—5 mm. long, 6-celled, densely scaly, glabrous; style long, straight or curved in the upper part, as long as the corolla or slightly shorter, rather densely scaly in the lower ¾ its length, glabrous. *Capsule* conoid or oblong-oval, oblique at the base, 1.4 cm. long, 1 cm. broad, ribbed, densely scaly, glabrous, calyx persistent.

R. carneum was described by Hutchinson in 1915 from a living plant raised by Col. F.B. Longe, Holly Lodge, Thorpe, Norwich, from a supply of seed sent by Major C.W. Browne, of the Survey of India. The plant is a native of the Northern Shan States, Northern Burma, and is said to grow on open grassy hillsides away from any large trees, preferring western slopes, at an elevation of about 2,288 m. (7,500 ft.).

A diagnostic feature of this plant is the pink or rose corolla. In this respect it is usually distinguished from its nearest ally, *R. ciliicalyx*. It also differs in that the calyx is minute, 1 mm. long, the corolla is usually smaller, scaly all over the outside, and the petiole and branchlets are not bristly.

In its native home, *R. carneum* grows to a height of about 3 feet. In cultivation it is a somewhat lax, broadly upright shrub up to 6 feet in height. The species has a long flowering season which extends from March or sometimes from the middle of February, to the end of May. Along the west coast it is successfully grown outdoors in well-sheltered gardens in mild localities, but along the east coast it is tender and is suitable for a cool greenhouse. The plant was given an Award of Merit when exhibited by Mr. Lionel de Rothschild, Exbury, in 1927.

Epithet. Flesh-coloured.
Hardiness 1—2. February—May.

R. ciliicalyx Franch. in Bull. Soc. Bot. France, XXXIII (1886) 233.
Illustration. Bot. Mag. Vol. 127 t. 7782 (1901).
A somewhat lax, broadly upright shrub, sometimes epiphytic, 80 cm.—3 m. (2½—10 ft.) high; *branchlets* moderately or rather densely scaly, *bristly* or sometimes not bristly. *Leaves* oblong-lanceolate, elliptic-lanceolate, oblanceolate, obovate, obovate-lanceolate, oblong-obovate, elliptic or obovate-elliptic, lamina coriaceous, 5—10.3 cm. long, 1.6—3.6 cm. broad, apex acute or obtuse, mucronate, base obtuse or cuneate; upper surface dark green, somewhat shining, not scaly or rarely sparsely scaly, midrib grooved, primary veins 8—12 on each side, deeply impressed; margin not bristly or rarely bristly; under surface glaucous green or pale glaucous green, scaly, the scales unequal, large, brown, 1½ times, or sometimes 1—2 times, or rarely ½ their own diameter apart, midrib prominent, primary veins raised; petiole 0.5—1.6 cm. long, grooved above, moderately or rather densely scaly, *moderately or sparsely bristly* or rarely not bristly. *Inflorescence* terminal, umbellate, 2—4-flowered; rhachis 2—4 mm. long, scaly, pubescent; pedicel 0.5—1.3 cm. long, thick, densely or rarely moderately scaly, not bristly or rarely bristly. *Calyx* 5-lobed, oblique, *1—7 mm. long*, lobes ovate or triangular or oblong, outside sparsely or moderately scaly, *margin moderately* or rarely slightly *bristly*. *Corolla* widely funnel-shaped or funnel-shaped, 4.6—7.8 cm. long, 5-lobed, margins of lobes entire, white or rarely white faintly flushed rose on exterior, or rarely rose, with a yellow blotch at the base, *outside not scaly* or rarely scaly along one side, or rarely laxly scaly all over the outside, pubescent at the base of the tube outside or rarely glabrous. *Stamens* 10 or rarely 11, unequal, 2.8—6 cm. long, shorter than the corolla; filaments rather densely pilose in the lower ¼—⅓ their length. *Ovary* conoid or rarely oblong, apex truncate, 4—6 mm. long, 6- or rarely 5- or 7-celled, densely scaly, glabrous; style long, straight or curved in

the upper part, as long as the corolla, or slightly shorter or longer, scaly in the lower ¼—½ its length, rarely at the base or in the lower ⅔ its length, glabrous or rarely pubescent at the base. *Capsule* oblong-oval, oblong or oval, oblique at the base, 1.2—2.8 cm. long, 0.7—1.5 cm. broad, ribbed, densely scaly, glabrous, calyx-lobes persistent.

This species was discovered by the Abbé Delavay in 1884 on Mt. Peechaho, near Mo-so-yn, Yunnan. It was later found by him again, and by other collectors in different localities in the same region. The plant grows on the sides of rocky hills and in woods, at elevations of 1,800—4,000 m. (5,902—13,111 ft.).

R. *ciliicalyx* was described by Franchet in 1886. Subsequently distinct specific names were given to similar plants, namely, R. *missionarum* Léveillé (1915), R. *pseudociliicalyx* Hutch. (1919), R. *atentsiense* Hand.-Mazz. (1921), and R. *yungchangense* Cullen (1978). In *The Species of Rhododendron* 1930, R. *atentsiense* correctly appears in synonymy under R. *ciliicalyx*. When the specimens under the other three names are examined, it will be seen that in height of growth, in the shape and size of the leaves, in the shape, size and colour of the flowers, and in all other morphological details, they are also identical with R. *ciliicalyx*. It is apparent that the whole material under these names represents a single variable unit. R. *ciliicalyx*, being the oldest described species, is the valid name.

A marked feature of R. *ciliicalyx* is the bristly calyx margin, to which the specific name refers. The species varies considerably in height of growth, in leaf shape and size, and in the size of the calyx. It is allied to R. *carneum*; the relationship between them is discussed under the latter.

R. *ciliicalyx* was first introduced by the Abbé Delavay to Paris, and thence to Kew in 1892. It was later reintroduced by Forrest from Yunnan, and by Kingdon-Ward from The Triangle, North Burma. In its native home it grows up to 10 feet high; in cultivation it is a somewhat lax, broadly upright shrub usually 3—5 feet high or rarely up to about 8 feet. The plant is free-flowering, and provides a fine display with its white or rarely white faintly flushed rose flowers in trusses of two to four. As it grows at elevations of 5,902—13,111 feet in its native home, its hardiness varies considerably in cultivation. Along the west coast it succeeds admirably in well-sheltered gardens, but along the east coast it needs the protection of a cool greenhouse. It received an Award of Merit when shown by Oxford Botanic Garden in 1923, and again the same Award when exhibited by Mr. G. Gorer, Sunte House, Haywards Heath, in 1975.

Epithet. Fringed calyx.
Hardiness 1—2. March—May.

R. ciliipes Hutch. in Notes Roy. Bot. Gard. Edin., Vol. 16 (1931) 177.

A shrub, 1.53—2.14 m. (5—7 ft.) high; *branchlets* scaly, *bristly*. *Leaves ovate-lanceolate or ovate*, lamina coriaceous, 6—8 cm. long, 2.4—3.6 cm. broad, apex acuminate, mucronate, base rounded; upper surface dark green, not scaly, midrib grooved, primary veins 8—10 on each side, deeply impressed; margin not bristly; under surface pale green, scaly, the scales unequal, medium-sized and small, brown, shining, 1½—2 times their own diameter apart, midrib prominent, primary veins raised; *petiole* 0.6—1.2 cm. long, grooved above, moderately or rather densely scaly, *bristly*. *Inflorescence* terminal, umbellate, *1—2-flowered*; rhachis 1—2 mm. long, scaly; pedicel 0.9—1.4 cm. long, somewhat thick, rather densely or moderately scaly, not bristly. *Calyx* 5-lobed, oblique, *4—6 mm. long*, reddish-purple, lobes oblong-oval or oval or ovate, outside scaly, margin hairy with long hairs. *Corolla* funnel-shaped, 5.5—6.8 cm. long, 5-lobed, margins of lobes entire, fragrant, white with a green blotch at the base, scaly all over the outside, pubescent at the base of the tube outside. *Stamens* 10, unequal, 3—4.5 cm. long, shorter than the corolla; filaments densely pubescent in the lower ⅓—½ their length. *Ovary* conoid, apex truncate, 4—5 mm. long, 6-celled, densely scaly, glabrous; style long, straight or curved in the upper part, as long as the corolla, scaly in the lower half, glabrous. *Capsule:*—

R. ciliipes is known from a single gathering made in May 1925 by Forrest in the Shweli-Salwin divide, mid-west Yunnan. It grows on cliffs and humus-covered boulders in side valleys at an elevation of 3,050 m. (10,000 ft.).

The original diagnosis makes no reference to its affinity. The species shows a certain degree of resemblance to *R. supranubium*, but is readily distinguished by the shape of the leaves, the large calyx, and usually the bristly petioles and branchlets. The plant has not been introduced into cultivation.

Epithet. Fringed at the base.

Not in cultivation.

R. coxianum Davidian in The Royal Horticultural Society's Rhododendrons (1972) 51.

A broadly upright or somewhat straggly shrub, sometimes epiphytic at least when young, 92 cm.—3 m. (3—10 ft.) high; branchlets scaly, moderately or sparsely bristly. *Leaves oblanceolate,* lamina coriaceous, 5.3—11.5 cm. long, *1.5—3 cm. broad, apex abruptly acute or acuminate,* mucronate, base tapered, decurrent or not decurrent on the petiole; upper surface green, shining, not scaly or sparsely scaly, not bristly or sparsely bristly; margin not bristly; *under surface* pale glaucous green, scaly, the *scales* unequal, medium-sized, brown, *2—5 times their own diameter apart;* petiole 0.5—1 cm. long, with or without narrow wings at the margins, grooved above, scaly, not bristly or slightly bristly. *Inflorescence* terminal, umbellate, 3-flowered; rhachis 2 mm. long, not scaly, sparsely bristly; pedicel somewhat stout, 1.2—1.4 cm. long, scaly, not bristly. *Calyx* 5-lobed, oblique, unequal, *4—5 mm. long,* lobes ovate-oblong or ovate, outside rather densely or moderately scaly, glabrous, margin sparsely scaly or not scaly, moderately or sparsely hairy with long hairs. *Corolla tubular-funnel shaped,* ventricose, 7.3—7.5 cm. long, 5-lobed, margins of lobes entire, *white without or with a faint yellow blotch at the base,* outside scaly, pubescent at the base of the tube. *Stamens* 10, unequal, 3.4—5.3 cm. long, shorter than the corolla; filaments densely pubescent in the lower third. *Ovary* conoid, 4—5 mm. long, 7-celled, densely scaly; style long, slender, straight or curved in the upper part, 6—7 cm. in length, as long as the corolla or a little shorter, scaly in the lower half, glabrous. *Capsule* oblong-oval, oblique at the base, 1.3 cm. long, 8 mm. broad, ribbed, straight, densely scaly, calyx-lobes persistent.

This species was discovered by Cox and Hutchison in April 1965 south-east of Apa Tani valley, Subansiri division, Assam. It grows in soft and boggy ground, at the edge of sub-tropical rain forest at an elevation of 1,647 m. (5,400 ft.).

R. coxianum is a distinct species. It is easily recognised by the long, narrow, oblanceolate leaves, abruptly acute or acuminate at the apex, by the widely spaced scales on the lower surface of the leaves, 2—5 times their own diameter apart, by the calyx 4—5 mm. long, and by the tubular-funnel shaped ventricose white corolla without or with a faint yellow blotch at the base. It shows a certain degree of resemblance to *R. formosum*, from which it differs markedly in distinctive features.

The species was introduced by Cox and Hutchison in 1965 (No. 475B — the Type number). In cultivation it grows up to 3—4 feet high (and is likely to grow a few feet taller), although in its native home it occasionally reaches a height of 10 feet. As it grows at a low elevation of 5,400 feet in Assam, in cultivation along the east coast it is only suitable for a cool greenhouse. The plant is free-flowering, and makes a fine show with its large flowers in trusses of three.

Epithet. After E.H.M. Cox, Glendoick.

Hardiness 1. April—May.

R. cubittii Hutch. in Notes Roy. Bot. Gard. Edin., Vol. 12 (1919) 78.

Illustration. Bot. Mag. Vol. 160 t. 9502 (1937).

A broadly upright, or upright spreading shrub, 1.53—2.44 m. (5—8 ft.) high; *stem and branches with smooth, brown, flaking bark; branchlets* scaly, *moderately or sparsely bristly* or not bristly. *Leaves oblong-lanceolate*, lamina coriaceous, 9—10.8 cm. long, 2.5—3.7 cm. broad, apex acute or acuminate, mucronate, base tapered or obtuse; upper surface dark green, somewhat shining, scaly or not scaly, midrib grooved, primary veins 10—12 on each side, deeply impressed; margin not bristly; under surface pale green or bright green or pale glaucous green, scaly, the scales unequal, large and medium-sized, brown, 1½—5 times their own diameter apart, midrib prominent, primary veins raised; *petiole* 0.8—1.8 cm. long, grooved above, rather densely or moderately scaly, *moderately or sparsely bristly*. *Inflorescence* terminal, umbellate, 2—3-flowered; rhachis 2—4 mm. long, scaly; pedicel 0.4—1.6 cm. long, thick, densely or moderately scaly, not bristly. *Calyx* 5-lobed, oblique, minute, 1 mm. long, lobes ovate or triangular, outside scaly, margin sparsely or moderately bristly. *Corolla* widely funnel-shaped or funnel-shaped, *6—8.3 cm. long*, 5-lobed, margins of lobes entire or somewhat undulate, white, or white flushed rose with or without a reddish band on the back of the lobes and tube, with a yellowish blotch at the base and brown spots, outside scaly on the tube and on the lobes, pubescent at the base of the tube outside. *Stamens* 10, unequal, 4.2—5.5 cm. long, shorter than the corolla; filaments pubescent in the lower half. *Ovary* conoid, apex truncate, 4—5 mm. long, 6-celled, densely scaly, glabrous; style long, straight or curved in the upper part, 6—6.1 cm. in length, shorter than the corolla, scaly in the lower ¼—⅓ its length, glabrous. *Capsule* oblong-oval or oval, oblique at the base, 1.5—2 cm. long, 1—1.3 cm. broad, ribbed, densely scaly, glabrous, calyx persistent.

The only collection of this species was made by G.E.S. Cubitt in the Bhamo Division of North Burma in March 1909 at an elevation of 1,678 m. (5,500 ft.).

R. cubittii is a remarkably distinct species and cannot be confused with any other species of its Series. The original diagnosis associated it with *R. veitchianum*. From this species it differs markedly in distinctive features. The main distinctions between them are that in *R. cubittii* the stem and branches have a smooth, brown, flaking bark, the petioles and usually the branchlets are bristly, the leaves are oblong-lanceolate, the under surface is pale green or bright green or pale glaucous green, the corolla is usually large up to 8.3 cm. long, and the margin of the calyx is moderately or sparsely bristly; whereas in *R. veitchianum* the stem and branches have a rough bark, the petioles and branchlets are not bristly, the leaves are usually obovate, elliptic, oblong-obovate or elliptic-lanceolate, the under surface is very glaucous, the corolla is usually smaller, up to 7 cm. long, and the margin of the calyx is usually not bristly. *R. cubittii* has also been associated with *R. formosum*; from this species it is remote. In some respects, it resembles *R. supranubium* from Yunnan, but is readily distinguished by well-marked characters. The plant is a diploid with 26 chromosomes.

R. cubittii was introduced by G.E.S. Cubitt in 1909. The original diagnosis makes no reference to its habit and height of growth in its native home. In cultivation it is a broadly upright or upright spreading shrub up to 6 feet or sometimes 8 feet high, fairly well-filled with dark green foliage. It is one of the largest-flowered species in its Subseries. The flowers are usually widely funnel-shaped up to about 4½ inches across. A most remarkable feature is the smooth, brown, flaking bark of the stem and branches, which always attracts attention. Along the west coast, the plant is cultivated outdoors in mild localities, but along the east coast it needs a cool greenhouse. The species is an early flowerer, the flowers appearing in March or sometimes February. Like all other species of the Maddenii Series, it is easy to root from cuttings. It is free-flowering, and provides an admirable display with its white or white flushed rose flowers in trusses of two to three. The species was given an Award of Merit when shown by Lt.-Col. E.H.W. Bolitho, Penzance, in 1935, and a First Class Certificate for a form 'Ashcombe' when exhibited by the Crown Estate Commissioners, Windsor Great Park, in 1962.

Epithet. After G.E.S. Cubitt, who collected in North Burma.

Hardiness 1—2. February—April. Plate 44.

R. cuffeanum Craib ex Hutch. in Bot. Mag. Vol. 143 t. 8721 (1917).

A lax broadly upright shrub, 1.53—1.83 m. (5—6 ft.) high; *branchlets* scaly, *not bristly.* *Leaves* oblong-lanceolate, oblanceolate or oblong-oblanceolate, lamina coriaceous, 0.7—12.3 cm. long, 2.5—4.4 cm. broad, apex acuminate, mucronate, base obtuse or cuneate; upper surface dark green, somewhat shining, sparsely scaly or not scaly, midrib grooved, primary veins 6—10 on each side, deeply impressed; margin not bristly; *under surface* pale glaucous green or pale green, scaly, the *scales* unequal, large and medium-sized, brown, *1½—2 times their own diameter apart*, midrib prominent, primary veins raised; *petiole* 1.2—2.5 cm. long, grooved above, moderately or densely scaly, *not bristly.* *Inflorescence* terminal, umbellate, *4—5-flowered*; rhachis 3—4 mm. long, scaly; pedicel 1—1.5 cm. long, thick, rather densely scaly, not bristly. *Calyx* 5-lobed, oblique, 2—5 mm. or sometimes up to 1 cm. long, lobes unequal, ovate or rounded or oblong-oval, outside scaly, margin sparsely or moderately hairy with long hairs. *Corolla tubular-campanulate or tubular-funnel shaped*, 6—7.3 cm. long, 5-lobed, margins of lobes entire, white with a yellow blotch at the base, *outside laxly scaly on the tube and on the lobes*, pubescent at the base of the tube outside. *Stamens* 10, unequal, 4.5—6.3 cm. long, shorter than the corolla; filaments rather densely pubescent in the lower ⅓—½ their length. *Ovary* oblong, apex truncate, 0.6—1 cm. long, 6-celled, densely scaly, glabrous; style long, straight or curved in the upper part, 6—7 cm. in length, longer than the corolla, scaly in the lower ⅓—½ its length, glabrous. *Capsule* oblong or oblong-oval, oblique at the base, 1.8—2 cm. long, 1.2—1.6 cm. broad, ribbed, densely scaly, glabrous, calyx-lobes persistent.

R. cuffeanum was discovered by Lady Wheeler Cuffe on Mt. Victoria, Burma. The young plants which she collected were presented to the Royal Botanic Gardens, Glasnevin, in August 1913. The species was described from one of these plants which flowered in May 1915.

It shows a strong resemblance to *R. inaequale* from Assam, but differs in that the branchlets are not bristly, the calyx is large, 2—5 mm. or sometimes up to 1 cm. long, and the corolla is tubular-campanulate or tubular-funnel shaped.

In cultivation it is a lax broadly upright shrub, up to 6 feet high, with large flowers produced freely in trusses of 4—5. The plant is tender and is suitable for a cool greenhouse. It is rare in cultivation.

Epithet. After Lady Wheeler Cuffe.

Hardiness 1. April—May.

R. dendricola Hutch. in Notes Roy. Bot. Gard. Edin., Vol. 12 (1919) 60.

A somewhat lax, broadly upright shrub, often epiphytic, 1.22—1.83 m. (4—6 ft.) high; branchlets scaly, not bristly. *Leaves elliptic or oblong-elliptic*, lamina coriaceous, 8—11.7 cm. long, 3.5—5.7 cm. broad, *apex abruptly acuminate*, mucronate, base rounded or obtuse; upper surface dark green or bright green, somewhat shining, not scaly, midrib grooved, primary veins 7—12 on each side, deeply impressed; margin not bristly; under surface pale glaucous green or pale green, scaly, the scales unequal, medium-sized, or medium-sized and large, reddish-brown, ½—3 times their own diameter apart, midrib prominent, primary veins raised; petiole 1—1.3 cm. long, grooved above, moderately or rather densely scaly, not bristly. *Inflorescence* terminal, umbellate, 3—5-flowered; rhachis 2—3 mm. long, scaly; pedicel 1—1.5 cm. long, thick, moderately or rather densely scaly, not bristly. *Calyx* an undulate rim, oblique, minute, 1 mm. long, outside scaly, margin sparsely hairy with long hairs or glabrous. *Corolla funnel-shaped, 5.8—7.2 cm. long*, 5-lobed, margins of lobes entire, fragrant, white tinged pink, or white, with an orange or yellow blotch at the base, scaly all over the outside, pubescent at the base of the tube outside, or glabrous. *Stamens* 10, unequal, *3.5—5 cm. long*, shorter than the corolla; filaments densely hairy in the lower ⅓—½ their length. *Ovary* conoid or oblong, apex truncate, 5—8 mm. long, 5—6-celled, densely scaly, glabrous; *style* long, straight or curved in the upper part, *4.8—6 cm. in length*, as long as the corolla, scaly in the lower

⅓—½ its length, glabrous. *Capsule* oblong-oval or oval, oblique at the base, 1.5—2 cm. long, 1.1—1.3 cm. broad, ribbed, densely scaly, glabrous, calyx persistent.

This species was first collected by Kingdon-Ward in May 1914 in the Nwai Valley, North Burma. It was afterwards found by Forrest in north-east Upper Burma. The plant grows in forests and on the margins of open thickets, often as an epiphyte, at elevations of 2,135—3,050 m. (7,000—10,000 ft.).

R. dendricola resembles *R. lasiopodum* in general appearance, but is distinguished by the smaller corolla, by the shorter stamens and style, and usually by the narrower leaves.

It was first introduced by Forrest in 1918 under No. 17227, and again in 1925 under Nos. 26441, 26462, and 27687; in *The Rhododendron Handbook* 1980, the last three numbers have been wrongly recorded as *R. taronense*. There is no record of its occurrence outdoors along the west coast; along the east coast it is tender and needs the protection of a greenhouse. It is a lax broadly upright shrub with white tinged pink flowers in trusses of three to five. The plant is rare in cultivation. It received a First Class Certificate when exhibited by Mr. L. de Rothschild in 1935 under the name *R. taronense*.

Epithet. Dweller on trees.

Hardiness 1. April—May.

R. fleuryi Dop in Chevalier, Rév. Bot. Appl. Agric. Trop. 9 (1929) 255.

A shrub, *5 m. (16 ft.) high*; branchlets scaly, not bristly. *Leaves* elliptic or oblong-elliptic, lamina coriaceous, 6—7.6 cm. long, 2.8—4 cm. broad, apex obtuse or acute, mucronate, base obtuse; upper surface not scaly, not bristly, midrib grooved, primary veins 10—12 on each side, deeply impressed; margin slightly recurved, not bristly; under surface not glaucous, densely scaly, the scales unequal, large and medium-sized, dark brown, overlapping or contiguous, midrib prominent, primary veins slightly raised; petiole 0.7—1 cm. long, grooved above, densely scaly, sparsely bristly or not bristly. *Inflorescence* terminal, shortly racemose, 3—5-flowered; rhachis 3—5 mm. long, scaly, glabrous, not bristly; pedicel 0.7—1.5 cm. long, thick, densely scaly, not bristly. *Calyx* 5-lobed or undulately 5-lobed, oblique, 1—2 mm. long, lobes ovate, outside rather densely or moderately scaly, margin scaly or not scaly, glabrous. *Corolla tubular*, with spreading lobes, *small, 3.6—4.5 cm. long*, 5-lobed, margins of lobes entire, white, outside scaly all over the tube and lobes, glabrous. *Stamens* 10, unequal, 2.3—3.8 cm. long, shorter than the corolla; filaments densely pubescent in the lower ¼ their length. *Ovary* oblong-conoid, apex somewhat tapered into the style, 4 mm. long, 5-celled, densely scaly, glabrous; style long, straight or curved in the upper part, as long as the corolla or slightly longer, scaly in the lower ¼—½ its length, glabrous. *Capsule:*—

This plant was discovered by Chevalier in February 1914 on the peak of Langbian, near the village of Beneur, Vietnam. In May 1922, M. Poilane collected it in the forest in the province of Nhatrang, in the same region. It grows at elevations of 2,000—2,500 m. (6,557—8,197 ft.).

The species bears a strong resemblance to *R. smilesii* from northern Thailand, but is distinguished by the shape of the leaves and usually by their larger size, the longer pedicel, and by the glabrous rhachis of the inflorescence. The plant has not been introduced into cultivation.

Epithet. After Fleury.

Not in cultivation.

R. formosum Wallich, Pl. Asiat. Rar. III t. 207 (1832) 3.

Illustration. Bot. Mag. Vol. 75 t. 4457 (1849).

A lax broadly upright, or broadly upright and spreading, or compact, or straggly shrub, 92 cm.—3 m. (3—10 ft.) high; branchlets moderately or rather densely scaly, moderately or rather densely bristly or sometimes not bristly. *Leaves oblanceolate, oblong-*

obovate or lanceolate, lamina coriaceous, 2—7.6 cm. long, 0.6—2.4 cm. broad, apex acute or abruptly acute or obtuse, mucronate, *base* tapered, *decurrent or slightly decurrent on the petiole*; upper surface dark green, somewhat shining, not scaly or scaly, midrib grooved, primary veins 5—8 on each side, deeply impressed; margin bristly or not bristly; under surface pale glaucous green or glaucous or pale green, scaly, the scales unequal, medium-sized, or medium-sized and large, brown, 1—2 times their own diameter apart, midrib prominent, primary veins slightly raised; *petiole* 3—8 mm. long, grooved above, *with narrow wings or ridges at the margins*, moderately or rather densely scaly, bristly or sometimes not bristly. *Inflorescence* terminal, umbellate, 2—3-, rarely 1- or 4-flowered; rhachis 1—3 mm. long, scaly; pedicel 0.5—2.1 cm. long, somewhat thick or thick, densely or moderately scaly, not bristly. *Calyx* an undulate rim or 5-lobed, oblique, minute, 1 mm. long, when lobed, lobes ovate, outside scaly, margin sparsely hairy with long hairs or glabrous. *Corolla* funnel-shaped, 4—6.5 cm. long, 5-lobed, margins of lobes not crinkled or slightly crinkled, fragrant or not fragrant, white with or without 5 pale or deep red bands outside along the middle of the tube and lobes, and with a yellow blotch at the base; or white with or without a yellow blotch at the base; scaly all over the outside, pubescent at the base of the tube ouside or glabrous. *Stamens* 10, unequal, 2.5—5.8 cm. long, shorter than the corolla; filaments densely pubescent in the lower half. *Ovary* conoid or oblong, apex truncate, 3—5 mm. long, 6-celled, densely scaly, glabrous; style long, straight or curved in the upper part, 4—6.8 cm. in length, as long as the corolla or longer, scaly in the lower ½—¾ its length, glabrous. *Capsule* oblong, oblique at the base, 1.5—2 cm. long, 6—8 mm. broad, ribbed, densely scaly, glabrous, calyx persistent.

R. formosum was discovered by a Mr. Smith in 1815 on the Khasia Hills, Assam, and was described by Wallich in 1832. Further gatherings by other collectors show that the plant is distributed in Assam and north-west Upper Burma. It grows among forest trees, on windswept hillsides, on steep banks and stream sides, and on cliffs, at elevations of 763—2,196 m. (2,500—7,200 ft.).

In 1837, Mr. J. Gibson, a collector employed by the then Duke of Devonshire, found a plant on the Khasia Hills, and it was described and figured as *R. gibsonii* by Paxton in his *Magazine of Botany*, viii, t. 217 (1841). In *Notes Roy. Bot. Gard. Edin.*, (1919), Hutchinson made the name synonymous with *R. formosum*.

R. formosum is a distinctive species, and is unlikely to be confused with any species of its Subseries. It is allied to *R. iteophyllum* which it resembles in some features, but differs markedly in that the leaves are usually oblanceolate or oblong-obovate, 1.3—1.6 cm. broad.

The species was first introduced by Mr. J. Gibson, who brought plants in 1845 under the name *R. gibsonii*. It first flowered in a greenhouse in 1849 in the Duchess of Northumberland's garden, and in the Royal Gardens by Mr. Low of Clapton. The species was reintroduced several times by other collectors. Along the west coast it succeeds in well-sheltered gardens situated in mild localities, but along the east coast it requires greenhouse conditions. Three forms are in cultivation: Form 1. Corolla 5—5.3 cm. long, white with 5 pale pink bands along the middle of the tube and lobes, and with a yellow blotch at the base, stamens 3—4.5 cm. long, style 5.2—5.5 cm. long, stigma green. Form 2. Corolla larger, 6.5—6.7 cm. long, same colour as Form 1 but without a blotch, stamens and style longer, stigma red. Form 3. Corolla 6 cm. long, pure white, without pink bands, without a blotch, stigma red. The species is fairly fast-growing and is most attractive when covered with its funnel-shaped flowers in clusters of 2—3. It received an Award of Merit when exhibited by The Royal Botanic Garden, Edinburgh, in 1960.

Epithet. Beautiful.
Hardiness 1—2. April—June.

R. horlickianum Davidian\in The Royal Horticultural Society's Rhododendrons (1972) 53.

A broadly upright or compact shrub, sometimes epiphytic, 92 cm.—3 m. (3—10 ft.) high; *branchlets* rather densely or moderately scaly, *not bristly*. *Leaves* elliptic-lanceolate, oblong-lanceolate, oblanceolate or obovate-lanceolate, lamina coriaceous, 5.3—11.5 cm. long, 1.8—4.5 cm. broad, *apex acutely or shortly acuminate*, mucronate, base obtuse or tapered; upper surface dark green, shining, not scaly, not bristly; margin not bristly or sparsely bristly; under surface pale glaucous green, scaly, the scales large, unequal, brown or dark brown, 1—3 times their own diameter apart; petiole 0.4—1.6 cm. long, grooved above, densely or moderately scaly, bristly or not bristly. *Inflorescence* terminal, umbellate, 2—3-flowered; rhachis 2 mm. long, densely or moderately scaly, not bristly; pedicel stout, 5—8 mm. long, densely scaly, not bristly. *Calyx* 5-lobed or a mere rim, oblique, minute, 1 mm. long, when lobed, lobes rounded, outside densely or moderately scaly, not bristly, margin densely or moderately scaly, sparsely bristly or not bristly. *Corolla* widely funnel-shaped, 6.5—7 cm. long, 5-lobed, margins of lobes not crinkled, white or creamy-white, with pink bands outside the lobes, and a yellow blotch at the base, not scented or scented, *outside* sparsely or moderately scaly, *rather densely or moderately pubescent*. *Stamens* 10—11, unequal, 3.2—5.2 cm. long, shorter than the corolla; filaments pubescent in the lower third. *Ovary* conoid, 5—6 mm. long, 6-celled, densely scaly; style long, slender, straight or curved in the upper part, as long as the corolla or a little shorter, scaly at the base. *Capsule* oblong or oval, oblique at the base, 1.2—2.5 cm. long, 0.9—1.1 cm. broad, straight, scaly, calyx persistent.

Kingdon-Ward discovered this plant in January 1931 along the Adung river, Northern Burma. He found it again in the same region later in the year. It grows in thickets, on cliffs, and sometimes as an epiphyte in the rain forest, at elevations of 1,220—2,135 m. (4,000—7,000 ft.).

It is allied to *R. inaequale*, but differs markedly in that the leaf-apex is usually long acuminate, the corolla is white or creamy-white with pink bands outside the lobes, densely or moderately pubescent all over the outside, the branchlets are not bristly, and the style is as long as the corolla or a little shorter. Moreover, it occupies a different geographical area.

R. horlickianum was introduced by Kingdon-Ward in 1931 (No. 9403 — the Type number). In its native home it grows up to 10 feet high, but in cultivation it is a broadly upright shrub, reaching a height of only 6 feet. Along the east coast it is suitable for a cool greenhouse. As it grows at elevations of up to 7,000 feet in Northern Burma, it is likely to succeed outdoors in cultivation in mild areas along the west coast. The species is free-flowering, and like many members of its Subseries, it has the added advantage of flowering at a young age when raised from seed.

Epithet. After Sir James Horlick.
Hardiness 1—2. April—May. Plate 47.

R. inaequale (C.B. Clarke) Hutch. in Notes Roy. Bot. Gard. Edin., Vol. 12 (1919) 15, 75.
Illustration. Bot. Mag. n. s. Vol. 171 t. 295 (1957).

A somewhat lax broadly upright or straggly shrub, sometimes epiphytic, 92 cm.—3 m. (3—10 ft.) high; *branchlets* moderately or rather densely scaly, *bristly* or rarely not bristly. *Leaves* oblong-lanceolate, elliptic-lanceolate or oblong-obovate, lamina coriaceous, 6—11 cm. long, 1.5—4 cm. broad, apex acute or acuminate or obtuse, mucronate, base obtuse or cuneate; upper surface dark green, somewhat shining, not scaly or rarely scaly, midrib grooved, primary veins 8—12 on each side, deeply impressed; margin not bristly; *under surface* pale green, scaly, the *scales* unequal, medium-sized, or medium-sized and large, brown, 2—3 *times their own diameter apart*, midrib prominent, primary veins raised; petiole 0.8—1.5 cm. long, grooved above, moderately or densely scaly, not bristly or rarely sparsely bristly. *Inflorescence* terminal, umbellate, 1—6-flowered; rhachis

2—3 mm. long, scaly; pedicel 0.5—1.5 cm. long, thick, densely scaly, not bristly. *Calyx* undulately 5-lobed, oblique, 1—2 mm. long, outside scaly, margin ciliate or hairy with long hairs. *Corolla* widely funnel-shaped or funnel-shaped, 5.5—7.5 cm. long, 5-lobed, margins of lobes not crinkled, not fragrant or fragrant, *white* with a yellow or green blotch at the base, outside laxly or sparsely scaly on the tube and on the lobes, glabrous or pubescent at the base of the tube outside. *Stamens* 10, unequal, 3.7—5.4 cm. long, shorter than the corolla; filaments densely pubescent in the lower third. *Ovary* conoid, apex truncate, 5—7 mm. long, 6-celled, densely scaly, glabrous; *style* long, straight or curved in the upper part, 6—8.3 cm. in length, *longer than the corolla*, scaly in the lower ⅓—½ its length, glabrous. *Capsule* oblong or oblong-oval, oblique at the base, 1.8—2.8 cm. long, 0.8—1.3 cm. broad, ribbed, densely scaly, glabrous, calyx persistent.

This plant was discovered by Griffith in 1837 on the summit of Kollong Rock, in the Khasia Hills, Assam. On 8th. July and 23rd. October 1850, J.D. Hooker and T. Thomson collected fruiting specimens of the plant in the same locality, and these were described in 1882 as *R. formosum* Wall. var. *inaequalis* by C.B. Clarke in Hook. f. *Fl. Brit. India*, 3, 473. In 1885 C.B. Clarke collected the plant in fruit on Kollong, and again in 1886 with withered corollas. In 1919, Hutchinson described the plant as *R. inaequale* in *Notes Roy. Bot. Gard. Edin.*, Vol. 12, p. 75. Later in November 1927, Kingdon-Ward found the plant in fruit at Japvo, Naga Hills, Assam. N.L. Bor collected it in flower in April 1944 at Shillong, Khasia Hills, and in 1965 Cox and Hutchison found it in flower and in fruit on the Khasia Hills, Assam. It grows on the hills, at the margins of forests, on cliffs, in open situations in grass, and in moist shady places on the sides of a gorge, sometimes as an epiphyte, at elevations of 1,220—2,135 m. (4,000—7,000 ft.).

R. inaequale is related to *R. veitchianum* which it resembles in general features, but differs in that the lower surfaces of the leaves are pale green, the leaves are usually oblong-lanceolate or elliptic-lanceolate, the calyx margin is ciliate or hairy with long hairs, the branchlets are usually bristly, and the margins of the corolla-lobes are not crinkled. It also shows a resemblance to *R. horlickianum* from Northern Burma. The relationship between them is discussed under the latter.

The species was first introduced by Kingdon-Ward in 1927 (No. 7717). It was reintroduced by Cox and Hutchison in 1965. In cultivation the plant grows well in the open in the milder parts of the west coast, but along the east coast it needs the protection of a greenhouse. The flowers are white with a yellow or green blotch at the base, and are produced freely in trusses of up to six. The species was given an Award or Merit when shown by Lord Aberconway, Bodnant, in 1947.

Epithet. Of unequal size.

Hardiness 1—2. March—May.

R. iteophyllum Hutch. in Notes Roy. Bot. Gard. Edin., Vol. 12 (1919) 83.

Illustration. Bot. Mag. n. s. Vol. 177 t. 563 (1970).

A lax broadly upright, upright, straggly, somewhat compact or sometimes compact shrub, 92 cm.—2.44 m. (3—8 ft.) high; *branchlets* rather densely or moderately scaly, *bristly* or rarely not bristly. *Leaves linear, linear-lanceolate, linear-oblanceolate, lanceolate or oblanceolate*, lamina coriaceous, 2.6—8 cm. long, 0.5—1.5 cm. broad, apex acute, mucronate, *base* tapered, *decurrent on the petiole*; upper surface dark green, somewhat shining, not scaly or scaly, midrib grooved, primary veins 5—8 on each side, deeply impressed; margin bristly or not bristly; under surface pale green, scaly, the scales unequal, medium-sized, or medium-sized and large, brown, ½—2 times their own diameter apart, midrib prominent, primary veins raised or obscure; *petiole* 0.5—1 cm. long, grooved above, *with narrow wings at the margins*, moderately or rather densely scaly, moderately or sparsely bristly. *Inflorescence* terminal, or rarely terminal and axillary in the uppermost 3—4 leaves, umbellate, 1—4-flowered; rhachis 1—3 mm. long, scaly; pedicel 0.4—1.8 cm. long, somewhat thick or thick, rather densely or moderately scaly, not bristly. *Calyx* an undulate rim or 5-lobed, oblique, minute, 0.5—1 mm. long, when lobed, lobes ovate, outside scaly, margin glabrous or hairy with long hairs. *Corolla* funnel-shaped, 4.8—6 cm. long, 5-lobed, margins of lobes not crinkled, not fragrant or fragrant, white or white tinged pink, with or without a yellow blotch at the base, outside moderately or laxly scaly on the tube and lobes, pubescent at the base of the tube or all over the tube and lobes outside or glabrous outside. *Stamens* 10 or rarely 12, unequal, 4—5.3 cm. long, shorter than the corolla; filaments densely pubescent in the lower ⅓—½ their length. *Ovary* conoid or oblong, apex truncate, 4—5 mm. long, 6- or rarely 5-celled, densely scaly, glabrous; style long, straight or curved in the upper part, 5—6 cm. in length, longer than the corolla, scaly in the lower ⅓—½ its length, glabrous. *Capsule* oblong-oval or oblong, oblique at the base, 1.6—1.8 cm. long, 6—8 mm. broad, ribbed, straight, densely scaly, glabrous, calyx persistent.

The distribution of *R. iteophyllum* is restricted to Assam. It was first collected by J.D. Hooker and T. Thomson in October 1850, at Bor-Panee, Khasia Hills. Subsequently it was found by other collectors in the same region. It grows on rocks and along streams, at elevations of 610—1,830 m. (2,000—6,000 ft.). N.L. Bor records it as being common at Shillong at 6,000 feet.

R. iteophyllum is easily recognised by its linear, linear-lanceolate, narrowly lanceolate or oblanceolate leaves, usually 0.5—1.2 cm. broad. In these respects it is readily distinguished from its nearest ally *R. formosum*. A characteristic feature is the decurrent leaf-base, with narrow wings at the margins of the petiole. It may be noted that the branchlets are moderately bristly or rarely not bristly, the petioles are moderately or sparsely bristly, and the margins of the leaves are bristly or not bristly.

The species was introduced by Thomas Lobb, a collector. In its native home, it varies considerably in habit and height of growth; it is a lax broadly upright or upright, straggly or compact shrub, and it grows from three up to eight feet high. In cultivation it is usually a rather compact or broadly upright and somewhat spreading shrub, up to about 4½ feet high and 3—4 feet across. The plant is successfully grown outdoors in the mildest parts of the west coast, but in the east coast it requires a greenhouse. The species varies in its flowering period; the flowers are often produced in March, April or May, occasionally in June, but during the past two years it flowered indoors towards the middle of February. It is free-flowering, with white or white tinged pink flowers in trusses of one to four. The clone 'Lucy Elizabeth' received an Award of Merit when exhibited by Mrs. Elizabeth MacKenzie, Fessingfield, Diss, Norfolk, in 1979.

Epithet. Willow-leaved.
Hardiness 1—2. February—June.

R. johnstoneanum Watt ex Hutch. in Notes Roy. Bot. Gard. Edin., Vol. 12 (1919) 72.
A lax broadly upright, straggly, bushy or somewhat compact and spreading shrub, 1.22—3.70 m. (4—12 ft.) high; *branchlets* scaly, *bristly. Leaves elliptic, obovate or oblong-elliptic,* lamina coriaceous, 5—10 cm. long, 2—4.6 cm. broad, *apex obtuse or rounded,* mucronate, base obtuse, not decurrent on the petiole; upper surface dark green, shining, not scaly or scaly, midrib grooved, primary veins 8—12 on each side, deeply impressed; *margin bristly* or not bristy; *under surface* pale green, *densely scaly,* the *scales* unequal, large, or medium-sized and large, brown or dark brown, *contiguous to ½ their own diameter apart,* midrib prominent, primary veins raised; *petiole* 0.5—1.3 cm. long, grooved above, rounded, without narrow wings at the margins, densely scaly, *moderately or rather densely bristly. Inflorescence* terminal, umbellate, 3—4-flowered; rhachis 2—3 mm. long, scaly; pedicel 0.6—2.3 cm. long, somewhat thick, densely scaly, not bristly. *Calyx* 5-lobed or an undulate rim, oblique, minute, 1 mm. long, when lobed, lobes ovate, outside moderately or densely scaly, margin bristly or rarely not bristly. *Corolla* funnel-shaped, 4.6—6 cm. long, 5-lobed, margins of lobes not crinkled, fragrant, yellow, pale yellow, white tinged yellow, pale creamy-white, white, white tinged pink or white with pink bands along the

middle of the lobes outside, with or without a yellow blotch at the base, and with or without red spots, outside scaly all over, pubescent at the base of the tube outside. *Stamens* 10, unequal, 3—4 cm. long, shorter than the corolla; filaments densely pubescent in the lower ¼—½ their length. *Ovary* conoid or oblong, apex truncate, 4—6 mm. long, 6-celled, densely scaly, glabrous; style long, straight or curved in the upper part, 4—4.8 cm. in length, as long as the corolla or longer, scaly in the lower ½—⅔ its length, glabrous. *Capsule* oblong or oblong-oval, oblique at the base, 1.5—2 cm. long, 0.7—1 cm. broad, ribbed, straight, densely scaly, glabrous, calyx persistent.

R. *johnstoneanum* was discovered by Sir George Watt in January 1882, in Manipur Assam. It was collected by him again later in the same year in other localities in the same region. In May 1918, Kingdon-Ward found the plant at Japvo, Naga Hills, Assam. It grows on the grassy summits of the mountains, along the margins of forests, amongst open scrub, in open places, and on cliffs in deep shade, at elevations of 1,830—3,355 m. (6,000—11,000 ft.). Sir George Watt records both the pink and white forms as being common at 2,745 m. (9,000 ft.) at Keyeng. According to Kingdon-Ward it is fairly common at 2,745—3,050 (9,000—10,000 ft.) at Japvo, Naga Hills.

The plant was at first regarded as R. *formosum* Wall. var. *johnstonianum*, Brandis, *Ind. Trees*, 411 (1906). In 1919 Hutchinson described it as a species.

A diagnostic feature is the densely or moderately bristly branchlets, petioles, and usually leaf-margins. Another distinctive character is the densely scaly lower surface of the leaves, the scales being contiguous to ½ their own diameter apart. It is allied to R. *lyi*, but is readily distinguished by the broad elliptic, obovate or oblong-elliptic leaves, obtuse or rounded at the apex.

R. *johnstoneanum* was first introduced by Sir George Watt in January 1882. All the seedlings raised from this introduction eventually died off. The species was reintroduced by Kingdon-Ward in December 1927 from Japvo Hills, Assam (No. 7732), and again several times later from the same region. The plant varies in hardiness. It grows well outdoors along the west coast and in gardens in the south, but along the east coast it is usually grown under glass. There is a remarkable group of three plants at Brodick Castle Gardens, Isle of Arran, somewhat compact and spreading, up to about five feet high and about fifteen feet across. It may be of interest to note that the flower colour of this species is very variable in cultivation. It is yellow, pale yellow, white tinged yellow, pale creamy-white, white, white tinged pink, or white with pink bands along the middle of the lobes outside, with or without a yellow blotch at the base, and with or without red spots. A form with pale creamy-white flowers and with a yellow blotch at the base, under Kingdon-Ward No. 7732, received an Award of Merit when exhibited by Lt.-Col. L.C.R. Messel, Nymans, Sussex, in 1934. The same Award was given when shown by Lt.-Col. E.H.W. Bolitho, Trengwainton, Cornwall, in 1941 to a form under the name 'Rubeotinctum' with white flowers bearing deep pink stripes along the middle of the lobes and having a pinkish-yellow blotch at the base, also under Kingdon-Ward No. 7732, and again when exhibited by Sir Giles Loder, Leonardslee, Sussex, in 1975 to a form 'Demi-John' with white flowers flushed yellow-green at the throat.

In cultivation R. *johnstoneanum* has produced plants with double or semi-double flowers.

Epithet. After Mrs. Johnstone, wife of the Political Agent, Manipur, 1882.

Hardiness 1—3. April—June. Plate 51.

R. lasiopodum Hutch. in Notes Roy. Bot. Gard. Edin., Vol. 12 (1919) 58.

A broadly upright shrub, sometimes epiphytic, 1.83—4.58 m. (6—15 ft.) high; branchlets moderately or rather densely scaly, not bristly or rarely bristly. *Leaves elliptic or oblong-elliptic*, lamina coriaceous, 6—12.3 cm. long, 3—6.8 cm. broad, apex abruptly acute or acuminate, mucronate, base rounded or obtuse; upper surface dark green, shining, not scaly, midrib grooved, primary veins 8—12 on each side, deeply impressed;

margin not bristly; under surface pale glaucous green or pale green, scaly, the scales large and medium-sized, brown, ½—3 times their own diameter apart, midrib prominent, primary veins raised; petiole 0.7—1.5 cm. long, grooved above, densely or moderately scaly, not bristly or rarely slightly bristly. *Inflorescence* terminal, umbellate, 2—5-flowered; rhachis 2—3 mm. long, scaly, apex densely pubescent or glabrous; pedicel 0.6—1.4 cm. long, thick, densely scaly, not bristly. *Calyx* an undulate rim or 5-lobed, oblique, minute, 1 mm. long, when lobed, lobes ovate or triangular, outside scaly, margin glabrous or hairy with long hairs. *Corolla* funnel-shaped, *7—8.5 cm. long*, 5-lobed, margins of lobes not crinkled, fragrant, white or white flushed purple-rose, with or without a yellow blotch at the base, laxly or moderately scaly all over the outside, pubescent at the base of the tube outside or rarely glabrous. *Stamens* 10, unequal, *4.6—6.8 cm. long*, shorter than the corolla; filaments densely pubescent in the lower ⅓—½ their length. *Ovary* oblong or conoid, apex somewhat tapered into the style or truncate, 5—7 mm. long, 5-celled, densely scaly, glabrous; style long, straight or curved in the upper part, *7—9 cm. in length*, as long as the corolla or longer, scaly in the lower ½—⅔ its length, glabrous. *Capsule* oblong or oval, oblique at the base, 1.4—2.5 cm. long, 0.8—1 cm. broad, densely scaly, glabrous, calyx persistent.

Forrest discovered this plant in May 1913 in the Shweli-Salwin divide, Western Yunnan. He found it again in May—June 1918 in the same region, and in April and November 1925 in North-east Upper Burma. Kingdon-Ward collected it later in West Central Burma. It grows in pine forest, at the margins of open mixed forests, on ledges and at the base of cliffs in forests, at elevations of 2,135—2,745 m. (7,000—9,000 ft.). According to Forrest, it is rare in North-east Upper Burma. Kingdon-Ward records it as being not uncommon in West Central Burma.

R. lasiopodum is a remarkably distinct species and cannot be confused with any other species of its Subseries. The diagnostic features of this plant are the large corolla 7—8.5 cm. long, the long stamens 4.6—6.8 cm. long, and the long style 7—9 cm. long. In these respects it is readily distinguished from its allies, *R. dendricola* and *R. roseatum*; it also differs from the latter in the shape of the leaves.

It was introduced by Forrest from Western Yunnan in 1913 (No. 9919 — the Type number). In cultivation it is undoubtedly one of the finest species in its Series. In its native home it grows 6—15 feet high, but in cultivation it reaches a height of only 6 feet. The plant has not been cultivated in the open, but along the east coast it flourishes under glass. As it has been introduced from an elevation of 8,000—9,000 feet, it should succeed outdoors in sheltered gardens along the east coast and in the south. In the glasshouse it is a broadly upright shrub, well-filled with dark green foliage, and is of exquisite beauty when covered with large, white flowers in trusses of two to five. The species is rare in cultivation, but is worthy of being widely grown.

Epithet. Woolly-footed.
Hardiness 1. May—June.

R. ludwigianum Hosseus in Beihefte Bot. Centralbl. XXVIII (1911) 422.

A broadly upright shrub, 1—1.50 m. (3⅓—5 ft.) high; *branchlets closely or widely warted with leaf-scars*, densely or moderately scaly, not bristly. *Leaves obovate, ovate or elliptic, lamina very thick, leathery, rigid*, 3—12 cm. long, 1.5—6 cm. broad, apex rounded or obtuse, mucronate, base cuneate or obtuse or rounded; upper surface dark green or bright green, (*in old leaves both surfaces and petiole usually turn crimson-purple*), somewhat matt, not scaly or scaly, midrib grooved, primary veins 5—12 on each side, deeply impressed; margin not bristly; under surface pale green, scaly, the scales unequal, large, brown, ½—1½ times their own diameter apart, midrib prominent, primary veins raised; petiole 0.4—1.8 cm. long, grooved above, densely or moderately scaly, not bristly. *Inflorescence* terminal, umbellate, 2—4-flowered; rhachis 2—3 mm. long, scaly, densely hairy or glabrous; pedicel 0.3—1 cm. long, thick, densely scaly, not bristly. *Calyx* an undulate rim or 5-lobed, oblique, 1—3 mm. long, when lobed, lobes ovate, outside densely or moderately scaly, margin hairy with long hairs. *Corolla* funnel-shaped, 5.2—9.3 cm. long, 5-lobed, margins of lobes not crinkled or crinkled, not fragrant, white with or without pale pink bands outside along the middle of the tube and lobes, or sometimes rose, with or without a yellow blotch at the base, very laxly or moderately scaly all over the outside, pubescent at the base of the tube outside or densely pubescent all over the outside. *Stamens* 10, unequal, 3.2—6.8 cm. long, shorter than the corolla; filaments densely pubescent in the lower third. *Ovary* conoid, apex truncate, 5—6 mm. long, 6-celled, densely scaly, glabrous; style long, straight or curved in the upper part, 4.8—8.3 cm. in length, as long as the corolla or longer, scaly in the lower ⅓—⅔ its length, glabrous. *Capsule* oblong-oval, oblique at the base, 1.6 cm. long, 6 mm. broad, ribbed, densely scaly, glabrous, calyx persistent.

This species was first collected by Hosseus in 1905 at Doi Chiengdao, Thailand. It was later found by other collectors in the same region. The plant grows on open ridges on limestone rocks, at elevations of 1,600—2,180 m. (5,246—7,148 ft.).

R. ludwigianum is easily recognised by the very thick, leathery, rigid, obovate, ovate or elliptic leaves, densely scaly on the lower surface, the scales being ½—1½ times their own diameter apart, by the branchlets being closely or widely warted with leaf-scars, by the small calyx with margins fringed with long hairs, and by the white or sometimes rose flowers. It shows a certain degree of resemblance to *R. dendricola* from Northern Burma, but differs in well-marked characters.

The species has been in cultivation for some time. It is a greenhouse plant, a fairly robust grower up to four or five feet high, and is most pleasing when laden with white flowers in trusses of two to four. A characteristic feature is that the old leaves usually turn crimson-purple in autumn. The species is uncommon in cultivation, but is well worth a place in every collection of rhododendrons.

Epithet. After Ludwig Hosseus, father of a collector in Thailand.

Hardiness 1. April—May.

R. lyi Léveillé in Fedde Repert., XIII (1914) 147, fig. 7.

Illustration. Bot. Mag. Vol. 150 t. 9051 (1924).

A broadly upright or somewhat straggly shrub, 92 cm.—2.44 m. (3—8 ft.) high; *branchlets* scaly, *moderately or rarely rather densely* bristly. *Leaves* oblanceolate, oblong-oblanceolate, oblong-lanceolate, lanceolate or rarely oblong-obovate, lamina coriaceous, 3.2—9.5 cm. long, 1.3—3.5 cm. broad, *apex acute or shortly acute or abruptly acute*, mucronate, base cuneate or tapered or obtuse, not decurrent or decurrent on the petiole; upper surface dark green, shining, not scaly, midrib grooved, primary veins 8—12 on each side, deeply impressed; margin not bristly or bristly; under surface pale glaucous green or pale green, densely scaly, the scales unequal, large, or large and medium-sized, brown, contiguous to their own diameter apart, midrib prominent, primary veins raised; *petiole* 0.5—1 cm. long, grooved above, rounded or with narrow wings at the margins, densely scaly, *moderately or rarely rather densely bristly* or rarely not bristly. *Inflorescence* terminal, umbellate, 3—6- or rarely 2-flowered; rhachis 2—6 mm. long, scaly, not bristly; pedicel 0.5—2 cm. long, thick or somewhat thick, densely or rarely moderately scaly, not bristly. *Calyx* 5-lobed, oblique, 1—2 mm. long, lobes ovate, outside densely or moderately scaly, margin bristly or rarely not bristly. *Corolla* funnel-shaped, 4.6—6 cm. long, 5-lobed, margins of lobes not crinkled, fragrant or not fragrant, *white*, with or without a yellowish or greenish blotch at the base, scaly all over the outside, pubescent at the base of the tube outside. *Stamens* 10, unequal, 2.3—5.3 cm. long, shorter than the corolla; filaments densely pubescent in the lower ⅓—½ their length. *Ovary* conoid, apex somewhat tapered, 3—6 mm. long, 5—6-celled, densely scaly, glabrous; style long, straight or curved in the upper part, 5—6.3 cm. in length, longer than the corolla, scaly in the lower

½—⅔ its length, glabrous. *Capsule* oblong or oblong-oval, oblique at the base, 1.4—2.5 cm. long, 8—9 mm. broad, ribbed, densely scaly, glabrous, calyx persistent.

R. lyi was discovered by J. Cavalérie in April 1912 at Gan Chouen, Kweichow. Subsequently it was found by other collectors in the same region. It grows on limestone plateau and in dense woods, at elevations of 2,000 m. (6,557 ft.).

The characteristic features of this plant are the lanceolate, oblanceolate or oblong-lanceolate leaves, with acute or abruptly acute apex, densely scaly on the lower surface, the scales being contiguous to their own diameter apart, the bristly branchlets and petioles, and the small calyx 1—2 mm. long, bristly at the margins. Stapf in the *Botanical Magazine* t. 9051, aptly associates it with *R. ciliicalyx* which it resembles in general appearance, but is distinguished by the densely scaly lower surface of the leaves, often by the shape of the leaves, usually by the smaller calyx and corolla, and by the corolla being scaly all over the outside. It also shows a resemblance to *R. johnstoneanum* from which it differs markedly in the shape of the leaves. The plant is a diploid with 26 chromosomes.

R. lyi was introduced into cultivation to Paris by Vilmorin. A good example of the species growing outdoors is to be seen at Lamellen, Major E.W.M. Magor's garden, Cornwall. Along the east coast it is tender and is suitable for a cool greenhouse where it grows up to three or four feet high, with white flowers bearing a yellow blotch at the base, in trusses of 3—4. The plant is uncommon in cultivation.

Epithet. After J. Ly, a Chinese collector.
Hardiness 1—2. April—June.

R. notatum Hutch. in The Species of Rhododendron (1930) 469.

A small or medium-sized shrub or bush, usually epiphytic; branchlets scaly, not bristly. *Leaves obovate, oblong-obovate, obovate-elliptic or elliptic*, lamina coriaceous, 5—10 cm. long, 2.5—4.5 cm. broad, *apex abruptly acute*, mucronate, base obtuse or cuneate; upper surface dark green, somewhat shining, not scaly or sparsely scaly, midrib grooved, primary veins 8—10 on each side, deeply impressed; margin not bristly; under surface pale green or pale glaucous green, laxly scaly, the scales unequal, medium-sized, brown, 3—5 times their own diameter apart, midrib prominent, primary veins raised; petiole 0.8—1.2 cm. long, grooved above, scaly, not bristly. *Inflorescence* terminal, umbellate, 2—3-flowered; rhachis 2—3 mm. long, scaly, not bristly; *pedicel* 0.9—1.3 cm. long, somewhat thick or thick, scaly, not bristly, *glabrous*. *Calyx* a mere rim, oblique, minute, 1 mm. long, outside scaly, margin glabrous. *Corolla* funnel-shaped or funnel-campanulate, 4.8—5.3 cm. long, 5-lobed, margins of lobes not crinkled, fragrant, *white, with purplish-pink bands on the angles outside, with a yellow blotch at the base*, laxly scaly all over the outside, pubescent at the base of the tube outside. *Stamens* 10, unequal, 4.8—5.3 cm. long, shorter than the corolla; filaments densely pubescent in the lower ⅓—½ their length. *Ovary* conoid, apex truncate, 4 mm. long, 5-celled, densely scaly, glabrous; style long, straight or curved in the upper part, 4.5—4.8 cm. in length, as long as the corolla, scaly in the lower ⅓—½ its length, glabrous. *Capsule* oblong or oblong-oval, oblique at the base, 1—2 cm. long, 0.8—1 cm. broad, straight, densely scaly, glabrous, calyx persistent.

Kingdon-Ward first found this plant in May 1926 in the Valley of the Nam Tamai, North-east Upper Burma. Later in the same year he collected it again in other localities in the same region. It grows in rhododendron thickets, in the rain forest, on rocks and boulders in the river bed, usually as an epiphyte, at elevations of 1,068—2,135 m. (3,500—7,000 ft.). Kingdon-Ward records it as being abundant in the rain forest, and on big boulders in the river bed.

R. notatum bears a resemblance to *R. taronense* in its appearance, but differs in that the leaves are usually obovate, oblong-obovate or obovate-elliptic, the apex is abruptly acute, the corolla is white with purplish-pink bands on the angles outside, with a yellow blotch at the base, the pedicel is not puberulous, and the scales on the lower surface of the leaves are smaller, being medium-sized. The species has not been introduced into cultivation.

Epithet. Marked.
Not in cultivation.

R. pachypodum Balf. f. et W.W. Sm. in Notes Roy. Bot. Gard. Edin., Vol. 9 (1916) 254.

A lax broadly upright shrub, 60 cm.—1.83 m. (2—6 ft.) or rarely 30 cm. (1 ft.) high, or sometimes a tree 7.63 m. (25 ft.) high; branchlets moderately or rather densely scaly, not bristly. *Leaves oblong-obovate, obovate, obovate-elliptic, elliptic, elliptic-oblanceolate or oblong-lanceolate*, lamina coriaceous, 5—10 cm. long, 2—4 cm. broad, apex acuminate or acute, mucronate, base cuneate or tapered or obtuse; upper surface dark green, somewhat shining, not scaly, midrib grooved, primary veins 6—10 on each side, deeply impressed; margin not bristly; *under surface* pale glaucous green, *densely scaly*, the *scales* unequal, large, or large and medium-sized, brown or dark brown, nearly *contiguous or ½ their own diameter apart*, midrib prominent, primary veins raised; petiole 0.5—1.6 cm. long, grooved above, densely scaly, not bristly or slightly bristly or rarely moderately bristly. *Inflorescence* terminal, umbellate, 1—5-flowered; rhachis 1—3 mm. long, scaly, moderately or densely pubescent or glabrous; pedicel 0.5—1 cm. long, thick, densely scaly, not bristly. *Calyx* 5-lobed, oblique, 1—2 mm. or rarely 3 mm. long, lobes ovate or triangular, outside moderately or densely scaly, margin bristly or rarely not bristly. *Corolla* funnel-shaped, *4.6—6.3 cm. or rarely 2.8 cm. long*, 5-lobed, margins of lobes not crinkled, fragrant, yellow, or white with a yellowish-brown blotch at the base, or white tinged pink with or without a pale lemon-yellow blotch at the base, or white with a streak of yellow on the upper lobe, or pink, or purplish, scaly all over the outside, pubescent at the base of the tube outside. *Stamens* 10 or rarely 11—13, unequal, 2.8—4.8 cm. or rarely 2.3 cm. long, shorter than the corolla; filaments densely hairy in the lower ⅓—½ their length. *Ovary* conoid, apex truncate, 4—5 mm. long, 5—6-celled, densely scaly, glabrous; style long, straight or curved in the upper part, 4.2—5.5 cm. or rarely 3 cm. in length, as long as the corolla or longer, scaly in the lower ⅓—⅔ its length, glabrous. *Capsule* oblong, oblong-oval or oval, oblique at the base, 1.2—2 cm. long, 0.7—1 cm. broad, ribbed, densely scaly, glabrous, calyx-lobes persistent.

This species was first collected by Forrest in August 1913, on the western flank of the Tali Range, Western Yunnan. It was afterwards found by him again and by other collectors in the same region. The plant grows in open stony pasture, in open scrub, among pine trees, and in forests, at elevations of 2,135—3,050 m. (7,000—10,000 ft.).

In 1919, *R. pilicalyx* Hutch. was described from a specimen (No. 10524) collected by A. Henry at Mengtsz, south-east Yunnan. The species is identical with *R. pachypodum* in its height of growth, in leaf shape and size, in flower shape, size and colour, and in all other respects they agree. It is clear that the retention of the specific name *R. pilicalyx* cannot be justified.

R. pachypodum is closely related to *R. supranubium* which it resembles in general characters but is distinguished usually by the shape of the leaves, by the densely scaly lower surface of the leaves, and often by the smaller corolla. It is also allied to *R. carneum* from which it differs in well-marked characters.

The species was first introduced by Forrest in 1913 (No. 11547 — the Type number), and again in 1917 (No. 16032). It was reintroduced by Kingdon-Ward in 1921 (No. 3776). In its native home it is a shrub or tree usually 2—25 feet high, but in cultivation it is a lax broadly upright shrub, and reaches a height of only four to five feet. As it grows at an elevation of 9,000—10,000 feet, it has been cultivated successfully in the open along the west coast in sheltered places. Along the east coast it is a greenhouse plant. It was given a

First Class Certificate when shown by Mr. L. de Rothschild, Exbury, in 1936. The species is rare in cultivation.

Epithet. Thick-footed.

Hardiness 1—2. March—May.

R. parryae Hutch. in Gard. Chron. Vol. 93 (1933) 386—7.

A broadly upright, or somewhat rounded and spreading shrub, or a small tree, sometimes epiphytic, 1.53—3 m. (5—10 ft.) high; stem and branches with smooth, pinkish-purple bark; branchlets moderately or rather densely scaly, not bristly or bristly. *Leaves* elliptic, oblong-elliptic or somewhat rounded, lamina coriaceous, 6—14 cm. long, 3—5.8 cm. broad, apex acuminate, obtuse or rounded, mucronate, base cuneate, obtuse or rounded; upper surface dark green, shining, scaly or not scaly, midrib grooved, primary veins 10—12 on each side, deeply impressed; margin not bristy; *under surface* pale glaucous green, scaly, the *scales* unequal, large and medium-sized, brown, *1—2 times their own diameter apart*, midrib prominent, primary veins raised; petiole 1—1.8 cm. long, grooved above, densely or moderately scaly, not bristly. *Inflorescence* terminal, umbellate, 3—5-flowered; rhachis 2—4 mm. long, scaly, pubescent or glabrous; pedicel 0.7—2.5 cm. long, thick or somewhat thick, densely or moderately scaly, glabrous or rarely puberulous, not bristly. *Calyx* 5-lobed, oblique, minute, 1 mm. long, lobes ovate, outside densely or moderately scaly, margin ciliate. *Corolla* funnel-shaped, *7—8.2 cm.* or rarely *5.5—6.5 cm. long*, 5-lobed, margins of lobes not crinkled, fragrant, white, with a yellow-orange or yellow blotch at the base, without or sometimes with greenish spots, laxly scaly all over the outside, pubescent on the tube outside. *Stamens* 10, unequal, 4—6.4 cm. long, shorter than the corolla; filaments densely pubescent in the lower 2/5 their length. *Ovary* conoid or oblong, apex truncate, 6—8 mm. long, 5—6-celled, densely scaly, glabrous; style long, straight or curved in the upper part, 5.8—6.8 cm. in length, as long as the corolla, scaly in the lower ⅔ its length or at the base, glabrous. *Capsule* oblong or oval, oblique at the base, 1.2—2.4 cm. long, 0.6—1 cm. broad, densely scaly, glabrous, calyx persistent.

R. parryae was described by Hutchinson in 1933 from a plant grown in the glasshouse at Kew, and raised from seeds taken from a fruiting specimen (No. 146) collected by Mrs. A.D. Parry in February 1927, on the Blue Moutain, Lushai Hills, Assam, at an elevation of 1,830 m. (6,000 ft.). In April 1965, Cox and Hutchison collected the plant in the south-east of the Apa Tani valley, Assam, growing as an epiphyte in the rain forest at 1,769—2,135 m. (5,800—7,000 ft).

In general appearance, it shows a resemblance to *R. lasiopodum*, but is distinguished usually by the somewhat smaller corolla, by the shorter style, very often by the lobed calyx, and usually by the more widely spaced scales on the lower surface of the leaves.

R. parryae was also introduced by Cox and Hutchison in 1965 (No. 373). It is one of the largest-flowered species in the Ciliicalyx Subseries. Two distinct forms are in cultivation. Form 1. A somewhat rounded and spreading shrub up to 5 feet high and as much across with somewhat rounded leaves. Form 2. A broadly upright shrub up to 6 or 7 feet high with oblong-elliptic leaves. It is worth noting that the plant flowers at a young age when raised from seed; the seeds of the Type plant (Parry No. 146) were sown in the summer of 1927, and the flowers first appeared in June 1933. The plant is a vigorous grower, and provides an admirable display with its white flowers with a yellow blotch at the base, produced freely in trusses of three to five. Along the west coast it succeeds in the open in well-sheltered gardens, but along the east coast it is a greenhouse plant. Form 1 grown under glass, received an Award of Merit when exhibited by the Royal Botanic Garden, Edinburgh in 1957; another form was given a First Class Certificate when shown by Geoffrey Gorer, Sunte House, Haywards Heath, Sussex, in 1973.

Epithet. After Mrs. A.D. Parry, wife of an officer in the Assam Civil Service.

Hardiness 1—2. April—May.

R. roseatum Hutch. in Notes Roy. Bot. Gard. Edin., Vol. 12 (1919) 57.

A broadly upright shrub, 92 cm.—3.70 m. (3—12 ft.) high; branchlets moderately or rather densely scaly, not bristly. *Leaves ovate, ovate-elliptic* or rarely elliptic, lamina coriaceous, 6—9.8 cm. long, 2.8—4.8 cm. broad, apex acuminate or abruptly acute, mucronate, base rounded or obtuse; upper surface dark green, somewhat shining, not scaly or rarely sparsely scaly, midrib grooved, primary veins 6—10 on each side, deeply impressed; margin not bristly; *under surface* pale glaucous green, *densely scaly,* the *scales* large, or large and medium-sized, brown or dark brown, ½ *or rarely their own diameter apart,* midrib prominent, primary veins raised; petiole 0.6—1 cm. long, grooved above, densely scaly, not bristly or rarely bristly. *Inflorescence* terminal, umbellate, 2—4-flowered; rhachis 2—3 mm. long, scaly, pubescent; pedicel 0.5—1 cm. long, thick, densely scaly, not bristly. *Calyx* 5-lobed, oblique, minute, 1 mm. long, lobes ovate or triangular, outside scaly, margin hairy with long hairs or rarely glabrous. *Corolla* funnel-shaped, *5.6—6.8 cm. long,* 5-lobed, margins of lobes not crinkled, fragrant, white, or white flushed with rose or faintly flushed with purple outside, or white with a yellowish blotch at the base, scaly all over the outside, glabrous or pubescent at the base of the tube outside. *Stamens* 10, unequal, 3.5—4.2 cm. long, shorter than the corolla; filaments densely pubescent in the lower ⅓ their length. *Ovary* conoid, apex truncate, 5—6 mm. long, 6-celled, densely scaly, glabrous; style long, straight or curved in the upper part, 5.3—6.5 cm. in length, as long as the corolla, scaly in the lower half, glabrous. *Capsule* oblong, oblong-oval or oval, oblique at the base, 1.3—2.2 cm. long, 0.8—1 cm. broad, ribbed, densely scaly, glabrous, calyx persistent.

This species was discovered by Forrest in May 1913 in the Shweli-Salwin divide, Western Yunnan. It was afterwards found by him again on several occasions in the same region and in mid-west Yunnan. The plant grows in open scrub, in open thickets, on open rocky slopes, and at the margins of open pine forests, at elevations of 2,440—2,745 m. (8,000—9,000 ft.).

The diagnostic features of this plant are usually the ovate or ovate-elliptic leaves, densely scaly on the lower surface, the scales being usually one-half their own diameter apart. In these respects, it is readily distinguished from its nearest ally *R. dendricola.* It also differs in that the corolla is usually smaller, and the calyx is lobed.

R. roseatum was first introduced by Forrest in 1918 (No. 17559) from the Shweli-Salwin divide, Western Yunnan. He reintroduced it in 1925 (No. 27685) from the hills west of Hsiao-sheen-Kai, mid-west Yunnan. It may be observed that in *The Rhododendron Handbook* 1980, p. 236, *R. roseatum* has been wrongly recorded as not in cultivation. Moreover, on p. 298 in the same *Handbook,* Forrest No. 27685 has been wrongly identified as *R. dendricola;* the dried specimen under this number is *R. roseatum.*

In its native home *R. roseatum* reaches a height of 12 feet, but in cultivation it is a broadly upright shrub only 3—4 feet high. As it has been introduced from an elevation of 9,000 feet, it should succeed along the west coast in the open in sheltered gardens; along the east coast it requires the shelter of a cool greenhouse. The plant is rare in cultivation.

Epithet. Rosy.

Hardiness 1. April—May.

R. rufosquamosum Hutch. in Notes Roy. Bot. Gard. Edin., Vol. 12 (1919) 63.

A shrub, 92 cm. (3 ft.) high; *branchlets* moderately or rather densely scaly, *not bristly. Leaves oblanceolate,* lamina coriaceous, 7—12 cm. long, 1.8—4 cm. broad, apex acuminate, mucronate, base tapered; upper surface dark green, not scaly or sparsely scaly, midrib grooved, primary veins 8—10 on each side, deeply impressed; margin not bristly; *under surface* pale glaucous green, *densely scaly,* the *scales* unequal, medium-sized, brown, ½ *their own diameter apart,* midrib prominent, primary veins raised; *petiole* 0.8—1.3 cm. long, grooved above, densely scaly, *not bristly. Inflorescence* terminal; umbellate, 2—3-flowered; rhachis 2—3 mm. long, scaly, pubescent; pedicel 5—7 mm. long, thick, densely scaly, not bristly. *Calyx 5-lobed, oblique, minute, 1 mm. long, lobes ovate or triangular,* outside densely scaly, margin bristly. *Corolla tubular-funnel shaped, 6—7 cm. long,* 5-lobed, margins of lobes not crinkled, *white,* (pink in bud), scaly all over the outside, pubescent at the base of the tube outside. *Stamens* 10, unequal, 4.3—5.4 cm. long, shorter than the corolla; filaments densely pubescent in the lower ¼ their length. *Ovary* conoid, apex truncate, 5 mm. long, 6-celled, densely scaly, glabrous; style long, straight or curved in the upper part, 4.9—5.1 cm. in length, as long as the corolla, scaly in the lower ¾ its length, glabrous. *Capsule:—*

R. *rufosquamosum* is represented by a single gathering, A.Henry No. 11983. It was found on the Szemao Hills in south-west Yunnan, at an elevation of 1,464 m. (4,800 ft.), and was described by Hutchinson in 1919.

It is a distinctive species and is characterised by the oblanceolate leaves, laminae 7—12 cm. long, 1.8—4 cm. broad, and by the tubular-funnel shaped corolla, 6—7 cm. long. Other notable features are the densely scaly lower surface of the leaves, the scales being one-half their own diameter apart, the corolla scaly all over the outside, and the non-bristly branchlets and petioles. The species is related to R. *supranubium* and R. *ciliicalyx,* but is distinguished from both by marked characteristics. The plant has not been introduced into cultivation.

Epithet. With reddish scales.

Not in cultivation.

R. scopulorum Hutch. in The Species of Rhododendron (1930) 475.

Illustration. Bot. Mag. Vol. 158 t. 9399 (1935).

A broadly upright or bushy shrub or rarely a tree, 92 cm.—4.58 m. (3—15 ft.) high; branchlets scaly, not bristly or rarely bristly. *Leaves oblong-obovate, obovate, obovate-oblanceolate or oblong-oblanceolate,* lamina coriaceous, *rigid,* 4—8.2 cm. long, 1.6—3.6 cm. broad, *apex rounded or obtuse,* mucronate, base cuneate or obtuse; upper surface dark green or green, shining, often convex, midrib grooved, primary veins 8—10 on each side, deeply impressed; margin not bristly; *under surface* pale glaucous green, *laxly scaly,* the *scales* unequal, medium-sized or small, brown, 2—4 *times their own diameter apart,* midrib prominent, primary veins slightly raised; petiole 0.8—1.3 cm. long, grooved above, moderately or rather densely scaly, not bristly or rarely sparsely bristly. *Inflorescence* terminal, umbellate, 2—4-flowered; rhachis 2—3 mm. long, scaly, glabrous; pedicel 0.8—1.8 cm. long, thick or somewhat slender, moderately or rather densely scaly, not bristly. *Calyx* 5-lobed, oblique, 2 mm. long, lobes ovate, outside scaly, margin scaly or not scaly, not bristly or rarely sparsely bristly. *Corolla* funnel-shaped, 4.5—6.2 cm. long, 5-lobed, margins of lobes somewhat crinkled, fragrant, white without or with faint pink bands along the lobes outside, or apple blossom pink, with or without a golden or yellowish-orange blotch at the base, *scaly and pubescent all over the outside. Stamens* 10 or rarely 10—11, unequal, 2.4—4.7 cm. long, shorter than the corolla; filaments densely pubescent in the lower ¼—⅓ their length. *Ovary* conoid, apex truncate, 4—5 mm. long, 6-celled, densely scaly, glabrous; style long, straight or curved in the upper part, 3.8—5.6 cm. in length, as long as the corolla, moderately or sparsely scaly at the base, or moderately scaly in the lower ⅓ its length, glabrous or rarely hairy at the base. *Capsule* oblong or oblong-oval, oblique at the base, 1.2—2 cm. long, 1—1.2 cm. broad, ribbed, densely scaly, glabrous, calyx-lobes persistent.

Kingdon-Ward discovered this plant in November 1924 in the Tsangpo Gorge, Eastern Tibet. He found it again about a week later in the same region. Ludlow, Sherriff and Elliot collected it in 1947 in various localities in south-east Tibet. It grows on boulder screes fully exposed to the sun, in thickets, on steep rocky slopes, on steep pine-covered slopes, and in mixed forest, at elevations of 1,830—2,440 m. (6,000—8,000 ft.). Ludlow, Sherriff and Elliot record it as being common in the Lower Po-Tsangpo Valley.

252

23. R. scopulorum
nat. size

a. petals. b. flower. c. stamen. d. ovary, style. e. capsule.

A diagnostic feature of the species is the corolla, which is scaly and pubescent all over the outside. Another distinctive character is the oblong-obovate, obovate or oblong-oblanceolate leaves, rigid in texture, and laxly scaly on the lower surface, the scales being 2—4 times their own diameter apart. The plant shows a certain degree of resemblance to *R. notatum*, from which it differs markedly in distinctive characters.

The species was first introduced by Kingdon-Ward in 1924 (No. 6325), and again in the same year (No. 6354 — the Type number). It was reintroduced by Ludlow, Sherriff and Elliot in 1947 (No. 12231). In its native home, it is a shrub or rarely a tree, 3—15 feet high, but in cultivation it is a broadly upright shrub up to only 3 or 4 feet high. Two colour forms are in cultivation: Form 1. Corolla white with a yellow blotch at the base. Form 2. Corolla white with pink bands along the lobes outside, with a yellow blotch at the base. It is a greenhouse plant, but it succeeds in the open in well-sheltered gardens. It is a pleasing species and is most effective when covered with funnel-shaped flowers in trusses of two to four. One of its chief merits is that it flowers quite young when raised from seed. It was given an Award of Merit when shown by Mr. L. de Rothschild, Exbury, in 1936.

Epithet. Of the crags.
Hardiness 1—2. April—May.

R. scottianum Hutch. in Notes Roy. Bot. Gard. Edin., Vol. 12 (1919) 64.
Illustration. Bot. Mag. Vol. 154 t. 9238 (1931).

A broadly upright shrub, 60 cm.—3.70 m. (2—12 ft.) high; branchlets moderately or rather densely scaly, not bristly or rarely bristly. *Leaves obovate*, elliptic, *oblong-obovate* or oblong-elliptic, lamina coriaceous, 5.5—10 cm. long, 2.5—4.2 cm. broad, *apex abruptly acute*, mucronate, base obtuse or rounded; upper surface dark green, shining, midrib grooved, primary veins 8—10 on each side, deeply impressed; margin not bristly; *under surface* pale glaucous green, *densely scaly*, the *scales* unequal, large, dark brown or brown, ½ *or rarely their own diameter apart*, midrib prominent, primary veins raised; petiole 0.5—1.4 cm. long, grooved above, densely scaly, not bristly or rarely sparsely bristly. *Inflorescence* terminal, umbellate, 2—4-flowered; rhachis 2—3 mm. long, scaly, pubescent or glabrous; pedicel 0.6—1.5 cm. long, thick, densely scaly, not bristly. *Calyx* an undulate rim or 5-lobed, oblique, 1—2 mm. long, when lobed, lobes ovate, outside moderately or densely scaly, margin bristly. *Corolla* funnel-shaped or funnel-campanulate, 6—8.2 cm. long, 5-lobed, margins of lobes not crenulate or somewhat crenulate, fragrant, white, or white flushed rose or crimson outside, with a yellow blotch at the base, *scaly all over the outside*, pubescent at the base of the tube outside. *Stamens* 10, unequal, 3.8—5.9 cm. long, shorter than the corolla; filaments densely or rarely moderately hairy in the lower ¼ their length. *Ovary* conoid, apex truncate, 4—6 mm. long, 5—7-celled, densely scaly, glabrous; style long, straight or curved in the upper part, 6—7 cm. in length, as long as the corolla, scaly in the lower ½—⅔ its length, glabrous. *Capsule* oblong, oblique at the base, 1.3—1.6 cm. long, 6—7 mm. broad, ribbed, straight, densely scaly, glabrous, calyx pesistent.

R. scottianum was first collected by Forrest in May 1912 on the hills north-west of Tengyueh, in Western Yunnan. It was found by him again in 1913 and 1922 in other localities in the same region. In 1932 Rock collected it between Talifu and Yunnanfu, Western Yunnan. The plant grows on cliffs, amongst scrub, on rocky situations, and on the shady flanks of ravines, at elevations of 1,830—2,288 m. (6,000—7,500 ft.).

In general appearance *R. scottianum* shows a resemblance to *R. dendricola* and *R. ciliicalyx*. It is distinguished from the former usually by the obovate or oblong-obovate leaves, abruptly acute at the apex, usually by the densely scaly lower surface of the leaves, and by the moderately bristly margin of the calyx; and from the latter usually by the non-bristly petioles and branchlets, by the densely scaly lower surface of the leaves, the scales being usually one-half their own diameter apart, usually by the smaller calyx, and by the corolla being scaly all over the outside.

R. *scottianum* was first introduced by Forrest in 1912 (No. 7516). It was reintroduced by Rock in 1932 (No. 25235). In cultivation it is a broadly upright shrub up to 4 or 5 feet high fairly densely filled with dark green foliage, although in its native home it reaches 12 feet. The plant has been grown outdoors along the west coast, particularly in Cornwall, but essentially it is a tender species and is suitable for a cool greenhouse. It is a fairly robust grower, and makes a fine show with its white flowers in trusses of two to four.

Epithet. After Munro B. Scott, a Kew botanist, killed at Arras; 1889—1917.

Hardiness 1—2. May—June.

R. smilesii Hutch. in Notes Roy. Bot. Gard. Edin., Vol. 12 (1919) 71.

A tree, 6.10 m. (20 ft.) high; branchlets scaly, with a few bristly hairs. *Leaves obovate-oblanceolate or oblong-oblanceolate*, lamina rather thinly and rigidly coriaceous, 4.5—6.5 cm. long, 1.8—2.5 cm. broad, apex obtuse, mucronate, narrowed to an obtuse base; upper surface glabrous, matt, midrib grooved, primary veins about 6 on each side, deeply impressed; under surface densely scaly, the scales dark brown, less than their own diameter apart, papillous between the scales, midrib prominent, primary veins slightly raised; petiole 5 mm. long, grooved above, densely scaly. *Inflorescence* terminal, umbellate, 3-flowered; *rhachis villous; pedicel about 3 mm. long*, scaly. *Calyx* obscurely lobed, small, 1.5 mm. long, outside scaly, margin not ciliate. *Corolla* funnel-shaped, small, about *4 cm. long*, 5-lobed, white, scaly nearly all over the outside. *Stamens* 10, unequal, shorter than the corolla; filaments pubescent in the lower ¼ their length. *Ovary* densely scaly, 5-celled; style long, straight, 3 cm. in length, scaly in the lower half. *Capsule: —*

This species is known from a single gathering made in April 1893 by F.H. Smiles, at Pu Sai Lai Leng, Northern Thailand.

The original diagnosis associated it with R. *supranubium*. From this species it is distinguished by the smaller corolla, often by the smaller leaves, and by the eciliate margin of the calyx. It also shows a resemblance to R. *veitchianum*, but differs in the pale glaucous green and densely scaly lower surface of the leaves, the scales being less than their own diameter apart, in the obtuse leaf-apex, and in the smaller corolla. There is no record of its occurrence in cultivation.

Epithet. After F.H. Smiles, its discoverer in 1893.

Not in cultivation.

R. supranubium Hutch. in Notes Roy. Bot. Gard. Edin., Vol. 12 (1919) 68.

A broadly upright shrub, sometimes epiphytic, 60 cm.—2.44 m. (2—8 ft.) high; branchlets moderately or rather densely scaly, slightly or moderately bristly or not bristly. *Leaves oblanceolate, lanceolate or oblong-lanceolate*, lamina coriaceous, 3—11.8 cm. long, 1.3—3.3 cm. broad, *apex acute or acuminate*, mucronate, base obtuse or tapered; upper surface dark green, somewhat shining, not scaly, midrib grooved, primary veins 8—12 on each side, deeply impressed; margin not bristly; under surface glaucous or pale glaucous green, scaly, the scales unequal, large, brown or dark brown, ½—4 times their own diameter apart, midrib prominent, primary veins raised; petiole 0.5—1 cm. long, grooved above, densely scaly, slightly or rarely moderately bristly, or not bristly. *Inflorescence* terminal, umbellate, 1—5-flowered; rhachis 2—3 mm. long, scaly, pubescent or glabrous; pedicel 0.5—1.3 cm. long, somewhat thick, densely or rarely moderately scaly, glabrous or rarely puberulous, not bristly. *Calyx* 5-lobed, oblique, 1—2 mm. long, lobes ovate or broadly ovate, outside scaly, margin hairy with long hairs or glabrous. *Corolla* funnel-shaped, 5—6.5 cm. long, 5-lobed, margins of lobes somewhat crenulate or entire, fragrant, white flushed rose or purplish outside, or white, with or without a yellow or greenish-yellow blotch at the base, *scaly all over the outside*, pubescent at the base of the tube outside or rarely pubescent all over the tube outside. *Stamens* 10, unequal, 3.2—5 cm. long, shorter than the corolla; filaments densely pubescent in the lower ⅓—½ their length. *Ovary* conoid or oblong, apex somewhat tapered into the style or truncate, 5—7 mm. long, 6-celled, densely scaly, glabrous; style long, straight or curved in the upper part, 4.5—7 cm. in length, as long as the corolla or rarely longer, scaly in the lower ½ or rarely ⅓ its length, glabrous. *Capsule* oblong or oblong-oval, oblique at the base, 1.4—2.5 cm. long, 7—9 mm. broad, ribbed, straight, densely scaly, glabrous, calyx-lobes peristent.

R. *supranubium* was discovered by Forrest in June—July 1906 on the eastern flank of the Tali range, Western Yunnan. It was afterwards found by him again on several occasions in other localities in the same region and in mid-west Yunnan. In 1919 Farrer and E.H.M. Cox collected it at Hpimaw, in the N'Maikha-Salwin Divide, Upper Burma, and in 1953 Kingdon-Ward found it in the North Triangle, Kachin State, North Burma. It grows on ledges of cliffs, in dry rocky situations, on rocky slopes, on rocks, and as an epiphyte in mixed forests, at elevations of 1,220—3,660 m. (4,000—12,000 ft.). According to Kingdon-Ward, it is an epiphyte, sometimes 25—31 m. (80—100 ft.) from the ground up on trees in the North Triangle.

In 1978, R. *pseudociliipes* Cullen was described from a specimen (No. 17900) collected by Forrest in May 1919 on the Eastern flank of the N'Maikha-Salwin Divide, Western Yunnan. When this specimen under R. *pseudociliipes* is examined it will be seen that in general characters and in every morphological detail it is identical with R. *supranubium* under which it will now appear in synonymy.

R. *supranubium* is a distinct species and is unlikely to be confused with any species of its Subseries. A characteristic feature is the oblanceolate, lanceolate or oblong-lanceolate leaves with acute or acuminate apex. The species is related to R. *pachypodum* which it resembles in some features, but is distinguished by the shape of the leaves, usually by the larger corolla, and often by the laxly scaly lower surface of the leaves. It also bears a resemblance to R. *cilliicalyx*, but differs usually in the shape of the leaves, in the corolla being scaly all over the outside, and usually in the smaller calyx. The species is a diploid with 26 chromosomes.

It was first introduced by Forrest in 1910 from an elevation of 11,000—12,000 feet (No. 6764 — the Type number), and again in 1919 from 8,000 feet (No. 17900). Farrer and E.H.M. Cox reintroduced it in 1919 from 7,000—9,000 feet (No. 848). In 1953, Kingdon-Ward sent seeds from 4,000—6,000 feet (No. 21512). As it grows at elevations of 4,000—12,000 feet, its hardiness varies considerably in cultivation. Forrest's form introduced from 11,000—12,000 feet has proved hardy outdoors in sheltered gardens. All the other forms are tender and require a cool greenhouse. In cultivation R. *supranubium* is a broadly upright shrub up to eight feet high, usually well-filled with dark green foliage. Two colour forms are grown in gardens: Form 1. Corolla white. Form 2. Corolla white flushed rose with a yellow blotch at the base. It is a vigorous grower, and is most attractive when laden with funnel-shaped flowers in trusses of one to five. Like all the other species in its Series, it is easy to increase from cuttings. An added advantage is that it flowers at a young age when raised from seed.

Epithet. Above the clouds.
Hardiness 1—2. April—May.

R. surasianum Balf. f. et Craib in Notes Roy. Bot. Gard. Edin., Vol. 10 (1917) 160.

A shrub, 1.22—4 m. (4—13 ft.) high; branchlets rather densely scaly, not bristly or slightly bristly. *Leaves* oblong-lanceolate, oblong-elliptic, ovate, elliptic, oblong-oval or rarely lanceolate, lamina coriaceous, 6—11.6 cm. long, 2.2—5.4 cm. broad, apex acute or acuminate or rarely rounded, mucronate, base obtuse, tapered or rounded; upper surface olive-green or dark green, matt or somewhat shining, not scaly, midrib grooved, primary veins 6—10 on each side, deeply impressed; margin not bristly or sometimes bristly; *under surface densely scaly*, the *scales* unequal, large or medium-sized, brown or dark brown, *overlapping or contiguous or ½ their own diameter apart*, with or without larger dark brown scales widely or closely scattered, midrib prominent, primary veins raised; petiole 0.8—1.5 cm. long, grooved above, densely scaly, not bristly or bristly. *Inflorescence* terminal, umbellate, 2—3-flowered; rhachis 2—3 mm. long, scaly, pubescent or glabrous; pedicel 0.9—1.5 cm. long, thick, densely scaly, not bristly. *Calyx* 5-lobed, oblique, 1—2 mm. long, lobes ovate, outside densely or moderately scaly, margin bristly or sometimes not bristly. *Corolla* funnel-shaped, 5.5—8 cm. long, 5-lobed, margins of lobes entire or somewhat crenulate, *pale pink*, scaly all over the outside, pubescent at the base of the tube outside or rarely glabrous. *Stamens* 10, unequal, 4—5.7 cm. long, shorter than the corolla; filaments densely pubescent at the base or in the lower ⅓ their length. *Ovary* conoid, apex somewhat tapered into the style or truncate, 4—7 mm. long, 5-celled, densely scaly, glabrous; style long, straight or curved in the upper part, 5.2—7 cm. in length, as long as the corolla or longer, scaly in the lower ½—⅔ its length, glabrous. *Capsule:*—

The distribution of this species is restricted to Thailand. It was first found by Dr. A.F.G. Kerr in June 1914 at Chiengmai, Doi Sutep. Subsequently it was collected by him again, and by Put and Garrett in other localities in the same region. The plant grows on rocky ground in open evergreen jungle and forest, at elevations of 1,400—1,560 m. (4,590—5,115 ft.).

In some respects, the species resembles *R. ludwigianum* also from Thailand, but is distinguished usually by the acute or acuminate leaf-apex, usually by the densely scaly lower surface of the leaves, the scales being overlapping or contiguous or one-half their own diameter apart, and by the longer pedicel. It is also related to *R. pachypodum* from which it differs in the longer pedicel, usually in the larger corolla and in flower colour.

R. surasianum has been in cultivation for a long time. In its native home it grows up to 13 feet high, but in cultivation it is broadly upright and reaches a height of only 4 or 5 feet. As it grows in its native home at the low elevation of 4,590—5,115 feet, in cultivation it is suitable only for a cool greenhouse. It is a fairly robust grower, and makes a fine show with its pale pink flowers in trusses of 2—3. Moreover, it is a useful plant in that it is a late flowerer, the flowers appearing in June or July. The species is rare in cultivation.

Epithet. After C.P. Surasi, Thailand.

Hardiness 1. June—July.

R. taronense Hutch. in The Species of Rhododendron (1930) 480.

A bushy or lax broadly upright shrub, usually epiphytic, 60 cm.—4.58 m. (2—15 ft.) high; stem and branches usually with smooth, brown, flaking bark; branchlets sparsely or moderately scaly, not bristly. *Leaves elliptic, elliptic-lanceolate or oblong-lanceolate,* lamina coriaceous, 8.7—11.5 cm. long, 2.4—4.5 cm. broad, *apex acuminate or acutely acuminate or acute,* mucronate, base cuneate, obtuse or tapered; upper surface dark green or pale green, somewhat shining, not scaly, midrib grooved, primary veins 10—16 on each side, deeply impressed; margin not bristly; *under surface* pale green or pale glaucous green, *laxly scaly,* the *scales* unequal, large, brown, *3—5 times their own diameter apart,* midrib prominent, primary veins raised; petiole 0.8—1.4 cm. long, grooved above, densely or moderately scaly, not bristly. *Inflorescence* terminal, umbellate, 3—5-flowered; rhachis 2—3 mm. long, scaly, pubescent; *pedicel* 0.5—1.3 cm. long, thick, densely or moderately scaly, *rather densely puberulous,* not bristly. *Calyx* a mere rim or 5-lobed, oblique, minute, 1 mm. long, when lobed, lobes broadly ovate, outside scaly, margin glabrous. *Corolla* funnel-shaped, *4.5—5.4 cm. long,* 5-lobed, margins of lobes not crinkled, slightly fragrant or not fragrant, white, with or without a yellow blotch at the base, and with or without yellow spots, moderately or laxly scaly all over the outside, pubescent at the base of the tube outside. *Stamens* 10, unequal, 3.6—5.6 cm. long, shorter than the corolla; filaments densely pubescent in the lower half. *Ovary* conoid, apex truncate, 4—5 mm. long, 6-celled, densely scaly, glabrous; style long, straight or curved in the upper part, 4.6—6 cm. in length, longer than the corolla, scaly in the lower ⅓—½ its length, glabrous. *Capsule* oblong-oval, oblique at the base, 1—3 cm. long, 0.8—1.5 cm. broad, ribbed, densely scaly, glabrous, calyx persistent.

Kingdon-Ward discovered this plant in November 1922 in the Taron Valley, Yunnan. He found it again in November 1937 in Nam Tamai Valley, Upper Burma. Later in 1938, Yü collected it in the Kiukiang Valley, Taron, Yunnan. The plant grows in woods and in dense thickets on rocks, usually as an epiphyte, at elevations of 1,220—1,600 m. (4,000—5,246 ft.). Kingdon-Ward first found it growing as an epiphyte about 40 feet from the ground. Yü records it as being casual in the Kiukiang Valley.

The marked characteristics of this species are the small corolla, 4.5—5.4 cm. long, and the laxly scaly lower surface of the leaves, the scales being 3—5 times their own diameter apart. The plant shows a certain degree of resemblance to *R. notatum*, but is readily distinguished by the shape of the leaves, by the rather densely puberulous pedicel, by the colour of the corolla, and by the larger scales on the lower surface of the leaves.

It may be remarked that the plant (raised from Forrest's seed No. 27687) figured in the *Botanical Magazine*, n. s. Vol. 165 t. 1 (1948) and which received a First Class Certificate in 1935, has been wrongly named as *R. taronense*. The specimen under Forrest No. 27687 is *R. dendricola*.

R. taronense was introduced by Yü in 1938 (No. 21005). As it comes from an elevation of 5,246 feet, it is too tender in the open, but it has been grown successfully in the protection of the glasshouse. In cultivation it is a lax broadly upright shrub, 4 or 5 feet high, although in its native home it grows up to 15 feet in height. It is fairly fast-growing, with white flowers produced freely in trusses of three to five. The plant is now rare in cultivation.

Epithet. From the Taron Gorge, Yunnan.
Hardiness 1. April—May.

R. veitchianum Hook. Bot. Mag. Vol. 83 t. 4992 (1857).

A broadly upright or spreading shrub or sometimes a small tree, sometimes epiphytic, 92 cm.—3.70 m. (3—12 ft.) high; branchlets moderately or rather densely scaly, not bristly. *Leaves* oblong-obovate, oblong-oblanceolate, elliptic-lanceolate, obovate or elliptic, *lamina* coriaceous, 5—10 cm. long, 2—4.6 cm. broad, *apex abruptly acuminate or abruptly acute*, mucronate, base tapered, obtuse or cuneate; upper surface dark green, shining, not scaly, midrib grooved, primary veins 6—12 on each side, deeply impressed; margin not bristly; *under surface very glaucous,* scaly, the scales unequal, large or medium-sized, brown, 1—3 times their own diameter apart, midrib prominent, primary veins raised; petiole 0.5—1.5 cm. long, grooved above, densely scaly, not bristly. *Inflorescence* terminal, umbellate, 2—5-flowered; rhachis 2—3 mm. long, scaly, glabrous; pedicel 3—8 mm. long, thick or somewhat thick, densely scaly, not bristly. *Calyx* 5-lobed, oblique, minute, 1 mm. or rarely 2 mm. long, lobes ovate or triangular, outside scaly, margin not bristly or rarely sparsely bristly. *Corolla* funnel-shaped, sometimes split along one side, 5.8—7 cm. long, 5-lobed, *margins of lobes usually crinkled,* fragrant, white, or white tinged pink or green outside, with or without a yellowish-green or yellow blotch at the base, moderately or laxly scaly all over the outside, or scaly only at the base of the tube, moderately or rarely slightly pubescent at the base of the tube outside. *Stamens* 10—11 or sometimes 12—14, unequal, 3.5—5.8 cm. long, shorter than the corolla; filaments densely hairy at the base or in the lower half, or rarely moderately hairy at the base. *Ovary* conoid, apex tapered into the style or truncate, 4—5 mm. long, 5-celled, densely scaly, glabrous; style long, straight or curved in the upper part, 5.5—6.8 cm. in length, longer or shorter than the corolla, scaly in the lower ⅓—½ its length, glabrous. *Capsule* oblong-oval, oblique at the base, 1.5—3 cm. long, 1—1.3 cm. broad, ribbed, moderately or densely scaly, glabrous, calyx persistent.

R. veitchianum was described by W.J. Hooker in 1857 from a plant raised in Veitch's nursery at Exeter. It was introduced by Thomas Lobb for Messrs. Veitch about 1850 from the mountains east of Moulmein, and was exhibited by them in May 1857. The species was later collected in other localities in central and Lower Burma, Thailand, and Laos. It grows in evergreen forest, in open scrub, and on rocks, sometimes as an epiphyte, at elevations of 1,220—2,288 m. (4,000—7,500 ft.). It is said to be common in evergreen jungle near the top of Doi Sootep, Thailand.

It is easily recognised by the very glaucous lower surfaces of the leaves, the scales being 1—3 times their own diameter apart, by the abruptly acuminate or abruptly acute leaf-apex, usually by the crinkled margin of the corolla-lobes, and by the white or white tinged pink flowers. The species bears a resemblance to *R. dendricola* in some features, but differs markedly in distinctive features. The plant is a diploid, 2n = 26.

The species has been reintroduced a few times within recent years. In cultivation it is one of the finest species in its Series. In its native home it is a shrub or sometimes a small tree, up to 12 feet high, but in cultivation it reaches a height of about 6 feet. It is a tender plant and is suitable for the cool greenhouse. Three distinct growth forms are in cultivation. Form 1. A broadly upright shrub 5—6 feet high with somewhat short branchlets, and fairly well-filled with foliage. Form 2. A rounded spreading shrub, 2—3 feet high and almost as much across with short branchlets. Form 3. A lax straggly shrub with long branchlets. Forms 1 and 2 are exceedingly charming when adorned with a profusion of funnel-shaped flowers in trusses of two to five. A clone 'Margaret Mead' recieved an Award of Merit when exhibited by Geoffrey Gorer, Sunte House, Haywards Heath, Sussex, in 1978.

Epithet. After the famous family Nurserymen.

Hardiness 1. May—June. Plate 45.

R. walongense Ward in Gard. Chron. CXXXIII (1953) 5.

A small tree or large shrub, sometimes epiphytic, 2—3 m. (6½—10 ft.) high; branchlets scaly, not bristly. *Leaves* oblong-lanceolate, oblanceolate or oblong-elliptic, *lamina* coriaceous, *10—13 cm. long*, 3—4.4 cm. broad, apex acuminate or abruptly acuminate, mucronate, base cuneate; upper surface dark green, somewhat shining, not scaly, midrib grooved, primary veins 10—14 on each side, impressed; margin not bristly; under surface pale glaucous green or pale green, scaly, the scales unequal, large, brown or dark brown, 1—3 times their own diameter apart, midrib prominent, primary veins raised; petiole 0.8—1 cm. long, grooved above, densely scaly, not bristly or slightly bristly. *Inflorescence* terminal, umbellate, 3—6-flowered; rhachis 2—3 mm. long, scaly, pubescent; pedicel 0.8—1.5 cm. long, thick, densely scaly, not bristly. *Calyx* 5-lobed, oblique, minute, 1 mm. long, outside scaly, margin hairy with long hairs or glabrous. *Corolla* funnel-shaped, 6—7 cm. long, 5-lobed, margins of lobes somewhat crenulate or entire, very fragrant, *creamy or creamy-white*, with a greenish blotch at the base, scaly all over the outside, *pubescent all over the tube* outside. *Stamens* 10, unequal, 3.5—5 cm. long, shorter than the corolla; filaments densely hairy in the lower ⅓—½ their length. *Ovary* conoid or oblong, apex truncate, 5—6 mm. long, 6-celled, densely scaly, glabrous; style long, straight, 6—7 cm. in length, longer than the corolla, scaly in the lower half, glabrous. *Capsule* oblong-oval, oblique at the base, 1.7 cm. long, 8—9 mm. broad, ribbed, densely scaly, glabrous, calyx persistent.

This species was first collected by Kingdon-Ward in April 1928 in Assam. It was found by him again in March 1950 near Rima, Tibet. The plant grows in forests in the ravines, on rocky slopes in mixed forest, on rocks and cliffs, at elevations of 1,525—2,135 m. (5,000—7,000 ft.).

R. walongense is allied to *R. supranubium* which it resembles in some features, but is readily distinguished usually by the larger leaves, by the larger corolla being pubescent all over the tube outside, and usually by the flower colour.

The species was first introduced by Kingdon-Ward in 1928 (No. 8016), and again in 1950 (No. 19259 — the Type number). It will be seen that in *The Rhododendron Handbook* 1980, p. 311, *R. walongense* has been wrongly recorded as Q (not in cultivation). Moreover, in the same Handbook on p. 232, Kingdon-Ward No. 8016 has been wrongly identified as *R. dendricola*. The specimen under this number is *R. walongense*.

In its native home *R. walongense* is a small tree or large shrub up to 10 feet high, but in cultivation it is a small shrub only about 3 feet in height. The plant is too tender to be grown in the open, but it succeeds in a cool greenhouse. The species is rare in cultivation.

Epithet. After the last Indian outpost in the Lohit Valley close to where it was discovered.

Hardiness 1. April—May.

MADDENII SUBSERIES

General characters: shrubs or sometimes small trees, 92 cm.—4.58 m. (3—15 ft.) or rarely 60 cm. (2 ft.) high. Leaves lanceolate, oblong-lanceolate, oblanceolate, oblong, elliptic, ovate-lanceolate, obovate, oblong-obovate or sometimes almost oval, lamina 5.3—18.6 cm. long, 2—8.2 cm. broad; under surface densely scaly, the scales overlapping or contiguous or ½, rarely up to 2—3 times, their own diameter apart; *petiole* 0.8—3.5 cm. long, *grooved above*. Inflorescence 2—6- or sometimes up to 9-flowered; pedicel 0.5—1.5 cm. or sometimes 2 cm. long, thick. Calyx 5-lobed or rarely an undulate rim, 0.1—2 cm. or rarely 0.5 mm. long, margin eciliate or rarely slightly ciliate. Corolla tubular-funnel shaped or sometimes tubular-campanulate, 4.5—11 cm. long, 5-lobed, usually fragrant, white, creamy-white, white tinged pink or red, rosy-white, rose-pink or pink, with or without a yellow or pale orange or greenish or pink blotch inside towards the base, rather densely scaly all over the outside, glabrous outside. *Stamens 15—25* or rarely 12; filaments glabrous or moderately or rather densely hairy with broad membranous flake-like hairs in the lower ⅓—⅔ their length. *Ovary* conoid or ovoid, *apex tapered or somewhat tapered into the style* (except in *R. odoriferum* and *R. polyandrum*, apex truncate), 0.5—1 cm. or rarely 1.5 cm. long, *10—12-celled* (except in *R. excellens*, 5-celled); style long, straight or curved in the upper part. Capsule oblong, oblong-oval or oval, 1—4 cm. long, 0.7—1.6 cm. broad, densely scaly.

KEY TO THE SPECIES

A. Stamens (filaments) glabrous.
>**B.** Under surface of the leaves densely scaly, the scales overlapping or contiguous or ½ their own diameter apart; leaves lanceolate, oblong-lanceolate, elliptic-lanceolate, oblanceolate or rarely oblong-obovate.
>>**C.** Stamens 15—22; calyx 5-lobed, 2—9 mm. or rarely 1.5 cm. long; inflorescence 2—4-flowered; corolla tubular-funnel shaped .... *maddenii* (part)
>>**C.** Stamens 15; calyx an undulate rim, 0.5—1 mm. long; inflorescence 6—7-flowered; corolla narrowly tubular-funnel shaped .... *odoriferum*
>
>**B.** Under surface of the leaves laxly scaly, the scales 2—3 times their own diameter apart; leaves obovate .... *calophyllum*

A. Stamens (filaments) moderately or rather densely hairy in the lower ⅓—⅔ their length.
>**D.** Stem and branches with smooth, brown, flaking bark .... *maddenii* (part)
>
>**D.** Stem and branches with rough bark.
>>**E.** Corolla 4.5—4.8 cm. long; stamens 2.6—3.1 cm. long; style 3—4 cm. long, often half as long as the corolla; corolla pink or white tinged red .... *brachysiphon*
>>**E.** Corolla usually 5—11 cm. long; stamens 3.6—8 cm. long; style usually 4.5—9 cm. long, a little shorter than, or as long as, the corolla; corolla white, white tinged pink, or pink.
>>>**F.** Stamens 20—25; calyx 2—4 mm. long; corolla 4.8—7 cm. long, narrowly tubular-funnel shaped (narrow trumpet shaped); leaves (laminae) usually 6—8.5 cm. long, usually oblong-lanceolate, lanceolate or oblanceolate .... *polyandrum*
>>>**F.** Stamens 12—21; calyx 6 mm.—2 cm. long; corolla usually 7—11 cm. long, tubular-funnel shaped; leaves (laminae) usually 8—18.6 cm. long, almost oval, oblong-oval, elliptic, obovate to oblong-lanceolate or lanceolate.
>>>>**G.** Anthers 3—6 cm. long; petiole 1—2.8 cm. long; pedicel 0.5—1.5 cm. long; primary veins on the upper surface of the leaves 8—16 on each side; stamens usually 15—21; style 3.6—8 cm. long; ovary 10—12-celled.
>>>>>**H.** Leaves (laminae) usually 2.3—4.8 cm. broad, often oblong-lanceolate, lanceolate or oblong-oblanceolate; ovary 10- or rarely 11-celled; chromosome number 2 n = 52 or 2 n = 78 .... *crassum*
>>>>>**H.** Leaves (laminae) usually 5—8.2 cm. broad, almost oval, oblong-oval, elliptic or oblong-elliptic; ovary 12-celled; chromosome number 2 n = 78 or 2 n = 156 .... *manipurense*
>>>>**G.** Anthers 1—1.3 cm. long; petiole 2.5—3.5 cm. long; pedicel 2 cm. long; primary veins on the upper surface of the leaves 18—20 on each side; stamens 12—15; style 8.5—9 cm. long; ovary 5-celled ... . *excellens*

DESCRIPTION OF THE SPECIES

R. brachysiphon Balf. f. in Notes Roy. Bot. Gard. Edin., Vol. 12 (1919) 24.

A broadly upright or somewhat rounded shrub, 1.83—2.44 m. (6—8 ft.) high; stem and branches with rough bark; branchlets moderately or rather densely scaly, not bristly. *Leaves obovate or elliptic*, lamina coriaceous, 5.5—12.5 cm. long, 2.5—6.4 cm. broad, apex rounded, mucronate, base cuneate; upper surface dark green, somewhat bullate, shining, not scaly, midrib grooved, primary veins 6—8 on each side, deeply impressed; margin not bristly; under surface densely scaly, the scales unequal, medium-sized, dark brown, nearly contiguous or ½ their own diameter apart, midrib prominent, primary veins raised; petiole 1—1.3 cm. long, grooved above, densely scaly, not bristly. *Inflorescence* terminal, umbellate, 2—7-flowered; rhachis 2 mm. long, scaly; pedicel 0.5—1 cm. long, thick, rather densely scaly, not bristly. *Calyx* 5-lobed, oblique, 7 mm. long, red, lobes ovate, outside scaly at the base, margin eciliate. *Corolla* tubular-campanulate, *4.5—4.8 cm. long*, 5-lobed, fragrant, *pink or white tinged red*, scaly all over the outside, glabrous outside. *Stamens* 20, unequal, *2.6—3.1 cm. long*, ⅔ *the length of the corolla*; filaments hairy with broad membranous flake-like hairs in the lower ⅓ or ½ their length; anthers 3—4 mm. long. *Ovary* ovoid or conoid, apex somewhat tapered, 5 mm. long, 10-celled, densely scaly, glabrous; *style* straight, *short*, 3—4 cm. long, ½ or ⅔ *as long as the corolla*, scaly in the lower half. *Capsule* oval, 1—1.5 cm. long, 0.9—1.2 cm. broad, ribbed, densely scaly, glabrous, calyx-lobes much enlarged, persistent.

R. brachysiphon was discovered by R.E. Cooper in May 1915 at Punakha, Bhutan, growing on steep hillsides, at elevations of 1,830—2,135 m. (6,000—7,000 ft.).

The diagnostic features of this plant are the short corolla 4.5—4.8 cm. long, the short style 3—4 cm. long, ½ or ⅔ as long as the corolla, and the short stamens 2.6—3.1 cm. long, ⅔ the length of the corolla. Other marked characteristics are the obovate or elliptic leaves, the pink or white tinged red corolla, and the stem and branches with rough bark. The species is allied to *R. maddenii* and *R. crassum*, but differs markedly in distinctive features.

R. brachysiphon has been in cultivation for a long time, and was possibly introduced by Cooper from Bhutan. It has proved hardy outdoors along the west coast and in well-sheltered positions in some gardens along the east coast. A fine example of this species is to be seen growing in the open in the Royal Botanic Garden, Edinburgh; it is a broadly upright shrub somewhat compact and spreading, 8 feet high, densely filled with dark green shining foliage, and is of great beauty with its white tinged red flowers produced freely in trusses of four to seven. It sets good fertile seed in plenty, and is easy to increase from cuttings.

Epithet. Short-tubed.
Hardiness 1—3. May—June.

R. calophyllum Nutt. in Hook. Kew Journ. Bot. Vol.5 (1853) 362.

A broadly upright shrub, 1.22—1.83 m. (4—6 ft.) high; branchlets scaly, not bristly. *Leaves obovate*, lamina coriaceous, 8—9.5 cm. long, 4.5—4.8 cm. broad, apex rounded, mucronate, base cuneate; upper surface dark green, somewhat shining, not scaly, midrib grooved, primary veins 6—8 on each side, deeply impressed; margin not bristly; *under surface* very glaucous, *laxly scaly*, the *scales* unequal, small, brown, *2—3 times their own diameter apart*, midrib prominent, primary veins raised; petiole about 1 cm. long, grooved above, scaly, not bristly. *Inflorescence* terminal, umbellate, 4—5-flowered; rhachis 2—3 mm. long, scaly; pedicel 1 cm. long, thick, rather densely scaly, not bristly. *Calyx* 5-lobed, oblique, short, 1—3 mm. long, lobes ovate, unequal, outside scaly, glabrous. *Corolla* tubular-campanulate, 7 cm. long, 5-lobed, probably white, densely scaly all over the outside, glabrous outside. *Stamens* 15, unequal, 6.2—6.5 cm. long, reaching to about the middle of the corolla lobes; filaments glabrous; anthers about 7 mm. long. *Ovary* and style not known. *Capsule* cylindric-ovate, 10-celled.

This species is known only from a single rather inadequate specimen collected by Booth on the southern slope of the Oola Mountain, Bhutan, at an elevation of 1,830—2,135 m. (6,000—7,000 ft.), and was described by Nuttall in 1853.

R. calophyllum shows a strong resemblance to *R. maddenii* in general appearance, but is distinguished by the laxly scaly lower surface of the leaves, the scales being small, 2—3 times their own diameter apart, by the broadly obovate leaves, and usually by the smaller corolla.

It should be noted that the specimen figured in the *Botanical Magazine* Vol. 83 t. 5002 (1857), is not *R. calophyllum*, since the scales on the lower surface of the leaf are shown to be almost contiguous, whereas in the Type specimen of *R. calophyllum* they are widely spaced, 2—3 times their own diameter apart. The illustration is possibly of *R. maddenii*.

True *R. calophyllum* has not been introduced into cultivation. Some plants which have been labelled as *R. calophyllum*, are in fact forms of *R. maddenii*. One of these cultivated plants growing in Eire resembles *R. calophyllum* in general characters but differs markedly in the distribution of the scales on the lower surface of the leaves.

Epithet. With a beautiful leaf.

Not in cultivation.

R. crassum Franch. in Bull. Soc. Bot. France, XXXIV (1887) 282.

Illustration. Bot. Mag. Vol. 164 t. 9673 (1946).

A broadly upright, or upright somewhat compact and spreading shrub, 92 cm.—4.58 m. (3—15 ft.) or sometimes 60 cm. (2 ft.) high, or sometimes a small tree 3—6.10 m. (10—20 ft.) high; *stem and branches with rough bark*; branchlets densely or moderately scaly, not bristly. *Leaves* oblong-lanceolate, lanceolate, oblong-oblanceolate, oblong-elliptic, elliptic, oblong-obovate or obovate, lamina thick, coriaceous, 6—18 cm. long, 2.3—6.2 cm. broad, apex obtuse, shortly acute, acute, acuminate or rounded, mucronate, base obtuse or cuneate; upper surface dark green, shining, scaly or not scaly, midrib grooved, primary veins 8—14 on each side, deeply impressed; margin not bristly; under surface densely scaly, the scales unequal, small, or medium-sized, or medium-sized and large, or large, brown or dark brown, ½ or their own diameter apart or nearly contiguous, midrib prominent, primary veins raised; petiole 1—2.6 cm. long, grooved above, densely scaly, not bristly. *Inflorescence* terminal, umbellate, 3—5- or rarely up to 7-flowered; rhachis 2—4 mm. long, scaly; pedicel 0.6—1.5 cm. long, thick, densely scaly, not bristly. *Calyx* 5-lobed, 0.6—2 cm. long, lobes oblong, ovate, oblong-oval, oval or sometimes lanceolate, outside not scaly or sometimes sparsely scaly at the base, margin not scaly, glabrous. *Corolla* tubular-funnel shaped, 6—10 cm. or rarely 5—5.8 cm. long, 5-lobed, fleshy, margins of the lobes entire, fragrant or rarely not fragrant, white, creamy-white, white tinged pink, rosy-white or pink, without or rarely with a yellow blotch at the base, rather densely scaly all over the outside, glabrous outside. *Stamens* 15—21, unequal, 4.8—7.2 cm. long, shorter than the corolla; *filaments moderately or rarely rather densely hairy* with broad membranous flake-like hairs *in the lower ⅓—½ their length* except at the base; anthers 3—6 mm. long. *Ovary* conoid or ovoid, apex tapered or somewhat tapered into the style or truncate, 5—9 mm. long, 10- or rarely 11-celled, densely scaly, glabrous; style long, straight or curved in the upper part, 3.6—8 cm. in length, a little shorter than the corolla, scaly to near the apex or in the lower ¾ its length, stigma disc-like. *Capsule* oblong, oblong-oval or oval, oblique at the base, 1.5—3.2 cm. long, 0.8—1.6 cm. broad, ribbed, densely scaly, glabrous, calyx-lobes persistent.

This species was first found by the Abbé Delavay about 1885 in the Tali range, Western Yunnan. Further gatherings by him and other collectors show that the area of distribution of the species extends from mid-west, west, and north-west Yunnan to North Burma, south and south-east Tibet. It grows in very varied habitats, in thickets, amongst scrub, on rocks, boulders, the ledges of cliffs, and on rocky slopes, in open conifer forests, on pine and oak covered slopes, in pine, Abies, and spruce forests, and among bamboo growths, at elevations of 1,600—4,280 m. (5,245—14,000 ft.). The species is said to be common in north-west Yunnan.

R. crassum is a very variable plant due to the various environmental conditions in which it is found. It is a shrub or sometimes a small tree, 2—20 feet high; the leaves are lanceolate, elliptic to oblong-obovate or obovate, laminae 6—18 cm. long, 2.3—6.2 cm. broad; the calyx is 6 mm.—2 cm. long; and the corolla is usually 6—10 cm. long.

It shows a strong resemblance to *R. maddenii* in its general appearance. The main distinctions between them are that in *R. crassum* the stem and branches have a rough bark, and the stamens are pubescent in the lower ⅓—½ their length; whereas in *R. maddenii* the stem and branches have a smooth, brown flaking bark, and the stamens are glabrous or sometimes pubescent in the lower ⅓ their length. Moreover, they difer in their geographical distribution. *R. crassum* is a native of Yunnan, North Burma, south and south-east Tibet, but *R. maddenii* is found in Sikkim and Bhutan. *R. crassum* is tetraploid 2 n = 52, or hexaploid 2 n = 78.

R. crassum was first introduced by Forrest in 1906. It was reintroduced many times by him and other collectors. The plant first flowered in 1914 with E.J.P. Magor, Lamellen, Cornwall. As it grows at elevations of 5,245—14,000 feet, its hardiness is very variable in cultivation. In the west coast the plant flourishes in the open. Along the east coast, plants introduced from the higher elevations have proved hardy outdoors in well-sheltered positions in some gardens, but most plants from low elevations are suitable only for the cool greenhouse. However, it may be of interest to note that a plant under Yü No. 21031, introduced from the Kiukiang Valley, Yunnan at a low elevation of 5,245 feet, and another plant under the Ludlow, Sherriff and Elliot No. 12248 introduced from Tsakchugong, Pome Province, south-east Tibet also from a low elevation of 6,500 feet, are successfully grown outdoors in well-sheltered positions in the Royal Botanic Garden, Edinburgh. The former is upright, 5 feet high; the latter is somewhat compact and spreading, 4 feet high and almost as much across.

R. crassum shows considerable variation in cultivation. At least twelve different forms are grown in various gardens. The more distinctive forms are: Form 1. Leaves medium-sized, oblong-lanceolate, laminae 9 cm. long; corolla medium-sized 8 cm. long. Form 2. Leaves small, laminae 6—7 cm. long; corolla small 6—7 cm. long. Form 3. Leaves large, oblong-lanceolate, laminae 15 cm. long; corolla large 10 cm. long. Form 4. Leaves broadly obovate, medium-sized 10 cm. long; corolla large 10 cm. long. Form 5. Small somewhat compact spreading shrub 4—5 feet high and almost as much across. Form 6. A large bushy or broadly upright shrub 12 feet high and 6—8 feet across. Form 7. A tall shrub 8 feet high with broadly elliptic leaves, late flowerer, the flowers being produced in August. All the foregoing plants have usually white or creamy-white flowers. Form 8. A medium-sized shrub with pink flowers.

It is to be noted that *R. crassum* has a long flowering period. Some plants produce the flowers in April, many others in May, June and July. Form 7 opens its flowers almost regularly during the first week in August.

R. crassum is a robust grower, and easy to root from cuttings. Most forms produce good fertile seed nearly every year. The plant is easy to grow, and is most attractive when covered with tubular-funnel shaped fragrant flowers in trusses of three to five. It received an Award of Merit when exhibited by T.H. Lowinsky, Sunninghill, Berks., in 1924.

Epithet. Fleshy.
Hardiness 1—3. April—August.

R. excellens Hemsl. et Wils. in Kew Bull. (1910) 113.

A shrub, 3.30 m. (11 ft.) high; branchlets dark purple, rather densely scaly. *Leaves* oblong-elliptic, lamina coriaceous, 15—18 cm. long, 4—5.5 cm. broad, apex obtuse or rounded, mucronate, base rounded; upper surface dark green, matt, not scaly, midrib grooved, *primary veins 18—20 on each side*, impressed; margin not bristly; under surface somewhat glaucous, densely scaly, the scales unequal, brown, about their own or a little less than their own diameter apart, midrib prominent, primary veins raised; *petiole 2.5—3.5 cm. long*, grooved above, dark purple, scaly, not bristly. *Inflorescence* terminal, umbellate, 3—4-flowered; rhachis 3—4 mm. long, scaly; *pedicel 2 cm. long*, thick, densely scaly, not bristly. *Calyx* 5-lobed, 1—1.5 cm. long, lobes rounded, outside scaly at the base, margin slightly ciliate or eciliate. *Corolla* tubular-funnel shaped, *10—11 cm. long*, 5-lobed, margins of the lobes entire, emarginate, white, rather densely scaly all over the outside, glabrous outside. *Stamens 12—15*, unequal, 5.2—6.3 cm. long, half the length of the corolla; filaments pubescent in the lower ½—⅔ their length; *anthers 1—1.3 cm. long*. *Ovary* conoid, tapering into the style, 1.5 cm. long, 5-celled, densely scaly, glabrous; *style long, straight, 8.5—9 cm. in length*, shorter than the corolla, scaly in the lower ⅓—½ its length, stigma large, disc-like. *Capsule:—*

R. excellens is represented by a single gathering, A. Henry No. 13666. It was found south of the Red River from Mengtze, South Yunnan. The plant is said to be rare in its native home.

It resembles *R. crassum* in general characters, but is distinguished by the longer pedicel, petiole, anther, ovary and style, by the 5-celled ovary, usually by the smaller number of stamens, and often by the longer corolla. The plant has not been introduced into cultivation.

Epithet. Superb.
Not in cultivation.

R. maddenii Hook. f. Rhod. Sikkim Himal. t. 18 (1851).
Illustration. Bot. Mag. Vol. 80 t. 4805 (1854).

A broadly upright, or bushy, or upright somewhat compact and spreading shrub, 92 cm.—3.70 m. (3—12 ft.) high; *stem and branches with smooth, brown, flaking bark;* branchlets moderately or densely scaly, not bristly. *Leaves* lanceolate, oblong-lanceolate, elliptic-lanceolate, oblong-obovate or ovate-lanceolate, lamina coriaceous, 5.3—14.5 cm. long, 2—5.6 cm. broad, apex acuminate, acute or obtuse, mucronate, base obtuse, cuneate or rounded; upper surface dark green or bright green, somewhat shining or matt, scaly or not scaly, midrib grooved, primary veins 8—14 on each side, deeply impressed; margin not bristly; under surface densely scaly, the scales unequal, small or large or medium-sized, brown or dark brown, ½ their own diameter apart or overlapping or contiguous, midrib prominent, primary veins raised; petiole 1—2.5 cm. long, grooved above, densely scaly, not bristly. *Inflorescence* terminal, umbellate, 2—6-flowered; rhachis 2—3 mm. long, scaly; pedicel 0.9—1.5 cm. long, thick or somewhat thick, densely or moderately scaly, not bristly. *Calyx* 5-lobed, 2—9 mm. or rarely 1.5 cm. long, lobes ovate or oblong, outside moderately or rather densely scaly at the base or in the lower half, or sometimes moderately scaly all over, margin eciliate or sometimes slightly ciliate. *Corolla* tubular-funnel shaped, 6.5—10 cm. long, 5-lobed, margins of the lobes entire, fleshy, fragrant, white, white flushed rose, rose-pink, pale pink, or apple blossom pink, with or without a yellow or greenish or pink blotch in the tube, rather densely scaly all over the outside, glabrous outside. *Stamens 15—22*, unequal, 4—8 cm. long, shorter than the corolla; *filaments glabrous, or sometimes hairy* with broad membranous flake-like hairs *in the lower ⅓ their length* except at the base; anthers 3—5 mm. long. *Ovary* conoid or ovoid, apex tapered into the style or truncate, 0.6—1 cm. long, 10-celled, densely scaly, glabrous; style long, straight or curved in the upper part, 5—8 cm. in length, a little shorter than, or as long as, the corolla, scaly to near the apex or in the lower ¾ its length, stigma lobulate. *Capsule* oval or oblong-oval, oblique at the base, 1.3—2.5 cm. long, 0.7—1.6 cm. broad, ribbed, densely scaly, glabrous, calyx-lobes persistent.

This species was discovered by J.D. Hooker in 1849 at Choongtam in Sikkim. It was afterwards found by other collectors in various localities in Sikkim and Bhutan. The plant grows in thickets, on dry hillsides, in scrub jungle, in oak and rhododendron jungle, among oak trees, and in forests, at elevations of 1,525—2,745 m. (5,000—9,000 ft.). Ludlow, Sherriff and Elliot record it as being common near Tashigong, Bhutan, at 2,440 m. (8,000 ft.).

Other plants which were subsequently described as *R. jenkinsii* Nutt. and varieties *aciphyllum*, *platyphyllum*, *undulatum*, and *R. maddenii* Hook. f. var. *longiflora* W. Watson, are identical with *R. maddenii*.

The characteristic features of the plant are the stem and branches with smooth, brown, flaking bark, and usually the glabrous stamens. The leaves are lanceolate to ovate-lanceolate, densely scaly on the lower surfaces, the scales being one-half their own diameter apart or overlapping or contiguous. The calyx is variable, 2—9 mm. or rarely 1.5 cm. long. The corolla is 6.5—10 cm. long, rather densely scaly all over the outside. *R. maddenii* is closely allied to *R. crassum*. The distinctions between them are discussed under the latter. The plant is tetraploid with 52 chromosomes or hexaploid with 78 chromosomes.

The species was first introduced by J.D. Hooker in 1849. It was reintroduced by Cooper, and by Ludlow and Sherriff, who also collected it with Hicks, from Bhutan. In cultivation it is an upright somewhat compact and spreading shrub up to eight feet high, well-filled with dark green foliage. Some plants grown under the name *R. maddenii*, are in fact, forms of *R. crassum*. Two flower colour forms are in cultivation, white and pink. As the plant grows at elevations of up to 9,000 feet in its native home, it should succeed in the open in well-sheltered positions in cultivation. Essentially it is a species for the cool greenhouse. The species is a late flowerer, the flowers appearing in May and June. A well-grown plant four or five feet high makes a fine show when laden with large tubular-funnel shaped fragrant flowers in trusses of two to six. It was given an Award of Merit when shown by Lt.-Col. E.H.W. Bolitho, Trengwainton, Cornwall, in 1938, and again for another form 'Ascreavie' (Ludlow and Sherriff No. 1141) when exhibited by Major A.E. Hardy, Sandling Park, Hythe, in 1978.

Epithet. After Lt.-Col. E. Madden, traveller in India; d. 1856.
Hardiness 1—2. May—June.

R. manipurense Balf. f. et Watt in Notes Roy. Bot. Gard. Edin., Vol. 10 (1917) 119.
Illustration. Bot. Mag. Vol. 134 t. 8212 (1908). Figured as *R. maddenii* var. *obtusifolium*.

A broadly upright, or bushy, or broadly upright spreading shrub, or a small tree, or rarely epiphytic, 1.53—4.58 m. (5—15 ft.) high; stem and branches with rough bark; branchlets densely or moderately scaly, not bristly. *Leaves elliptic, oblong-elliptic, oblong-oval or sometimes almost oval,* lamina thick, coriaceous, 9—18.6 cm. long, *3.6—8.2 cm. broad,* apex rounded, obtuse or acute, mucronate, base rounded or obtuse; upper surface dark green, shining, scaly or not scaly, midrib grooved, primary veins 10—16 on each side, deeply impressed; margin not bristly; under surface densely scaly, the scales unequal, medium-sized, or medium-sized and large, or large, dark brown or brown, contiguous or nearly contiguous or ½ their own diameter apart, midrib prominent, primary veins raised; petiole 1—2.8 cm. long, grooved above, densely scaly, not bristly. *Inflorescence* terminal, umbellate, 3—5- or rarely up to 9-flowered; rhachis 2—4 mm. long, scaly; flower-bud scales glabrous or rather densely puberulous at the margins; pedicel 0.5—1.3 cm. long, thick, densely scaly, not bristly. *Calyx* 5-lobed, 0.6—1.5 cm. long, lobes oblong or oval, outside not scaly or scaly at the base, margin not scaly, glabrous. *Corolla* tubular-funnel shaped, 7—10 cm. long, 5-lobed, margins of the lobes entire, fragrant, white or white tinged red, without or sometimes with a yellow blotch at the base, rather densely scaly all over the outside, glabrous outside. *Stamens* 17—20 or rarely 14, unequal, 4.5—8 cm. long, shorter than the corolla; filaments hairy with broad membranous flake-like hairs in the lower ⅓—½ their length except at the base; anthers 4—5 mm. long. *Ovary* conoid or ovoid, apex tapered into the style or truncate, 5—8 mm. long, 12-celled, densely scaly, glabrous; style long, straight or curved in the upper part,

5.3—7.5 cm. in length, a little shorter than the corolla, scaly to near the apex or in the lower ¾ its length, stigma lobulate. *Capsule* oval, oblong-oval or oblong, oblique at the base, 1.6—4 cm. long, 1—1.5 cm. broad, ribbed, densely scaly, glabrous, calyx-lobes persistent.

This species was discovered by Sir George Watt in March 1882 at Japvo, Naga Hills, Assam. It was found by him again later in the same year in other localities in the same region.

In 1908, *R. maddenii* var. *obtusifolium* was described by Hutchinson in the *Botanical Magazine*, t. 8212 from a plant cultivated at Kew, raised from seeds which were sent by Sir George Watt. In 1917—1918, the plant was given specific status, *R. manipurense*, by Sir Isaac Bayley Balfour and Sir George Watt in *Notes Roy. Bot. Gard. Edin.*, Vol. 10, p. 119.

R. manipurense was later found by Kingdon-Ward in Upper Burma and on the Burma-Tibet Frontier, by Forrest in north-west Yunnan, and by Farrer in Upper Burma. It grows in thickets, on open ridges in Tsuga-Rhododendron forest, in cane and mixed thickets, amongst scrub, on rocky slopes, on ledges of cliffs, in open forest, and on damp shady limestone cliffs, at elevations of 2,440—3,660 m. (8,000—12,000 ft.). Sir George Watt records it as being an extremely common plant forming a dense jungle at Japvo, Assam. According to Kingdon-Ward it is common on rocks in the river bed in the Adung Valley, Burma-Tibet Frontier. Forrest points out that it forms thickets at 3,050—3,355 m. (10,000—11,000 ft. in the Shweli-Salwin Divide, north-west Yunnan.

The diagnostic features of the species are the large broadly elliptic, oblong-oval or almost oval leaves, usually 5—8.2 cm. broad, and the 12-celled ovary. In these respects it is readily distinguished from its nearest ally, *R. crassum*. The corolla varies from 7 to 10 cm. in length, white or white tinged red, without or sometimes with a yellow blotch at the base. The leaves are densely scaly on the lower surface, the scales being contiguous to one-half their own diameter apart. The species is hexaploid, $2n = 78$, or dodecaploid, $2n = 156$.

The species was reintroduced by Kingdon-Ward, by Forrest, and by Ludlow, Sherriff and Taylor. In its native home it grows up to 15 feet high, but in cultivation it is a broadly upright shrub and reaches a height of some 10 feet. As it grows at elevations of up to 12,000 feet in its native home, it is hardy in the open in cultivation, although some forms are tender along the east coast and require the protection of the greenhouse. It is a valuable plant in that it is a late flowerer, extending the flowering season into May or June. The plant has proved to be of sturdy habit, fairly fast-growing, and is of great beauty when covered with large white flowers.

Epithet. From Manipur.
Hardiness 1—3. May—June.

R. odoriferum Hutch. in Gard. Chron. Vol. 82 (1927) 32.

A broadly upright shrub up to about 1.53 m. (5 ft.) high with stout branchlets; branchlets scaly, young shoots purplish. *Leaves* oblong-lanceolate, elliptic-lanceolate, elliptic or oblanceolate, lamina coriaceous, up to 10 cm. long, and 6 cm. broad, apex obtuse or acute, mucronate, base obtuse or cuneate; upper surface dark green, shining, not scaly or scaly, midrib grooved, primary veins about 12 on each side, deeply impressed; margin not bristly; under surface densely scaly, the scales unequal, large, brown, contiguous or nearly contiguous, midrib prominent, primary veins raised; petiole about 1 cm. long, grooved above, densely scaly, not bristly. *Inflorescence* terminal, umbellate, *6—7-flowered;* rhachis 2—3 mm. long, scaly; pedicel 1—1.5 cm. long, thick, scaly, not bristly, usually with a thin, linear, brownish bracteole at the base, or sometimes adnate up to the calyx and resembling calyx-lobes. *Calyx an undulate rim, 0.5—1 mm. long,* outside scaly, margin eciliate. *Corolla narrowly tubular-funnel shaped,* 7 cm. long, 5-lobed, margins of the lobes entire, fragrant, white, slightly flushed rose outside, the tube inside tinged green, rather densely scaly all over the outside, glabrous outside. *Stamens* 15, unequal, 3.5—4 cm. long, shorter than the corolla; filaments glabrous. *Ovary* ovoid, apex truncate, 5 mm. long, 10—11-celled, densely scaly, glabrous; style long, straight or curved in the upper part, 5—6.8 cm. in length, shorter than, or nearly as long as, the corolla, scaly to near the apex, stigma lobulate. *Capsule:* —

R. odoriferum was described by Hutchinson in 1927 from a cultivated plant raised at Kew from seed collected by Bailey (No. 2) in the Upper Nyamsang Valley, southern Tibet, at an elevation of 2,440 m. (8,000 ft.).

The original diagnosis associates it with *R. maddenii* which it resembles in general appearance, but differs in that the calyx is an undulate rim 0.5—1 mm. long, the stamens are 15, the inflorescence is 6—7-flowered, and the corolla is narrowly tubular-funnel shaped.

In cultivation it is a broadly upright shrub up to about five feet high with dark green leaves, densely scaly on the lower surface, the scales being contiguous or nearly contiguous. It is a tender plant and is suitable for a cool greenhouse. The plant is free-flowering, and provides a fine display with its large white flushed rose flowers. It is uncommon in cultivation.

Epithet. Fragrant.
Hardiness 1. April—May.

R. polyandrum Hutch. in Notes Roy. Bot. Gard. Edin., Vol. 12 (1919) 25.
A broadly upright, or upright somewhat spreading shrub, or bush, or small tree, 92 cm.—4.58 m. (3—15 ft.) high; stem and branches with rough bark; branchlets densely or moderately scaly, not bristly. *Leaves oblong-lanceolate, lanceolate, oblong, oblanceolate* or oblong-obovate, *lamina* thick, coriaceous, *6—12 cm. long*, 2.4—4.5 cm. broad, apex acute, obtuse or abruptly acute, mucronate, base obtuse or tapered; upper surface dark green, shining, not scaly or scaly, midrib grooved, primary veins 6—12 on each side, deeply impressed; margin not bristly; under surface densely scaly, the scales unequal, medium-sized or large, brown or dark brown, contiguous or nearly contiguous or ½ their own diameter apart, midrib prominent, primary veins slightly raised; petiole 0.8—1.8 cm. long, grooved above, densely scaly, not bristly. *Inflorescence* terminal, umbellate, 3—6-flowered; rhachis 2—3 mm. long, scaly; pedicel 0.8—2 cm. long, thick, moderately or densely scaly, not bristly. *Calyx* 5-lobed, *2—4 mm. long*, lobes ovate, outside scaly, margin scaly or not scaly, glabrous. *Corolla narrowly tubular-funnel shaped* (narrow trumpet shaped), *4.8—7 cm. long*, 5-lobed, margins of the lobes entire, white, or white tinged pink, or rose-pink, with or without a pale orange or yellow blotch inside towards the base, rather densely scaly all over the outside, glabrous outside. *Stamens 20—25*, unequal, 3.6—5.6 cm. long, shorter than the corolla; filaments rather densely or moderately hairy with broad membranous flake-like hairs in the lower ⅓—½ their length except at the base; anthers 3—4 mm. long. *Ovary* conoid or ovoid, apex truncate, 5—7 mm. long, 12-celled, densely scaly, glabrous; style long, straight or curved in the upper part, 4.5—5.2 cm. in length, a little shorter than, or as long as, the corolla, scaly to near the apex, stigma lobulate. *Capsule* oblong or oblong-oval, 1.5—3.5 cm. long, 0.8—1.5 cm. broad, ribbed, densely scaly, glabrous, calyx-lobes persistent.

This species was first found by R.E. Cooper in July 1914 at Chapcha Timpu, Bhutan. In February 1925 Kingdon-Ward collected it at the border of north-west Bhutan, and again in June 1938 in Assam. It grows on hill tops, in Tsuga forest, and in rocky situations, at elevations of 2,135—3,050 m. (7,000—10,000 ft.).

A diagnostic feature of the plant is the large number of stamens, 20—25, to which the specific name refers. Another characteristic is the small lanceolate to oblong leaf, densely scaly on the lower surface, the scales being contiguous to one-half their own diameter apart. The corolla is narrowly tubular-funnel shaped, varying from 4.8 to 7 cm. long, and is rather densely scaly all over the outside. The species is closely related to R. *maddenii*, but is distinguished usually by the larger number of stamens, by the rough bark of the stem and branches, and usually by the smaller leaves and smaller narrowly tubular-funnel shaped flowers. It is also allied to R. *crassum* but differs in notable characters. The species is hexaploid, 2 n = 78.

R. *polyandrum* was first introduced by R.E. Cooper in 1915 under seed No. 3061. It was reintroduced by Kingdon-Ward in 1925 (No. 6413). In its native home it is a shrub or a small tree up to 15 feet high; in cultivation it is a medium-sized shrub reaching 5—10 feet. Two colour forms are grown in gardens, white and rose-pink, with a yellow blotch at the base. The species is one of the hardiest of its Series. It is successfully grown outdoors in sheltered positions, but some plants are tender along the east coast and need greenhouse conditions. A form with white flowers received an Award of Merit in 1933, and again the same Award was given in 1938 for a form with rose-pink flowers, when exhibited on both occasions by Lt.-Col. L.C.R. Messel, Nymans, Handcross, Sussex.

Epithet. With many stamens.

Hardiness 1—3. May—June.

MEGACALYX SUBSERIES

General characters: shrubs or sometimes small trees, often epiphytic, 1—9.15 m. (3⅓—30 ft.) or sometimes 15—92 cm. (6 in.—3 ft.) high. Leaves oblong, oblong-obovate, oblanceolate, oblong-oval, obovate, elliptic, oblong-elliptic or rarely oval, lamina 4—26.5 cm. long, 2—13.1 cm. broad; under surface densely or laxly scaly, the scales ½—4 or rarely 5 times their own diameter apart; *petiole* 0.7—3.5 cm. or rarely 3—5 mm. long, *convex, not grooved above* (except in R. *megacalyx* and rarely in R. *basfordii*, grooved above). Inflorescence 1—8- or rarely up to 12-flowered; pedicel 0.8—3.5 cm. long, thick or somewhat thick. *Calyx* 5-lobed, *0.7—2.6 cm. long*, margin glabrous or densely or moderately fringed with hairs. *Corolla* tubular-campanulate or sometimes funnel-shaped, 4.5—13.6 cm. long, 5-lobed, usually fragrant, white, creamy-white, creamy, yellow; white or cream tinged pink, greenish or rose; rarely pink, with or without a golden or orange or yellowish or yellow blotch at the base, outside rather densely to sparsely scaly at the base of the tube, or rather densely or moderately scaly all over the outside, or not scaly, *glabrous* or rarely pubescent on the tube *outside*. Stamens 10 or rarely 8; filaments densely or rarely moderately hairy in the lower ¼—½ their length, anthers 0.2—1.3 cm. long. *Ovary* oblong, oblong-ovate, oblong-oval, ovate or conoid, *tapered into the style* (except in R. *megacalyx* and rarely in R. *nuttallii*, apex truncate), 0.5—1 cm. or rarely 1.5 cm. long, 5-celled; style long, straight or curved in the upper part. Capsule oblong, sometimes oblong-oval, conoid, ovoid or ovate, rarely oblong-ovate or oval, 1.8—7.2 cm. or rarely 0.9 cm. long, 0.8—2.5 cm. or rarely 5—6 mm. broad, densely scaly.

KEY TO THE SPECIES

A. Pedicel and calyx not scaly; calyx broadly campanulate, divided to about the middle, lobes very broad, 1.2—1.8 cm. broad; capsule very short, 1.8—2.5 cm. long, shorter than the calyx, completely enclosed by the calyx-lobes; petiole grooved above; ovary truncate at the apex; style scaly at the base .... *megacalyx*

A. Pedicel densely or moderately scaly, calyx scaly outside along the middle or at the base or all over the outside (except in *R. lindleyi* and *R. grothausii*, not scaly or rarely sparsely scaly at the base); calyx not campanulate, divided to the base, lobes narrow 4 mm.—1 cm. or rarely 1.2—1.4 cm. broad; capsule usually longer, 3—7.2 cm. long (except in *R. basfordii* 9 mm.—1.2 cm. long), longer than the calyx, not enclosed by the calyx-lobes; petiole convex, usually not grooved above; ovary tapered into the style; style often scaly in the lower ¼—⅔ its length.

    B. Under surface of the leaves conspicuously wrinkled, primary veins thick, markedly raised, prominently looped and branched; upper surface of the leaves strongly bullate; anthers large, usually 1—1.3 cm. long .... *nuttallii*

    B. Under surface of the leaves not wrinkled, primary veins usually thin, slightly raised, not looped, not branched; upper surface of the leaves reticulate, not bullate (except in *R. grothausii* and *R. taggianum*, moderately bullate); anthers small, 2—9 mm. long (except in *R. dalhousiae* and *R. rhabdotum* 0.7—1.3 cm. long).

        C. Pedicel rather densely or sometimes moderately pubescent.

            D. Corolla white, yellow or white tinged rose, without five red stripes outside .... *dalhousiae*

            D. Corolla cream, pale yellow or white, marked with five conspicuous red stripes outside .... *rhabdotum*

        C. Pedicel not pubescent (glabrous).

            E. Leaves large, laminae 14.5—24.5 cm. long, 5.8—12 cm. broad, under surface pale green; calyx 1.6—2 cm. long ..... *goreri*

            E. Leaves smaller, laminae usually 4—14 cm. long, 2—5.5 cm. broad (rarely broader in *R. taggianum*), under surface glaucous or pale glaucous-green; calyx 7 mm.—1.5 cm. long (rarely longer in *R. lindleyi* and *R. taggianum*).

                F. Leaves (laminae) 4—5 cm. long; petiole 3—5 mm. long; stamens 8, 2.5 cm. long; Kiangsi species .. *kiangsiense*

                F. Leaves (laminae) usually 5.5—14 cm. long; petiole 7 mm.—3.5 cm. long; stamens 10, 2.6—7.2 cm. long.

                    G. Petioles, and often branchlets, basal half of the margins or the base of the leaves (laminae) bristly; both ends of the leaf rounded; Kwantung species .... *levinei*

                    G. Petioles and branchlets usually not bristly, margins of the leaves (laminae) not bristly; usually both ends of the leaf not rounded.

                        H. Corolla rather densely or moderately scaly all over the outside; style rather densely or moderately scaly usually in the lower half.

                          I. Corolla 8.2—9 cm. long, rather densely scaly all over the outside, margins of the lobes entire; capsule 2.6—4.5 cm. long, 1.2—1.3 cm. broad; style 6—6.4 cm. long; anthers 6—7 mm. long; Kweichow species .... *liliiflorum*

     I. Corolla 5.8—7 cm. long, moderately scaly all over the outside, margins of the lobes crinkled; capsule 0.9—1.2 cm. long, 5—6 mm. broad; style 4.8—5.2 cm. long; anthers 3 mm. long; Bhutan species .... *basfordii*

H. Corolla not scaly outside, or rather densely or moderately scaly only at the base of the tube; style moderately scaly only at the base or in the lower ¼—⅓ its length.

     J. Large, somewhat robust shrub or sometimes a small tree, usually 1.20—4.58 m. high; leaves usually 3.2—6.8 cm. broad, margins flat, base not decurrent on the petiole.

          K. Margins of calyx-lobes not hairy; leaves usually broadly elliptic or elliptic or oblong-elliptic .... *taggianum*

          K. Margins of calyx-lobes densely or moderately fringed with white hairs; leaves usually oblong or oblong-lanceolate.

               L. Upper surface of the leaves not bullate, laminae usually 3.8—5.5 cm. broad; corolla usually 7.8—11.6 cm. long; flower-bud pale green .... *lindleyi*

               L. Upper surface of the leaves bullate, laminae usually 2.8—3.8 cm. broad; corolla 5.3—7.5 cm. long; flower-bud reddish-brown .... *grothausii*

     J. Small or dwarf, somewhat slender shrub, 15 cm.—1 m. high; leaves usually 2—3 cm. broad, margins recurved, base slightly decurrent on the petiole .... *headfortianum*

DESCRIPTION OF THE SPECIES

R. basfordii Davidian in The Royal Horticultural Society's Rhododendrons with Magnolias and Camellias (1979—80) 61.

A broadly upright shrub, 1.53—2.44 m. (5—8 ft.) high; branchlets scaly, sparsely bristly or not bristly. *Leaves* evergreen, oblong, oblong-lanceolate or oblong-elliptic, lamina coriaceous, 5.5—10.5 cm. long, 2—3.9 cm. broad, apex rounded, obtuse or acute, mucronate, base obtuse or rounded, slightly decurrent on the petiole; upper surface dark green, shining, not bullate, not scaly, midrib grooved, primary veins 8—10 on each side, deeply impressed; margin not bristly; under surface glaucous-green, scaly, the scales unequal, medium-sized and large, brown, ½—2 times their own diameter apart, midrib prominent, primary veins raised; *petiole* 0.7—2 cm. long, *convex, not grooved* or rarely grooved *above*, densely or moderately scaly, slightly bristly or not bristly. *Inflorescence* terminal, umbellate, flower-bud pale green, 3—4-flowered; rhachis 3—4 mm. long, scaly, not bristly; pedicel 1.4—1.7 cm. long, somewhat thick, rather densely or moderately scaly, not bristly. *Calyx* 5-lobed, *0.8—1.1 cm. or rarely 1.4—1.8 cm. long*, reddish-green or green, lobes ovate-oblong, ovate, oval or oblong, outside scaly in the lower half or at the base, glabrous, margin hairy with long hairs. *Corolla funnel-shaped, 5.8—7 cm. long*, 5-lobed, fleshy, *lobes* rounded, *margins crinkled,* slightly scented, white, with a small yellowish-green blotch at the base, *scaly all over the outside*, glabrous or pubescent at the base of the tube outside. *Stamens* 10, unequal, *3.2—5.4 cm. long*, shorter than the corolla; filaments densely hairy in the lower ⅓ their length; *anthers 3 mm. long.* Ovary oblong, tapered into the style, 7—8 mm. long, 5-celled, densely scaly, glabrous; style long, straight or curved in the upper part, 4.8—5.2 cm. in length, shorter than the corolla, scaly in the lower ⅓—½ its length, *stigma 1—3 mm. in diameter*, disc-like. *Capsule* oblong or oblong-oval, *0.9—1.2 cm. long*, 5—6 mm. broad, straight or slightly curved, ribbed, densely scaly, glabrous, calyx-lobes persistent.

This species was discovered by Ludlow, Sherriff and Hicks in fruit in October 1949 at Rudo La, Bhutan, growing in rhododendron and Abies forest at an elevation of 2,593 m. (8,500 ft.).

R. basfordii shows a resemblance to *R. lindleyi* in some features, but differs markedly in that the corolla is usually smaller, funnel-shaped, scaly all over the outside, the margins of the lobes are crinkled, the lower surface of the leaves is usually densely scaly, the calyx, stamens, anthers, stigmas, and the capsules are smaller, and the calyx is scaly in the lower half or at the base.

The species was introduced by Ludlow, Sherriff and Hicks in 1949 (No. 19848 — the Type number), and it flowered for the first time at Brodick Castle, Isle of Arran. In cultivation it is broadly upright up to 6 feet high, fairly densely filled with dark green leaves, shining on the upper surface. It is successfully grown in the open at Brodick Castle along the west coast. The species is a vigorous grower, and very often it produces fertile seed in plenty. Like all other species of its Series, it is easy to root from cuttings. Moreover, when raised from open-pollinated seed, the seedlings usually come true to type. The plant is a late flowerer, prolonging the flowering season to the end of May or June. It is free-flowering, and provides an admirable display with its white flowers in trusses of three to four.

Epithet. After John Basford, Brodick Castle Garden, Isle of Arran.

Hardiness 1—2. May—June.

R. dalhousiae Hook f. Rhod. Sikkim Himal. t. 1 (1849).

Illustration. Bot. Mag. Vol. 79 t. 4718 (1853).

A straggly or lax upright shrub, often epiphytic, 92 cm.—3 m. (3—10 ft.) or rarely up to 6.10 m. (20 ft.) high; branchlets scaly, not bristly or sometimes moderately or sparsely bristly. *Leaves* oblong, oblong-obovate or oblanceolate, lamina coriaceous, 6.5—14.8 cm. long, 2.3—6 cm. broad, apex rounded or obtuse, mucronate, base cuneate or obtuse; *upper surface slightly bullate*, dark green or bright green, somewhat shining, not scaly or sometimes scaly, midrib grooved, primary veins 8—15 on each side, deeply impressed; margin not bristly; under surface glaucous-green or pale glaucous-green, scaly, the scales unequal, small or sometimes medium-sized, brown or dark brown, 1—3 times their own diameter apart, midrib prominent, primary veins raised; petiole 1—1.5 cm. long, convex, not grooved above, moderately or rather densely scaly, not bristly or sparsely or moderately bristly. *Inflorescence* terminal, umbellate, 2—5- or sometimes up to 7-flowered; rhachis 2—3 mm. long, scaly, not bristly or rarely sparsely bristly; *pedicel* 0.8—2.3 cm. long, thick, rather densely scaly, *rather densely or sometimes moderately pubescent. Calyx* 5-lobed, 0.7—1.1 cm. or rarely 1.5—1.7 cm. long, lobes oblong, oblong-oval, ovate or ovate-oblong, outside sparsely or moderately scaly at the base or rarely moderately scaly along the middle of the lobes, hairy along the middle of the lobes, margin eciliate or rarely ciliate. *Corolla tubular-campanulate*, 7—9.5 cm. or rarely up to 11.8 cm. long, 5-lobed, margins of the lobes entire, fragrant, white, cream, creamy-white, yellow, or at first creamy-yellow or yellow fading to creamy-white, or white tinged rose, without spots, sparsely or moderately scaly at the base of the tube outside or not scaly, glabrous outside. *Stamens* 10, unequal, 6—9 cm. or rarely up to 10.6 cm. long, shorter than the corolla; filaments densely hairy in the lower ¼—⅓ their length; anthers large, 0.8—1.3 cm. long, chocolate-brown. *Ovary* oblong, tapered into the style, 0.7—1 cm. long, 5-celled, densely scaly, glabrous; style long, straight or curved in the upper part, 5.8—9 cm. or rarely 10 cm. in length, slightly shorter or slightly longer than the corolla, scaly at the base to ½ or rarely ⅔ its length, stigma large, disc-like. *Capsule* oblong, 3—4.8 cm. long, 1.3—2 cm. broad, straight, ribbed, rather densely scaly, glabrous, calyx-lobes persistent.

272

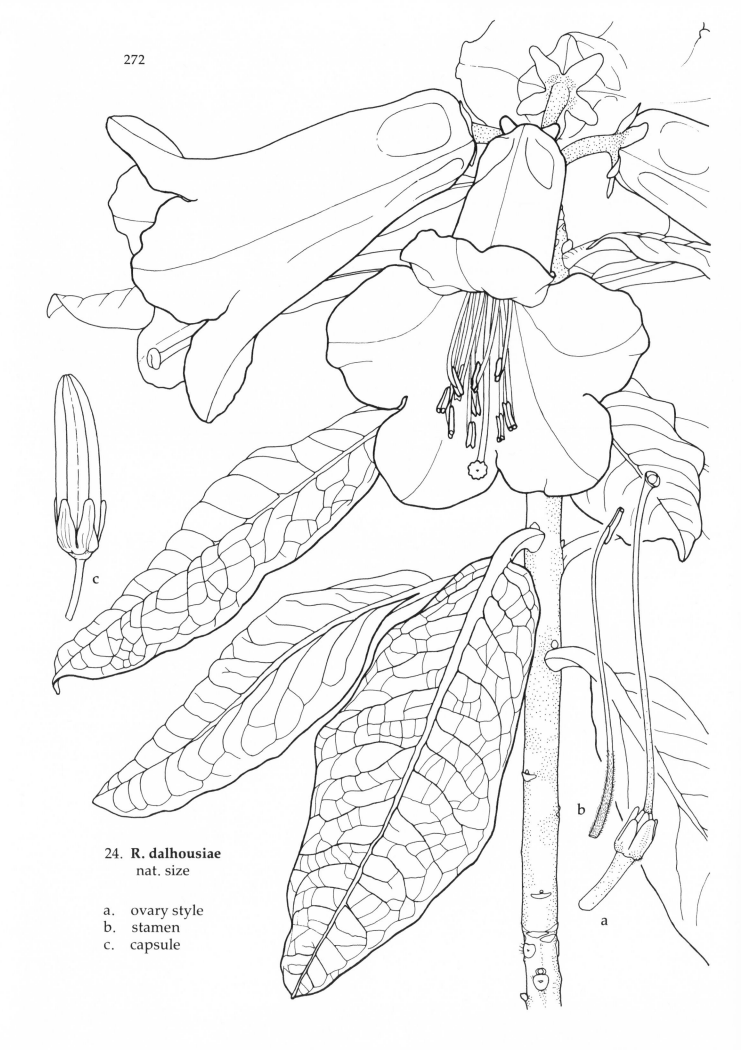

24. **R. dalhousiae**
    nat. size

a. ovary style
b. stamen
c. capsule

R. dalhousiae was discovered by J.D. Hooker in 1848 in Sikkim. Subsequently it was found by other collectors in Nepal, Sikkim and Bhutan. It grows in forests, on steep dry hillsides, on rocks, in rocky soil in jungle, and on boulders, often as an epiphyte on large trees, at elevations of 1,830—2,898 m. (6,000—9,500 ft.). The plant is recorded as being of frequent occurrence in some localities in Sikkim.

The species is easily recognised by the tubular-campanulate yellow or creamy-white corolla, 7—11.8 cm. long, by the oblong to oblong-obovate leaves, slightly bullate above, usually laxly scaly below, the scales being 1—3 times their own diameter apart, and by the rather densely or sometimes moderately pubescent pedicel. A distinct feature of the species (and all the members of its Subseries except *R. megacalyx* and rarely *R. nuttallii*) is the ovary tapered into the style. *R. dalhousiae* resembles *R. rhabdotum* in general features, but is readily distinguished by the flower colour. The species is diploid, 2 n = 26.

The species was first introduced by J.D. Hooker in the spring of 1850. It was first flowered three years later in March 1853, at Dysart House, Kirkcaldy, Fife, Scotland, by Mr. John Laing, gardener to the Earl of Rosslyn. The flowers were 4½ inches long; the same plant was figured by W.J. Hooker in the *Botanical Magazine* t. 4718 (1853). In cultivation and in its native home, the flower is usually smaller. The species is tender in cultivation, and is suitable for a cool greenhouse. It is free-flowering, and is of exquisite beauty when adorned with large yellow or creamy-white flowers in trusses of three to five. The species was given an Award of Merit when shown by Adm. A. Walker Heneage-Vivian, Clyne Castle, Swansea, in 1930. The same Award was given for a form 'Tom Spring-Smyth' in 1974, and a First Class Certificate for a form 'Frank Ludlow' (Ludlow, Sherriff and Taylor No. 6694) also in 1974 when exhibited on both occasions by Major A.E. Hardy, Sandling Park, Hythe.

Epithet. After Lady Dalhousie, wife of the Governor-General of India.

Hardiness 1—2. April—June. Plate 50.

R. goreri Davidian in Quart. Bull. Amer. Rhod. Soc. Vol. 34, October (1980) 213.

A lax upright shrub, or tree, 1.22—4.58 m. (4—15 ft.) high; older stem and branches with dark purplish bark; branchlets rather densely scaly with very large scales, not bristly. *Leaves* elliptic, oblong-oval, oblong-elliptic or ovate-oblong, lamina coriaceous, 14.5—24.5 cm. long, 5.8—12 cm. broad, apex rounded or obtuse, mucronate, base obtuse or rounded; *upper surface pale green, (young growths pale green), not bullate or somewhat bullate*, reticulate, somewhat shining, scaly or not scaly, midrib grooved, primary veins 14—18 on each side, deeply impressed; margin not bristly; *under surface pale green, not wrinkled or slightly wrinkled*, densely scaly, the scales unequal, small, or medium-sized and large, with widely scattered large scales, brown or dark brown, ½ to their own diameter apart, midrib prominent, *primary veins* thin or thick, raised, *not looped and not branched*; petiole 2—3.1 cm. long, thick, convex, not grooved above, densely scaly with very large scales, not bristly. *Inflorescence* terminal, umbellate, 3—5-flowered; rhachis 3—5 mm. long, scaly, not bristly; pedicel 2.8—3 cm. long, lengthening considerably in fruit, very thick, scaly, glabrous, not bristly. *Calyx* 5-lobed to the base, 1.6—2 cm. long, green, lobes oblong-oval or oval, 7—9 mm. or rarely 1.2 cm. broad, outside scaly with very large scales, glabrous, margin eciliate. *Corolla* tubular-campanulate, *7—7.6 cm. long*, fleshy, 5-lobed, lobes rounded, margins slightly crinkled, creamy-white, yellowish at the base of the tube within, scaly all over the outside, glabrous outside. *Stamens* 10, unequal, *3.6—4.3 cm. long*, shorter than the corolla-tube; filaments densely hairy in the lower ⅓ their length; *anthers 2—3 mm. long*. *Ovary* ovate, tapered into the style, 8—9 mm. long, 5-celled, densely scaly, glabrous; style long, straight or curved in the upper part, 4.8—5 cm. in length, shorter than the corolla, scaly in the lower ⅓—½ its length, stigma 5—6 mm. in diameter, disc-like. *Capsule* oblong, 4—5 cm. long, 1.3—2 cm. broad, slightly curved or straight, ribbed, rather densely scaly, glabrous, longer than the calyx, not enclosed by the calyx-lobes.

This species was first found by Ludlow, Sherriff and Elliot in January 1947 at Trulung, Pome province, south-east Tibet. It was collected by them again in June of the same year in the Po-Tsangpo Valley in the same region. The plant grows in dense mixed forest at elevations of 2,135—2,288 m. (7,000—7,500 ft.).

R. goreri resembles *R. nuttallii* in some features, but differs markedly in that the upper surface of the leaf is pale green, not bullate or somewhat bullate, the lower surface is pale green, not wrinkled or slightly wrinkled, the primary veins are not markedly raised, not looped and not branched, the young growths are pale green, the pedicel and the outside of the calyx are not pubescent, the corolla is smaller, the stamens are shorter, and the anthers are smaller.

The species was introduced by Ludlow, Sherriff and Elliot in 1947 (No. 12117). In its native home it is a shrub or tree up to 15 feet high; in cultivation it is a lax upright shrub and grows up to 5 feet. The plant is tender, and is suitable for a cool greenhouse. It is a robust grower, and makes a fine show with its tubular-campanulate flowers in trusses of three to five. The species received an Award of Merit when exhibited by the Sunningdale Nurseries, Windlesham, Surrey in 1955 as *R. sinonuttallii* (L.S & E. No. 12117).

Epithet. After G.E. Gorer, Sunte House, Haywards Heath, Sussex.
Hardiness 1. May—June. Plate 49.

R. grothausii Davidian in Quart. Bull. Amer. Rhod. Soc. Vol. 34, October (1980) 211.

A broadly upright or upright shrub, sometimes epiphytic, 1.22—4.58 m. (4—15 ft.) high; branchlets moderately or rather densely scaly, not bristly. *Leaves* oblong or oblong-lanceolate, lamina coriaceous, 6.5—11.5 cm. long, 2.8—4.4 cm. broad, apex rounded or obtuse, mucronate, base rounded or obtuse; *upper surface* dark green, shining or somewhat shining, *bullate*, scaly or not scaly, midrib grooved, primary veins 8—10 on each side, deeply impressed; margin not bristly; under surface glaucous, laxly scaly, the scales unequal, medium-sized or large, brown or dark brown, 2—4 times their own diameter apart, midrib prominent, primary veins raised; petiole 1—2 cm. long, convex, not grooved above, densely or moderately scaly, not bristly. *Inflorescence* terminal, umbellate, *flower-bud reddish-brown* (the upper half of the bud-scales) *turning crimson-purple later*, 3—8-flowered; rhachis 2—5 mm. long, scaly, not bristly; pedicels 0.8—1.8 cm. long, thick or somewhat thick, rather densely scaly, not bristly. *Calyx* 5-lobed, 1—1.5 cm. long, pale green, green or pink, lobes oblong-oval, oblong or oval, outside not scaly or rarely sparsely scaly at the base, glabrous, margin moderately or rarely densely fringed with white hairs. *Corolla* narrowly tubular-campanulate or tubular-campanulate, slightly ventricose, *5.3—7.5 cm. long*, 5-lobed, lobes rounded, emarginate or not emarginate, margins of the lobes entire, fragrant, white, or white tinged pink on a few petals, or cream, or pink, with a yellowish-orange or orange or yellowish blotch at the base, outside not scaly or scaly at the base of the tube or rarely scaly all over the outside, glabrous outside. *Stamens* 10, unequal, 3—5.2 cm. long, shorter than the corolla; filaments densely hairy in the lower ¼—⅓ their length; anthers 4—5 mm. long. *Ovary* oblong, tapered into the style, 8—9 mm. long, 5-celled, densely scaly, glabrous; style long, straight or curved in the upper part, 3—5.5 cm. in length, shorter than the corolla, scaly in the lower ¼—⅓ its length, stigma 4 mm. in diameter, disc-like. *Capsule* oblong, 4—4.4 cm. long, 1.3—1.5 cm. broad, straight or slightly curved, ribbed, rather densely scaly, glabrous, calyx-lobes persistent.

This plant has for long been confused with *R. lindleyi*. It was discovered by Ludlow and Sherriff in March 1936 at Migyitun, Tsari Chu, south Tibet. They found it again later in Bhutan, and with Hicks in another locality also in Bhutan. It grows hanging over cliffs or river banks, and in Tsuga forest, sometimes as an epiphyte on trees, at elevations of 2,593—2,745 m. (8,500—9,000 ft.). Ludlow and Sherriff record it as being common at Migyitun, south Tibet at 2,593 m. (8,500 ft.).

The species is allied to *R. lindleyi* from which it differs markedly in that the corolla is smaller, 5.3—7.5 cm. long, the leaves (laminae) are usually smaller, bullate on the upper surfaces, and the flower-buds are reddish-brown turning crimson-purple later.

It was introduced by Ludlow and Sherriff in 1936. In cultivation it has proved hardy outdoors along the west coast, and flourishes in several gardens. A remarkable collection of the species is found at Glenarn, Rhu, Dunbartonshire, in the garden of the Gibson family. Along the east coast it is well represented in Mr. and Mrs. Hamish Gunn's greenhouse, at Colinton, Edinburgh. In its native home it grows 4—15 feet high; in cultivation it is broadly upright and reaches 6 or 7 feet, usually with oblong leaves. One of its chief merits is that it flowers at an early age when raised from seed. The species is a late flowerer, the flowers appearing in May or June. It is free-flowering, and is of great beauty with its tubular-campanulate flowers in trusses of three to eight. A form strongly flushed pink and named 'Geordie Sherriff' was given an Award of Merit when shown by Messrs. A.C. and J.F.A. Gibson, Glenarn, Rhu, Dunbartonshire, in 1969.

Epithet. After Mr. & Mrs. Louis C. Grothaus, Lake Oswego, Oregon, U.S.A.
Hardiness 1—3. May—June. Plate 48.

R. headfortianum Hutch. in Bot. Mag. Vol. 163 t. 9614 (1942).

A *small or dwarf, somewhat slender, upright shrub,* often epiphytic, *15 cm.—1.22 m. (6 in.—4 ft.)* high; branchlets scaly, not bristly. *Leaves narrowly oblong or oblong-lanceolate,* lamina coriaceous, 7—12 cm. long, *2—4.5 cm. broad,* apex obtuse or rounded, mucronate, *base* cuneate or obtuse, *slightly decurrent on the petiole;* upper surface dark green or bright green, somewhat shining, not scaly or scaly, midrib grooved, primary veins 8—10 on each side, deeply impressed; *margin recurved;* under surface glaucous, scaly, the scales unequal, large and medium-sized, brown, 2—3 times their own diameter apart, midrib prominent, primary veins raised; petiole 1.5—2 cm. long, convex, not grooved above, margins slightly ridged at the apex, scaly, not bristly. *Inflorescence terminal, umbellate, 1—3-flowered;* rhachis 2—3 mm. long, densely scaly; pedicel 1.3—2 cm. long, thick, densely scaly, glabrous. *Calyx* 5-lobed, 1.3—1.5 cm. long, lobes oblong-oval or ovate-elliptic, outside scaly along the middle of the lobes, glabrous, margin sparsely scaly or not scaly, glabrous. *Corolla* tubular-campanulate, *5.5—7 cm. long,* 5-lobed, margins of the lobes entire, *creamy-yellow,* or creamy slightly tinged pink outside the top of the tube, outside rather densely scaly at the base of the tube, not scaly above, glabrous outside. *Stamens* 10, unequal, 4.6—4.8 cm. long, shorter than the corolla; filaments densely hairy in the lower ⅓ their length; anthers 5 mm. long. *Ovary* oblong, tapered into the style, 5—7 mm. long, 5-celled, densely scaly, glabrous; style long, straight or curved in the upper part, 4.7—5 cm. in length, shorter than the corolla, scaly in the lower ¼ its length, stigma large, lobulate. *Capsule* oblong, 4.3—5 cm. long, 8—9 mm. broad, straight, ribbed, densely scaly, glabrous, calyx-lobes persistent.

Kingdon-Ward discovered this plant in fruit (No. 6310) in November 1924 in the Tsangpo Gorge, south-east Tibet. He found it again in fruit (No. 8546) in 1928 in Assam. The plant grows on gneiss cliffs, on boulders, in thickets, and amongst scrub, at elevations of 2,135—2,745 m. (7,000—9,000 ft.). It is recorded also as an epiphyte, fairly widespread in the forest.

The species was described by Hutchinson in 1942 from a cultivated plant raised by Lord Headfort in County Meath, Eire, from Kingdon-Ward seed No. 6310.

R. headfortianum is a distinct species and cannot be confused with any other species of its Subseries. It is a dwarf or small, slender shrub, 6 inches to 4 feet high. The leaves are a diagnostic feature, being narrowly oblong or oblong-lanceolate, usually 2—3 cm. broad, slightly decurrent on the petiole, with recurved margins, laxly scaly on the lower surface, the scales 2—3 times their own diameter apart. Other characteristic features are the 1—3-flowered inflorescence, and the creamy-yellow flowers, 5.5—7 cm. long. The species shows a certain degree of resemblance to *R. grothausii,* but differs markedly in distinctive features.

In its native home, *R. headfortianum* grows from 6 inches to 3 feet high, but in cultivation it reaches a height of 3—4 feet. Since it grows at elevations of up to 8,000—9,000 feet, the plant succeeds in sheltered gardens along the west coast, particularly in Northern Ireland, but along the east coast it needs the protection of the glasshouse. The plant is uncommon in cultivation.

Epithet. After the late Marquess of Headfort.

Hardiness 1—2. May.

R. kiangsiense Fang in Acta Phytotax. Sinica, Vol. VII, May (1958) 192.

A shrub, 1 m. (3⅓ ft.) high; stem and branches with rough bark, branchlets green or pale green, scaly. *Leaves oblong-elliptic, lamina coriaceous, 4—5 cm. long,* 2—2.5 cm. broad, apex obtuse, mucronate, base obtuse or narrowed; upper surface green, not scaly, midrib grooved, primary veins 8—9 on each side, deeply impressed; margin slightly recurved; under surface pale glaucous-green, scaly, the scales golden, 1—2 times their own diameter apart, midrib raised, primary veins raised; *petiole 3—5 mm. long,* upper surface flat, under surface rounded, scaly, sparsely pilose. *Inflorescence* terminal, subumbellate, 2-flowered; pedicel 1—1.4 cm. long, robust, brown, densely scaly. *Calyx* 5-lobed, 7—8 mm. long, lobes ovate, outside scaly, margin wavy. *Corolla widely funnel-shaped, 6—6.2 cm. long,* 4 cm. in diameter, 5-lobed, lobes rounded, margin wavy, white, *outside sparsely scaly. Stamens 8, 2.5 cm. long;* filaments pubescent in the lower ⅓ their length; anthers oblong-linear. *Ovary* conoid, 6 mm. long, densely scaly; *style 3.5 cm. long,* scaly at the base, stigma capitate. *Capsule: —*

This species was described by Fang in 1958 from a plant collected in 1954 on the slopes of the hills in Kiangsi, at an elevation of 1,100 m. (3,607 ft.).

In the original diagnosis, it is associated with *R. liliiflorum*. From this plant it is readily distinguished by the smaller oblong-elliptic leaves, the shorter petioles, the smaller corolla sparsely scaly on the outside, the 8 shorter stamens 2.5 cm. long, and by the shorter style. The species has not been introduced into cultivation.

Epithet. From Kiangsi, China.

Not in cultivation.

R. levinei Merrill in Philipp. Journ. Sci. XIII (1918) 153.

A shrub or small tree, 2—4 m. (6½—13 ft.) high; *branchlets scaly, bristly or not bristly. Leaves oblong or oblong-oval,* lamina coriaceous, 5—7.3 cm. long, 2—3.6 cm. broad, *apex rounded,* mucronate, *base rounded;* upper surface dark green, somewhat shining, scaly or not scaly, midrib grooved, primary veins 8—10 on each side, deeply impressed; *margin* recurved or flat, *bristly in the basal half or at the base* or not bristly; under surface densely scaly, the *scales* unequal, medium-sized and large, brown or dark brown, *their own diameter apart,* midrib prominent, primary veins raised; *petiole* 0.8—1.3 cm. long, convex, not grooved above, moderately or rather densely scaly, *bristly. Inflorescence* terminal, umbellate, 1—3-flowered; rhachis 1—3 mm. long, scaly, not bristly; pedicel 0.8—1.5 cm. long, thick, densely scaly, glabrous. *Calyx* 5-lobed, 0.7—1 cm. long, lobes ovate, oval or oblong-oval, outside scaly along the middle or at the base, glabrous, margin not scaly, glabrous. *Corolla tubular-campanulate, 4.5—7 cm. long,* 5-lobed, margins of the lobes entire, fragrant, white or creamy-white, outside moderately or sparsely scaly, glabrous. *Stamens* 10, unequal, 2.6—5 cm. long, shorter than the corolla; filaments densely or moderately hairy in the lower ⅓—½ their length; anthers 5 mm. long. *Ovary* oblong-ovate, tapered into the style, 5 mm. long, 5-celled, densely scaly, glabrous; style long, straight or curved in the upper part, 3.5—4.5 cm. in length, shorter than the corolla, scaly in the lower ¼ its length, stigma small, 3 mm. in diameter, lobulate. *Capsule: —*

R. levinei was described by Merrill in 1918 from fruiting material collected in 1917 on Loh Fau Mountain, Kwantung. It grows at an elevation of 900—950 m. (2,951—3,115 ft.).

The diagnostic features of the species are the oblong or oblong-oval leaves, rounded at the apex and base, the bristly petiole and often the bristly branchlets and margins of the leaves. Other distinguishing characters are the tubular-campanulate corolla, 4.5—7 cm. long, the calyx 0.7—1 cm. long, and the densely scaly lower surface of the leaves, the scales being their own diameter apart. The species resembles *R. kiangsiense* in some features, but is distinguished by well-marked characters. The plant has not been introduced into cultivation.

Epithet. After Mr. Levine, a collector.

Not in cultivation.

R. liliiflorum Léveillé in Fedde Repert. XII (1913) 102.

A shrub or tree, 3—8 m. (10—26 ft.) high; branchlets moderately or rather densely scaly, not bristly. *Leaves oblong-lanceolate or oblong,* lamina coriaceous, *7—16 cm. long,* 2—5.1 cm. broad, apex obtuse or rounded, mucronate, base cuneate, obtuse or rounded; upper surface dark green, somewhat matt, not scaly, midrib grooved, primary veins 10—18 on each side, deeply impressed; margin not bristly; under surface pale glaucous-green, scaly, the scales unequal, medium-sized or large or small, brown, 1—3 times their own diameter apart, midrib prominent, primary veins raised; petiole 1.5—3 cm. long, convex, not grooved above, moderately or rather densely scaly, not bristly. *Inflorescence* terminal, umbellate, 2—3-flowered; rhachis 3—4 mm. long, scaly, not bristly; pedicel 1.2—1.6 cm. long, thick, densely scaly, glabrous. *Calyx* 5-lobed, 0.8—1 cm. long, lobes oblong-oval or oval, outside scaly or scaly at the base, glabrous, margin scaly or not scaly, glabrous. *Corolla* tubular-campanulate, *8.2—9 cm. long,* 5-lobed, margins of the lobes entire, fragrant, white, *rather densely scaly all over the outside,* glabrous outside. *Stamens* 10, unequal, 4.8—5.7 cm. long, shorter than the corolla; filaments densely hairy in the lower ⅓ their length; *anthers 6—7 mm. long. Ovary* oblong, tapered into the style, 1 cm. long, 5-celled, densely scaly, glabrous; *style* long, straight or curved in the upper part, *6—6.4 cm. in length,* shorter than the corolla, rather densely scaly in the lower half, stigma large, 5 mm. in diameter, lobulate. *Capsule* oblong, oblique at the base, *2.6—4.5 cm. long,* *1.2—1.3 cm. broad,* curved or straight, ribbed, densely scaly, glabrous, calyx-lobes persistent.

R. liliiflorum was first collected by Cavalérie in June 1902 at Fin-Fa, Kweichow. It was later found by other collectors in different localities in the same region. The plant grows in open ridges, in scrubs, in woods, and on rocky shaded slopes, at elevations of 600—1,400 m. (1,967—4,590 ft.).

The main features of the species are the oblong-lanceolate or oblong leaves (laminae) 7—16 cm. long, the large corolla 8.2—9 cm. long, rather densely scaly all over the outside, and the large capsule 2.6—4.5 cm. long. It is allied to *R. kiangsiense.* The distinctions between them are discussed under the latter. It also shows a resemblance to *R. basfordii* but differs in the larger corolla, rather densely scaly all over the outside, the margins of the lobes being entire, in the larger capsule, and in the longer anthers and style. It further differs in its geographical distribution. There is no record of the species in cultivation.

Epithet. With lily-like flowers.

Not in cultivation.

R. lindleyi T. Moore in Gard. Chron. (1864) 364.

Illustration. Bot. Mag. n. s. Vol. 173 t. 363 (1960—62).

A straggly or upright shrub, often epiphytic, 76 cm.—3.66 m. (2½—12 ft.) or rarely up to 4.58 m. (15 ft.) high; branchlets moderately or rather densely scaly, not bristly. *Leaves* oblong or oblong-lanceolate, rarely oblong-elliptic or oblong-obovate, *lamina* coriaceous, *6.5—14 cm. or rarely up to 19.6 cm. long, 2.1—5.5 cm. or rarely up to 6 cm. broad,* apex rounded or obtuse, mucronate, base obtuse, cuneate or rounded; *upper surface* dark green, somewhat shining or matt, *reticulate, not bullate,* not scaly, midrib grooved, primary veins 10—14 on each side, deeply impressed; margin not bristly; under surface glaucous or pale glaucous-green, laxly scaly, the scales unequal, medium-sized or large, brown or dark brown, 2—4 times their own diameter apart, midrib prominent, primary veins raised; petiole 1—2 cm. or rarely 3 cm. long, convex, not grooved above, rather densely or moderately scaly, not bristly. *Inflorescence* terminal, umbellate, *flower-bud pale green*, 3—6-flowered; rhachis 3—5 mm. long, scaly, not bristly; pedicel 1—2.5 cm. long, somewhat thick or thick, densely or moderately scaly, glabrous. *Calyx* 5-lobed, 1—2 cm. long, lobes oblong, oblong-oval or oblong-ovate, outside finely striate, not scaly or rarely sparsely scaly at the base, glabrous, margin not scaly, densely or sometimes moderately fringed with white hairs. *Corolla broadly tubular-campanulate, 7—11.6 cm. long*, 5-lobed, lobes rounded, emarginate or not emarginate, margins of the lobes entire, fragrant, white or rarely yellow-white, with or without a golden or golden-yellow blotch at the base, outside scaly at the base of the tube or not scaly, glabrous or rarely pubescent at the base of the tube outside. *Stamens* 10, unequal, 4.5—7.2 cm. long, shorter than the corolla; filaments densely hairy in the lower ⅓ their length; anthers large, 5—9 mm. long. *Ovary* oblong, tapered into the style, 0.8—1 cm. long, 5-celled, densely scaly, glabrous; style long, straight or curved in the upper part, 5—7.2 cm. in length, shorter than the corolla, scaly at the base or in the lower ⅓ its length, stigma 4—6 mm. in diameter, disc-like. *Capsule* oblong, 4.2—5 cm. long, 1.2—1.4 cm. broad, straight or slightly curved, ribbed, rather densely scaly, glabrous, calyx-lobes persistent.

J.D. Hooker discovered this plant in 1848—49 in Sikkim, but he confused it with *R. dalhousiae*. An account of the confusion is given by Hutchinson in *Notes Roy. Bot. Gard. Edin.*, Vol. 12 (1919) 10—11. The species was described by Thomas Moore in 1864 from a plant grown in Standish's nursery at Ascot, raised from seeds collected in Bhutan. T.J. Booth, who was in Bhutan in 1849—1860, is said to have collected the seeds. Further gatherings by other collectors show that the plant is distributed in Nepal, Sikkim, Bhutan, Assam, and south Tibet. It grows in dense mixed forest, in mossy rain-forest, and on rocks, at elevations of 2,135—3,355 m. (7,000—11,000 ft.). Sir George Watt records it as being common in Magnolia forests in Sikkim. According to Ludlow and Sherriff it makes a wonderful show on big rocks in south Tibet. Kingdon-Ward points out that it is common in Tsuga-Rhododendron forest, and is also a common epiphyte in the upper temperate rain-forest in Assam.

The diagnostic features of the species are the large corolla usually 7.8—11.6 cm. long, the long leaves (laminae) usually 9—14 cm. in length, the upper surface reticulate, not bullate, and the pale green flower-buds. In these respects, it is readily distinguished from its ally *R. grothausii*. It is also closely related to *R. taggianum*, but differs in that the leaves are oblong or oblong-lanceolate, the upper surface is reticulate, not bullate, and the margin of the calyx-lobes is densely or sometimes moderately fringed with white hairs. The plant is a diploid with 26 chromosomes. *R. bhotanicum* C.B. Clarke is a synonym of *R. lindleyi*.

Some plants in cultivation under the name *R. lindleyi* introduced by Ludlow and Sherriff, are in fact forms of *R. grothausii*. In its native home it grows 2½—12 feet or rarely up to 15 feet high, but in cultivation it reaches a height of only 8 feet. Along the west coast the plant succeeds outdoors in a few well-sheltered gardens, but along the east coast it requires the protection of the greenhouse. It is an exceptionally fine plant with its broadly tubular-campanulate fragrant flowers produced freely in trusses of three to six. It is worth noting that the true *R. lindleyi* with large flowers about 11.6 cm. long and long oblong-lanceolate leaves, (laminae) about 14 cm. long, is uncommon in cultivation. The species received an Award of Merit when exhibited by Mr. L. de Rothschild in 1935, and again the same Award was given to a form 'Dame Edith Sitwell' when shown by Mr. G.E. Gorer, Sunte House, Haywards Heath, in 1965. It received a First Class Certificate when exhibited by Adm. A. Walker Heneage-Vivian, Clyne Castle, Swansea, in 1937.

Epithet. After Dr. John Lindley, 1799—1865 botanist and Secretary to the R.H.S.
Hardiness 1—2. May—June.

R. megacalyx Balf. f. et Ward in Notes Roy. Bot. Gard. Edin., Vol. 9 (1916) 246.

Illustration. Bot. Mag. Vol. 156 t. 9326 (1933).

A straggly or bushy or broadly upright shrub or tree, 1.22—7.63 m. (4—25 ft.) high; branchlets dark brownish-purple or sometimes green, scaly, not bristly. *Leaves* oblong-oval, oblong-obovate, obovate, oblong, elliptic or oblong-elliptic, lamina coriaceous, 9.8—16.8 cm. long, 3—7.5 cm. broad, apex rounded or sometimes broadly obtuse, with a sunken mucro, base rounded or obtuse; *upper surface* bright green or olive-green, matt or somewhat matt, *bullate* or somewhat bullate, not scaly or scaly, midrib grooved, primary veins 14—16 on each side, deeply impressed; margin not bristly; *under surface* glaucous, densely scaly, the scales unequal, medium-sized, or medium-sized and large, or small, brown or dark brown, sunken, ½ to their own diameter apart, midrib prominent, *primary veins thick, markedly raised; petiole* 1—2.5 cm. long, rounded, *grooved above*, dark purple or sometimes green, densely scaly, not bristly. *Inflorescence* terminal, very shortly racemose, 3—6- or rarely 7-flowered; rhachis 4—8 mm. long, not scaly, not bristly; *pedicel* 1.8—3.2 cm. long, thick, lengthening considerably in fruit, dark purple or purple or green, glaucous or not glaucous, *not scaly*, not bristly. *Calyx broadly campanulate, divided to about the middle*, 5-lobed, 1.7—2.6 cm. long, dark purple or sometimes pale green, *lobes* oval or oblong-oval, *1.2—1.8 cm. broad*, outside glaucous or sometimes not glaucous, *not scaly*, glabrous, margin glabrous. *Corolla* tubular-campanulate, 7.5—11 cm. long, 5-lobed, lobes rounded, margins entire, fragrant, white or white flushed purplish-rose or creamy-white or cream tinged pink, outside scaly, glabrous. *Stamens* 10, unequal, 3—5.8 cm. long, shorter than the corolla-tube; filaments densely hairy in the lower ¼—⅓ their length; anthers 4—5 mm. long. *Ovary* oblong-oval, ovate or broadly conoid, *apex truncate*, 7—9 mm. long, 5-celled, densely scaly, glabrous; style long, straight or curved in the upper part, 5—8 cm. in length, shorter than the corolla, scaly at the base, stigma 4—6 mm. in diameter, disc-like. *Capsule* oblong-oval or oval, *1.8—2.5 cm. long*, 1—1.5 cm. broad, *shorter than the calyx*, ribbed, densely scaly, glabrous, *enclosed by the persistent calyx-lobes.*

R. *megacalyx* was first collected by Kingdon-Ward in June 1914 in the Nwai Valley, north-east Upper Burma. Subsequently it was found by other collectors in north-east and north Burma, eastern Tibet, and in west and mid-west Yunnan. It grows in the rain forest by streams, in scrub, on cliffs, in open thickets and cane brakes, on the margins of forests, and in woods, at elevations of 1,830—3,965 m. (6,000—13,000 ft.). According to Farrer, it is abundant in masses overhanging a sheer granite cliff at one point of a gorge, above Nyitadi, north-east Upper Burma.

A striking character of this plant is the large broadly campanulate calyx, divided to about the middle, with very large lobes 1.2—1.8 cm. broad. Another diagnostic feature is the short capsule, shorter than the calyx, and completely enclosed by the calyx-lobes. Other distinctive features are the petiole grooved above, the non-scaly pedicel, and the ovary truncate at the apex. In all these respects R. *megacalyx* is readily distinguished from all other members of its Subseries. Other marked characteristics are the bullate or somewhat bullate upper surface of the leaves, the thick lateral veins markedly raised on the lower surface of the leaves, the large tubular-campanulate corolla, 7.5—11 cm. long, and the non-scaly calyx. The plant is a diploid with 26 chromosomes.

The species was first introduced by Forrest in 1917 (No. 15774) from western Yunnan at 11,000—12,000 feet. It was reintroduced on many occasions by Forrest, Farrer, Kingdon-Ward, Rock, and Yü from elevations of 6,000—13,000 feet. In its native home it is a shrub or tree 4—25 feet high; in cultivation it is a broadly upright or bushy shrub and grows up to 8 feet. Along the west coast it is successfully cultivated in well-sheltered gardens, but along the east coast it needs greenhouse conditions. The plant is exceedingly charming when laden with large tubular-campanulate very fragrant flowers. It received an Award of Merit when exhibited by Adm. Walker Heneage-Vivian, Clyne Castle, Swansea, in 1937.

Epithet. Large calyx.
Hardiness 1—2. April—June.

R. nuttallii Booth in Hook. Kew Journ. Bot. Vol. 5 (1853) 355.
Illustration. Bot. Mag. Vol. 85 t. 5146 (1859).

A straggly or upright shrub or tree, sometimes epiphytic, 1.22—9.15 m. (4—30 ft.) high; stem and branches with smooth, dark purplish-brown bark; branchlets rather densely or moderately scaly with very large scales, not bristly. *Leaves* elliptic or oblong-elliptic, lamina coriaceous, 13.2—26.5 cm. long, 5—13.1 cm. broad, apex rounded or obtuse or abruptly acute, mucronate, base rounded or obtuse; *upper surface* dark green, (*young growths crimson-purple*), *strongly bullate*, reticulate, somewhat matt, not scaly or scaly, midrib grooved, primary veins 12—18 on each side, deeply impressed; margin not bristly; *under surface* pale glaucous-green, *conspicuously wrinkled*, scaly, the scales unequal, small and medium-sized, or medium-sized, with closely or widely scattered large scales, brown or dark brown, ½—1½ or sometimes 2 times their own diameter apart, midrib prominent, *primary veins thick, markedly raised, prominently looped and branched*; petiole 1.5—2.9 cm. long, thick, convex, not grooved above, rather densely or moderately scaly with very large scales, not bristly. *Inflorescence* terminal, umbellate, 3—7- or rarely up to 12-flowered; rhachis 3—6 mm. long, scaly, not bristly; *pedicel* 1.4—3.5 cm. long, lengthening considerably in fruit, very thick, scaly with very large scales, *moderately or rather densely pubescent* or rarely glabrous, not bristly. *Calyx* 5-lobed to the base, 1.6—2.6 cm. long, pale green, lobes oblong-oval or oblong, upright, 0.7—1.4 cm. broad, *outside* scaly with very large scales or rarely slightly scaly at the base or rarely not scaly, *rather densely pubescent* or rarely glabrous, margin eciliate or rarely ciliate. *Corolla* tubular-campanulate, *8.7—13.6 cm. long*, fleshy, 5-lobed, lobes rounded, margins slightly crinkled or rarely entire, fragrant, white; or creamy-white suffused greenish, the petals or the corolla tinged pink; or white flushed rose; with a yellow or golden-orange blotch at the base, moderately or rarely rather densely scaly all over the outside or rarely sparsely scaly, outside glabrous or rarely pubescent on the tube. *Stamens* 10, unequal, *4.5—9.5 cm. long*, as long as, or shorter than, the corolla-tube; filaments densely hairy in the lower ⅓—½ their length; *anthers 0.7—1.3 cm. long*, dark brown. *Ovary* oblong, oblong-oval, conoid or ovoid, tapered or rarely somewhat tapered into the style, 0.8—1.5 cm. long, 5-celled, densely scaly, glabrous; style long, straight or curved in the upper part, 6.2—9 cm. in length, shorter than the corolla, scaly in the lower ⅓—½ its length or rarely at the base, stigma 6—9 mm. in diameter, disc-like. *Capsule* oblong or sometimes oval, oblique at the base, 1.8—7.2 cm. long, 1.3—2.5 cm. broad, longer or rarely shorter than the calyx, slightly curved or straight, ribbed, rather densely scaly, glabrous, calyx-lobes persistent.

This species was discovered by T.J. Booth in 1849—50 in the Duphla Hills, Assam, growing on the banks of the Papoo, amongst yews and oaks. Further gatherings by other collectors show that the plant has a wide area of distribution, extending from Bhutan and Assam to south-east and east Tibet, Upper Burma and north-west Yunnan. It grows in swampy ground, in mossy wet ground, on boulders, on cliffs and rocky slopes, in open conifer and spruce forests, in thickets, and on the margins of mixed forest, at elevations of 1,220—4,423 m. (4,000—14,500 ft.). Kingdon-Ward records it as being fairly common in the Taron Valley, north-west Yunnan, at 1,830—2,135 m. (6,000—7,000 ft.).

In 1920, *R. sinonuttallii* Balf. f. et Forrest was described from a specimen (No. 18939) collected by Forrest in the Salwin-Kiu-Chiang divide, south-east Tibet. The ample material now available and plants in cultivation show that the species is identical in general characters with *R. nuttallii* under which it will now appear in synonymy.

R. nuttallii is easily recognised by the dark green leaves, the upper surfaces being strongly bullate, the lower surfaces conspicuously wrinkled, and the primary veins markedly raised and prominently looped and branched. It is also distinguished by the crimson-purple young growths, by the pedicel and the outside of the calyx which are usually rather densely or moderately pubescent, by the large corolla, and the long stamens. In these respects, the species differs markedly from its ally *R. goreri*. A notable characteristic is the large elliptic or oblong-elliptic leaf, 13.2—26.5 cm. long, 5—13.1 cm. broad. The species is a diploid with 26 chromosomes.

R. nuttallii was first introduced by T.J. Booth in 1852 from Assam. It was reintroduced many times by Forrest, Kingdon-Ward, Rock, and Yü from south-east Tibet, Assam, north-east Upper Burma, and north-west Yunnan from 1,600—3,660 m. (5,245—12,000 ft.). Although the plant comes from high elevations, it is tender and needs the protection of a cool greenhouse. It first flowered in 1858 with Otto Forster of Augsberg. In May 1859, it flowered at Kew when 9 feet high; one of the branches is recorded as having a truss of 12 flowers. In cultivation the plant is straggly or upright up to 10 feet high or more, although in its native home it is a shrub or tree, sometimes epiphytic, 4—30 feet in height. An attractive feature is the smooth, dark purplish-brown bark of the stem and branches. Among the most remarkable characteristics are the crimson-purple young growths which always attract attention. The flowers are large, 8.7—13.6 cm. long, white or creamy-white with a yellow blotch at the base, for which the large dark green foliage provides an effective contrast. *R. nuttallii* is a most charming plant, and is generally regarded as being one of the best of its Series. It was given a First Class Certificate when shown by the Victoria Nursery, Highgate, in 1864.

Epithet. After Thomas Nuttall, botanist and traveller, 1786—1859.

Hardiness 1. April—May.

R. nuttallii Booth var. **stellatum** Hutch. in Gard. Chron. Vol. CI, February (1937) 119.

The variety was described by Hutchinson in 1937 from a plant grown by Mr. Lionel de Rothschild at Exbury House. It was raised from seeds collected by Kingdon-Ward under No. 6333 in December 1924 in the Tsangpo Gorge, Tibet. The plant grows in thickets and on the margins of the lower forest at elevations of 1,525—1,830 m. (5,000—6,000 ft.). Kingdon-Ward states that it is a small tree 4.58—6.10 m. (15—20 ft.) high with smooth coppery-purple bark.

The variety differs from the species in its spreading calyx and smaller sweetly-scented flowers. It received an Award of Merit when exhibited by Mr. Lionel de Rothschild in 1936 (K.W. No. 6333).

Epithet of the variety. Stellate, referring to spreading calyx-lobes.

Hardiness 1. April—May.

R. rhabdotum Balf. f. et Cooper in Notes Roy. Bot. Gard. Edin., Vol. 10 (1917) 141.

Illustration. Bot. Mag. Vol. 159 t. 9447 (1936).

A straggly or lax upright shrub, or tree, often epiphytic, 92 cm.—3.66 m. (3—12 ft.) high; stem and older branches with reddish-brown bark; branchlets scaly, moderately or sparsely bristly. *Leaves* oblong or obovate, rarely oval or elliptic, lamina coriaceous, 5.2—17 cm. long, 2.2—7.4 cm. broad, apex rounded or obtuse, mucronate, base cuneate, rounded or obtuse; *upper surface* bright green or dark green, *slightly bullate*, somewhat shining, not scaly, midrib grooved, primary veins 9—12 on each side, deeply impressed; margins not bristly or bristly in the lower half or at the base; under surface glaucous or glaucous-green, scaly, the scales unequal, medium-sized and large, or small and medium-sized, brown or dark brown, 2—3 times or rarely their own diameter apart, midrib prominent, primary veins raised; petiole 0.8—1.8 cm. long, convex, not grooved above, moderately or rather densely scaly, not bristly or moderately or sparsely bristly. *Inflorescence* terminal, umbellate, 2—5-flowered; rhachis 2—3 mm. long, scaly, not bristly or rarely bristly; *pedicel* 0.8—1.8 cm. long, thick, rather densely or moderately scaly, *rather densely or sometimes moderately pubescent*, not bristly or rarely sparsely bristly. *Calyx* 5-lobed, 0.7—1.8 cm. long, lobes oblong, oblong-oval or ovate-oblong, 4—8 mm. broad, outside scaly at the base or sometimes along the middle of the lobes, hairy along the middle of the lobes or rarely glabrous, margin glabrous. *Corolla* tubular-campanulate,

7—11 cm. long, 5-lobed, lobes rounded, margins entire, fragrant, cream, pale yellow or white, *marked with five conspicuous red stripes outside*, with or without a golden blotch at the base of the tube within, not scaly or rarely scaly at the base of the tube outside, glabrous outside. *Stamens* 10, unequal, 5—9.5 cm. long, as long as, or longer than, the corolla-tube; filaments densely hairy in the lower ¼—⅓ their length; anthers large, 0.7—1.2 cm. long, chocolate-brown. *Ovary* oblong, oblong-ovate or ovate, tapered into the style, 0.8—1 cm. long, 5-celled, densely scaly, glabrous; style long, straight or curved in the upper part, 6.5—10 cm. in length, slightly shorter than, or as long as, the corolla, scaly in the lower ½—⅔ its length or at the base, stigma 4—8 mm. in diameter, disc-like. *Capsule* oblong, 4.2—5.3 cm. long, 1.4—2 cm. broad, slightly curved or straight, rather densely scaly, glabrous, calyx-lobes persistent.

R. *rhabdotum* was first collected by R.E. Cooper in May 1915 at Punakka, Bhutan. It was afterwards found by other collectors in Bhutan, Assam and south Tibet. The plant grows on rocks and boulders, in rhododendron and deciduous forests, in pine and oak forests, and on open hillsides, often as an epiphyte, at elevations of 1,525—2,783 m. (5,000—9,125 ft.). According to Ludlow and Sherriff, it is common at Muktur, south Tibet at 2,440 m. (8,000 ft.), and in the rain forest at Rudo La, Bhutan at 2,288—2,593 m. (7,500—8,500 ft.).

A diagnostic feature of R. *rhabdotum* is the cream or pale yellow or white corolla, marked with five conspicuous red stripes outside. In this respect, the species is readily distinguished from its nearest ally R. *dalhousiae* and from all other members of its Series. Other characteristics of the plant are the oblong or oblong-obovate leaves, laxly scaly on the lower surface, the scales being usually 2—3 times their own diameter apart, and the rather densely or sometimes moderately pubescent pedicel.

R. *rhabdotum* was first introduced by Kingdon-Ward in 1925 from the border between Bhutan and Assam at 2,135—2,440 m. (7,000—8,000 ft.) (No. 6415). It was first flowered in August 1931 by Lord Aberconway. The species was reintroduced by Ludlow and Sherriff in 1936 (No. 2917) from south Tibet, and with Hicks in 1949 (No. 21257) from 2,593 m. (8,500 ft.) Bhutan. Along the west coast it succeeds outdoors in a few well-sheltered gardens, but along the east coast it is tender and requires greenhouse conditions. In cultivation it is a lax upright shrub up to 6 feet high, and makes a fine show with its large tubular-campanulate flowers produced freely in trusses of two to five. It is a late flowerer, prolonging the flowering season into June or July. The species was given an Award of Merit when shown by Lady Aberconway and the Hon. H.D. McLaren, Bodnant, in 1931, and a First Class Certificate when exhibited by Mr. L. de Rothschild, Exbury, in 1934.

Epithet. Striped.
Hardiness 1—2. May—July. Plate 46.

R. taggianum Hutch. in The Species of Rhododendron (1930) 499.
Illustration. Bot. Mag. Vol. 163 t. 9612 (1942).
A broadly upright or upright shrub or a small tree, sometimes epiphytic, 1.53—2.50 m. (5—8 ft.) high; branchlets rather densely or moderately scaly, not bristly. *Leaves* oblong, oblong-lanceolate, *oblong-elliptic, elliptic or broadly elliptic*, lamina coriaceous, 7—16.3 cm. long, 2.5—6.8 cm. broad, apex rounded or obtuse, mucronate, base rounded or obtuse; *upper surface* dark green, shining, reticulate, *bullate*, scaly or not scaly, midrib grooved, primary veins 12—16 on each side, deeply impressed; margin not bristly; under surface glaucous, laxly scaly, the scales unequal, medium-sized and large, or large, brown or dark brown, 2—5 times their own diameter apart, midrib prominent, primary veins raised; petiole 1—3.5 cm. long, convex, not grooved above, rather densely or moderately scaly, not bristly. *Inflorescence* terminal, umbellate, flower-bud pale green, 2—4-flowered; rhachis 2—4 mm. long, scaly, not bristly; pedicel 1.5—2.8 cm. long, thick or somewhat thick, rather densely or moderately scaly, glabrous. *Calyx* 5-lobed to the

base, 1.3—2 cm. long, pale green, lobes oblong-oval, oval, ovate or ovate-oblong, outside finely striate, 0.9—1.2 cm. broad, scaly at the base or rarely all over the outside or rarely not scaly, *margin glabrous. Corolla* broadly tubular-campanulate, 6.8—9.5 cm. long, 5-lobed, lobes rounded, not emarginate, margins entire, fragrant, white, with a yellow blotch at the base, outside moderately or rather densely scaly at the base of the tube, glabrous. *Stamens* 10, unequal, 4—6.2 cm. long, as long as, or shorter than, the corolla-tube; filaments densely hairy in the lower ⅓—½ their length; anthers 5—6 mm. long. *Ovary* oblong, tapered into the style, 0.8—1 cm. long, 5-celled, densely scaly, glabrous; style long, straight or curved in the upper part, 4.2—6.2 cm. in length, as long as, or longer than, the stamens, scaly at the base or in the lower ⅓ its length, stigma 3—7 mm. in diameter, disc-like. *Capsule* oblong, 3—5 cm. long, 1.3—1.5 cm. broad, slightly curved or straight, ribbed, rather densely scaly, glabrous, calyx-lobes persistent.

The discovery of *R. taggianum* has been wrongly credited to Forrest. It was first found by Farrer in April 1920 at Kum La Bum, north-east Upper Burma (No. 1520). Four and a half years later, in September 1924, Forrest collected it (No. 25865) in the Salwin Kiu-Chiang divide, north-west Yunnan, and again in 1925 in north-east Upper Burma (Nos. 26440 and 27638). It was later found by Kingdon-Ward in Upper Burma and on the Burma-Tibet Frontier, and by Rock in north-west Yunnan. The species was described in 1930, but there is no reference to Farrer's collection. It grows in open conifer forests, on the margins of thickets, and in spruce forest, at elevations of 1,830—3,700 m. (6,000—12,131 ft.).

R. taggianum shows a strong resemblance to *R. lindleyi* in its appearance, but differs markedly in that the leaves are usually elliptic or broadly elliptic or oblong-elliptic, the upper surfaces are bullate, and the margin of the calyx-lobes is glabrous. It is a diploid with 26 chromosomes.

The species was first introduced by Forrest in September 1924 from north-west Yunnan (No. 25865), and again in 1925 from north-east Upper Burma. It was re-introduced by Kingdon-Ward in June 1926 from Upper Burma (No. 6809), and from the Burma-Tibet Frontier in April 1931 (No. 9402). As it comes from elevations of up to 11,000 feet, the plant is hardy in the open in sheltered gardens along the west coast, but along the east coast it is tender and is grown under glass. It flowered for the first time in May 1930 in the glasshouse in the Royal Botanic Garden, Edinburgh, raised from Forrest's 1925 seed (No. 26440 = 27638) when the plant was only 1½ feet high. Two forms are in cultivation: Form 1. Leaves oblong, corolla 7—8 cm. long. Form 2. Leaves broadly elliptic, corolla larger up to 9.5 cm. long. The species is free-flowering and is most attractive with its broadly tubular-campanulate flowers in trusses of two to four. It received an Award of Merit when exhibited by the Marquess of Headfort, Kells, in 1932, and a First Class Certificate when shown by Murray Adams-Acton in 1943.

Epithet. After H.F. Tagg, 1874—1933, botanist at the Royal Botanic Garden, Edinburgh.

Hardiness 1—2. April—May.

MICRANTHUM SERIES

General characters: a shrub, 60 cm.—2.50 m. (2—8 ft.) high; branchlets thin, scaly. Leaves evergreen, oblanceolate, lanceolate or rarely oblong, lamina 1.5—3.8 cm. or rarely 5.9 cm. long, 0.4—1.5 cm. broad; under surface densely scaly, the scales overlapping or contiguous or ½ their own diameter apart. *Inflorescence* terminal, or terminal and axillary in the uppermost 1—3 leaves, *racemose, 10—28-flowered*; rhachis 1—2.6 cm. long; pedicel 0.7—1.3 cm. long. Calyx 5-lobed, minute, 0.5—1 mm. long. *Corolla* campanulate, *small, 4—6 mm. long*, 5-lobed, white, outside scaly. Stamens 10. Ovary conoid, 1—2 mm. long, 5—6-celled, densely scaly; *style* slender, straight, *short, shorter than, or as long as, the stamens*, twice or three times as long as the ovary. Capsule oblong, 4—8 mm. long, 2—3 mm. broad, moderately or rather densely scaly.

Distribution: north and central China, Manchuria, and Korea.

The Series consists of a single very distinct species, bearing no close affinity with the species of other Series.

DESCRIPTION OF THE SPECIES

R. micranthum Turcz. in Bull. Soc. Nat. Mosc. (1837) 155.

Illustration. Bot. Mag. Vol. 134 t. 8198 (1908).

A bushy shrub, 60 cm.—2.50 m. (2—8 ft.) high; branchlets thin, scaly, moderately or rather densely minutely puberulous. *Leaves* evergreen, oblanceolate, lanceolate or rarely oblong, lamina coriaceous, 1.5—3.8 cm. or rarely 5.9 cm. long, 0.4—1.5 cm. broad, apex obtuse, acute or rounded, mucronate, base tapered or obtuse, decurrent on the petiole or not decurrent; upper surface dark green, shining, moderately or sparsely scaly or not scaly, midrib minutely puberulous or glabrous; under surface densely scaly, the scales medium-sized, unequal, brown or dark brown, overlapping or contiguous or ½ their own diameter apart; petiole 2—8 mm. long, margin ridged on each side or not ridged, moderately or rather densely scaly, moderately or rather densely minutely puberulous. *Inflorescence* terminal, or terminal and axillary in the uppermost 1—3 leaves, *racemose, 10—28-flowered,* flower-bud scales deciduous; *rhachis 1—2.6 cm. long,* not scaly, rather densely pubescent; pedicel 0.7—1.3 cm. long, slender, moderately or densely scaly, glabrous. *Calyx* 5-lobed, minute, 0.5—1 mm. long, lobes lanceolate or linear or triangular, outside scaly, margin ciliate. *Corolla* campanulate, *small 4—6 mm. long,* 5-lobed, white, outside scaly, glabrous. *Stamens* 10, unequal, 4—8 mm. long, as long as the corolla or slightly longer; filaments glabrous. *Ovary* conoid, 1—2 mm. long, 5—6-celled, densely scaly, glabrous; *style* slender, straight, short, *as long as the corolla or shorter, shorter than or as long as the stamens,* twice or three times as long as the ovary, not scaly or rarely scaly at the base, glabrous. *Capsule* oblong, 4—8 mm. long, 2—3 mm. broad, straight, moderately or rather densely scaly, glabrous, calyx persistent.

R. micranthum was described by Turczaninov in 1837 from a specimen collected on the mountains north of Peking. It is widely distributed in north and central China, Manchuria, and Korea. The plant grows in thickets, on cliffs, in dry gorges, and on ridges, at elevations of 1,600—3,000 m. (5,246—9,836 ft.).

A remarkable feature of this plant is the distinctly racemose inflorescence of 10—28 flowers, with a rhachis 1—2.6 cm. long. Other noteworthy characters are the small, campanulate, white corolla, 4—6 mm. long, and the short, slender, straight style, as long as the corolla or shorter. The plant is a diploid with 26 chromosomes.

The species was first introduced by Wilson from western Hupeh in 1901 (No. 1218). It was reintroduced by him from the same region in 1907 (No. 660), and from western Szechuan in 1908 (Nos. 1200 and 1320) and again in 1910 (No. 4262). It first flowered in May 1904 in Messrs. Veitch and Sons' nursery at Coombe Wood. In cultivation it is a bushy, somewhat spreading shrub, up to 8 feet high and often as much across. It is a useful plant in that it is a late flowerer, prolonging the flowering season into June or July. The plant is hardy and free-flowering.

Epithet. Small-flowered.

Hardiness 3—4. May—July.

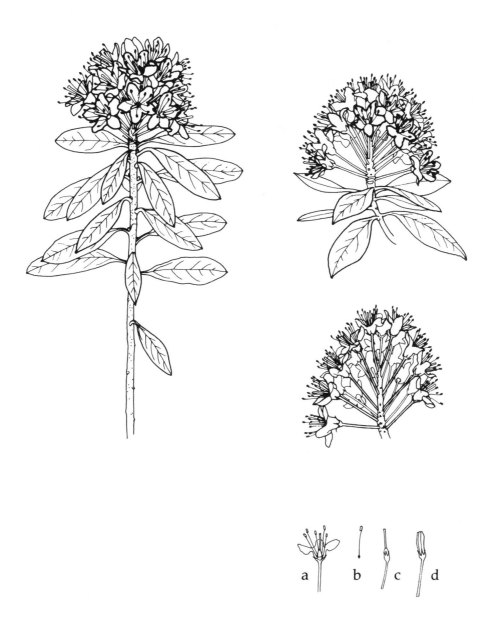

25. **R. micranthum**
nat. size
a. section. b. stamen. c. ovary, style. d. capsule.

MOUPINENSE SERIES

General characters: shrubs, sometimes epiphytic, 35 cm.—1.22 m. (1.14—4 ft.) or rarely 1.53 m. (5 ft.) high; *branchlets* scaly, *moderately or rather densely bristly. Leaves* evergreen, elliptic, ovate-elliptic, oblong-elliptic, ovate or oval, lamina *thick, rigid,* 0.9—4.6 cm. long, 0.4—2.3 cm. broad; margin recurved; under surface densely scaly, the scales slightly overlapping to their own diameter apart; petiole scaly, moderately or rather densely bristly. *Inflorescence* terminal, *1—2- flowered;* pedicel 2—9 mm. long, bristly or not bristly. Calyx 5-lobed, 1—4 mm. long. Corolla widely funnel-shaped, 2—4.8 cm. long, 5-lobed, bright rosy-red, white, or white tinged pink or red, with or without purple or crimson spots, outside not scaly. Stamens 10. Ovary conoid or ovoid, 2—4 mm. long, 5-celled, densely scaly; style slender, straight, shorter or longer than the stamens. Capsule oblong-oval or oval, 1.3—2.1 cm. long, 0.8—1.1 cm. broad.

Distribution: western Szechuan.

A small Series of three species allied to the Ciliatum Series.

KEY TO THE SPECIES

A. Leaves (laminae) 2—4.6 cm. long, 1.1—2.3 cm. broad; style long, longer than the stamens; corolla 3—4.8 cm. long .... *moupinense*

A. Leaves (laminae) 0.9—1.6 cm. long, 0.4—1 cm. broad; style short, shorter than the stamens; corolla 2—2.5 cm. long.

    B. Corolla bright rosy-red; scales on the under surface of the leaves one-half or their own diameter apart .... *dendrocharis*

    B. Corolla white; scales on the under surface of the leaves slightly overlapping or contiguous .... *petrocharis*

DESCRIPTION OF THE SPECIES

R. dendrocharis Franch. in Bull. Soc. Bot. France XXXIII (1886) 233.

Usually an epiphytic shrub, 35—70 cm. (1.16—2.33 ft.) high; branchlets scaly, moderately or rather densely bristly, leaf-bud scales deciduous. *Leaves* evergreen, elliptic or oval, *lamina* coriaceous, thick, rigid, *0.9—1.6 cm. long*, 0.4—1 cm. broad, apex obtuse or rounded, mucronate, base obtuse or rounded; upper surface bright green, somewhat matt, not scaly, glabrous; margin recurved; *under surface densely scaly*, the *scales* small or somewhat medium-sized, unequal, brown or dark brown, *one-half their own diameter apart*; petiole 2—6 mm. long, scaly, bristly. *Inflorescence* terminal, umbellate, 1- or rarely 2-flowered, flower-bud scales persistent or deciduous; rhachis 1 mm. long, scaly, not bristly; pedicel 2—3 mm. long, scaly, glabrous or rather densely minutely puberulous, bristly. *Calyx* 5-lobed, 1—3 mm. long, lobes oval or ovate, outside sparsely or moderately scaly, glabrous or minutely puberulous, margin moderately or rather densely hairy with long hairs. *Corolla* widely funnel-shaped, 2—2.5 cm. long, 2.3—3 cm. across, 5-lobed, *bright rosy-red*, outside not scaly, glabrous, inside rather densely pubescent in the tube. *Stamens* 10, unequal, 1.2—1.5 cm. long, shorter than the corolla; filaments rather densely pubescent in the lower one-third or one-half. *Ovary* conoid or ovoid, 2—3 mm. long, 5-celled, densely scaly, glabrous; *style* slender, straight, *somewhat short, 8 mm. long*, shorter than the corolla, *shorter than the stamens*, 3 times as long as the ovary, not scaly, glabrous or rather densely pubescent at the base. *Capsule* 1.3 cm. long, laxly scaly.

R. dendrocharis was described by Franchet in 1886. It is a native of Western Szechuan, growing in forests, usually as an epiphyte on Abies and Tsuga, at elevations of 2,600—3,000 m. (8,525—9,836 ft.).

The species shows a strong resemblance to *R. petrocharis* in general characters, but is distinguished by the bright rosy-red corolla, and usually by the less densely scaly lower surface of the leaves. The plant has not been introduced into cultivation.

Epithet. Tree-adorning.

Not in cultivation.

R. moupinense Franch. in Bull. Soc. Bot. France XXXIII (1886) 237.

Illustration. Bot. Mag. Vol. 141 t. 8598 (1915).

A somewhat compact rounded, or lax straggly somewhat rounded and spreading, or broadly upright shrub, often epiphytic, 60 cm.—1.22 m. (2—4 ft.) or rarely 1.53 m. (5 ft.) high; branchlets scaly, glabrous or minutely puberulous, bristly, leaf-bud scales deciduous. *Leaves* evergreen, elliptic, ovate-elliptic, oblong-elliptic, ovate or oval, *lamina* coriaceous, thick, *rigid, 2—4.6 cm. long, 1.1—2.3 cm. broad*, apex obtuse or rounded, mucronate, base rounded or cordulate or obtuse; upper surface dark green, shining, not scaly, glabrous, midrib glabrous or pubescent; margin recurved; under surface pale green, densely scaly, the scales medium-sized or small, unequal, brown, their own diameter apart; petiole 3—9 mm. long, scaly, glabrous or minutely puberulous, bristly. *Inflorescence* terminal, umbellate, 1—2-flowered, flower-bud scales persistent; rhachis 1—2 mm. long, scaly, pubescent or glabrous, not bristly; pedicel 6—9 mm. long, moderately

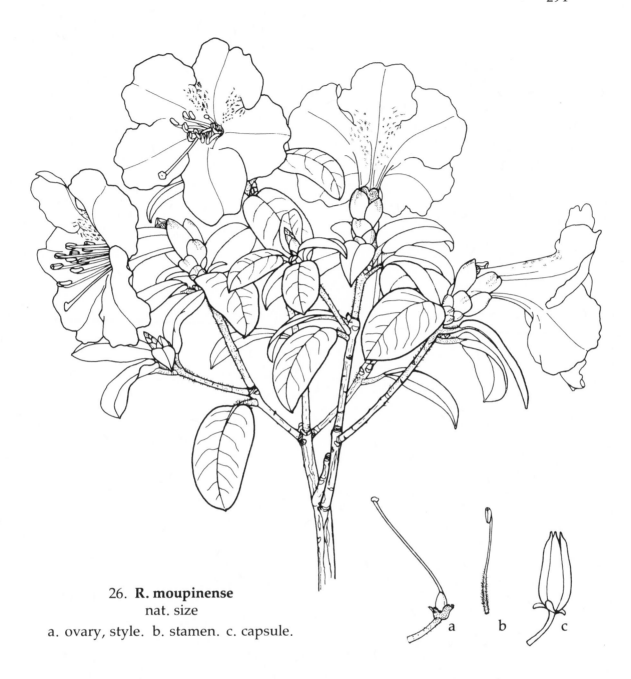

26. **R. moupinense**
nat. size

a. ovary, style. b. stamen. c. capsule.

or rather densely scaly, rather densely puberulous or glabrous, not bristly. *Calyx* 5-lobed, 1—4 mm. long, lobes ovate or rounded or triangular, outside rather densely or moderately scaly, puberulous or glabrous, margin ciliate or eciliate, inside puberulous or glabrous. *Corolla* widely funnel-shaped, *3—4.8 cm. long*, 3.5—4.8 cm. across, 5-lobed, white, or white tinged pink or red, with purple or crimson spots, outside not scaly, glabrous, inside pubescent in the tube. *Stamens* 10, unequal, 1.8—2.8 cm. long, shorter than the corolla; filaments densely or moderately pubescent in the lower one-half or one-third or at the base. *Ovary* conoid or ovoid, 3—4 mm. long, 5-celled, densely scaly, glabrous or puberulous at the apex; *style long*, slender, straight, shorter than the corolla, *longer than the stamens,* not scaly or scaly at the base, glabrous or puberulous at the base. *Capsule* oblong-oval or oval, 1.6—2.1 cm. long, 0.8—1.1 cm. broad, densely scaly, glabrous, calyx-lobes persistent.

R. moupinense is a native of Western Szechuan. It was described by Franchet in 1886. The plant grows often as an epiphyte on oaks and other trees; it is also found on rocks, on cliffs, and in woods, at elevations of 2,000—3,300 m. (6,557—10,820 ft.).

The diagnostic features of this plant are the thick, rigid, ovate to oval leaves, (laminae) 2—4.6 cm. long, the 1—2-flowered inflorescence with persistent flower-bud scales, and the widely funnel-shaped corolla with a long tube and spreading lobes. It is allied to *R. dendrocharis* and *R. petrocharis*, but is readily distinguished by the larger leaves, larger corolla and longer style.

The species was first introduced by Wilson in 1909. Three growth forms are in cultivation. Form 1. A somewhat compact, rounded shrub up to 3 feet high and as much across. Form 2. A lax straggly somewhat rounded and spreading shrub up to 3 feet high and as much across. Form 3. A broadly upright shrub up to 3 or 4 feet high. The flower colour is white, or white tinged pink or red, with or without purple or crimson spots. The species is an early flowerer, the flowers appearing towards the end of February or sometimes early in the same month. When it escapes the frost, it heralds Spring with a blaze of white tinged red, or white flowers. Although the plant comes from relatively low elevations in Szechuan, it is perfectly hardy in cultivation and is easily adaptable to any position in the garden. It often sets good fertile seed. Nearly all the seedlings raised from open -pollinated seed come true to type. It is an exceedingly charming plant, and should be a valuable acquisition to any rock garden. A form with white flowers, exhibited in 1914, by Miss Willmott, Great Warley, received an Award of Merit. A form with rose-pink flowers when shown by Lord Aberconway, Bodnant, in 1937, received the same Award.

Epithet. From Moupin, i.e. Paoksing-hsien, W. China.
Hardiness 3—4. February—March. Plate 52.

R. petrocharis Diels in Fedde Repert. XVII (1921) 196.

A small shrub; branchlets scaly, glabrous or minutely puberulous, bristly. *Leaves* evergreen, elliptic or ovate-elliptic, lamina coriaceous, thick, rigid, 1—1.3 cm. long, 5—7 mm. broad, apex obtuse or rounded, mucronate, base obtuse or rounded; upper surface bright green, somewhat matt, sparsely scaly or not scaly, glabrous, midrib hairy or glabrous; margin recurved; *under surface densely scaly*, the *scales* medium-sized, unequal, brown or dark brown, *slightly overlapping or contiguous*; petiole 2—7 mm. long, scaly, moderately or rather densely bristly. *Inflorescence* terminal, umbellate, 1—2-flowered, flower-bud scales persistent or deciduous; rhachis 1 mm. long, scaly, bristly; pedicel 4 mm. long, scaly, minutely puberulous, bristly. *Calyx* 5-lobed, 2—3 mm. long, lobes ovate or ovate-oblong, outside scaly, glabrous, margin hairy. *Corolla* widely funnel-shaped, 2—3 cm. long, 3.5 cm. across, 5-lobed, *white*, outside not scaly, glabrous, inside nearly glabrous. *Stamens* 10, unequal, about 1.5 cm. long, shorter than the corolla; filaments hairy above the base. *Ovary* conoid, 3 mm. long, 5-celled, densely scaly, glabrous; style slender, straight, short, 0.6—1 cm. long, shorter than the corolla, shorter than the stamens or about the length of the shortest stamen, 3 times as long as the ovary, not scaly, glabrous. *Capsule:* —

This plant was found by Limpricht in April 1914 in Szechuan, growing on rocks at an elevation of 1,800 m. (5,902 ft.).

It is very similar to *R. dendrocharis* in the shape and size of the leaves, and in the shape of the corolla, but differs in that the corolla is white, and the scales on the lower surface of the leaves are slightly overlapping or contiguous. There is no record of its occurrence in cultivation.

Epithet. Gracing the rocks.
Not in cultivation.

SALUENENSE SERIES

General characters: dwarf or small, broadly upright, cushion or prostrate shrubs, 3 cm.—1.22 m. (1 in.—4 ft.) or sometimes up to 1.53 m. (5 ft.) high; branchlets densely or moderately scaly, moderately or densely bristly or not bristly. *Leaves* evergreen, oval, oblong-oval, nearly orbicular, ovate-elliptic, elliptic, lanceolate or linear, lamina 0.4—3.6 cm. long, 0.1—2.4 cm. broad; *under surface densely scaly with overlapping Crenulate scales;* petiole moderately or densely scaly, bristly or not bristly. Inflorescence terminal, 1—4- or sometimes up to 7-flowered; pedicel 0.7—3.2 cm. long, moderately or rather densely scaly, moderately or rather densely bristly or not bristly. Calyx 5-lobed to base, 0.3—1 cm. long, lobes pinkish-purple, purple, crimson, scarlet or rarely green, outside densely or slightly scaly along the middle or not scaly, margin fringed with long or short hairs. *Corolla widely funnel-shaped, sometimes rotate or saucer-shaped,* 1.3—3 cm. long, purple, pinkish-purple, purplish-rose, deep rose, deep crimson-rose or crimson, with or rarely without crimson spots at the base of the upper three lobes, *outside* moderately or rather densely scaly along the middle of the lobes or sometimes not scaly, *moderately or rather densely pubescent* or rarely glabrous. Stamens 10; filaments densely villous towards the base. Ovary conoid, 2—3 mm. long, 5-celled, densely scaly, glabrous or rarely puberulous, or puberulous at the base. Capsule conoid or ovoid, 0.4—1 cm. long, densely scaly, enclosed or partly enclosed by the persistent calyx-lobes.

Distribution: north-east Upper Burma, Upper Burma, west and north-west Yunnan, south-west Szechuan, south-east and east Tibet.

A well-defined Series of closely allied species, related to the Lapponicum Series.

KEY TO THE SPECIES

A. Branchlets and petioles moderately or densely bristly.
  B. Outside of calyx, ovary and capsule not bristly.
    C. Usually broadly upright or rounded shrub, up to 1.50 m. high; leaves (laminae) up to 3.6 cm. long; upper surface of the leaves rather densely or moderately scaly or not scaly.
      D. Shrub usually 60 cm.—1.50 high; leaves (laminae) large, usually 2—3.6 cm. long; upper surface of the leaves rather densely or moderately scaly, in young leaves dark green .... *saluenense*
      D. Shrub 5—60 cm. high; leaves (laminae) small, 0.5—2 cm. long; upper surface of the leaves not scaly or sometimes moderately scaly, in young leaves purplish-crimson or margins deep purple .... *chameunum*
    C. Protrate spreading or sometimes compact spreading shrub, 3—60 cm. high; leaves (laminae) 0.4—1.5 cm. long (rarely longer); upper surface of the leaves not scaly .... *prostratum*
  B. Outside of calyx, ovary and capsule bristly .... *charidotes*
A. Branchlets and petioles not bristly.
      E. Upper surface of the leaves matt, densely scaly, the scales overlapping (rarely ½ their own diameter apart), pale green, pale silvery-bluish, pale greyish or bluish-green, in young leaves pale bluish-white or sometimes pale bluish-green .... *calostrotum*
      E. Upper surface of the leaves shining, not scaly or sparsely or moderately or sometimes rather densely scaly, not overlapping, (the scales ½—8 times their own diameter apart), in both adult and young leaves dark green or bright green.
        F. Broadly upright shrub 30—45 cm. high; flowers appearing late, in June, July, August .... *nitens*
        F. Very compact rounded spreading, or semi-prostrate, or completely prostrate creeping shrub 3—45 cm. high; flowers appearing earlier, in May, June.
          G. Very compact rounded spreading shrub 15—45 cm. (or sometimes semi-prostrate up to 15 cm.) high; leaves oblong, elliptic, ovate-elliptic or oblong-oval, (rarely lanceolate), up to twice as long as broad .... *keleticum*
          G. Completely prostrate creeping shrub 2—3 cm. high (or sometimes forming a low compact mound 20 cm. high with creeping outer branches); leaves linear, lanceolate, narrowly oblanceolate or narrowly oblong, 3—5 times as long as broad ......
              .... *radicans*

DESCRIPTION OF THE SPECIES

R. calostrotum Balf. f. et Ward in Notes Roy. Bot. Gard. Edin., Vol. 13 (1920) 35.
    Illustration. Bot. Mag. Vol. 149 t. 9001 (1924).
    A cushion or compact rounded or compact spreading, broadly upright, prostrate or matted shrub, rarely epiphytic, 8—92 cm. (3 in.—3 ft.) or rarely 1.22—1.53 m. (4—5 ft.) high; *branchlets* densely scaly with flaky stalked scales, *not bristly*, leaf-bud scales deciduous. *Leaves* elliptic, ovate-elliptic, oblong-elliptic, obovate, oval, oblong-oval or nearly orbicular, lamina coriaceous, 1.3—2.5 cm. or sometimes up to 3.5 cm. long, 0.5—1.5 cm. broad, apex rounded or obtuse, with a reflexed mucro, base rounded or obtuse; *upper surface pale green, pale silvery-bluish, pale greyish or bluish-green (in young leaves pale bluish-white* or sometimes pale bluish-green), *matt, densely scaly, the scales overlapping* (or rarely

27. R. calostrotum

nat. size

a. ovary, style. b. stamen. c. capsule. d. capsule enclosed.
e. leaf (lower surface).

½ their own diameter apart); margin not bristly or rarely bristly; under surface densely scaly, the scales brown, dark brown or cinnamon-coloured, overlapping; *petiole* 2—5 mm. long, densely scaly, *not bristly*. *Inflorescence* terminal, umbellate, 1—3- or rarely up to 5-flowered, flower-bud scales deciduous; *pedicel* 0.9—2.6 cm. long, longer or shorter than the corolla, rather densely scaly, *not bristly*. *Calyx* 5-lobed to base, 3—8 mm. long, lobes pinkish-purple or crimson, oblong-oval, oval, ovate, elliptic or nearly orbicular, outside glabrous or sometimes puberulous, densely or sometimes sparsely scaly along the middle, margin long - or short - ciliate. *Corolla* widely funnel-shaped or saucer-shaped or rotate, 1.3—2.5 cm. long, 5-lobed, purple, pinkish-purple, bright rosy-purple, deep rose-purple, claret, crimson-purple or rich purple-crimson, with crimson spots at the base of the upper three lobes, outside rather densely or moderately pubescent or rarely glabrous, rather densely or moderately scaly along the middle of the lobes or rarely not scaly. *Stamens* 10, slightly unequal, long-exserted, 0.6—1.7 cm. long; filaments densely villous towards the base. *Ovary* conoid, 2—3 mm. long, 5-celled, densely scaly, glabrous or sometimes puberulous; style red, longer than the stamens, glabrous or puberulous at the base. *Capsule* conoid or ovoid, 4—8 mm. long, densely scaly, enclosed by the persistent calyx-lobes.

This species was discovered by Kingdon-Ward in July 1914 on the Ridge of Naung-Chaung, Mwai divide, north-east Upper Burma. Further gatherings by other collectors show that the plant is widely distributed in north-east and east Upper Burma, north-west Yunnan, south-east Tibet and Assam. It grows in open stony meadows, on boulders, cliffs, crags, rocks, and hillsides, in rocky moorland, and by the side of streams, at elevations of 3,050—4,880 m. (10,000—16,000 ft.). Farrer records it as forming a close carpet covering the tops of the mountains in north-east Upper Burma. Ludlow and Sherriff have found it growing in a swamp, and as an epiphyte about one foot high in south-east Tibet.

R. calostrotum varies considerably in general features. It is a cushion or compact rounded, broadly upright or prostrate shrub, 3 inches to 3 or 4 feet high, the leaves are elliptic, obovate to oval or nearly orbicular, (laminae) 1.3—2.5 cm. long, and the corolla is 1.3—2.5 cm. long. It is allied to *R. saluenense*. The main distinctions between them are that in *R. calostrotum* the branchlets, petioles, and pedicels are not bristly, and the upper surfaces of the leaves are pale green, pale silvery-bluish or pale greyish, (in young leaves pale bluish-white), matt, densely scaly, the scales usually overlapping; whereas in *R. saluenense* the branchlets and petioles are moderately or densely bristly, the pedicels are often sparsely to rather densely bristly, and the upper surfaces of the leaves in both the adult and young leaves are dark green, shining, scaly, the scales ½—6 times their own diameter apart.

The species was first introduced by Farrer and Cox in 1919 (No. 1045). It was re-introduced many times by Forrest and other collectors. Six distinct forms are in cultivation: Form 1. A low compact spreading shrub with pale silvery-bluish leaves and rose-crimson flowers, known as the 'Gigha' form. Form 2. A broadly upright shrub up to one foot high with claret flowers, sometimes known as the "claret" form. Form 3. A compact rounded shrub 2½ feet high and as much across with pale greyish leaves. Form 4. A broadly upright shrub 3 feet high with fairly large leaves and rosy-purple flowers. Form 5. An upright lax somewhat straggly shrub, 2 feet high with small flowers, which was known as *R. riparium* (now a synonym of *R. calostrotum*). Form 6. A large somewhat rounded shrub 4—5 feet high, with large leaves, upper surface bluish-green, and with crimson-purple flowers, known as "Rock's" form.

In cultivation most forms of *R. calostrotum* are extremely free-flowering and provide a fine display with their large widely funnel-shaped, saucer-shaped or rotate flowers, completely hiding the foliage. The species has a long flowering period, extending from April to the end of June. A most distinctive feature is the young foliage, pale bluish-white in colour, which always attracts attention. Some forms produce good fertile seed in profusion. The plant flowers quite young when grown from seed. A plant raised from seed of Form 4 above, flowered when it was only two years old. The species is very hardy, and is easily adaptable to any position in the rock garden. It was given an Award of Merit when shown by Lt.-Col. L.C.R. Messel, Nymans, Sussex in 1935 (Forrest No. 27065 = 27497). A form 'Gigha' raised at Tower Court, gained a First Class Certificate when exhibited by Glendoick Gardens Ltd. in 1971. It was given an Award of Garden Merit in 1969.

Epithet. With a beautiful covering.
Hardiness 3—4. April—June. Plate 53.

R. calostrotum Balf. f. et Ward var. **calciphilum** (Hutch. et Ward) Davidian in The Rhododendron and Camellia Year Book (1954) 87.

Syn. *R. calciphilum* Hutch. et Ward in Notes Roy. Bot. Gard. Edin., Vol. 16 (1931) 179.

This plant was first collected by Kingdon-Ward in June 1926, at Seinghku Wang, Upper Burma. It was later found by Yü in the Upper Kiukiang Valley, north-west Yunnan. The plant grows on limestone ridge, and in thickets on open rocky slopes, at elevations of 3,700—4,270 m. (12,131—14,000 ft.). Yü records it as being common usually forming dense thickets in north-west Yunnan.

The variety differs from the species in its smaller leaves, 0.5—1.2 cm. long. The flowers are pale pinkish or rosy-purple, with deep purple spots at the base of the upper three lobes.

The plant was first introduced by Kingdon-Ward in 1926 (No. 6984 — the Type number). It was reintroduced by Yü in 1938. In cultivation it is a spreading or broadly upright shrub up to 2 feet high, with pale greyish leaves and saucer-shaped flowers produced in May. The plant is hardy, easy to grow, and well worth a place in every rock garden.

Epithet of the variety. Lime-loving.
Hardiness 3. May. Plate 54.

R. chameunum Balf. f. et Forrest in Notes Roy. Bot. Gard. Edin., Vol. 13 (1920) 37.

A *rounded, spreading, cushion,* broadly upright, *prostrate* or matted *shrub, 5—60 cm. (2 in.—2 ft.) high; branchlets* densely or moderately scaly with flaky stalked scales, *moderately or densely bristly,* leaf-bud scales subpersistent or deciduous. *Leaves* oblong-oval, oval, elliptic, oblong-elliptic, obovate or ovate-elliptic, *lamina* coriaceous, *0.5—2 cm. long,* 0.4—1.1 cm. broad, apex rounded or sometimes obtuse, with a reflexed or straight mucro, base rounded or obtuse; *upper surface* dark green, (*in young leaves purplish-crimson or margins deep purple*), shining, *not scaly* or sometimes moderately or rarely rather densely scaly, the scales ½—6 times their own diameter apart; margin bristly or not bristly; under surface densely scaly, the scales fawn, yellowish, brown or dark brown, overlapping; *petiole* 1—5 mm. long, scaly, *bristly* or rarely not bristly. *Inflorescence* terminal, umbellate, 1—3- or sometimes 4—6-flowered, flower-bud scales persistent or deciduous; *pedicel* 0.7—2.2 cm. long, shorter than the corolla, scaly, *moderately or rather densely bristly* or rarely not bristly. *Calyx* 5-lobed to base, 0.3—1 cm. long, lobes pinkish-purple, purple, scarlet or crimson, lanceolate, ovate-elliptic or ovate, outside rather densely or moderately puberulous or glabrous, not bristly, not scaly or sparsely or moderately scaly along the middle, margin fringed with long or short hairs. *Corolla* widely funnel-shaped, 1.7—2.9 cm. long, 5-lobed, purple-rose, deep purplish-rose, deep rose or purple-crimson, with crimson spots at the base of the upper three lobes, outside rather densely or moderately pubescent, sparsely or moderately or rarely rather densely scaly along the middle of the lobes. *Stamens* 10, slightly unequal, long-exserted, 0.9—1.8 cm. long; filaments densely villous towards the base. *Ovary* conoid, 2—3 mm. long, 5-celled, densely scaly, moderately or rarely densely puberulous, or glabrous, not bristly; style red, longer than the stamens, glabrous or puberulous at the base. *Capsule* conoid or ovoid, 4—8 mm. long, densely scaly, enclosed or partly enclosed by the persistent calyx-lobes.

R. chameunum was first collected by Forrest in June 1914 on the mountains of the Chungtien plateau, west Yunnan. Subsequently it was found by him again and by other collectors in west and north-west Yunnan, north-east Upper Burma, south-west Szechuan, and south-east Tibet. It grows in open stony pasture, on hillsides, cliffs, boulders, granite screes, and in moist alpine moorland, at elevations of 3,355—4,575 m. (11,000—15,000 ft.). Yü records it as being common in thickets at Atuntze, north-west Yunnan. Kingdon-Ward found it forming much of the carpet on sheltered granite slopes at Pai-ma-shan, on the Yunnan-Tibet-Burma Border.

The species resembles *R. saluenense* in its moderately or densely bristly branchlets, petioles and pedicels, but differs markedly in that it is usually a small cushion, rounded or prostrate shrub, 2 inches to 2 feet high, the upper surfaces of the leaves are often not scaly, and the young leaves are purplish-crimson or with deep purple margins.

The plant was first introduced by Forrest in 1914 (No. 12968). It was reintroduced by him several times and by Rock from north-west Yunnan. In cultivation it is a somewhat compact rounded or broadly upright shrub, 1—2 feet high, with leaves shining above. During the fruiting stage in summer, an attractive feature is the enlarged oval crimson calyx at the end of the lengthened pedicel. The plant is very hardy, free-flowering, and would be well worth acquiring for every rock garden.

Epithet. Lying on the ground.
Hardiness 3. April—May.

R. charidotes Balf. f. et Farrer in Notes Roy. Bot. Gard. Edin., Vol. 13 (1922) 242.

A *prostrate or rounded shrub, 8—30 cm. (3 in.—1 ft.)* high; *branchlets* moderately or rather densely scaly with flaky stalked scales, *moderately or rather densely bristly,* leaf-bud scales deciduous or subpersistent. *Leaves* elliptic, oblong-elliptic, oblong-oval or oval, lamina coriaceous, 0.9—1.8 cm. long, 0.4—1 cm. broad, apex rounded or obtuse, with a straight or reflexed mucro, base obtuse or rounded; upper surface dark green, (in young leaves dark green), shining, rather densely or moderately scaly or not scaly; margin bristly or not bristly; under surface densely scaly, the scales dark brown, overlapping, midrib bristly or sometimes not bristly; *petiole* 1—3 mm. long, scaly, *bristly. Inflorescence* terminal, umbellate, 1—3-flowered, flower-bud scales persistent or deciduous; *pedicel* 1—2 cm. long, scaly, *rather densely bristly. Calyx* 5-lobed to base, 0.5—1 cm. long, lobes purple or crimson-purple, ovate, oval or nearly orbicular, *outside* not pubescent or rather densely pubescent, *bristly,* not scaly or scaly along the middle, margin bristly. *Corolla* widely funnel-shaped, 1.8—2 cm. long, 5-lobed, magenta-crimson or purple-crimson, with crimson spots at the base of the upper three lobes, outside rather densely or moderately pubescent, rather densely or moderately scaly along the middle of the lobes. *Stamens* 10, unequal, long-exserted, 0.9—1.5 cm. long; filaments villous towards the base. *Ovary* conoid, 2—3 mm. long, 5-celled, densely scaly, not puberulous, *bristly;* style red, longer than the stamens, glabrous. *Capsule* conoid, 4—6 mm. long, densely scaly, *bristly,* enclosed or partly enclosed by the persistent calyx-lobes.

R. charidotes was discovered by Farrer in July 1920 in the Chawchi Pass, north-east Upper Burma, growing at an elevation of 3,660 m. (12,000 ft.).

It shows a certain degree of similarity to *R. chameunum* from which it is readily distinguished by the bristly calyx, ovary and capsule, and by the dark green young leaves. It further differs in cultivation in its habit and height of growth.

The plant has been in cultivation for a long time, and was possibly introduced by Farrer. In its native home is grows from 3 to 12 inches high; in cultivation it is a rounded shrub of about 10 inches with dark green adult and young leaves, and purple-crimson flowers. It is hardy, free-flowering, and is well suited for the rock garden. The plant is rare in cultivation.

Epithet. Giving joy.
Hardiness 3. April—May.

R. keleticum Balf. f. et Forrest in Notes Roy. Bot. Gard. Edin., Vol. 13 (1920) 50.

A *very compact, rounded spreading shrub, 15—45 cm. (6 in.—1½ ft.) high* and up to 1.22 m. (4 ft.) wide; *or a semi-prostrate* or prostrate or matted *shrub, 8—15 cm. (3—6 in.)* or rarely 3—5 cm. (1—2 in.) high; *branchlets* densely scaly with flaky stalked scales, *not bristly* or rarely sparsely bristly, leaf-bud scales subpersistent. *Leaves oblong, oblong-elliptic, elliptic, ovate-elliptic, oblong-oval* or lanceolate, lamina coriaceous, 0.7—2.1 cm. long, 3—9 mm. broad, apex rounded, obtuse or acute, with a long straight or reflexed mucro, base rounded, obtuse or tapered; upper surface dark green, (in young leaves dark green), shining, not scaly or moderately or rather densely scaly, the scales ½—6 times their own diameter apart; margin bristly or not bristly; under surface densely scaly, the scales brown or fawn, overlapping; *petiole* 1—4 mm. long, densely or moderately scaly, *not bristly* or rarely sparsely bristly. *Inflorescence* terminal, umbellate, 1—3-flowered, flower-bud scales persistent or subpersistent; pedicel 1.5—3.2 cm. long, longer than the corolla or equalling it, moderately or rather densely scaly, bristly or not bristly. *Calyx* 5-lobed to base, 5—8 mm. long, lobes pinkish or crimson, ovate, oval, ovate-oblong, oblong-oval or ovate-lanceolate, outside glabrous or rarely puberulous, not bristly or rarely bristly, moderately or densely scaly along the middle, margin fringed with long hairs. *Corolla* widely funnel-shaped, 1.6—3 cm. long, 5-lobed, deep purplish-crimson or deep purplish-rose, with crimson spots at the base of the upper three lobes, outside rather densely pubescent, moderately or rather densely scaly along the middle of the lobes. *Stamens* 10, slightly unequal, long-exserted, 0.9—2 cm. long; filaments densely villous towards the base. *Ovary* conoid, 2—3 mm. long, 5-celled, densely scaly; style red, longer than the stamens, glabrous. *Capsule* conoid, 5—8 mm. long, densely scaly, enclosed or partly enclosed by the persistent calyx-lobes.

This species was discovered by Forrest in August 1919 in the Salwin-Kiu-chiang Divide, south-east Tibet. It was afterwards found by other collectors in south-east and east Tibet, and in north-east Upper Burma. The plant grows in peaty stony pasture, on cliffs and screes, in corries, and in moist stony moorland, at elevations of 3,965—4,575 m. (13,000—15,000 ft.). Kingdon-Ward found it forming mats on schistose rocks on the Yunnan-Burma border. Yü records it as being common in north-west Yunnan.

The non-bristly branchlets and petioles are a distinctive feature of this plant. In this respect it is similar to *R. radicans* from which it is readily distinguished by its habit of growth, usually by the leaf shape, and by the broader leaves. It is also allied to *R. chameunum*, but differs markedly in its habit of growth, in the non-bristly branchlets and petioles, in the green young foliage, and often in leaf shape.

R. keleticum was first introduced by Forrest in 1919 from eastern Tibet (No. 18918 — the Type number). It was reintroduced by him several times from the same region, and by Kingdon-Ward from north-east Upper Burma. Rock sent seeds in 1948 under No. 58 from north-west Yunnan. In cultivation it is easily recognised by its very compact habit of growth, forming a mound 1—1½ feet high and up to 2 feet across. It is worth noting that a low compact spreading form, possibly introduced by Forrest, links the species with *R. radicans*. Although the species is hardy, early severe frosts along the east coast are apt to damage the plant. In May or June it makes a fine show with its deep purplish-crimson flowers produced with freedom. The species received an Award of Merit when exhibited by Messrs. Gill, Falmouth, in 1928.

Epithet. Charming.
Hardiness 3. May—June.

R. nitens Hutch. in Gard. Chron., Vol. 99 (1936) 10.

A *broadly upright shrub*, 30—45 cm. (1—1½ ft.) high; branchlets scaly with flaky stalked scales, *not bristly*; leaf-bud scales subpersistent or deciduous. *Leaves* oblong-obovate or oblong-elliptic, lamina coriaceous, 0.7—2.4 cm. long, 0.4—1.1 cm. broad, apex rounded with a reflexed mucro, base rounded or obtuse; upper surface bright green or dark green, (*in young leaves bright green*), shining, sparsely or moderately scaly, the scales 1—8 times their own diameter apart; margin bristly or not bristly; under surface densely scaly, the scales brown or fawn, overlapping; *petiole* 2—3 mm. long, scaly, *not bristly* or rarely sparsely bristly. *Inflorescence* terminal, umbellate, 1—3-flowered, flower-bud scales persistent or subpersistent; *pedicel* 1.4—2.5 cm. long, shorter than the corolla, rather densely scaly, *not bristly*. *Calyx* 5-lobed to base, 6—8 mm. long, lobes pinkish-purple, ovate-oblong or lanceolate, outside puberulous or glabrous, rather densely scaly along the middle or not scaly, margin fringed with long or short hairs. *Corolla* widely funnel-shaped or rotate, 1.8—2.8 cm. long, 5-lobed, deep pinkish-purple or deep pink-magenta, with crimson spots at the base of the upper three lobes, outside moderately or rather densely pubescent, scaly along the middle of the lobes. *Stamens* 10, unequal, long-exserted, 0.7—1.7 cm. long; filaments densely villous towards the base. *Ovary* conoid, 2—3 mm. long, 5-celled, densely scaly; style red, longer than the stamens, glabrous. *Capsule* ovoid, 5—6 mm. long, densely scaly, enclosed or partly enclosed by the persistent calyx-lobes.

R. nitens was described in 1936 from living specimens growing at Tower Court, Ascot, raised from Kingdon-Ward seed No. 5842. The corresponding specimen in fruit was collected at Tara Tru, north-east Upper Burma, growing on sloping granite slabs and under bamboos along the edge of thickets at an elevation of 3,660 m. (12,000 ft.).

The species resembles *R. chameunum* to a certain degree, but is readily distinguished by its habit of growth, by the non-bristly branchlets, petioles and pedicels, and by the bright green young foliage. From *R. keleticum* it differs markedly in its habit of growth.

In cultivation, *R. nitens* is a broadly upright shrub, 1—1½ feet high, bearing a profusion of large pinkish-purple flowers. One of its chief merits is that it flowers at a remarkably early age when raised from seed. From all the other members of its Series it differs in its time of flowering, being a late flowerer, extending the flowering season into July or sometimes August. It has proved to be most attractive in flower, and should be grown in every rock gaden.

Epithet. Shining.
Hardiness 3. June—August.

R. prostratum W. W. Sm. in Notes Roy. Bot. Gard. Edin., Vol. 8 (1914) 202.
Illustration. Bot. Mag. Vol. 144 t. 8747 (1918).

A *prostrate or semi-prostrate spreading or sometimes compact spreading* shrub, *3—30 cm. (1 in.—1 ft.)* or sometimes up to 60 cm. (2 ft.) high; branchlets moderately or rather densely scaly with flaky stalked scales, *moderately or rather densely bristly*, leaf-bud scales deciduous or persistent. *Leaves* oval, oblong-oval, nearly orbicular, elliptic or oblong-elliptic, *lamina* coriaceous, *0.4—1.5 cm. (or rarely up to 2.3 cm.) long*, 3—9 mm. (or rarely 1.2 cm.) broad, apex rounded with a reflexed or straight mucro, base rounded or obtuse; *upper surface* dark green, (in young leaves dark green) shining, *not scaly* or rarely sparsely scaly; margin moderately or slightly bristly; under surface densely scaly, the scales brown, overlapping; *petiole* 1—3 mm. long, scaly, *moderately or slightly bristly*. *Inflorescence* terminal, umbellate, 1—3-flowered, flower-bud scales deciduous or persistent; *pedicel* 0.8—2.3 cm. long, shorter than the corolla or equalling it, scaly, *moderately or rather densely or rarely slightly bristly*. *Calyx* 5-lobed to base, 5—7 mm. long, lobes crimson or pinkish-purple, oval, oblong-oval, ovate or ovate-oblong, outside puberulous or glabrous, not bristly, sparsely or moderately scaly along the middle, or not scaly, margin bristly. *Corolla* widely funnel-shaped, 1.6—2.3 cm. long, 5-lobed, crimson or deep purple-rose, with crimson spots at the base of the upper three lobes, outside moderately or rather densely pubescent, not scaly or sometimes scaly along the middle of the lobes. *Stamens* 10, slightly unequal, long-exserted, 1—1.5 cm. long; filaments densely villous towards the base. *Ovary* conoid, 2—3 mm. long, 5-celled, densely scaly, glabrous or sometimes minutely puberulous; style red, longer than the stamens, glabrous or rarely puberulous at the base. *Capsule* conoid or ovoid, 5—6 mm. long, densely scaly, puberulous or glabrous, enclosed or partly enclosed by the persistent calyx-lobes.

This species was discovered by Forrest in June 1910 on the eastern flank of the Lichiang Range, Yunnan. Further gatherings by him and other collectors show that the plant is distributed in west and north-west Yunnan, south-west Szechuan and south-east Tibet. It grows on rocks and peaty moist soil, on boulders, and in open stony alpine pasture, almost at the limit of vegetation, at elevations of 3,660—5,335 m. (12,000—17,491 ft.).

R. prostratum is similar to *R. saluenense* and *R. chameunum* in the moderately or rather densely bristly branchlets and petioles. It is distinguished from the former by its habit and height of growth, by the smaller leaves, and by the absence of scales on the upper surface of the leaves, and from the latter by its habit and usually by its height of growth, by the dark green young foliage, and often by the smaller leaves. The plant is a tetraploid with 52 chromosomes.

The species was first introduced by Forrest in 1910 (No. 5862 — the Type number). It was reintroduced by him in 1912 and 1930. Rock sent seeds in 1948 from north-west Yunnan. Two distinct forms are in cultivation. Form 1. A prostrate spreading shrub, 2—3 inches high. Form 2. A compact spreading cushion, 8 inches high and 1½ feet across, rare in cultivation. The plant is a slow grower, and requires several years before it flowers freely. It is very hardy, and a well-grown plant covered with crimson flowers is most effective in April—May. The species is easy to grow, and is a charming plant for the rock garden.

Epithet. Low growing.
Hardiness 3. April—May.

R. radicans Balf. f. et Forrest in Notes Roy. Bot. Gard. Edin., Vol. 13 (1922) 290.

A completely prostrate matted or creeping shrublet 3 cm. (1 in.) high or sometimes forming a low compact mound 20 cm. (8 in.) high with creeping outer branches, branchlets moderately or densely scaly with flaky stalked scales, *not bristly,* leaf-bud scales subpersistent or deciduous. *Leaves linear, lanceolate, narrowly oblanceolate or narrowly oblong,* lamina coriaceous, 0.6—1.7 cm. long, 1—6 mm. broad, apex acute or obtuse, with a straight or reflexed mucro, base tapered or obtuse; upper surface dark green, (in young leaves dark green), shining, not scaly or scaly, the scales 2—4 times their own diameter apart; margin bristly or not bristly; under surface densely scaly, the scales fawn or brown, overlapping; *petiole* 1—2 mm. long, scaly, *not bristly. Inflorescence* terminal, umbellate, 1-flowered, flower-bud scales persistent; *pedicel* 1.4—3 cm. long, longer than the corolla or equalling it, moderately or rather densely scaly, *not bristly* or rarely bristly. *Calyx* 5-lobed to base, 4—7 mm. long, lobes crimson or green, ovate, ovate-lanceolate, oval or lanceolate, outside glabrous, not bristly, moderately or rather densely scaly along the middle, margin fringed with long or short hairs. *Corolla* widely funnel-shaped, 1.5—2 cm. long, 5-lobed, dark rosy-purple or purple, with or without crimson spots at the base of the upper three lobes, outside moderately or rather densely pubescent, scaly along the middle of the lobes. *Stamens* 10, unequal, long-exserted, 0.6—1.1 cm. long; filaments densely villous towards the base. *Ovary* conoid, 2 mm. long, 5-celled, densely scaly; style red, longer than the stamens, glabrous. *Capsule* ovoid or conoid, 5—6 mm. long, densely scaly, enclosed by the persistent calyx-lobes.

Forrest first found this plant in August 1921 in the Salwin-Kiu-chiang Divide, eastern Tibet. He collected it again later in the same region. In 1923 Rock found it in the Salwin-Irrawadi watershed, south-eastern Tibet. It grows in open alpine moors and in open stony moorland, at elevations of 4,270—4,575 m. (14,000—15,000 ft.).

R. radicans is a distinctive species. It is easily recognised by its prostrate creeping habit of growth, and by the narrow, linear, lanceolate, narrowly oblanceolate or narrowly oblong leaves, being 3—5 times as long as broad. In these respects it is readily distinguished from its allies *R. keleticum* and *R. prostratum*. It further differs from the latter in the absence of bristles from the branchlets, petioles and pedicels.

The species was first introduced by Forrest in 1921 (No. 19919 — the Type number). It was reintroduced by him from the same region, under Nos. 20235 and 20861. Two distinct forms are in cultivation. Form 1. A completely prostrate creeping shrub, 1 inch

28. R. radicans
nat. size

a. section. b. ovary, style. c. capsule.

high. Form 2. A small shrublet forming a low compact mound 8 inches high, with creeping outer branches. A distinct feature in both forms is the rooting of the branches as they creep along the ground. Although the species is hardy, it is liable to be damaged by severe spring frosts along the east coast, but the damage is usually repaired by new growths later in the growing season. It is usually free-flowering, and provides an admirable display with its dark rosy-purple flowers in May and June. It is a charming plant for the rock garden, although in cultivation it has not received the wide recognition it deserves. A completely prostrate form, under Forrest No. 19919, was given an Award of Merit when shown by J.B. Stevenson, Tower Court, Ascot, in 1926.

Epithet. Rooting.

Hardiness 3. May—June. Plate 55.

R. saluenense Franch. in Journ. de Bot. XII (1898) 263.

Illustration. Bot. Mag. Vol. 151 t. 9095 (1926).

A broadly upright, upright, spreading, somewhat rounded or compact rounded shrub, *60 cm.—1.53 m. (2—5 ft.)* or sometimes 30 cm. (1 ft.) high; *branchlets* densely scaly with flaky stalked scales, *moderately or densely bristly*, leaf-bud scales deciduous or subpersistent. *Leaves* oval, oblong-oval, nearly orbicular, ovate-elliptic or oblong-elliptic, aromatic, *lamina* coriaceous, *1.4—3.6 cm. long*, 0.8—2.4 cm. broad, apex rounded with a reflexed or straight mucro, base rounded or obtuse; *upper surface dark green, (in young leaves dark green), shining* or rarely matt, *rather densely or moderately scaly*, the scales ½—6 times their own diameter apart, sparsely or rarely moderately bristly or not bristly; margin bristly or not bristly; under surface densely scaly, the scales yellowish-brown or brown, overlapping; *petiole* 3—6 mm. long, moderately or rather densely scaly, *bristly. Inflorescence* terminal, umbellate, 1—4- or sometimes 5—7-flowered, flower-bud scales subpersistent or persistent; *pedicel* 0.8—2.5 cm. long, shorter than the corolla, moderately or rather densely scaly, *sparsely to rather densely bristly* or sometimes not bristly. *Calyx* 5-lobed to base, 5—8 mm. long, lobes pinkish-purple or crimson, ovate, oval, ovate-elliptic or oblong-oval, ouside puberulous or rarely glabrous, rather densely to slightly scaly along the middle or rarely not scaly, margin fringed with long hairs. *Corolla* widely funnel-shaped, 2.1—3 cm. long, 5—lobed, purplish-rose, deep purple, deep rose, deep crimson-rose, very deep plum-purple or deep purple-crimson, with or rarely without crimson spots at the base of the upper three lobes, outside rather densely or moderately pubescent, rather densely or moderately scaly along the middle of the lobes. *Stamens* 10, slightly unequal, long-exserted, 1—2.4 cm. long; filaments densely villous towards the base. *Ovary* conoid, 2—3 mm. long, 5-celled, densely scaly, glabrous or rarely puberulous; style red, longer than the stamens, puberulous at the base or glabrous. *Capsule* conoid or ovoid, 0.6—1 cm. long, densely scaly, enclosed or partly enclosed by the persistent calyx-lobes.

This species was discovered by the Abbé Soulié in 1894 at Dong in the valley of the Upper Mekong, and in June 1895 at Sela in the Mekong-Salwin Divide, eastern Tibet. It was later found by other collectors in east and south-east Tibet, north-west Yunnan and south-west Szechuan. The plant grows in open alpine pastures, in open stony meadows, on hillsides, on ledges of limestone cliffs, on rocky slopes, amongst rocks, on boulders, in boggy moorland meadows, at the margins of conifer forests, and by streams, at elevations of 3,050—4,270 m. (10,000—14,000 ft.). Yü records it as being common in north-west Yunnan. Kingdon-Ward found it forming thickets on alpine slopes in south-east Tibet.

R. saluenense is a very variable palnt. It is a broadly upright, upright, spreading, somewhat rounded or compact rounded shrub, and grows from 2 to 5 feet (or sometimes 1 foot) high; the leaves (laminae) are 1.4—3.6 cm. long, 0.8—2.4 cm. broad, and the inflorescence is 1—4- or sometimes 5—7-flowered. A striking feature of this plant is the moderately or densely bristly branchlets and petioles. It is allied to *R. chameunum* which it resembles in the bristly character, but differs in that it is usually a larger shrub with larger leaves, the young leaves are dark green, and the upper surface of the leaves is rather densely or moderately scaly. It is also related to *R. calostrotum*; the distinctions between them are discussed under the latter. The plant is a diploid with 26 chromosomes or tetraploid with 52 chromosomes.

The species was first introduced by Forrest in 1914 (No. 12934). It was reintroduced many times by him, by Kingdon-Ward, Rock, and Yü. Five distinct forms are in cultivation: Form 1. A large somewhat rounded shrub, 5 feet high and as much across, with large shiny leaves and purplish-rose flowers. Form 2. A small spreading shrub, densely branched, 2 feet high and 3 feet across, with medium-sized very shiny leaves, and deep purple-crimson flowers. Form 3. A broadly upright shrub, 3 feet high with bristly, greyish leaves, matt above. Form 4. A compact rounded shrub 2 or 3 feet high and as much across with shiny leaves. Form 5. An upright shrub, somewhat lax and straggly, 2 or 3 feet high, with small leaves. The species has a long flowering season which extends from April to the end of June. Some plants, particularly Form 2, produce the flowers twice during the year, in May and again later in August or September. The species is free-flowering, and one of its chief merits is that it flowers at a remarkably early age. It is very hardy, a robust grower, and is not particular as to position in the garden. The smaller forms up to 2 or 3 feet high are well suited for the rock garden. The species received an Award of Merit when exhibited by E. de Rothschild, Exbury, in 1945.

Epithet. From the Salwin River.

Hardiness 3. April—June.

SCABRIFOLIUM SERIES

General characters: small, medium-sized or large shrubs or sometimes small trees, 15 cm.—4.58 m. (6 in.—15 ft.) high; branchlets bristly or not bristly, *rather densely pubescent* or sometimes glabrous, moderately or rather densely scaly. Leaves lanceolate, linear, oblong-lanceolate, oblanceolate, oblong, obovate or sometimes oval, lamina 1—9.5 cm. long, 0.2—4.5 cm. broad; upper surface bristly or not bristly, *rather densely or moderately pubescent* or sometimes glabrous; *under surface* pale green (in *R. hemitrichotum* and *R. racemosum* glaucous), *rather densely or moderately pubescent* (in *R. hemitrichotum* and *R. racemosum* glabrous except sometimes midrib pubescent), scaly, the scales ½—4 times their own diameter apart; *petiole* bristly or not bristly, *rather densely pubescent* (in *R. racemosum* glabrous or puberulous). Inflorescence axillary, 1—4- (or rarely 5-) flowered; *pedicel* 0.4—1.9 cm. long, bristly or not bristly, *densely or moderately pubescent* (in *R. racemosum* glabrous or sometimes minutely puberulous). *Calyx* 0.5—5 mm. long, *outside rather densely or moderately pubescent* (in *R. hemitrichotum* and *R. racemosum* usually glabrous), margin often pubescent. Corolla widely funnel-shaped or narrowly tubular-funnel shaped or tubular, 0.8—2.8 cm. long, rose, pink, white, reddish-purple, crimson or rarely yellowish, with or without purple or crimson spots. Stamens 10 or rarely 8. Ovary oval, ovate, conoid or oblong, densely pubescent or sometimes glabrous; style long, straight. Capsule oval, oblong-oval or oblong, 0.4—1.5 cm. long, densely or moderately pubescent or sometimes glabrous.

Distribution: south-west Szechuan, north-west, west, mid-west and southern Yunnan, and Kweichow.

The Series contains six species allied to the Virgatum Series, with a general tendency towards the Triflorum Series.

KEY TO THE SPECIES

A. Under surface of the leaves glaucous, not pubescent except sometimes midrib.
  B. Branchlets and petioles rather densely pubescent; upper surface of the leaves rather densely or moderately pubescent; pedicels and capsules puberulous; leaves lanceolate, oblanceolate, oblong-lanceolate or oblong ....
  .... *hemitrichotum*
  B. Branchlets and petioles glabrous or puberulous; upper surface of the leaves glabrous or rarely puberulous; pedicels glabrous or sometimes minutely puberulous, capsule glabrous; leaves oval, elliptic, obovate, oblong-elliptic, oblong-obovate, oblong or oblong-lanceolate .... *racemosum*
A. Under surface of the leaves pale green, rather densely or sometimes moderately pubescent.
    C. Corolla tubular, contracted at the upper end; stamens usually glabrous; upper surface of the leaves usually not bristly .... *spinuliferum*
    C. Corolla widely funnel-shaped or narrowly tubular-funnel shaped; stamens usually puberulous towards the base; upper surface of the leaves bristly or not bristly.
      D. Corolla widely funnel-shaped, not oblique, 1—1.7 cm. long; upper surface of the leaves bristly, rough (rarely not bristly), margins bristly (rarely not bristly); calyx 5-lobed, 0.5—5 mm. long; branchlets moderately or rather densely bristly.
        E. Leaves (laminae) usually 3.5—9.5 cm. long, 1—2.8 cm. broad, lanceolate, oblong-lanceolate or elliptic .... *scabrifolium*
        E. Leaves (laminae) usually 1.2—3 cm. long, 2—8 mm. broad, linear, linear-lanceolate, lanceolate to oblong-obovate ....
        .... *spiciferum*
      D. Corolla narrowly tubular-funnel shaped, oblique, 1.7—3.4 cm. long; upper surface of the leaves not bristly, not rough (rarely sparsely bristly), margins not bristly; calyx cupular or 5-lobed, 0.5—1 mm. long; branchlets not bristly or sparsely or moderately bristly .... *mollicomum*

DESCRIPTION OF THE SPECIES

R. hemitrichotum Balf. f. et Forrest in Notes Roy. Bot. Gard. Edin., Vol. 12 (1920) 115.

A broadly upright shrub, 25 cm.—2.44 m. (10 in.—8 ft.) high; *branchlets* not bristly or rarely bristly, *rather densely pubescent*, moderately or rather densely scaly. *Leaves* lanceolate, oblanceolate, oblong-lanceolate or oblong, lamina 1.2—4.5 cm. long, 0.3—1.3 cm. broad, apex acute or sometimes obtuse, mucronate, base tapered or sometimes obtuse; *upper surface* not scabrid, not bristly or rarely bristly, *rather densely or sometimes moderately pubescent*, moderately or sparsely scaly; margin recurved, not bristly, not pubescent; *under surface glaucous*, not pubescent, midrib not pubescent or sometimes pubescent, scaly, the scales medium-sized, unequal, brown or pale brown, their own diameter apart or sometimes ½ their own diameter apart; *petiole* 2—4 mm. long, not bristly or rarely bristly, *rather densely* (or rarely moderately) *pubescent*, scaly. *Inflorescence* axillary in the uppermost few leaves, flowers usually in several clusters or rarely forming a raceme along the branchlet, umbellate or shortly racemose, 1—3-flowered; rhachis 0.5—2 mm. long, pubescent, not bristly, scaly or not scaly, flower-bud scales persistent during flowering; *pedicel* 0.4—1 cm. long, *puberulous* or rarely glabrous, not bristly, scaly. *Calyx* 5-lobed or a mere rim or cupular, 0.5 mm. long, lobes triangular or ovate, outside puberulous or glabrous, not bristly, densely or moderately scaly, margin puberulous or glabrous, ciliate or eciliate. *Corolla* widely funnel-shaped, 5-lobed, 0.9—1.4 cm. long, pale rose or pink or deep pink, or white edged with pink, with or without purple spots, outside scaly. *Stamens* 8—10, unequal, 0.8—1.5 cm. long; filaments puberulous towards the base or rarely glabrous. *Ovary* conoid, 2 mm. long, 5-celled, puberulous or glabrous, densely scaly; style long, straight, longer than the stamens, glabrous or rarely sparsely puberulous at the base. *Capsule* oblong or sometimes oblong-ovate, 5—8 mm. long, 2—3 mm. broad, *puberulous* or rarely glabrous, rather densely scaly, calyx persistent.

R. hemitrichotum was first collected by Forrest in June 1918 on the Muli mountains, south-west Szechuan. Subsequently it was found by him again and by other collectors in various localities in the same region and in west Yunnan. It grows in open rocky pasture, on dry rocky slopes amongst scrub, in open thickets in side valleys, in dry open meadows, in dry pine forests, and in dry oak forests, at elevations of 2,440—3,965 m. (8,000—13,000 ft.).

The species shows a resemblance to *R. racemosum*, particularly in the glaucous lower surfaces of the leaves. The distinctions between them are that in *R. hemitrichotum* the branchlets and petioles are rather densely pubescent, the upper surfaces of the leaves are rather densely or moderately pubescent, and the pedicels and capsules are puberulous; in *R. racemosum* the branchlets and petioles are glabrous or puberulous, the upper surfaces of the leaves are glabrous or rarely puberulous, the pedicels are glabrous or sometimes minutely puberulous, and the capsule is glabrous. Moreover, in *R. hemitrichotum* the leaves are lanceolate, oblanceolate, oblong-lanceolate or oblong; in *R. racemosum* they are oval, elliptic, obovate to oblong or oblong-lanceolate. *R. hemitrichotum* is also allied to *R. spiciferum* which differs mainly in that the branchlets and leaves are bristly, and the lower surfaces of the leaves are pale green and rather densely pubescent.

R. hemitrichotum was first introduced by Forrest in 1918 from south-west Szechuan (No. 16250 — the Type number). It was reintroduced several times by him, by Kingdon-Ward, and by Yü. In cultivation it is a broadly upright shrub up to 5 or 6 feet high. It is hardy, free-flowering, and easy to grow.

Epithet. Half-hairy.
Hardiness 3. April—May.

R. mollicomum Balf. f. et W.W. Sm. in Notes Roy. Bot. Gard. Edin., Vol. 9 (1916) 249.

A broadly upright shrub, 60 cm.—1.83 m. (2—6 ft.) high; branchlets not bristly or bristly, rather densely pubescent, scaly. *Leaves* lanceolate or rarely oblong, lamina 1.2—3.6 cm. long, 0.3—1.3 cm. broad, apex acute or obtuse, mucronate, base tapered or obtuse; *upper surface not scabrid, not bristly* or rarely sparsely bristly, rather densely pubescent, scaly; *margin* recurved, *not bristly*, pubescent; under surface pale green, rather densely pubescent, scaly, the scales medium-sized, unequal, pale brown or brown, 1—3 times their own diameter apart; petiole 3—5 mm. long, not bristly or bristly, rather densely pubescent, scaly. *Inflorescence* axillary in the uppermost few leaves, flowers usually in several clusters, umbellate or shortly racemose, 1—3-flowered; rhachis 1—2 mm. long, pubescent, not bristly, sparsely scaly or not scaly, flower-bud scales persistent during flowering; pedicel 0.5—1.4 cm. long, rather densely pubescent, not bristly, scaly. *Calyx cupular or 5-lobed, 0.5—1 mm. long,* lobes rounded or triangular, outside rather densely or rarely sparsely pubescent, not bristly, moderately or rather densely scaly, margin not bristly or sometimes sparsely bristly, pubescent. *Corolla narrowly tubular-funnel shaped, oblique, 5-lobed, 1.7—2.8 cm. long,* pale or deep rose, without spots, outside scaly. *Stamens* 10 or rarely 8, unequal, 1.3—3 cm. long; filaments puberulous towards the base. *Ovary* oblong or conoid, 2—4 mm. long, 5-celled, rather densely or rarely sparsely pubescent, densely scaly; style long, straight, longer than the stamens, pubescent at the base or in the lower ⅓ of its length. *Capsule* oblong, 0.6—1 cm. long, 2—4 mm. broad, rather densely or rarely moderately pubescent, rather densely scaly, calyx persistent.

Forrest discovered this plant in July 1913 on the mountains in the north-east of the Yangtze bend, north-west Yunnan. He found it again in other localities in the same region, and in south-west Szechuan. Rock collected it on the eastern slopes of the Lichiang Snow Range in 1922. It grows in open thickets, in open scrub, in open situations amongst scrub on the margins of pine forests, and amongst scrub on bouldery hillsides, at elevations of 2,440—3,355 m. (8,000—11,000 ft.).

R. mollicomum is allied to *R. spiciferum* which it resembles in general appearance, but is distinguished mainly by the shape and size of the corolla, and by the non-bristly upper surfaces and margins of the leaves.

The species was first introduced by Forrest in 1913 from north-west Yunnan (No. 10347—the Type number). It was reintroduced by him a few times from the same region. In cultivation it is a broadly upright shrub, up to 6 feet high. It is hardy with narrowly tubular-funnel shaped deep rose flowers in axillary clusters of 1—3 produced with great freedom. Although uncommon in cultivation, it is a pleasing shrub, fairly fast-growing, and is well worth a place in every collection of rhododendrons. It received an Award of Merit when exhibited by Lady Aberconway and the Hon. H.D. McLaren, Bodnant, in 1931.

Epithet. Soft-haired.
Hardiness 3. April—May.

R. mollicomum Balf. f. et W.W. Sm. var. **rockii** Tagg in Notes Roy. Bot. Gard. Edin., Vol. 15 (1926) 114.

This plant was first collected by Rock in April 1923 on the western slope of the Lichiang Snow Range, Yunnan. It was later found by Forrest in the Chienchuan-Mekong divide, mid-west Yunnan. The plant grows in forests on steep slopes, and amongst scrub on rocky hillsides, at elevations of 2,745—3,050 m. (9,000—10,000 ft.).

The variety differs from the species in the larger corolla 2.7—3.4 cm. long, in the longer stamens up to 3.5 cm. long, and in the longer gynoecium 3.5—5 cm. long. The flowers are reddish-purple, reddish or pale rose. The plant has not been introduced into cultivation.

Epithet of the variety. After J.F. Rock, an American collector in China.
Not in cultivation.

R. racemosum Franch. in Bull. Soc. Bot. France, XXXIII (1886) 235.

Illustration. Bot. Mag. Vol. 119 t. 7301 (1893).

A compact rounded, or cushion, or widely branched, or broadly upright, or lax upright shrub, 15 cm.—4.58 m. (6 in.—15 ft.) high; *branchlets glabrous or minutely puberulous*, moderately or rather densely scaly, the scales often peltate. *Leaves* elliptic, oblong-elliptic, obovate, oblong-obovate, oval, oblong or oblong-lanceolate, lamina 1—5.4 cm. long, 0.4—2.6 cm. broad, apex obtuse or rounded or rarely acute, mucronate, base obtuse or rounded or rarely tapered; *upper surface* not scabrid, *glabrous* or rarely puberulous, scaly or not scaly, midrib glabrous or puberulous; margin moderately or slightly recurved, glabrous; *under surface glaucous* or rarely not glaucous, glabrous, midrib glabrous or rarely minutely puberulous, scaly, the scales medium-sized or small, unequal, pale brown to dark brown, ½ to their own diameter apart or sometimes twice their own diameter apart; *petiole* 2—6 mm. long, *glabrous or puberulous*, scaly. *Inflorescence* axillary in the uppermost few leaves, flowers usually in several clusters or sometimes forming a raceme along the branchlet, umbellate or shortly racemose, 1—4-flowered; rhachis 0.5—2 mm. long, minutely puberulous or glabrous, scaly or not scaly, flower-bud scales persistent during flowering or rarely deciduous; *pedicel* 0.4—1.7 cm. long, *glabrous or sometimes minutely puberulous*, moderately or rather densely scaly. *Calyx* cupular or a mere rim or 5-lobed, 0.5 mm. long, lobes rounded or triangular, outside glabrous, densely or moderately scaly, margin not bristly or sometimes bristly, eciliate or rarely ciliate, not puberulous or rarely puberulous, densely or moderately scaly. *Corolla* widely funnel-shaped, 5-lobed, 0.8—2.3 cm. long, pale or deep rose, pink, reddish-pink or white, without or sometimes with crimson spots, outside scaly or rarely not scaly. *Stamens* 10, unequal, 0.8—2.3 cm. long; filaments puberulous towards the base or sometimes glabrous. *Ovary* conoid or sometimes oblong, 2—3 mm. long, 5-celled, glabrous, densely scaly; style long, straight, longer than, or sometimes as long as, the stamens, glabrous or sometimes sparsely puberulous at the base, not scaly. *Capsule* oblong or sometimes oblong-ovate, 0.4—1 cm. long, 2—4 mm. broad, *glabrous*, rather densely scaly, calyx persistent.

This well-known species is widely distributed in mid-west and north-west Yunnan, and south-west Szechuan. It was discovered by the Abbé Delavay in April 1884, on He-chan mountain, above Lan Kong, Yunnan. It grows in very varied habitats, in open scrub, on dry limestone hills, in open mountain pastureland, in dry stony and open rocky situations, amongst boulders, on ledges of cliffs, in peaty boggy ground, in thickets and in oak and pine forests, at elevations of 1,830—4,270 m. (6,000—14,000 ft.). According to Forrest, the species covers large tracts in open situations and is abundant in open pine forests in north-west Yunnan. Kingdon-Ward records it as being a dwarf shrub less than a foot in height, growing in matted carpets, on the steep, rocky slopes of the valley, east of the Yangtze bend.

In *The Species of Rhododendron, R. racemosum* appeared in the Virgatum Series; it is an aberrant species in that Series. It closely resembles the species of the Scabrifolium Series to which it was transferred in 1963 (*The Rhododendron and Camellia Year Book*, p. 104 (1963)).

R. racemosum shows considerable variation, particularly in habit and height of growth, and in leaf shape and size. It is a compact rounded, spreading, broadly upright or upright shrub, 6 inches to 15 feet high; the leaves are oval, obovate to oblong-lanceolate, 1—5.4 cm. long, 0.4—2.6 cm. broad. The glaucous lower surfaces of the leaves are a distinctive feature. In this respect it is similar to *R. hemitrichotum*, its nearest ally. The relationship between them is discussed under the latter.

The species was first introduced by the Abbé Delavay from Yunnan. It was then raised in the Jardin des Plantes in 1889, and thence introduced to Kew in November of the same year. It was reintroduced many times by other collectors. Several forms are in cultivation, including: Form 1. A dwarf compact rounded shrub, 2 feet high and as much across, with reddish-pink flowers, introduced by Forrest under No. 19404. Form 2. A somewhat compact spreading shrub, 3 feet high and 4 feet across with rose flowers. Form 3. A broadly upright shrub, 6 feet high with deep pink flowers. Form 4. A lax upright shrub, 9 feet high with white tinged pink flowers. The species is free-flowering, and in some forms up to 10 inches of the upper parts of the branchlets are covered with axillary 1—4-flowered inflorescences. Most of the plants produce good fertile seed in plenty, and the capsules often persist on the plant for a year or more. The species is very hardy, and it flowers at an early age when raised from seed. Form 1, a dwarf compact shrub up to 2 feet high (Forrest No. 19404) is a charming plant, and is well suited for the rock garden. The species was given a First Class Certificate when shown by J. Veitch & Son, Chelsea in 1892. An Award of Merit was given to a form 'Rock Rose', 4 or 5 feet high with bright pink flowers, when exhibited by Hydon Nurseries in 1970, the original plant having been raised at Tower Court. A tall-growing form with deep pink flowers shown from Glendoick, also received an Award of Merit, and the same Award was given to a form 'White Lace' with white flowers when exhibited from Glendoick in 1974. It was also given an Award of Garden Merit in 1930.

Epithet. Flowers in racemes.

Hardiness 3. March—May. Plate 56.

R. scabrifolium Franch. in Bull. Soc. Bot. France, XXXIII (1886) 236.

Illustration. Bot. Mag. Vol. 117 t. 7159 (1891).

A low spreading, or upright shrub, 23 cm.—3 m. (9 in.—10 ft.) high; branchlets moderately or rather densely bristly, densely pubescent, scaly. *Leaves* lanceolate, oblong-lanceolate or sometimes elliptic, *lamina 2.3—9.5 cm. long, 0.6—2.8 cm.* broad, apex acute or obtuse or rarely acuminate, mucronate, base obtuse or tapered; *upper surface* bullate, *scabrid, bristly* or rarely not bristly, rather densely or moderately pubescent, sparsely scaly or not scaly; *margin moderately* or slightly recurved, *bristly* or rarely not bristly, pubescent; under surface pale green, rather densely or moderately pubescent, scaly, the scales medium-sized, unequal, pale brown or brown, 1—4 times (rarely ½) their own diameter apart, primary veins raised; petiole 3—8 mm. long, moderately or rather densely bristly, rather densely pubescent, scaly. *Inflorescence* axillary in the uppermost few leaves, flowers usually in several clusters, umbellate or shortly racemose, 1—3-flowered; rhachis 1—3 mm. long, pubescent, bristly or not bristly, not scaly or sparsely scaly, flower-bud scales persistent during flowering or rarely deciduous; pedicel 0.5—1.9 cm. long, densely pubescent, bristly or not bristly, scaly. *Calyx* 5-lobed, 0.5—5 mm. long, lobes rounded, lanceolate, ovate or triangular, outside densely pubescent, not bristly or rarely bristly, sparsely or moderately scaly, margin bristly, pubescent. *Corolla* widely funnel-shaped, 5-lobed, 1—1.7 cm. long, rose, crimson, deep reddish, pink, white, or white faintly flushed pink, outside scaly. *Stamens* 10, unequal, 0.7—2.3 cm. long; filaments puberulous towards the base or rarely glabrous. *Ovary* oval or ovate or rarely oblong, 2—3 mm. long, 5-celled, densely or rarely moderately pubescent, moderately or densely scaly; style long, straight, longer than the stamens, puberulous at the base or rarely glabrous. *Capsule* oval or oblong-oval or oblong, 4—8 mm. long, 3—4 mm. broad, densely pubescent, moderately or rather densely scaly, calyx-lobes persistent.

This species is a native of Yunnan. It was first collected by the Abbé Delavay in June 1887 on Heechanmen mountain above Lankong. Subsequently it was found by other collectors in various localities in the same region. It grows in thickets, in scrub, amongst rocks, in pine and oak scrub, and in pine forests, at elevations of 1,800—3,355 m. (5,902—11,000 ft.).

R. scabrifolium varies considerably in height of growth, ranging from 9 inches to 10 feet high. It is very similar to *R. spiciferum* in the bristly and pubescent branchlets and leaves, and in the shape, size and colour of the flowers, but differs usually in the size and often in the shape of the leaves. It also shows a resemblance to *R. spinuliferum* from which it is readily distinguished by the shape of the corolla, by the bristly upper surface of the leaves, usually by the larger calyx, and very often by the stamens which are puberulous towards the base.

The species was first introduced by Delavay in 1885. It was reintroduced by Forrest, Kingdon-Ward, Rock, and McLaren's collectors. In cultivation it is a low spreading, or upright shrub. Although in its native home it grows up to 10 feet high, in cultivation it reaches a height of only 5 or sometimes 6 feet. A broadly upright form up to 4 feet high provides a fine display with its axillary deep reddish flowers produced in great profusion. The species varies in hardiness, and to be able to grow it satisfactorily, particularly along the east coast and in gardens inland, a well-sheltered position should be provided.

Epithet. With rough leaves.
Hardiness 3. March—May.

R. spiciferum Franch. in Journ. de Bot. IX (1895) 400.
Illustration. Bot. Mag. Vol. 156 t. 9319 (1933). Figured as *R. pubescens.*
A low spreading, or upright shrub, 15 cm.—1.53 m. (6 in.—5 ft.) high; branchlets moderately or rather densely bristly or rarely not bristly, densely or rarely moderately pubescent, scaly. *Leaves linear, linear-lanceolate, lanceolate, oblanceolate, oblong or oblong-obovate, lamina 1.2—3.5 cm. long, 0.2—1.3 cm. broad,* apex acute or obtuse or rounded, mucronate, base tapered or obtuse or rarely rounded; *upper surface scabrid, bristly* or rarely not bristly, rather densely or moderately pubescent, scaly or not scaly; *margin* recurved, *bristly* or rarely not bristly, pubescent; under surface pale green, rather densely

or sometimes moderately pubescent, scaly, the scales medium-sized, unequal, pale brown or brown, 1—2 or rarely 3 times their own diameter apart; petiole 1—3 mm. long, moderately or rarely sparsely bristly, densely pubescent, sparsely or moderately scaly. *Inflorescence* axillary in the uppermost few leaves, flowers usually in several clusters, or rarely forming a raceme along the branchlet, umbellate or shortly racemose, 1—4-flowered; rhachis 1—3 mm. long, pubescent or rarely glabrous, not bristly or rarely bristly, not scaly or sparsely scaly, flower-bud scales persistent during flowering or rarely deciduous; pedicel 0.4—1 cm. long, rather densely or rarely moderately pubescent, not bristly or bristly, scaly. *Calyx* 5-lobed, 0.5—1 mm. or sometimes 2—4 mm. long, lobes ovate or triangular or lanceolate, outside rather densely or moderately pubescent or rarely glabrous, not bristly, scaly, margin bristly, pubescent or not pubescent. *Corolla* widely funnel-shaped, 5-lobed, 1—1.5 cm. long, pink or deep pink or rose or white, outside scaly. *Stamens* 10, unequal, 0.6—1.8 cm. long; filaments puberulous towards the base or rarely glabrous. *Ovary* ovate, oval or oblong, 1—2 mm. long, 5-celled, densely or rarely moderately pubescent, moderately or densely scaly; style long, straight, longer than the stamens, pubescent at the base or glabrous. *Capsule* oblong or oblong-ovate, 5—8 mm. long, 2—4 mm. broad, densely or moderately pubescent, rather densely or moderately scaly, calyx persistent.

R. spiciferum was discovered by the Abbé Delavay in March 1891 near Yunnansen, Yunnan. It was later found by other collectors in west and north-west Yunnan, Kweichow, and south-west Szechuan. The plant grows in thickets, amongst scrub, amongst rocks, and in pine woods, at elevations of 1,525—3,200 m. (5,000—10,492 ft.)

In 1920, *R. pubescens* Balf. f. et Forrest was described from a specimen (No. 16812) collected by Forrest in August 1918 on the Muli mountains, south-west Szechuan. The species is identical with *R. spiciferum* in every respect, and in *The Rhododendron and Camellia Year Book*, 1964, it was placed in synonymy under *R. spiciferum*.

R. spiciferum is very variable in height of growth, from 6 inches to 5 feet high, and in leaf shape from linear to oblong-obovate. It is very closely allied to *R. scabrifolium*, but differs usually in the size and often in the shape of the leaves. It is also related to *R. racemosum*, from which it is distinguished mainly by the bristly and pubescent branchlets and leaves, and by the pale green lower surfaces of the leaves.

The species was first introduced by Kingdon-Ward in 1921 under No. 3952A. Two distinct growth forms are in cultivation: Form 1. A low spreading shrub, 2 feet high and 3—4 feet across. Form 2. An upright shrub, 4—5 feet high. The smaller forms with axillary rose flowers produced with freedom, are well worth growing in the rock garden. A clone, 'Fine Bristles' received an Award of Merit when exhibited under the name *R. pubescens* by the Crown Estate Commissioners, Windsor Great Park, in April 1955.

Epithet. Breaking spikes.
Hardiness 3. April—May.

R. spinuliferum Franch. in Journ. de Bot. IX (1895) 399.
Illustration. Bot. Mag. Vol. 137 t. 8408 (1911).
A broadly upright shrub or sometimes a small tree, 60 cm.—4.58 m. (2—15 ft.) high; branchlets moderately or rather densely bristly, rather densely pubescent, scaly. *Leaves* lanceolate, oblong-lanceolate, oblanceolate, obovate, oblong-elliptic or elliptic, lamina 2.4—9.5 cm. long, 0.6—4.5 cm. broad, apex acuminate, acutely acuminate, acute, obtuse or rarely rounded, mucronate, base obtuse or tapered; *upper surface bullate*, not scabrid or rarely scabrid, *not bristly* or rarely bristly, puberulous or glabrous, sparsely or moderately scaly; margin recurved or flat, bristly or sometimes not bristly, pubescent or sometimes not pubescent; under surface rather densely pubescent, midrib not bristly or rarely sparsely bristly, scaly, the scales medium-sized, unequal, brown or pale brown, ½—3 times their own diameter apart, primary veins raised; petiole 0.3—1 cm. long, bristly, rather densely pubescent, scaly. *Inflorescence* axillary in the uppermost few leaves, or

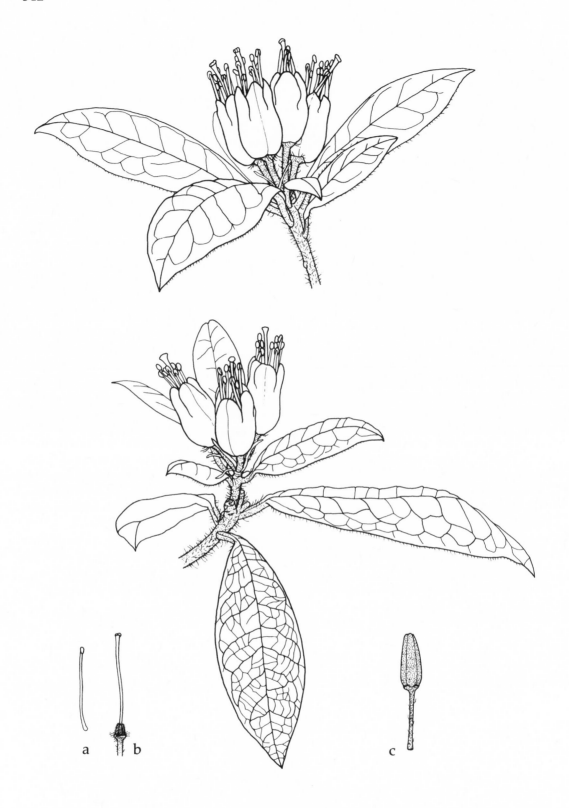

29. R. spinuliferum
nat. size

a. stamen. b. ovary, style. c. capsule.

terminal, flowers sometimes in several clusters, umbellate or shortly racemose, 1—4- (or rarely 5-) flowered; rhachis 1—3 mm. long, pubescent, not bristly or rarely sparsely bristly, sparsely scaly or not scaly, flower-bud scales deciduous during flowering or persistent; pedicel 0.4—1.2 cm. long, densely pubescent, not bristly or rarely bristly, scaly or not scaly. *Calyx* cupular or 5-lobed, *0.5 mm. long*, lobes triangular or rounded, outside densely pubescent, not bristly, scaly or not scaly, margin bristly or rarely not bristly, pubescent. *Corolla tubular, contracted at the upper end*, 5-lobed, 1.4—2.5 cm. long, crimson-red, red, pink or yellowish, outside not scaly or sometimes scaly. *Stamens* 10, unequal, 1.2—3 cm. long; *filaments glabrous* or sometimes puberulous towards the base. *Ovary* conoid or rarely oblong, 3—4 mm. long, 5-celled, densely tomentose, densely or moderately scaly; style long, straight, longer than the stamens, glabrous or puberulous at the base. *Capsule* oblong or oblong-oval, 0.7—1.5 cm. long, 4—5 mm. broad, densely tomentose, rather densely scaly, calyx persistent.

The distribution of this species is restricted to Yunnan. It was first collected by the Abbé Delavay in July 1891 above Tonghay, southern Yunnan. The plant was afterwards found by other collectors in the same region. It grows in woods and shady thickets at elevations of 800—2,440 m. (2,623—8,000 ft.).

R. spinuliferum is a unique species in that the tubular corolla is contracted at the upper end with protruding stamens and style. In this respect, it is readily distinguished from all other members of its Series. The upright flowers in clusters of 1—5 are a characteristic feature. The species is allied to *R. scabrifolium* which it resembles in the shape and size of the leaves, in the bristly and pubescent branchlets and petioles, and in the pubescent lower surface of the leaves, but is readily distinguished by the shape of the corolla, by the non-bristly upper surface of the leaves, usually by the glabrous stamens, and the smaller calyx.

The species was first introduced to France by Maurice de Vilmorin in 1907, and thence it reached Kew in 1910. It was reintroduced by Rock in 1932, and several times by McLaren in the same year. In its native home it is a shrub or sometimes a small tree, and grows from 2 feet up to 15 feet high; in cultivation it is a broadly upright shrub 5—7 feet in height. The species varies in hardiness. Although the plant comes from relatively low elevations in Yunnan, it has proved hardy along the east coast in well-sheltered positions, except in one or two very cold gardens with heavy frosts. It is fairly fast-growing, and provides a fine show with its tubular, crimson-red or red flowers produced freely in clusters of 1—5. A form 'Jack Hext' was given an Award of Merit when shown by Nigel T. Holman, Chyverton, Truro, Cornwall, in 1974, and again the same Award to another form 'Blackwater' when exhibited by Brodick Castle Gardens, Isle of Arran, in 1977.

Epithet. Bearing spines.

Hardiness 2—3. April—May.

TEPHROPEPLUM SERIES

General characters: small, medium-sized or tall shrubs, sometimes epiphytic, 30 cm.—3 m. (1—10 ft.) or rarely 4.58 m. (15 ft.) high; branchlets moderately or rather densely scaly, glabrous. Leaves evergreen, lanceolate, oblong-lanceolate, ovate-lanceolate, oblong or oblong-obovate, lamina 2.7—13 cm. long, 0.8—4 cm. broad; under surface pale green, pale glaucous green or glaucous, densely scaly, the scales ½ to their own diameter apart or nearly contiguous or sometimes 3—4 times their own diameter apart; petiole moderately or densely scaly, glabrous. Inflorescence terminal, or terminal and axillary in the uppermost one or two leaves, 3—9-flowered; pedicel 0.5—2.5 cm. or rarely 3 cm. long, moderately or densely scaly, glabrous. Calyx 5-lobed, 3—8 mm. long, (in *R. chrysolepis* an undulate rim, minute, 0.5—1 mm. long). Corolla tubular-campanulate or sometimes campanulate, 1.8—3.4 cm. long, 5-lobed, yellow, sulphur-yellow, lemon-yellow, rose, pink, purplish or rarely white. Stamens 10. Ovary conoid, ovoid or oblong, 2—5 mm. long, 5-celled (in *R. chrysolepis* 5—6-celled), densely scaly; *style long, slender and straight*, scaly at the base or to two-thirds of its length. Capsule oblong-oval, oval or oblong, 0.5—1.5 cm. long, 4—7 mm. broad, densely scaly.

Distribution: east and south-east Tibet, north-west and west Yunnan, north-east and Upper Burma, and Assam.

In *The Species of Rhododendron*, the species of this Series are placed in the Boothii Series, but they have little in common with this Series. The main features of these species are the tubular-campanulate corolla and the long, slender and straight style. In these respects they differ markedly from the Boothii Series with rotate or broadly campanulate corolla and short, stout and sharply bent style. Moreover, they do not fit well into any known Series. Accordingly, these species are now placed in a new Series, Tephropeplum Series.

The affinity of the Tephropeplum Series is with the Cinnabarinum Series, and less closely with the Ciliatum Series.

KEY TO THE SPECIES

A. Calyx an undulate rim, minute, 0.5—1 mm. long; under surface of the leaves laxly scaly, the scales 3—4 times their own diameter apart; corolla-tube and lobes with bands of scales outside .... *chrysolepis*

A. Calyx 5-lobed, large, leafy, 3—8 mm. long; under surface of the leaves densely scaly, the scales one-half to their own diameter apart or nearly contiguous; scales on corolla-tube and lobes scattered or absent.

    B. Corolla yellow, sulphur-yellow or lemon-yellow, outside rather densely or moderately scaly on the tube and lobes.

        C. Calyx lobes reflexed; stem and branches with brown, smooth, flaking bark; scales on the under surface of the leaves small, with closely scattered large scales .... *auritum*

        C. Calyx lobes erect; stem and branches with rough bark; scales on the under surface of the leaves small, without or sometimes with widely scattered large scales .... *xanthostephanum*

    B. Corolla rose, pink, purplish or rarely white, outside not scaly on the tube and lobes, or sometimes scaly only on the lobes .... *tephropeplum*

DESCRIPTION OF THE SPECIES

R. auritum Tagg in Rhod. Soc. Notes, Vol. 3 (1929—31) 278.

A broadly upright or upright or bushy shrub, 92 cm.—3 m. (3—10 ft.) high; *stem and branches* coppery-red *with brown, smooth, flaking bark*; branchlets rather densely scaly, glabrous, leaf-bud scales deciduous. *Leaves* evergreen, oblong, lanceolate or oblong-lanceolate, lamina coriaceous, 2.7—6.6 cm. long, 1—2.7 cm. broad, apex obtuse or acute, mucronate, base obtuse or tapered; upper surface bright green or dark green, shining, moderately or rather densely scaly, glabrous; *under surface* pale glaucous green, *densely scaly*, the *scales* very unequal in size, *small*, brown or dark brown, one-half to their own diameter apart or nearly contiguous, *with closely scattered large scales*; petiole 5—8 mm. long, densely scaly, glabrous. *Inflorescence* terminal, or terminal and axillary in the uppermost one or two leaves, umbellate, 4—7-flowered, flower-bud scales deciduous; rhachis 1—2 mm. long, scaly, glabrous; pedicel 0.5—1.3 cm. long, densely scaly, glabrous. *Calyx* 5-lobed, 3—5 mm. long, *lobes reflexed*, oblong, ovate or nearly orbicular, outside sparsely or moderately scaly, margin scaly, eciliate. *Corolla* tubular-campanulate, 1.8—2.5 cm. long, 5-lobed, *sulphur-yellow, yellow sometimes tinged red, creamy-yellow, or creamy-white with a slight tinge of pink on the lobes*, outside rather densely or moderately scaly on the tube and lobes, glabrous. *Stamens* 10, unequal, 1—2 cm. long, slightly shorter or longer than the corolla; filaments pubescent towards the base or towards the lower half. *Ovary* conoid or ovoid, 2—4 mm. long, 5-celled, densely scaly, glabrous; style long, slender and straight, as long as the corolla or longer, scaly in the lower one-third or one-half of its length, glabrous. *Capsule* oblong-oval, 0.8—1 cm. long, 4—5 mm. broad, densely scaly, glabrous, calyx-lobes persistent.

Kingdon-Ward discovered this plant in fruit in November 1924 in the Tsangpo Gorge, near Pemako-chung, south-eastern Tibet. The species was described by Tagg in 1931. The description of the truss and flowers is based upon cultivated specimens under Kingdon-Ward No. 6278 — the Type number, which first flowered in 1930 grown by Sir John Ramsden, at Bulstrode Gardens, Gerrards Cross, Bucks., and also upon specimens under the same number which flowered in the same year at the Royal Botanic Garden, Edinburgh. Kingdon-Ward records it as being abundant on gneiss cliffs and boulders in open situations along the river side in the Tsangpo Gorge, at an elevation of 2,440 m. (8,000 ft.). In April 1947, Ludlow, Sherriff and Elliot collected it in the Po-Tsangpo Valley, Pome, growing on open stony banks at 2,135 m. (7,000 ft.), and later in the same month they found it again in the Tsangpo Gorge, Kongbo, on rock cliffs at 2,593 m. (8,500 ft.).

The diagnostic features of the plant are the brown, smooth, flaking bark of the stem and branches, and the reflexed lobes of the calyx. In these respects, the species is readily distinguished from its nearest ally, *R. xanthostephanum*.

In its native home *R. auritum* grows from 3 up to 10 feet high; in cultivation it is a broadly upright or upright or bushy shrub 3—6 feet high, fairly densely filled with bright green leaves. In a well-grown plant, a conspicuous feature is the brown, smooth, flaking bark of the stem and branches which always attracts attention. The flowers are tubular-campanulate, creamy-yellow, and are produced freely in terminal, or terminal and axillary trusses of four to seven. The plant is hardy outdoors, but along the east coast and in gardens inland it should be given a sheltered position for the best results to be obtained; in fact in a few very cold gardens it is difficult to establish. It was given an Award of Merit when shown by Mr. Lionel de Rothschild, Exbury, in 1931 (K.W. No. 6278).

Epithet. With long ears.
Hardiness 2—3. April—May.

R. chrysolepis Hutch. et Ward in The Species of Rhododendron (1930) 161.

A small or fair-sized epiphytic shrub with long or short branches; *stem and branches with deep red brown, smooth, flaking bark*; branchlets scaly, glabrous, leaf-bud scales deciduous. *Leaves* evergreen, lanceolate, oblong-lanceolate or ovate-lanceolate, lamina coriaceous, 5.4—10.7 cm. long, 1.9—3.5 cm. broad, apex acute, mucronate, base tapered or rounded; upper surface dark green, not scaly, glabrous; *under surface* pale green, scaly, the *scales* unequal, large, golden-yellow or brown, 3—4 *times their own diameter apart*; petiole 0.8—1.3 cm. long, grooved above, scaly, glabrous. *Inflorescence* terminal, umbellate, 4—6-flowered, flower-bud scales deciduous; rhachis 1—2 mm. long, scaly or not scaly, glabrous; pedicel 0.7—1.3 cm. long, moderately or rather densely scaly with golden-yellow scales, glabrous. *Calyx an undulate rim, 5-lobed, minute, 0.5—1 mm. long,* lobes ovate or triangular, outside moderately or densely scaly, margin eciliate or slightly ciliate. *Corolla* tubular-campanulate or campanulate, *2.6—3.4 cm. long,* 5-lobed, bright canary yellow or yellow, *outside with bands of scales on the tube and lobes,* tube pubescent outside towards the base or glabrous. *Stamens* 10, unequal, 1.5—2.6 cm. long, shorter than, or as long as, the corolla; filaments densely hairy at the base. *Ovary* oblong or conoid, 4—5 mm. long, 5—6-celled, densely scaly wih golden-yellow scales, glabrous; style long, slender and straight, longer than the corolla, scaly in the lower two-thirds of its length, glabrous, stigma large. *Capsule* oblong or oblong-oval, 1—1.5 cm. long, 5—7 mm. broad, densely scaly with large, brown scales, calyx persistent.

This species was first collected by Kingdon-Ward in June 1926 at Seinghku Wang, Upper Burma. It was found by him again later in September of the same year in the valley of the Seinghku, and in November 1937 in the Nam Tamai Valley, in the same region. It is an epiphytic shrub growing in the rain forest or sometimes on trees in the river bed, at elevations of 2,135—2,440 m. (7,000—8,000 ft.). Kingdon-Ward records it as being fairly abundant in the rain forest at about 2,135 m. (7,000 ft.).

The conspicuous characters of the plant are the minute calyx which is an undulately lobed rim, the large corolla with bands of scales on the tube and lobes, and the laxly scaly lower surfaces of the leaves, the scales being large 3—4 times their own diameter apart. In these features, it differs markedly from all its allies in its Series. It also shows a certain degree of affinity with *R. chrysodoron* in the Boothii Series but is readily distinguished by the long, slender and straight style; in *R. chrysodoron* it is stout and sharply bent.

R. chrysolepis was first introduced by Kingdon-Ward in 1926 (No. 7455). It was reintroduced by him in 1937 (No. 13500). The plant first flowered in The Royal Horticultural Society's Garden at Wisley raised from Kingdon-Ward seed No. 13500. It is

now possibly lost to cultivation.
    Epithet. With golden scales.
    Hardiness 2. May—June.

R. tephropeplum Balf. f. et Farrer in Notes Roy. Bot. Gard. Edin., Vol. 13 (1922) 302.
    Illustration. Bot. Mag. Vol. 157 t. 9343 (1934).
    A somewhat compact, rounded, bushy, spreading, broadly upright or upright shrub,
30 cm.—1.22 m. (1—4 ft.) or rarely 1.83—2.44 m. (6—8 ft.) high; stem and branches with
rough bark; branchlets moderately or rather densely scaly, glabrous, leaf-bud scales
deciduous. *Leaves* evergreen, lanceolate, oblong or oblong-obovate, lamina coriaceous,
3—13 cm. long, 0.8—4 cm. broad, apex acute, obtuse or rounded, mucronate, base
tapered or obtuse; upper surface dark green, shining, scaly, glabrous; margin recurved;
under surface pale glaucous, densely scaly, the scales unequal, small, black or brown,
one-half to their own diameter apart, with or without widely scattered large scales;
petiole 0.5—1.3 cm. long, moderately or densely scaly, glabrous. *Inflorescence* terminal,
or sometimes terminal and axillary in the uppermost one or two leaves, umbellate,
3—9-flowered, flower-bud scales deciduous; rhachis 1—4 mm. long, scaly, glabrous;
pedicel 1—2.5 cm. or rarely 3 cm. long, rather densely or moderately scaly, glabrous.
Calyx 5-lobed, leafy, 4—8 mm. long, lobes erect or spreading, nearly orbicular, oval or
oblong-oval, outside slightly or moderately scaly at the base, or sometimes moderately
scaly outside, margin ciliate or eciliate. *Corolla* tubular-campanulate, 1.8—3.2 cm. long,
5-lobed, *dark or pale rose, rose, carmine-rose, pink, purplish, rosy-crimson, crimson-purple or
rarely white*, without spots, *outside not scaly, or sometimes sparsely or moderately scaly on the
lobes*, glabrous. *Stamens* 10, unequal, 1—2.3 cm. long, shorter than the corolla; filaments
densely or moderately pubescent towards the base or to two-thirds of their length. *Ovary*
conoid, 3—4 mm. long, 5-celled, densely scaly, glabrous; style long, slender and
straight, slightly shorter or longer than the corolla, longer than the stamens, scaly at the
base or to two-thirds of its length or not scaly, glabrous. *Capsule* oval or oblong-oval,
0.5—1 cm. long, 5—6 mm. broad, densely scaly, glabrous, enclosed by the persistent
calyx-lobes.

    R. tephropeplum was discovered by Farrer in May 1920 at Chawchi Pass, north-east
Upper Burma. Further gatherings by him and other collectors show that the species is
distributed in north-east Upper Burma, north-west Yunnan, eastern Tibet, and Assam.
It grows on rocks and cliffs, in cane brakes, in stony alpine meadows, on rocky slopes, in
Abies forest, and amongst scrub, at elevations of 2,440—4,300 m. (8,000—14,098 ft.).
Farrer records it as being very abundant on rocks and cliffs, forming wide and often
procumbent masses at the Chawchi Pass, north-east Upper Burma at 3,173 m. (10,500
ft.). According to Kingdon-Ward it is fairly common in the sub-alpine region, Tsangpo
Gorge, south-east Tibet, growing in Abies forest at 3,050 m. (10,000 ft.).
    In 1930 *R. deleiense* Hutch. et Ward was described from a plant (No. 8165) collected by
Kingdon-Ward in 1928 in the Delei Valley, Assam. In 1948, the name was placed in
synonymy under *R. tephropeplum* (*The Rhododendron Year Book*, 1948, p. 75).
    The species varies considerably in habit and height of growth, in leaf shape and size,
and in flower size and colour. It resembles *R. xanthostephanum* in some features but
differs markedly in flower colour, and in its corolla usually not scaly outside.
    R. tephropeplum was first introduced by Forrest in 1921 from eastern Tibet at 4,270 m.
(14,000 ft.) (No. 20230). It was reintroduced by him on several occasions. Kingdon-Ward
sent seeds a few times. Rock also introduced it in 1929 from north-west Yunnan. In its
native home it grows usually 1—4 feet high, but Kingdon-Ward found a plant in the
Tsangpo Gorge 6—8 feet in height. Several forms are in cultivation. At one extreme the
species is a large somewhat rounded shrub 4 feet high, with large oblong-obovate leaves,
laminae 10 cm. long, 4 cm. broad, and with large rosy-crimson corolla 3.2 cm. long; at the
other extreme it is a small broadly upright shrub 2 feet high, with small lanceolate leaves,

laminae 3 cm. long, 0.8 cm. broad, and with small pink corolla 1.8 cm. long. These extremes are linked with several intermediates varying in habit and height of growth, in leaf shape and size, and in flower size and colour. Two features common to all these forms are the densely scaly lower surface of the leaves with small black or brown scales, ½ to their own diameter apart, and the large leafy erect or spreading calyx 4—8 mm. long. The species is free-flowering, and is a delightful plant particularly a rounded form, 3 feet high with large carmine-rose flowers for which the large dark green leaves provide an excellent contrast. This form and a low spreading form are well suited for the rock garden. Although the species is hardy along the east coast and inland, a sheltered position should be provided. It was given an Award of Merit in 1929 when shown by Lady Aberconway and the Hon. H.D. McLaren, Bodnant, and again in 1935 when exhibited as *R. deleiense* by Lord Swaythling, Townhill Park, Hants. The same Award was given in 1975 to a form 'Butcher Wood' when shown by Major A.E. Hardy, Sandling Park (K.W. No. 20844).

Epithet. With ash-grey covering.
Hardiness 2—3. April—May. Plate 57.

R. xanthostephanum Merr. in Brittonia Vol. 4 (1941) 148.
    Syn. *R. aureum* Franch. in Journ. de Bot. IX (1895) 394.
    Illustration. Bot. Mag. Vol. 147 t. 8882 (1938).
    A broadly upright or upright or bushy shrub, 30 cm.—3 m. (1—10 ft.) or rarely 4.58 m. (15 ft.) high; branchlets rather densely scaly, glabrous, leaf-bud scales deciduous. *Leaves* evergreen, lanceolate, oblong-lanceolate or oblong, lamina coriaceous, 5—10.4 cm. long, 1.3—3.4 cm. broad, apex acute, obtuse or rounded, mucronate, base obtuse or tapered; upper surface bright green or dark green, somewhat shining, scaly, glabrous; under surface glaucous, densely scaly, the scales unequal, small or somewhat small, brown or dark brown, one-half to their own diameter apart, with or without widely scattered large scales; petiole 0.5—1.3 cm. long, densely scaly, glabrous. *Inflorescence* terminal, or rarely terminal and axillary in the uppermost one or two leaves, umbellate, 3—5-or rarely 8-flowered, flower-bud scales deciduous or persistent; rhachis 1—5 mm. long, scaly, glabrous; pedicel 0.5—1.8 cm. long, densely scaly, glabrous. *Calyx* 5-lobed, 3—6 mm. long, *lobes erect*, nearly orbicular, oval, oblong-oval, ovate or oblong, outside sparsely to rather densely scaly, margin eciliate or rarely ciliate. *Corolla* tubular-campanulate, 2—2.6 cm. long, 5-lobed, *bright yellow, deep lemon-yellow, lemon-yellow, yellow or canary yellow, outside rather densely or moderately scaly on the tube and lobes*, glabrous. *Stamens* 10, unequal, 1.2—2.8 cm. long, longer or shorter than the corolla; filaments densely or moderately hairy at the base or to one-half of their length. *Ovary* conoid, 2—3 mm. long, 5-celled, densely scaly, glabrous; style long, slender and straight, longer than the corolla and the stamens, scaly at the base, glabrous. *Capsule* oblong-oval, oblong or oval, 0.5—1 cm. long, 4—5 mm. broad, densely scaly, glabrous, calyx-lobes persistent.

R. xanthostephanum was first collected by the Abbé Delavay in September 1890 on Tsang-shan above Tali, Yunnan, and was described by Franchet in 1895 under the name *R. aureum*. It was afterwards found by other collectors in west and north-west Yunnan, north-east Upper Burma, Assam, and south-east and east Tibet. The plant grows on open alpine slopes, on cliffs, in cane and rhododendron scrub, in stony pasture, in cane thickets, at the margins of thickets and forests, in spruce and pine forests, and in woods, at elevations of 1,830—4,118 m. (6,000—13,500 ft.). According to Kingdon-Ward it is locally abundant in the Rong Tö Valley, Upper Burma. Yü records it as being common in woods and in dense forest in the Kiukiang Valley, north-west Yunnan.

In 1941, Merrill came to the conclusion that it was necessary for Franchet's species *R. aureum* to have a new name; he called it *R. xanthostephanum* (*Brittonia*, Vol. 4, No. 1, Dec. 1941, p. 148). He pointed out that the name *R. aureum* Georgi is the valid name for the Siberian species known as *R. chrysanthum* Pallas.

R. xanthostephanum is allied to *R. auritum* and *R. tephropeplum*. It is distinguished from the former by its erect calyx, and by its stem and branches with rough bark; from the latter by the flower colour, and by the corolla which is rather densely or moderately scaly outside. From *R. sulfureum* in the Boothii Series it differs markedly in that the style is long, slender and straight.

The species was first introduced by Forrest in 1906 from west Yunnan at an elevation of 2,745—3,050 m. (9,000—10,000 ft.) (No. 4135). He later sent seeds on several occasions from south-east and east Tibet and from north-west Yunnan. It was also introduced by Kingdon-Ward, Rock, Ludlow, Sherriff and Taylor, and Yü. In its native home, it usually grows 1—6 or rarely 9 feet high, although Kingdon-Ward found a slender plant 10—15 feet in height in a river gorge in north-east Upper Burma. In cultivation it is a broadly upright shrub up to 4 or 5 feet high with bright green leaves. Along the west coast it succeeds outdoors in a few well-sheltered gardens in mild areas; along the east coast it is tender and suited to a cool greenhouse. In passing it may be noted that the species has also been introduced from very high elevations, including Forrest No. 20880 from 3,660—3,965 m. (12,000—13,000 ft.), and Rock No. 22014 from 4,118 m. (13,500 ft.); these plants are possibly now lost to cultivation. *R. xanthostephanum* is a pleasing shrub, free-flowering, and provides an admirable display when covered with yellow flowers in trusses of three to five. A clone 'Yellow Garland' received an Award of Merit when exhibited by the Crown Estate Commissioners, Windsor Great Park, in 1961, raised from Forrest seed No. 21707 (= 22652).

Epithet. Yellow garland.
Hardiness 1—2. April—May.

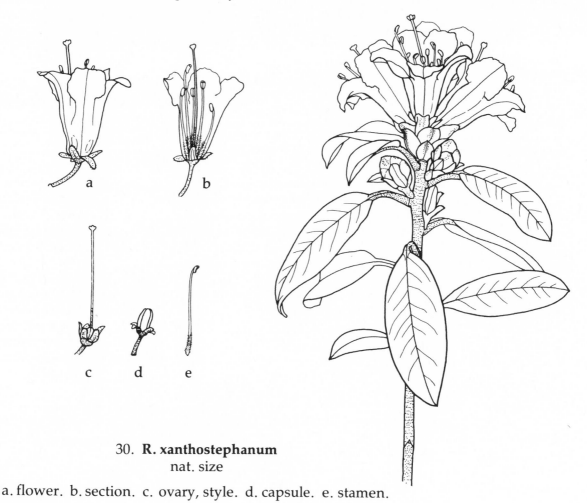

30. **R. xanthostephanum**
nat. size

a. flower. b. section. c. ovary, style. d. capsule. e. stamen.

TRICHOCLADUM SERIES

General characters: small to medium-sized shrubs, 30 cm.—2.44 m. (1—8 ft.) high; branchlets scaly, bristly or not bristly, puberulous or not puberulous. *Leaves deciduous* or rarely semi-deciduous, *or evergreen*, obovate, oblong-obovate, oblong-oval, oval, elliptic, oblong-elliptic, oblong or lanceolate, lamina 1.6—6.3 cm. long, 0.6—3.4 cm. broad; upper surface scaly or not scaly, bristly or not bristly; margin bristly or not bristly; under surface scaly, the *scales Vesicular*, 1—6 times their own diameter apart, bristly or not bristly, midrib bristly or not bristly; petiole 0.2—1.2 cm. long, scaly, bristly or sometimes not bristly, puberulous or not puberulous. Inflorescence terminal, or sometimes terminal and axillary in the uppermost one to three leaves, 1—6-flowered; pedicel 0.8—3.5 cm. long, scaly or rarely not scaly, bristly or not bristly. Calyx 0.5—7 mm. long, outside not bristly or sometimes bristly, margin bristly or not bristly. Corolla campanulate or rarely tubular-campanulate, or funnel-campanulate or widely funnel-shaped, zygomorphic or not zygomorphic, 1.3—2.8 cm. long, sulphur-yellow, yellow, greenish-yellow, pale lemon-yellow, creamy-white, reddish-yellow or rarely reddish, with or without greenish or crimson spots on the posterior side. Stamens 10 or rarely 8. Ovary conoid or oblong, 2—5 mm. long; style long, thick or slender, sharply bent or bent or straight. Capsule oblong, conoid or rarely oblong-oval, 0.5—1 cm. long, 2—6 mm. broad.

Distribution: mid-west, west, and north-west Yunnan, north-east and east Upper Burma, south, south-east and east Tibet.

A very distinct Series of four deciduous and five evergreen species with *Vesicular scales*, showing no particular affinity with any other Series.

KEY TO THE SPECIES

A. Leaves deciduous; flowers precocious.
    B. Calyx margin densely fringed with long hairs; pedicels, branchlets and petioles rather densely or moderately bristly; margin of the leaves bristly . . . . *trichocladum*
    B. Calyx margin not hairy or sometimes moderately hairy with long hairs; pedicels, branchlets, and petioles not bristly or sparsely or moderately bristly; margin of the leaves not bristly or bristly.
        C. Scales on the under surface of the leaves closely spaced, usually 1—3 times their own diameter apart; corolla yellow, pale yellow tinged green, lemon-yellow, dark greenish-orange, greenish-yellow, dark olive-yellow greenish at base, with or without darker greenish or orange spots; calyx 0.5—7 mm. long.
            D. Upper surface of the leaves slightly glaucous, under surface somewhat glaucous; margin of the leaves (laminae) not bristly (or rarely sparsely bristly); corolla yellow, with or without orange spots; midrib on the under surface of the leaves not bristly or slightly bristly . . . . *melinanthum*
            D. Upper and usually the lower surface of the leaves not glaucous; margin of the leaves (laminae) moderately bristly or sometimes not bristly; corolla pale yellow tinged green, lemon-yellow, dark greenish-orange, greenish-yellow, dark olive-yellow greenish at base or sometimes yellow, with or' without darker greenish spots; midrib on the under surface of the leaves moderately bristly or not bristly . . . . *mekongense*
        C. Scales on the under surface of the leaves widely spaced, 4—6 times their own diameter apart; corolla pale sulphur-yellow; calyx 1 mm. long . . . . *lithophilum*
A. Leaves evergreen or sometimes semi-evergreen; flowers not precocious.
        E. Ovary, under surface of the leaves and midrib, corolla-tube outside, calyx outside, and capsule bristly; leaf-bud scales persistent; branchlets and petioles rather densely bristly. . . . . *lepidostylum*
        E. Ovary, under surface of the leaves and usually midrib, corolla-tube outside, calyx outside, and capsule not bristly; leaf-bud scales deciduous; branchlets and petioles moderately bristly or not bristly.
            F. Corolla creamy-yellow or creamy-white, lined and flushed rose on the outside, or reddish-yellow with numerous crimson spots on the posterior side; inflorescence terminal and axillary in the uppermost one to three leaves, or sometimes terminal.
                G. Corolla creamy-yellow or creamy-white, lined and flushed rose on the outside; upper surface of the adult and young leaves olive-green, not glaucous, under surface not glaucous; pedicels and branchlets not bristly . . . . *rubrolineatum*
                G. Corolla reddish-yellow, with numerous crimson spots on the posterior side; upper surface of the adult leaves bluish, glaucous, in young leaves markedly bluish glaucous, under surface glaucous; pedicels moderately or rather densely bristly, branchlets moderately bristly... *rubroluteum*
            F. Corolla yellowish-green, pale yellowish-green or yellow, with greenish spots on the posterior side; inflorescence terminal.

H. Under surface of the leaves markedly glaucous, laxly scaly, scales 2—5 times their own diameter apart; branchlets and pedicels not bristly (or rarely moderately bristly) .... *caesium*

H. Under surface of the leaves pale green, not glaucous or slightly glaucous, scaly, scales 1—3 times their own diameter apart; branchlets moderately or rather densely bristly; pedicels moderately bristly (or rarely not bristly) .... *viridescens*

DESCRIPTION OF THE SPECIES

R. caesium Hutch. in Gard. Chron. Vol. 94 (1933) 102.

A rounded or broadly upright shrub, 92 cm.—1.53 m. (3—5 ft.) high; *branchlets* moderately or sparsely scaly, *not bristly* or rarely bristly, not puberulous, leaf-bud scales deciduous. *Leaves evergreen*, oblong, oblong-lanceolate or elliptic, lamina coriaceous, 2.3—5 cm. long, 1.2—3.4 cm. broad, apex obtuse or rounded, mucronate, base obtuse or rounded; upper surface olive-green or bright green, not glaucous, (in young leaves pale bluish-green, slightly glaucous), not scaly, not bristly, not puberulous, midrib not bristly, glabrous; margin recurved or flat, bristly or not bristly; *under surface markedly glaucous* or rarely slightly glaucous, scaly, the *scales* unequal, large, brown, *2—5 times their own diameter apart*, not bristly, midrib bristly or not bristly, not puberulous; petiole 2—6 mm. long, scaly, sparsely or moderately bristly or not bristly, not puberulous. *Inflorescence* terminal, umbellate or shortly racemose, 3—5-flowered, flower-bud scales deciduous; rhachis 2—3 mm. long, scaly, not bristly, glabrous; *pedicel* 1—2 cm. long, scaly, *not bristly* or rarely bristly, not puberulous. *Calyx* 5-lobed, 1 mm. or rarely 4 mm. long, lobes ovate or rarely oblong, outside scaly, glabrous, margin scaly, slightly or moderately bristly. *Corolla* funnel-campanulate, zygomorphic, 1.5—2.5 cm. long, 5-lobed, yellowish-green, with greenish spots on the posterior side, margins tinged or not tinged red, outside scaly on the tube and lobes, glabrous. *Stamens* 10, unequal, exserted, 0.9—2.1 cm. long; filaments villous towards the base. *Ovary* conoid or oblong, 3—5 mm. long, 5-celled, densely scaly, glabrous; style long, slender and straight, longer than, or as long as, the corolla, not scaly, glabrous. *Capsule* oblong or conoid, 5—8 mm. long, 2—3 mm. broad, rather densely scaly, glabrous, calyx-lobes persistent.

This species was described by Hutchinson in 1933 from a living plant raised from Forrest's seed No. 26798, by Mr. Lionel de Rothschild, at Exbury, Southampton. Forrest first collected the plant in fruit in June 1925 on the hills around Lung-fan, mid-west Yunnan. He found it again later in November that year in the same region. It grows on rocky slopes amongst scrub in side valleys, at elevations of 2,440—3,050 m. (8,000—10,000 ft.).

R. caesium was at first placed in the Triflorum Series. But it shows a marked similarity to the species of the Trichocladum Series, particularly in its Vesicular type of scales on the lower surface of the leaves, and in 1963 it was transferred to the latter Series (*The Rhododendron and Camellia Year Book,* 1963). It may be remarked that the Vesicular type of scale is one of the main diagnostic features of the Trichocladum Series. In the Triflorum Series, the scale is of the usual Entire type.

The species is allied to *R. viridescens* which it resembles in general features and in the evergreen leaves, but is readily distinguished by the markedly glaucous lower surface of the leaves, and usually by the non-bristly branchlets and pedicels.

In cultivation *R. caesium* is a rounded or broadly upright shrub with olive-green or bright green leaves. The flowers are funnel-campanulate, yellowish-green, produced freely in clusters of 3—5. Although hardy, it should be given a sheltered position along the east coast and in gardens inland. The plant is uncommon in cultivation.

Epithet. Dullish blue, alluding to the lower leaf surface.

Hardiness 3. May—June.

R. lepidostylum Balf. f. et Forrest in Notes Roy. Bot. Gard. Edin., Vol. 12 (1920) 124.

A compact rounded, or spreading or sometimes broadly upright shrub, 30 cm.—1.22 m. (1—4 ft.) high; *branchlets* scaly, *rather densely bristly*, not puberulous, *leaf-bud scales persistent. Leaves evergreen*, obovate, oblong-obovate, oblong-oval or oval, lamina coriaceous, 2—4.3 cm. long, 1—2 cm. broad, apex rounded or obtuse, mucronate, base rounded or obtuse; upper surface olive-green or bluish-green, not glaucous, (in young leaves bluish-green, markedly glaucous), not scaly, not bristly, not puberulous, midrib glabrous; margin recurved, bristly; *under surface* somewhat glaucous or glaucous, scaly, the scales unequal, large, brown, 1—4 times their own diameter apart, *bristly, midrib bristly*, not puberulous; *petiole* 0.4—1.2 cm. long, scaly, *rather densely bristly*, not puberulous. *Inflorescence* terminal, umbellate, 1—3-flowered, flower-bud scales persistent; rhachis 1—2 mm. long, scaly, not bristly, glabrous; pedicel 2—3 cm. long, scaly, bristly, not puberulous. *Calyx* 5-lobed, 1—7 mm. long, lobes lanceolate, oblong, oval or ovate, *outside* scaly, *bristly*, not puberulous, margin not scaly, bristly. *Corolla* funnel-campanulate, zygomorphic, 2—2.8 cm. long, 5-lobed, pale yellow or yellow, with or without numerous orange or greenish spots on the posterior side, outside scaly on the tube and lobes, not puberulous, *tube bristly outside*, lobes not bristly outside. *Stamens* 10, unequal, exserted, 1—2.5 cm. long; filaments villous towards the base. *Ovary* conoid, 3—4 mm. long, 5-celled, densely scaly, *bristly*; style long, slender and straight, as long as the corolla or longer, scaly at the base or not scaly, glabrous or puberulous at the base. *Capsule* conoid or oblong, 6—9 mm. long, 3—5 mm. broad, rather densely scaly, *bristly*, not puberulous, calyx-lobes persistent.

This species has a comparatively restricted distribution in west and mid-west Yunnan. It was discovered by Forrest in June 1919 on the summit of the Jangtzow Shan, Shweli-Salwin divide. This gathering was in foliage only. Forrest found it again later in the same year. It grows in open situations on cliffs, on humus-covered boulders, and in the crevices of cliffs in ravines, at elevations of 3,050—3,660 m. (10,000—12,000 ft.).

R. lepidostylum is a distinct species with evergreen leaves. The characteristic features of this plant are the rather densely or moderately bristly branchlets, leaves, pedicels, calyx, corolla, ovary and capsule. The lower surfaces of the leaves are somewhat glaucous or moderately glaucous. In this respect it shows a resemblance to *R. caesium*, but differs markedly in distinctive features.

The species was introduced by Forrest in 1924 (No. 24633). In its native home it grows from one foot or less up to three feet. In cultivation it is a compact rounded or spreading shrub 2—3 feet high and up to 5 feet across. When planted in the woodland with a fair amount of shade, the plant often tends to grow broadly upright up to about 4 feet in height. The outstanding feature of the species is its exceptionally fine young leaves, bluish-green and markedly glaucous. The flowers are widely funnel-shaped, pale yellow or yellow, and are often produced freely in clusters of 1—3. The species is a fairly robust grower, and is easy to increase from cuttings. It is hardy, but to be able to grow it satisfactorily, particularly along the east coast and in gardens inland, protection from wind is essential. The plant was given an Award of Merit when shown by Capt. Collingwood Ingram, Benenden, in 1969.

Epithet. With scaly styles.

Hardiness 3. May—June. Plate 58.

R. lithophilum Balf. f. et Ward in Notes Roy. Bot. Gard. Edin., Vol. 13 (1922) 275.

A broadly upright shrub, *60—92 cm. (2—3 ft.)* high; branchlets sparsely scaly, not bristly, not puberulous, leaf-bud scales deciduous. *Leaves deciduous,* obovate, lamina coriaceous, 2.1—3 cm. long, 1—1.8 cm. broad, apex rounded, notched or entire, mucronate, base obtuse or rounded; upper surface green, not glaucous, not scaly, not bristly, glabrous, midrib glabrous; margin bristly; *under surface* not glaucous, *laxly scaly,* the *scales* unequal, large, brown, *4—6 times their own diameter apart,* not bristly, midrib not bristly or rarely slightly bristly; petiole 3—4 mm. long, scaly, sparsely bristly, not puberulous. *Inflorescence* terminal, umbellate, 2—4-flowered, *flowers precocious,* flower-bud scales deciduous; rhachis 2 mm. long, scaly, not bristly, glabrous; pedicel 0.9—1 cm. long, scaly, not bristly, glabrous. *Calyx* 5-lobed, *1 mm. long,* lobes ovate, outside sparsely scaly or not scaly, glabrous, margin not scaly, bristly. *Corolla* campanulate, 1.5—1.8 cm. long, 5-lobed, *pale sulphur-yellow,* outside scaly on the tube and lobes, glabrous. *Stamens* 10, unequal, exserted, 0.9—1.3 cm. long; filaments villous or puberulous towards the base. *Ovary* conoid, 4 mm. long, 5-celled, densely scaly, glabrous; style long, slender, bent or straight, shorter than the corolla, not scaly, glabrous. *Capsule:*—

This species is known from a single collection made in July 1919 by Kingdon-Ward on the western spur of Imaw Bum, north-east Burma. It grows amongst large granite boulders in bamboo thickets at elevations of 3,355—3,660 m. (11,000—12,000 ft.). It is recorded as being not common in its native home.

R. lithophilum is a small plant 2 or 3 feet high. It is similar to *R. mekongense* in general appearance, but differs in that the corolla is pale sulphur-yellow, the scales on the lower surface of the leaves are large, widely spaced, 4—6 times their own diameter apart, and the calyx is minute, 1 mm. long.

The species was introduced by Kingdon-Ward in 1919 (No. 3305 — the Type number). Its dwarf habit of growth makes it suitable for the rock garden. It always was a rare plant, and has possibly now been lost to cultivation.

Epithet. Stone-loving.

Hardiness 3. May—June.

R. mekongense Franch. in Journ. de Bot. XII (1898) 263.

A broadly upright shrub, 30 cm.—2.44 m. (1—8 ft.) high; branchlets moderately or sparsely scaly, bristly or not bristly, minutely puberulous or not puberulous, leaf-bud scales deciduous. *Leaves deciduous,* oblong-obovate, obovate, oval, oblong-elliptic or rarely oblanceolate, lamina coriaceous, 1.6—4.6 cm. long, 0.8—2.6 cm. broad, apex rounded or obtuse, mucronate, base obtuse or rounded; *upper surface* dark green or olive-green, *not glaucous,* not scaly, not bristly, glabrous or rarely puberulous, midrib puberulous or glabrous; margin bristly or not bristly; *under surface* slightly glaucous or *not glaucous,* scaly, the scales small or rarely large, brown, pale or dark brown, 1—4 times their own diameter apart, not bristly, midrib not bristly or bristly, not puberulous; petiole 2—5 mm. long, scaly, moderately or sparsely bristly or rarely not bristly, minutely puberulous or not puberulous. *Inflorescence* terminal, umbellate, 2—5-flowered, *flowers precocious,* flower-bud scales deciduous; rhachis 1—3 mm. long, scaly or not scaly, not bristly, puberulous or rarely glabrous; pedicel 1—2.5 cm. long, moderately or slightly scaly, not bristly or sparsely or moderately bristly, not puberulous or minutely puberulous. *Calyx* 5-lobed, 0.5—7 mm. long, lobes lanceolate, oblong, ovate, rounded or triangular, outside moderately or sparsely scaly or not scaly, glabrous, margin scaly or not scaly, hairy with long hairs or glabrous. *Corolla* campanulate or tubular-campanulate, 1.4—2.3 cm. long, 5-lobed, *yellow, pale yellow tinged green, lemon-yellow, dark greenish-orange, greenish-yellow or dark olive-yellow greenish at base,* with or without darker greenish spots, tube not scaly or sometimes scaly outside, lobes scaly or rarely not scaly, glabrous outside. *Stamens* 10 or sometimes 8, unequal, exserted, 0.7—2.2 cm. long;

filaments villous or puberulous towards the base. *Ovary* conoid or oblong, 3—4 mm. long, 5-celled, densely scaly, glabrous; style long, thick or slender, straight or bent or sharply bent, shorter than, or as long as, the corolla, or rarely longer, not scaly, glabrous. *Capsule* oblong or conoid, 0.5—1 cm. long, 3—6 mm. broad, densely or moderately scaly, glabrous, calyx-lobes persistent.

R. mekongense was discovered by the Abbé Soulié in June 1895 in the Mekong valley at Sela, eastern Tibet. Subsequently it was found by other collectors in south-east Tibet, north-west Yunnan and north-east Burma. It grows on the margins of forests and thickets, in open situations in pine forests, amongst scrub, on open grassy slopes and rocks, at elevations of 2,745—4,270 m. (9,000—14,000 ft.). Ludlow, Sherriff and Elliot record it as growing in a swamp in south-east Tibet.

During the years 1920—1922, three other species were described, namely, *R. chloranthum* Balf. f. et Forrest from a specimen collected by Forrest in north-west Yunnan, *R. semilunatum* Balf. f. et Forrest from a specimen also collected by Forrest in the same region, and *R. brachystylum* Balf. f. et Ward found by Kingdon-Ward in north-east Burma. It will be seen that in *The Species of Rhododendron* 1930, *R. brachystylum* has been placed in synonymy under *R. trichocladum* Franch. The adequate material now available and plants in cultivation show that the diagnostic criteria which were used in separating these species are not constant, and the whole material under these names represents a single variable unit, *R. mekongense*.

The species shows a resemblance to *R. melinanthum* in its appearance, but differs in that the calyx is usually large, 1—7 mm. long, the margin of the leaves is often bristly, the corolla is usually greenish-yellow, lemon-yellow, pale yellow tinged green or sometimes yellow, and the upper and usually the lower surfaces of the leaves are not glaucous.

R. mekongense has been in cultivation for a long time. It was first introduced by Forrest in 1917 (No. 13900). It was reintroduced by him a few times in 1917 and 1922. Kingdon-Ward sent seeds in 1925. Rock reintroduced it in 1948 from north-west Yunnan. In cultivation it is a broadly upright shrub 3—4 feet high, although in its native home it grows up to 8 feet. It is fairly fast-growing with deciduous leaves, often with greenish-yellow flowers produced freely in clusters of 2—5. The plant is very hardy, and is easily adaptable to any position in the garden.

Epithet. From the Mekong River, China.
Hardiness 3. May.

R. melinanthum Balf. f. et Ward in Trans. Bot. Soc. Edin., Vol. 27 (1916) 85.

An upright or bushy shrub, 1.53—2.44 m. (5—8 ft.) high; branchlets sparsely or moderately scaly, not bristly or bristly, not puberulous or puberulous, leaf-bud scales deciduous. *Leaves* deciduous or sometimes semi-deciduous, oblong-obovate, oblanceolate or elliptic, lamina coriaceous, 3.2—5.2 cm. long, 1.4—2.5 cm. broad, apex rounded or obtuse, mucronate, base tapered or obtuse; *upper surface* dark green or bluish-green, *slightly glaucous*, not scaly, *not bristly*, glabrous, midrib glabrous or minutely puberulous; *margin not bristly* or sparsely bristly; *under surface somewhat glaucous*, scaly, the scales small or medium-sized, brown, 1—3 times their own diameter apart, not bristly, *midrib not bristly* or slightly bristly, not puberulous; petiole 2—4 mm. long, moderately or sparsely scaly, bristly or not bristly, not puberulous or puberulous. *Inflorescence* terminal, umbellate, 3—5-flowered, flowers precocious, flower-bud scales deciduous; rhachis 1—3 mm. long, sparsely or moderately scaly, not bristly, puberulous or glabrous; pedicel 1.6—2.1 cm. long, moderately or sparsely scaly, bristly or not bristly, not puberulous. *Calyx* 5-lobed, 1—2 mm. long, lobes ovate or triangular, outside scaly, glabrous, margin not scaly or scaly, glabrous or hairy with long hairs. *Corolla* campanulate or widely funnel-campanulate, 1.8—2.4 cm. long, 2—3 cm. across, 5-lobed, *yellow, with or without orange spots*, outside scaly on the tube and lobes, glabrous. *Stamens* 10, unequal, exserted, 0.8—1.7 cm. long; filaments villous towards the base. *Ovary* conoid or oblong, 2—4 mm.

long, 5-celled, densely scaly, glabrous; style long, slender, straight or bent, as long as the corolla or longer, not scaly, glabrous. *Capsule* oblong or conoid, 6—9 mm. long, 3 mm. broad, densely scaly, glabrous, calyx-lobes persistent.

This plant was discovered by Kingdon-Ward in June 1913 at the Ka-gwr-pw glacier valley, east Upper Burma, growing in Abies forest at elevations of 3,660—4,270 m. (12,000—14,000 ft.).

A plant which has been figured as *R. melinanthum* in the *Botanical Magazine* Vol. 147 t. 8903 (1938), is in fact *R. trichocladum*.

R. melinanthum is a deciduous or sometimes semi-deciduous shrub. It is allied to *R. trichocladum* which it resembles in some features. The main distinctions between them are that in *R. melinanthum* the margin of the leaves (laminae) is not bristly (or rarely slightly bristly), the midrib on the lower surface is not bristly (or rarely slightly bristly), the upper surface is not bristly, the pedicels and calyx margin are not bristly or bristly, and both surfaces of the leaves are somewhat glaucous; whereas in *R. trichocladum* the margin of the leaves (laminae) and the midrib on the lower surface are moderately bristly, the upper surface is bristly or not bristly, the pedicels and calyx margin are densely or moderately pilose, and both surfaces of the leaves are not glaucous. *R. melinanthum* is also related to *R. mekongense*; the distinctions between them are discussed under the latter.

R. melinanthum was first introduced by Kingdon-Ward in 1913 (No. 406 — the Type number), and was reintroduced by him in 1922. In cultivation it is a deciduous shrub with precocious flowers. Although in its native home it is a bushy shrub up to 8 feet high, in cultivation it is an upright shrub, usually only up to 5 or 6 feet. It is a pleasing shrub, and gives a delightful colour display with its widely funnel-campanulate or campanulate yellow flowers in clusters of 3—5. Moreover, it is a valuable plant in that it is a late flowerer, the flowers appearing in May—June. The species received an Award of Merit when exhibited as *R. mekongense* by R.N. Stephenson Clarke in 1979 (Kingdon-Ward No. 406 — the Type number).

Epithet. Honey-flowered.
Hardiness 3. May—June.

R. rubrolineatum Balf. f. et Forrest in Notes Roy. Bot. Gard. Edin., Vol. 12 (1920) 160.

A broadly upright shrub, 60 cm.—1.53 m. (2—5 ft.) high; *branchlets* scaly, *not bristly*, not puberulous, leaf-bud scales deciduous. *Leaves evergreen or semi-evergreen*, elliptic, oblong-elliptic or oblong, lamina coriaceous, 2.4—6.3 cm. long, 1.3—2.6 cm. broad, apex obtuse, mucronate, base obtuse; *upper surface olive-green, not glaucous*, moderately or sparsely scaly, not bristly, not puberulous, midrib puberulous or glabrous; margin slightly or moderately recurved, crenulate or not crenulate, not bristly; *under surface not glaucous*, scaly, the scales large or small, brown or pale brown, 1—3 times their own diameter apart, not bristly, midrib not bristly, glabrous; *petiole* 2—6 mm. long, scaly, *not bristly* or slightly bristly, puberulous above or glabrous. *Inflorescence terminal and axillary in the uppermost two or three leaves*, umbellate or shortly racemose, 3—5-flowered, flower-bud scales deciduous; rhachis 2—6 mm. long, scaly, not bristly, puberulous or glabrous; *pedicel* 1—1.8 cm. long, scaly, *not bristly*, glabrous. *Calyx* 5-lobed, minute, 1 mm. long, lobes rounded or triangular, outside scaly, glabrous, margin scaly or not scaly, slightly hairy with long hairs or ciliate or glabrous. *Corolla* campanulate or funnel-campanulate, 1.3—1.9 cm. long, 5-lobed, *creamy-yellow or creamy-white, lined and flushed rose on the outside*, scaly on the tube and lobes outside, glabrous. *Stamens* 10, unequal, exserted, 1—1.8 cm. long; filaments villous towards the base. *Ovary* conoid, 2—3 mm. long, 5-celled, densely scaly, glabrous; style long, slender, straight or sharply bent, as long as the corolla or longer, not scaly, glabrous. *Capsule* oblong or conoid, 0.9—1 cm. long, 4—5 mm. broad, densely scaly, glabrous, calyx-lobes persistent.

R. rubrolineatum was discovered by Forrest in May 1917 on the Tali Range, mid-west Yunnan, growing in open pasture at an elevation of 3,355 m. (11,000 ft.). This specimen is without a number. The species is recorded as being very rare in its native home.

The diagnostic features of this plant are the evergreen or semi-evergreen leaves, the creamy-yellow or creamy-white corolla lined and flushed rose on the exterior, and the terminal and axillary inflorescence in the uppermost two or three leaves. In these respects it is readily distinguished from its ally *R. lithophilum*. It also differs in that the scales on the lower surfaces of the leaves are 1—3 times their own diameter apart. The species is also allied to *R. viridescens* but is distinguished by the colour of the corolla, by the inflorescence, and by the non-bristly branchlets, petioles and pedicels.

The species was introduced by Forrest in 1917 (No. 19912). In cultivation it is a broadly upright shrub up to 5 feet high with olive-green leaves. The plant seeds itself in milder areas along the west coast. It is hardy, a fairly robust grower, with campanulate or funnel-campanulate flowers produced freely in clusters of 3—5.

Epithet. Lined with red.
Hardiness 3. May—June.

R. rubroluteum Davidian in Quart. Bull. Amer. Rhod. Soc. Vol. 29, July (1975) 144-145.

A broadly upright shrub, 92 cm.—1.70 m. (3—5½ ft.) high; branchlets scaly, bristly, leaf-bud scales deciduous. *Leaves evergreen*, obovate, oblong or oblong-elliptic, lamina coriaceous, 3—5.8 cm. long, 1.3—2.6 cm. broad, apex rounded or obtuse, mucronate, base rounded, obtuse or cordulate; *upper surface bluish, glaucous, (in young leaves markedly bluish glaucous)*, matt, not scaly or slightly scaly, not bristly; margin not bristly; under surface pale glaucous green, scaly, the scales unequal, minute, dark or pale brown, 2—3 times their own diameter apart, not bristly; petiole 2—3 mm. long, scaly, sparsely bristly or not bristly. *Inflorescence* terminal, or terminal and axillary in the uppermost one or two leaves, shortly racemose, 3—5-flowered, flower-bud scales deciduous; rhachis 3—5 mm. long, scaly, pubescent or glabrous, sparsely bristly or not bristly; *pedicel* 2—2.4 cm. long, scaly, *moderately or rather densely bristly. Calyx* 5-lobed, minute, 0.5—1 mm. long, lobes ovate, outside scaly or not scaly, not bristly, *margin* scaly or not scaly, *rather densely bristly. Corolla widely funnel-shaped*, zygomorphic, 1.8—2 cm. long, 5-lobed, *reddish-yellow, with numerous crimson spots on the posterior side*, outside scaly, glabrous. *Stamens* 10, unequal, long-exserted, 1—1.7 cm. long; filaments densely pubescent at the base or up to one-half of their length. *Ovary* conoid or ovoid, 2—4 mm. long, 5-celled, densely scaly, glabrous; style bent or straight, not scaly, glabrous. *Capsule* oblong, 6—9 mm. long, 3—4 mm. broad, straight, densely scaly, glabrous, calyx persistent.

This species was discovered by Kingdon-Ward in the course of his expedition of 1922 to Yunnan, Szechuan, Tibet and north-east Upper Burma. The exact locality of the plant has not been recorded. It grows in grassy pastures and on open granite slopes at an elevation of 3,660 m. (12,000 ft.).

R. rubroluteum is a remarkably distinct species. It is allied to *R. melinanthum*, but differs markedly in that the corolla is reddish-yellow with numerous crimson spots on the posterior side, widely funnel-shaped, zygomorphic, the leaves are evergreen, bluish glaucous on the upper surfaces, the pedicel and calyx margin are rather densely bristly.

The species was introduced by Kingdon-Ward in 1922 (No. 5489 — the Type number). In *The Rhododendron Handbook* 1980, this number has been wrongly recorded as "*R. mekongense* (as *melinanthum*)". In cultivation it is a broadly upright shrub up to about 5 feet high. A most striking feature is the markedly bluish glaucous young growths which are of great beauty and attract attention. It is fairly fast-growing, with widely funnel-shaped flowers produced with great freedom in clusters of three to five. The plant sets good fertile seed in plenty. Moreover, it is a valuable plant in that it is a late flowerer, prolonging the flowering season into June and July. It is hardy, and well worth a place in every collection of rhododendrons.

Epithet. Reddish-yellow.
Hardiness 3. June—July.

R. trichocladum Franch. in Bull. Soc. Bot. France, XXXIII (1886) 234.

Illustration. Bot. Mag. Vol. 151 t. 9073 (1925).

A rounded somewhat lax, or upright shrub, 30 cm.—1.83 m. (1—6 ft.) high; *branchlets* moderately or sparsely scaly, *moderately or rather densely bristly* or rarely not bristly, not puberulous or rarely puberulous, leaf-bud scales deciduous. *Leaves deciduous,* obovate, oblong-obovate, oblong-oval, elliptic or oblong, rarely lanceolate or oblong-lanceolate, lamina coriaceous, 1.6—5.6 cm. long, 0.6—2.6 cm. broad, apex rounded, obtuse or rarely acute, mucronate, base obtuse, rounded or rarely tapered; upper surface olive-green or dark green, sparsely or moderately scaly or not scaly, sparsely or moderately bristly or not bristly, pubescent or not pubescent; margin bristly; *under surface* scaly, the scales large or sometimes small, pale or dark brown, 1—6 times their own diameter apart, not bristly or sometimes bristly, *midrib bristly,* not puberulous or rarely puberulous; *petiole* 2—5 mm. long, moderately or sparsely scaly, *densely or moderately bristly,* not puberulous or rarely puberulous. *Inflorescence* terminal, umbellate, 2—5-flowered, *flowers precocious,* flower-bud scales deciduous or persistent; rhachis 1—2 mm. long, not scaly or rarely scaly, not bristly, not puberulous or puberulous; *pedicel* 0.8—3.5 cm. long, moderately or sparsely scaly or sometimes not scaly, *rather densely or moderately pilose,* not puberulous. *Calyx* 5-lobed, 1—4 mm. long, lobes ovate, oblong, oblong-lanceolate or rarely lanceolate, outside moderately or sparsely scaly, not hairy or rarely hairy with long hairs, *margin* not scaly, *fringed with long hairs. Corolla* campanulate or funnel-campanulate, 1.5—2.3 cm. long, 5-lobed, sulphur-yellow, pale yellow, bright yellow, pale greenish-yellow, greenish-yellow or pale lemon-yellow, with or without green spots, outside scaly on the tube and lobes, not bristly or rarely bristly. *Stamens* 10, unequal, exserted, 0.8—1.7 cm. long; filaments villous (or rarely puberulous) towards the base. *Ovary* conoid or oblong, 2—4 mm. long, 5-celled, densely scaly, not bristly, rarely moderately or rather densely bristly, not puberulous or rarely puberulous at the base; style long, thick or rarely slender, sharply bent or bent or rarely straight, not scaly, glabrous or rarely puberulous at the base. *Capsule* oblong, conoid or oblong-oval, 0.5—1 cm. long, 3—5 mm. broad, rather densely or moderately scaly, glabrous, calyx-lobes persistent.

R. trichocladum was first collected by the Abbé Delavay in June 1885 on Tsangchan mountain above Tali, Yunnan. It was later found by other collectors in west and central Yunnan, north-east Upper Burma, Burma-Tibet Frontier, and south-east Tibet. Stainton collected it in the Arun Valley, Nepal, far away from its native home. It grows on open rocky slopes, cliffs and open grassy slopes, in meadows, among scrub, in thickets, and in fir forests, at elevations of 2,000—4,270 m. (6,557—14.000 ft.). Ludlow, Sherriff and Elliot record it as sprawling over rocks, 1—2 feet high, in south-east Tibet. Yü found it common in the Salwin-Kiukiang Divide, Yunnan.

In 1916 *R. xanthinum* Balf. f. et W.W. Sm. was described from a specimen collected by Forrest in Yunnan. In *The Species of Rhododendron* 1930, it correctly appears in synonymy under *R. trichocladum.* In 1922, a description of *R. oulotrichum* Balf. f. et Forrest was based on a specimen collected by Forrest in western Yunnan, and in 1930 *R. lophogynum* (Balf. f. et Forrest) Hutch. was described from a specimen also collected by Forrest in the same region. The ample material now available and plants in cultivation show that these species are identical with *R. trichocladum* under which they will now appear in synonymy.

R. trichocladum is a deciduous shrub with precocious flowers. It is easily recognised by the moderately or rather densely bristly branchlets, petioles, margins of the leaves and midrib on the lower surface, pedicels, and calyx margin. It is allied to *R. melinanthum;* the distinctions between them are discussed under the latter.

The species was first introduced by Forrest in 1910 (No. 6755). It was reintroduced later several times by him, and by Kingdon-Ward, and Rock. Two distinct growth forms are in cultivation: Form 1. A rounded shrub, somewhat lax, 4—5 feet high and as much across. Form 2. An upright shrub, 4—5 feet high, with rigid branchlets. The plant is a

31. R. trichocladum
nat. size

a. flower. b. petals.
c. section d. ovary, style.
e. stamens. f. capsule.
g. leaf (upper surface).

vigorous grower, and makes a fine show with its sulphur-yellow or greenish-yellow flowers, with or without green spots, produced freely in clusters of 2—5. It is a useful plant in that it has a long flowering season, from April to about the end of July. The plant is hardy, easy to grow, and worth being more widely cultivated. It was given an Award of Merit when shown under the name *R. lophogynum*, by the Crown Estate Commissioners, Windsor Great Park, in 1971.

Epithet. With hairy twigs.
Hardiness 3. April—July.

R. trichocladum Franch. var. **longipilosum** Cowan in Notes Roy. Bot. Gard. Edin., Vol. 19 (1936) 186.

This plant was first found by Kingdon-Ward in July 1935 at Migyitun, south-east Tibet. It was afterwards collected by Ludlow and Sherriff at Tsari, south Tibet. The plant grows on rocks in open places, among scrub, and in deciduous forest, at elevations of 3,050—3,355 m. (10,000—11,000 ft.).

The variety differs from the species in that the upper surfaces of the leaves are rather densely bristly.

The plant was introduced by Kingdon-Ward in 1935 (No. 11915 — the Type number). Ludlow and Sherriff record it as being a shrub about 2 feet high, but in cultivation it reaches a height of 4 feet. It is hardy and free-flowering.

Epithet of the variety. With very long hairs.
Hardiness 3. April—May.

R. viridescens Hutch. in Gard. Chron. Vol. 94 (1933) 116.

A somewhat compact, rounded or spreading shrub, 30 cm.—1.53 m. (1—5 ft.) high; *branchlets* scaly, *moderately or rather densely bristly*, not puberulous or puberulous, leaf-bud scales deciduous. *Leaves evergreen*, obovate, oval, oblong-obovate, elliptic or oblong-elliptic, lamina coriaceous, 2.3—6.7 cm. long, 1.3—3 cm. broad, apex rounded or obtuse, mucronate, base obtuse or rounded; upper surface olive-green or bright green, not glaucous, (in young leaves pale bluish-green, glaucous), not scaly, not bristly, glabrous, midrib not bristly, glabrous; margin flat, not bristly or sparsely bristly at the base; *under surface pale green, not glaucous or slightly glaucous*, scaly, the scales large or medium-sized, brown, 1—3 times their own diameter apart, not bristly, midrib not bristly or rarely sparsely bristly at the base, not puberulous or rarely puberulous; petiole 2—4 mm. long, scaly, moderately or sparsely bristly, not puberulous or rarely puberulous. *Inflorescence* terminal, umbellate or shortly racemose, 3—6-flowered, flower-bud scales deciduous; rhachis 1—8 mm. long, scaly, not bristly or bristly, glabrous or puberulous; *pedicel* 1.4—3 cm. long, scaly, *bristly* or rarely not bristly, not puberulous. *Calyx* 5-lobed, 1—2 mm. long, lobes ovate or rounded, outside scaly, glabrous, margin not scaly, bristly. *Corolla* funnel-campanulate, zygomorphic, 1.6—2.4 cm. long, 5-lobed, pale yellowish-green or yellow, with greenish spots on the posterior side, margins tinged or not tinged with pale crimson, outside scaly on the tube and lobes, glabrous. *Stamens* 10, unequal, exserted, 0.8—2 cm. long; filaments villous towards the base. *Ovary* conoid, 2—4 mm. long, 5-celled, densely scaly, glabrous; style long, slender, straight or sharply bent, longer than, or as long as, the corolla, not scaly, glabrous or rarely puberulous at the base. *Capsule* oblong or conoid, 6—8 mm. long, 3—4 mm. broad, rather densely scaly, glabrous, calyx-lobes persistent.

R. viridescens was described by Hutchinson in 1933 from a plant raised from Kingdon-Ward's seed No. 5829, by Mr. Lionel de Rothschild at Exbury, Southampton. It was discovered by Kingdon-Ward in June 1924 at Doshong La, south-east Tibet. In February 1947, Ludlow, Sherriff and Elliot found it in fruit (No. 12505) in the Showa Valley, Pome, in the same region (this specimen has been wrongly labelled *R. trichocladum*). The plant grows in boggy pastures, along the banks of streams, and in alpine valleys at elevations of 2,898—3,355 m. (9,500—11,000 ft.).

The species is an evergreen shrub. It shows a resemblance to *R. caesium* in general appearance and in the evergreen leaves, but differs markedly in that the lower surface of the leaves is pale green, and the branchlets and pedicels are moderately or rather densely bristly.

R. viridescens was first introduced by Kingdon-Ward in 1924 (No. 5829 — the Type number). It was reintroduced by Ludlow, Sherriff and Elliot in 1947 (No. 12505). Kingdon-Ward records it as being an undershrub 12—15 inches high forming low clumps, although Ludlow, Sherriff and Elliot have seen it 3—4 feet high. In cultivation it is a somewhat compact, rounded or spreading shrub 3—5 feet in height and as much across. It is a pleasing plant with remarkable pale bluish-green glaucous, young foliage. The species is hardy, free-flowering, with funnel-campanulate yellow flowers with greenish spots, in clusters of 3—6. An additional asset is that it flowers late, the blooms appearing in May—June. The plant is uncommon in cultivation but is very desirable for inclusion in every collection of rhododendrons. A clone 'Doshong La' (K.W. No. 5829) received an Award of Merit when shown from Glendoick, in 1972.

Epithet. Becoming green.
Hardiness 3. May—June. Plate 59.

TRIFLORUM SERIES

General characters: small, medium-sized or large shrubs or sometimes trees, 15 cm.—10.60 m. (6 in.—34 ft.) high; branchlets usually scaly, glabrous or pubescent or sometimes bristly. Leaves evergreen, or sometimes semi-deciduous or completely deciduous, lanceolate, oblong-lanceolate, oblong, elliptic, obovate or almost orbicular, lamina 1.6—12.8 cm. long, 0.6—5.5 cm. broad; upper surface glabrous, or sometimes pubescent or bristly; under surface scaly, the scales Entire, overlapping to 8 times their own diameter apart, glabrous, or sometimes pubescent or bristly, midrib glabrous or hairy ⅓ to its entire length; petiole 0.2—2 cm. long, puberulous or glabrous, bristly or not bristly. Inflorescence terminal, or terminal and axillary in the uppermost few leaves, shortly or distinctly racemose, 1—15-flowered; pedicel 0.3—3 cm. long, glabrous or puberulous or sometimes bristly. Calyx 0.5—1 mm. (sometimes up to 5 mm.) long. Corolla usually widely funnel-shaped, zygomorphic, "butterfly-shaped", 0.8—4.8 cm. long, white, pink, yellow, purple, lavender-blue to intense violet. Stamens 10. Ovary oblong, conoid or sometimes oval, 2—6 mm. long. Style long, slender (in *R. afghanicum* sharply bent or deflexed or straight). Capsule usually oblong, ovoid or oblong-oval.

Distribution: west and east Yunnan, Kweichow, west and east Szechuan, Hupeh, Shensi, east and south-east Tibet, Upper Burma, Assam, Nepal, Sikkim, Bhutan; one species represented in Japan and one in Afghanistan.

A large Series of 35 species, divided into 4 Subseries. The diagnostic features of the Series are the widely funnel-shaped zygomorphic corolla, "butterfly-shaped", the long protruding stamens and long, slender and straight style, and usually the minute calyx 0.5—1 mm. long. The species are diploids (2n = 26), tetraploids (2n = 52) or hexaploids (2n = 78).

KEY TO THE SUBSERIES

A. Inflorescence distinctly racemose, 5—15-flowered, rhachis 0.8—5 cm. long; calyx 5-lobed, 1—4 mm. long .... *Hanceanum Subseries*

A. Inflorescence umbellate or shortly racemose, 3- (rarely up to 10-) flowered, rhachis 1—5 mm. (rarely up to 1 cm.) long; calyx a mere rim or 5-lobed, often 0.5—1 mm. long.

    B. Flowers pale or deep yellow or greenish-yellow .... *Triflorum Subseries*

    B. Flowers white, pink, purple, lavender to intense violet (except *R. zaleucum* var. *flaviflorum*).

        C. Midrib on the under surface of the leaves hairy ..... *Augustinii Subseries*

        C. Midrib on the under surface of the leaves not hairy .... *Yunnanense Subseries*

AUGUSTINII SUBSERIES

General characters: shrubs, 1—7.63 m. (3⅓—25 ft.) high; branchlets scaly, rather densely or moderately pubescent or not pubescent, not bristly or densely or moderately bristly. Leaves lanceolate, oblong-lanceolate, oblong, elliptic or obovate, lamina 3.1—12 cm. long, 1.1—4.5 cm. broad; upper surface glabrous or pubescent or bristly; *under surface* scaly, the scales ½—5 times their own diameter apart, glabrous or pubescent or bristly, *midrib hairy ⅓ to its entire length.* Inflorescence usually terminal, shortly racemose, 2—6-flowered; pedicel 0.4—2.7 cm. long, glabrous or puberulous or bristly. Calyx usually 0.5—1 mm. long, outside glabrous or puberulous or moderately or rather densely bristly. Corolla widely funnel-shaped, zygomorphic, 2—4.3 cm. long, white tinged pink, pale lavender-rose to intense violet or dark purple. Stamens 10. Ovary oblong or conoid, 3—4 mm. long; style long, slender and straight. Capsule oblong, 0.8—2 cm. long, 3—5 mm. broad.

KEY TO THE SPECIES

A. Branchlets, petioles, upper surface of the leaves, pedicels, calyx, corolla-tube and ovary not bristly (petiole hairy with long hairs in *R. bergii* and often in *R. augustinii*), pubescent or not pubescent.

    B. Leaves evergreen.

        C. Corolla 2.2—4.3 cm. long; leaves usually lanceolate, oblong-lanceolate or oblong, apex usually acuminate or acute, laminae 3.3—12 cm. long; flowers pink, white, lilac-purple, pale or deep lavender-rose to intense violet, or red; stamens hairy towards the base.

            D. Flowers pink, white, lilac-purple, pale or deep lavender-rose to intense violet; broadly upright or spreading shrub; upper surface of the leaves matt. (In cultivation it flowers in April—May) .... *augustinii*

            D. Flowers red; compact shrub; upper surface of the leaves shining. (In cultivation it flowers in March or early April, three or four weeks before *R. augustinii* has opened its flowers) .... *bergii*

        C. Corolla 2 cm. long; leaves obovate or elliptic, apex obtuse, laminae 3.1—3.8 cm. long; flowers rose; stamens glabrous .... *bivelatum*

    B. Leaves completely deciduous or semi-deciduous.

            E. Flowers white, or rarely greenish-white faintly tinged lavender with yellowish or greenish spots at the base; leaves completely deciduous or almost deciduous; pedicel 1.2—3 cm. long; calyx 0.5—3 mm. long; stamens 2.4—3 cm. long .... *hardyi*

          E. Flowers whitish-rose, apparently not spotted; leaves semi-deciduous; pedicel 0.4—1.2 cm. long; calyx 0.5—1 mm. long; stamens 1.9—2.2 cm. long .... *hirsuticostatum*

A. Branchlets, petioles, upper surface of the leaves bristly, often pubescent, pedicels, calyx, corolla-tube and ovary bristly, not pubescent ....*trichanthum*

DESCRIPTION OF THE SPECIES

R. augustinii Hemsl. in Journ. Linn. Soc., XXVI (1889) 19.
Illustration. Bot. Mag. Vol. 139 t. 8497 (1913).

A shrub, 1—7.63 m. (3⅓—25 ft.) high; *branchlets* scaly, *rather densely pubescent* or sometimes glabrous. *Leaves* evergreen, lanceolate, oblong-lanceolate, oblong, oblong-elliptic or elliptic-obovate, lamina 3.3—12 cm. long, 1.1—4.5 cm. broad, apex acuminate, acute or obtuse, mucronate; base obtuse or tapered; upper surface scaly or not scaly, pubescent or glabrous, midrib pubescent or sometimes minutely puberulous or glabrous; *under surface* scaly, the scales unequal, medium-sized and large, brown, ½—5 times their own diameter apart, glabrous or sometimes pubescent, *midrib hairy ⅓ to its entire length; petiole* 0.5—1.4 cm. long, scaly, *moderately or rather densely pubescent and often with long hairs*, or sometimes glabrous. *Inflorescence* terminal, shortly racemose or umbellate, 2—6-flowered; rhachis 2—8 mm. long, scaly or not scaly, pubescent or glabrous; pedicel 0.6—2.7 cm. long, scaly, puberulous or glabrous. *Calyx* 5-lobed or a mere rim, minute, 0.5—1 mm. (rarely 2—4 mm.) long, lobes rounded or triangular, outside sparsely to densely scaly, glabrous or pubescent, margin ciliate or rarely eciliate. *Corolla* widely funnel-shaped, zygomorphic, 2—4.3 cm. long, 5-lobed, pink, rose, pale lavender-rose, purple, lilac-purple, deep lavender-purple, pale or dark lavender-blue, intense violet, or white tinged pink, with yellowish-green or olive-green or brownish spots, outside moderately or sparsely scaly, glabrous or pubescent on the tube. *Stamens* 10, unequal, long-exserted, 1.3—4.5 cm. long; filaments villous towards the base. *Ovary* oblong or conoid, 3—4 mm. long, 5-celled, densely scaly, pubescent or glabrous; style long, slender, not scaly, puberulous at the base or glabrous. *Capsule* oblong, 0.8—2 cm. long, 3—5 mm. broad, moderately or rather densely scaly, calyx persistent.

This species was discovered by Augustine Henry in 1886 in the Patung district of Hupeh. Subsequently it was found by other collectors in the same region, and in western Szechuan, east and south-east Tibet, and north-west Yunnan. It grows at the margins of woods, in woodlands, thickets, in spruce and pine forests, in rocky situations, and on cliffs, at elevations of 1,300—3,400 m. (4,262—11,148 ft.). Wilson records it as being an exceedingly common species in Hupeh.

R. augustinii is very variable in general features due to its wide geographical distribution, altitudinal range, and diverse habitats in which it is found. It grows from 3 to 25 feet high; the leaves are lanceolate, oblong-lanceolate, oblong, oblong-elliptic or obovate-elliptic, laminae 3.3—12 cm. long, 1.1—4.5 cm. broad, the upper surface is pubescent or glabrous; the corolla is 2—4.3 cm. long; and the flower colour is pink, rose, pale lavender-rose, purple, lilac-purple, deep lavender-purple, pale or dark lavender-blue, intense violet, or white tinged pink. It is a tetraploid with 52 chromosomes.

A diagnostic feature of the species and all the members of its Subseries is the rather densely hairy midrib, ⅓ to its entire length, on the lower surfaces of the leaves.

R. augustinii was first introduced to France by the French missionary Farges. In 1900 Wilson sent seed from western Hupeh (No. 598). The species was reintroduced several times by other collectors. In its native home it reaches a height of 25 feet, but in cultivation it usually grows up to 10 or 12 feet high or sometimes up to 15 feet. The plant varies considerably in leaf size and particularly in flower colour. It may be noted that some of the finest dark lavender-blue forms including "Magor's form", "Tower Court form" and "Exbury form" were produced by crossing some of the best lavender-blue forms in cultivation. The dark lavender-blue forms are exceptionally fine plants, but some of the lavender-purple or lavender-rose forms are also exceedingly attractive when the plants are laden with masses of large widely funnel-shaped flowers. The flower colour of the same individual plant, particularly the lavender blue forms, sometimes varies considerably in the course of years. Some forms often produce a second flush of flowers in October or November. Coming as it does from a wide altitudinal range, from

32. **R. augustinii**
nat. size

a. petals. b. section. c. stamen. d. ovary, style.
e. capsule. f. leaf (lower surface).
g. leaf (lower surface hairy on midrib only).

4,262 to 11,148 feet, the species varies a great deal in hardiness, irrespective of flower colour. It has been pointed out that the darker the blue flower colour, the more tender is the plant. This remark conflicts with the fact that some of the dark blue forms raised from cultivated seed are very hardy along the east coast and west coast. The species was given an Award of Merit when exhibited by Dame Alice Godman, Horsham, Sussex, in 1926. It received an Award of Garden Merit in 1924.

Epithet. After Augustine Henry, 1857—1930, Medical Officer in Chinese Customs, later Professor of Forestry, Dublin.

Hardiness 2—3. April—May.

R. augustinii Hemsl. var. **chasmanthum** (Diels) Davidian in The Rhododendron and Camellia Year Book, 1963, p. 164.

Syn. *R. chasmanthum* Diels in Notes Roy. Bot. Gard. Edin., Vol. 5 (1912) 212.

Illustration. Bot. Mag. n.s. Vol. 166 t. 79 (1949). Figured as *R. chasmanthum*.

This plant has long been known under the name *R. chasmanthum* Diels. In 1963 it was reduced to varietal status in *The Rhododendron and Camellia Year Book* 1963, p. 164. In the same publication, *R. augustinii* Hemsl. f. *grandifolia* Franch., *R. augustinii* Hemsl. f. *subglabra* Franch., and *R. chasmanthoides* Balf. f. et Forrest were placed in synonymy under the above variety.

R. augustinii var. *chasmanthum* was first collected by the Abbé Soulié in 1895 at Tsekou, above Mekong, eastern Tibet. Further gatherings by other collectors show that the plant is distributed in east and south-east Tibet and in north-west Yunnan. It grows in rocky situations, amongst scrub, in thickets, at the margins of Abies and mixed forests, and in spruce and pine forests, at elevations of 2,440—3,660 m. (8,000—12,000 ft.).

The variety differs from the species in that the corolla lobes are markedly reflexed, and the inflorescence is compact, 5—6-flowered.

The plant was first introduced by Forrest in 1919 from south-east Tibet (No. 15004). It was reintroduced by him several times from north-west Yunnan. The plant grows up to about 10 feet high, and is of great beauty when covered with lavender-blue or lavender-rose flowers. It is hardy, easy to grow, and worthy of being widely grown. The plant received an Award of Merit and a First Class Certificate when shown by Mr. Lionel de Rothschild, Exbury, in 1930 and 1932 respectively.

Epithet of the variety. With gaping flowers.

Hardiness 2—3. April—May.

R. bergii Davidian in Quart. Bull. Amer. Rhod. Soc., Vol. 30 (1976) 210—211. Also illustration, front cover.

Syn. *R. augustinii* Hemsl. var. *rubrum* Davidian in The Rhododendron and Camellia Year Book, 1963, p. 165.

A *compact shrub*, 1.50—2.75 m. (5—9 ft.) high; branchlets moderately or rather densely scaly, sparsely hairy with long hairs or glabrous; leaf-bud scales deciduous. *Leaves* evergreen, lanceolate, oblong-lanceolate or oblong, lamina coriaceous, 4—7.8 cm. long, 1.6—3.3 cm. broad, apex acute or acuminate, mucronate, base obtuse or tapered; *upper surface* dark green, *shining*, scaly or not scaly, glabrous or sparsely puberulous, midrib puberulous; *under surface* pale green, scaly, the scales unequal, medium-sized or large, brown, 1—3 times their own diameter apart, glabrous, *midrib rather densely or moderately pubescent*; petiole 0.6—1.6 cm. long, scaly, pubescent or not pubescent, hairy with long hairs. *Inflorescence* terminal, or terminal and axillary in the uppermost one to three leaves, umbellate, 3—5-flowered, flower-bud scales persistent or deciduous; rhachis 2—3 mm. long, scaly, glabrous; pedicel 0.7—2 cm. long, rather densely scaly, glabrous. *Calyx* 5-lobed or a mere rim, minute, 0.5—1 mm. long, lobes rounded or ovate, outside densely scaly, glabrous, margin ciliate. *Corolla* widely funnel-shaped, zygomorphic, 2.7—3 cm. long, 5-lobed, *red, with deep red spots on the upper lobes*, outside scaly, glabrous or puberulous on the tube. *Stamens* 10, unequal, long-exserted, 1.2—2.5 cm. long; filaments pubescent towards the base. *Ovary* oblong or conoid, 2—3 mm. long, 5-celled, densely scaly, glabrous; style long, slender and straight, as long as the corolla or longer, not scaly, glabrous. *Capsule* oblong, 0.7—1 cm. long, 4 mm. broad, densely scaly, glabrous, calyx persistent.

This plant was first described as *R. augustinii* var. *rubrum*. It is so distinct in cultivation, that in 1976 it was given specific rank. The name "Rubra" in binary combination, has already been used in naming several hybrids. In order to avoid confusion, the Yunnan plant had to receive a new name.

R. bergii was discovered by Forrest in October 1924 at Shui-lu Shan, north-west Yunnan, growing in thickets and amongst scrub in side valleys on rocky slopes at an elevation of 3,965 m. (13,000 ft.).

The species is allied to *R. augustinii*, from which it is readily distinguished by the red flowers, by the compact habit of growth, and by the shining upper surface of the leaves. Moreover, in cultivation it flowers in March or early April, three or four weeks before *R. augustinii* has opened its flowers.

The plant was introduced by Forrest in 1924 (No. 25914 — the Type number). In cultivation it grows from 4 to 9 feet high. It often sets good fertile seed; moreover, it is easy to increase from cuttings. The plant is free-flowering, and provides an admirable display with its red flowers in clusters of three to five. It is hardy, and is a most desirable plant for every collection of rhododendrons. A clone 'Papillon' was given an Award of Merit when shown by R.N. Stephenson Clarke in 1978 (Forrest No. 25914).

Epithet. After Mr. and Mrs. Warren E. Berg, Kent, Washington, U.S.A.

Hardiness 3. March—early April. Plate 63.

R. bivelatum Balf. f. in Notes Roy. Bot. Gard. Edin., Vol. 10 (1917) 85.

A shrub; branchlets scaly, puberulous. *Leaves obovate or elliptic,* lamina 3.1—3.8 cm. long, 1.5—2 cm. broad, apex broadly obtuse or rounded, mucronate, base obtuse; upper surface not scaly, midrib pubescent ½ of its length; *under surface* scaly, the scales medium-sized, brown, ½ to their own diameter apart, pubescent, *midrib pubescent;* petiole 3—5 mm. long, scaly, puberulous, sometimes slightly bristly. *Inflorescence* terminal, shortly racemose, 2—3-flowered; rhachis 2 mm. long, scaly, pubescent; pedicel 0.7—1 cm. long, scaly, puberulous. *Calyx* 5-lobed, minute, 1—1.5 mm. long, lobes rounded or triangular, outside scaly, glabrous or moderately or slightly puberulous, margin moderately or slightly ciliate. *Corolla* funnel-shaped, *2 cm. long,* 5-lobed, *rose,* outside scaly, glabrous. *Stamens* 10, unequal, exserted, 1.6—2.1 cm. long; *filaments glabrous.* Ovary conoid, 3 mm. long, 5-celled, densely scaly, with a tuft of hairs at the apex; style slender, not scaly, glabrous. *Capsule* not seen.

R. bivelatum is known only from a single gathering made in 1913 by E.E. Maire on dry hills behind Mo-tsou, north-east Yunnan, at an elevation of 854 m. (2,800 ft.).

In the original diagnosis it was associated with *R. siderophyllum,* in the Yunnanense Subseries. From this species it is readily distinguished by well-marked characters. In *The Species of Rhododendron,* it has been placed in the Augustinii Subseries on account of the hairy midrib on the lower surface of the leaves. Apart from this character it does not conform to the species of this Subseries.

R. bivelatum shows a strong resemblance to *R. tatsienense* in the Yunnanense Subseries, particularly in the shape and size of the leaves, and in the shape, size and colour of the flowers. In both plants the leaf epidermis is said to be two-layered. Although its closest relationship would appear to be with *R. tatsienense,* it will have to remain in its present Subseries until more adequate material is available. There is no record of its occurrence in cultivation.

Epithet. Twice covered.

Not in cultivation.

R. hardyi Davidian in Rhododendrons with Magnolias and Camellias (1974) 46—47.

A shrub, 1.22—3 m. (4—10 ft.) high; branchlets scaly, minutely puberulous or glabrous. *Leaves completely deciduous or almost deciduous*, lanceolate or oblong-lanceolate, lamina 4.5—8.2 cm. long, 1.8—2.9 cm. broad, apex acute or acuminate, mucronate, base obtuse or tapered; upper surface dark green, shining, scaly, glabrous, midrib puberulous; *under surface* scaly, the scales unequal, medium-sized and large, brown or pale brown, 3—6 times their own diameter apart, glabrous, *midrib hairy ⅔ to its entire length*; petiole 5—9 mm. long, scaly, minutely puberulous or glabrous. *Inflorescence* terminal, or terminal and axillary in the uppermost one or two leaves, shortly racemose, 2—4-flowered; rhachis 2—5 mm. long, sparsely scaly or not scaly, minutely puberulous or glabrous; pedicel 1.2—3 cm. long, scaly, minutely puberulous or glabrous. *Calyx* 5-lobed, 0.5—3 mm. long, lobes ovate or triangular, outside scaly or not scaly, glabrous or rarely hairy, margin scaly or not scaly, ciliate. *Corolla* widely funnel-shaped, zygomorphic, 2.3—3.3 cm. long, 5-lobed, *white, or rarely greenish-white faintly tinged lavender, with yellowish or greenish spots at the base*, outside scaly, glabrous or hairy towards the base of the tube. *Stamens* 10, unequal, long-exserted, 2.4—3 cm. long; filaments densely pubescent towards the base. *Ovary* oblong or conoid, 3—4 mm. long, 5-celled, densely scaly, glabrous, or densely pubescent at the apex or at the base; style long, slender, not scaly, glabrous or rarely pubescent at the base. *Capsule* oblong, 0.8—1.2 cm. long, 4—5 mm. broad, densely scaly, calyx persistent.

R. hardyi was first found by the Abbé Soulié in 1895 at Tsekou, east Tibet. It was afterwards collected by Forrest at Shui-lu Shan, north-west Yunnan in June 1924, and by Rock on the Tsarung Border, Yunnan—south-east Tibet, in May—June 1932. The plant grows in thickets and in spruce forests, at elevations of 3,355—3,660 m. (11,000—12,000 ft.).

The species is allied to *R. augustinii* from which it is readily distinguished by the completely deciduous or almost deciduous leaves, and by the white flowers.

R. hardyi was introduced by Rock in 1949. Although in its native home it grows up to 10 feet high, in cultivation it reaches a height of only 6 feet. It is broadly upright, somewhat compact, and is most attractive when covered with white flowers in clusters of two to four. The plant is hardy, and is well worth a place in every collection of rhododendrons.

Epithet. After Major A.E. Hardy.

Hardiness 3. April—May.

R. hirsuticostatum Hand.-Mazz. in Wien Akad. Anzeig., No. 27 (1920).

A shrub, 1.50 m. (5 ft.) high; branchlets scaly, puberulous or glabrous. *Leaves semi-deciduous*, lanceolate or oblong-lanceolate, lamina 3.3—5.5 cm. long, 1.2—2 cm. broad, apex acuminate or acute, mucronate, base rounded or obtuse; upper surface not scaly or slightly scaly, midrib puberulous; *under surface* scaly, the scales large, brown, 2—4 times their own diameter apart, *midrib hairy ½ of its length*; petiole 4—5 mm. long, scaly, puberulous. *Inflorescence* terminal and axillary in the uppermost one or two leaves, shortly racemose, 2—4-flowered; rhachis 3—4 mm. long, scaly or not scaly, puberulous or glabrous; pedicel 0.4—1.2 cm. long, scaly, glabrous or puberulous. *Calyx* almost a mere rim, minute, 0.5—1 mm. long, outside densely scaly, margin scaly, eciliate. *Corolla* widely funnel-shaped, zygomorphic, 2.3—2.5 cm. long, 5-lobed, *whitish-rose*, apparently not spotted, outside sparsely or moderately scaly, glabrous. *Stamens* 10, unequal, 1.9—2.2 cm. long, exserted; filaments densely pubescent towards the base. *Ovary* oblong, 3 mm. long, 5-celled, densely scaly; style slender, not scaly, pubescent at the base. *Capsule* not seen.

This plant is represented by a single gathering, Handel-Mazzetti No. 1353. It was collected in April 1914 in Ningyüen region, south-west Szechuan, at an elevation of 2,200—2,700 m. (7,213—8,852 ft.).

R. hirsuticostatum resembles *R. augustinii* in the hairy midrib on the lower surface of the leaves, but is distinguished by its semi-deciduous leaves. It is also very similar to *R. yunnanense* in general characters and in minor details, but differs in the hairy midrib below. The original diagnosis associates it with *R. stereophyllum* (now *R. tatsienense*). From this plant it is readily distinguished by its general appearance. In *The Species of Rhododendron*, Hutchinson points out aptly that it is "very closely allied to *R. yunnanense*, but with a hairy midrib . . . " Whether this one distinction is of sufficient importance by which to regard *R. hirsuticostatum* as specifically distinct is a matter of some doubt. Nevertheless the name may be allowed to stand until more is known of this plant. There is no record of it in cultivation.

Epithet. With hairy ribs.
Not in cultivation.

R. trichanthum Rehder in Journ. Arn. Arb., XXVI (1945) 480.
Syn. *R. villosum* Hemsl. et Wils. in Kew Bull. Misc. Inform. (1910) 119.
Illustration. Bot. Mag. Vol. 147 t. 8880 (1938). Figured as *R. villosum*.

A broadly upright shrub, 1—6 m. (3⅓—20 ft.) high; *branchlets scaly, densely or moderately bristly and often pubescent. Leaves* oblong-lanceolate or lanceolate or ovate-lanceolate, lamina 4—11 cm. long, 1.5—3.7 cm. broad, apex acuminate or acutely acuminate, mucronate, base obtuse, rounded or cordulate; *upper surface scaly, bristly and often pubescent,* midrib pubescent; under surface scaly, the scales unequal, large or medium-sized, brown, 1—4 times their own diameter apart, bristly or pubescent, midrib rather densely bristly or pubescent ½ to its entire length; *petiole* 0.4—1 cm. long, scaly, *moderately or rather densely bristly and often pubescent. Inflorescence* terminal, shortly racemose, 3—5-flowered; rhachis 3—5 mm. long, scaly or not scaly, bristly or rarely not bristly; *pedicel* 1—1.5 cm. long, scaly, *moderately or rather densely bristly. Calyx* 5-lobed, minute, 0.5—1 mm. long, lobes rounded, *outside* moderately or slightly scaly, *moderately or rather densely bristly, margin bristly. Corolla* widely funnel-shaped, zygomorphic, 2.8—3.8 cm. long, 5-lobed, light to dark purple or rose, outside scaly, *bristly on the tube. Stamens* 10, unequal, long-exserted, 2—3.3 cm. long; filaments densely villous towards the base. *Ovary* oblong, 4 mm. long, 5-celled, densely scaly, *moderately or densely bristly;* style long, slender, not scaly, glabrous or rarely puberulous at the base. *Capsule* oblong, 1.4—1.9 cm. long, 4—5 mm. broad, densely scaly, hairy or rarely glabrous, calyx persistent.

This species was discovered by Wilson in 1904 in west Szechuan. Subsequently it was found by him again, and by McLaren's collectors, by Rock, and by Chu in various localities in the same region and in south-west Szechuan. It grows in thickets and woodlands at elevations of 1,600—3,650 m. (5,245—11,967 ft.). Wilson records it as being a very common species, often forming dense thickets.

R. trichanthum is a unique species in its Series in that the branchlets, leaves, pedicels, calyx, corolla-tube and ovary are moderately or rather densely bristly. In the shape and size of the leaves it resembles *R. augustinii*. From this species and from all the other members of its Series it differs markedly in the bristly characters.

The species was first introduced by Wilson in 1904 (No. 1862) and again in 1908 and in 1910. In its native home it grows up to 20 feet high, but in cultivation it is a medium-sized shrub usually reaching a height of 6—8 feet. According to Wilson the flowers are very variable in colour in western Szechuan, but in cultivation they are very often dark purple or sometimes light purple. The plant is a late flowerer, the flowers appearing in May and June. Although hardy, it should be given a sheltered position, particularly along the east coast and in gardens inland. The species is uncommon in cultivation, but is worth being more widely grown. A clone, 'Honey Wood' was given an Award of Merit when exhibited by Major A.E. Hardy, Sandling Park, in June 1971.

This plant has been known under the name *R. villosum* Hemsl. et Wils., described in 1910. In the *Journal of the Arnold Arboretum*, XXVI, pp. 480, 481 (1945), Rehder changed this name to *R. trichanthum*, pointing out that at an earlier date (1807) A.W. Roth had applied the name *R. villosum* to another plant, and that the same name is now a synonym of *Clerodendrum fragrans* Jacquin. The change in nomenclature is regrettable, but is strictly in accordance with the *International Code Of Botanical Nomenclature*.

Epithet. With hairy flowers.

Hardiness 3. May—June.

HANCEANUM SUBSERIES

General characters: shrubs, 15 cm.—1.50 m. (6 in.—5 ft.) high; branchlets scaly. Leaves lanceolate, oblong-lanceolate, ovate-lanceolate, obovate or ovate, lamina 3—12.8 cm. long, 1—5.5 cm. broad, upper surface scaly or not scaly; under surface scaly, the scales nearly contiguous to 5 times their own diameter apart. *Inflorescence* terminal, *racemose, 5—15-flowered, rhachis 0.8—5 cm. long*; pedicel 0.6—1.4 cm. long. Calyx 1—4 mm. long. *Corolla* campanulate or funnel-campanulate, 0.8—2.1 cm. long, *whitish-green, creamy-white, pale yellow, yellow or white*. Stamens 10. Ovary oblong or oval, 2—3 mm. long; style sharply bent or deflexed, or long, slender, straight. Capsule ovoid or oblong-oval, 6—8 mm. long, 4—5 mm. broad.

KEY TO THE SPECIES

A. Style sharply bent or deflexed or straight; corolla 0.8—1.3 cm. long, campanulate; scales on the under surface of the leaves contiguous to their own diameter apart; leaves lanceolate, oblong-lanceolate or oblong; rhachis of the inflorescence 1.3—5 cm. long .... *afghanicum*

A. Style long, slender and straight; corolla 1.3—2.1 cm. long, funnel-campanulate; scales on the under surface of the leaves 1½—5 times their own diameter apart; leaves ovate, obovate or ovate-lanceolate; rhachis of the inflorescence 0.8—2 cm. long .... *hanceanum*

DESCRIPTION OF THE SPECIES

R. afghanicum Aitch. et Hemsl. in Journ. Linn. Soc. XVIII (1881) 75.

Illustration. Bot. Mag. Vol. 147 t. 8907 (1938).

A low-growing or straggly or semi-prostrate or creeping poisonous shrub up to 50 cm. (1⅔ ft.) high; branchlets scaly, glabrous. *Leaves lanceolate, oblong-lanceolate or oblong*, lamina coriaceous, 3—8 cm. long, 1—2.3 cm. broad, apex obtuse or acute, mucronate, base obtuse or tapered, slightly decurrent on the petiole; upper surface olive-green or bright green or bluish-green, sparsely scaly or not scaly; *under surface* scaly, the *scales* unequal, large and medium-sized, yellowish or pale brown, *nearly contiguous to their own diameter apart*; petiole 0.6—1.2 cm. long, scaly. *Inflorescence* terminal, *distinctly racemose*, 8—15-flowered; *rhachis 1.3—5 cm. long*, scaly, rather densely puberulous; pedicel 0.6—1.5 cm. long, as long as the corolla or longer, moderately or densely scaly, glabrous. *Calyx* 5-lobed, 1—5 mm. long, lobes rounded, oval, ovate or lanceolate, outside and margin moderately or densely scaly, glabrous. *Corolla campanulate, small, 0.8—1.3 cm. long*, 5-lobed, whitish-green, creamy-yellow or white, outside not scaly or slightly scaly, glabrous. *Stamens* 10, unequal, long-exserted, 1—1.5 cm. long; filaments densely villous towards the base. *Ovary* oblong or oval, 2—3 mm. long, 5-celled, densely scaly; *style sharply bent or deflexed or straight*, not scaly. *Capsule* ovoid or oblong-oval, 6—8 mm. long, 4—5 mm. broad, moderately or rather densely scaly, glabrous, calyx-lobes persistent.

R. afghanicum is an outlier from the known area of distribution of its Series. It was discovered by Dr. J.E.T. Aitchison in 1879 in the Kurrum Valley, at Shendtoi and Kaiwas, Afghanistan. (Shendtoi is now on the Pakistan side of the frontier). For a period of ninety years after its discovery, there was no record of this plant having been collected again in its native home. In June 1969, however, I. Hedge and P. Wendelbo collected the plant on Mt. Sikaram, Safed Kuh, province of Paktiva, and again later in July of the same year, at Alishang valley in the province of Laghman, north-east of Kabul. It grows on rocks, on limestone rocks in Abies forest, on ledges and crevices of cliffs, at elevations of 2,135—3,000 m. (7,000—9,836 ft.). Aitchison records it as being abundant at Shendtoi and Kaiwas. According to Hedge and Wendelbo it is locally common in Abies forest on Mt. Sikaram.

The species has long been confused with *R. collettianum* Aitch. et Hemsl., also from Afghanistan. From this species, *R. afghanicum* differs markedly in important features.

The plant varies considerably in habit of growth, in the many-flowered inflorescence, in the length of the rhachis, and in the shape of the style which may be sharply bent or deflexed or straight. It shows a strong resemblance to the smaller forms of *R. hanceanum* in general features, but is distinguished by the shape and often the size of the corolla, often by the sharply bent or deflexed style, and the shape of the leaves, by the distribution of the scales on the lower surface of the leaves, and often by the longer rhachis of the inflorescence.

The species was first introduced by Aitchison in 1880. The plants from this introduction were grown in several gardens; some of these plants persisted until 1919, while a few others were still in cultivation in 1946. Aitchison records the species as being "a poisonous shrub"; moreover, Hedge points out that the local nomads in Afghanistan knew the plant and "that it was a poisonous shrub fatal to sheep if they grazed on it". It was due to this poisonous nature of *R. afghanicum* that soon after the Second World War a healthy group of plants, the last remnants of this species, growing at Tower Court, Ascot, were lifted and destroyed. All the plants from the first introduction by Aitchison, were now lost to cultivation. In 1969, Hedge and Wendelbo reintroduced the species from Sikaram and Alishang, Afghanistan. In cultivation it is a low-growing shrub up to 1⅔ feet high with olive-green or bluish-green leaves, and racemose inflorescences of up to 15 flowers. It is hardy, but to be able to grow it satisfactorily a well-sheltered position should be provided. The plant is rare in cultivation.

Epithet. From Afghanistan.

Hardiness 3. April—May. Plate 66.

R. hanceanum Hemsl. in Journ. Linn. Soc. Bot., XXVI (1889) 24.

Illustration. Bot. Mag. Vol. 142 t. 8669 (1916).

A broadly upright, or somewhat rounded; or compact and spreading or dome-shaped shrub, 30 cm.—1.53 m. (1—5 ft.) high; branchlets scaly. *Leaves ovate-lanceolate, ovate or obovate, lamina rigid,* 3.5—12.8 cm. long, 1.6—5.5 cm. broad, apex acutely acuminate or acute, mucronate, base rounded or obtuse; upper surface bright green or olive-green, moderately or slightly scaly; *under surface* scaly, the *scales* unequal, large and medium-sized, brown, *1½—5 times their own diameter apart;* petiole 0.4—1.4 cm. long, scaly. *Inflorescence terminal, racemose,* 5—11-flowered; *rhachis 0.8—2 cm. long,* scaly, glabrous; pedicel 0.8—1.4 cm. long, scaly, glabrous or sometimes minutely puberulous. *Calyx* 5-lobed, 2—4 mm. long, lobes oblong or oval, outside scaly or not scaly, margin ciliate or eciliate. *Corolla funnel-campanulate, 1.3—2.1 cm. long,* 5-lobed, creamy-white, pale yellow or white, outside scaly or not scaly. *Stamens* 10, unequal, long-exserted, 1.4—2.6 cm. long; filaments pilose towards the base. *Ovary* ovoid, 2—3 mm. long, 5-celled, densely scaly; *style long, slender and straight,* not scaly, glabrous or rarely puberulous at the base. *Capsule* ovoid or oblong-oval, 6—8 mm. long, 4—5 mm. broad, densely scaly, calyx-lobes persistent.

The distribution of this species is restricted to south-west Szechuan. It was first collected by the Rev. Ernest Faber about 1886 on Mt. Omei. The plant grows on cliffs, in rocky places, and in thickets, at elevations of 1,220—3,000 m. (4,000—9,836 ft.). Wilson records it as being locally very common, forming dense thickets.

The plant is easily recognised usually by its rounded or compact habit of growth, by the rigid ovate-lanceolate, ovate or obovate leaves, laxly scaly on the lower surface, the scales being 1½—5 times their own diameter apart, and by the distinctly racemose inflorescence of 5—11 funnel-campanulate, creamy-white, pale yellow or white flowers. It resembles to an extent *R. afghanicum* from Afghanistan in general appearance. The distinctions between them are discussed under the latter.

R. hanceanum was first introduced by Wilson in 1909 (Nos. 882 and 882A), and again in 1910 (No. 4255). Two distinct forms are in cultivation: Form 1. A large, broadly upright or somewhat rounded shrub, 3—4 feet high, with large leaves, laminae 6.8—12 cm. long, 3—5.5 cm. broad. Form 2. A small compact, and spreading or dome-shaped shrub, 1—2 feet high, and as much across, with smaller leaves, laminae 3.8—5.5 cm. long, 1.8—2.2 cm. broad. Form 1 is rare in cultivation. The species is a slow grower, with bright green or olive-green leaves. The young growths, bronzy-brown in colour are an attractive feature. The plant is hardy, free-flowering, and seldom fails to display the beauty of its creamy-white or pale yellow flowers in clusters of 5—11. Form 2 is a charming plant for the rock garden and should be in every collection of rhododendrons. A small form with cream flowers, which was later known as 'Canton Consul', received an Award of Merit when shown by the Crown Estate Commissioners, Windsor Great Park, in 1957.

Epithet. After H.F. Hance, 1827—86, Consul at Canton, etc.

Hardiness 3. April—May.

R. hanceanum Hemsl. 'Nanum.'

This plant has long been known as *R. hanceanum* var. *nanum*. It appeared in cultivation among seedlings raised from *R. hanceanum* seed (No. 4255) collected by Wilson in south-west Szechuan.

The true 'Nanum' is a dwarf compact shrub, 8—15 cm. (3—6 in.) high, and up to 25 cm. (10 in.) wide, with small leaves 2—3.5 cm. long, 1—1.6 cm. broad, and with yellow flowers. It is free-flowering, and is exceedingly charming when covered with funnel-campanulate flowers in clusters of four to seven. It is hardy, and although a slow grower, is an excellent plant for the rock garden.

Epithet of the cultivar. Dwarf habit.

Hardiness 3. April—May. Plate 67.

TRIFLORUM SUBSERIES

General characters: shrubs or rarely trees, 60 cm.—6 m. (2—20 ft.) high; branchlets scaly. Leaves lanceolate, oblong-lanceolate, ovate-lanceolate or elliptic; lamina 1.5—9.3 cm. long, 0.8—3.7 cm. broad; under surface glaucous or not glaucous, scaly, the scales ½—5 times their own diameter apart, rarely contiguous. Inflorescence terminal, or terminal and axillary in the uppermost few leaves, shortly racemose, 1—7-flowered; pedicel 0.4—2 cm. long. Calyx 0.5—1 mm. (rarely up to 4 mm.) long. *Corolla* widely funnel-shaped or sometimes flat saucer-shaped, zygomorphic, rarely tubular or tubular-campanulate, 1.3—3.4 cm. long, *pale or deep yellow, or greenish-yellow*. Stamens 10. Ovary oblong or conoid, 2—5 mm. long; style long, slender and straight. Capsule oblong or sometimes oblong-oval, 0.6—1.8 cm. long, 3—5 mm. broad.

KEY TO THE SPECIES

A. Inflorescence axillary in the uppermost few leaves and terminal; corolla rather densely or sometimes moderately pubescent outside; leaf apex markedly acutely acuminate .... *lutescens*

A. Inflorescence terminal (rarely axillary and terminal); corolla not pubescent outside (except sometimes in *R. triflorum* and *R. bauhiniiflorum*); leaf apex obtuse, acute or acuminate.

    B. Corolla not scaly outside or sometimes scaly; leaf apex broadly obtuse or rounded; leaves (laminae) up to 3 cm. long, and up to 1.5 cm. broad .. *wongii*

    B. Corolla moderately or rather densely scaly outside, leaf apex acuminate or acute or obtuse; leaves (laminae) up to 8 cm. long, and up to 3.2 cm. broad.

        C. Scales on the under surface of the leaves densely set, contiguous to their own diameter apart.

            D. Corolla flat, saucer-shaped, 3.8—4.3 cm. across .... *bauhiniiflorum*

            D. Corolla widely funnel-shaped, usually 1.5—3.6 cm. across.

                E. Under surface of the leaves usually glaucous; petiole not bristly; usually large shrub up to 5.8 m. high; (Himalayan and Chinese species).

                    F. Scales on the under surface of the leaves minute, more or less equal in size, similar in colour, dark or pale brown; midrib on the upper surface of the leaves not hairy; stem and branches with smooth, reddish-brown flaking bark .... *triflorum*

                    F. Scales on the under surface of the leaves large, of different sizes, dissimilar in colour, yellowish-brown and blackish, or yellowish-brown and dark brown; midrib on the upper surface of the leaves hairy; stem and branches with rough bark .... *ambiguum*

                E. Under surface of the leaves usually pale green, not glaucous; petiole bristly or not bristly; small or medium-sized shrub, 30 cm.—1.80 m. high; (Japanese species) .... *keiskei* (part)

        C. Scales on the under surface of the leaves widely spaced, 2—5 times their own diameter apart.

                G. Under surface of the leaves intensely glaucous .... *zaleucum* var. *flaviflorum* (Yunnanense Subseries)

                G. Under surface of the leaves pale green or pale glaucous green or sometimes glaucous.

                    H. Corolla widely funnel-shaped; under surface of the leaves usually pale green; midrib on the upper surface of the leaves puberulous; petiole bristly or not bristly; inflorescence 3—6-flowered; (Japanese species) ... *keiskei* (part)

                    H. Corolla tubular-campanulate or tubular; under surface of the leaves pale glaucous green; midrib on the upper surface of the leaves not puberulous; petiole not bristly; inflorescence 2—3-flowered; (Assam and Tibet species).

                      I. Calyx a mere rim or 5-lobed, 0.5 mm. long; corolla tubular-campanulate .. *kasoense*

                      I. Calyx distinctly 5-lobed, 4 mm. long; corolla broadly tubular or tubular-campanulate .... *flavantherum*

DESCRIPTION OF THE SPECIES

R. ambiguum Hemsl. in Bot. Mag. Vol. 137 t. 8400 (1911).

A rounded or broadly upright shrub, 60 cm.—5.80 m. (2—19 ft.) high; *stem and branches with rough bark*; branchlets densely or moderately scaly. *Leaves* lanceolate, oblong-lanceolate, ovate-lanceolate or elliptic, lamina 2.3—8 cm. long, 1.2—3.2 cm. broad, apex obtuse, acuminate or acute, mucronate, base rounded or obtuse; *upper surface* scaly, *midrib hairy* or rarely glabrous; *under surface glaucous*, scaly, the scales unequal, large and medium-sized, *yellowish-brown*, dark brown or *blackish*, contiguous to their own diameter apart; petiole 0.5—1.3 cm. long, scaly. *Inflorescence* terminal, or rarely terminal and axillary in the uppermost leaf, shortly racemose, 2—7-flowered; rhachis 2—4 mm. long, scaly, puberulous or glabrous; pedicel 0.6—2 cm. long, moderately or rarely densely scaly. *Calyx* 5-lobed, minute, 0.5—1 mm. long, lobes triangular or rounded, outside scaly, margin puberulous or bristly or glabrous. *Corolla* widely funnel-shaped, zygomorphic, 2—3.4 cm. long, 5-lobed, yellow or greenish-yellow, with green spots on the posterior side, outside scaly. *Stamens* 10, unequal, long-exserted, 1.4—3.4 cm. long; filaments villous towards the base. *Ovary* conoid or oblong, 2—5 mm. long, 5-celled, densely scaly; style long, slender, not scaly. *Capsule* oblong or oblong-oval, 0.6—1.3 cm. long, 3—5mm. broad, densely scaly, calyx persistent.

R. ambiguum was discovered by Wilson in 1904 in western Szechuan. It was later found by other collectors in various localities in the same region. The plant grows on rocks in woods, in thickets and woodlands, at elevations of 2,300—4,500 m. (7,541—14,754 ft.). It is recorded as being very abundant in thickets and rocky exposed places.

In 1942, *R. chengshienianum* Fang was described from a specimen (No. 229) collected by C.L. Sun on Mt. Omei, west Szechuan. The isotype and the ample material now available show that *R. chengshienianum* is identical with *R. ambiguum* in every respect (*The Rhododendron and Camellia Year Book*, 1963, p. 174).

R. ambiguum varies considerably in height of growth and in the size of the leaves. It is related to *R. triflorum* and *R. bauhiniiflorum,* but is distinguished from both by the large, unequal, differently coloured scales on the lower surfaces of the leaves, by the hairy midrib on the upper surfaces, and by the rough bark of the stem and branches; it also differs from the latter in the shape of the flowers. From *R. concinnum* in the Yunnanense Subseries, to which it shows a resemblance, it is readily distinguished by the yellow or greenish-yellow flowers, with green spots on the posterior side. It is a tetraploid with 52 chromosomes.

The species was first introduced by Wilson in 1904 (No. 1879), and again later in 1908 and 1910. In its native home it reaches a height of 19 feet, but in cultivation it is a rounded or broadly upright shrub and grows up to 5, or sometimes up to 10 feet high. It is hardy, free-flowering, and a well-grown plant, laden with yellow or greenish-yellow flowers, with green spots, is most effective in April or May. A clone 'Jane Banks' was given an Award of Merit when shown by W.L. and R.A. Banks, Hergest Croft, Kington, Hereford-shire, in 1976.

Epithet. Doubtful.
Hardiness 3. April—May. Plate 69.

R. bauhiniiflorum Watt ex Hutch. in The Species of Rhododendron (1930) 785.

A lax shrub, 1.53—1.83 m. (5—6 ft.) high; *stem and branches with smooth, brown, flaking bark*; branchlets scaly. *Leaves* oblong-lanceolate or ovate-lanceolate, lamina 3.8—6. cm. long, 1.4—2.6 cm. broad, apex acuminate or acute, mucronate, base rounded, obtuse or cordulate; upper surface bluish-green, not scaly, glabrous; *under surface* glaucous or not glaucous, densely scaly, the *scales very small*, more or less equal, dark or pale brown, one-half their own diameter apart; petiole 0.6—1 cm. long, scaly. *Inflorescence* terminal, shortly racemose, 2—3-flowered; rhachis 2—3 mm. long, scaly; pedicel 0.6—1.2 cm.

long, rather densely scaly, not hairy or rarely hairy. *Calyx* 5-lobed, 0.5—2 mm. long, lobes rounded, triangular or oblong, outside densely scaly, margin ciliate. *Corolla flat, saucer-shaped*, zygomorphic, 2.2—2.8 cm. long, *3.8—4.3 cm. across*, 5-lobed, deep or pale yellow or greenish-yellow, with or without yellowish-green spots on the posterior side, outside rather densely scaly, glabrous or hairy on the tube. *Stamens* 10, unequal, long-exserted, 1—2.3 cm. long; filaments villous towards the base. *Ovary* oblong or conoid, 3—4 mm. long, 5-celled, densely scaly; style long, slender, not scaly. *Capsule* oblong, 1—1.2 cm. long, 3—4 mm. broad, densely scaly, calyx persistent.

This species was discovered by Sir George Watt at Japvo, Ching Sow and Keyang, Manipur, Assam, during the Government Demarcation Survey of 1881—1882. It was again collected by him at Japvo in 1895, in leaf. The plant grows at elevations of 2,440—2,898 m. (8,000—9,500 ft.). It is recorded as being one of the most common plants on Mt. Japvo.

R. bauhiniiflorum is closely allied to *R. triflorum* which it resembles in height and habit of growth, in the shape and size of the leaves, and in the size and colour of the flowers. There is one fairly constant criterion between them, namely, the fact that the corolla in *R. bauhiniiflorum* is flat, saucer-shaped, 3.8—4.3 cm. across, while in *R. triflorum* it is funnel- or widely funnel-shaped, usually 2—3.6 cm. across.

The species was introduced by Kingdon-Ward from Mt. Japvo, Assam, in 1928 (No. 7731). In cultivation it is a lax shrub 6—10 feet high, with bluish-green leaves. A characteristic feature is the smooth, brown, flaking bark of the stem and branches. The plant often sets good and plentiful fertile seed. One of its chief merits is that it flowers at a young age when raised from seed. It is hardy and free-flowering, although in cultivation it has not received the wide recognition it deserves.

Epithet. With *bauhinia*-like flowers.
Hardiness 3. April—June.

R. flavantherum Hutch. et Ward in The Species of Rhododendron (1930) 786.

A shrub, 1.83—3 m. (6—10 ft.) high; branchlets scaly. *Leaves* oblong-elliptic, lamina 3—4 cm. long, 1.3—2 cm. broad, apex obtuse, mucronate, base rounded; upper surface scaly, under surface scaly, the scales unequal, medium-sized and large, pale brown, 2—3 times their own diameter apart; petiole 5—8 mm. long, scaly. *Inflorescence* terminal, shortly racemose, 3-flowered; rhachis 2 mm. long, scaly; pedicel 6—8 mm. long, scaly. *Calyx 5-lobed, 4 mm. long*, lobes rounded or oblong-ovate, outside scaly, margin eciliate. *Corolla tubular or tubular-campanulate*, 1.5—2 cm. long, 5-lobed, bright clear yellow, outside scaly. *Stamens* 10, unequal, exserted, 1.3—1.8 cm. long; filaments densely pilose at the base. *Ovary* oblong, 3 mm. long, 5-celled, densely scaly; style long, slender, scaly in the lower half. *Capsule* oblong, 1 cm. long, 3—4 mm. broad, densely scaly, calyx-lobes persistent.

The only collection of this species was made by Kingdon-Ward in November 1924, in the Tsangpo Gorge, near Churung Confluence, Tibet. It was found on vertical cliffs, flowering a second time, at elevations of 2,440—2,745 m. (8,000—9,000 ft.).

It is a shrub 6—10 feet high, with oblong-elliptic leaves, and a broadly tubular or tubular-campanulate, bright clear yellow corolla.

R. flavantherum is an aberrant species in the Triflorum Series on account of its broadly tubular or tubular-campanulate corolla. The original diagnosis makes no reference to its affinity. In *The Species of Rhododendron*, it has been placed in the Triflorum Subseries, Triflorum Series. In the shape and size of the leaves, in the shape and colour of the corolla, and in the size of the calyx, *R. flavantherum* shows a strong resemblance to *R. xanthostephanum* in the Tephropeplum Series. The herbarium material of this plant is scanty. Although the species would be better placed in the Tephropeplum Series, it may, meanwhile, have to remain in its present Series until further material is available. The plant has not been introduced into cultivation.

Epithet. With yellow anthers.

Not in cultivation.

R. kasoense Hutch. et Ward in The Species of Rhododendron (1930) 787.

A lanky or compact shrub, sometimes epiphytic, 30 cm.—2.44 m. (1—8 ft.) high; branchlets scaly. *Leaves* lanceolate or oblong-lanceolate, lamina 3—7.3 cm. long, 1—2.8 cm. broad, apex acute, acuminate or obtuse, mucronate, base obtuse or tapered; upper surface scaly; under surface scaly, the scales unequal, large and medium-sized, pale brown, 1½—3 times their own diameter apart; petiole 0.5—1.5 cm. long, scaly. *Inflorescence* terminal, shortly racemose, 2—3-flowered; rhachis 1—2 mm. long, scaly; pedicel 4—6 mm. long, rather densely scaly. *Calyx 5-lobed or a mere rim, minute, 0.5 mm. long,* lobes triangular, outside densely scaly, margin densely scaly, eciliate. *Corolla tubular-campanulate,* 1.6—2 cm. long, 5-lobed, yellow, outside scaly, glabrous. *Stamens* 10, unequal, exserted, 0.8—1.9 cm. long; filaments densely villous in the lower one-third or one-half their lengths. *Ovary* oblong, 3—4 mm. long, 5-celled, densely scaly; style long, slender, not scaly. *Capsule* oblong, 0.9—1.8 cm. long, 3—4 mm. broad, densely scaly, calyx persistent.

This plant was first collected by Kingdon-Ward in August 1928 on Kaso Peak, Assam. It was later found by Ludlow, Sherriff and Taylor at Nyug La, south-east Tibet. The plant grows in thickets, on rocks, and as an epiphyte in dense mixed forests, at elevations of 2,135—2,745 m. (7,000—9,000 ft.). According to Kingdon-Ward it is a lanky shrub in the shade, 6—8 feet high, but is more common in the open on gneiss rocks where it is a compact shrublet 1—2 feet high.

In the original diagnosis its affinity was stated to be with *R. lutescens*. From this species it differs markedly in that the inflorescence is terminal, and the corolla is tubular-campanulate, glabrous outside.

R. kasoense is very closely allied to *R. flavantherum*. The two species are very much alike in general features. The main distinction between them is that in *R. kasoense* the calyx is a mere rim or minutely 5-lobed, 0.5 mm. long, whereas in *R. flavantherum* it is distinctly 5-lobed, 4 mm. long. It is very doubtful whether this criterion will prove constant when more specimens are available. For the present the name *R. kasoense* has to be retained until more is known of the species.

The plant is said to have been introduced by Kingdon-Ward. There is no record of its occurrence in cultivation.

Epithet. From Kaso Peak, Delei Valley, Assam.

Not in cultivation.

R. keiskei Miq. in Ann. Mus. Bot. Lugd. Bat., (1866) 163.

Illustration. Bot. Mag. Vol. 136 t. 8300 (1910).

A broadly upright, lax upright, rounded, low compact or prostrate shrub, 30 cm.—1.83 m. (1—6 ft.) or sometimes 5—8 cm. (2—3 in.) high; branchlets sparsely or moderately scaly, glabrous or puberulous. *Leaves* lanceolate, oblong-lanceolate, oblong-oval, oval or ovate, lamina 2.3—8.5 cm. long, 0.8—3.5 cm. broad, apex acute, acuminate, obtuse or rounded, mucronate, base obtuse, tapered, or slightly cordulate, or rounded; upper surface olive-green or bright green, scaly or not scaly, not bristly or rarely bristly, midrib moderately or rather densely puberulous; margin not bristly or rarely bristly; *under surface pale green or green or sometimes glaucous,* scaly, the *scales* more or less equal, large or medium-sized, brown or dark brown, *½—5 times their own diameter apart;* petiole 0.2—1.2 cm. long, moderately or rather densely scaly, sparsely bristly or not bristly, not puberulous or sometimes puberulous. *Inflorescence* terminal, shortly racemose, 3—6-flowered; rhachis 2—4 mm. long, scaly; pedicel 0.5—1.2 cm. long, scaly. *Calyx* 5-lobed or a mere rim, 0.5—1 mm. long, lobes rounded, ovate or triangular, outside densely scaly, margin puberulous or not puberulous, moderately or slightly bristly or not bristly. *Corolla* widely funnel-shaped, zygomorphic, 1.4—3 cm. long, 1.6—4.5 cm. across, 5-lobed, pale yellow or lemon-yellow, not spotted, outside scaly, glabrous. *Stamens* 10, unequal, long-exserted, 1—3.2 cm. long; filaments moderately or rather densely puberulous or rarely villous towards the base. *Ovary* oblong or conoid, 2—4 mm. long, 5-celled, densely scaly; style long, slender, longer than the stamens and the corolla, not scaly. *Capsule* oblong or slender, 0.6—1.3 cm. long, 2—4 mm. broad, densely scaly, calyx persistent.

R. keiskei was described by Miquel in 1866. It is a native of Japan where it is widely distributed, from the main island south-westwards to Yakushima. It grows on hills and rocks, sometimes as an epiphyte, at elevations of 610—1,830 m. (2,000—6,000 ft.).

The species shows considerable variation, particularly in habit and height of growth, and in leaf shape and size. It is a broadly upright, lax upright, rounded, low compact or prostrate shrub, from a few inches up to 6 feet in height; the leaves are lanceolate, oblong-lanceolate, oblong-oval, oval or ovate, laminae 2.3—8.5 cm. long, 0.8—3.5 cm. broad.

It is related to *R. triflorum* from which it is distinguished usually by the habit and height of growth, usually by the green lower surface of the leaves, and by the moderately or rather densely puberulous midrib on the upper surface. Moreover, it differs markedly from its ally in that the scales on the lower surface of the leaves are large or medium-sized, and are usually widely spaced. The bristly petiole which is given as a distinguishing factor in *The Species of Rhododendron*, is not constant.

R. keiskei was first introduced in 1908. Several forms are in cultivation, including: Form 1. A broadly upright shrub, 4 feet high with lanceolate leaves, laminae up to 7 cm. long, and up to 2 cm. broad. Form 2. A lax upright shrub up to 3 feet high with smaller lanceolate or oblong-lanceolate leaves, laminae up to 4 cm. long, and up to 1.5 cm. broad. Form 3. A rounded spreading lax shrub, 2 feet high and as much across with lanceolate leaves. Form 4. A compact spreading shrub, 1—2 feet high with oblong-oval, oval or ovate leaves. Form 5. A prostrate shrub with oval leaves known as var. *cordifolia*. Form 6. A very prostrate clone, a few inches high, named 'Yaku Fairy'. In some forms a remarkable feature is the bronzy-brown young foliage. The flowers are widely funnel-shaped, pale yellow or lemon-yellow without spots, and are usually produced freely in clusters of three to six. The smaller plants, up to about 2 feet high, are charming shrubs for the rock garden. The species varies in hardiness. It is to be noted that the dwarf forms are very hardy, much hardier than the taller forms. To be able to grow the taller forms successfully, particularly along the east coast and in gardens inland, a well-sheltered position should be provided. It was given an Award of Merit when exhibited by Mr. Harry White, Windlesham, Surrey, in 1929. The same Award for the prostrate clone, 'Yaku Fairy' Plate 35, was gained when shown by Mr. B.N. Starling in 1970.

Epithet. After Ito Keisuke, 1803—1900, a Japanese botanist.
Hardiness 2—3. April—May. Plate 34.

R. lutescens Franch. in Bull. Soc. Bot. France, XXXIII (1886) 235.
Illustration. Bot. Mag. Vol. 146 t. 8851 (1920).
A lax broadly upright shrub, 92 cm.—6 m. (3—20 ft.) high with long branches; *stem and branches with smooth, brown, flaking bark*; branchlets scaly; *young growths bronzy-brown. Leaves* lanceolate, oblong-lanceolate or ovate-lanceolate, lamina 4.8—9.3 cm. long, 1.3—3.7 cm. broad, *apex acutely acuminate*, mucronate, base rounded or obtuse; upper surface bright green or olive-green, moderately or sparsely scaly, midrib glabrous or rarely puberulous; under surface scaly, the scales large, unequal, yellowish or brown, ½—5 times their own diameter apart; petiole 0.6—1.2 cm. long, scaly. *Inflorescence terminal and axillary in the uppermost few leaves*, umbellate or shortly racemose, 1—3-flowered; rhachis

33. **R. lutescens**
nat. size
a. capsule. b. ovary, style. c. stamen.

1—2 mm. long, scaly; pedicel 0.4—1.5 cm. long, rather densely or moderately scaly, glabrous or rarely minutely puberulous. *Calyx* 5-lobed or a mere rim, minute, 0.5—1 mm. long, lobes rounded or triangular, outside densely scaly, margin ciliate or eciliate. *Corolla* widely funnel-shaped, zygomorphic, 1.3—2.6 cm. long, 2—4.5 cm. across, 5-lobed, pale yellow (rarely white), with green spots, *outside* scaly or not scaly, *rather densely or sometimes moderately pubescent*, rarely slightly pubescent. *Stamens* 10, unequal, long-exserted, 1—3.5 cm. long; filaments densely villous towards the base. *Ovary* oblong or sometimes conoid, 2—4 mm. long, 5-celled, densely scaly, glabrous or sometimes ciliate at the apex; style long, slender, not scaly. *Capsule* oblong, 0.8—1.1 cm. long, 3—4 mm. broad, densely scaly, calyx persistent.

This species was described by Franchet in 1886 from a plant collected at Mupin, west Szechuan about the year 1870. It was afterwards found by various collectors in other localities in the same region and in north-west Yunnan. The plant grows in woods and thickets, and on hill slopes, at elevations of 800—3,000 m. (2,623—9,836 ft.). Wilson records it as being very common in thickets and margins of woods in west Szechuan.

During the years 1895—1914, three other plants which were collected in the same regions, were described as *R. costulatum* Franch., *R. lemeei* Lévl., and *R. blinii* Lévl., and in *The Species of Rhododendron* 1930, the names correctly appear in synonymy under *R. lutescens*.

R. lutescens is a distinct species, and is readily distinguished from all the other members of its Subseries by the terminal and axillary inflorescence in the uppermost few leaves, by the long acutely acuminate leaf apex, and usually by the corolla which is rather densely or sometimes moderately pubescent outside. It is allied to *R. triflorum*, *R. keiskei* and *R. ambiguum*, but differs markedly in distinctive features.

The species was first introduced by Wilson in 1904 (No. 1875). It was first raised by Messrs. Veitch in their nursery at Coombe Wood. In its native home it reaches a height of 20 feet, but in cultivation it grows up to only 10 feet high. It is a lax broadly upright shrub with long branches and bright green or olive-green leaves. A remarkable feature is the smooth, brown, flaking bark of the stem and branches. The young growths, of a bronzy-brown colour, are another prominent character. The species blooms early, the flowers appearing in February, March or April, and when it escapes the frost it provides a fine display with its pale yellow or lemon-yellow flowers in clusters of one to three. A form 'Exbury' with clear lemon-yellow flowers received a First Class Certificate when shown by Mr. Lionel de Rothschild, Exbury, in 1938, and an Award of Merit was given to a form 'Bagshot Sands' with primrose-yellow flowers, when exhibited by Mrs. R.M. Stevenson, Tower Court, Ascot, in 1953. It was given an Award of Garden Merit in 1969.

Epithet. Becoming yellow.
Hardiness 3. February—March—April.

R. triflorum Hook. f. Rhod. Sikkim Himal., t. XIX (1851).

A lax broadly upright shrub, 45 cm.—4.58 m. (1½—15 ft.) high with slender branches; *stem and branches with smooth, reddish-brown, flaking bark*; branchlets scaly. *Leaves* lanceolate, oblong-lanceolate, ovate-lanceolate, elliptic or oval, lamina 3—7.8 cm. long, 1.3—3.3 cm. broad, apex acuminate, acute or obtuse, mucronate, base rounded, obtuse or cordulate; upper surface bright green or dark green, not scaly, glabrous; *under surface glaucous* or sometimes pale green, densely scaly, the *scales very small, more or less equal*, dark or pale brown, one-half to their own diameter apart; petiole 0.5—1.3 cm. long, scaly. *Inflorescence* terminal, shortly racemose, 2—4-flowered; rhachis 3—5 mm. long, scaly; pedicel 0.6—1.6 cm. long, moderately or densely scaly. *Calyx* 5-lobed, minute, 0.5—1 mm. long, lobes rounded, ovate or triangular, outside densely or sometimes moderately scaly, margin ciliate or puberulous or rarely glabrous. *Corolla funnel-shaped or widely funnel-shaped*, zygomorphic, 2—3.3 cm. long, 2—3.6 cm. or rarely up to 4 cm. across, pale yellow, sulphur-yellow, greenish-yellow, yellow or rarely yellow tinged pink, with greenish-yellow or olive-green spots, outside rather densely scaly, pubescent or glabrous. *Stamens* 10, unequal, long-exserted, 1.2—2.8 cm. long; filaments villous towards the base. *Ovary* oblong or conoid, 3—5 mm. long, 5-celled, densely scaly; style long, slender, not scaly, glabrous or rarely puberulous at the base. *Capsule* oblong, 1—1.3 cm. long, 3—4 mm. broad, densely scaly, calyx persistent.

This species is one of J.D. Hooker's discoveries in the Sikkim Himalaya in 1849. Further gatherings by other collectors show that the area of distribution of this species extends from Nepal, Sikkim, Bhutan to Assam, south and south-east Tibet, and the Burma-Tibet Frontier. It is found in very varied habitats, on dry or damp hillsides, on sandy soil, in rhododendron and holly forest, in mixed and pine forests, in birch and shrub jungle, in thickets, along the banks of streams, and on river edge, at elevations of 2,135—3,965 m. (7,000—13,000 ft.). It is recorded as being very common in pine forests in south-east Tibet, and at the edge of forests in Bhutan.

R. triflorum varies considerably in general features. It grows from 2 up to 15 feet high, although Stainton found a plant (No. 187) just 1½ feet in height on a large rock in the Arun Valley, Nepal; the leaves are lanceolate, oblong-lanceolate, ovate-lanceolate, elliptic or oval, laminae 3—7.8 cm. long, 1.3—3.3 cm. broad; the corolla is 2—3.3 cm. long, 2—3.6 cm. or rarely up to 4 cm. across. It is a diploid with 26 chromosomes.

A diagnostic feature of the species is usually the glaucous lower surface of the leaves, densely scaly with minute scales, one-half to their own diameter apart. *R. triflorum* is very closely allied to *R. bauhiniiflorum*. There is a definite resemblance between them in habit and height of growth, and in the shape and size of the leaves. The distinctions given in the Key in *The Species of Rhododendron*, as to the size and colour of the scales on the under surface of the leaves, and the number of flowers in the inflorescences, are not constant. However, there is one fairly constant distinguishing mark between them, namely the fact that the corolla in *R. triflorum* is funnel- or widely funnel-shaped, usually 2—3.6 cm. across, while in *R. bauhiniiflorum* it is flat, saucer-shaped, 3.8—4.3 cm. across. Moreover, in the former the corolla is pale yellow, yellow or greenish-yellow, whilst in the latter it is often deep yellow.

R. triflorum was first introduced by Hooker in 1850 from the Sikkim Himalaya. It was reintroduced by other collectors from Bhutan and south Tibet. In cultivation it is a lax, broadly upright shrub usually up to 8 feet high with slender branches and bright or dark green leaves. Several forms are grown in gardens, varying in height of growth, in leaf shape and size, and in flower size. The best form is 5—6 feet high with large yellow flowers 3.3 cm. long, produced freely in clusters of two to four. An attractive feature is the smooth, reddish-brown, flaking bark of the stem and branches. The species is hardy and late-flowering, prolonging the flowering season into May and June.

Epithet. Three-flowered.
Hardiness 3. May—June.

R. triflorum Hook. f. var. **mahogani** Hutch. in Gard. Chron., C1 (1937) 135.

This plant was discovered by Kingdon-Ward in May 1924 at Lusha, south-east Tibet. It was found by him again later in October that year in the same region. Ludlow and Sherriff collected it in 1936 at Mola, south-east Tibet, and again later with Elliot in other localities in the same region. It grows in birch copse, beside streams, on open hill slopes, and in dry bracken-covered moorland, at elevations of 2,745—3,813 m. (9,000—12,500 ft.). Kingdon-Ward records it as being abundant in birch copse on the mountains. According to Ludlow, Sherriff and Elliot it is very common, usually close to streams, in the Tsangpo Valley.

The variety differs from the species in that the corolla has a mahogany coloured blotch and spots, or is suffused mahogany, or is of mahogany colour.

The plant was first introduced by Kingdon-Ward in 1924 (Nos. 5687, 6263). In its native home it grows up to 8 feet or more in height. Ludlow and Sherriff record it as being one foot high on hill slopes. In cultivation it is a medium-sized shrub, broadly upright, 4—8 feet high. Three flower colour forms are grown in gardens: Form 1. Corolla white, slightly tinged mahogany, with a pale greenish-mahogany blotch at the base. Form 2. Corolla white, tinged mahogany, with a large mahogany blotch. Form 3. Corolla mahogany all over, with a large mahogany blotch. Form 3 is generally considered to be the best; it is free-flowering, and is extremely charming with its mahogany-coloured flowers produced in great profusion.

Epithet of the variety. With mahogany-coloured flowers.

Hardiness 3. May—June.

R. wongii Hemsl. et Wils. in Kew Bull., (1910) 118.

A rounded or broadly upright shrub, 60 cm.—2 m. (2—6½ ft.) high; stem and branches with rough bark; branchlets rather densely scaly, glabrous. *Leaves* oblong, elliptic or oblong-elliptic, *lamina 1.5—3 cm. long, 0.8—1.5 cm. broad, apex broadly obtuse, obtuse, rounded* or sometimes acute, mucronate, base broadly obtuse, obtuse or rounded; upper surface dark green or pale green or olive-green, moderately or densely scaly; margin slightly recurved; under surface slightly glaucous or not glaucous, densely scaly, the scales large, or large and medium-sized, pale brown or brown or dark brown, nearly contiguous or one-half or their own diameter apart; petiole 3—5 mm. long, moderately or densely scaly, glabrous. *Inflorescence* terminal, umbellate or shortly racemose, 2—5-flowered; rhachis 0.5—1 mm. long, scaly; pedicel 0.4—1 cm. long, moderately or rather densely scaly, glabrous. *Calyx* 5-lobed, minute, 0.5—1 mm. long, lobes ovate or rounded or triangular, outside scaly, margin ciliate or eciliate. *Corolla* widely funnel-shaped or funnel-shaped, zygomorphic, *1.6—2.2 cm. long*, 5-lobed, cream-coloured or yellow, *outside not scaly* or sometimes scaly, not puberulous or sometimes puberulous at the base of the tube. *Stamens* 10, unequal, long-exserted, 1.5—2 cm. long; filaments villous towards the base. *Ovary* conoid, 2—3 mm. long, 5-celled, densely scaly, glabrous; style long, slender, straight, longer than the corolla, not scaly, minutely puberulous at the base or glabrous. *Capsule* oblong, 0.8—1 cm. long, 3—4 mm. broad, straight, rather densely or moderately scaly, glabrous, calyx persistent.

This plant was first collected by Wilson in June 1904 on a mountain side near Tatsienlu, western Szechuan, at an elevation of 3,650 m. (11,967 ft.). It was afterwards found by F.T. Wang on Mt. Omei and vicinity, Szechuan, in 1930.

It is a small or medium-sized shrub 2—6½ feet high with cream-coloured or yellow flowers. The original diagnosis associates it with *R. flavidum* and *R. concinnum*. From these species, and particularly from the former, it differs markedly in general characters.

R. wongii shows a strong resemblance to *R. ambiguum* in its general appearance, but is distinguished by the smaller corolla usually not scaly outside, and usually by the smaller leaves broadly obtuse or rounded at the apex. It further differs in its hardiness.

The species was introduced possibly by Wilson in 1904. In its native home it grows up to 6½ feet high, but in cultivation it is a small rounded or broadly upright shrub up to only about 2 or 3 feet high with pale yellow or yellow flowers in clusters of 2—5. The plant is extremely hardy, much hardier than *R. ambiguum*, and is successfully grown outdoors in the colder parts of Scandinavia and Eastern U.S.A. It is uncommon in cultivation, but should be a valuable acquisition to the rock garden.

Epithet. After Y.C. Wong, Ichang, friend and helper of E.H. Wilson.

Hardiness 4. April—May.

R. hormophorum, Muli mountains, south-west Szechuan. Photo J.F. Rock

YUNNANENSE SUBSERIES

General characters: shrubs or sometimes trees, 26 cm.—10.60 m. (11 in.—34 ft.) high; branchlets moderately or rather densely scaly or sometimes not scaly, glabrous or puberulous or sometimes bristly. Leaves evergreen, or sometimes semi-deciduous or completely deciduous, lanceolate, oblong-lanceolate, oblong, elliptic or almost orbicular; lamina 1.6—10.4 cm. long, 0.6—4.2 cm. broad; under surface scaly, the scales overlapping to 8 times their own diameter apart. Inflorescence terminal, or terminal and axillary in the uppermost one or two leaves, shortly racemose, 1—10-flowered; pedicel 0.3—3 cm. long. Calyx 0.5—1 mm. (sometimes up to 5 mm.) long. Corolla usually widely funnel-shaped, zygomorphic, 1.2—4.8 cm. long, white, pink, rose-purple, lavender-blue to dark reddish-purple. Stamens 10. Ovary oblong or conoid, 2—6 mm. long; style long, slender. Capsule oblong or rarely conoid, 0.5—2 cm. long.

KEY TO THE SPECIES

A. Under surface of the leaves markedly glaucous.
    B. Scales on the under surface of the leaves widely spaced, 1½—4 times their own diameter apart; corolla moderately scaly outside; under surface of the leaves intensely glaucous .... *zaleucum*
    B. Scales on the under surface of the leaves closely spaced ½ or rarely their own diameter apart; corolla not scaly or rarely only tube scaly outside; under surface of the leaves bluish-glaucous .... *searsiae*
A. Under surface of the leaves pale green or brown or pale glaucous green.
    C. Flowers purple, dark purple, reddish-purple or purplish-violet; corolla moderately or rather densely scaly outside (except in *R. apiculatum*, only lobes sparsely scaly outside).
        D. Leaves lanceolate, oblong-lanceolate or oblanceolate, 3—4 times as long as broad; scales on the under surface of the leaves overlapping or contiguous; scales on the branchlets and usually on the under surface of the leaves flaky .... *polylepis*
        D. Leaves oval, ovate, elliptic, ovate-lanceolate or sometimes oblong-lanceolate, usually as long as broad or up to twice as long as broad; scales on the under surface of the leaves ½ to their own diameter apart or contiguous; scales on the branchlets and on the under surface of the leaves not flaky.
        E. Petioles bristly; branchlets, pedicels and calyx bristly or not bristly .... *amesiae*
        E. Petioles, branchlets, pedicels and calyx not bristly.
            F. Corolla widely funnel-shaped, 1.5—3.5 cm. long; (Szechuan and Yunnan species).
                G. Upper surface of the leaves scaly; the scales on the under surface of the leaves contiguous to their own diameter apart; branchlets, petioles and pedicels rather densely or moderately scaly .....
                .... *concinnum*
(part)
                G. Upper surface of the leaves not scaly; the scales on the under surface of the leaves 1½—2 times their own diameter apart; branchlets not scaly or sparsely scaly, petioles and pedicels sparsely scaly .... *apiculatum*
            F. Corolla tubular-campanulate, 1.6—2.6 cm. long; (Assam species) .... *concinnoides*
    C. Flowers white, pink, rose or pale lavender; corolla not scaly or sparsely or moderately scaly outside.
            H. Upper surface of the leaves and/or margins and/or petiole bristly.
                I. Leaves completely deciduous ....
                .... *hormophorum*
(part)
                I. Leaves evergreen or semi-deciduous.
                    J. Scales on the under surface of the leaves widely spaced, usually 2—6 times their own diameter apart; leaves evergreen or semi-deciduous; corolla not scaly or sparsely or moderately scaly outside; pedicels not pubsecent.

K. Margins of the leaves usually sparsely bristly or not bristly, usually not rough to the touch; upper surface of the leaves green or pale green, under surface pale glaucous green or green; corolla pink, white, deep rose, pale rose-lavender or lavender ... *yunnanense* (part)

K. Margins of the leaves usually rather densely bristly, rough to the touch; upper surface and usually the under surface of the leaves dark green; corolla ivory-white or ivory-white flushed rose .... *suberosum*

J. Scales on the under surface of the leaves closely spaced, usually ½—1½ times their own diameter apart; leaves evergreen; corolla moderately scaly outside; pedicels often pubescent .... *vilmorinianum* (part)

H. Upper surface of the leaves and margins, and petioles not bristly.

 L. Scales on the under surface of the leaves closely set, usually contiguous to their own diameter apart.

  M. Leaves lanceolate, oblong-lanceolate or narrowly oblong.

   N. Corolla small, usually 1.2—1.5 cm. long .... *hypophaeum*

   N. Corolla large, usually 1.8—3.5 cm. long.

    O. Upper surface of the leaves pale greyish-green, matt; inflorescence terminal and axillary in the uppermost one or two leaves; pedicel usually densely scaly .... *siderophyllum* (part)

    O. Upper surface of the leaves dark or bright green, usually shining; inflorescence terminal, or terminal and axillary in the uppermost one or two leaves; pedicel usually moderately scaly.

     P. Lamina of leaf V-shaped with the midrib in cross section or flat; pedicel not pubescent; calyx margin often eciliate; ovary not bristly .... *davidsonianum*

     P. Lamina of leaf flat; pedicel often pubescent, calyx margin often ciliate or bristly; ovary bristly at the apex or not bristly .... *vilmorinianum* (part)

  M. Leaves orbicular, oval, ovate, elliptic, obovate or ovate-lanceolate.

    Q. Corolla moderately or rather densely scaly all over the tube and lobes outside .... *concinnum* (part)

    Q. Corolla usually not scaly or sparsely scaly or sometimes only the lobes moderately scaly outside.

     R. Upper surface of the leaves pale greyish-green, matt; inflorescence terminal and axillary in the uppermost one or two leaves; flowers usually in several clusters towards the apex of the branchlets; leaf apex often acuminate or acute .... *siderophyllum* (part)

R. Upper surface of the leaves usually dark green or green or sometimes bluish-green, often shining; inflorescence terminal, or terminal and axillary in the uppermost one or two leaves; flowers often in only one or two clusters towards the apex of the branchlets; leaf apex usually rounded or obtuse.

 S. Leaves not rigid; branchlets green or deep pink, often not scaly or sparsely scaly; upper surface of the leaves often not scaly or sparsely scaly; under surface of the leaves often pale glaucous green; corolla 1.8—4 cm. long, often not scaly .... *oreotrephes* (part)

 S. Leaves rigid; branchlets deep crimson or deep crimson-purple, moderately or rather densely scaly; upper surface of the leaves moderately or rather densely scaly; under surface of the leaves usually pale green; corolla usually 1.4—2.3 cm. long, often moderately scaly outside .... *tatsienense*

L. Scales on the under surface of the leaves widely spaced, 2—8 times their own diameter apart.

 T. Leaves completely deciduous .... *hormophorum* (part)

 T. Leaves evergreen or semi-deciduous.

  U. Leaves lanceolate, oblong-lanceolate or narrowly oblanceolate.

   V. Leaf apex markedly long acuminate .... *bodinieri*

   V. Leaf apex acute, shortly acuminate or obtuse.

    W. Corolla widely funnel-shaped, large, usually 1.8—3.4 cm. long; leaves 1.3 cm. broad; calyx a mere rim or 5-lobed, 0.5—1 mm. long.

     X. Upper surface of the adult and young leaves green; leaves evergreen or semi-deciduous; branchlets, petioles and midrib on the upper surface of the leaves usually puberulous; branchlets moderately or sparsely scaly; pedicel moderately or sparsely scaly or not scaly; under surface of the leaves pale green or pale glaucous green .... *yunnanense* (part)

     X. Upper surface of the adult leaves bluish-green, in young leaves glaucous bluish-green; leaves evergreen; branchlets, petioles and midrib on the upper surface of the leaves usually not puberulous; branchlets usually not scaly or sparsely scaly; pedicel not scaly or rarely sparsely scaly; under surface of the leaves pale glaucous green .... *rigidum* (part)

    W. Corolla tubular-funnel shaped, small, usually 1.3—1.6 cm. long; leaves 0.6—1.5 cm. broad; calyx 5-lobed, usually 2—3 mm. long .... *longistylum*

  U. Leaves orbicular, oval, ovate, elliptic or oblong.

   Y. Upper surface of the leaves dark green or sometimes bluish-green; scales on the under surface of the leaves usually 2—3 times their own diameter apart .... *oreotrephes* (part)

   Y. Upper surface of the leaves bluish-green; scales on the under surface of the leaves 4—8 times their own diameter apart .... *rigidum* (part)

DESCRIPTION OF THE SPECIES

R. amesiae Rehd. et Wils. in Plantae Wilsonianae (1913) 523.

Illustration. Bot. Mag. Vol. 154 t. 9221 (1930).

A broadly upright spreading shrub, 2—4 m. (6½—13 ft.) high; *branchlets* moderately or rather densely scaly, *bristly* or not bristly. *Leaves* ovate, ovate-elliptic, oblong-elliptic or elliptic, lamina 2.8—7 cm. long, 1.5—3.4 cm. broad, apex obtuse or acute, mucronate, base rounded or broadly obtuse; upper surface dark green, moderately or rather densely scaly, pubescent or glabrous, midrib pubescent; under surface pale green, densely scaly, the scales unequal, medium-sized and large, pale or dark brown, or yellowish-brown, one-half to their own diameter apart; *petiole* 0.5—1.1 cm. long, moderately or rather densely scaly, *bristly*. *Inflorescence* terminal, shortly racemose, 2—5-flowered; rhachis 2—3 mm. long, scaly, puberulous or glabrous; *pedicel* 0.8—1.8 cm. long, scaly, *bristly* or not bristly, puberulous or glabrous. *Calyx* 5-lobed, minute, 0.5—1 mm. long, lobes rounded or ovate or triangular, *outside* scaly, *bristly* or not bristly, pubescent or glabrous, *margin* not scaly or scaly, *bristly* or not bristly, pubescent or glabrous. *Corolla* widely funnel-shaped, zygomorphic, 2.8—4 cm. long, 5-lobed, purple or dark reddish-purple, with or without darker spots on the posterior side, outside moderately or sparsely scaly, glabrous or sometimes hairy on the tube outside. *Stamens* 10, unequal, 1.8—3.6 cm. long, exserted; filaments densely villous towards the base. *Ovary* oblong or conoid, 3—4 mm. long, 5-celled, densely scaly, glabrous or sparsely hairy at the apex; style long, slender, not scaly. *Capsule* oblong, 1.2—1.8 cm. long, 3—6 mm. broad, moderately or rather densely scaly, calyx persistent.

R. amesiae was discovered by Wilson in 1908 at Mupin, western Szechuan. It was found by him again later in October 1910 in the same region. He records it as being local in its distribution, growing in woods, at elevations of 2,300—3,000 m. (7,541—9,836 ft.).

In the original diagnosis *R. amesiae* was associated with *R. searsiae, R. villosum* (now *R. trichanthum*), and *R. augustinii*. From these plants it differs markedly in general characters. Its kinship is undoubtedly with *R. concinnum* which it resembles in habit and height of growth, in the shape and size of the leaves, and in the shape, size and colour of the flowers. In *R. amesiae,* the colour of the scales, which has been given as a diagnostic criterion in the description and in the Key in *The Species of Rhododendron,* varies from dark brown to pale yellowish-brown. The species is distinguished from *R. concinnum* by the bristly petioles and sometimes by the bristly branchlets, pedicels, and calyx. Whether *R. amesiae,* on these distinctions, merits specific rank, is very doubtful. Nevertheless, the specific status of this plant will have to stand until more adequate material is available. The plant is a tetraploid with 52 chromosomes.

R. amesiae was introduced by Wilson in 1910 (No. 4233). Although in its native home it grows up to 13 feet in height, in cultivation it is medium-sized, 6—7 feet high. It is a broadly upright spreading shrub, fairly well-filled with dark green foliage, and with dark reddish-purple flowers produced freely in clusters of two to five. It is hardy, a robust grower, and easy to cultivate. The plant is rare in cultivation.

Epithet. After Mary S. Ames, of North Easton, Mass.

Hardiness 3. May.

R. apiculatum Rehd. et Wils. in Plantae Wilsonianae (1913) 520.

A shrub, 1.50 m. (5 ft.) high; branchlets not scaly or sparsely scaly. *Leaves* oval or broadly elliptic, lamina 2.8—5 cm. long, 1.8—3.2 cm. broad, apex rounded or broadly obtuse, mucronate, base rounded, truncate or cordulate; upper surface not scaly; *under surface* scaly, the *scales* more or less equal, large and medium-sized, brown, *1½—2 times their own diameter apart*; petiole 6—8 mm. long, sparsely scaly. *Inflorescence* terminal, shortly racemose, 2—3-flowered; rhachis 2 mm. long; pedicel 0.7—1 cm. long, sparsely scaly at the apex. *Calyx* 5-lobed, minute, 1 mm. long, lobes triangular or rounded, scaly.

Corolla funnel-campanulate, 3—3.5 cm. long, 5-lobed, *dark purple*, not scaly or lobes sparsely scaly outside. *Stamens* 10, unequal, 1.8—2 cm. long; filaments pubescent towards the base. *Ovary* conoid, 5 mm. long, 5-celled, densely scaly; style glabrous. *Capsule* not seen.

R. apiculatum is represented by a single rather inadequate specimen. It was collected by Wilson in July 1908 near Wen-ch'uan Hsien, western Szechuan, growing in thickets and margins of woods at elevations of 2,500—3,000 m. (8,197—9,836 ft.).

The original diagnosis associated it with *R. yanthinum* (now *R. concinnum*). When this specimen under *R. apiculatum* is examined, it will be seen that it agrees with *R. oreotrephes* in general characters and in morphological details, but differs only in the dark purple colour of the flowers. There would appear to be no significant difference between these two plants but the scanty material is insufficient as conclusive evidence. The plant has not been introduced into cultivation.

Epithet. With pointed leaves.

Not in cultivation.

R. bodinieri Franch. in Journ. de Bot., XII (1898) 257.

A small shrub; branchlets sparsely scaly, glabrous. *Leaves* evergreen, *lanceolate*, lamina 4.6—6 cm. long, 1—1.5 cm. broad, *apex markedly long acuminate*, mucronate, base tapered; upper surface not scaly or sparsely scaly, glabrous, midrib glabrous; margins glabrous; *under surface* scaly, the *scales* unequal, medium-sized, brown, *4—6 times their own diameter apart*; petiole 0.5—1 cm. long, scaly, glabrous. *Inflorescence* terminal and axillary in the uppermost one or two leaves, shortly racemose, 5—8-flowered; rhachis 2—3 mm. long, slightly scaly or not scaly, glabrous; pedicel 0.8—1.3 cm. long, sparsely scaly or not scaly. *Calyx* a mere rim or 5-lobed, minute, 0.5 mm. long, lobes rounded or triangular, outside not scaly, margin scaly, glabrous. *Corolla* widely funnel-shaped, zygomorphic, 2.3—3 cm. long, 5-lobed, rose with purple spots, not scaly or lobes slightly scaly outside. *Stamens* 10, unequal, 1.6—2.5 cm. long, exserted; filaments glabrous or puberulous towards the base. *Ovary* oblong, 4 mm. long, 5-celled, densely scaly, glabrous, style long, slender, not scaly. *Capsule* not seen.

R. bodinieri was found by R.P. Bodinier in April 1897, growing between Ma Kay and Se-Tsong-hien, in east Yunnan, and is known by a single collection.

It is very closely related to *R. yunnanense*. There is a strong similarity between them in leaf shape and size, and in the distribution of the scales on the lower surface, in the terminal and axillary inflorescence in the uppermost one or two leaves, and in flower shape, size and colour. *R. bodinieri* differs from its ally in that the leaf apex is markedly long acuminate. Whether this one distinction justifies a separate specific rank is very doubtful. Meanwhile, the name *R. bodinieri* will have to be retained until further specimens are available. There is no record of its occurrence in cultivation.

Epithet. After Emile Bodinier, French missionary in China; 1824—1901.

Not in cultivation.

R. concinnoides Hutch. et Ward in The Species of Rhododendron (1930) 780.

A small lax shrub, often epiphytic; branchlets rather densely or moderately scaly. *Leaves* elliptic or obovate-elliptic, lamina 2.3—4.5 cm. long, 1—2.5 cm. broad, apex obtuse, mucronate, base obtuse; upper surface scaly, midrib glabrous; under surface densely scaly, the scales unequal, medium-sized and large, dark brown, one-half their own diameter apart or almost contiguous; petiole 3—6 mm. long, densely scaly. *Inflorescence* terminal, shortly racemose, 3-flowered; rhachis 1—2 mm. long, scaly; pedicel 0.5—1 cm. long, densely or moderately scaly. *Calyx* 5-lobed, minute, 1 mm. long, lobes rounded or triangular, outside scaly, margin scaly, eciliate or ciliate. *Corolla tubular-campanulate, slightly oblique, compressed laterally, 1.6—2.6 cm. long*, 5-lobed, lobes and upper part of corolla pinkish-purple fading to white at the base, with darker spotting inside, outside rather densely scaly. *Stamens* 10, unequal, 1.6—2.5 cm. long; filaments densely villous towards the base. *Ovary* oblong, 4 mm. long, 5-celled, densely scaly; style slender, not scaly. *Capsule:* —

This species was first collected by Kingdon-Ward in May 1928 in the Delei Valley, Assam. It was found by him again later in August of that year in the same region. The plant grows as an epiphyte on conifers in rhododendron forests, also on rocks and on tree stumps in rhododendron thickets, at elevations of 2,440—3,355 m. (8,000—11,000 ft.).

R. concinnoides is an aberrant species in the Triflorum Series in view of its tubular-campanulate corolla. In the original diagnosis it was associated with *R. concinnum*. From this species it appears to be very remote. The corolla is slightly oblique, compressed laterally as in most members of the Maddenii Series. In some respects it shows a resemblance to the species of the Tephropeplum Series. Until more is known of this plant, it will be kept in its present Series. The plant has not been introduced into cultivation.

Epithet. Like *R. concinnum*.
Not in cultivation.

R. concinnum Hemsl. in Journ. Linn. Soc. XXVI (1889) 21.
Illustration. Bot. Mag. Vol. 141 t. 8620 (1915); ibid. Vol. 135 t. 8280 (1909), figured as *R. coombense*; ibid. Vol. 147 t. 8912 (1938), figured as *R. concinnum* f. *laetevirens*.

A rounded, broadly upright, or broadly upright and spreading shrub or small tree, 1—4.50 m. (3⅓—15 ft.) high; branchlets rather densely or moderately scaly. *Leaves* oblong-lanceolate, oblong, elliptic, ovate or ovate-lanceolate, lamina 2.5—8.5 cm. long, 1.2—3.5 cm. broad, apex acute or obtuse or rarely shortly acuminate, mucronate, base obtuse or rounded; upper surface dark green, moderately or sometimes sparsely scaly, midrib rather densely or moderately puberulous; *under surface* pale glaucous green or green, densely scaly, the *scales* unequal, medium-sized and large, *yellowish*, pale or dark brown, or *yellowish-brown, one-half their own diameter apart or contiguous* or rarely their own diameter apart; petiole 0.5—1.3 cm. long, densely scaly. *Inflorescence* terminal, or terminal and axillary in the uppermost one or two leaves, shortly racemose, 2—5-flowered; rhachis 2—5 mm. long, scaly, glabrous or puberulous; pedicel 0.4—1.8 cm. long, rather densely or moderately scaly. *Calyx* 5-lobed or rarely a mere rim, minute, 0.5—1½ mm. (rarely 4—6 mm.) long, lobes rounded or triangular or rarely lanceolate, outside scaly or rarely not scaly, margin scaly, eciliate or ciliate. *Corolla* widely funnel-shaped, zygomorphic, 1.5—3.2 cm. long, 5-lobed, deep or pale purple, purple, deep rosy-purple, purplish-lavender, deep pinkish, creamy-white tinged purple, or white, with or without brownish or crimson spots, *outside moderately or rather densely scaly* or rarely not scaly, glabrous or sometimes sparsely hairy towards the base. *Stamens* 10, unequal, 1—3.1 cm. long, exserted; filaments densely villous towards the base. *Ovary* conoid or oblong, 2—5 mm. long, 5-celled, densely scaly; style long, slender, not scaly, glabrous or rarely puberulous at the base. *Capsule* oblong, 1—1.5 cm. long, 3—4 mm. broad, rather densely scaly, calyx persistent.

R. concinnum is distributed in western Szechuan, western Hupeh and Shensi. It grows in thickets, in and at the margins of woodlands, on cliffs, by streams, and on mountain slopes, at elevations of 1,600—4,150 m. (5,245—13,606 ft.). Wilson records it as being a very common species in the margins of woods and thickets throughout western Szechuan, although comparatively rare in Hupeh.

The species was described by Hemsley in 1889 from a plant collected by the Rev. Ernest Faber in 1886 on Mount Omei. Subsequently distinctive names were given to various forms, namely, *R. yanthinum* Bur. et Franch. (1891), *R. coombense* Hemsl. (1909), (*R. laetevirens*, Balf. f. nomen, *R. atroviride* Dunn. nomen, *R. subcoombense* Balf. f. nomen),

R. benthamianum Hemsl. (1910), *R. yanthinum* Bur. et Franch. var. *lepidanthum* Rehd. et Wils. (1913), *R. ioanthum* Balf. f. (1922), *R. pseudoyanthinum* Balf. f. ex Hutch. (1930), *R. concinnum* Hemsl. f. *laetevirens* Cowan (1938), *R. concinnum* Hemsl. var. *lepidanthum* (Rehd. et Wils.) Rehd. (1939), and *R. hutchinsonianum* Fang 1953. It will be seen that in *The Species of Rhododendron* 1930, the first two names and *R. laetevirens* Balf. f. nomen, correctly appear in synonymy under *R. concinnum*. Moreover, in *The Rhododendron and Camellia Year Book* 1963, *R. benthamianum* and *R. pseudoyanthinum* were reduced to varietal status; *R. ioanthum* was referred to *R. siderophyllum*, and all the other names, also *R. atroviride* Dunn. nomen and *R. subcoombense* Balf. f. nomen, were placed in synonymy under *R. concinnum*.

R. concinnum varies considerably in height of growth, in leaf size, and in flower size and colour. The main features of the plant are its ovate to oblong-lanceolate dark green leaves, usually the large yellowish scales on the lower surface of the leaves densely set one-half their own diameter apart or contiguous, and usually the dark purple or purple corolla, moderately or rather densely scaly outside. The plant is a tetraploid with 52 chromosomes. It is closely allied to *R. amesiae*; the relationship between them is discussed under the latter.

The species was first introduced by Wilson in 1904 (No. 1433 — as *R. yanthinum*). It was reintroduced by him several times from western Szechuan. In its native home it is a shrub or small tree, 3—15 feet high; in cultivation it is a medium-sized rounded or broadly upright, or broadly upright and spreading shrub, usually attaining a height of 4—8 feet, much branched, and somewhat densely filled with foliage. Five flower colour forms are grown in gardens: Form 1. Deep purple. Form 2. Purple. Form 3. Deep pinkish. Form 4. Creamy-white tinged purple. Form 5. White. Forms 3, 4 and 5 are rare in cultivation. The species is free-flowering and is most attractive when covered with flowers in clusters of two to five. It is hardy, a vigorous grower, and is easily adaptable to any position in the garden.

It may be remarked that in cultivation some plants which have been named *R. concinnum*, would appear to be natural hybrids. In the Royal Botanic Garden, Edinburgh and elsewhere, some forms which are said to have been raised from Szechuan seed of *R. concinnum*, have intermediate features which suggest that the plants are possibly natural hybrids between *R. concinnum* and *R. augustinii*, *R. davidsonianum* and *R. ambiguum*.

Epithet. Neat.

Hardiness 3. April—May. Plate 61.

R. concinnum Hemsl. var. **benthamianum** (Hemsl.) Davidian in The Rhododendron and
    Camellia Year Book, 1963, p. 194.

    Syn. *R. benthamianum* Hemsl. in Kew Bull. (1907) 319.

This plant was first described by Hemsley in 1907 from a cultivated specimen raised by Messrs. James Veitch & Sons, from Wilsons's seed No. 1878 which had been collected in western Szechuan.

The variety differs from the species in that the flowers are lavender-purple, and the scales on the lower surfaces of the leaves are dissimilar in colour, being dark brown and yellowish.

In cultivation it is a somewhat rounded spreading shrub up to 5 or 6 feet high with olive-green or bright green leaves. It is hardy, flowers freely, and is well worth growing.

Epithet of the variety. After Bentham.

Hardiness 3. April—May.

R. concinnum Hemsl. var. **pseudoyanthinum** (Balf. f. ex Hutch.) Davidian in The
    Rhododendron and Camellia Year Book, 1963, p. 194.

    Syn. *R. pseudoyanthinum* Balf. f. ex Hutch. in The Species of Rhododendron 1930, p. 783.

This plant was first described as *R. pseudoyanthinum* in *The Species of Rhododendron*,

1930. It is a native of western Szechuan. The plant is a tetraploid with 52 chromosomes.

The variety is readily distinguished by its deep ruby-red flowers (R.H.S. Colour Chart Ruby Red 827/2) and often by its larger oblong-lanceolate leaves.

The plant has long been in cultivation under the name *R. pseudoyanthinum* Red Form, possibly introduced by Wilson from western Szechuan. It is a broadly upright shrub, 4—6 feet high, with rigid branchlets and dark green foliage. The plant is hardy, and is extremely charming with its large widely funnel-shaped flowers produced in great profusion. It received an Award of Merit when shown as *R. pseudoyanthinum* by The Royal Horticultural Society's Garden, Wisley, in 1951.

Epithet of the variety. Like *R. yanthinum*.

Hardiness 3. April—May.

R. davidsonianum Rehd. et Wils. in Plantae Wilsonianae (1913) 515.

Illustration. Bot. Mag. Vol. 141 t. 8605 (1915); ibid Vol. 144 t. 8759 (1918), figured as *R. siderophyllum.*

A broadly upright,or broadly upright and spreading shrub, or small tree, 60 cm.—5 m. (2—16 ft.) high; branchlets moderately or rarely rather densely scaly, minutely puberulous or glabrous. *Leaves lanceolate*, rarely oblong-lanceolate or oblong, *lamina* 2.3—7.8 cm. long, 0.8—2.6 cm. broad, apex acute or sometimes obtuse, mucronate, base tapered or obtuse; *often V-shaped;* upper surface dark green or bright green, sparsely or moderately scaly, midrib puberulous or glabrous; *under surface* scaly, the *scales* unequal, medium-sized and large, pale or dark brown, *nearly contiguous to their own diameter apart* or rarely up to 4 times their own diameter apart; petiole 0.3—1 cm. long, moderately or densely scaly, minutely puberulous or glabrous. *Inflorescence* terminal, or terminal and axillary in the uppermost one or two leaves, shortly racemose, 3—6- (rarely up to 10-) flowered; rhachis 2—4 mm. long, scaly or not scaly, glabrous or sometimes puberulous; pedicel 0.6—1.8 cm. long, moderately or rarely rather densely scaly, glabrous or rarely minutely puberulous. *Calyx* 5-lobed or a mere rim, minute, 0.5—1 mm. long, lobes rounded or triangular, outside moderately or densely scaly, margin eciliate or sometimes ciliate. *Corolla* widely funnel-shaped, zygomorphic, 1.9—3.3 cm. long, 5-lobed, white, white tinged pink, pink, deep pink, rose, pale lavender, purple or pale purplish-pink, with or without purple or red spots, outside scaly or not scaly. *Stamens* 10, unequal, exserted, 1.3—3.6 cm. long; filaments puberulous towards the base. *Ovary* oblong or conoid, 2—4 mm. long, 5-celled, densely scaly; style long, slender, not scaly, glabrous or sometimes puberulous at the base. *Capsule* oblong, 0.6—1.8 cm. long, 3—6 mm. broad, rather densely scaly, calyx persistent.

R. davidsonianum was first collected by the Abbé Soulié in April 1892 at Tatsienlu, western Szechuan. Subsequently, it was found by other collectors in western and south-western Szechuan, and in north-western Yunnan. It grows in thickets and woodlands, in pine forests, on cliffs, and amongst rock and scrub in dry situations, at elevations of 2,000—3,580 m. (6,557—11,738 ft.). Wilson records it as being very common in sunny situations in western Szechuan, and that it is very floriferous, the flowers almost hiding the foliage.

In 1916, *R. charianthum* Hutch. was described from a plant raised from Wilson's seed No. 1274. The herbarium specimen under the same number is true *R. davidsonianum. R. charianthum* is said to differ in its densely red-spotted corolla and in the style pubescent at the base. These characteristics are shared by *R. davidsonianum*. It is clear that the retention of the specific name *R. charianthum*, cannot be justified, and in *The Rhododendron and Camellia Year Book* 1963, p. 195, it was placed in synonymy under *R. davidsonianum*.

A marked feature of *R. davidsonianum* is the bending up of the two halves of the leaf, forming a V with the midrib in cross section, although this is not a constant character. The species is allied to *R. yunnanense* which it resembles in general features, but differs markedly in that the leaves and branchlets are not bristly, and the lower surfaces of the leaves are densely scaly, the scales being nearly contiguous to their own diameter apart. The plant is a hexaploid with 78 chromosomes.

R. davidsonianum was first introduced by Wilson in 1904 (Nos. 1535, 1779). In cultivation it is a broadly upright, or broadly upright and spreading shrub up to 10 feet in height, although in its native home it is a shrub or small tree, 2—16 feet high. Several forms are grown in gardens, including: Form 1. A plant with narrowly lanceolate small leaves, laminae up to 4 cm. long, the two halves of the leaf forming a V with the midrib in cross section, and with white flowers. Form 2. A plant with broadly lanceolate, large leaves, laminae 7—8 cm. long, flat, with white flowers. Form 3. A plant with lanceolate leaves, with several trusses clustered together forming a large compact rounded, compound inflorescence of 15—30 white flowers. Form 4. A plant very similar to Form 3 with compound inflorescence of 15—30 flowers, deep pink in colour. Form 5. A plant with deep pink flowers closely dispersed. All these forms are attractive plants. Forms 3 and 4 are generally considered to be the best; they are exceedingly charming when adorned with a profusion of white or deep pink flowers. The species is a vigorous grower, and one of its chief merits is that it flowers quite young when raised from seed. It is hardy, but along the east coast and inland, it should be well sheltered from wind. A form with pink flowers was given an Award of Merit when exhibited by Lord Aberconway, Bodnant, in April 1935, and a First Class Certificate was awarded to a pink form when shown by Lord Aberconway and the National Trust, Bodnant, in May 1955. It received an Award of Garden Merit in 1969.

Epithet. After Dr. W.H. Davidson, Friends Mission in China.
Hardiness 3. April—May. Plate 65.

R. hormophorum Balf. f. et Forrest in Notes Roy. Bot. Gard. Edin., Vol. 12 (1920) 117.

A broadly upright, or broadly upright and spreading shrub, 25 cm.—4.90 m. (10 in.—16 ft.) high; branchlets scaly, puberulous or rarely glabrous. *Leaves completely deciduous*, lanceolate or oblanceolate, lamina 2.8—7.3 cm. long, 1—2.4 cm. broad, apex acute, mucronate, base tapered; upper surface dark green or bright green, moderately or sparsely scaly, bristly or not bristly, puberulous or glabrous, midrib puberulous or glabrous; margins bristly or not bristly; under surface pale glaucous green or green, scaly, the scales unequal, medium-sized, brown or yellowish, 3—6 times (rarely twice) their own diameter apart; petiole 0.3—1 cm. long, scaly, bristly or not bristly, puberulous. *Inflorescence* terminal, or terminal and axillary in the uppermost one or two leaves, shortly racemose, 3—6-flowered, *flowers precocious*; rhachis 2—4 mm. long, scaly or not scaly, puberulous or glabrous; pedicel 0.3—2.1 cm. long, scaly or not scaly. *Calyx* a mere rim or 5-lobed, minute, 0.5 mm. long, lobes rounded or triangular, outside densely or moderately scaly or not scaly, margin scaly or not scaly, glabrous or puberulous or ciliate. *Corolla* widely funnel-shaped, zygomorphic, 1.6—3.1 cm. long, 1.8—4.5 cm. across, 5-lobed, rose, white, white tinged pink, rose-lilac or lavender, with or without crimson, olive-green, olive-brown, rose or orange spots, not scaly or sparsely scaly or sometimes lobes moderately scaly outside. *Stamens* 10, unequal, 1—3.4 cm. long, exserted; filaments densely pubescent towards the base. *Ovary* oblong or rarely conoid, 2—4 mm. long, 5-celled, densely scaly, glabrous; style long, slender, not scaly. *Capsule* oblong, 0.8—1.3 cm. long, 3—5 mm. broad, rather densely scaly, calyx persistent.

This species was discovered by Forrest in June 1918, on the Muli mountains, in the Valley of the Litang, south-west Szechuan. It was later collected by him again and by other collectors in the same region and in north-west Yunnan. The plant grows in stony pasture, in pine, oak, and spruce forests, amongst scrub, in thickets, in dry open situations, and on the ledges of cliffs, at elevations of 2,440—3,965 m. (8,000—13,000 ft.).

R. chartophyllum Franch. f. *praecox* Diels, a plant from north-west Yunnan, is identical with *R. hormophorum* in every morphological detail.

R. hormophorum shows a strong resemblance to *R. yunnanense* in habit and height of growth, in the shape and size of the leaves, and in the shape, size and colour of the flowers, but differs markedly in that the leaves are completely deciduous, and the flowers are precocious; in *R. yunnanense* the leaves are evergreen or sometimes semi-deciduous, and the flowers are not precocious.

The species was first introduced by Forrest in 1918 from south-west Szechuan (No. 16816). It flowered in the Royal Botanic Garden, Edinburgh, for the first time in 1924. In its native home it grows 10—18 inches high in open dry stony pasture, but up to 16 feet in other habitats; in cultivation it is a shrub of 8 to 10 feet. Two forms are grown in gardens: Form 1. A plant with closely dispersed flowers. Form 2. A plant with several trusses clustered together forming a large compact rounded, compound inflorescence of 15—30 flowers. The latter is the better form, but is rare in cultivation. It will be observed that the leaves are shed gradually in March or April, and by about the end of May the whole plant is completely deciduous. The species is perfectly hardy, extremely free-flowering, and provides an admirable display with its white or white tinged pink flowers, although in cultivation it has not gained the wide recognition it deserves. A form with white flowers and a few spots received an Award of Merit when shown by Lord Digby, Minterne, Dorset, in May 1943.

Epithet. Bearing a necklace.
Hardiness 3. May. Plate 60.

R. hypophaeum Balf. f. et Forrest in Notes Roy. Bot. Gard. Edin., Vol. 12 (1920) 120.

A broadly upright and spreading shrub, 1.22—5 m. (4—16 ft.) high; branchlets moderately or rather densely scaly, glabrous. *Leaves* lanceolate or rarely oblong, lamina 2.4—6.2 cm. long, 0.8—2.4 cm. broad, apex acute or rarely obtuse, mucronate, base obtuse or tapered; *upper surface olive-green*, scaly, midrib puberulous or glabrous; *under surface pale glaucous green*, scaly, the scales unequal, medium-sized and small, brown, ½—1½ times their own diameter apart; petiole 0.5—1 cm. long, scaly, glabrous or rarely puberulous. *Inflorescence* terminal, or terminal and axillary in the uppermost one or two leaves, shortly racemose, 3—5-flowered; rhachis 2—3 mm. long, scaly, glabrous; pedicel 0.6—1.5 cm. long, scaly. *Calyx* 5-lobed or a mere rim, minute, 0.5—1 mm. long, lobes rounded or triangular, outside scaly or not scaly, margin scaly or not scaly, glabrous or puberulous. *Corolla* widely funnel-shaped, zygomorphic, *1.2—1.9 cm. long*, 5-lobed, white faintly tinged rose, or pink, deep purplish-pink, purplish-blue, purple or pale lavender, outside not scaly or sparsely scaly. *Stamens* 10, unequal, 0.8—2 cm. long, exserted; filaments puberulous towards the base. *Ovary* conoid, 2—3 mm. long, 5-celled, densely scaly; style long, slender, not scaly, glabrous or sparsely puberulous at the base. *Capsule:* not seen.

This species was first collected by Forrest in June 1918 on the mountains around the Muli Valley of the Litang river, south-west Szechuan. It was later found by Rock in north-west Yunnan in 1923, and in south-west Szechuan in 1929. The plant grows in and on the margins of pine forests, and along streams, at elevations of 3,080—3,355 m. (10,098—11,000 ft.).

R. hypophaeum is one of the small-flowered members of its Series. In general appearance it shows a resemblance to *R. davidsonianum* and *R. longistylum*. It is distinguished from the former mainly by the smaller flowers, and from the latter by the widely funnel-shaped corolla, often by the broader leaves, by the closely spaced scales on the lower surfaces of the leaves, usually by the smaller calyx, and by the glabrous branchlets and petioles.

The species was introduced by Forrest in 1918 (No. 16249 — the Type number). In its native home it reaches a height of 16 feet; in cultivation it is a medium-sized shrub of 5—6 feet, with olive-green leaves and white tinged rose flowers in clusters of three to five. It is hardy, free-flowering, and easy to grow. The plant is rare in cultivation, but is worthy of being widely grown.

Epithet. Grey beneath.

Hardiness 3. May.

R. longistylum Rehd. et Wils. in Plantae Wilsonianae (1913) 514.

A broadly upright shrub, 50 cm.—2.14 m. (1⅔—7 ft.) high; branchlets not scaly or scaly, minutely puberulous or rarely glabrous. *Leaves* evergreen, oblanceolate, lanceolate or oblong-lanceolate, lamina 1.6—6 cm. long, 0.6—1.5 cm. broad, apex acute, mucronate, base tapered or obtuse; upper surface dark green, not scaly or scaly, midrib glabrous; under surface scaly, the scales unequal, medium-sized and small, brown, 2—4 times their own diameter apart; petiole 2—6 mm. long, scaly, minutely puberulous. *Inflorescence* terminal, or terminal and axillary in the uppermost one or two leaves, shortly racemose, 3—10-flowered or more; rhachis 0.3—1 cm. long, scaly, minutely puberulous; pedicel 0.6—1.5 cm. long, scaly, glabrous or minutely puberulous. *Calyx* 5-lobed, *2—3 mm.* (rarely 1 mm.) *long,* lobes oblong, lanceolate or oval, outside sparsely scaly or not scaly, margin ciliate. *Corolla tubular-funnel shaped,* zygomorphic, 1.3—1.6 cm. (rarely up to 2 cm.) *long,* 5-lobed, white or white tinged pink, not scaly or rarely slightly scaly on the lobes outside. *Stamens* 10, unequal, 0.9—2.3 cm. long, exserted; filaments pubescent towards the base. *Ovary* conoid, 2—3 mm. long, 5-celled, densely scaly, glabrous or rarely minutely puberulous; style long, slender, not scaly. *Capsule* conoid, 5—8 mm. long, 4—5 mm. broad, rather densely scaly, calyx-lobes persistent.

R. longistylum was discovered by Wilson in 1908 in western Szechuan, and was again gathered by him in 1910 in the same region. It grows in thickets, on cliffs and scrub-clad rocky slopes, at elevations of 1,000—2,300 m. (3,279—7,541 ft.).

According to Rehder and Wilson, the inflorescence of this plant varies from 10 to 20 or more flowers, but in cultivation it consists of 3—10 flowers only.

The original diagnosis associated it with *R. micranthum.* From this plant it differs markedly in distinctive features. It is allied to *R. yunnanense* which it resembles in general appearance, but is distinguished by the tubular-funnel shaped corolla which is usually smaller, often by the non-bristly leaves, and usually by the larger calyx. In some respects, it shows a resemblance to *R. hypophaeum;* the distinctions between them are discussed under the latter.

R. longistylum was first introduced by Wilson in 1908 (No. 1204 — the Type number). He sent seeds again in 1910 (No. 4726). In cultivation it is a broadly upright shrub up to 7 feet high with dark green foliage. The species varies in hardiness, and to be able to obtain the best results, particularly along the east coast and in gardens inland, a well-sheltered position should be provided. It flowers freely, but is uncommon in cultivation.

Epithet. Long-styled.

Hardiness 2—3. April—May.

R. oreotrephes W.W. Sm. in Notes Roy. Bot. Gard. Edin., Vol. 8 (1914) 201.

Illustration. Bot. Mag. Vol. 144 t. 8784 (1918).

A broadly upright or compact shrub or tree, 60 cm.—7.62 m. (2—25 ft.) high; branchlets not scaly or sparsely or moderately (rarely densely) scaly, glabrous or puberulous. *Leaves* evergreen or sometimes semi-deciduous, oblong-elliptic, elliptic, oblong, ovate, oval or almost orbicular, lamina coriaceous, 1.8—8.9 cm. long, 1.2—4.2 cm. broad, apex obtuse or rounded or rarely acute, mucronate, base rounded or obtuse or cordulate; upper surface dark green or green or sometimes bluish-green, not glaucous or glaucous, (in young leaves sometimes markedly glaucous), not scaly or sparsely or moderately (rarely densely) scaly, midrib glabrous or sometimes puberulous; *under surface* glaucous or pale glaucous-green or brown, scaly, the *scales* more or less equal, medium-sized, brown, *contiguous to 3* (rarely 4) *times their own diameter apart;* petiole 0.5—2 cm.

long, not scaly or scaly, glabrous or puberulous. *Inflorescence* terminal, or sometimes terminal and axillary in the uppermost one or two leaves, shortly racemose, 3—10-flowered; rhachis 1—8 mm. (rarely 1 cm.) long, scaly or not scaly, glabrous or sometimes puberulous; pedicel 0.5—3 cm. long, scaly or not scaly. *Calyx* a mere rim or 5-lobed, minute, 0.5—1 mm. (rarely 2 mm.) long, lobes rounded, oblong or triangular, outside scaly or not scaly, margin scaly or not scaly, eciliate or rarely ciliate. *Corolla* widely or narrowly funnel-shaped or sometimes funnel-campanulate, usually zygomorphic, 1.8—4 cm. long, 5-lobed, whitish-pink, rose, deep rose, deep pink, pale or deep lavender-rose, purple, grey-lavender or lavender-blue, (rarely white or apricot yellow), with or without crimson or brownish-crimson spots, outside not scaly or sparsely scaly. *Stamens* 10, unequal, 1—3.6 cm. long, exserted; filaments densely pubescent towards the base. *Ovary* conoid or oblong, 3—6 mm. long, 5-celled, densely scaly; style long, slender, not scaly. *Capsule* oblong, 0.8—1.6 cm. long, 3—5 mm. broad, rather densely or moderately scaly, calyx persistent.

Forrest discovered this plant in June 1910 on the western flank of the Lichiang Range in north-west Yunnan. Further gatherings by him and by Rock, Ludlow, Sherriff and Elliot, McLaren's collectors, Kingdon-Ward, and Yü show that the species is widely distributed from mid-west and north-west Yunnan and north-east Upper Burma to south-west Szechuan and south-east Tibet. It grows in rhododendron, pine, Abies and spruce forests, in cane brakes, in open pastures, on cliffs and rocky slopes, in thickets, amongst scrub, and along streams, at elevations of 2,745—4,880 m. (9,000—16,000 ft.). Kingdon-Ward records it as being abundant, forming thickets by itself in south-east Tibet. It is said to be common at the margins of Abies forest in north-west Yunnan. Ludlow, Sherriff and Elliot found it by the side of a swamp growing as a tree 10—15 feet high in south-east Tibet, and by the banks of a torrent, as a shrub of 3 feet.

As would be expected from the wide distribution, different habitats and altitudinal range, *R. oreotrephes* varies considerably in general features. It is a shrub or tree, 2—25 feet high; the leaves are oblong, elliptic, ovate, oval or almost orbicular, laminae 1.8—8.9 cm. long, 1.2—4.2 cm. broad; the inflorescence is 3—10-flowered; and the corolla is 1.8—4 cm. long.

During the years 1917—1919, Forrest collected a number of closely similar plants in south-east Tibet and north-west Yunnan. In the *Notes Roy. Bot. Gard. Edin.*, Vol. 13, 1922, these were described as *R. depile* Balf. f. et Forrest, *R. hypotrichotum* Balf. f. et Forrest, *R. phaeochlorum* Balf. f. et Forrest, *R. artosquameum* Balf. f. et. Forrest, *R. cardioeides* Balf. f. et Forrest, *R. pubigerum* Balf. f. et Forrest, and *R. trichopodum* Balf. f. et Forrest. It will be seen that in *The Species of Rhododendron* 1930, the first three names and *R. oreotrephoides* Balf. f. nomen appear in synonymy under *R. oreotrephes*, and the last three names under *R. artosquameum*. Moreover, in 1920, *R. timeteum* Balf. f. et Forrest was described from a plant collected by Forrest in south-west Szechuan; in 1932, *R. exquisetum* Hutch. was founded on a cultivated specimen raised from Forrest's seed No. 20489; and in 1935 the specific name *R. siderophylloides* Hutch. was given to a similar plant. It is worth noting that in *The Rhododendron and Camellia Year Book* 1963, pp. 200—201, *R. artosquameum* and its synonyms, also *R. timeteum*, *R. exquisetum* and *R. siderophylloides* were relegated to synonymy under *R. oreotrephes*.

R. oreotrephes is allied to *R. tatsienense* from which it differs in that the leaves are not rigid, they are usually glaucous beneath, the corolla is usually larger, the upper surface of the leaves, the corolla and the branchlets are often not scaly. It is a hexaploid with 78 chromosomes.

The plant was first introduced by Forrest in 1910 (No. 5873 — the Type number). It was reintroduced by him and by Kingdon-Ward, Rock, and McLaren on many occasions. Several forms are in cultivation, including: Form 1. A compact shrub 5 feet high and almost as much across, densely filled with leaves, and with deep pink flowers. Form 2. A tall broadly upright shrub 7 feet high, with deep rose flowers. Form 3. A medium-sized shrub with several trusses clustered together forming a large compact rounded, compound inflorescence of 15—30 flowers. Form 4. A medium-sized shrub with dark green glaucous foliage, and with markedly glaucous young leaves. Form 5. A medium-sized shrub with reddish-purple branchlets and petioles, bluish-green glaucous foliage, and with markedly glaucous young leaves. Form 6. A shrub with semi-deciduous leaves and white tinged pink flowers. All these forms are extremely charming plants. It should be noted that in hardiness of constitution, freedom of flower, beauty of habit, of leaves, and flower, in general adaptability to various situations, and in ease of cultivation, this species and its forms have all the essential qualities of ideal garden plants and deserve the widest possible recognition.

A form with rosy-purple flowers received an Award of Merit when exhibited under the name *R. timeteum* by Mr. Lionel de Rothschild, Exbury, in 1932. Another form with bright pinkish-mauve flowers and darker spots, also got the same Award when shown as *R. siderophylloides* by J.J. Crosfield, Embley Park, Hants., in 1935.

Epithet. Mountain bred.

Hardiness 3. April—May. Plate 70.

R. oreotrephes W.W. Sm. 'Exquisetum'.

Syn *R. exquisetum* Hutch. in Gard. Chron. XCII (1932) 98.

Illustration. Bot. Mag. Vol. 162 t. 9597 (1940). Figured as *R. exquisetum*.

This plant has long been known as *R. exquisetum* Hutch. which was described in 1932 from a cultivated plant raised from Forrest's seed No. 20489. The herbarium specimen under the same number was collected by Forrest in south-west Szechuan in July 1921 at an elevation of 3,050—3,355 m. (10,000—11,000 ft.).

R. exquisetum is very similar to *R. oreotrephes* in leaf shape and size, in flower shape, size and colour, and in all other respects also, they agree. However, the cultivated plant under Forrest's seed No. 20489 with large leaves and large flowers is so distinct that it will now be regarded as a cultivar. It was given an Award of Merit when shown as *R. exquisetum* by Mr. L. de Rothschild, Exbury, in 1937.

Epithet of the cultivar. Exquisite.

Hardiness 3. April—May.

R. polylepis Franch. in Bull. Soc. Bot. France, XXXIII (1886) 232.

Illustration. Bot. Mag. Vol. 136 t. 8309 (1910). Figured as *R. harrovianum*.

An upright lax shrub or sometimes small tree, 92 cm.—5 m. (3—16 ft.) high; *branchlets* densely scaly *with flaky scales. Leaves oblong-lanceolate, lanceolate or oblanceolate,* lamina 4.5—10.2 cm. long, 1.2—3.7 cm. broad, apex acute or shortly acuminate, mucronate, base tapered; upper surface dark green, sparsely scaly or not scaly, midrib glabrous; *under surface densely scaly,* the *scales* unequal, large, dark brown or brown, dry *flaky, overlapping or contiguous* or rarely one-half their own diameter apart, usually *with larger scattered flaky scales;* petiole 0.5—1 cm. long, densely scaly. *Inflorescence* terminal, or rarely terminal and axillary in the uppermost one or two leaves, shortly racemose, 3—5-flowered; rhachis 2—6 mm. long, scaly, glabrous or rarely puberulous; pedicel 0.6—2 cm. long, moderately or densely scaly. *Calyx* 5-lobed, minute, 0.5—1 mm. long, lobes rounded or triangular, outside densely scaly, margin densely scaly, eciliate or rarely ciliate. *Corolla* widely funnel-shaped, zygomorphic, 2.1—3.5 cm. long, 5-lobed, pale or deep purple or purplish-violet, with or without yellowish spots on the posterior side, outside rather densely or moderately scaly. *Stamens* 10, unequal, 1.8—3.8 cm. long, exserted; filaments densely villous towards the base. *Ovary* oblong or conoid, 3—4 mm. long, 5-celled, densely scaly, glabrous or puberulous at the apex; style long, slender, not scaly, glabrous or sometimes puberulous at the base. *Capsule* oblong, 1—1.6 cm. long, 3—4 mm. broad, rather densely scaly, calyx persistent.

R. polylepis was described by Franchet in 1886. It is distributed in south-west and western Szechuan. The plant grows in thickets and woodlands, and on cliffs, at elevations of 2,000—3,447 m. (6,557—11,300 ft.). Wilson records it as being an exceedingly common species in western Szechuan.

In some respects, *R. polylepis* resembles *R. concinnum*, from which it is distinguished by the lanceolate, oblanceolate or oblong-lanceolate leaves, and usually by the overlapping scales with larger scattered ones on the under surfaces of the leaves. It further differs in that the scales on the branchlets and on the under surfaces of the leaves are flaky. The leaf epidermis is said to be two-layered in *R. polylepis*, but one-layered in *R. concinnum*. Moreover, *R. polylepis* is a diploid with 26 chromosomes, whereas *R. concinnum* is a tetraploid with 52 chromosomes.

The species was first introduced by Wilson in 1904 (Seed No. 1857). It was reintroduced by him in 1908 and in 1911. In cultivation it is an upright, lax shrub up to 12 feet high with long, slender branchlets and dark green leaves. Two colour forms are grown in gardens, purple and dark purple. The flowers are produced freely in clusters of three to five. The plant is very hardy, and fairly fast-growing.

Epithet. With many scales.

Hardiness 3. April—May.

R. rigidum Franch. in Bull. Soc. Bot. France, XXXIII (1886) 233.

A compact or broadly upright or rounded somewhat lax shrub or small tree, 60 cm.—10 m. (2—33 ft.) high; *branchlets* not scaly or sometimes scaly, *glabrous* or rarely puberulous. *Leaves* evergreen, elliptic, oblong-elliptic, oblong-lanceolate, oblanceolate, oblong or lanceolate, lamina 2.5—6.8 cm. long, 1—3.2 cm. broad, apex obtuse, acute, shortly acuminate or rounded, mucronate, base tapered, obtuse or rounded; *upper surface bluish-green*, (*in young leaves glaucous bluish-green*), not scaly or rarely scaly, *midrib glabrous* or rarely puberulous; *under surface* pale glaucous green, scaly, the *scales* unequal, large and medium-sized, brown, 4—8 (rarely 2—3) *times their own diameter apart; petiole* 0.2—1.2 cm. long, not scaly or sparsely or moderately scaly, *glabrous* or rarely puberulous. *Inflorescence* terminal, or terminal and axillary in the uppermost one or two leaves, shortly racemose, 2—6-flowered; rhachis 2—4 mm. long, scaly or not scaly, glabrous; pedicel 0.5—2 cm. long, not scaly, rarely sparsely or moderately scaly. *Calyx* 5-lobed or a mere rim, minute, 0.5—1 mm. long, lobes rounded or triangular, outside not scaly or scaly, margin not scaly or scaly, glabrous or rarely puberulous. *Corolla* widely funnel-shaped, zygomorphic, 1.8—3.1 cm. long, 5-lobed, pink, deep rose-lavender or white, with olive-brown or purple spots, outside not scaly or rarely scaly. *Stamens* 10, unequal, 1.2—3.8 cm. long, exserted; filaments densely pubescent towards the base. *Ovary* conoid or oblong, 2—5 mm. long, 5-celled, densely scaly, glabrous or rarely puberulous at the apex; style long, slender, not scaly. *Capsule* oblong, 0.8—1 cm. long, 3—4 mm. broad, scaly, calyx persistent.

This species was first collected by the Abbé Delavay in April 1884 at Lan-kien-ho, near Mosoyn, north-west Yunnan. It was later found by other collectors in the same region and in west Yunnan. The plant grows amongst scrub, in mixed forests, at the margins of forests, in open thickets, on cliffs and rocky slopes, and amongst boulders, at elevations of 800—3,355 m. (2,623—11,000 ft.).

R. rigidum was described by Franchet in 1886. Subsequently distinct specific names were given to similar plants, namely, *R. caeruleum* Lévl. (1913), *R. rarosquameum* Balf. f. (1917), *R. sycnanthum* Balf. f. et W.W. Sm. (1917), *R. hesperium* Balf. f. et Forrest (1922), and *R. eriandrum* Lévl. ex Hutch. (1930). It will be seen that in *The Rhododendron Society Notes* 1928, *R. rarosquameum* has been referred to *R. caeruleum*, while in *The Species of Rhododendron* 1930, the same name has been placed in synonymy under *R. eriandrum*. Moreover, afterwards in the latter work, p. 851, *R. caeruleum* has been referred to *R. eriandrum* as a doubtful synonym. It should be noted that in *The Rhododendron and*

Camellia Year Book 1963, p. 206, all the above names were relegated to synonymy under *R. rigidum*.

R. rigidum is allied to *R. yunnanense* but differs in the glabrous leaves and branchlets, in the bluish-green foliage, and often in the shape of the leaves. Moreover, *R. rigidum* is a diploid with 26 chromosomes, while *R. yunnanense* is a hexaploid with 78 chromosomes or sometimes tetraploid with 52 chromosomes.

The species has been in cultivation for a long time, having been introduced by Forrest, Rock, and McLaren. In its native home it is a shrub or tree ranging from 2 up to 33 feet high, but in cultivation it reaches a height of only 12 feet. Three distinct forms are grown in gardens, namely: Form 1. A compact shrub 5—6 feet high with short branchlets, and several trusses clustered together forming a large compact rounded, compound inflorescence of 15—30 flowers. Form 2. A broadly upright or rounded somewhat lax shrub 5—6 feet high, with closely dispersed flowers. Form 3. A tall broadly upright shrub 10—12 feet high with long, oblong-lanceolate or lanceolate leaves. All these forms are most charming plants; form 1 is undoubtedly the best. A distinctive feature of the species in cultivation is the glaucous bluish-green young leaves. The flowers are usually white or sometimes pink, with purple spots. In some plants the protruding anthers are dark brown or almost black for which the white corolla provides a most effective contrast. The species is free-flowering, and it has the added advantage of producing the flowers at a young age when raised from seed. It produces plentiful good fertile seed. It is hardy, and a most desirable plant for every collection of rhododendrons. The species received an Award of Merit in 1933 when shown as *R. eriandrum* with white flowers slightly flushed pink (Rock No. 59207 = 11288) by H. White, Sunningdale Nurseries, and again in May 1939 when exhibited as *R. caeruleum* with white flowers, spotted red (also Rock No. 59207 = 11288) by Mr. Lionel de Rothschild. A form 'Louvecienne' was given the same Award when shown by Mr. Edmund de Rothschild in May 1975.

Epithet. Stiff.
Hardiness 3. April—May. Plate 64.

R. searsiae Rehd. et Wils. in Plantae Wilsonianae (1913) 522.

Illustration. Bot. Mag. Vol. 149 t. 8993 (1924).

A somewhat compact rounded, or broadly upright and spreading shrub, 1.53—5 m. (5—16 ft.) high; branchlets moderately or rarely densely scaly. *Leaves* lanceolate, oblong-lanceolate, oblanceolate or rarely oblong-elliptic, lamina 2.5—8 cm. long, 1—2.6 cm. broad, apex acuminate or acutely acuminate or acute, mucronate, base tapered or obtuse; upper surface dark green or pale green, scaly, midrib puberulous or rarely glabrous; *under surface bluish-glaucous, densely scaly,* the *scales* unequal, medium-sized and large, *yellowish* or pale brown, *one-half their own diameter apart* or rarely their own diameter apart, *with larger dark brown scattered scales;* petiole 0.3—1 cm. long, rather densely or moderately scaly. *Inflorescence* terminal, or rarely terminal and axillary in the uppermost leaf, shortly racemose, 3—8-flowered; rhachis 3—6 mm. long, scaly or rarely not scaly, puberulous or glabrous; pedicel 0.5—1.6 cm. long, moderately or rarely densely scaly. *Calyx* 5-lobed, minute, 0.5—1 mm. or rarely 4—5 mm. long, lobes rounded or triangular or rarely oblong, outside scaly, margin scaly, eciliate or rarely ciliate. *Corolla* widely funnel-shaped, zygomorphic, 2—3.4 cm. long, 5-lobed, white or pale rose-purple, with light green spots on the posterior side, *not scaly,* or rarely tube scaly *outside. Stamens* 10, unequal, 1.1—3.4 cm. long, exserted; filaments densely pubescent towards the base. *Ovary* oblong or conoid, 3—5 mm. long, 5-celled, densely scaly; style long, slender, not scaly, glabrous or rarely puberulous at the base. *Capsule* oblong, 1—1.4 cm. long, 3—4 mm. broad, rather densely scaly, calyx persistent.

Wilson discovered this plant in June 1908 at Wa-shan, western Szechuan. He found it again in that locality in the same month. In May 1932, Yü collected it at O-pien Hsien in the same region. It grows in thickets and woods, at elevations of 2,300—3,000 m. (7,541—9,836 ft.).

The marked features of this species are the bluish-glaucous lower surfaces of the leaves, being densely scaly with yellowish scales, usually one-half their own diameter apart, with larger dark brown scattered scales. In these respects, it is readily distinguished from its allies *R. polylepis* and *R concinnum*. It further differs from both in that the corolla is not scaly or rarely scaly on the tube outside, and often from the latter by the lanceolate to oblanceolate leaves. It is also allied to *R. zaleucum* which, however, differs in that the lower surface of the leaves is intensely glaucous, with widely spaced scales of one kind, 1½—4 times their own diameter apart, and the corolla is moderately scaly outside. *R. searsiae* is a tetraploid with 52 chromosomes.

The species was introduced by Wilson in 1908 (No. 1343 — the Type number). In cultivation it grows up to 12 feet high, although in its native home it reaches 16 feet. Two distinct forms are grown in gardens. Form 1. A somewhat compact, rounded shrub, 5—6 feet high and almost as much across, with small narrowly lanceolate leaves, laminae 3.5—4 cm. long, and small flowers 2 cm. long. Form 2. A tall broadly upright and spreading shrub, 12 feet high, with large broadly lanceolate leaves, laminae 6—7.5 cm. long, and large flowers 2.8—3 cm. long. The species is hardy, free-flowering, and easy to grow.

Epithet. After Sarah C. Sears, an American artist.

Hardiness 3. April—May.

R. siderophyllum Franch. in Journ. de Bot., XII (1898) 262.

A broadly upright or compact rounded shrub, or tree, 92 cm.—8 m. (3—26 ft.) high; branchlets rather densely or rarely moderately scaly, glabrous or rarely puberulous. *Leaves* oblong-lanceolate, ovate-lanceolate, lanceolate, elliptic, oblong-oval or almost orbicular, lamina 3—9 cm. long, 1.5—4.1 cm. broad, apex acuminate, acute or obtuse, mucronate, base tapered, rounded or obtuse; *upper surface pale greyish-green, matt,* scaly, midrib puberulous or glabrous; under surface scaly, the scales unequal, medium-sized and large, or medium-sized and small, brown or dark brown, almost contiguous to 1½ times their own diameter apart; petiole 0.6—1.5 cm. long, densely scaly. *Inflorescence terminal and axillary in the uppermost one or two leaves,* rarely terminal, shortly racemose, 3—6-flowered; rhachis 2—4 mm. long, scaly, glabrous or sometimes puberulous; *pedicel* 0.4—1.5 cm. (rarely 2.1 cm.) long, *densely* or rarely moderately *scaly,* glabrous or rarely puberulous. *Calyx* a mere rim or sometimes 5-lobed, minute, 0.5—1 mm. (rarely 2 mm.) long, lobes rounded, triangular or lanceolate, outside and margin densely or moderately scaly, margin eciliate or rarely ciliate. *Corolla* widely funnel-shaped, zygomorphic, 1.5—3 cm. long, 5-lobed, white, very pale pink, pink, rose, purple or pale lavender-blue, with or without yellow or rose spots, not scaly or lobes moderately or sparsely scaly outside, rarely both tube and lobes scaly. *Stamens* 10, unequal, 0.6—2.4 cm. long, exserted; filaments puberulous towards the base or sometimes glabrous. *Ovary* conoid or oblong, 3—4 mm. long, 5-celled, densely scaly; style long, slender, not scaly, glabrous or rarely puberulous at the base. *Capsule* oblong, 1—1.5 cm. long, 4—6 mm. broad, rather densely scaly, calyx persistent.

R. siderophyllum was first collected by Bodinier and Ducloux in March 1897, on the mountains at Yunnansen, south-west Yunnan. It was afterwards found by other collectors in the same region, and in Kweichow, also in south-west Szechuan. The plant grows on dry wooded hills, on open ridges, in mixed thickets by streams, and in dry scrub on hills, at elevations of 840—3,355 m. (2,754—11,000 ft.).

This species was described by Franchet in 1898. Subsequently distinctive names were given to closely similar plants, namely, *R. rubropunctatum,* Lévl. et Van. (1911), *R. leucandrum* Lévl. (1913), *R. jahandiezii* Lévl. (1914), *R. ioanthum* Balf. f. (1922), and *R. obscurum* Franch. ex Balf. f. (1922). In *The Species of Rhododendron* 1930, (pp. 781, 809, 852,

853), these names have been referred to *R. siderophyllum*, *R. bodinieri*, and *R. concinnum*. It will be seen that in *The Rhododendron and Camellia Year Book* 1963, p. 210, all these names were placed in synonymy under *R. siderophyllum*. The plant which was figured in the *Botanical Magazine*, Vol. 144, t. 8759 (1918) as *R. siderophyllum*, is correctly referred to *R. davidsonianum* in *The Species of Rhododenron* 1930, p. 797.

R. siderophyllum is a very variable plant. It is a shrub or tree, 3—26 feet high. The leaves are oblong-lanceolate, ovate-lanceolate, lanceolate, elliptic, oblong-oval or almost orbicular, laminae 3—9 cm. long, 1.5—4.1 cm. broad, and the corolla is 1.5—3 cm. long. The plant is a hexaploid with 78 chromosomes.

The species shows a resemblance to *R. davidsonianum* and *R. yunnanense*. It is distinguished from the former usually by the shape and size and by the pale greyish-green, matt upper surfaces of the leaves; from the latter usually by the non-bristly leaves, by the densely scaly lower surfaces of the leaves, the scales being almost contiguous to 1½ times their own diameter apart, and often by the shape and size of the leaves.

R. siderophyllum was first introduced possibly by Forrest in 1918 (No. 15129). It was reintroduced by him in 1921 (No. 20648). McLaren's collectors sent seeds in 1932 (McLaren No. AA 16). In its native home it is a shrub or tree 3—26 feet high. Two distinct forms are in cultivation: Form 1. A compact, rounded shrub, 3—4 feet high and as much across, densely filled with oblong-lanceolate leaves. Form 2. A broadly upright shrub, 6 feet high with smaller leaves. A distinctive feature of the species is the pale greyish-green, matt upper surfaces of the leaves. It is hardy, free-flowering, and provides a fine display with its white flowers in clusters of three to six. The plant was given an Award of Merit when shown by Mr. Edmund de Rothschild, Exbury, in March 1945.

Epithet. Rusty-coated leaves.
Hardiness 3. May.

R. suberosum Balf. f. et Forrest in Notes Roy. Bot. Gard. Edin., Vol. 13 (1922) 301.

A broadly upright or bushy shrub, 92 cm.—3 m. (3—10 ft.) high; branchlets scaly, bristly or not bristly, not puberulous. *Leaves* evergreen, lanceolate, narrowly lanceolate or oblong-lanceolate, *lamina* chartaceous, 3.5—7.3 cm. long, 1—2.2 cm. broad, apex acuminate or acute, mucronate, base tapered or obtuse; *upper surface dark green*, shining, not scaly or scaly, not bristly or bristly, midrib puberulous or glabrous; *margin erose, rough to the touch, rather densely or sometimes moderately bristly*, slightly recurved or flat; *under surface dark green* or sometimes pale green, scaly, the scales unequal, medium-sized, 2—5 times their own diameter apart; petiole 4—7 mm. long, moderately or rather densely scaly, bristly, not puberulous. *Inflorescence terminal and axillary in the uppermost 2—7 leaves*, shortly racemose, 1—3-flowered; rhachis 1—3 mm. long, scaly, glabrous; *flower-bud scales* deciduous or *persistent*; pedicel 0.5—1.5 cm. long, moderately or rather densely scaly, not bristly, not puberulous. *Calyx* a mere rim or 5-lobed, minute, 0.5—1 mm. long, lobes ovate or triangular, outside moderately or rather densely scaly, margin scaly or not scaly, bristly or not bristly, not puberulous. *Corolla* funnel-shaped, zygomorphic, 1.7—3 cm. long, 5-lobed, white faintly flushed rose or *ivory-white flushed rose or ivory-white*, with deep rose or green spots on the posterior side, outside scaly. *Stamens* 10, unequal, 1.6—2.6 cm. long, exserted; filaments densely or moderately pubescent towards the base. *Ovary* conoid or oblong, 2—4 mm. long, 5-celled, densely scaly, glabrous; style long, slender and straight, longer than the corolla and the stamens, not scaly, glabrous. *Capsule* oblong, 0.7—1 cm. long, 3—4 mm. broad, straight, densely scaly, glabrous, calyx persistent.

Forrest discovered this plant in May 1919 on the eastern flank of the N'Maikha-Salwin Divide, west Yunnan. He found it again in 1919, 1924 and 1925 in other localities in west and mid-west Yunnan, and in Upper Burma. Rock collected it in south-west Szechuan in 1932. It grows in open scrub by streams and in side valleys, and in thickets on rocky slopes, at elevations of 3,355—3,965 m. (11,000—13,000 ft.).

R. suberosum is allied to *R. yunnanense* from which it is distinguished by the dark green leaves with very bristly and rough margins, usually by the terminal and axillary inflorescence in the uppermost two to seven leaves, and usually by the ivory-white corolla with green spots. It also differs in that it is a diploid with 26 chromosomes, while *R. yunnanense* is a hexaploid with 78 chromosomes.

The species was first introduced by Forrest in 1919 (No. 18000 — the Type number). It was reintroduced by him on several occasions. In cultivation it is a broadly upright or bushy shrub 5—8 feet high with erect branchlets, and fairly well-filled with dark green foliage. A characteristic feature of the cultivated plants is the ivory-white corolla with green spots. The species is very hardy, flowers freely, and is worth being more widely grown.

Epithet. Slightly gnawed.

Hardiness 3. April—May. Plate 62.

R. tatsienense Franch. in Journ. de Bot., IX (1895) 394.

A lax or broadly upright shrub, 30 cm.—2.75 m. (1—9 ft.) high; *branchlets deep crimson or deep crimson-purple*, moderately or rather densely scaly, glabrous or sometimes puberulous. *Leaves* elliptic, obovate, oval, ovate, oblong or oblong-lanceolate; *lamina rigid* or somewhat rigid, 1.6—6 cm. long, 1—3.1 cm. broad, apex rounded, obtuse or rarely acute, mucronate, base obtuse, rounded or rarely truncate; upper surface dark green, shining, moderately or rather densely scaly or rarely not scaly, midrib puberulous or glabrous; *under surface pale green* or pale glaucous green, scaly, the scales unequal, medium-sized or small, brown or dark brown, one-half to their own diameter apart, rarely up to twice their own diameter apart; petiole 0.3—1.4 cm. long, moderately or densely scaly, glabrous or rarely puberulous. *Inflorescence* terminal, or terminal and axillary in the uppermost 1—3 leaves, umbellate or shortly racemose, 1—6-flowered; rhachis 2—3 mm. long, scaly, glabrous or rarely puberulous; pedicel 0.4—1.9 cm. long, moderately or rarely densely scaly, glabrous or rarely minutely puberulous. *Calyx* 5-lobed or a mere rim, minute, 0.5—1 mm. long, lobes rounded or triangular, outside scaly, margin scaly or rarely not scaly, glabrous or rarely ciliate. *Corolla* widely funnel-shaped, zygomorphic, *1.4—2.3 cm.* (rarely 3 cm.) *long*, 5-lobed, purple, rose, pale rose, rose-lavender or rose-pink, with or without red spots, outside moderately or sparsely scaly or rarely not scaly. *Stamens* 10, unequal, 0.5—2.5 cm. long, exserted; filaments densely pubescent towards the base. *Ovary* oblong or conoid, 2—4 mm. long, 5-celled, densely scaly; style long, slender, not scaly, glabrous or sometimes puberulous at the base. *Capsule* oblong, 0.6—1.4 cm. long, 4—5 mm. broad, rather densely scaly, calyx persistent.

This species was first collected by the Abbé Soulié in 1893 near Tatsienlu, in the valley of Jerikkou, western Szechuan. It was later found by Forrest, Maire, Rock, and Lee in other localities in the same region and in north-west and mid-west Yunnan. The plant grows amongst scrub, in thickets, stony meadows, in open dry situations, on rocky dry slopes, on the margins of forests, and in pine forests, at elevations of 2,135—4,270 m. (7,000—14,000 ft.).

R. tatsienense was described by Franchet in 1895. During the years 1915—1933, distinct specific names were given to four other plants, namely, *R. tapelouense* Lévl. (1915), *R. stereophyllum* Balf. f. et W.W. Sm. (1916), *R. leilungense* Balf. f. et Forrest (1922), and *R. heishuiense* Fang (1933). It will be seen that *R. tapelouense* has been correctly referred to *R. tatsienense* in *The Species of Rhododendron* 1930, p. 853. Moreover, in *The Rhododendron and Camellia Year Book* 1963, p. 212, all the other names were placed in synonymy also under *R. tatsienense*.

R. tatsienense shows a certain degree of resemblance to *R. oreotrephes*, but differs in that the leaves are rigid, they are usually pale green beneath, the branchlets are deep crimson or deep crimson-purple, the upper surface of the leaves, the branchlets and petioles are often rather densely scaly, and the corolla is usually smaller and is often moderately scaly outside.

The species was first introduced by Forrest in 1917 (Nos. 15204, 15263). It was reintroduced by him in 1921 and 1922. Several forms are in cultivation, including: Form 1. A small lax shrub, 2—3 feet high with long branchlets, and with terminal and axillary inflorescences in the uppermost few leaves. Form 2. A large broadly upright shrub 5—6 feet high with somewhat short branchlets. A well-marked character of the cultivated plants is the deep crimson or deep crimson-purple branchlets. The species has proved to be of sturdy habit, fairly fast-growing, and is easily adaptable to any position in the garden.

Epithet. From Tatsienlu, now Kang-ting, W. China.

Hardiness 3. April—May.

R. vilmorinianum Balf. f. in Notes Roy. Bot. Gard. Edin., Vol. 12 (1920) 181.

A broadly upright shrub, 92 cm.—1.50 m. (3—5 ft.) high; branchlets deep crimson or deep crimson-purple, scaly, rather densely pubescent or glabrous, not bristly or sparsely bristly. *Leaves* lanceolate, oblong, oblong-lanceolate or oblong-obovate, lamina 2.4—6.6 cm. long, 0.8—2.6 cm. broad, apex acute or obtuse, mucronate, base tapered, obtuse or rounded; upper surface dark green, shining, not scaly or scaly, midrib pubescent or rarely glabrous, margins bristly or not bristly; under surface scaly, the scales unequal, medium-sized and large, brown, one-half to their own diameter apart, or rarely twice their own diameter apart; petiole 3—9 mm. long, scaly, bristly or sometimes not bristly, pubescent or sometimes glabrous. *Inflorescence* terminal, or terminal and axillary in the uppermost 1—3 leaves, shortly racemose, 2—4-flowered; rhachis 2—3 mm. long, scaly, moderately or rather densely puberulous or sometimes glabrous; *pedicel* 0.8—1.8 cm. long, scaly, *pubescent* or sometimes glabrous. *Calyx* 5-lobed, 0.5—2 mm. long, lobes rounded or triangular or oblong, outside scaly, margin scaly, ciliate or bristly or sometimes glabrous. *Corolla* widely funnel-shaped, zygomorphic, 1.8—3.5 cm. long, 5-lobed, yellowish-white or pink, with or without brownish spots on the posterior side, outside scaly. *Stamens* 10, unequal, 1.5—3.5 cm. long, exserted; filaments densely villous towards the base. *Ovary* oblong, 2—4 mm. long, 5-celled, densely scaly, bristly at the apex or not bristly; style long, slender, not scaly, puberulous at the base or glabrous. *Capsule* oblong, 0.8—1.1 cm. long, 2—4 mm. broad, densely scaly, calyx-lobes persistent.

This plant raised by M. de Vilmorin from seed probably collected by the Abbé Farges in east Szechuan, was described by Sir Isaac Bayley Balfour in 1920. It has sometimes been known as the white-flowered form of *R. augustinii*.

R. vilmorinianum is allied to *R. davidsonianum* which it resembles in general features, but is distinguished often by the flat lamina of the leaf and the pubescent pedicels, and ciliate or bristly calyx margin. Moreover, *R. vilmorinianum* is usually a smaller plant. It is also related to *R. yunnanense* from which it differs in that the scales on the lower surfaces of the leaves are closely spaced, the corolla is scaly all over the outside, and the pedicels are often pubescent.

It is a broadly upright shrub with dark green leaves and yellowish-white or pink flowers produced freely in clusters of 2—4. It is hardy, and well worth a place in every garden.

Epithet. After the famous French seedsman.

Hardiness 3. May.

R. yunnanense Franch. in Bull. Bot. Soc. France, XXXIII (1886) 232.

Illustration. Bot. Mag. Vol. 124 t. 7614 (1898).

A somewhat lax broadly upright, or lax upright, or broadly upright and spreading shrub, 30 cm.—3.66 m. (1—12 ft.) high; branchlets moderately or sparsely scaly, not bristly or sometimes bristly, puberulous or sometimes glabrous. *Leaves evergreen or sometimes semi-deciduous,* oblanceolate, oblong-lanceolate or lanceolate, lamina 2.5—10.4 cm. long, 0.8—2.8 cm. broad, apex shortly acuminate, acute or obtuse, mucronate, base tapered or obtuse, upper surface green, moderately or sparsely scaly or sometimes not scaly, sparsely or rarely moderately bristly, or not bristly, glabrous or sometimes puberulous, midrib puberulous or rarely glabrous, margins sparsely or sometimes moderately bristly, or not bristly; *under surface* pale glaucous green or green, scaly, the *scales* unequal, medium-sized, brown, *2—6 times their own diameter apart,* rarely their own diameter apart; petiole 0.3—1.1 cm. long, moderately or sparsely or sometimes rather densely scaly, bristly or not bristly, puberulous or rarely glabrous. *Inflorescence* terminal, or terminal and axillary in the uppermost 1—3 leaves, shortly racemose, 3—5-flowered; rhachis 2—3 mm. long, scaly, puberulous or glabrous; pedicel 0.5—2 cm. long, moderately or sparsely scaly or not scaly. *Calyx* a mere rim or 5-lobed, minute, 0.5—1 mm. long, lobes rounded or triangular, outside scaly or not scaly, margin scaly or sometimes not scaly, glabrous or puberulous or ciliate. *Corolla* widely funnel-shaped, zygomorphic, 1.8—3.4 cm. long, 2—4 cm. across, 5-lobed, pale pink, pink, white, pale purplish-pink, deep rose, pinkish-lavender, pale rose-lavender, lavender or blue-lavender, with or rarely without deep crimson, brownish-crimson, deep rose, olive-brown, green or deep green spots, not scaly or scaly or sometimes only lobes moderately scaly outside. *Stamens* 10, unequal, 1.4—4 cm. long, exserted; filaments densely or moderately pubescent towards the base. *Ovary* oblong, 3—5 mm. long, 5-celled, densely scaly, glabrous or rarely puberulous at the apex; style long, slender, not scaly. *Capsule* oblong, 0.6—2 cm. long, 3—5 mm. broad, rather densely scaly, calyx persistent.

This plant was discovered by the Abbé Delavay in April 1883 at Houang-li-pin, western Yunnan. Further gatherings by other collectors show that the species has a wide geographical distribution, extending from mid-west, west and north-west Yunnan and west Kweichow to north-east Upper Burma, south-west Szechuan and south-east Tibet. It is found in thickets, in pine and spruce forests, on cliffs, amongst boulders by streams, in open moorland, amongst scrub, in cane brakes, in rocky meadows, and on rocky slopes, at elevations of 1,983—4,270 m. (6,500—14,000 ft.), rarely at 890 m. (2,918 ft.).

R. yunnanense is very variable in general features due to the various environmental conditions in which it is found. It grows from 1 foot to 12 feet high; the leaves (laminae) are 2.5—10.4 cm. long, 0.8—2.8 cm. broad; the corolla ranges from 1.8 cm. to 3.4 cm. long; and the flower colour is white, pink to lavender, usually with deep crimson, brownish-crimson, deep rose, olive-brown, green or deep green spots.

It may be observed that the names *R. chartophyllum* Franch. (1895), *R. seguini* Lévl. (1914), *R. strictum* Lévl. nomen, *R. aechmophyllum* Balf. f. et Forrest (1922), and *R. pleistanthum* Balf. f. ex Hutch. (1930), were placed in synonymy under *R. yunnanense* in *The Rhododendron and Camellia Year Book* 1963, p. 215.

R. yunnanense is closely allied to *R. hormophorum* which, however, has completely deciduous leaves. It is also related to *R. davidsonianum* from which it differs in that the leaves are often bristly, and the lower surfaces of the leaves are laxly scaly, the scales being 2—6 times their own diameter apart.

The species was first introduced by Delavay to Paris in 1889. It was reintroduced by Forrest, Rock, Kingdon-Ward, and Yü on many occasions. Several forms are in cultivation, varying in habit and height of growth, in leaf shape and size, in the degree of hairiness of the leaves, in flower size and colour, and in the colour of the spots of the corolla. At one extreme the species is a medium-sized, upright and lax shrub, 5—6 feet high with small leaves (laminae) 2.5 cm. long, and small flowers 1.8 cm. long; at the other extreme it is a large shrub, broadly upright and spreading, 12 feet high, with large leaves (laminae) 8 cm. long, and large flowers 3.4 cm. long. These extremes, however, are linked by intergrading forms. It should be noted that differences in flower size and colour, and in leaf size, cannot always be correlated with the habit and height of the plants. A large broadly upright spreading form with fairly large leaves and large white flowers 3.4 cm. long and about 4 cm. across is generally regarded as being one of the best forms. The species is hardy, free-flowering, and is extremely charming when laden with white or pink flowers in clusters of 3—5. It received an Award of Merit when exhibited by Mr. F.W. Moore, from Glasnevin, Dublin, in May 1903. It was given an Award of Garden Merit in July 1934.

Epithet. From Yunnan.

Hardiness 3. May. Plate 68.

R. zaleucum Balf. f. et W.W. Sm. in Notes Roy. Bot. Gard. Edin., Vol. 10 (1917) 163.

Illustration. Bot. Mag. Vol. 147 t. 8878 (1938).

A broadly upright or bushy shrub, or tree, 30 cm.—10.68 m. (1—35 ft.) high; branchlets scaly. *Leaves* lanceolate or oblong-lanceolate, rarely oblong, elliptic or obovate, lamina 3.2—8.8 cm. long, 1—3 cm. broad, apex acuminate, acutely acuminate or acute, rarely broadly obtuse or rounded, mucronate, base tapered, obtuse or rounded; upper surface pale green or olive-green, not scaly or rarely scaly, midrib puberulous or sometimes glabrous, margins sparsely bristly or not bristly; *under surface markedly glaucous* or rarely not glaucous, scaly, the *scales* unequal, *large*, brown, *1½—4 times their own diameter apart*, midrib glabrous or minutely puberulous; petiole 0.4—1.5 cm. long, scaly. *Inflorescence* terminal, or terminal and axillary in the uppermost leaf, shortly racemose, 3—5-flowered; rhachis 2—5 mm. long, scaly, glabrous or rarely puberulous; pedicel 0.8—2.8 cm. long, scaly. *Calyx* 5-lobed, minute, 0.5—1 mm. or rarely 2 mm. long, lobes rounded or triangular or rarely oblong, outside densely or moderately scaly, margin scaly or rarely not scaly, glabrous, or slightly or moderately bristly, or ciliate. *Corolla* funnel-shaped, zygomorphic, 2.6—4.8 cm. long, 5-lobed, white, white flushed rose, pink, rose, lavender-rose, pale purple or purple, with or without crimson spots, *outside scaly*, tube hairy in the lower half outside or glabrous. *Stamens* 10, unequal, 1.3—3.3 cm. long, exserted; filaments pubescent towards the base. *Ovary* conoid or oblong, 3—5 mm. long, 5-celled, densely scaly; style long, slender, glabrous or rarely pubescent at the base. *Capsule* oblong, 0.8—1.5 cm. long, 3—5 mm. broad, rather densely scaly, calyx persistent.

R. zaleucum was discovered by Forrest in August 1912 on the western flank of the Shweli-Salwin Divide, west Yunnan. It was afterwards found by him and other collectors in other localities in the same region and in mid-west and north-west Yunnan, also in north-east and east Upper Burma. The plant grows in rhododendron, pine, and spruce forests, and in open deciduous forests, in thickets, amongst dwarf scrub, amongst boulders in side valleys, and on rocky slopes at elevations of 1,830—3,965 m. (6,000—13,000 ft.).

It is to be noted that in 1920 *R. erileucum* Balf. f. et Forrest was described from a specimen No. 17593 collected by Forrest in June 1918 also on the Shweli-Salwin Divide, west Yunnan. In *The Rhododendron and Camellia Year Book* 1963, p. 218, it was placed in synonymy under *R. zaleucum*.

A diagnostic feature of *R. zaleucum* is the intensely glaucous lower surface of the leaves, by which the species is readily distinguished from *R. searsiae,* its nearest ally, and from all the other members of its Series. It further differs from its ally in that the scales on the lower surface of the leaves are large and widely spaced, 1½—4 times their own diameter apart, and the corolla is moderately scaly outside. It is a tetraploid with 52 chromosomes.

The species was first introduced by Forrest in 1912 (No. 8923 — the Type number). It was reintroduced by him in 1924 and 1925, and by Farrer in 1919. In its native home it is a shrub or tree ranging from 1 to 35 feet high; in cultivation it is a broadly upright shrub 5 to 10 feet in height. It is a pleasing species with rose or lavender-rose flowers produced freely in clusters of three to five. The plant varies in hardiness, but to be able to grow it satisfactorily, particularly along the east coast and in gardens inland, a well-sheltered position should be provided. It was given an Award of Merit when shown by Col. R. Stephenson Clarke, Borde Hill, Haywards Heath, in 1932.

Epithet. Very white.

Hardiness 2—3. April—May.

R. zaleucum Balf. f. et W. W. Sm. var. **flaviflorum** Davidian in Quart. Bull. Amer. Rhod. Soc. Vol. 32, Spring, No. 2 (1978) 84.

Kingdon-Ward discovered this plant in May 1953 at Uring Bum, above Ahkail, North Triangle, North Burma, at an elevation of 2,745 m. (9,000 ft.). He records it as being common along the exposed ridge.

The variety differs from the species in its yellow flowers, and in the larger leaves, laminae up to 10 cm. long.

It was introduced by Kingdon-Ward in 1953 (No. 20837 — the Type number). In its native home, it is a small tree up to 25 feet high, but in cultivation it is a broadly upright shrub reaching only up to 8 feet in height, fairly well-filled with foliage. It is a vigorous grower, and is of great beauty when covered with large funnel-shaped yellow flowers. The plant varies in hardiness. In the west coast it is successfully grown in the open. Along the east coast it should be given a well-sheltered position; in a few very cold gardens, it has proved tender outdoors.

Epithet of the variety. With yellow flowers.

Hardiness 2—3. April—May.

UNIFLORUM SERIES

General characters: dwarf, prostrate spreading, compact or broadly upright shrubs, 3—92 cm. (1.2 in.—3 ft.) high (*R. monanthum* up to 1.22 m. [4 ft.]). Leaves evergreen, lanceolate, oblanceolate to oval or almost orbicular, lamina 0.8—3.8 cm. (rarely up to 5 cm.) long, 0.4—1.5 cm. (rarely up to 2.5 cm.) broad; under surface scaly, the scales ½—6 times their own diameter apart. *Inflorescence* terminal, *1—2-* (rarely 3-) *flowered*; pedicel 1—2.6 cm. (rarely 4—6 mm.) long. Calyx 5-lobed (in *R. monanthum* undulate-lobulate), 1—3 mm. (in *R. ludlowii* 5—7 mm.) long. *Corolla* widely funnel-shaped or campanulate or tubular-campanulate, 5-lobed, 0.8—3.5 cm. long, purple, rose, pink or yellow, *outside rather densely pubescent* (in *R. monanthum* glabrous), usually scaly. Stamens 10. Ovary 5-celled; *style long* (in *R. pumilum* short), *slender, and straight*. Capsule 0.4—1.3 cm. (rarely 1.6 cm.) long.

Distribution: Upper and north-east Burma, north-west Yunnan, south and south-east Tibet, Assam, Bhutan, and Nepal.

A homogeneous Series of closely allied species with one aberrant species, *R. monanthum*. It shows affinity with the Tephropeplum Series, and less closely with the Lepidotum Series.

KEY TO THE SPECIES

A. Leaf margin crenulate-undulate, distinctly notched; calyx large, 5—7 mm. long; corolla large for the size of the leaves, yellow with reddish-brown spots .. *ludlowii*

A. Leaf margin entire; calyx minute 1—2 mm., rarely 3—4 mm. long; corolla not large for the size of the leaves, purple, rose or pink (in *R. monanthum* bright yellow).

    B. Corolla bright yellow, outside not pubescent; scales on the under surface of the leaves markedly different in size, mostly large, densely set, one-half their own diameter apart; small or medium-sized broadly upright or spreading shrub, sometimes epiphytic, up to 1.20 m. high; leaves large, laminae usually 2.6—5 cm. long, 1.3—2.5 cm. broad .... *monanthum*

    B. Corolla purple, rose or pink, outside rather densely pubescent; scales on the under surface of the leaves small, uniform (in *R. pemakoense* varying), usually laxly spaced, 2—6 times (in *R. pemakoense* ½—1½ times) their own diameter apart; dwarf, prostrate or compact or broadly upright shrub, usually 3—60 cm. high; leaves small, laminae usually 0.8—2.6 cm. long, 0.4—1.3 cm. broad.

        C. Corolla small, 0.8—1.9 cm. long, campanulate; style about one-half as long as the corolla; leaves oval, elliptic, almost orbicular or obovate .... *pumilum*

        C. Corolla large, 2.2—3.5 cm. long, widely funnel-shaped (in *R. pemakoense* tubular-campanulate or tubular-funnel shaped); style as long as the corolla or longer or two-thirds the length of the corolla; leaves lanceolate, oblanceolate, obovate to oval.

            D. Leaves obovate, oblong-obovate, oblong-oval or oval, apex rounded or obtuse, upper surface usually bright green; rounded shrub forming a mound or broadly upright or upright or a low compact spreading shrub, 30—90 cm. high.

                E. Corolla tubular-campanulate or tubular-funnel shaped; scales on the under surface of the leaves closely spaced, ½—1½ times their own diameter apart; style as long as the corolla or longer; leaves obovate or oblong-obovate ..... *pemakoense*

                E. Corolla widely funnel-shaped; scales on the under surface of the leaves widely spaced, 3—6 times their own diameter apart; style about two-thirds the length of the corolla; leaves oblong-oval, oval, obovate or oblong-obovate .. *uniflorum*

            D. Leaves lanceolate or oblanceolate, apex usually acute, upper surface dark green; completely prostrate or prostrate shrub, 3—10 cm. high, with spreading or creeping branches, mat-forming .... *imperator*

DESCRIPTION OF THE SPECIES

R. imperator Hutch. et Ward in The Species of Rhododendron (1930) 440.

    Illustration. Bot. Mag. n.s. Vol. 176 t. 514 (1967).

    A dwarf, *completely prostrate or prostrate shrub, 3—10 cm. (1.2—4 in.) high, with spreading or creeping branches,* mat-forming; branchlets scaly, minutely puberulous or glabrous. *Leaves lanceolate or oblanceolate,* lamina coriaceous, 1.3—3.8 cm. long, 0.4—1 cm. broad, *apex acute* or sometimes rounded, mucronate, base tapered; *upper surface dark green,* scaly or not scaly, under surface pale glaucous green or pale green, scaly, the scales small, brown, 1—6 times their own diameter apart; petiole 1—5 mm. long, scaly. *Inflorescence* terminal, 1—2-flowered; pedicel 1—2.5 cm. long, scaly. *Calyx* 5-lobed, 1—2 mm. long, lobes ovate or lanceolate, outside scaly, margin ciliate or eciliate. *Corolla widely funnel-shaped,* 5-lobed, 2.3—3.2 cm. long, dark purple, rich purple, bright purple, deep pinkish-purple or purple, with or without deep crimson spots, outside rather densely pubescent, sparsely or moderately scaly or not scaly. *Stamens* 10, unequal, 1—2.5 cm. long, shorter than the corolla; filaments moderately or rather densely pubescent towards the base. *Ovary* conoid or ovoid, 2—3 mm. long, 5-celled, densely scaly; style long, slender and straight, longer than the corolla or equalling it, glabrous. *Capsule* oblong or oblong-oval, 1—1.3 cm. long, rather densely scaly with very small scales, calyx-lobes persistent.

This plant was discovered by Kingdon-Ward in June 1926 at Seinghku Wang, Upper Burma. It forms flat mats with other species on bare ledges of granite cliffs in a well-shaded gully where it receives very little sun, at elevations of 3,050—3,355 m. (10,000—11,000 ft.). It is recorded as being very rare. No other collector has found this plant in its native home.

In May 1928, Kingdon-Ward collected a plant (No. 8260) on the Mishmi Hills, Assam Frontier. He records it as being an absolutely creeping species, growing in extensive drifts on steep slopes and rocks, fully exposed, at elevations of 3,355—3,660 m. (11,000—12,000 ft.), and the plant was given the specific name *R. patulum* Ward. When this specimen under *R. patulum* is examined, it will be seen that in habit and height of growth, in leaf shape and size, in flower shape, size and colour, and in other details, it is identical with *R. imperator*. The only distinction between them is that in *R. imperator* the scales on the lower surface of the leaves are 2—6 times their own diameter apart; in *R. patulum* they are 1—1½ times their own diameter apart. On this distinction alone, *R. patulum* does not merit specific status, and it will now appear under *R. imperator* in synonymy. It is worth noting that some plants in cultivation under the name *R. patulum* are, in fact, forms of *R. pemakoense*.

R. imperator is a distinctive species, and is unlikely to be confused with any species of its Series. It is allied to *R. pemakoense*. The main distinctions between them are that *R. imperator* is a completely prostrate or prostrate shrub, a few inches high with spreading or creeping branches, mat-forming, the leaves are usually lanceolate acute at the apex, dark green above, and the corolla is widely funnel-shaped, dark purple, bright purple to purple in colour; whereas *R. pemakoense* is a rounded shrub forming a mound, or a low compact spreading, or broadly upright, or upright shrub, 1—2 feet high, the leaves are obovate or oblong-obovate, rounded or sometimes obtuse at the apex, bright green, pale- or greyish-green above, and the corolla is tubular-campanulate or tubular-funnel shaped, pinkish-purple, pale purple or pale pink in colour. *R. imperator* is a diploid with 26 chromosomes.

The species was introduced by Kingdon-Ward in 1926 (No. 6884 — the Type number), and it first flowered in 1929. In cultivation it is a prostrate shrub, a few inches high with spreading or creeping branches. A broadly upright plant 1 foot high which has been named *R. imperator* in cultivation, would appear to be a "rogue". The species is a slow grower, and many years are needed before it forms a fairly large plant. In some gardens along the east coast and inland, it is a difficult plant and will hardly establish; in other gardens it is satisfactorily grown whether it is raised from seed or cuttings. The plant succeeds well on the peat walls in the Royal Botanic Garden, Edinburgh. One of the chief merits of the species is that it flowers at a remarkably early age. The plant occasionally produces good fertile seed, and when sown the seeds germinate freely. In some plants the leaves provide good crimson-purple autumn colour. The species varies in hardiness, and to be able to grow it successfully a well-sheltered position and shade are essential. A well-grown plant about 10 inches in diameter is of exquisite beauty when covered with large widely funnel-shaped single or paired flowers. It well deserved the Award of Merit which it received when exhibited by Lord Swaythling, Townhill Park, Southampton, in 1934 (K.W. No. 6884).

Epithet. Emperor.
Hardiness 2—3. April—May. Plate 74.

34. R. ludlowii

nat. size

a. section. b. stamen. c. ovary, style. d. capsule.

R. ludlowii Cowan in Notes Roy. Bot. Gard. Edin., Vol. 19 (1937) 243.

Illustration. Bot. Mag. n.s. Vol. 174 t. 412 (1963).

A dwarf, prostrate shrub a few cms. (in.) high with spreading or creeping long branches, or a rounded or broadly upright shrub up to 30 cm. (1 ft.) high with short branches; branchlets scaly, glabrous. *Leaves* obovate, oval or rounded, lamina coriaceous, 1.2—1.4 cm. long, 0.8—1 cm. broad, apex rounded, mucronate, base obtuse; upper surface dark green, scaly; *margin crenulate-undulate, distinctly notched; under surface* pale glaucous green or pale green, scaly, the *scales* large, brown, 2—3 *times their own diameter apart;* petiole 1—2 mm. long, scaly. *Inflorescence* terminal, 1—2-flowered; pedicel 1.5—1.9 cm. long, scaly. *Calyx* deeply 5-lobed, large, leafy, *5—7 mm. long,* lobes rounded or ovate, outside rather densely or moderately scaly, margin ciliate. *Corolla broadly campanulate,* 5-lobed, 1.5—2.5 cm. long, *yellow with reddish-brown spots inside the tube,* outside scaly, rather densely pubescent. *Stamens* 10, unequal, 0.7—1.5 cm. long, shorter than the corolla; filaments densely pubescent towards the base. *Ovary* ovate, 2—3 mm. long, 5-celled, densely scaly; style slender, straight, longer than the stamens, shorter than the corolla, glabrous. *Capsule* rounded, 4—5 mm. long, scaly, calyx-lobes persistent.

R. ludlowii was discovered by Ludlow and Sherriff in July 1936 at Lo La, Pachakshiri District, south-east Tibet, growing on a rocky hillside, at an elevation of 4,118 m. (13,500 ft.). Along with George Taylor they found it on Tsari Sama, Tibet, in 1938.

It is easily recognised by its obovate, oval or rounded leaves, laminae 1.2—1.4 cm. long, with crenulate-undulate distinctly notched margins, laxly scaly on the lower surface, the scales being 2—3 times their own diameter apart, by the large rounded or ovate leafy calyx 5—7 mm. long, and by the broadly campanulate corolla, 1.5—2.5 cm. long, yellow with reddish-brown spots. The species is related to *R. pumilum,* but differs in distinctive features.

The plant was introduced by Ludlow, Sherriff and Taylor in 1938 (No. 6600). In its native home it is a prostrate shrub a few inches high with spreading or creeping long branches. In cultivation it shows a distinct change in its habit and height of growth; it forms a rounded or broadly upright shrub up to 1 foot high with short branches. It is laxly foliaged, but a striking feature is the corolla, very large for the size of the leaves. The plant is reputed to be difficult, and it has been grown successfully in only two or three cold gardens; in several gardens it has failed to establish. It is a very slow grower, although it flowers at a very young age. The species produces good fertile seed. It is a charming little plant and provides a fine display with its single or paired large flowers.

Epithet. After F. Ludlow, who collected widely in the Himalayas.

Hardiness 2—3. April—May. Plate 73.

R. monanthum Balf. f. et W.W. Sm. in Notes Roy. Bot. Gard. Edin., Vol. 9 (1916) 250.

A small spreading shrub, sometimes epiphytic, 30 cm.—1.22 m. (1—4 ft.) high; branchlets scaly, slightly bristly or not bristly. *Leaves* elliptic, oblong-elliptic or oblong, *lamina* coriaceous, *2—5 cm. long, 1—2.5 cm. broad,* apex obtuse or sometimes acute, mucronate, base obtuse or narrowed; upper surface scaly; *under surface* glaucous, *densely scaly,* the *scales varying much in size, mostly large,* brown, *one-half their own diameter apart;* petiole 4—8 mm. long, scaly. *Inflorescence* terminal, solitary; pedicel curved or straight, 4—6 mm. long, densely scaly. *Calyx* very small, undulate-lobulate, 5-lobed, 1—2 mm. long, outside densely scaly, margin not ciliate. *Corolla* campanulate, 5-lobed, 1.6—2.3 cm. long, *bright yellow, outside* scaly, *not hairy. Stamens* 10, unequal, 1—2.2 cm. long, longer or slightly shorter than the corolla; filaments densely pubescent towards the base. *Ovary* conoid, 3—4 mm. long, 5-celled, densely scaly; style long, slender and straight, longer than the corolla, glabrous. *Capsule* oblong, 0.8—1.6 cm. long, 4—5 mm. broad, densely scaly, calyx-lobes persistent.

This plant was first collected by Forrest in 1905 in the Lupo Pass, in the Mekong-Salwin Divide, north-west Yunnan. It was later found by him, and by Kingdon-Ward, Rock, and Yü in other localities in Yunnan and south-east Tibet. Farrer collected it in north-east Upper Burma. It grows in shady situations on the margins of pine forests, on rocky slopes, amongst scrub, and on cliffs, at elevations of 2,745—4,423 m. (9,000—14,500 ft.). The original gathering was placed under the name *R. sulfureum* by Diels but this same plant was afterwards described as a new species, *R. monanthum*.

In *The Species of Rhododendron*, *R. monanthum* was included in the Boothii Series, but it differs markedly from the typical members of that Series by its solitary flower and long, slender, straight style. Accordingly, in *The Rhododendron Year Book* 1948, it was placed in the Uniflorum Series. It is an aberrant species and does not conform to the members of any Series. The species shows a certain degree of affinity with the Tephropeplum Series, but its closest relationship would appear to be with the species of the Uniflorum Series. It differs from the species of its Series in its larger leaves, in the large scales markedly different in size on the lower surfaces, in the thick short pedicel, in the corolla being glabrous outside, and usually in the taller habit of growth. The plant has not been introduced into cultivation.

Epithet. One-flowered.

Not in cultivation.

R. pemakoense Ward in Gard. Chron., LXXXVIII (1930) 298.

A dwarf rounded shrub forming a mound, or broadly upright, or upright, 30—60 cm. (1—2 ft.) high, or a low compact spreading shrub 30 cm. (1 ft.) high, 60—75 cm. (2—2½ ft.) across, often stoloniferous; branchlets scaly, minutely puberulous or glabrous. *Leaves obovate or oblong-obovate*, lamina coriaceous, 1—3 cm. long, 0.5—1.5 cm. broad, apex rounded or sometimes obtuse, mucronate, base obtuse or tapered; upper surface bright green, pale- or greyish-green, scaly; *under surface* pale glaucous green or glaucous, scaly, the *scales* unequal in size, brown, *½—1½ times their own diameter apart*; petiole 1—4 mm. long, scaly. *Inflorescence* terminal, 1—2-flowered; pedicel 1.3—2.5 cm. long, lengthening in fruit up to 3.8 cm. or more, scaly. *Calyx* 5-lobed, small, 1—3 mm. (rarely 4 mm.) long, crimson-purple, reddish-purple, purple, pink or pale greenish, lobes lanceolate, oblong or ovate, outside scaly, margin ciliate or eciliate. *Corolla tubular-campanulate or tubular-funnel shaped*, 5-lobed, 2.5—3.5 cm. long, pinkish-purple, purple, pale purple or pale pink, outside scaly, rather densely pubescent. *Stamens* 10, unequal, 1.2—2.8 cm. long, shorter than the corolla; filaments densely pubescent towards the base. *Ovary* ovate or conoid, 2—3 mm. long, 5-celled, densely scaly; style long, slender and straight, about as long as the corolla or longer, not scaly or rarely scaly at the base, glabrous or rarely pubescent at the base. *Capsule* oblong or conoid, 0.6—1 cm. long, densely scaly, calyx-lobes persistent.

Kingdon-Ward discovered this plant in fruit in November 1924 at Pemakochung, in the Tsangpo gorge, south-east Tibet. He found it again ten days later, above the Tsangpo gorge, on Namcha Barwa and Sanglung, and he described the species in 1930 from specimens cultivated at the Royal Botanic Garden, Edinburgh. In May 1947, Ludlow, Sherriff and Elliot collected it at Pemakochung, and a month later they found it again near Showa Dzong, Pome, south-east Tibet. The plant forms carpets on steep damp moss-covered slabs of rock, and it also grows on ravine slopes. Kingdon-Ward records it as being fairly common on cliffs above the Tsangpo gorge. It is found at an elevation of 2,898—3,050 m. (9,500—10,000 ft.).

The species is allied to *R. uniflorum*. The main distinctions between them are that in *R. pemakoense* the corolla is tubular-campanulate or tubular-funnel shaped, the lower surfaces of the leaves are densely scaly, the scales being ½—1½ times their own diameter apart, and the plant is rounded forming a mound, or compact spreading, broadly upright or upright; whereas in *R. uniflorum* the corolla is widely funnel-shaped, the lower

35. R. pemakoense
nat. size

a. petals. b. section. c. ovary, style. d. stamen. e. calyx. f. capsule.
g. leaf (upper surface). h. leaf (lower surface).

surfaces of the leaves are laxly scaly, the scales being 3—6 times their own diameter apart (rarely less), and the plant is usually broadly upright in growth. *R. pemakoense* is also related to *R. imperator*; the distinctions between them are discussed under the latter. The plant is a tetraploid with 52 chromosomes or diploid with 26 chromosomes.

R. pemakoense was introduced by Kingdon-Ward in 1924 (No. 6301 — the Type number). In cultivation it varies considerably in habit of growth and in leaf size, laminae 1—3 cm. long, 0.5—1.5 cm. broad. Four distinct growth forms are found in gardens: Form 1. A rounded shrub forming a mound 1—1½ feet high. Form 2. A broadly upright shrub 1½ feet high. Form 3. A stoloniferous broadly upright or upright shrub, (spreading by underground runners). Form 4. A low compact spreading shrub, 1 foot high and 2—2½ feet across. All these forms (except Form 4) which vary in habit and height of growth and in leaf size, are recorded as having been introduced under one number K.W. 6301. According to Kingdon-Ward some of the seeds came from his first gathering on November 21, 1924, but the bulk of the seeds was collected ten days later on November 30. The extreme variation of the plant in cultivation shows that the seeds must have been collected from two or three or more different plants, and were placed in one bag under No. 6301.

In cultivation *R. pemakoense* is somewhat densely branched, and well-filled with bright green, pale- or greyish-green foliage. It is an early flowerer, the flowers appearing in March or April. Unfortunately, the flowers and flower-buds are liable to be destroyed by early spring frosts. The plant is very free-flowering and, when it escapes the frost, provides a mass of colour with its single or paired pale pink flowers, often hiding the foliage. A notable feature is the pedicel elongating in fruit up to 3.8 cm. or more. It is not difficult to increase from cuttings, and an interesting feature is that it flowers freely at a very young age. The plant is hardy in sheltered positions, and is an excellent plant for the rock garden. It was given an Award of Merit when shown by Sir John Ramsden, Bulstrode, Gerrards Cross, in 1933 (K.W. No 6301).

Epithet. From the province of Pemako, E. Tibet.

Hardiness 3. March—April. Plate 71.

R. pumilum Hook. f. in Rhod. Sikkim Himal., t. 14 (1851).

A dwarf, lax or slender shrub 5—10 cm. (2—4 in.) high, with long prostrate spreading or creeping branches up to 13 cm. (5 in.) long; or a low compact prostrate shrub 8—13 cm. (3—5 in.) high and up to 25 cm. (10 in.) across; or a lax broadly upright shrub up to 20 cm. (8 in.) or sometimes up to 60 cm. (2 ft.) high; branchlets scaly, minutely puberulous. *Leaves oval, elliptic, almost orbicular or obovate*, lamina coriaceous, 0.8—1.9 cm. long, 0.4—1.1 cm. broad, apex rounded or obtuse, mucronate, base obtuse or rounded; upper surface dark green, scaly or not scaly; under surface pale green or pale glaucous green, scaly, the scales small, dark brown or brown, 2—3 times or sometimes their own diameter apart; petiole 1—2 mm. long, scaly. *Inflorescence* terminal, 1—3-flowered; pedicel 1—2.6 cm. long, lengthening in fruit up to 5.8 cm. long, densely scaly. *Calyx* deeply 5-lobed, 1—3 mm. long, crimson-purple, purplish-red or reddish-brown, lobes ovate, oval or oblong-oval, outside scaly, margin ciliate or eciliate. *Corolla campanulate*, 5-lobed, *0.8—1.9 cm. long*, pink, pale pink, rose, pinkish-purple or purple, outside rather densely pubescent, slightly or moderately scaly. *Stamens* 10, unequal, 5—7 mm. long, shorter than the style or equalling it; filaments pubescent towards the base. *Ovary* ovate, 2—3 mm. long, 5-celled, densely scaly; *style* straight, *short, about half as long as the corolla*, glabrous. *Capsule* ovate, oval or oblong-oval, 0.5—1.3 cm. long, densely scaly, calyx-lobes persistent.

This species was first collected by J.D. Hooker in 1849 in the Sikkim Himalaya. Subsequently it was found by other collectors in Nepal, Bhutan, south and south-east Tibet, Assam, and north-east Upper Burma. It grows on open hillsides, rocks, steep slopes, and alpine turf slopes, at elevations of 3,508—4,270 m. (11,500—14,000 ft.).

Kingdon-Ward records it as forming hassocks and mats on steep alpine slopes at Doshong La, south Tibet.

R. pumilum is easily recognised by its prostrate habit of growth, by the small oval, almost orbicular, elliptic or obovate leaves, laminae 0.8—1.9 cm. long, 0.4—1.1 cm. broad, by the small campanulate corolla, 0.8—1.9 cm. long, and by the short straight style about half as long as the corolla. It differs from its allies in distinctive characters.

This species was probably first introduced by J.D. Hooker in 1850. It was reintroduced by Kingdon-Ward in 1924 (No. 5856) and in 1926 (No. 6961), also by Ludlow and Sherriff, and by Stainton. In its native home, it grows from 3 up to 8 inches high or sometimes up to 2 feet. Three distinct growth forms are in cultivation: Form 1. A lax slender shrub, 2—4 inches high, with long prostrate spreading or creeping branches up to 5 inches long. Form 2. A low compact shrub 3 to 5 inches high and up to 10 inches or more across, without or sometimes with a few prostrate spreading branches. Form 3. A lax broadly upright shrub up to 4 or 5 inches high. The species is a slow grower, but one of its chief merits is that it flowers at a young age when raised from seed. It is free-flowering, and is extremely charming when adorned with pink campanulate flowers in clusters of one to three. Kingdon-Ward called this plant (No. 6961) "Pink Baby" "with shell pink flowers hoisted above the leaves". A characteristic feature is the pedicel lengthening considerably in fruit up to 5.8 cm. (2⅓ in.). Some plants produce plentiful good fertile seed. The plant varies in hardiness; in some gardens along the east coast, it is somewhat tender, but is successfully grown in the Royal Botanic Garden, Edinburgh. It requires protection from wind and some shade for the best results to be obtained. The plant received an Award of Merit when exhibited by Lord Swaythling, Townhill Park, Southampton, in 1935 (K.W. No. 6961).

Epithet. Dwarfish.
Hardiness 2—3. April—May.

R. uniflorum Hutch. et Ward in The Species of Rhododendron (1930) 446.

A dwarf low-growing shrub with subprocumbent branches up to 30 cm. (1 ft.) high, or a broadly upright shrub up to 92 cm. (3 ft.) high; branchlets scaly, minutely puberulous or glabrous. *Leaves oblong-oval, oval, obovate or oblong-obovate*, lamina coriaceous, 1.3—2.4 cm. long, 0.6—1.2 cm. broad, apex rounded or sometimes obtuse, mucronate, base obtuse or cuneate; upper surface dark green or bright green, scaly or not scaly; *under surface* glaucous or pale glaucous green or pale green, laxly scaly, the *scales* small, brown, *3—6 times their own diameter apart* (rarely less); petiole 1—4 mm. long, scaly. *Inflorescence* terminal, 1—2-flowered; pedicel 1.3—2.2 cm. long, lengthening in fruit up to 3.5 cm. long, scaly. *Calyx* 5-lobed, small, 1—2 mm. long, lobes ovate or oval, outside scaly, margin ciliate or eciliate. *Corolla widely funnel-shaped*, 5-lobed, 2.2—2.8 cm. long, purple, outside rather densely pubescent, scaly. *Stamens* 10, unequal, 0.8—1.6 cm. long, shorter than the corolla; filaments pubescent towards the base. *Ovary* conoid or ovoid, 2—3 mm. long, 5-celled, densely scaly; *style* slender, straight, *about two-thirds the length of the corolla*, glabrous. *Capsule* oblong-oval or oblong, 6—9 mm. long, densely scaly, calyx-lobes persistent.

R. uniflorum was discovered by Kingdon-Ward in June 1924 at Doshong La, above the gorge of the Tsangpo, southern Tibet. It grows in clumps on steep grassy slopes at elevations of 3,355—3,660 m. (11,000—12,000 ft.). The plant is rare in its native home.

The main features of this species are its widely funnel-shaped corolla, the oval to obovate leaves, the lower surfaces laxly scaly, the scales being 3—6 times their own diameter apart, and usually the broadly upright habit of growth up to 3 feet high. It is allied to *R. pemakoense*; the distinctions between them are discussed under the latter.

R. uniflorum was introduced by Kingdon-Ward in 1924 (No. 5876 — the Type number). It first flowered in 1927 in the Royal Botanic Garden, Edinburgh, when it was only 1—2 inches high, with widely funnel-shaped flowers. It may be of interest to note that the same plant produced two capsules later in the autumn of the same year. In its native home it is a dwarf low-growing shrub with ascending branches up to one foot high; in cultivation it is a broadly upright shrub up to three feet in height. It is fairly fast-growing, and seldom fails to display the beauty of its single or paired flowers produced with freedom. A striking feature is the lengthening of the pedicel in fruit, up to 3.5 cm. The plant has proved hardy, and should be a most valuable acquisition to any rock garden.

Epithet. One-flowered.
Hardiness 2—3. April—May. Plate 72.

VACCINIOIDES SERIES

General characters: small shrubs, usually epiphytic, 15—92 cm. (6 in.—3 ft.) or sometimes up to 1.53 m. (5 ft.) high; *branchlets rather densely or moderately scabrid with warts* (except in *R. kawakamii*, not scabrid, without warts), scaly. Leaves evergreen, oblong-obovate, spatulate-obovate, obovate, oblanceolate or obovate-lanceolate, lamina 0.7—5 cm. long, 0.4—2.4 cm. broad, apex emarginate or sometimes not emarginate, *base* tapered, *decurrent on the petiole*; margin recurved; *under surface* scaly, the scales *2—5 times their own diameter apart*; petiole 1—8 mm. long, *narrowly winged on each side* or rarely not winged. Inflorescence terminal or rarely axillary in the uppermost leaf, 1—7-flowered; pedicel 0.7—2.5 cm. long. Calyx 5-lobed or sometimes rim-like, 0.5—4 mm. long. *Corolla campanulate, 0.6—1.5 cm. long*, 5-lobed, white, creamy-white, white tinged pink, pink, lilac-pink, red, bright orange or yellow, outside scaly. Stamens 10. Ovary conoid or ovoid or sometimes oblong, 2—3 mm. or sometimes 5 mm. long, 5-celled, densely scaly, glabrous or densely pubescent; *style short*, thick, bent or straight, *shorter than*, or rarely as long as, *the stamens*, or rarely longer, 1½—3 times as long as the ovary or equalling it, or rarely shorter. *Capsule slender*, 1.2—3.4 cm. long, 3—5 mm. broad, straight or slightly curved, moderately or rather densely scaly, glabrous or sometimes densely or moderately pubescent, dehiscing from the top downwards; *seeds with a long tail at each end*.

Distribution: north and north-east Upper Burma, north-west and west Yunnan, Kweichow, Taiwan, Assam, south-east and east Tibet, Nepal, Sikkim, and Bhutan.

A distinct Series, usually epiphytic, with short style and linear capsule. A characteristic feature is the seed with a long tail at each end.

Four plants from the Philippine Islands, *R. quadrasianum* Vidal, *R. malindangense* Merr., *R. rosmarinifolium* Vidal, and *R. vidalii* Rolfe belong to the Malaysian rhododendrons, and are now excluded from the Vaccinioides Series.

KEY TO THE SPECIES

A. Leaf apex acuminate or acute, not emarginate; leaves obovate-lanceolate; style shorter than the ovary .... *santapaui*
A. Leaf apex rounded or rarely obtuse, emarginate; leaves oblong-obovate, obovate or rarely oblanceolate; style 1½—3 times as long as the ovary or equalling it.
    B. Inflorescence 1—2-flowered.
        C. Leaves (laminae) usually 0.7—1.7 cm. long, 4—9 mm. broad .. *vaccinioides*
        C. Leaves (laminae) usually 1.8—4 cm. long, 1—2 cm. broad.
            D. Corolla 7—8 mm. long, pale pink .... *asperulum*
                (part)
            D. Corolla 1—1.5 cm. long, bright orange or yellow.
                E. Corolla bright orange; ovary and capsule moderately or rather densely pubescent .... *insculptum*
                E. Corolla yellow; ovary and capsule glabrous or rarely pubescent
                    F. Leaves (laminae) 1.5—2 cm. broad; stamens 5 mm. long .... *emarginatum*
                    F. Leaves (laminae) 0.6—1.5 cm. broad; stamens 1—1.5 cm. long .... *euonymifolium*
    B. Inflorescence 3—7-flowered.
            G. Corolla 1—1.2 cm. long, white or yellow; branchlets not scabrid, without warts; inflorescence 3—7-flowered .... *kawakamii*
            G. Corolla 7—8 mm. long, pale pink; branchlets very scabrid, rather densely covered with warts; inflorescence 3-flowered .... *asperulum*
                (part)

DESCRIPTION OF THE SPECIES

R. asperulum Hutch. et Ward in The Species of Rhododendron (1930) 818.

A small shrub, often epiphytic; branchlets rather densely scabrid with warts, scaly, glabrous, leaf-bud scales persistent or deciduous. *Leaves* evergreen, oblong-obovate, *lamina* coriaceous, *2—3.5 cm. long, 1—2 cm. broad*, apex rounded, emarginate, mucronate, base tapered, decurrent on the petiole; upper surface dark or bright green, somewhat matt, scaly or not scaly; margin recurved, entire or somewhat crenulate in the upper half; under surface scaly, the scales somewhat small or medium-sized, unequal, brown, 2—5 times their own diameter apart; petiole 2—3 mm. long, narrowly winged on each side, scaly. *Inflorescence* terminal, umbellate, 1—3-flowered, flower-bud scales persistent or deciduous; rhachis 0.5—1 mm. long, scaly or not scaly, glabrous; pedicel 1.3—2.2 cm. long, scaly, glabrous. *Calyx* 5-lobed, 2—4 mm. long, lobes oval, ovate or oblong, outside scaly or scaly at the base, or not scaly, margin scaly or not scaly, glabrous. *Corolla* campanulate, *7—8 mm. long*, 5-lobed, pale pink, outside scaly. *Stamens* 10, unequal, 5—7 mm. long, as long as the corolla or shorter; filaments densely pubescent in the lower two-thirds. *Ovary* conoid or ovoid, 2—3 mm. long, tapered into the style, 5-celled, densely scaly, glabrous; style short thick, straight or bent, shorter than the corolla, shorter than the stamens, twice as long or as long as the ovary, scaly at the base, glabrous. *Capsule* slender, 2—2.5 cm. long, 3 mm. broad, slightly curved, scaly, glabrous, calyx-lobes persistent, dehiscing from the top downwards; seeds with a long tail at each end.

R. asperulum was discovered by Kingdon-Ward in May 1926 at Seinghku Wang, Upper Burma. It was found by him again later in July of the same year in the Valley of the Di Chu, same region. It grows as an epiphyte on alder and other trees in open pastures and on mossy boulders in the lower forest, at elevations of 1,983—2,135 m. (6,500—7,000 ft.).

The main features of this plant are its large leaves, laminae 2—3.5 cm. long, 1—2 cm. broad, lower surfaces laxly scaly, the scales being 2—5 times their own diameter apart, and the small corolla 7—8 mm. long. The species is allied to *R. vaccinioides*, but is readily distinguished by its large leaves. The plant has not been introduced into cultivation.

Epithet. Slightly roughened.

Not in cultivation.

R. emarginatum Hemsl. et Wils. in Kew Bull. (1910) 118.

A shrub, 60 cm. (2 ft.) high, with spreading branches, branchlets scabrid, scaly, leaf-bud scales deciduous. *Leaves* evergreen, in whorls, obovate or oblong-obovate, *lamina* coriaceous, 3—4 cm. long, *1.5—2 cm. broad*, apex rounded, emarginate, mucronate, base tapered, decurrent on the petiole; upper surface dark green, somewhat shining, sparsely scaly or not scaly, primary veins 3—4 on each side, deeply impressed; margin recurved; under surface scaly, the scales somewhat small, unequal, brown, 2—3 times their own diameter apart, primary veins raised; petiole 3—5 mm. long, narrowly winged on each side, scaly. *Inflorescence* terminal, umbellate, 1—2-flowered; rhachis 0.5—1 mm. long; pedicel 2 cm. long, scaly. *Calyx* 5-lobed, minute, lobes triangular, unequal, outside scaly. *Corolla* campanulate, 1.3 cm. long, 5-lobed, *yellow*, outside scaly. *Stamens* 10, unequal, *5 mm. long*, shorter than the corolla; filaments pubescent about the middle. *Ovary* ovoid, 2 mm. long, densely scaly; *style* short, straight, shorter than the corolla, *longer than the stamens*, 2 or 2½ times as long as the ovary, glabrous. *Capsule:* —

This species is known from a single collection made by A. Henry about 1900 on the mountains south-west of Mengtsze, Yunnan, at an elevation of 2,000 m. (6,557 ft.).

It shows a resemblance to *R. asperulum* in its appearance. The main distinctions between them are that in *R. emarginatum* the calyx is minute with triangular lobes, the corolla is 1.3 cm. long, yellow, and the style is longer than the stamens; whereas in *R. asperulum* the calyx is 2—4 mm. long with oval, ovate or oblong lobes, the corolla is 7—8 mm. long, pale pink, and the style is shorter than the stamens. There is no record of its occurrence in cultivation.

Epithet. Notched at the apex.

Not in cultivation.

R. euonymifolium Lévl. in Fedde Repert. XII (1913) 103.

A small shrub, branchlets rather densely or sparsely scabrid with warts, scaly, glabrous, leaf-bud scales deciduous. *Leaves* evergreen, oblong-obovate, oblanceolate or obovate, *lamina* coriaceous, 1.9—3.5 cm. long, *0.6—1.5 cm. broad*, apex rounded, emarginate, mucronate, base tapered or cuneate, decurrent on the petiole; upper surface dark green, somewhat matt, sparsely scaly or not scaly; margin recurved, entire or somewhat crenulate in the upper half; under surface scaly, the scales small, unequal, brown, 2—5 times their own diameter apart, primary veins not raised or slightly raised; petiole 2—3 mm. long, narrowly winged on each side, slightly or moderately scaly. *Inflorescence* terminal, umbellate, 1-flowered, flower-bud scales persistent or deciduous; rhachis 0.5—1 mm. long, scaly or not scaly, glabrous; pedicel 1.4—2.3 cm. long, scaly, glabrous. *Calyx* 5-lobed, minute, 0.5—1 mm. long, lobes ovate, triangular or oblong, outside scaly, margin scaly or not scaly, glabrous. *Corolla* campanulate, 1—1.5 cm. long, 5-lobed, *yellow*, outside scaly. *Stamens* 10, unequal, *1—1.5 cm. long*, as long as the corolla or shorter; filaments densely pubescent in the middle one-third or towards the lower two-thirds. *Ovary* conoid or oblong, 3 mm. long, not tapered or tapered into the style, 5-celled, moderately or densely scaly, densely pubescent or glabrous; *style* short, thick, bent or straight, shorter than the corolla, *shorter than the stamens*, 1½ times or twice as long as the ovary, not scaly, glabrous. *Capsule* slender, 1.3—1.6 cm. long, 3 mm. broad, straight, rather densely scaly, glabrous, calyx persistent.

This plant was first found by J. Cavalérie in August 1902 at Pin-Fa, Kweichow. In 1905 it was collected by Esquirol, and in 1930 by Y. Tsiang at Na-kan, in the same region. It grows on rocks and in dense woods.

R. euonymifolium is very closely related to *R. emarginatum*. There is a strong similarity between them in general characters. *R. euonymifolium* differs from its ally in that the leaves are usually narrower, 0.6—1.5 cm. broad, and the stamens are longer, 1—1.5 cm. long. Whether *R. euonymifolium*, on these distinctions, merits specific rank is very doubtful. Nevertheless, the name will have to stand until more is known of this plant. The plant has not been introduced into cultivation.

Epithet. With *Euonymus*-like leaves.

Not in cultivation.

R. insculptum Hutch. et Ward in The Species of Rhododendron (1930) 821.

A small upright or straggly epiphytic shrub; branchlets rather densely scabrid with warts, scaly, glabrous, leaf-bud scales deciduous. *Leaves* evergreen, whorled, obovate-spatulate, lamina coriaceous, 1.8—4 cm. long, 1—1.8 cm. broad, apex rounded, emarginate, mucronate, base tapered, decurrent on the petiole; upper surface dark green, somewhat matt, not scaly, primary veins 2—3 on each side, deeply impressed; margin recurved, entire; under surface scaly, the scales somewhat small, unequal, brown, 2—3 times their own diameter apart, primary veins raised; young foliage crimson; petiole 2—3 mm. long, narrowly winged on each side, scaly. *Inflorescence* axillary in the uppermost leaf or terminal, umbellate, 1—2-flowered, flower-bud scales persistent; rhachis 0.5—1 mm. long, scaly or not scaly, glabrous; pedicel 1—2.3 cm. long, scaly, glabrous. *Calyx* 5-lobed, 1—3 mm. long, lobes ovate, triangular or oblong, outside scaly, margin scaly or not scaly, glabrous. *Corolla* campanulate, *1—1.3 cm. long*, 5-lobed, *bright orange*, outside scaly. *Stamens* 10, unequal, 0.6—1 cm. long, shorter than the corolla; filaments densely pubescent in the lower two-thirds. *Ovary* oblong, 3 mm. long, not tapered into the style, 5-celled, densely scaly, *moderately or rather densely pubescent; style short*, thick, bent, shorter than the corolla, shorter than the stamens, *as long as the ovary*, not scaly, glabrous. *Capsule* slender, 1.8—2.5 cm. long, 3 mm. broad, straight or slightly curved, moderately or rather densely scaly, *moderately or rather densely pubescent*, calyx-lobes persistent, dehiscing from the top downwards.

Kingdon-Ward discovered this plant in May 1926 at Seinghku Wang, Upper Burma. He found it again in April 1931 in the Adung Valley, in the same region. It is a common epiphyte on trees growing on ridges, or on cliffs, or on trees overhanging rivers, in the temperate rain forest, at elevations of 1,830—2,135 m. (6,000—7,000 ft.).

R. insculptum is closely allied to *R. asperulum*. There is a definite resemblance between them in habit and height of growth, in leaf shape and size, in the inflorescence, in the size of the calyx, and in the shape of the corolla. The main distinctions between them are that in *R. insculptum* the corolla is 1—1.3 cm. long, bright orange, and the ovary and capsule are moderately or rather densely pubescent; whereas in *R. asperulum* the corolla is 7—8 mm. long, pale pink, and the ovary and capsule are glabrous. *R. insculptum* is also related to *R. emarginatum*, but differs in distinctive features. There is no record of the species in culture.

Epithet. Carved.

Not in cultivation.

R. kawakamii Hayata in Journ. Coll. Sci. Tokyo XXX (1911) 171.

A lax upright shrub, 92 cm.—1.53 m. (3—5 ft.) high with *long branches*, usually epiphytic; *branchlets not scabrid, without warts*, scaly, glabrous, leaf-bud scales deciduous. *Leaves* evergreen, oblong-obovate or obovate, lamina thick, leathery, rigid, 2—5 cm. long, 0.9—2.4 cm. broad, apex rounded or obtuse, entire, mucronate, base tapered or cuneate, decurrent on the petiole; upper surface dark green or bright green, shining, sparsely scaly or not scaly; margin recurved, entire or somewhat crenulate in the upper half; under surface yellowish-green, scaly, the scales small, unequal, brown, 2—3 times their own diameter apart, primary veins slightly raised or not raised; petiole 2—8 mm. long, narrowly winged on each side or not winged, moderately or slightly scaly. *Inflorescence* terminal, umbellate, *3—7-flowered*, flower-bud scales persistent or deciduous; rhachis 1—2 mm. long, scaly or not scaly, glabrous; pedicel 0.8—2.5 cm. long, scaly, rather densely minutely puberulous or glabrous. *Calyx* 5-lobed, 1—2 mm. long, lobes ovate or triangular, outside moderately or rather densely scaly, minutely puberulous or glabrous, margin scaly, ciliate or eciliate. *Corolla* campanulate, *1—1.2 cm. long*, 5-lobed, *white or yellow*, outside scaly. *Stamens* 10, unequal, 6—7 mm. long, as long as the corolla or shorter; filaments densely pubescent towards the lower one-half or two-thirds. *Ovary* ovoid or conoid, 2—3 mm. long, not tapered into the style, 5-celled, densely scaly, *densely pubescent*; style short, thick, straight or bent, shorter than the corolla, as long as the stamens or shorter, 2 or 3 times as long as the ovary, not scaly, glabrous or pubescent in the lower half. *Capsule* cylindric, 1.2 cm. long, 5 mm. broad, minutely scaly, *densely pubescent*, calyx-lobes persistent.

R. kawakamii is a native of Taiwan, and was first collected by T. Kawakami and U. Mori in October 1906 on Mount Morrison. It grows on the temperate mountains, in rain-forest, in Chamaecyparis forest or in thickets, usually as an epiphyte, at elevations of 2,000—2,135 m. (6,557—7,000 ft.).

In the original diagnosis it is associated with *R. emarginatum*. From this plant it differs markedly in its 3—7-flowered inflorescence, often in its larger leaves, in the larger calyx, and in the densely pubescent ovary and capsule.

R. kawakamii was introduced by John Patrick and Hsu in 1969, and was reintroduced by them in 1970. In its native home it grows up to 5 feet; in cultivation it is a lax upright shrub with long branches and oblong-obovate or obovate, dark green or bright green leaves. It is suitable for a cool greenhouse, although it may prove somewhat hardy outdoors in well-sheltered gardens.

Epithet. After T. Kawakami, collector in Taiwan.

Hardiness 1—2. April—May.

R. santapaui Sastry, Kataki, P. Cox, Patricia Cox & P. Hutchison in Journ. Bombay Nat. Hist. Soc. XV. (1969) 744.

An epiphytic shrub up to 60 cm. (2 ft.) high; branchlets sparsely or moderately scabrid with warts, scaly, glabrous, leaf-bud scales deciduous. *Leaves* evergreen, *obovate-lanceolate*, lamina coriaceous, 2.5—4 cm. long, 1.1—1.5 cm. broad, *apex acuminate or acute, not emarginate*, mucronate, base tapered, decurrent on the petiole; upper surface bright green, somewhat matt, sparsely scaly or not scaly, primary veins 3—4 on each side, deeply impressed; margin recurved, entire or somewhat crenulate in the upper half; under surface pale green, scaly, the scales medium-sized, unequal, brown, 2—3 times their own diameter apart, primary veins slightly raised; petiole 2—6 mm. long, narrowly winged on each side, scaly. *Inflorescence* terminal, umbellate, 2—3-flowered, flower-bud scales deciduous; rhachis 1—2 mm. long, scaly or not scaly, glabrous; pedicel 1.6—2 cm. long, scaly, glabrous. *Calyx* 5-lobed, minute, 1 mm. long, lobes ovate or triangular, outside scaly, margin scaly or not scaly, glabrous. *Corolla* campanulate, 1.2—1.3 cm. long, 5-lobed, *creamy-white*, outside scaly. *Stamens* 10, unequal, 1—1.2 cm. long, shorter than the corolla; filaments densely pubescent in the middle one-third. *Ovary* conoid, 5 mm. long, 5-celled, densely scaly, glabrous; *style* short, stout, bent, 4 mm. long, shorter than the corolla and the stamens, *shorter than the ovary,* not scaly, glabrous. *Capsule* slender, 2.8—3.4 cm. long, 3—4 mm. broad, straight or slightly curved, rather densely scaly, glabrous, dehiscing from the top downwards, calyx persistent.

This plant was discovered by Cox and Hutchison in April 1965 in the south-east of the Apa Tani Valley, Assam, growing as an epiphyte on trees in sub-tropical rain-forest, at an elevation of 1,647 m. (5,400 ft.).

R. santapaui shows a certain degree of resemblance to *R. emarginatum* from which it differs in that the leaves are obovate-lanceolate, the apex is acuminate or acute, not emarginate, the corolla is creamy-white, the stamens are longer, 1—1.2 cm. long, the ovary is longer, 5 mm. long, and the style is shorter than the ovary. It is also related to *R. asperulum,* but is distinguished by notable characteristics.

The species was introduced by Cox and Hutchison in 1965. In cultivation it is a lax shrub with bright green foliage and creamy-white flowers in clusters of two to three. It is a slow grower, and a late flowerer. Along the east coast and inland, the plant is tender and is suited to a cool greenhouse. It is rare in cultivation.

Epithet. After Rev. H. Santapau, India.
Hardiness 1. July—August.

R. vaccinioides Hook. f. Rhod. Sikkim Himal. Part ii (1851) 3.
Illustration. Bot. Mag. Vol. 158 t. 9407 B (1935).
A small compact, bushy, straggly upright or upright shrub, often epiphytic, 15—92 cm. (6 in.—3 ft.) high; *branchlets rather densely scabrid with warts,* scaly, glabrous, leaf-bud scales persistent or deciduous. *Leaves* evergreen, oblong-obovate, spathulate-obovate or obovate, *lamina* coriaceous, *0.7—2 cm. long, 0.4—1.1 cm. broad,* apex rounded, emarginate, mucronate, base tapered, decurrent on the petiole; upper surface dark or bright green, somewhat shining, not scaly; margin recurved, entire or somewhat crenulate in the upper half; under surface scaly, the scales somewhat small or medium-sized, unequal, brown, 2—5 times their own diameter apart, primary veins not raised; petiole 1—3 mm. long, narrowly winged on each side, scaly. *Inflorescence* terminal, umbellate, 1—2- or rarely 3-flowered, flower-bud scales persistent or deciduous; rhachis 0.5—1 mm. long, scaly or not scaly, glabrous; pedicel 0.7—2 cm. long, scaly, glabrous. *Calyx* 5-lobed, 1—2 mm. long, lobes ovate or oblong, outside scaly or scaly at the base, margin scaly or not scaly, glabrous. *Corolla* campanulate, 0.6—1.1 cm. long, 5-lobed, white, creamy-white, white tinged pink, pink or lilac-pink, outside sparsely or moderately scaly. *Stamens* 10, unequal, 0.6—1.1 cm. long, as long as the corolla; filaments densely pubescent in the lower two-thirds. *Ovary* conoid or ovoid, 2 mm. long, tapered into the style or not tapered, 5-celled, densely scaly, glabrous; style short, thick, straight or sharply bent, shorter than the corolla and the stamens, twice or 1½ times as long as the ovary or equalling it, not scaly or scaly at the base, glabrous. *Capsule* slender, 1.4—3 cm. long, 3—4 mm. broad, straight or slightly curved, scaly, glabrous, calyx-lobes persistent, dehiscing from the top downwards, seeds with a long tail at each end.

R. vaccinioides was first found by J.D. Hooker in 1849 in the Sikkim Himalaya. Further gatherings by various collectors show that the species has a wide area of distribution, extending from Nepal, Sikkim and Bhutan to Assam, south-east and east Tibet, north and north-east Upper Burma, north-west and west Yunnan. It grows on granite cliffs, rocks, ledges of cliffs, and humus-covered boulders, in shady and moist places, and often as an epiphyte on forest trees, at elevations of 1,800—4,270 m. (5,902—14,000 ft.). Kingdon-Ward records it as being a common epiphyte in the forests in East Manipur, Assam.

The species shows a strong resemblance to *R. asperulum* in general characters, but is readily distinguished by the smaller leaves. It is a diploid with 26 chromosomes.

It was first introduced by J.D. Hooker in 1850, and it was reintroduced by other collectors on several occasions. In cultivation it is a compact spreading or straggly upright shrub with dark or bright green foliage and small, creamy-white or white tinged pink, single or paired flowers. A distinctive feature of the species and its allies is the rather densely or moderately scabrid branchlets with warts, rough to the touch. The species is a slow grower. It has a long-flowering season; some plants produce the flowers in April—May, other plants in June—July. A diagnostic character of the species and all the members of its Series is the minute seed with a long tail at each end. As the plant comes from elevations of 5,902—14,000 feet in its native habitats, it varies in hardiness in cultivation. In some gardens it has been sucessfully grown outdoors; in other gardens the plant is tender and is only suitable for a cool greenhouse.

Epithet. Like *Vaccinium*.

Hardiness 1—2. April—July.

VIRGATUM SERIES

General characters: shrub, 30 cm.—2.44 m. (1—8 ft.) high; branchlets moderately or rather densely scaly. Leaves lanceolate, oblong-lanceolate, oblong to oblong-oval, lamina 1.8—8 cm. long, 0.5—2 cm. broad; under surface scaly, the scales flaky, ½—2 or rarely 3—4 times their own diameter apart. *Inflorescence axillary, 1—2-flowered.* Calyx 0.5—2 mm. or rarely 3 mm. long. Corolla funnel-shaped or tubular-funnel shaped, 1.4—3.9 cm. long, pink, rose, purple or white, outside rather densely or moderately pubescent. Stamens 10. Ovary conoid or ovate; style long, straight. Capsule oblong or oblong-ovate, 0.5—1.2 cm. long.

Distribution: Nepal, Sikkim, Bhutan, Assam, south-east Tibet, north-west and mid-west Yunnan.

The Series consists of a single species, with single or paired axillary inflorescence.

DESCRIPTION OF THE SPECIES

R. virgatum Hook. f. Rhod. Sikkim Himal., t. 26A (1851).
  Illustration. Bot. Mag. Vol. 84 t. 5060 (1858); ibid. Vol. 145 t. 8802 (1919), figured as *R. oleifolium*.
  A lax broadly upright or upright shrub, 30 cm.—2.44 m. (1—8 ft.) high with long branches; branchlets moderately or rather densely scaly, glabrous. *Leaves* lanceolate, oblong-lanceolate, oblong, oblong-obovate, oblong-oval or rarely obovate, lamina coriaceous, 1.8—8 cm. long, 0.5—2 cm. broad, apex obtuse or acute or rounded, mucronate, base tapered or obtuse or rounded; upper surface dark green, scaly or not scaly, glabrous; margin moderately or slightly recurved; under surface pale green or pale glaucous green, scaly, the scales flaky, medium-sized, unequal, brown or dark brown, one-half to their own diameter apart, sometimes twice or rarely 3—4 times their own

diameter apart, with large peltate scales widely or closely separated, glabrous; petiole 3—8 mm. long, densely or moderately scaly, glabrous. *Inflorescence axillary in the upper 1—12 leaves, 1- (or sometimes 2-) flowered*; rhachis 0.5—1 mm. long, scaly or not scaly, glabrous; flower-bud scales persistent during flowering, outside densely puberulous or glabrous, not scaly, margin densely puberulous, not scaly; pedicel 2—8 mm. long, densely scaly, glabrous. *Calyx* 5-lobed, 0.5—2 mm. or rarely 3 mm. long, lobes rounded, outside scaly or rarely not scaly, glabrous, margin not scaly or rarely scaly, puberulous or glabrous. *Corolla* funnel-shaped or tubular-funnel shaped, 5-lobed, 1.4—3.9 cm. long, pink, pale or deep pink, rose, pale rose, white flushed rose, purple or white, *outside scaly, rather densely or moderately pubescent. Stamens* 10, unequal, 0.9—3.8 cm. long; filaments pubescent towards the base. *Ovary* conoid or ovate, 2—3 mm. or rarely 4 mm. long, 5-celled, densely scaly, glabrous; style long, straight, longer than the stamens, scaly at the base or up to one-half its length or not scaly, pubescent at the base or up to one-half its length or glabrous. *Capsule* oblong or oblong-ovate, 0.5—1.2 cm. long, 3—5 mm. broad, densely scaly, glabrous, calyx-lobes persistent.

This plant was discovered by J.D. Hooker in 1849 in the Lachen Valley, Sikkim Himalaya. Subsequent gatherings by other collectors show that the species is widely distributed from Nepal, Sikkim, Bhutan, Assam, to south-east Tibet, north-west and mid-west Yunnan. It grows in very varied habitats, on rocks, cliffs, grassy slopes, and the banks of streams, in dry open pastureland, amongst scrub, in thickets, cane brakes, and in pine and spruce forests, at elevations of 1,830—3,813 m. (6,000—12,500 ft.). Ludlow, Sherriff and Elliot record it from Pome Province, south-east Tibet as being common, up to 10,000 feet, always growing together with pines.

R. virgatum is a very variable plant. It grows from 1 to 8 feet high; the leaves are lanceolate, oblong to oblong-oval, laminae 1.8—8 cm. long, 0.5—2 cm. broad; the inflorescence is axillary in the upper 1—12 leaves, and the corolla is 1.4—3.9 cm. long.

In 1886, *R. oleifolium* Franch. was described from a specimen collected by the Abbé Delavay in Yunnan. The ample material now available and plants in cultivation show that *R. oleifolium* agrees with *R. virgatum* in height and habit of growth, in the shape and size of the leaves, in the axillary inflorescence, in the shape, size and colour of the flowers, and in all other respects they are also identical. It may be noted that in *The Rhododendron and Camellia Year Book*, 1964, p. 131, *R. oleifolium* was placed under *R. virgatum* in synonymy.

R. virgatum was first introduced by J.D. Hooker in 1850. It was reintroduced several times by other collectors. In cultivation it is a lax broadly upright or upright shrub up to 5 feet high with long annual growths up to 12 inches or more in length. In some plants an interesting feature is the change in habit of growth; when raised from seed or cuttings, for a period of 6—8 years the plant forms a somewhat compact rounded shrub about 10 inches high and as much across, with short branches, fairly well-filled with foliage; it then develops into a lax broadly upright shrub up to 3 or 4 feet high with long branches. A characteristic feature is the single or paired flowers axillary in the uppermost 1—6 or more leaves; or sometimes they occur in the leaf-axils along the entire length of the branch up to 12 inches long. In cultivation the flower colour is usually pink or rose; a white form is known to have been cultivated. As it has a wide altitudinal range from 6,000 to 12,500 feet, the species varies in hardiness. Along the west coast it grows well in the open; along the east coast it is successfully grown in the rock garden of the Royal Botanic Garden, Edinburgh, and in a few other gardens in well-sheltered positions, although some forms are tender and very difficult in other gardens. The species is free-flowering, and easy to increase from cuttings. The smaller forms up to about 2 feet high are well worth a place in every rock garden. The plant was given an Award of Merit when shown by Major A.E. Hardy, Sandling Park, in 1973.

Epithet. With willowy twigs.
Hardiness 1—3. April—May.

Forests on the Tali Range, Yunnan. Photos J.F. Rock

List of Synonyms

achroanthum Balf. f. et W.W. Sm.	=	RUPICOLA
acraium Balf. f. et W.W. Sm.	=	PRIMULIFLORUM
acuminatum Hort.	=	MUCRONULATUM var. ACUMINATUM
adamsii Rehd.	=	PRIMULIFLORUM
aechmophyllum Balf. f. et Forrest	=	YUNNANENSE
ALPICOLA Rehd. et Wils. var. *strictum* Rehd. et Wils.	=	ALPICOLA
amaurophyllum Balf. f. et Forrest	=	SALUENENSE
amphichlorum Ingram	=	CREMASTUM
ANTHOPOGON D. Don subsp. ANTHOPOGON	=	ANTHOPOGON
ANTHOPOGON D. Don var. *haemonium* (Balf. f. et Cooper) Cowan et Davidian	=	HYPENANTHUM
ANTHOPOGON D. Don subsp. *hypenanthum* (Balf. f.) Cullen	=	HYPENANTHUM
artosquameum Balf. f. et Forrest	=	OREOTREPHES
atentsiense Hand.-Mazz.	=	CILIICALYX
atroviride Dunn, nomen nudum	=	CONCINNUM
AUGUSTINII Hemsl. subsp. AUGUSTINII	=	AUGUSTINII
AUGUSTINII Hemsl. var. *azureus* Chen. ex Laum.	=	AUGUSTINII
AUGUSTINII Hemsl. subsp. *chasmanthum* (Diels) Cullen	=	AUGUSTINII var. CHASMANTHUM
AUGUSTINII Hemsl. f. *grandifolia* Franch.	=	AUGUSTINII var. CHASMANTHUM
AUGUSTINII Hemsl. subsp. *hardyi* (Davidian) Cullen	=	HARDYI
AUGUSTINII Hemsl. var. *rubrum* Davidian	=	BERGII
AUGUSTINII Hemsl. subsp. *rubrum* (Davidian) Cullen	=	BERGII
AUGUSTINII Hemsl. f. *subglabra* Franch.	=	AUGUSTINII var. CHASMANTHUM
AUGUSTINII Hemsl. var. *yüi* Fang	=	AUGUSTINII
aureum Franch.	=	XANTHOSTEPHANUM
Azalea lapponica Linn.	=	LAPPONICUM
batangense Balf. f.	=	STICTOPHYLLUM
benthamianum Hemsl.	=	CONCINNUM var. BENTHAMIANUM
bhotanicum Clarke	=	LINDLEYI
blandfordiiflorum W.J. Hooker	=	CINNABARINUM var. BLANDFORDIIFLORUM
blinii Lévl.	=	LUTESCENS
BRACHYANTHUM Franch. subsp. BRACHYANTHUM	=	BRACHYANTHUM
BRACHYANTHUM Franch. subsp. *hypolepidotum* (Franch.) Cullen	=	BRACHYANTHUM var. HYPOLEPIDOTUM
brachystylum Balf. f. et Ward	=	MEKONGENSE
brevistylum Franch.	=	HELIOLEPIS
brevitubum Balf. f. et Cooper non J.J. Smith	=	BRACHYSIPHON
bullatum Franch.	=	EDGEWORTHII
butyricum Ward, nomen nudum	=	CHRYSODORON
caeruleo-glaucum Balf. f. et Forrest	=	CAMPYLOGYNUM var. CHAROPOEUM
caeruleum Lévl.	=	RIGIDUM
calciphilum Hutch. et Ward	=	CALOSTROTUM var. CALCIPHILUM
CALOSTROTUM Balf. f. et Ward subsp. CALOSTROTUM	=	CALOSTROTUM

CALOSTROTUM Balf. f. et Ward subsp.
  keleticum (Balf. f. et Forrest) Cullen   = KELETICUM
CALOSTROTUM Balf. f. et Ward subsp.
  riparioides Cullen   = CALOSTROTUM
CALOSTROTUM Balf. f. et Ward subsp.
  riparium (Ward) Cullen   = CALOSTROTUM
CAMPYLOGYNUM Franch. var. *cremastum*
  (Balf. f. et Forrest) Davidian   = CREMASTUM
CAMPYLOGYNUM Franch. var.
  eupodum Ingram   = CAMPYLOGYNUM
CAMPYLOGYNUM Franch. var.
  leucanthum Ingram   = CAMPYLOGYNUM 'Leucanthum'
cantabile Balf. f.   = RUSSATUM
cardioeides Balf. f. et Forrest   = OREOTREPHES
catapastum Balf. f. et Forrest   = DESQUAMATUM
cephalanthoides Balf. f. et W.W. Sm.   = PRIMULIFLORUM var. CEPHALANTHOIDES
CEPHALANTHUM Franch. subsp.
  CEPHALANTHUM   = CEPHALANTHUM
CEPHALANTHUM Franch. var.
  crebreflorum (Hutch. et Ward)
  Cowan et Davidian   = CREBREFLORUM
CEPHALANTHUM Franch. var. *nmaiense*
  (Balf. f. et Ward)
  Cowan et Davidian   = NMAIENSE
CEPHALANTHUM Franch. var.
  platyphyllum Franch. ex Diels   = PLATYPHYLLUM
CEPHALANTHUM Franch. subsp.
  platyphyllum (Franch. ex Diels) Cullen   = PLATYPHYLLUM
cerasiflorum Ward, nomen nudum   = CAMPYLOGYNUM
cerinum Balf. f. et Forrest   = SULFUREUM
chamaetortum Balf. f. et Ward   = CEPHALANTHUM
chamaezelum Balf. f. et\Forrest   = CHRYSEUM
charianthum Hutch.   = DAVIDSONIANUM
CHARITOPES Balf. f. et Farrer
  subsp. CHARITOPES   = CHARITOPES
CHARITOPES Balf. f. et Farrer
  subsp. *tsangpoense* (Hutch.et
  Ward) Cullen   = TSANGPOENSE
charitostreptum Balf. f. et Ward   = BRACHYANTHUM var. HYPOLEPIDOTUM
charopoeum Balf. f. et Farrer   = CAMPYLOGYNUM var. CHAROPOEUM
chartophyllum Franch.   = YUNNANENSE
chartophyllum Franch. f. *praecox*
  Diels   = HORMOPHORUM
chasmanthoides Balf. f. et Forrest   = AUGUSTINII var. CHASMANTHUM
chasmanthum Diels   = AUGUSTINII var. CHASMANTHUM
cheilanthum Balf. f. et Forrest   = CUNEATUM
chengshienianum Fang   = AMBIGUUM
chloranthum Balf. f. et Forrest   = MEKONGENSE
CILIATUM Hook. f. var.
  roseo-album W.J. Hooker   = CILIATUM
cinereum Balf. f., nomen nudum   = CUNEATUM
CINNABARINUM Hook. f. subsp.
  CINNABARINUM   = CINNABARINUM
CINNABARINUM Hook. f. subsp.
  xanthocodon (Hutch.) Cullen   = XANTHOCODON
CINNABARINUM Hook. f. subsp.
  tamaense (Davidian) Cullen   = TAMAENSE
clivicola Balf. f. et W.W. Sm.   = PRIMULIFLORUM
colobodes Balf. f., nomen nudum   = CHAMEUNUM
commodum Balf. f. et Forrest   = SULFUREUM
CONCINNUM Hemsl. f. *laetevirens*
  Cowan   = CONCINNUM
CONCINNUM Hemsl. var. *lepidanthum*
  (Rehd. et Wils.) Rehd.   = CONCINNUM

coombense Hemsl.	=	CONCINNUM
cooperi Balf. f.	=	CAMELIIFLORUM
cosmetum Balf. f. et Forrest	=	CHAMEUNUM
costulatum Franch.	=	LUTESCENS
cremnastes Balf. f. et Farrer	=	LEPIDOTUM
cremnophilum Balf. f. et W.W. Sm.	=	PRIMULIFLORUM
crenatum Lévl.	=	RACEMOSUM
curvistylum Ward, nomen nudum	=	TSANGPOENSE var. CURVISTYLUM
cuthbertii Small	=	MINUS
dahuricum DC.	=	DAURICUM
DALHOUSIAE Hook. f. var. DALHOUSIAE	=	DALHOUSIAE
DALHOUSIAE Hook. f. var. *rhabdotum* (Balf. f. et Cooper) Cullen	=	RHABDOTUM
damascenum Balf. f. et Forrest	=	CAMPYLOGYNUM
daphniflorum Diels	=	RUFESCENS
DAURICUM Linn. var. *albiflorum* Nakai	=	DAURICUM var. ALBUM
DAURICUM Linn. var. *atrovirens* Hort.	=	DAURICUM var. SEMPERVIRENS
DAURICUM Linn. var. *mucronulatum* (Turcz.) Maxim.	=	MUCRONULATUM
deflexum Griffith	=	TRIFLORUM
deleiense Hutch. et Ward	=	TEPHROPEPLUM
depile Balf. f. et Forrest	=	OREOTREPHES
duclouxii Lévl.	=	SPINULIFERUM
elaeagnoides Hook. f.	=	LEPIDOTUM var. ELAEAGNOIDES
eriandrum Lévl., nomen nudum	=	RIGIDUM
eriandrum Lévl., ex Hutch.	=	RIGIDUM
erileucum Balf. f. et Forrest	=	ZALEUCUM
exquisetum Hutch.	=	OREOTREPHES 'Exquisetum'
FERRUGINEUM Linn. subsp. *kotschyi* (Simonkai) Hayek.	=	KOTSCHYI
FERRUGINEUM Linn. var. *myrtifolium* (Schott et Kotschy) Schroet.	=	KOTSCHYI
FERRUGINEUM Linn. subsp. *myrtifolium* (Schott et Kotschy) Hayek.	=	KOTSCHYI
fittianum Balf. f.	=	RACEMOSUM hybrid
FLAVIDUM Franch. var. FLAVIDUM	=	FLAVIDUM
FLAVIDUM Franch. var. *psilostylum* Rehd. et Wils.	=	FLAVIDUM
FORMOSUM Wall. var. FORMOSUM	=	FORMOSUM
FORMOSUM Wall. var. *inaequale* (Hutch.) Cullen	=	INAEQUALE
FORMOSUM Wall. var. *inaequalis* C.B. Clarke	=	INAEQUALE
FORMOSUM Wall. var. *johnstonianum* Brandis	=	JOHNSTONEANUM
FORMOSUM Wall. var. *salicifolium* C.B. Clarke	=	FORMOSUM
FORMOSUM Wall. var. *veitchianum* (Hooker) Kurz	=	VEITCHIANUM
fragrans Maxim.	=	PRIMULIFLORUM
fuchsiiflorum Lévl.	=	SPINULIFERUM
gemmiferum M.N. et W.R. Philipson	=	SCINTILLANS
gibsonii Paxton	=	FORMOSUM
glauco-aureum Balf. f. et Forrest	=	CAMPYLOGYNUM
GLAUCOPHYLLUM Rehder var. GLAUCOPHYLLUM	=	GLAUCOPHYLLUM
GLAUCOPHYLLUM Rehder var. *luteiflorum* Davidian	=	LUTEIFLORUM
GLAUCOPHYLLUM Rehder var. *tubiforme* Davidian	=	TUBIFORME
glaucum Hook. f.	=	GLAUCOPHYLLUM
glomerulatum Hutch.	=	YUNGNINGENSE
gymnomiscum Balf. f. et Ward	=	PRIMULIFLORUM

habaense Balf. f. et Forrest, nomen nudum	=	CUNEATUM
haemonium Balf. f. et Cooper	=	HYPENANTHUM
harrovianum Hemsl.	=	POLYLEPIS
hedyosmum Balf. f.	=	TRICHOSTOMUM var. HEDYOSMUM
heishuiense Fang	=	TATSIENENSE
HELIOLEPIS Franch. var. *brevistylum* (Franch.) Cullen	=	HELIOLEPIS
HELIOLEPIS Franch. var. HELIOLEPIS	=	HELIOLEPIS
hesperium Balf. f. et Forrest	=	RIGIDUM
HIPPOPHAEOIDES Balf. f. et W.W. Sm. var. HIPPOPHAEOIDES	=	HIPPOPHAEOIDES
HIPPOPHAEOIDES Balf. f. et W.W. Sm. var. *occidentale* Philipson et Philipson	=	WEBSTERIANUM
HIRSUTUM Linn. var. *album* Schinz et Kell	=	HIRSUTUM var. ALBIFLORUM
humicola Balf. f. nomen nudum	=	SALUENENSE
humifusum Balf. f. nomen nudum	=	CHAMEUNUM
hutchinsonianum Fang	=	CONCINNUM
hypolepidotum (Franch.) Balf. f. et Forrest	=	BRACHYANTHUM var. HYPOLEPIDOTUM
hypotrichotum Balf. f. et Forrest	=	OREOTREPHES
igneum Cowan	=	KEYSII
ioanthum Balf. f.	=	SIDEROPHYLLUM
iochanense Lévl., nomen nudum	=	RACEMOSUM
jahandiezii Lévl.	=	SIDEROPHYLLUM
jenkinsii Nutt. and var. *aciphyllum,* var. *platyphyllum,* and var. *undulatum*	=	MADDENII
KEISKEI Miq. var. *hypoglaucum* Suto et Suzuki	=	KEISKEI
KEISKEI Miq. f. *hypoglaucum* (Suto et Suzuki) Hara	=	KEISKEI
laetevirens Balf. f. nomen nudum	=	CONCINNUM
laticostum Ingram	=	KEISKEI
laticostum Ingram var. *lithophilum* Ingram, nomen nudum	=	KEISKEI
LAUDANDUM Cowan var. LAUDANDUM	=	LAUDANDUM
leclerei Lévl.	=	RUBIGINOSUM
ledebourii Pojark.	=	DAURICUM var. SEMPERVIRENS
ledoides Balf. f. et W.W. Sm.	=	TRICHOSTOMUM
leilungense Balf. f. et Forrest	=	TATSIENENSE
lemeei Lévl.	=	LUTESCENS
lepidanthum Balf. f. et W.W. Sm.	=	PRIMULIFLORUM
LEPIDOTUM Wall. var. *chloranthum* Hook. f.	=	LEPIDOTUM
leprosum Balf. f. nomen nudum	=	DESQUAMATUM
leucandrum Lévl.	=	SIDEROPHYLLUM
lochmium Balf. f.	=	natural hybrid of DAVIDSONIANUM and TRICHANTHUM
lophogynum Balf. f. et Forrest ex Hutch.	=	TRICHOCLADUM
luridum Ward, nomen nudum	=	RUSSATUM
macrocarpos Griffith	=	DALHOUSIAE
MADDENII Hook. f. var. *calophylla* C.B. Clarke	=	CALOPHYLLUM
MADDENII Hook. f. subsp. *crassum* (Franch.) Cullen	=	CRASSUM
MADDENII Hook. f. var. *longiflora* W. Watson	=	MADDENII
MADDENII Hook. f. subsp. MADDENII	=	MADDENII
MADDENII Hook. f. var. *obtusifolium* Hutch.	=	MANIPURENSE
MEKONGENSE Franch. var. *longipilosum* (Cowan) Cullen	=	TRICHOCLADUM var. LONGIPILOSUM

MEKONGENSE Franch. var.
   MEKONGENSE   = MEKONGENSE
MEKONGENSE Franch. var. *melinanthum*
   (Balf. f. et Ward) Cullen   = MELINANTHUM
MEKONGENSE Franch. var. *rubrolineatum*
   (Balf. f. et Forrest) Cullen   = RUBROLINEATUM
melanostictum Balf. f. et Forrest,
   nomen nudum   = CHRYSEUM
messatum Balf. f. et Forrest, nomen nudum = XANTHOSTEPHANUM
MINUS Michaux var. *chapmanii* (A. Gray)
   Duncan et Pullen   = CHAPMANII
MINUS Michaux var. MINUS   = MINUS
minyaense Philipson et Philipson = YUNGNINGENSE
mirabile Ward, nomen nudum   = GENESTIERIANUM
missionarum Lévl.   = CILIICALYX
modestum Hook. f.   = CILIATUM
motsouense Lévl.   = RACEMOSUM
MUCRONULATUM Turcz. var. *ciliatum*
   Nakai   = MUCRONULATUM
muliense Balf. f. et Forrest   = CHRYSEUM
myrtifolium Schott et Kotschy, not Lodd = KOTSCHYI
myrtifolium Lodd   = PONTICUM
myrtilloides Balf. f. et Ward = CAMPYLOGYNUM var. MYRTILLOIDES
nanum Lévl.   = FASTIGIATUM
NITIDULUM Rehd. et Wils. var.
   NITIDULUM   = NITIDULUM
NITIDULUM Rehd. et Wils. var.
   omeiense Philipson et Philipson = NITIDULUM
NIVALE Hook. f. subsp. NIVALE   = NIVALE
obovatum Hook. f.   = LEPIDOTUM var. OBOVATUM
obscurum Franch. ex Balf. f.   = SIDEROPHYLLUM
oleifolium Franch.   = VIRGATUM
oporinum Balf. f. et Ward   = HELIOLEPIS
oreinum Balf. f.   = ALPICOLA
oreotrephoides Balf. f., nomen nudum = OREOTREPHES
ORTHOCLADUM Balf. f. et Forrest
   var. *longistylum* Philipson et
   Philipson   = SCINTILLANS
ORTHOCLADUM Balf. f. et Forrest
   var. *microleucum* (Hutch.)
   Philipson et Philipson   = MICROLEUCUM
ORTHOCLADUM Balf. f. et Forrest
   var. ORTHOCLADUM   = ORTHOCLADUM
osmerum Balf. f. et Forrest, nomen nudum = RUSSATUM
oulotrichum Balf. f. et Forrest = TRICHOCLADUM
pallescens Hutch.   = natural hybrid of
                        RACEMOSUM and DAVIDSONIANUM
palustre Turcz.   = PARVIFOLIUM
pamprotum Balf. f. et Forrest,
   nomen nudum   = CHAMEUNUM
patulum Ward   = IMPERATOR
peramabile Hutch.   = INTRICATUM
phaeochlorum Balf. f. et Forrest = OREOTREPHES
pilicalyx Hutch.   = PACHYPODUM
plebeium Balf. f. et W.W. Sm. = HELIOLEPIS
pleistanthum Balf. f. ex Hutch. = YUNNANENSE
porrosquameum Balf. f. et Forrest = HELIOLEPIS
praeclarum Balf. f. et Farrer = PRIMULIFLORUM
PRIMULIFLORUM Bur. et Franch. var.
   lepidanthum (Balf. f. et W.W. Sm.)
   Cowan et Davidian   = PRIMULIFLORUM
primulinum Hemsl.   = FLAVIDUM
pritzelianum Diels   = MICRANTHUM

propinquum Balf. f. et Ward, nomen nudum	=	RUPICOLA
pseudociliicalyx Hutch.	=	CILIICALYX
pseudociliipes Cullen	=	SUPRANUBIUM
pseudoyanthinum Balf. f. ex Hutch.	=	CONCINNUM var. PSEUDOYANTHINUM
pubescens Balf. f. et Forrest	=	SPICIFERUM
pubigerum Balf. f. et Forrest	=	OREOTREPHES
pubitubum Balf. f. et W.W. Sm., nomen nudum	=	FASTIGIATUM
punctatum Ker	=	CAROLINIANUM
punctatum Andrews	=	MINUS
pycnocladum Balf. f. et W.W. Sm.	=	DIACRITUM
RACEMOSUM Franch. var. *rigidum* (Franch.) Rehnelt	=	RACEMOSUM
radinum Balf. f. et W.W. Sm.	=	TRICHOSTOMUM var. RADINUM
rarosquameum Balf. f.	=	RIGIDUM
ravum Balf. f. et W.W. Sm.	=	CUNEATUM
riparium Ward	=	CALOSTROTUM
rivulare Ward	=	CALOSTROTUM
rosthornii Diels	=	MICRANTHUM
roylei Hook. f.	=	CINNABARINUM var. ROYLEI
rubriflorum Ward, nomen nudum	=	CAMPYLOGYNUM
rubro-punctatum Lévl. et Vant	=	SIDEROPHYLLUM
RUPICOLA W.W. Sm. var. *chryseum* (Balf. f. et Ward) Philipson et Philipson	=	CHRYSEUM
RUPICOLA W.W. Sm. var *muliense* (Balf. f. et Forrest) Philipson et Philipson	=	CHRYSEUM
RUPICOLA W.W. Sm. var. RUPICOLA	=	RUPICOLA
salignum Hook. f.	=	LEPIDOTUM
SALUENENSE Franch. subsp. *chameunum* (Balf. f. et Forrest) Cullen	=	CHAMEUNUM
SALUENENSE Franch. subsp. SALUENENSE	=	SALUENENSE
SCABRIFOLIUM Franch. var. *pauciflora* Franch.	=	SPINULIFERUM
SCABRIFOLIUM Franch. var. SCABRIFOLIUM	=	SCABRIFOLIUM
SCABRIFOLIUM Franch. var. *spiciferum* (Franch.) Cullen	=	SPICIFERUM
sciaphyllum Balf. f. et Ward	=	EDGEWORTHII
semanteum Balf. f., nomen nudum	=	IMPEDITUM
semilunatum Balf. f. et Forrest	=	MEKONGENSE
sequini Lévl.	=	YUNNANENSE
sericocalyx Balf. f., nomen nudum	=	CHAMEUNUM
siderophylloides Hutch.	=	OREOTREPHES
sinolepidotum Balf. f.	=	LEPIDOTUM
sinonuttallii Balf. f. et Forrest	=	NUTTALLII
sinovaccinioides Balf. f. et Forrest	=	VACCINIOIDES
sinovirgatum Balf. f., nomen nudum	=	VIRGATUM
sordidum Hutch.	=	TSANGPOENSE
sparsiflorum Nutt.	=	CAMELLIIFLORUM
sphaeranthum Balf. f. et W.W. Sm.	=	TRICHOSTOMUM
spodopeplum Balf. f. et Farrer	=	TEPHROPEPLUM
squarrosum Balf. f., nomen nudum	=	RUBIGINOSUM
stenoplastum Balf. f. et Forrest	=	RUBIGINOSUM
stereophyllum Balf. f. et W.W. Sm.	=	TATSIENENSE
strictum Lévl., nomen nudum	=	YUNNANENSE
subcoombense Balf. f., nomen nudum	=	CONCINNUM
sycnanthum Balf. f. et W.W. Sm.	=	RIGIDUM
tapeinum Balf. f. et Farrer	=	MEGERATUM

tapelouense Lévl.	=	TATSIENENSE
taquetii Lévl.	=	MUCRONULATUM
temoense Ward, nomen nudum	=	LAUDANDUM var. TEMOENSE
theiochroum Balf. f. et W.W. Sm.	=	SULFUREUM
thyodocum Balf. f. et Cooper	=	BAILEYI
timeteum Balf. f. et Forrest	=	OREOTREPHES
trichocalyx Ingram	=	KEISKEI hybrid
trichophorum Balf. f.	=	natural hybrid of TRICHANTHUM and possibly AUGUSTINII
trichopodum Balf. f. et Forrest	=	OREOTREPHES
TRICHOSTOMUM Franch. var. *ledoides* (Balf. f. et W.W. Sm.) Cowan et Davidian	=	TRICHOSTOMUM
TRIFLORUM Hook. f. var. *bauhiniiflorum* (Watt ex Hutch.) Cullen	=	BAUHINIIFLORUM
TRIFLORUM Hook. f. var. TRIFLORUM	=	TRIFLORUM
TSANGPOENSE Hutch. et Ward var. *pruniflorum* (Hutch.) Cowan et Davidian	=	PRUNIFLORUM
tsarongense Balf. f. et Forrest	=	PRIMULIFLORUM
UNIFLORUM Hutch. et Ward var. *imperator* (Hutch. et Ward) Cullen	=	IMPERATOR
UNIFLORUM Hutch. et Ward var. UNIFLORUM	=	UNIFLORUM
vicarium Balf. f.	=	EDGARIANUM
villosum Hemsl. et Wils.	=	TRICHANTHUM
VIRGATUM Hook. f. subsp. *oleifolium* (Franch.) Cullen	=	VIRGATUM
VIRGATUM Hook. f. subsp. VIRGATUM	=	VIRGATUM
WEBSTERIANUM Rehd. et Wils. var. WEBSTERIANUM	=	WEBSTERIANUM
WEBSTERIANUM Rehd. et Wils. var. *yulongense* Philipson et Philipson	=	WEBSTERIANUM
xanthinum Balf. f. et W.W. Sm.	=	TRICHOCLADUM
yanthinum Bur. et Franch.	=	CONCINNUM
yanthinum Bur. et Franch. var. *lepidanthum* Rehd. et Wils.	=	CONCINNUM
yaragongense Balf. f.	=	RAMOSISSIMUM
yungchangense Cullen	=	CILIICALYX

New Taxa

Subseriei **Boothae** Cowan et Davidian, Subser. nov.

Frutices parvi vel medii. Foliorum lamina 2.6—12.6 cm. longa, infra pallide glauca-viridis vel pallide glauca, squamis patelliformis margine integris. Inflorescentia 3—10- (vel raro 2-) flora. Corolla late campanulata vel campanulata, lutea.

Typus subseriei: *R. boothii* Nutt.

Subseriei **Megeratae** Cowan et Davidian, Subser. nov.

Frutices parvi vel medii. Foliorum lamina 1.3—5 cm. longa, infra glauca, squamis vesicariis. Inflorescentia 1—2 (vel raro 3-) flora. Corolla campanulata, rotata vel fere patelliforma, lutea vel alba.

Typus subseriei *R. megeratum* Balf. f. et Forrest

Seriei **Ciliatae** Davidian, Ser. nov.

Frutices parvi vel medii, ramulis et petiolis moderate vel dense setulosis vel nonnunquam esetulosis. Folia sempervirentia; lamina 2—8.6 cm. longa. Inflorescentia 1—6- (vel raro 10-) flora. Calyx 0.5—1 cm. longus, lobis margine moderate vel dense setulosis vel raro paulo setulosis. Corolla tubuloso-campanulata vel tubulosa lobis expansus vel campanulata vel late infundibuliformis. Stylus gracilis rectus.

Typus seriei: *R. ciliatum* Hook. f.

Subseriei **Genestierianae** Cowan et Davidian, Subser. nov.

Frutices parvi vel medii vel nonnunquam arbuscula. Foliorum lamina 3—15.3 cm. longa, infra lepidota, squamis brunneis vel pallide brunneis. Inflorescentia 2—15-flora. Stylus brevis validus curvatus vel longus gracilis rectus.

Typus subseriei: *R. genestierianum* Forrest

Subseriei **Glaucophyllae** Cowan et Davidian, Subser. nov.

Frutices parvi vel medii. Foliis infra lepidotis, squamis minoribus pallide flavidis imbricatus vel inter se ad 10 diametris distantibus praedita, squamis majoribus atrobrunneis dispersis. Inflorescentia 3—10-flora. Stylus validus curvatus vel deflexus vel nonnunquam longus gracilis rectus.

Typus subseriei: *R. glaucophyllum* Rehder

Subseriei **Cuneatae** Davidian, Subser. nov.

Frutices plerumque magni, 30 cm.—3.70 m. altus. Foliorum lamina 1.4—7 cm. longa, infra dense lepidota, squamis contiguus vel imbricatus vel fere contiguus. Inflorescentia 1—6-flora. Calyx 0.4—1.2 cm. longus. Corolla 1.6—3.4 cm. longa.

Typus subseriei: *R. cuneatum* W.W. Sm.

Subseriei **Lapponicae** Davidian, Subser. nov.

Frutices nani vel parvi, 5 cm.—1.53 m. alti. Foliorum lamina 0.2—4 cm. longa, infra squamis imbricati vel inter se ad 2 diametris (raro 4—6 diametris) distantibus praedita. Inflorescentia 1—6- (vel raro ad 14-) flora; pedicelli 0.5—6 mm. longi. Calyx 0.5—6 mm. longus. Corolla 0.5—2 cm. longa.

Typus subseriei: *R. lapponicum* (L.) Wahlenb.

Subseriei **Baileyae** Cowan et Davidian, Subser. nov.

Frutices parvi vel medii. Folia sempervirentia, lamina 2.2—7 cm. longa, infra squamis crenulatis imbricatis. Inflorescentia racemosa, 5—12-vel nonnunquam ad 18-flora; rhachis 0.3—2.5 cm. longa. Corolla atropurpurea, purpurea vel atrokermesina.

Typus subseriei: *R. baileyi* Balf. f.

Subseriei **Lepidotae** Cowan et Davidian, Subser. nov.

Frutices parvi vel medii. Folia sempervirentia vel decidua, lamina 0.3—6 cm. longa, infra squamis imbricatus vel inter se ad 4 diametris distantibus praedita. Inflorescentia umbellata vel breviter racemosa, 1—2-vel nonnunquam ad 5-flora. Corolla rosea, purpurea, coccinea, kermesina, lutea vel alba.

Typus subseriei: *R. lepidotum* Wall.

Seriei **Tephropeplae** Davidian, Ser. nov.

Frutices nani vel medii vel magni, 30 cm.—3 m. vel raro 4.58 m. altus. Folia sempervirentia, infra pallide viridis vel pallide glauca-viridis vel glauca, dense vel nonnunquam laxe lepidota. Inflorescentia 3—9-flora. Corolla tubuloso-campanulata vel nonnunquam campanulata, 1.8—3.4 cm. longa, lutea, rosea, purpurea vel raro alba. Stamina 10. Stylus longus gracilis rectus.

Typus seriei: *R. tephropeplum* Balf. f. et Farrer

Seriei **Uniflorae** Cowan et Davidian, Ser. nov.

Frutices nani. Folia sempervirentia, lamina 0.8—3.8 cm. (raro ad 5 cm.) longa, infra squamis ½—6 diametris distantibus praedita. Inflorescentia 1—2- (vel raro 3-) flora. Corolla late infundibuliformis vel campanulata vel tubuloso-campanulata, 0.8—3.5 cm. longa, purpurea, rosea, pallide rosea vel lutea, extra dense pubescens (in *R. monanthum* glabra). Stamina 10. Stylus longus (in *R. pumilum* brevis) gracilis rectus.

Typus seriei: *R. uniflorum* Hutch. et Ward

Synopsis of Lepidote Rhododendron Species and Some of their Characteristics

Q = Not in cultivation

Species	Series	Subseries	Height	Flower colour	Hardiness	Month of flowering
afghanicum	Triflorum	Hanceanum	Up to 50 cm. (1⅔ ft.)	Whitish-green, creamy-yellow, white	3	April—May
alpicola	Lapponicum	Lapponicum	30 cm.—1.37 m. (1—4½ ft.)	Lavender-purple	3—4	April—May
amandum Q	Ciliatum	—	1.22—1.53 m. (4—5 ft.)	Pale lemon-yellow	—	—
ambiguum	Triflorum	Triflorum	60 cm.—5.80 m. (2—19 ft.)	Yellow, greenish-yellow	3	April—May
amesiae	Triflorum	Yunnanense	2—4 m. (6½—13 ft.)	Purple or dark reddish-purple	3	May
amundsenianum Q	Lapponicum	Lapponicum	30 cm. (1 ft.)	—	—	—
anthopogon	Anthopogon	—	15 cm.—1.53 m. (6 in.—5 ft.)	Pink, pale pink, deep rose, reddish, rarely crimson	3	April—May
anthopogon var. album	Anthopogon	—	30—92 cm. (1—3 ft.)	White	3	April—May
anthopogonoides	Anthopogon	—	92 cm.—1.83 m. (3—6 ft.)	Yellow, greenish, greenish-yellow, greenish-white, whitish-pink, white	3	April—May
apiculatum Q	Triflorum	Yunnanense	1.50 m. (5 ft.)	Dark purple	—	—
asperulum Q	Vaccinioides	—	Small shrub	Pale pink	—	—
augustinii	Triflorum	Augustinii	1—7.63 m. (3⅓—25 ft.)	Pink, rose, purple, lilac-purple, pale or dark lavender-blue, intense violet, white	2—3	April—May
augustinii var. chasmanthum	Triflorum	Augustinii	1.22—3 m. (4—10 ft.)	Lavender-blue, lavender-rose	2—3	April—May
auritum	Tephropeplum	—	92 cm.—3 m. (3—10 ft.)	Sulphur-yellow, yellow sometimes tinged red, creamy-yellow	2—3	April—May
baileyi	Lepidotum	Baileyi	60 cm.—1.83 m. (2—6 ft.), rarely 30 cm. (1 ft.)	Deep purple, deep reddish-purple	3	April—May
basfordii	Maddenii	Megacalyx	1.53—2.44 m. (5—8 ft.)	White	1—2	May—June
bauhiniiflorum	Triflorum	Triflorum	1.55—1.83 m. (5—6 ft.)	Deep or pale yellow, greenish-yellow	3	April—June
bergii	Triflorum	Augustinii	1.50—2.75 m. (5—9 ft.)	Red	3	March—early April
bivelatum Q	Triflorum	Augustinii	Medium-sized shrub	Rose	—	—
bodinieri Q	Triflorum	Yunnanense	Small shrub	Rose	—	—
boothii	Boothii	Boothii	1.53—2.44 m. (5—8 ft.), sometimes 3 m. (10 ft.)	Yellow, bright lemon-yellow, sulphur-yellow	1—2	April—May
brachyanthum	Glaucophyllum	Glaucophyllum	30 cm.—1.83 m. (1—6 ft.)	Yellow, pale or deep yellow, greenish-yellow, rarely white	3	May—June
brachyanthum var. hypolepidotum	Glaucophyllum	Glaucophyllum	60 cm.—1.53 m. (2—5 ft.)	Yellow, pale or deep yellow, greenish-yellow	3	May—June
brachysiphon	Maddenii	Maddenii	1.83—2.44 m. (6—8 ft.)	Pink, white tinged red	1—3	May—June
bracteatum	Heliolepis	—	92 cm.—3 m. (3—10 ft.)	White, white tinged pink	3	June—July

Species	Series	Subseries	Height	Flower colour	Hardiness	Month of flowering
bulu Q	Lapponicum	Lapponicum	30 cm.—1.53 m. (1—5 ft.)	Pure white, bright purple, magenta, deep violet-magenta, purplish, pinkish-purple	—	—
burjaticum Q	Lapponicum	Lapponicum	Up to 15 cm. (6 in.)	Rosy-violet	—	—
burmanicum	Ciliatum	—	92 cm.—1.83 m. (3—6 ft.)	Yellow, creamy-yellow, greenish-yellow, greenish-white	1—2	March—May
caesium	Trichocladum	—	92 cm.—1.53 m. (3—5 ft.)	Yellowish-green	3	May—June
calophyllum Q	Maddenii	Maddenii	1.22—1.83 m. (4—6 ft.)	Probably white	—	—
calostrotum	Saluenense	—	8—92 cm. (3 in.—3 ft.), rarely 1.22—1.53 m. (4—5 ft.)	Purple, pinkish-purple, bright rose-purple, deep rose-purple, claret, crimson-purple, rich purple-crimson	3—4	April—June
calostrotum var. calciphilum	Saluenense	—	Up to 61 cm. (2 ft.)	Pale pinkish, rosy-purple	3	May
camelliiflorum	Camelliiflorum	—	60 cm.—1.83 m. (2—6 ft.)	White, white tinged pink, red, deep wine red	1—2	May—July
campylogynum	Campylogynum	—	2.5—45 cm. (1 in.—1½ ft.)	Pale rose-purple, salmon-pink, carmine, deep plum-purple, almost black-purple	3	May—June
campylogynum var. celsum	Campylogynum	—	45 cm.—1.83 m. (1½—6 ft.)	Deep plum-purple, deep purple	3	May—June
campylogynum var. charopoeum	Campylogynum	—	46 cm. (1½ ft.)	Deep plum-purple, pale rose	3	May—June
campylogynum var. myrtilloides	Campylogynum	—	15—30 cm. (6 in.—1 ft.)	Black-purple, deep plum-purple, bright wine-red, rose-purple, rose, pink	3	May—June
capitatum	Lapponicum	Lapponicum	30—92 cm. (1—3 ft.)	Bluish-purple, deep purplish-red, purplish-lavender	3—4	April—May
carneum	Maddenii	Ciliicalyx	92 cm.—1.83 m. (3—6 ft.)	Pink, rose	1—2	February—May
carolinianum	Carolinianum	—	92 cm.—2.44 m. (3—8 ft.)	Pink, pale rosy-purple	3	May—June
carolinianum var. album	Carolinianum	—	Up to 1.22 m. (4 ft.)	White, whitish	3	May—June
cephalanthum	Anthopogon	—	5—92 cm. (2 in.—3 ft.), sometimes up to 1.53 m. (5 ft.)	White, rose, deep rose, pink, rose-crimson	3	April—May
chameunum	Saluenense	—	5—60 cm. (2 in.—2 ft.)	Purple-rose, deep purplish-rose, deep rose, purple-crimson	3	April—May
chapmanii	Carolinianum	—	60 cm.—2 m. (2—6½ ft.)	Pink, rose	1—2	April—May
charidotes	Saluenense	—	8—30 cm. (3 in.—1 ft.)	Magenta-crimson, purple-crimson	3	April—May
charitopes	Glaucophyllum	Glaucophyllum	23—92 cm. (9 in.—3 ft.), sometimes up to 1.53 m. (5 ft.)	Apple-blossom pink, rose, deep rose-crimson, rose-crimson	3	April—May
chryseum	Lapponicum	Lapponicum	15—92 cm. (6 in.—3 ft.), rarely up to 1.53 m. (5 ft.)	Bright yellow, yellow, greenish, golden-yellow, deep or pale yellow	3—4	April—May
chrysodoron	Boothii	Boothii	20 cm.—1.83 m. (8 in.—6 ft.)	Bright canary yellow, yellow	1—2	February—April
chrysolepis	Tephropeplum	—	Small or fair-sized	Bright canary yellow, yellow	2	May—June
ciliatum	Ciliatum	—	30 cm.—1.53 m. (1—5 ft.), rarely 1.83 m. (6 ft.)	White, white tinged pink or red, pale pink	3	March—May

Species	Series	Subseries	Height	Flower colour	Hardiness	Month of flowering
ciliicalyx	Maddenii	Ciliicalyx	80 cm.—3 m. (2½—10 ft.)	White, rarely white faintly flushed rose, rarely rose	1—2	March—May
ciliipes Q	Maddenii	Ciliicalyx	1.53—2.14 m. (5—7 ft.)	White	—	—
cinnabarinum	Cinnabarinum	—	1.22—5.49 m. (4—18 ft.)	Cinnabar-red, salmon-pink, yellow, rarely orange	3	April—July
cinnabarinum var. aestivale	Cinnabarinum	—	1.22—3.66 m. (4—12 ft.)	Cinnabar-red, salmon-pink	3	July
cinnabarinum var. blandfordiiflorum	Cinnabarinum	—	Up to 3 m. (10 ft.)	Red outside, yellow or greenish-yellow within	3	May—July
cinnabarinum var. breviforme	Cinnabarinum	—	1.22—1.53 m. (4—5 ft.)	Bright red outside, deep yellowish inside and at the margin of the lobes	3	June—July
cinnabarinum var. pallidum	Cinnabarinum	—	Up to 1.83 m. (6 ft.)	Rose, pale pinkish-purple	3	June—July
cinnabarinum var. purpurellum	Cinnabarinum	—	Up to 1.83—3.66 m. (6—12 ft.)	Rich plum-purple, bright pinkish-mauve,	3	May—July
cinnabarinum var. roylei	Cinnabarinum	—	Up to 5.49—6 m. (18—20 ft.)	Deep plum-crimson	3	May—July
cinnabarinum var. roylei f. magnificum	Cinnabarinum	—	1.53—2.44 m. (5—8 ft.)	Deep plum-crimson	3	June—July
collettianum	Anthopogon	—	Up to 1 m. (3⅓ ft.)	White, white tinged rose	3	April—May
compactum	Lapponicum	Lapponicum	70 cm.—1 m. (2⅓—3⅓ ft.)	Violet-mauve, purplish-mauve	3—4	April—May
complexum	Lapponicum	Lapponicum	30—60 cm. (1—2 ft.)	Deep rose-purple, very pale purple almost white, pink	3—4	April—May
concatenans	Cinnabarinum	—	1.53—2.14 m. (5—7 ft.)	Apricot, faintly tinged with pale purple or not tinged	3	April—May
concinnoides Q	Triflorum	Yunnanense	Small shrub	Lobes and upper part of corolla pinkish-purple fading to white at the base	—	—
concinnum	Triflorum	Yunnanense	1—4.50 m. (3⅓—15 ft.)	Deep or pale purple, purple, deep rosy-purple, purplish-lavender, deep pinkish, creamy-white tinged purple, white	3	April—May
concinnum var. benthamianum	Triflorum	Yunnanense	Up to 1.83 m. (6 ft.)	Lavender-purple	3	April—May
concinnum var. pseudoyanthinum	Triflorum	Yunnanense	1.22—1.83 m. (4—6 ft.)	Deep ruby-red	3	April—May
cowanianum	Lepidotum	Lepidotum	92 cm.—2.44 m. (3—8 ft.)	Reddish-purple, crimson-purple, pink	3	April—May
coxianum	Maddenii	Ciliicalyx	92 cm.—3 m. (3—10 ft.)	White	1	April—May
crassum	Maddenii	Maddenii	92 cm.—4.58 m. (3—15 ft.), sometimes 60 cm. (2 ft.) or up to 6.10 m. (20 ft.)	White, creamy-white, white tinged pink, rosy-white, pink	1—3	April—August
crebreflorum	Anthopogon	—	5—25 cm. (2—10 in.)	Pale pink, white tinged pink, deep rose, reddish	3	April—May
crenulatum Q	Ciliatum	—	1 m. (3⅓ ft.)	Pale yellow	—	—
cremastum	Campylogynum	—	60 cm.—1.83 m. (2—6 ft.)	Light plum-rose, bright red, deep wine-red	3	May—June
cubittii	Maddenii	Ciliicalyx	1.53—2.44 m. (5—8 ft.)	White, white flushed rose	1—2	February—April

Species	Series	Subseries	Height	Flower colour	Hardiness	Month of flowering
cuffeanum	Maddenii	Ciliicalyx	1.53—1.83 m. (5—6 ft.)	White	1	April—May
cuneatum	Lapponicum	Cuneatum	30 cm.—3.70 m. (1—12 ft.)	Rose-lavender, deep rose, rose, deep-rose purple, purple, lavender, purple-lavender, lavender-blue	3	April—May
dalhousiae	Maddenii	Megacalyx	92 cm.—3 m. (3—10 ft.), rarely up to 6.10 m. (20 ft.)	White, cream, creamy-white, yellow, at first creamy-yellow or yellow fading to creamy-white, white tinged rose	1—2	April—June
dasypetalum	Lapponicum	Lapponicum	30—76 cm. (1—2½ ft.)	Bright purplish-rose	3—4	April—May
dauricum	Dauricum	—	1.53—2.44 m. (5—8 ft.)	Pink, rose-purple, reddish-purple, dark purple	3—4	Jan.—Feb.—March, sometimes December
dauricum var. album	Dauricum	—	1.53—2.44 m. (5—8 ft.)	White	3—4	Jan.—Feb.—March
dauricum var. sempervirens	Dauricum	—	1.53—2.44 m. (5—8 ft.)	Pink, rose-purple, reddish-purple, dark purple	3—4	March—April
davidsonianum	Triflorum	Yunnanense	60 cm.—5 m. (2—16 ft.)	White, white tinged pink, pink, deep pink, rose, pale lavender, purple, pale purplish-pink	3	April—May
dekatanum Q	Boothii	Boothii	60 cm.—1.22 m. (2—4 ft.)	Bright lemon-yellow	—	—
dendricola	Maddenii	Ciliicalyx	1.22—1.83 m. (4—6 ft.)	White tinged pink, white	1	April—May
dendrocharis Q	Moupinense	—	35—70 cm. (1—2⅓ ft.)	Bright rosy-red	—	—
desquamatum	Heliolepis	—	1.53—8 m. (5—26 ft.)	Deep rose, pink, deep rose-lavender, deep purple-rose, intense bluish-purple, lavender-purple, lavender, purple, pinkish-purple, white	3	April—May
diacritum	Lapponicum	Lapponicum	8 cm.—1.07 m. (3 in.—3½ ft.)	Deep rose-purple, purplish-blue, deep blue-purple, purplish-red	3—4	April—May
drumonium	Lapponicum	Lapponicum	8 cm.—1.07 m. (3 in.—3½ ft.)	Deep purplish-blue, purple-blue, deep rose-purple,	3—4	April—May
edgarianum	Lapponicum	Lapponicum	30—92 cm. (1—3 ft.)	Rose-purple, purple, deep purplish-blue, purple-blue	3—4	April—June
edgeworthii	Edgeworthii	—	30 cm.—3.60 m. (1—12 ft.)	White, white tinged pink or rose	1—2	April—May
emarginatum Q	Vaccinioides	—	60 cm. (2 ft.)	Yellow	—	—
euonymifolium Q	Vaccinioides	—	Small shrub	Yellow	—	—
excellens Q	Maddenii	Maddenii	3.30 m. (11 ft.)	White	—	—
fastigiatum	Lapponicum	Lapponicum	15 cm.—1.22 m. (6 in.—4 ft.)	Lavender-rose, bright lavender-blue, purplish-blue, deep purple-blue, deep lavender, deep blue	3—4	April—May
ferrugineum	Ferrugineum	—	30 cm.—1.22 m. (1—4 ft.)	Crimson-purple, rose-scarlet, rose-purple, deep rose	3—4	June—July
ferrugineum var. album	Ferrugineum	—	Up to 60 cm. (2 ft.)	White	3—4	June—July

Species	Series	Subseries	Height	Flower colour	Hardiness	Month of flowering
ferrugineum var. atrococcineum	Ferrugineum	—	Up to 60 cm. (2 ft.)	Scarlet	3—4	June—July
fimbriatum	Lapponicum	Lapponicum	60 cm.—1.22 m. (2—4 ft.)	Deep mauve-purple, purple	3—4	April—May
flavantherum Q	Triflorum	Triflorum	1.83—3 m. (6—10 ft.)	Bright clear yellow	—	—
flavidum	Lapponicum	Lapponicum	45—92 cm. (1½—3 ft.), rarely 2 m. (6½ ft.)	Pale yellow	3—4	April—May
fletcherianum	Ciliatum	—	60 cm.—1.22 m. (2—4 ft.)	Pale yellow	3	March—May
fleuryi Q	Maddenii	Ciliicalyx	5 m. (16 ft.)	White	—	—
formosum	Maddenii	Ciliicalyx	92 cm.—3 m. (3—10 ft.)	White with or without 5 pale or deep red bands outside	1—2	April—June
fragariflorum	Lapponicum	Lapponicum	10—30 cm. (4 in.—1 ft.)	Purple, "crushed strawberry" colour, dark purple, plum-purple, pinkish-purple, purplish-crimson	3	May—June
fumidum	Heliolepis	—	1.53—2 m. (5—6½ ft.)	Pale violet, pale lavender-purple	3	May—June
genestierianum	Glaucophyllum	Genestierianum	1.22—4.58 m. (4—15 ft.)	Deep plum-purple	1—2	April—May
glaucophyllum	Glaucophyllum	Glaucophyllum	30 cm.—1.22 m. (1—4 ft.), sometimes 1.5 m. (5 ft.)	Pink, rose, pinkish-purple, reddish-purple	3	April—May
glaucophyllum var. album	Glaucophyllum	Glaucophyllum	46—92 cm. (1½—3 ft.)	White	3	April—May
goreri	Maddenii	Megacalyx	1.22—4.58 m. (4—15 ft.)	Creamy-white	1	May—June
grothausii	Maddenii	Megacalyx	1.22—4.58 m. (4—15 ft.)	White, white tinged pink on a few petals, cream, pink	1—3	May—June
grothausii 'Geordie Sherriff'	Maddenii	Megacalyx	1.22—3 m. (4—10 ft.)	White strongly flushed pink	1—3	May—June
hanceanum	Triflorum	Hanceanum	30 cm.—1.53 m. (1—5 ft.)	Creamy-white, pale yellow, white	3	April—May
hanceanum 'Nanum'	Triflorum	Hanceanum	8—15 cm. (3—6 in.)	Yellow	3	April—May
hardyi	Triflorum	Augustinii	1.22—3 m. (4—10 ft.)	White, rarely greenish-white faintly tinged lavender	3	April—May
headfortianum	Maddenii	Megacalyx	15 cm.—1.22 m. (6 in.—4 ft.)	Creamy-yellow, creamy slightly tinged pink outside the top of the tube	1—2	May
heliolepis	Heliolepis	—	60 cm.—5.49 m. (2—18 ft.)	Rose, deep rose, red, deep or pale lavender-rose, lavender-purple, purple, pink, white, white flushed rose	3	June—July
hemitrichotum	Scabrifolium	—	25 cm.—2.44 m. (10 in.—8 ft.)	Pale rose, pink, deep pink, white edged with pink	3	April—May
hippophaeoides	Lapponicum	Lapponicum	23 cm.—1.22 m. (9 in.—4 ft.), rarely 1.53 m. (5 ft.)	Lavender-blue, pale lavender-blue, purplish-blue, sometimes bright rose	3—4	April—May
hirsuticostatum Q	Triflorum	Augustinii	1.50 m. (5 ft.)	Whitish-rose	—	—
hirsutum	Ferrugineum	—	30 cm.—1 m. (1—3⅓ ft.)	Rose-pink, scarlet, crimson	3—4	June—July
hirsutum var. albiflorum	Ferrugineum	—	60—92 cm. (2—3 ft.)	White	3—4	June—July
hirsutum var. latifolium Q	Ferrugineum	—	60—92 cm. (2—3 ft.)	Rose-pink, scarlet, crimson	—	—
hirsuticostatum Q	Triflorum	Augustinii	1.50 m. (5 ft.)	Whitish-rose	—	—

Species	Series	Subseries	Height	Flower colour	Hardiness	Month of flowering
horlickianum	Maddenii	Ciliicalyx	92 cm.—3 m. (3—10 ft.)	White, creamy-white, with pink bands outside the lobes	1—2	April—May
hormophorum	Triflorum	Yunnanense	25 cm.—4.90 m. (10 in.—16 ft.)	Rose, white, white tinged pink, rose-lilac, lavender	3	May
hypenanthum	Anthopogon	—	15—92 cm. (6 in.—3 ft.)	Yellow, pale yellow, pale creamy-yellow, lemon-green	3	April—May
hypophaeum	Triflorum	Yunnanense	1.22—5 m. (4—16 ft.)	White faintly tinged rose, pink, deep purplish-pink, purplish-blue, purple, pale lavender	3	May
idoneum	Lapponicum	Lapponicum	15—45 cm. (6 in.—1½ ft.)	Deep purplish-blue, purplish-blue	3—4	April—May
impeditum	Lapponicum	Lapponicum	10—76 cm. (4 in.—2½ ft.)	Light or deep purplish-blue, pale or deep purple, pale or deep rose-purple, intense blue-purple, bright violet, lavender	3—4	April—May
imperator	Uniflorum	—	3—10 cm. (1—4 in.)	Dark purple, rich purple, bright purple, deep pinkish-purple, purple	2—3	April—May
inaequale	Maddenii	Ciliicalyx	92 cm.—3 m. (3—10 ft.)	White	1—2	March—May
insculptum Q	Vaccinioides	—	Small shrub	Bright orange	—	—
intricatum	Lapponicum	Lapponicum	15—92 cm. (6 in.—3 ft.)	Dark purplish-blue, dark blue, lavender-blue, pale lavender-blue, purple-blue, deep violet-mauve, rarely rose-pink	3—4	April—May
invictum Q	Heliolepis	—	1.22—2.14 m. (4—7 ft.)	Purple	—	—
iteophyllum	Maddenii	Ciliicalyx	92 cm.—2.44 m. (3—8 ft.)	White, white tinged pink	1—2	February—June
johnstoneanum	Maddenii	Ciliicalyx	1.22—3.70 m. (4—12 ft.)	Yellow, pale yellow, white tinged yellow, pale creamy-white, white, white tinged pink, white with pink bands along the middle of the lobes outside	1—3	April—June
kasoense Q	Triflorum	Triflorum	30 cm.—2.44 m. (1—8 ft.)	Yellow	—	—
kawakamii	Vaccinioides	—	92 cm.—1.53 m. (3—5 ft.)	White, yellow	1—2	April—May
keiskei	Triflorum	Triflorum	30 cm.—1.83 m. (1—6 ft.)	Pale yellow, lemon-yellow	2—3	April—May
keiskei 'Yaku Fairy'	Triflorum	Triflorum	5—12 cm. (2—5 in.)	Pale yellow, lemon-yellow	3	April—May
keleticum	Saluenense	—	8—45 cm. (3 in.—1½ ft.), rarely 3—5 cm. (1—2 in.)	Deep purplish-crimson, deep purplish-rose	3	May—June
keysii	Cinnabarinum	—	60 cm.—6 m. (2—20 ft.)	Orange, coral, salmon-pink, deep scarlet, with yellow or yellowish lobes	3	June—July
keysii var. unicolor	Cinnabarinum	—	60 cm.—6 m. (2—20 ft.)	Deep red, rarely the tips of the short erect lobes being slightly yellowish	3	June—July
kiangsiense Q	Maddenii	Megacalyx	1 m. (3⅓ ft.)	White	—	—

Species	Series	Subseries	Height	Flower colour	Hardiness	Month of flowering
kongboense	Anthopogon	—	15 cm.—2.44 m. (6 in.—8 ft.)	Rose, pink, almost white flushed pink, strawberry red, deep red, reddish-purple	3	April—May
kotschyi	Ferrugineum	—	30—45 cm. (1—1½ ft.)	Crimson-purple, scarlet-purple, rosy-pink, rarely white	3	May—July
lapponicum	Lapponicum	Lapponicum	5—45 cm. (2 in.—1½ ft.), sometimes 60—92 cm. (2—3 ft.)	Rose-purple, pinkish-purple, pink, purplish	3—4	March—April
lasiopodum	Maddenii	Ciliicalyx	1.83—4.58 m. (6—15 ft.)	White, white flushed purple-rose	1	May—June
laudandum Q	Anthopogon	—	15 cm.—1.22 m. (6 in.—4 ft.)	Pale pink, pink, white, rarely creamy-yellow	—	—
laudandum var. temoense	Anthopogon	—	15 cm.—1.22 m. (6 in.—4 ft.)	Pale pink, white	3	April—May
lepidostylum	Trichocladum	—	30 cm.—1.22 m. (1—4 ft.)	Pale yellow, yellow	3	May—June
lepidotum	Lepidotum	Lepidotum	5—92 cm. (2 in.—3 ft.), sometimes up to 1.53 m. (5 ft.)	Pink, purple, rose, scarlet, crimson, yellow	2—3	April—June
lepidotum var. album	Lepidotum	Lepidotum	30—60 cm. (1—2 ft.)	White, white slightly tinged pink	3	May—June
lepidotum var. elaeagnoides	Lepidotum	Lepidotum	5—30 cm. (2 in.—1 ft.)	Yellow, pale yellow, greenish-yellow	3	May—June
lepidotum var. minutiforme	Lepidotum	Lepidotum	30—60 cm. (1—2 ft.)	Red, crimson-purple	3	May—June
lepidotum var. obovatum	Lepidotum	Lepidotum	30 cm.—1.22 m. (1—4 ft.)	Purple, dark red, deep rose	3	May—June
leucaspis	Boothii	Megeratum	30—92 cm. (1—3 ft.), sometimes 1.22—1.53 m. (4—5 ft.)	White, sometimes with a pinkish tinge	2—3	February—April
levinei Q	Maddenii	Megacalyx	2—4 m. (6½—13 ft.)	White, creamy-white	—	—
liliiflorum Q	Maddenii	Megacalyx	3—8 m. (10—26 ft.)	White	—	—
lindleyi	Maddenii	Megacalyx	76 cm.—3.66 m. (2½—12 ft.), rarely up to 4.58 m. (15 ft.)	White, rarely yellow-white	1—2	May—June
litangense	Lapponicum	Lapponicum	30 cm.—1.22 m. (1—4 ft.)	Plum-purple, deep purplish-blue, bluish-purple, deep purple, purple, reddish-purple, lavender-blue	3—4	April—May
lithophilum	Trichocladum	—	60—92 cm. (2—3 ft.)	Pale sulphur-yellow	3	May—June
longistylum	Triflorum	Yunnanense	50 cm.—2.14 m. (1⅔—7 ft.)	White, white tinged pink	2—3	April—May
lowndesii	Lepidotum	Lepidotum	5—12 cm. (2—5 in.), rarely 30 cm. (1 ft.)	Pale yellow	3	May—June
lucidum Q	Camelliiflorum	—	Shrub	—	—	—
ludlowii	Uniflorum	—	A few cms. (in.) up to 30 cm. (1 ft.)	Yellow	2—3	April—May
ludwigianum	Maddenii	Ciliicalyx	1—1.50 m. (3⅓—5 ft.)	White with or without pale pink bands outside, sometimes rose	1	April—May
luteiflorum	Glaucophyllum	Glaucophyllum	60 cm.—1.53 m. (2—5 ft.)	Lemon-yellow, greenish-yellow	3	April—May
lutescens	Triflorum	Triflorum	92 cm.—6 m. (3—20 ft.)	Pale yellow, rarely white	3	Feb.—March—April
lyi	Maddenii	Ciliicalyx	92 cm.—2.44 m. (3—8 ft.)	White	1—2	April—June
lysolepis	Lapponicum	Lapponicum	45 cm.—1.22 m. (1½—4 ft.)	Purple-violet, pinkish-violet, dark purple, pinkish-purple	3—4	April—July

Species	Series	Subseries	Height	Flower colour	Hardiness	Month of flowering
maddenii	Maddenii	Maddenii	92 cm.—3.70 m. (3—12 ft.)	White, white flushed rose, rose-pink, pale pink, apple blossom pink	1—2	May—June
manipurense	Maddenii	Maddenii	1.53—4.58 m. (5—15 ft.)	White, white tinged red	1—3	May—June
megacalyx	Maddenii	Megacalyx	1.22—7.63 m. (4—25 ft.)	White, white flushed purplish-rose, creamy-white, cream tinged pink	1—2	April—June
megeratum	Boothii	Megeratum	8—92 cm. (3 in.—3 ft.), rarely 1.53—1.83 m. (5—6 ft.)	Yellow, deep yellow, pale lemon-yellow, creamy-yellow, rarely white	2—3	March—April
mekongense	Trichocladum	—	30 cm.—2.44 m. (1—8 ft.)	Yellow, pale yellow tinged green, lemon-yellow, dark greenish-orange, greenish-yellow, dark olive-yellow greenish at base	3	May
melinanthum	Trichocladum	—	1.53—2.44 m. (5—8 ft.)	Yellow	3	May—June
micranthum	Micranthum	—	60 cm.—2.50 m. (2—8 ft.)	White	3—4	May—July
microleucum	Lapponicum	Lapponicum	45—60 cm. (1½—2 ft.)	Pure white	3—4	April—May
micromeres	Glaucophyllum	Genestierianum	92 cm.—2 m. (3—6½ ft.)	Yellow, pale yellow, greenish-yellow, rarely white	1—2	May—June
minus	Carolinianum	—	1.22—6 m. (4—20 ft.), rarely 9.16 m. (30 ft.)	Pink, rose, pale pinkish-purple, sometimes white	3	May—June
mishmiense	Boothii	Boothii	Up to 1.22 m. (4 ft.)	Bright lemon-yellow, yellow, sulphur-yellow	1	April—May
mollicomum	Scabrifolium	—	60 cm.—1.83 m. (2—6 ft.)	Pale or deep rose	3	April—May
mollicomum var. rockii Q	Scabrifolium	—	60 cm.—1.83 m. (2—6 ft.)	Reddish-purple, reddish, pale rose	—	—
monanthum Q	Uniflorum	—	30 cm.—1.22 m. (1—4 ft.)	Bright yellow	—	—
moupinense	Moupinense	—	60 cm.—1.22 m. (2—4 ft.), rarely 1.53 m. (5 ft.)	White, white tinged pink or red	3—4	Feb.—March
mucronulatum	Dauricum	—	1—4 m. (3⅓—13 ft.), sometimes up to 30 cm. (1 ft.)	Rose, rose-purple, pale rose-purple, reddish-purple	3—4	Jan.—Feb.—March, sometimes in December
mucronulatum var. acuminatum	Dauricum	—	Up to 2.44 m. (8 ft.)	Pale pinkish-purple	3—4	March—April
mucronulatum var. albiflorum Q	Dauricum	—	1—4 m. (3⅓—13 ft.)	White	—	—
nigropunctatum	Lapponicum	Lapponicum	25—60 cm. (10 in.—2 ft.)	Pale purple, pink	3—4	April—May
nitens	Saluenense	—	30—45 cm. (1—1½ ft.)	Deep pinkish-purple, deep pink-magenta	3	June—August
nitidulum	Lapponicum	Lapponicum	60 cm.—1.53 m. (2—5 ft.)	Violet-purple	3—4	April—May
nitidulum var. nubigenum Q	Lapponicum	Lapponicum	10—30 cm. (4 in.—1 ft.)	Violet-purple	—	—
nivale	Lapponicum	Lapponicum	8—30 cm. (3 in.—1 ft.), sometimes 60—92 cm. (2—3 ft.), rarely up to 1.53 m. (5 ft.)	Reddish-purple, purple, lilac, deep purple, deep pink	3—4	April—May
nmaiense	Anthopogon	—	15—92 cm. (6 in.—3 ft.)	Sulphur-yellow, lemon-yellow, creamy-white, tube often deep yellow	3	April—May

Species	Series	Subseries	Height	Flower colour	Hardiness	Month of flowering
notatum Q	Maddenii	Ciliicalyx	Small or medium-sized shrub	White, with purplish-pink bands outside	—	—
nuttallii	Maddenii	Megacalyx	1.22—9.15 m. (4—30 ft.)	White; creamy-white suffused greenish, the petals or the corolla tinged pink; white flushed rose	1	April—May
nuttallii var. stellatum	Maddenii	Megacalyx	1.22—6.10 m. (4—20 ft.)	White, creamy-white suffused greenish, white flushed rose	1	April—May
odoriferum	Maddenii	Maddenii	Up to about 1.53 m. (5 ft.)	White, slightly flushed rose outside, the tube inside tinged green	1	April—May
oreotrephes	Triflorum	Yunnanense	60 cm.—7.62 m. (2—25 ft.)	Whitish-pink, rose, deep rose, deep pink, pale or deep lavender-rose, purple, grey-lavender, lavender-blue, rarely white or apricot yellow	3	April—May
oreotrephes 'Exquisetum'	Triflorum	Yunnanense	1.53—3 m. (5—10 ft.)	Whitish-pink, rose, deep rose, pale or deep lavender-rose	3	April—May
oresbium	Lapponicum	Lapponicum	15—60 cm. (6 in.—2 ft.)	Purple-blue, pinkish-lavender	3—4	April—May
orthocladum	Lapponicum	Lapponicum	30 cm.—1.22 m. (1—4 ft.)	Lavender, pale purplish-blue, deep blue-purple, purple	3—4	April—May
pachypodum	Maddenii	Ciliicalyx	60 cm.—1.83 m. (2—6 ft.), rarely 30 cm. (1 ft.), sometimes 7.63 m. (25 ft.)	Yellow, white, white tinged pink, white with a streak of yellow on the upper lobe, pink, purplish	1—2	March—May
paludosum	Lapponicum	Lapponicum	23—76 cm. (9 in.—2½ ft.)	Violet, lavender, bluish-purple, purple	3—4	April—May
parryae	Maddenii	Ciliicalyx	1.53—3 m. (5—10 ft.)	White	1—2	April—May
parvifolium	Lapponicum	Lapponicum	30—92 cm. (1—3 ft.)	Deep reddish, bright rose, rose-purple, pale rose-magenta	3—4	January—March
parvifolium var. albiflorum Q	Lapponicum	Lapponicum	30—92 cm. (1—3 ft.)	White	—	—
pemakoense	Uniflorum	—	30—75 cm. (1—2½ ft.)	Pinkish-purple, purple, pale purple, pale pink	3	March—April
pendulum	Edgeworthii	—	30—1.22 m. (1—4 ft.)	White, white tinged pink or pale yellow	1—3	April—May
petrocharis Q	Moupinense	—	Small shrub	White	—	—
pholidotum	Heliolepis	—	92 cm.—2.44 m. (3—8 ft.)	Rose-purple, rose, deep purple	3	June—July
platyphyllum Q	Anthopogon	—	15 cm.—1.53 m. (6 in.—5 ft.)	White, creamy-white, occasionally faintly flushed rose, pale rose, white flushed rose	—	—
pogonophyllum Q	Anthopogon	—	3—10 cm. (1—4 in.)	White, pale pink	—	—
polifolium	Lapponicum	Lapponicum	30—60 cm. (1—2 ft.)	Deep purplish-blue, purplish-blue	3—4	April—May
polyandrum	Maddenii	Maddenii	92 cm.—4.58 m. (3—15 ft.)	White, white tinged pink, rose-pink	1—3	May—June

Species	Series	Subseries	Height	Flower colour	Hardiness	Month of flowering
polycladum Q	Lapponicum	Lapponicum	Small shrub	Purple	—	—
polylepis	Triflorum	Yunnanense	92 cm.—5 m. (3—16 ft.)	Pale or deep purple, purplish-violet	3	April—May
primuliflorum	Anthopogon	—	5 cm.—1.83 m. (2 in.—6 ft.), rarely 2.44—2.75 m. (8—9 ft.)	White, white with yellow tube, pale rose, pink, deep rose-pink, white tinged orange at base, creamy-yellow, creamy-white, yellow	3	April—May
primuliflorum var. cephalanthoides	Anthopogon	—	60 cm.—1.53 m. (2—5 ft.)	White, white with yellow tube, pink, rose-pink, deep rose-pink, creamy-white	3	April—May
prostratum	Saluenense	—	3—30 cm. (1 in.—1 ft.), sometimes up to 60 cm. (2 ft.)	Crimson, deep purple-rose	3	April—May
pruniflorum	Glaucophyllum	Glaucophyllum	30—1.22 m. (1—4 ft.)	Nearly crimson, plum-purple, cerise-coloured, violet, lavender-purple, rarely pink	3	May—June
pumilum	Uniflorum	—	5—20 cm. (2—8 in.), sometimes up to 60 cm. (2 ft.)	Pink, pale pink, rose, pinkish-purple, purple	2—3	April—May
racemosum	Scabrifolium	—	15 cm.—4.58 m. (6 in.—15 ft.)	Pale or deep rose, pink, reddish-pink, white	3	March—May
radendum Q	Anthopogon	—	Up to 1 m. (3⅓ ft.)	Purplish-white	—	—
radicans	Saluenense	—	3 cm. (1 in.), sometimes 20 cm. (8 in.)	Dark rosy-purple, purple	3	May—June
ramosissimum	Lapponicum	Lapponicum	10 cm.—1 m. (4 in.—3⅓ ft.)	Dark purplish-blue, purplish-red, deep bluish, purple	3—4	April—May
rhabdotum	Maddenii	Megacalyx	92 cm.—3.66 m. (3—12 ft.)	Cream, pale yellow, white, marked with five conspicuous red stripes outside	1—2	May—July
rigidum	Triflorum	Yunnanense	60 cm.—10 m. (2—33 ft.)	Pink, deep rose-lavender, white	3	April—May
roseatum	Maddenii	Ciliicalyx	92 cm.—3.70 m. (3—12 ft.)	White, white flushed with rose or faintly flushed with purple	1	April—May
rubiginosum	Heliolepis	—	60 cm.—9.15 m. (2—30 ft.)	Pink, pale rose, lilac-rose, deep lavender-rose, deep lavender, purple, deep purple, pinkish-purple, lavender-purple, white	3	April—May
rubrolineatum	Trichocladum	—	60 cm.—1.53 m. (2—5 ft.)	Creamy-yellow, creamy-white, lined and flushed rose on the outside	3	May—June
rubroluteum	Trichocladum	—	92 cm.—1.70 m. (3—5½ ft.)	Reddish-yellow, with numerous crimson spots on the posterior side	3	June—July
rufescens Q	Anthopogon	—	30 cm.—1.25 m. (1—4 ft.)	White, rose	—	—
rufosquamosum Q	Maddenii	Ciliicalyx	92 cm. (3 ft.)	White	—	—

Species	Series	Subseries	Height	Flower colour	Hardiness	Month of flowering
rupicola	Lapponicum	Lapponicum	8 cm.—1.22 m. (3 in.—4 ft.)	Deep plum-purple, deep plum-crimson, plum-purple, black-purple, deep magenta-red, purplish-rose	3—4	April—May
russatum	Lapponicum	Lapponicum	15 cm.—1.53 m. (6 in.—5 ft.)	Deep purple-blue, deep rose-purple, rose-purple, deep violet-purple, light purple, violet	3—4	April—May
saluenense	Saluenense	—	60 cm.—1.53 m. (2—5 ft.)	Purplish-rose, deep purple, deep rose, deep crimson-rose, very deep plum-purple, deep purple-crimson	3	April—June
santapaui	Vaccinioides	—	Up to 60 cm. (2 ft.)	Creamy-white	1	July—August
sargentianum	Anthopogon	—	30—60 cm. (1—2 ft.)	Lemon-yellow, pale yellow, white	3	April—May
scabrifolium	Scabrifolium	—	23 cm.—3 m. (9 in.—10 ft.)	Rose, crimson, deep reddish, pink, white, white faintly flushed pink	3	March—May
scintillans	Lapponicum	Lapponicum	15 cm.—1.07 m. (6 in.—3½ ft.)	Lavender-blue, deep or pale purplish-blue, deep blue-purple, pale rose-purple, dark purplish-red	3—4	April—May
sclerocladum	Lapponicum	Lapponicum	92 cm.—1.53 m. (3—5 ft.)	Purplish-rose	3	April—May
scopulorum	Maddenii	Ciliicalyx	92 cm.—4.58 m. (3—15 ft.)	White without or with faint pink bands along the lobes outside, apple blossom pink	1—2	April—May
scottianum	Maddenii	Ciliicalyx	60 cm.—3.70 m. (2—12 ft.)	White, white flushed rose or crimson outside	1—2	May—June
searsiae	Triflorum	Yunnanense	1.53—5 m. (5—16 ft.)	White, pale rose-purple	3	April—May
seinghkuense	Edgeworthii	—	30—92 cm. (1—3 ft.)	Sulphur-yellow	1	March—April
setosum	Lapponicum	Lapponicum	15 cm.—1.22 m. (6 in.—4 ft.)	Purple, reddish-pink, pink, wine red, bright purple-pink, reddish-purple	3—4	April—May
shweliense	Glaucophyllum	Glaucophyllum	30—76 cm. (1—2½ ft.)	Pale pink tinged yellow, upper three lobes spotted pink	3	April—May
sichotense	Dauricum	—	1.22—1.83 m. (4—6 ft.)	Pale pinkish-purple, rose	3—4	March—April
siderophyllum	Triflorum	Yunnanense	92 cm.—8 m. (3—26 ft.)	White, very pale pink, pink, rose, purple, pale lavender-blue	3	May
smilesii Q	Maddenii	Ciliicalyx	6.10 m. (20 ft.)	White	—	—
spiciferum	Scabrifolium	—	15 cm.—1.53 m. (6 in.—5 ft.)	Pink, deep pink, rose, white	3	April—May
spilanthum	Lapponicum	Lapponicum	60—92 cm. (2—3 ft.)	Blue-purplish	3—4	April—May
spinuliferum	Scabrifolium	—	60 cm.—4.58 m. (2—15 ft.)	Crimson-red, red, pink, yellowish	2—3	April—May
stictophyllum	Lapponicum	Lapponicum	15—60 cm. (6 in.—2 ft.)	Deep purplish-blue, deep rose-purple, pale purple, rose	3—4	April—May
suberosum	Triflorum	Yunnanense	92 cm.—3 m. (3—10 ft.)	White faintly flushed rose, ivory-white flushed rose, ivory-white	3	April—May

Species	Series	Subseries	Height	Flower colour	Hardiness	Month of flowering
sulfureum	Boothii	Boothii	30 cm.—1.53 m. (1—5 ft.)	Bright or deep yellow, bright or deep sulphur-yellow, greenish-yellow, rarely greenish-orange	1—2	April—May
supranubium	Maddenii	Ciliicalyx	60 cm.—2.44 m. (2—8 ft.)	White flushed rose or purplish outside, white	1—2	April—May
surasianum	Maddenii	Ciliicalyx	1.22—4 m. (4—13 ft.)	Pale pink	1	June—July
taggianum	Maddenii	Megacalyx	1.53—2.50 m. (5—8 ft.)	White	1—2	April—May
tamaense	Cinnabarinum	—	92 cm.—1.83 m. (3—6 ft.)	Deep royal purple, purple, pale lavender	3	April—May
tapetiforme	Lapponicum	Lapponicum	12—60 cm. (5 in.—2 ft.)	Pink, pale purple, pale rose-purple, dark pale purple-blue, red	3—4	April—May
taronense	Maddenii	Ciliicalyx	60 cm.—4.58 m. (2—15 ft.)	White	1	April—May
tatsienense	Triflorum	Yunnanense	30 cm.—2.75 m. (1—9 ft.)	Purple, rose, pale rose, rose-lavender, rose-pink	3	April—May
telmateium	Lapponicum	Lapponicum	10—92 cm. (4 in.—3 ft.)	Rose-purple, deep rose-purple, lavender, purplish-blue, deep indigo blue	3—4	April—May
tephropeplum	Tephropeplum	—	30 cm.—1.22 m. (1—4 ft.), rarely 1.83—2.44 m. (6—8 ft.)	Dark to pale rose, carmine-rose, pink, purplish, rosy-crimson, crimson-purple, rarely white	2—3	April—May
thymifolium	Lapponicum	Lapponicum	30 cm.—1.22 m. (1—4 ft.)	Lavender-blue, purple, blue, purplish-lavender	3—4	April—May
trichanthum	Triflorum	Augustinii	1—6 m. (3⅓—20 ft.)	Light to dark purple, rose	3	May—June
trichocladum	Trichocladum	—	30 cm.—1.83 m. (1—6 ft.)	Sulphur-yellow, pale yellow, bright yellow, pale greenish-yellow, greenish-yellow, pale lemon-yellow	3	April—July
trichocladum var. longipilosum	Trichocladum	—	60 cm.—1.22 m. (2—4 ft.)	Sulphur-yellow, pale yellow, greenish-yellow	3	April—May
trichostomum	Anthopogon	—	20 cm.—1.22 m. (8 in.—4 ft.), rarely 2 m. (6½ ft.)	White, pink, rose, deep rose, rarely creamy-white tinged salmon-pink tube deep pink	3	May—June
trichostomum var. hedyosmum	Anthopogon	—	20 cm.—1.22 m. (8 in.—4 ft.)	White, pink, rose, deep rose	3	May—June
trichostomum var. radinum	Anthopogon	—	20 cm.—1.22 m. (8 in.—4 ft.)	White, pink, rose	3	May—June
triflorum	Triflorum	Triflorum	45 cm.—4.58 m. (1½—15 ft.)	Pale yellow, sulphur-yellow, greenish-yellow, yellow, rarely yellow tinged pink	3	May—June
triflorum var. mahogani	Triflorum	Triflorum	30 cm.—2.44 m. (1—8 ft.)	Pale yellow with mahogany coloured blotch and spots, or is suffused mahogany, or is of mahogany colour	3	May—June
tsai Q	Lapponicum	Lapponicum	30 cm. (1 ft.)	Purplish-white	—	—
tsangpoense	Glaucophyllum	Glaucophyllum	30 cm.—1.22 m. (1—4 ft.)	Pink, reddish-purple, pinkish-purple, rarely cerise	3	May—June

Species	Series	Subseries	Height	Flower colour	Hardiness	Month of flowering
tsangpoense var. curvistylum	Glaucophyllum	Glaucophyllum	15—60 cm. (6 in.—2 ft.)	Deep cerise-coloured	3	May—June
tubiforme	Glaucophyllum	Glaucophyllum	30 cm.—2.14 m. (1—7 ft.)	Pink, deep rose, pink with white lobes	3	April—May
uniflorum	Uniflorum	—	Up to 30 cm. (1 ft.)	Purple	2—3	April—May
vaccinioides	Vaccinioides	—	15—92 cm. (6 in.—3 ft.)	White, creamy-white, white tinged pink, pink, lilac-pink	1—2	April—July
valentinianum	Ciliatum	—	30 cm.—1.22 m. (1—4 ft.)	Bright yellow, bright sulphur-yellow	1—2	April—May
valentinianum var. changii Q	Ciliatum	—	30 cm.—1.22 m. (1—4 ft.)	Bright yellow	—	—
veitchianum	Maddenii	Ciliicalyx	92 cm.—3.70 m. (3—12 ft.)	White, white tinged pink or green outside	1	May—June
verruculosum	Lapponicum	Lapponicum	60—90 cm. (1—3 ft.)	Purple, deep purple	3—4	April—May
vilmorinianum	Triflorum	Yunnanense	92 cm.—1.50 m. (3—5 ft.)	Yellowish-white, pink	3	May
violaceum	Lapponicum	Lapponicum	23 cm.—1.22 m. (9 in.—4 ft.)	Violet-purple, pinkish-violet	3—4	April—May
virgatum	Virgatum	—	30 cm.—2.44 m. (1—8 ft.)	Pale to deep pink, rose, pale rose, white flushed rose, purple, white	1—3	April—May
viridescens	Trichocladum	—	30 cm.—1.53 m. (1—5 ft.)	Pale yellowish-green, yellow	3	May—June
walongense	Maddenii	Ciliicalyx	2—3 m. (6½—10 ft.)	Creamy, creamy-white	1	April—May
websterianum	Lapponicum	Lapponicum	30 cm.—1.37 m. (1—4½ ft.)	Rosy-purple, bright rose, rose-lavender, purple-blue, deep lavender-blue, lavender-blue	3—4	April—May
wongii	Triflorum	Triflorum	60 cm.—2 m. (2—6½ ft.)	Cream-coloured, yellow	3	April—May
xanthocodon	Cinnabarinum	—	1.53—2.14 m. (5—7 ft.)	Apricot, faintly tinged with pale purple outside or not tinged	3	April—May
xanthostephanum	Tephropeplum	—	30 cm.—3 m. (1—10 ft.), rarely 4.58 m. (15 ft.)	Bright yellow, deep lemon-yellow, lemon-yellow, yellow, canary yellow	1—2	April—May
yungningense	Lapponicum	Lapponicum	30 cm.—1.07 m. (1—3½ ft.)	Deep purple, deep blue-purple, pale bluish-purple, deep purplish-red	3—4	April—May
yunnanense	Triflorum	Yunnanense	30 cm.—3.66 m. (1—12 ft.)	Pale pink, pink, white, pale purplish-pink, deep rose, pinkish-lavender, pale rose-lavender, lavender, blue-lavender	3	May
zaleucum	Triflorum	Yunnanense	30 cm.—10.68 m. (1—35 ft.)	White, white flushed rose, pink, rose, lavender-rose, pale purple, purple	2—3	April—May
zaleucum var. flaviflorum	Triflorum	Yunnanense	2.44—7.63 m. (8—25 ft.)	Yellow	2—3	April—May

General Index

Index of Rhododendrons